11th International Conference on Natural Language Processing (ICON-2014)

Goa, India
18 – 21 December 2014

ISBN: 978-1-5108-3786-7

ICON-2014

11th International Conference on Natural Language Processing

Proceedings of the Conference

18-21 December 2014
Goa University, Goa, India

Preface

Research in Natural Language Processing (NLP) has taken a noticeable leap in the recent years. Tremendous growth of information on the web and its easy access has stimulated large interest in the field. India with multiple languages and continuous growth of Indian language content on the web makes a fertile ground for NLP research. Moreover, industry is keenly interested in obtaining NLP technology for mass use. The internet search companies are increasingly aware of the large market for processing languages other than English. For example, search capability is needed for content in Indian and other languages. There is also a need for searching content in multiple languages, and making the retrieved documents available in the language of the user. As a result, a strong need is being felt for machine translation to handle this large instantaneous use. Information Extraction, Question Answering Systems and Sentiment Analysis are also showing up as other business opportunities.

These needs have resulted in two welcome trends. First, there is much wider student interest in getting into NLP at both postgraduate and undergraduate levels. Many students interested in computing technology are getting interested in natural language technology, and those interested in pursuing computing research are joining NLP research. Second, the research community in academic institutions and the government funding agencies in India have joined hands to launch consortia projects to develop NLP products. Each consortium project is a multi-institutional endeavour working with a common software framework, common language standards, and common technology engines for all the different languages covered in the consortium. As a result, it has already led to development of basic tools for multiple languages which are inter-operable for machine translation, cross lingual search, hand writing recognition and OCR.

In this backdrop of increased student interest, greater funding and most importantly, common standards and interoperable tools, there has been a spurt in research in NLP on Indian languages whose effects we have just begun to see. A great number of submissions reflecting good research is a heartening matter. There is an increasing realization to take advantage of features common to Indian languages in machine learning. It is a delight to see that such features are not just specific to Indian languages but to a large number of languages of the world, hitherto ignored. The insights so gained are furthering our linguistic understanding and will help in technology development for hopefully all languages of the world.

For machine learning and other purposes, linguistically annotated corpora using the common standards have become available for multiple Indian languages. They have been used for the development of basic technologies for several languages. Larger set of corpora are expected to be prepared in near future.

This volume contains papers selected for presentation in technical sessions of ICON-2014 and short communications selected for poster presentation. We are thankful to our excellent team of reviewers from all over the globe who deserve full credit for the hard work of reviewing the high quality submissions with rich technical content. From 140 submissions, 54 papers were selected, 34 for full presentation and 20 for poster presentation, representing a variety of new and interesting developments, covering a wide spectrum of NLP areas and core linguistics.

We are deeply grateful to Aravind K. Joshi, Lori Levin and Sobha L for giving the three keynote lectures at ICON. We would also like to thank the members of the Advisory Committee and Programme Committee for their support and co-operation in making ICON 2014 a success.

We thank Vishal Goyal, Chair, Student Paper Competition and Sandipan Dandapat, Chair, NLP Tools Contest for taking the responsibilities of the events.

We convey our thanks to P V S Ram Babu, G Srinivas Rao and A Lakshmi Narayana, International Institute of Information Technology (IIIT), Hyderabad for their dedicated efforts in successfully handling the ICON Secretariat. We also thank IIIT Hyderabad team of Vasudeva Varma, Soma Paul, Radhika Mamidi, Manish Shrivastava, B Yegnanarayana, Kishore Prahallad and Suryakanth V Gangashetty and the team at Goa University lead by Ramdas Karmali and Ramrao Wagh along with large number of volunteers and many others for sharing the work and responsibilities of ICON. We also thank all those who came forward to help us in this task.

Finally, we thank all the researchers who responded to our call for papers and all the participants of ICON-2014, without whose overwhelming response the conference would not have been a success.

<table>
<tr><td>December 2014</td><td>Dipti Misra Sharma</td></tr>
<tr><td>Goa</td><td>Rajeev Sangal</td></tr>
<tr><td></td><td>Jyoti D. Pawar</td></tr>
</table>

Advisory Committee:

Aravind K Joshi, University of Pennsylvania, USA (Chair)
Junichi Tsujii, University of Tokyo, Japan
B Yegnanarayana, IIIT Hyderabad, India

Conference General Chair:

Rajeev Sangal, IIT (BHU), Varanasi, India

Programme Committee:

Jyoti D. Pawar, Goa University, Goa, India (Chair)
Dipti Misra Sharma, IIIT Hyderabad, India (Co-Chair)
Karunesh Arora, CDAC Noida, India
Sivaji Bandyopadhyay, Jadavpur University, India
Srinivas Bangalore, AT&T Research, USA
Peri Bhaskararao, IIIT Hyderabad, India
Rajesh Bhatt, University of Massachusetts, USA
Pushpak Bhattacharyya, IIT Bombay, India
Josef van Genabith, Dublin City University, Dublin
Amba P Kulkarni, University of Hyderabad, India
A Kumaran, Microsoft Research, India
Gurpreet Singh Lehal, Punjabi University, India
Hema A. Murthy, IIT Madras, India
Joakim Nivre, Uppsala University, Uppsala, Sweden
Kishore S. Prahallad, IIIT Hyderabad, India
Achla M Raina, IIT Kanpur, India
L Ramamoorthy, CIIL Mysore, India
Owen Rambow, Columbia University, USA
Sudeshna Sarkar, IIT Kharagpur, India
Shikhar Kr. Sarma, Gauhati University, India
Sobha L, AU-KBC Centre, Chennai, India
Keh-Yih Su, Institute of Information Science, Academia Sinica, Taiwan
Vasudeva Varma, IIIT Hyderabad, India
Bonnie Webber, University of Edinburgh, UK

Tools Contest Chair:

Sandipan Dandapat, CNGL, Dublin City University

Student Paper Competition Chair:

Vishal Goyal, Punjabi University, India

Organizing Committee:

Ramdas N. Karmali, Goa University, India (Chair)

Organized by

**International Institute of Information
Technology, Hyderabad**

**Natural Language Processing
Association, India**

Goa University, Goa

LDC-IL, CIIL Mysore

Sponsors

Microsoft Research, India

**Dept of Information Technology
Government of Goa**

Referees

We gratefully acknowledge the excellent quality of refereeing we received from the reviewers. We thank them all for being precise and fair in their assessment and for reviewing the papers in time.

Balamurali A R
Sivanand Achanta
Bharatt Ram Ambati
Gopalakrishna
Anumanchipalli
Karunesh Arora
Xabier Arregi
B Bajibabu
Rakesh Balabantaray
Kalika Bali
Sivaji Bandyopadhyay
Srinivas Bangalore
Mohit Bansal
Romil Bansal
Vijayaraghavan Bashyam
Riyaz Ahmad Bhat
Rajesh Bhatt
Brijesh Bhatt
Pushpak Bhattacharyya
Christian Boitet
Nicoletta Calzolari
Vineet Chaitanya
Sutanu Chakraborti
Somnath Chandra
Swapnil Chaudhari
Sriram Chaudhury
Monojit Choudhury
Sandipan Dandapat
Dipankar Das
Amitava Das
Niladri Sekhar Dash
Devadath V
Mathew Doss
Asif Ekbal
Veera Raghavendra Elluru
Suryakanth V Gangashetty
Kamal Deep Garg
Josef Van Genabith
Basil George
Sanjukta Ghosh
Dhananjaya Gowda
Vishal Goyal
Pawan Goyal
Parth Gupta
Bikash Gyawali
Samar Husain
Balaji Jagan

Girish Nath Jha
Aditya Joshi
Aravind Joshi
Sachin Joshi
Shreya Khare
Adam Kilgariff
Parameshwari
Krishnamurthy
Amba Kulkarni
Malhar Kulkarni
Pranaw Kumar
A Kumaran
Anoop Kunchukuttan
Bibekananda Kundu
Gurpreet Singh Lehal
Srikanth Madikeri
Radhika Mamidi
Gautam Mantena
Leena Mary
Michael Maxwell
Govind Menon
Abhijit Mishra
Hemant Misra
Vinay Kumar Mittal
K P Mohanan
Aditi Mukherjee
Hema Murthy
K Narayana Murthy
Sri Rama Murty
Vasudevan N
Bhuvana Narasimhan
Shashi Narayan
Sudip Kumar Naskar
Joakim Nivre
Kishorjit Nongmeikapam
Deepak S Padmanabhan
Sandeep Panem
Alok Parlikar
Ranjani Parthasarathi
Braja Gopal Patra
Soma Paul
Jyoti Pawar
Bhaskararao Peri
Kishore Prahallad
Lavanya Prahallad
Rashmi Prasad
Vikram Pudi

Rajeev Puri
Avinesh PVS
Priya Radhakrishnan
Preethi Raghavan
Achla Raina
S Rajendran
Aravind Ganapati Raju
Geetanjali Rakshit
Owen Rambow
Ankur Rana
Pattabhi Rk Rao
Preeti Rao
K. Sreenivasa Rao
G Umamaheshwara Rao
Srikanth Ronanki
Paolo Rosso
Rishiraj Saha Roy
Kunal Sachdeva
Niharika Sachdeva
K Samudravijaya
Baskaran Sankaran
Sudeshna Sarkar
Shikhar Kr Sarma
Dipti Misra Sharma
Himanshu Sharma
Raksha Sharma
Manish Shrivastava
Anil Kumar Singh
Bira Chandra Singh
Smriti Singh
Karan Singla
Rohit Sinha
Sunayana Sitaram
L Sobha
Priyanka Srivastava
Keh-Yih Su
K V Subbarao
ParthaTalukdar
Anil Thakur
Ashwini Vaidya
Andre Prisco Vargas
Vasudeva Varma
R. Vijay Sundar Ram
Sriram Venkatapathy
Bonnie Webber

Table of Contents

Conference Program

Friday, December 18, 2014

+ 10:00-11:00 Keynote Lecture 1 by Aravind K Joshi

Keynote Lecture 1: Complexity of Dependency Representations for Natural Languages
Aravind K Joshi

+ 11:00-11:20 Tea Break

+ 11:20-13:20 Technical Session I: Statistical Machine Translation

SMT from Agglutinative Languages: Use of Suffix Separation and Word Splitting
Prakash B. Pimpale, Raj Nath Patel and Sasikumar M.

Tackling Close Cousins: Experiences In Developing Statistical Machine Translation Systems For Marathi And Hindi
Raj Dabre, Jyotesh Choudhari and Pushpak Bhattacharyya

Correlating decoding events with errors in Statistical Machine Translation
Eleftherios Avramidis and Maja Popović

Supertag Based Pre-ordering in Machine Translation
Rajen Chatterjee, Anoop Kunchukuttan and Pushpak Bhattacharyya

+ 11:20-13:20 Technical Session II: Speech

Duration Modeling by Multi-Models based on Vowel Production characteristics
V Ramu Reddy, Parakrant Sarkar and K Sreenivasa Rao

Voice Activity Detection using Temporal Characteristics of Autocorrelation Lag and Maximum Spectral Amplitude in Sub-bands
Sivanand Achanta, Nivedita Chennupati, Vishala Pannala, Mansi Rankawat and Kishore Prahallad

Use of GPU and Feature Reduction for Fast Query-by-Example Spoken Term Detection
Gautam Mantena and Kishore Prahallad

Influence of Mother Tongue on English Accent
G. Radha Krishna and R. Krishnan

+ **13:20-14:15 Lunch**

+ **14:15-15:15 Keynote Lecture 2 by Sobha L**

Keynote Lecture 2: Text Analysis for identifying Entities and their mentions in Indian languages
Sobha L

+ **15:15-15:30 Tea Break**

+ **15:30-16:20 Poster Session and Demonstrations:**

HinMA: Distributed Morphology based Hindi Morphological Analyzer
Ankit Bahuguna, Lavita Talukdar, Pushpak Bhattacharyya and Smriti Singh

Roles of Nominals in Construing Meaning at the Level of Discourse
Soumya Sankar Ghosh and Samir Karmakar

Anou Tradir: Experiences In Building Statistical Machine Translation Systems For Mauritian Languages – Creole, English, French
Raj Dabre, Aneerav Sukhoo and Pushpak Bhattacharyya

How Sentiment Analysis Can Help Machine Translation
Santanu Pal, Braja Gopal Patra, Dipankar Das, Sudip Kumar Naskar, Sivaji Bandyopadhyay and Josef van Genabith

Introduction to Synskarta: An Online Interface for Synset Creation with Special Reference to Sanskrit
Hanumant Redkar, Jai Paranjape, Nilesh Joshi, Irawati Kulkarni, Malhar Kulkarni and Pushpak Bhattacharyya

LMSim : Computing Domain-specific Semantic Word Similarities Using a Language Modeling Approach
Sachin Pawar, Swapnil Hingmire and Girish K. Palshikar

Multiobjective Optimization and Unsupervised Lexical Acquisition for Named Entity Recognition and Classification
Govind, Asif Ekbal and Chris Biemann

Improving the accuracy of pronunciation lexicon using Naive Bayes classifier with character n-gram as feature: for language classified pronunciation lexicon generation
Aswathy P V, Arun Gopi, Sajini T and Bhadran V K

Learning phrase-level vocabulary in second language using pictures/gestures and voice
Lavanya Prahallad, Prathyusha Danda and Radhika Mamidi

Creating a PurposeNet Ontology: An insight into the issues encountered during ontology creation
Rishabh Srivastava and Soma Paul

Bundeli Folk-Song Genre Classification with kNN and SVM
Ayushi Pandey and Indranil Dutta

Word net based Method for Determining Semantic Sentence Similarity through various Word Senses
Madhuri A. Tayal, M. M. Raghuwanshi and Latesh Malik

Identification of Karaka relations in an English sentence
Sai Kiran Gorthi, Ashish Palakurthi, Radhika Mamidi and Dipti Misra Sharma

A Sentiment Analyzer for Hindi Using Hindi Senti Lexicon
Raksha Sharma and Pushpak Bhattacharyya

A Sandhi Splitter for Malayalam
Devadath V V, Litton J Kurisinkel, Dipti Misra Sharma and Vasudeva Varma

PaCMan : Parallel Corpus Management Workbench
Diptesh Kanojia, Manish Shrivastava, Raj Dabre and Pushpak Bhattacharyya

+ 16:20-17:50 Technical Session III: Machine Translation

How to Know the Best Machine Translation System in Advance before Translating a Sentence?
Bibekananda Kundu and Sanjay Kumar Choudhury

A Domain-Restricted, Rule Based, English-Hindi Machine Translation System Based on Dependency Parsing
Pratik Desai, Amit Sangodkar and Om P. Damani

Translation of TO infinitives in Anusaaraka Platform: an English Hindi MT system
Akshar Bharati, Sukhada and Soma Paul

Friday, December 18, 2014 (continued)

+ 16:20-17:50 Technical Session IV : Sentiment Analysis and Emotion Detection

Determing Trustworthiness in E-Commerce Customer Reviews
Dhruv Gupta and Asif Ekbal

Naturalistic Audio-Visual Emotion Database
Sudarsana Reddy Kadiri, P. Gangamohan, V.K. Mittal and B. Yegnanarayana

Discriminating Neutral and Emotional Speech using Neural Networks
Sudarsana Reddy Kadiri, P. Gangamohan and B. Yegnanarayana

+ 17:50-18:50 NLPAI Meeting

+ 19:00-20:00 Cultural Program

+ 20:00-20:30 Dinner

Saturday, December 20, 2014

+ 9:30-10:30 Keynote Lecture 3 by Lori Levin

Keynote Lecture 3: Modeling NonPropositional Semantics
Lori Levin

+ 10:30-10:50 Tea Break

+ 10:50-13:20 Technical Session V: Statistical Methods

Text Readability in Hindi: A Comparative Study of Feature Performances Using Support Vectors
Manjira Sinha, Tirthankar Dasgupta and Anupam Basu

Sangam: A Perso-Arabic to Indic Script Machine Transliteration Model
Gurpreet Singh Lehal and Tejinder Singh Saini

AutoParSe: An Automatic Paradigm Selector For Nouns in Konkani
Shilpa Desai, Neenad Desai, Jyoti Pawar and Pushpak Bhattacharyya

Continuum models of semantics for language discovery
Deepali Semwal, Sunakshi Gupta and Amitabha Mukerjee

Syllables as Linguistic Units?
Amitabha Mukerjee and Prashant Jalan

+ 10:50-13:20 Technical Session VI: Parsing

Accurate Identification of the Karta (Subject) Relation in Bangla
Arnab Dhar and Sudeshna Sarkar

Manipuri Chunking: An Incremental Model with POS and RMWE
Kishorjit Nongmeikapam, Thiyam Ibungomacha Singh, Ngariyanbam Mayekleima Chanu and Sivaji Bandyopadhyay

Segmentation of Navya-Nyya Expressions
Arjuna S. R. and Amba Kulkarni

Handling Plurality in Bengali Noun Phrases
Biswanath Barik and Sudeshna Sarkar

Making Verb Frames for Bangla Vector Verbs
Sanjukta Ghosh

+ 10:50-13:20 Technical Session VII: Student Paper Contest

English to Punjabi Transliteration using Orthographic and Phonetic Information
Kamaljeet Kaur and Parminder Singh

+ 14:20-16:50 Technical Session VIII: Lexical Resources and Corpora Annotation

Evaluating Two Annotated Corpora of Hindi Using a Verb Class Identifier
Neha Dixit and Narayan Choudhary

Hindi Word Sketches
Anil Krishna Eragani, Varun Kuchib Hotla, Dipti Misra Sharma, Siva Reddy and Adam Kilgarriff

Extracting and Selecting Relevant Corpora for Domain Adaptation in MT
Lars Bungum

Merging Verb Senses of Hindi WordNet using Word Embeddings
Sudha Bhingardive, Ratish Puduppully, Dhirendra Singh and Pushpak Bhattacharyya

Hierarchical Recursive Tagset for Annotating Cooking Recipes
Sharath Reddy Gunamgari, Sandipan Dandapat and Monojit Choudhury

+ 14:20-16:50 Technical Session IX: Emerging Areas

Named Entity Based Answer Extraction form Hindi Text Corpus Using n-grams
Lokesh Kumar Sharma and Namita Mittal

"ye word kis lang ka hai bhai?" Testing the Limits of Word level Language Identification
Spandana Gella, Kalika Bali and Monojit Choudhury

Identifying Languages at the Word Level in Code-Mixed Indian Social Media Text
Amitava Das and Björn Gambäck

Unsupervised Detection and Promotion of Authoritative Domains for Medical Queries in Web Search
Manoj K. Chinnakotla, Rupesh K. Mehta and Vipul Agrawal

Significance of Paralinguistic Cues in the Synthesis of Mathematical Equations
Venkatesh Potluri, SaiKrishna Rallabandi, Priyanka Srivastava and Kishore Prahallad

+ 14:20-16:50 Technical Session X: NLP Tools Contest

Keynote Lecture-1

Complexity of Dependency Representations for Natural Languages

Aravind K. Joshi
University of Pennsylvania, USA
joshi@seas.upenn.edu

Most of the formal issues about the complexity of dependency representations are studied via various types of phrase structure grammars and their capabilities for representing dependencies. We will consider a particular kind of phrase structure grammar, well suited to describe various levels of complexity in the context of dependencies. We will relate these representations to some key linguistic issues and the corresponding parsing complexities. We hope that this work will give some further insight into the limits of dependency representations as well as the associated processing complexities.

D S Sharma, R Sangal and J D Pawar. Proc. of the 11th Intl. Conference on Natural Language Processing, page 1,
Goa, India. December 2014. ©2014 NLP Association of India (NLPAI)

SMT from Agglutinative Languages:
Use of Suffix Separation and Word Splitting

Prakash B. Pimpale
KBCS, CDAC Mumbai
prakash@cdac.in

Raj Nath Patel
KBCS, CDAC Mumbai
rajnathp@cdac.in

Sasikumar M.
KBCS, CDAC Mumbai
sasi@cdac.in

Abstract

Marathi and Hindi both being Indo-Aryan family members and using Devanagari script are similar to a great extent. Both follow SOV sentence structure and are equally liberal in word order. The translation for this language pair appears to be easy. But experiments show this to be a significantly difficult task, primarily due to the fact that Marathi is morphologically richer compared to Hindi. We propose a Marathi to Hindi Statistical Machine Translation (SMT) system which makes use of compound word splitting to tackle the morphological richness of Marathi.

1 Introduction

Marathi is widely spoken in and around Maharashtra, India and also in other parts of the world. Hindi is widely spoken in Northern India and is understood in most parts of the nation. Hindi also has significant number of speakers across the world in countries where Indians have migrated. Marathi speaking areas host many important economic and social activity centers, where many times there is need for translation of content from Marathi to Hindi.

Marathi and Hindi both belong to the Indo-Aryan family of languages and have the same flexibility towards word order, canonically following the SOV structure. As both are written in Devanagari script and have many words which are either same or can be traced to same origin, they resemble each other to a great extent. This resemblance may make us to believe that Statistical Machine Translation will be an easier affair on this pair. But upon experiments it is observed that the morphological richness of Marathi makes it as difficult as any other Indian language to Indian language Machine Translation.

Marathi is agglutinative in nature which makes Marathi to Hindi SMT even more difficult. It is known that SMT produces more unknown words resulting in bad translation quality, if morphological divergence between source and target languages is high. Koehn & Knight (2003), Popovic & Ney (2004) and Popovic et al. (2006) have demonstrated ways to handle this issue with morphological segmentation of words before training the SMT system.

We demonstrate a better performing Marathi to Hindi SMT system which makes use of morphological segmentation on the source side prior to training. The proposed system shows significant improvement in translation quality compared to the baseline. We also present comparative study using BLEU (Papineni et al. 2002), NIST (Doddington, 2002), Position-independent Word Error Rate (Tillmann et al., 1997), Word Error Rate (Nießen et al., 2000), manual evaluations and 10-fold cross validation.

The rest of the paper is organized as follows. In Section 2, we discuss the similarities and dissimilarities in the language pair under study. In Section 3, we describe the experimental set up and splitting algorithm. Section 4 discusses experiments and results for splitting and constrained splitting. Analysis and discussion is done in section 5 with manual evaluation, 10-fold cross validation, error analysis and comparative study with similar work, followed by conclusion and future work in section 6.

2 Similarity Analysis of Marathi and Hindi

Marathi and Hindi both belong to Indo-Aryan family of languages and Marathi is Southern-most in this category. Being situated in such a geographical vicinity of India Marathi seems considerably influenced by Dravidian languages (Junghare, 2009). It makes frequent use of word compounding or post modifications to create meaningful words using prefixes and suffixes. Number of such derived words in Marathi is very high and this distinguishes Marathi from others in Indo-Aryan language family. Dabre et al.

2

D S Sharma, R Sangal and J D Pawar. Proc. of the 11th Intl. Conference on Natural Language Processing, pages 2–10,
Goa, India. December 2014. ©2014 NLP Association of India (NLPAI)

(2012) and Bhosale et al. (2011) have theoretically discussed the morphological richness of Marathi and compared it with Hindi.

We analyzed a parallel Marathi and Hindi translation corpus of size 48000 sentences for following parameters:

- Average Sentence Length: Considered number of words in a sentence as the sentence length. This parameter is captured to compare number of words a language needs to represent a concept, assuming a sentence is written to represent a concept.
- Word Count: Total number of words in the corpus. This is captured to affirm that a morphologically poorer language needs more words as compared to the richer.
- Unique Word Count: Number of distinct words in the corpus. This is computed to compare morphological richness of the languages.
- Average Word Frequency: Word frequency is number of times the word is repeated in corpus. This will help to demonstrate that word frequency is higher in morphologically poorer language.
- Average Word Length: Number of characters in a word is word length. This is measured to analyze the significant presence of compound words in Marathi.

The corpus analysis in Table 1 shows that a Hindi sentence needs on an average 17 words to represent a concept whereas Marathi sentence needs just 12 words to represent the same concept. The total number of words in Hindi corpus is 834417 and Marathi has just 602500 which affirm the fact that Marathi represents varied concepts with lesser number of words as compared to Hindi. We can also see that unique word count for Marathi is more than Hindi by 44474, which demonstrates that Marathi has larger vocabulary of surface forms to describe different meanings, and the same in case of Hindi is done by using different word combinations. As Hindi has less unique words it needs to repeat many of them for representing certain meanings and this is evident from the higher average word frequency of 19. Marathi has comparatively less word frequency as it doesn't need to do the same. The average word length for Marathi is higher and it shows that significant number of Marathi words carry more information than their Hindi counterparts. The length difference also demonstrates that the compound words are significantly high in Marathi and thus statistically affirms the morphological richness of Marathi compared to Hindi.

In Marathi there are words like 'हरिद्वारमध्येही' (*haridwarmadhyehi* – also in Haridwar) and 'पोहोचण्याकरिता' (*pohachanyakarita* – to reach) which when translated to Hindi will become 'हरिद्वार में भी' (*haridwar men bhi*) and 'पहुंचने के लिए' (*pahunchane ke liye*) respectively. Here the word 'हरिद्वारमध्येही' (*haridwarmadhyehi*) is formed by compounding a proper noun 'हरिद्वार' (*haridwar*), preposition 'मध्ये' (*madhye* - in) and an adverbial 'ही' (*hi* - also) and 'पोहोचण्याकरिता' (*pohachanyakarita*) is formed by compounding 'पोहोचण्या' (*pohachanya* - derived verb form of 'reach') and 'करिता' (*karita* - 'TO' infinitive equivalent in Marathi). Marathi follows different rules for derivation of such words by stacking together different surface forms and suffixes. In the process (called as *Sandhi*), it may modify the form of surface word.

As an example we can see word 'उपाहारगृहाप्रमाणे' (*upahargruhapramane*) is formed by combining 'उपाहारगृह' (*upahargruh* - restaurant) and 'प्रमाणे' (*pramane* – as per); but while combining these two words, ' ाा' (*aa*) letter is attached to 'उपाहारगृह' (*upahargruh*) as suffix to derive a new base form 'उपाहारगृहा'

	Average Sentence Length	Word Count	Unique Word Count	Average Word Frequency	Average Word Length
Hindi	17	834417	43342	19	6
Marathi	12	602500	87816	6	8

Table 1. Analysis of Marathi-Hindi Parallel Corpus (48000 Sentences)

Marathi Word	Hindi Translation	English Translation
उपाहारगृहाप्रमाणे (*upahargruhapramane*)	भोजनालय के अनुसार (*bhojanalay ke anusar*)	As per the restaurant
रेल्वेमार्गावर (*relwemargavar*)	रेल मार्ग पर (*rel marg par*)	On the railway route
परिवर्तनाशिवाय (*pariwartanashivay*)	परिवर्तन के सिवाय (*pariwartan ke siway*)	Without changes
त्यावेळेपर्यंत (*tyaveleparyant*)	उस समय तक (*us samay tak*)	By that time
घरापासून (*gharapasun*)	घर से (*ghar se*)	From home

Table 2. Marathi to Hindi Translation Examples

Common Words in Hindi and Marathi - CW	CW as % of Hindi Unique words	CW as % of Marathi Unique words
16693	38.51	19.00

Table 3. Marathi-Hindi Parallel Corpus Similarity Analysis

	Number of Bi-lingual Sentences	Number of Hindi Words	Number of Marathi Words
Training(TM)	49000	854995	644878
Training(LM)	72394	1475217	-
Testing	1000	17660	13372

Table 4. Corpus Distribution, TM-Translation Model, LM- Language Model

```
BEGIN
  INITIALISE suffixSet
  INITIALISE splits = {candidateWord, "NULL"}
  FOR suffix IN suffixSet:
    IF candidateWord ENDSWITH suffix AND candidateWord.LENGTH > suffix.LENGTH
    splits[0] = candidateWord.SUBSTRING(0, candidateWord.LASTINDEXOF(suffix))
    splits[1] = suffix
    RETURN splits
END
```

Figure 1. Splitting Algorithm

(*upahargruha*) and then word 'प्रमाणे' (*pramane*) is suffixed. More examples demonstrating this phenomenon have been provided in Table 2. We can observe that a single word in Marathi is translated to multiple words in Hindi and English and that's due to the morphological richness of Marathi compared to Hindi and English.

Another analysis presented in Table 3 shows that Marathi and Hindi have around 16693 words in common which are 38.51% of Hindi and 19.00% of Marathi vocabulary extracted from the corpus. Some of these words are common nouns like 'सचिव' (*sachiv*) and 'चित्र' (*chitra*), proper nouns like 'आकाश' (*akash*), 'नागापट्टिनम' (*nagapattinam*) and a few words from other languages transliterated in Devanagari script like 'इन्सुलिन' (insulin) and 'टेक्नोलॉजी' (technology). Many of these common words have their origin in Sanskrit and are used as it is or on derivation. We also need to notice that the foreign language words transliterated into Devanagari are part of this common words set as both the languages use Devanagari for representation.

3 Experimental Setup

In the following subsections we describe training corpus and SMT system setup for the experiments.

3.1 Corpus for SMT Training and Testing

A prime need for any SMT system is good quality bi-lingual corpus. We have used manually translated bi-lingual corpus of size 49000 sentences for training the translation model. The 49000 bi-lingual corpus of Health and Tourism domains contained 854995 Hindi words and 644878 Marathi words. Language model training was done using monolingual Hindi corpus of size 72394 sentences. A set of 1000 unseen sentences has been used for testing the systems. The test set contained 500 sentences from Health and Tourism each. Table 4 summarizes the Training and Testing data.

3.2 Splitting Marathi Words

To tackle the described morphological complexity of Marathi for the purpose of better SMT system we have devised an algorithm to split inflected and compound Marathi words. The splitting algorithm uses a list of suffix and commonly compounded words as suffixes, combinedly referred as suffix list hereafter. The list is created from the available bi-lingual and monolingual corpus.

3.2.1   Creating Suffix List

To develop the Marathi Splitter we trained an alignment (GIZA++; Och and Ney, 2003) model to get the Marathi-Hindi phrase alignments. Upon training we extracted Marathi words which align to multiple Hindi words from the alignment table. The extracted Marathi word set was then manually analyzed to develop a list of valid compound words. From the list of valid compound words, we further extracted high frequency suffixes. On manual analysis of these suffixes a valid list of suffixes for splitting (list 1) was developed. We also analyzed the Marathi corpus and extracted words with length more than 10 (as the average word length for Marathi is 8). These extracted words were then manually analyzed to get a comprehensive list of compound suffixes (list 2). The final set of 129 suffixes was a combination of list 1 and list 2.

3.2.2   Splitter Algorithm

The algorithm splits a given Marathi word if it contains a suffix from the list created. Figure 1 shows pseudo-code for Marathi Splitter. The algorithm will split Marathi word 'उपाहारगृहासारखी' (*upahargruhasarkhi* — like

restaurant) into 'उपाहारगृह' (*upahargruha* — restaurant) and 'ासारखी' (*aasarkhi*) which are valid and invalid dictionary words respectively. In case of 'ासारखी' (*aasarkhi*), 'ा' (*aa*) is a *Sandhi* marker and 'सारखी' (*sarkhi*) means 'like' in English. Word 'प्रसारमाध्यमकेंद्र' (*prasarmadhyamkendra* — media center) on splitting will give 'प्रसारमाध्यम' (*prasarmadhyam* - media) and 'केंद्र' (*kendra* – center) which are valid dictionary words. Though most of the splits give at least one valid dictionary word, there are cases where it fails to do so. Like in case of 'घेण्याचा' (*ghenyacha* – to take), the splits will be 'घेण्य' (*ghenya*) and 'ाचा' (*aacha*), where both are invalid dictionary words.

3.3 SMT System Setup

The baseline system was setup by using the phrase-based model (Och and Ney, 2003; Brown et al., 1990; Marcu and Wong, 2002; Koehn et al., 2003) and Koehn et al. (2007) was used for factored model. The language model (5-gram) was trained using KenLM (Heafield, 2011) toolkit with modified Kneser-Ney smoothing (Chen and Goodman, 1998). For factored SMT training source and target side stem has been used as alignment factor. Stemming has been done using Ramanathan and Rao (2003) lighweight stemmer for Hindi. The stemmer for Marathi has been developed by modifying Ramanathan and Rao (2003).

3.4 Evaluation Metrics

The different experimental systems have been evaluated using, BLEU (Papineni et al., 2002), NIST (Doddington, 2002), position-independent word error rate (Tillmann et al., 1997), word error rate (Nießen et al., 2000) and manual evaluations. For a MT system to be better, higher BLEU and NIST scores with lower position-independent word error rate (PER) and word error rate (WER) are desired.

4   Experiments and Results

In the following subsections we discuss different SMT systems and their performance. We also study the impact of splitting on output of SMT systems. Further we discuss methodologies to improve splitting and hence the translation quality.

4.1 Impact of Splitting

For training the translation model we used 49K bi-lingual corpus and language model was developed using 72.394K Hindi sentences. We used splitting discussed in section 3.2.2, as a pre-processing step for training phrase-based and factored SMT systems, MH3 and MH4 respectively. The systems are described in Table 5.

Results for the systems described in Table 5 are detailed in Table 6. Impact of splitting can be observed by comparing MH1 and MH3. We also notice that factored systems, MH2 and MH4 are performing better than phrase-based systems, MH1 and MH3 respectively. The significant improvements in all evaluation metrics demonstrate that splitting of Marathi words is helping to achieve better translation quality.

	MH1	MH2	MH3	MH4
BLEU	38.35	38.55	41.71	**42.01**
NIST	7.756	7.778	7.982	**8.023**
PER	42.08	42.15	39.58	**39.28**
WER	35.82	35.61	32.21	**31.91**

Table 6. Experiment Results (in %)

Upon analysis of the translations by MH4, we noticed that some of the words were getting wrongly translated. For example 'वरात' (*varat* – A marriage function) which should not have been split, was split into 'वर' (*var*) and ' ात' (*aat*) resulting into incorrect translation as 'पर हैं' (*par hai* – over/at). How to tackle such errors? Can we use length constraints to prohibit such words from splitting? Can POS (NNP) constrain help? These questions lead us to investigate further. We experimented various combinations of length and POS constraints which are described in following section.

4.2 Constrained Splitting

We use splitting discussed in section 3.2.2, as a pre-processing step for training various phrase-based and factored SMT systems. However, we apply constraints over word length and POS tag before splitting. The systems with different constraints are described in Table 7. For MH5, MH7, MH8 and MH9, words with character length at least five were considered for splitting. This particular length constraint was selected as it gave maximum BLEU score, on experimenting with different lengths ranging from 4 to 8. For MH5 and MH6 pre-processing was performed only once. To tackle words like 'आजारापासूनसुद्धा' (*aajaranpasunsuddha*), formed by compounding N multiple words, they need to be split N-1 times. We have tried to handle these cases in MH7, MH8 and MH9 by two level and multi-level splitting as detailed in Table 7. In MH7 a word was subjected to pre-processing twice, whereas in case of MH8 and MH9, the same was done as long as the word satisfies length criterion. Further, with the aim to prohibit splitting of named entities like 'परमेश्वर' (*parmeshwar*), 'पेशावर ' (*peshawar*) and 'खरात ' (*kharat*), we tried applying NNP POS tag constraint in MH6.

System	Description
MH1	Phrase-Based SMT System (Baseline)
MH2	Factored SMT System
MH3	Phrase-Based SMT System with Splitting (all words considered as candidates for splitting)
MH4	Factored MH3 (stem as alignment factor on source and target side)

Table 5. System Description

System	SMT Model	Splitting Candidate Criteria for A Word	Splitting Level
MH5	Phrase-Based	A word with character length >= 5	One
MH6	Phrase-Based	All words except proper nouns (NNP)	One
MH7	Phrase-Based	A word with character length >= 5	Two
MH8	Phrase-Based	A word with character length >= 5	Multi
MH9	Factored	A word with character length >= 5	Multi

Table 7. System Description

	MH3	MH4	MH5	MH6	MH7	MH8	MH9
BLEU	41.71	42.01	41.70	41.24	41.94	41.93	**42.06**
NIST	7.982	8.023	7.987	7.953	8.025	8.023	**8.029**
PER	39.58	39.28	39.53	39.83	39.25	39.20	39.26
WER	32.21	31.91	32.19	32.63	32.07	32.04	31.88

Table 8. Evaluation (in %)

Criteria	% Accuracy	Grade Scale
Syntactically well-formed / semantically high acceptance	80% and above	4 point grade scale
Syntactically well-formed / semantically low acceptance	60% - 79%	3 point grade scale
Syntactically well-formed / semantically unacceptable	40% - 59%	2 point grade scale
Syntactically ill-formed / semantically unacceptable	below 40%	1 point grade scale
No output / garbage output	-	0 point grade scale

Table 9. Grading Scheme

Table 8 details the results obtained on different evaluation metrics for the experimental systems. We can see that among all, the highest BLEU and NIST scores are achieved by MH9 which is factored SMT system and makes use of length constrained multi-level splitting. There is not much difference in BLEU for MH3 and MH5. But MH7 and MH8 show significant improvement in BLEU over MH3. BLEU for MH6 is slightly decreased, as many words like 'राजस्थानात' (*rajasthanat* – in Rajasthan) which are candidates for splitting are not getting split because of their NNP POS tag. Use of a Marathi NER may be experimented to tackle this issue in future. In next section, we have further analyzed and compared manual evaluation and 10-fold cross validation for some of these systems to better understand the performance difference.

5 Analysis and Discussion

We discuss here, manual evaluation, 10-fold cross validation and error analysis followed by comparative study with the existing work. MH1, MH3, MH5, MH8 and MH9 only have been considered for manual evaluation, as comparison of these systems is sufficient to understand the contribution of splitting to translation quality.

5.1 Manual Evaluation

Figure 2 shows manual evaluation of systems (MH1, MH3, MH5, MH8 and MH9) for 50 random sentences from the test set. For the evaluation, sentences were translated using systems under study and graded as per the scheme detailed in Table 9.

Figure 2 shows that among the systems compared, MH9 has highest number of sentences with accuracy more than 80%. We can also see that use of constraints on splitting in MH5 has helped reduce the number of sentences in grade 2 as compared to MH3. That shows, semantic acceptance of translations is increasing with the use of constrained splitting.

Table 11 describes with the help of an example, improvement in the quality of translation upon use of splitting. In the input sentence, words 'वलसाडच्या' (*valsadchya* – of Valsad) and 'किनाऱ्यावर' (*kinaryavar* – on the bank) are candidates for splitting. These words are split into 'वलसाड' (*valsad*) + 'च्या' (*chya*) and 'किनाऱ्या' (*kinarya*) + 'वर' (*var*), respectively. We can see that the MH1 is unable to translate the word 'वलसाडच्या' (*valsadchya*), whereas MH9 has correctly translated it into 'वलसाड के' (*valsad ke* – of Valsad) as expected in the reference translation.

5.2 10-Fold Cross Validation

To correctly compare the performance of the systems, we also did 10-fold cross validation. Results for the same are available in Table 10. We can see that significant BLEU increment in all folds of MH5 which makes use of splitting, is consistent in comparison to MH1. Also we can infer that multi-level (MH8) splitting is slightly better than two-level (MH7) and one-level (MH5) splitting.

5.3 Error Analysis

In the following subsections we analyze different errors in splitting.

5.3.1 Superfluous Splitting

With the splitting, Marathi word 'दिलावर' (*dilawar*) is getting split into 'दिला' (*dila*) + 'वर' (*war*) which is a wrong split. 'दिलावर' (*dilawar*) is a proper noun and hence should not have been split. We tried to overcome this error using NNP POS tag constraint, but that was stopping many other valid candidates from splitting. Many words like 'राजस्थानात' (*rajasthanat* – in Rajasthan) have NNP as POS tag and still are valid candidates for splitting; applying NNP POS constraint prohibits them from being split, which doesn't help in reducing sparsity in training.

5.3.2 Bad Split

Word like 'जर्मनीतील' (*jarmanitil*) is getting split into 'जर्मनीत' (*jarmanit*) + ' ‌ील ' (*il*) which actually should have been split into 'जर्मनी' (*jarmani*) + 'तील' (*til*). Similarly many words on splitting aren't giving any valid word which also doesn't help in reducing sparsity in training.

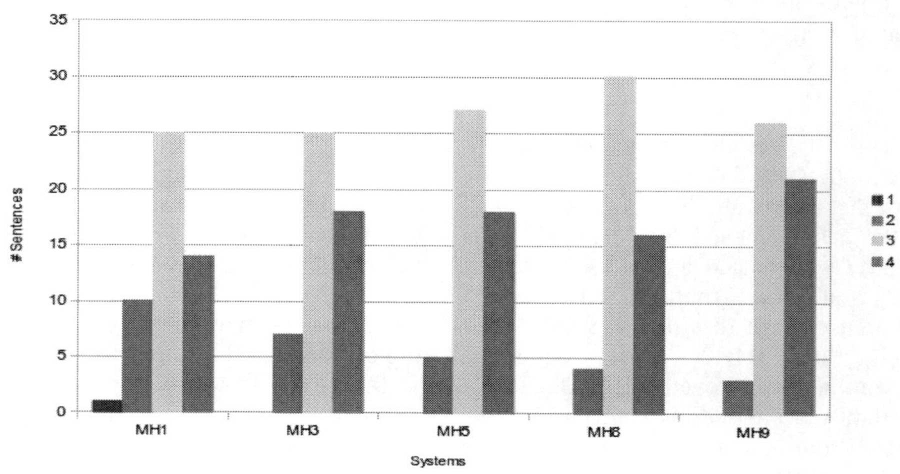

Figure 2. Manual Evaluation

	#1	#2	#3	#4	#5	#6	#7	#8	#9	#10	Avg
MH1	36.74	36.43	36.56	36.50	34.60	36.45	36.04	35.44	38.02	35.97	**36.26**
MH5	40.61	40.47	40.84	41.19	39.17	40.97	40.19	39.77	42.06	40.74	**40.60**
MH7	40.50	40.48	40.59	41.29	39.18	41.07	40.50	39.90	42.21	40.80	**40.65**
MH8	40.62	40.88	40.86	41.25	39.40	41.35	40.69	40.26	42.69	41.15	**40.90**

Table 10. 10-fold Cross Validation

Input	वलसाडच्या समुद्र किनार्‍यावर तिथल आणि उभराट अशी सुंदर नगरे आहेत. *valsadchya samudra kinaryavar tithal ani ubhrat ashi sundar nagare aahet.*
Split Input	वलसाड च्या समुद्र किनार्‍या वर तिथल आणि उभराट अशी सुंदर नगरे आहेत. *Valsad chya samudra kinarya var tithal ani ubhrat ashi sundar nagare aahet.*
MH1	वलसाडच्या समुद्र तट पर तिथल और उभराट ऐसे सुंदर नगर हैं । *valasadchya samudra tat par tithal aur ubharat aise sundar nagar hain.*
MH9	वलसाड के समुद्र तट पर तिथल और उभराट ऐसे सुंदर नगर हैं । *valasad ke samudra tat par tithal aur ubharat aise sundar nagar hain.*
Reference	वलसाड के समुद्र किनारे तिथल और उभराट जैसे सुंदर नगर हैं । *valasad ke samudra kinare par tithal aur ubharat jaise sundar nagar hain.*

Table 11. Comparison of Translation Systems

5.4 Comparative study with Similar Work

Not much work has been done for Marathi to Hindi Machine Translation and we compare our work with the existing systems in our knowledge. We found that the proposed system outperforms all the existing systems (Kunchukuttan et al., 2014; Shreelekha et al., 2013 and Bhosale et al., 2011). Table 13 details scores for the systems to be compared. To compare the manual evaluation we have used formula given in Figure 3 (Bhosale et al., 2011).

$$Accuracy = (1*N4 + 0.8*N3 + 0.6*N2)/N$$

N4: Number of score 4 sentences
N3: Number of score3 sentences
N2: Number of score 2 sentences
N: Total Number of sentences

Figure 3. Formula for Calculating Manual Accuracy

	BLEU	Accuracy
Bhosale et al., 2011	-	63.45%
Shreelekha et al., 2003	9.31	69.60%
Kunchukuttan et al., 2014	41.66	-
MH9	42.06	87.20%

Table 13. Comparison with Existing Work

6   Conclusion and Future Work

In this paper, we presented a factored Marathi to Hindi SMT system, which makes use of source side splitting and shows significantly higher accuracy than the baseline. More work remains to be done next to further take advantage of splitting by using sophisticated methodologies for the same. For example, suffix list can be enriched to include more suffixes, complex constraints can be applied to reduce negative impact of splitting, source language dictionary can be used to guide splitting and *sandhi* correction can also be exploited to generate valid words out of splitting. The same approach can be applied to other language pairs with similarities to Marathi and Hindi. SMT for Dravidian languages to Hindi is planned to be considered next.

Acknowledgments

We would like to thank the Technology Development for Indian Languages (TDIL) program and the Department of Electronics & Information Technology, Govt. of India for providing the ILCI corpus.

References

Bhosale, G., Kembhavi, S., Amberkar, A., Mhatre, S., Popale, L., & Bhattacharyya, P. (2011). Processing of Kridanta (Participle) in Marathi. In *Proceedings of ICON-2011: 9th International Conference on Natural Language Processing*. Macmillan Publishers, December 2011.

Brown, P. F., Cocke, J., Pietra, S. A. D., Pietra, V. J. D., Jelinek, F., Lafferty, J. D., Mercer R. L. & Roossin, P. S. (1990). A statistical approach to machine translation. *Computational linguistics, 16*(2), 79-85.

Chen, S. F., & Goodman, J. (1996, June). An empirical study of smoothing techniques for language modeling. In *Proceedings of the 34th annual meeting on Association for Computational Linguistics* (pp. 310-318). Association for Computational Linguistics.

Dabre, R., Amberkar, A., & Bhattacharyya, P. (2012). Morphological Analyzer for Affix Stacking Languages: A Case Study of Marathi. In *COLING (Posters)* (pp. 225-234).

Doddington, G. (2002, March). Automatic evaluation of machine translation quality using n-gram co-occurrence statistics. In *Proceedings of the second international conference on Human Language Technology Research* (pp. 138-145). Morgan Kaufmann Publishers Inc.

Franz Josef Och. 2003. Minimum error rate training in statistical machine translation. In *Proceedings of the 41st Annual Meeting on Association for Computational Linguistics-Volume* 1:pp. 160- 167.

Heafield, K. (2011, July). KenLM: Faster and smaller language model queries. In *Proceedings of the Sixth Workshop on Statistical Machine Translation* (pp. 187-197). Association for Computational Linguistics.

Junghare, I. Y. (2009). Syntactic Convergence: Marathi and Dravidian. *Bulletin of the Transilvania University of Braşov• Vol, 2*, 51.

Koehn, P., & Knight, K. (2003, April). Empirical methods for compound splitting. In *Proceedings of the tenth conference on European chapter of the Association for Computational Linguistics-Volume 1* (pp. 187-193). Association for Computational Linguistics.

Koehn, P., Och, F. J., & Marcu, D. (2003, May). Statistical phrase-based translation. In *Proceedings of the 2003 Conference of the North American Chapter of the Association for Computational Linguistics on Human Language Technology-Volume 1* (pp. 48-54). Association for Computational Linguistics.

Koehn, P., & Hoang, H. (2007, June). Factored Translation Models. In *EMNLP-CoNLL* (pp. 868-876).

Kunchukuttan, A., Mishra, A., Chatterjee, R., Shah, R., & Bhattacharyya, P. (2014). Sata-Anuvadak: Tackling Multiway Translation of Indian Languages. *Pan, 841*(54,570), 4-135.

Marcu, D., & Wong, W. (2002, July). A phrase-based, joint probability model for statistical machine translation. In *Proceedings of the ACL-02 conference on Empirical methods in natural language processing-Volume 10* (pp. 133-139). Association for Computational Linguistics.

Nießen, S., Och, F. J., Leusch, G., & Ney, H. (2000, May). An Evaluation Tool for Machine Translation: Fast Evaluation for MT Research. In *LREC*.

Och, F. J., & Ney, H. (2003). A systematic comparison of various statistical alignment models. *Computational linguistics, 29*(1), 19-51.

Papineni, K., Roukos, S., Ward, T., & Zhu, W. J. (2002, July). BLEU: a method for automatic evaluation of machine translation. In *Proceedings of the 40th annual meeting on association for computational linguistics* (pp. 311-318). Association for Computational Linguistics.

Popovic, M., & Ney, H. (2004, May). Towards the Use of Word Stems and Suffixes for Statistical Machine Translation. In *LREC*.

Popović, M., Stein, D., & Ney, H. (2006). Statistical machine translation of German compound words. In *Advances in Natural Language Processing* (pp. 616-624). Springer Berlin Heidelberg.

Ramanathan, A., & Rao, D. D. (2003, April). A lightweight stemmer for Hindi. In *the Proceedings of EACL*.

Sreelekha, S. , Dabre, R., & Bhattacharyya, P. Comparison of SMT and RBMT, The Requirement of Hybridization for Marathi–Hindi MT.

Tillmann, C., Vogel, S., Ney, H., Zubiaga, A., & Sawaf, H. (1997, September). Accelerated DP based search for statistical translation. In *Eurospeech*.

Tackling Close Cousins: Experiences In Developing Statistical Machine Translation Systems For Marathi And Hindi

Raj Dabre
CFILT
IIT Bombay
prajdabre
@gmail.com

Jyotesh Choudhari
CFILT
IIT Bombay
jyoteshrc
@gmail.com

Pushpak Bhattacharyya
CFILT
IIT Bombay
pushpakbh
@gmail.com

Abstract

In this paper we present our experiences in building Statistical Machine Translation (SMT) systems for the Indian Language pair Marathi and Hindi, which are close cousins. We briefly point out the similarities and differences between the two languages, stressing on the phenomenon of Krudantas (Verb Groups) translation, which is something Rule based systems are not able to do well. Marathi, being a language with agglutinative suffixes, poses a challenge due to lack of coverage of all word forms in the corpus; to remedy which, we explored Factored SMT, that incorporate linguistic analyses in a variety of ways. We evaluate our systems and through error analyses, show that even with small size corpora we can get substantial improvement of approximately 10-15% in translation quality, over the baseline, just by incorporating morphological analysis. We also indirectly evaluate our SMT systems by analysing and reporting the improvement in the quality of translations of a Marathi to Hindi Rule Based system (Sampark) by injecting SMT translations of Krudantas. We believe that our work will help researchers working with limited corpora on similar morphologically rich language pairs and relatable phenomena to develop quality MT systems.

1 Introduction

Marathi 1 and Hindi 2 are Indian languages ranking fourth and first 3 with respect to the number of speakers. Marathi has close to 72 million speakers whereas Hindi has close to 400 million speakers. Both Marathi and Hindi belong to the family of 'Indo-European languages' i.e. both have originated from Sanskrit and thus have some phonological, morphological and syntactic features in common.

1.1 Comparison of Marathi and Hindi

Marathi uses agglutinative, inflectional and analytic forms. It displays abundant amount of both derivational (wherein attachment of suffixes to a word form changes its grammatical category) and inflectional morphology. Hindi shares these properties of Marathi except that it is not agglutinative in nature. Both languages follow the S-O-V word order. Both languages have dative verbs. In both languages, when the agent in the sentence is in nominative case, the verb agrees with it in person, number and gender; however, when it is not in nominative case, the verb does not agree with it. These languages differ most in the participial and reported speech constructions.

1.2 Agglutination, Participials and Reported Speech constructions

The major factor in translating from Marathi (Mr) to Hindi (Hi) is handling the transfer of agglutinative morphemes. In the reverse case it is the generation of appropriate agglutinative morphological forms. Consider the translation of the Marathi word "माझ्याबरोबरच्यानेही" {majhya-barobar-chya-ne-hii} {the one with me also (nominative)} which is "मेरे साथ वाले ने भी", a whole phrase in Hindi. Marathi suffixes become Hindi post positions. Typically, in languages that have agglutinative suffixes there are millions to billions of possible surface forms and when all surface forms are not present in the parallel corpora, translation suffers from data sparsity. Also,

---

[1] http://en.wikipedia.org/wiki/Marathi_language
[2] http://en.wikipedia.org/wiki/Hindi
[3] http://en.wikipedia.org/wiki/Eighth_Schedule_to_the_Constitution

D S Sharma, R Sangal and J D Pawar. Proc. of the 11th Intl. Conference on Natural Language Processing, pages 11–19,
Goa, India. December 2014. ©2014 NLP Association of India (NLPAI)

the translation of morphemes does not merely involve independent dictionary substitution but require looking at neighboring morphemes.

An important aspect of our work involved handling of participial forms known as Krudantas and Akhyatas (Bhosale et al, 2011; Bapat et al. 2010) which are derivatives of verbs. Consider: "मी धावल्यानंतर असलेला व्यायाम करत आहे" {mi dhava-lya-nantar asa-le-la vyayam ka-ra-ta aahe} {I am doing the exercises that come after running} in which "धावल्यानंतर" and "असलेला" (both nominal forms and are 2 consecutive Krudantas) and "करत आहे" (Verb group indicating tense, aspect and mood of action) are participial constructions. The last auxiliary verb in the verb group, "आहे" dictates the tense of the sentence; present in this case.

Consider the translation of "धावल्याने" {dhava-lya-ne} {by running (nominative)}, a Krudanta in nominal form, which in Hindi is "भागने से" {bhaagne se} or "भागने की वजह से" {bhaagne ki wajah se}. When the suffixes are to be translated, "ल्या" {lya} is translated as {ने} {ne} and "ने" {ne} is translated as से {se}. Note that "ने" {ne} is also used as a nominative case marker and will be translated as "ने" {ne} in the case of the Krudanta "धावणाऱ्याने" {dhava-narya-ne} {the runner (nominative)} which in Hindi is दौड़ने वाले ने {daudne wale ne}. "ल्या" {lya} also has an alternate translation as "हुए" {hue} {became (dead for e.g.)} in the case of "मेलेल्याला" {melelyala} {the dead person (accusative)} which in Hindi is: "मरे हुए को" {mare hue ko}. This is sufficient to indicate that translating a verb group by using rules and bilingual dictionaries is a difficult and an involved process.

A construction of reported speech contains two sentences a sentential complement and a matrix sentence. Hindi, typically, positions the sentential complement (underlined) after the matrix sentence but Marathi can place this either before or after. The sentence "He says that he comes home at 8" is written in Hindi as: "वह कहता है की <u>वह आठ बजे घर आता है</u>" {vaha kahta hai ki vaha aath baje ghar aata hai} but in Marathi as "<u>तो घरी आठ वाजता येतो</u> असे तो म्हणतो" {to ghari aath vaj-ta ye-to ase to mhana-to} or "तो म्हणतो की <u>तो आठ वाजता घरी येतो</u>" {to mhana-to ki to aath vaj-ta ghari ye-to}. Due to Krudantas a Marathi sentence can have many possible Hindi equivalents.

All these examples serve to indicate that translation between Marathi and Hindi, inspite of their closeness, is quite challenging. Due to space constraints we do not elaborate further but those interested may look at the books of M.K. Damle (1970) and Dhongde et al. (2009). We now describe the various experiments conducted and SMT systems developed.

1.3 Related Work

Nair et al. (2013) developed a basic phrase based SMT system and compared it against a Rule based system, Sampark, for Marathi to Hindi translation. Their work lacked any kind of linguistic processing leading to only simple sentences being translated well. Bapat et al. (2011) had explored the impact of handling Krudanta forms via morphological analysis during translation in Sampark by using rules. We obtained the Sampark system and its source code so that we could convert it into a Hybrid system, by SMT phrase translation injection, to get an indirect evaluation of the quality of our SMT systems. Dabre et al. (2012) had worked on improving coverage and quality for their Marathi morphological analyzer which we exploit in the development of our SMT systems. The remainder of the paper is dedicated to the experiments conducted and evaluation.

2 SMT Systems and Experiments

We first describe the corpora used and then the SMT systems. The evaluation is in the following

Corpora	#Lines	#words
ILCI–Health–Marathi-Hindi	25000	
ILCI–Tourism– Marathi-Hindi	25000	Mr-85681
DIT–Health – Marathi-Hindi	20000	Hi -43102
DIT–Tourism– Marathi-Hindi	20000	
Wiki+News Web- Marathi	1968907	896430
Wiki+News Web-Hindi	1538429	558206

Table 1: Corpora details

section.

2.1 Corpora details

Table 1 below describes the sources and sizes of the corpora which come from 2 major projects namely ILCI (Indian Languages Corpora Initiative) and DIT (Department of Information Technology). We also crawled the web for monolingual corpora which we used for language modelling.

The crawl of Wikipedia (Wiki) by itself provided around 500000-600000 monolingual sentences. There are many Marathi and Hindi news websites amongst which we crawled only the prominent ones for our corpora. It must be noted that the parallel corpus, which is undergoing revisions, was not of high quality and contains duplicate sentence pairs.

2.2 Training and Technical details

In order to perform training we used IBM models (Brown et al., 1993) implementation in GIZA++ for alignment and Moses (Koehn et al., 2007, 2003) for phrase table extraction and decoding. In order to obtain factors for Marathi we used the Morphological analyzer and Part of speech tagger developed under the ILMT (Indian Language Machine Translation) project. For Hindi we used a freely available tool[4] that does Morphological analysis and POS tagging simultaneously. All non-factored systems took around 15-20 minutes of training time whereas inclusion of factors increased the time to around 30-50 minutes.

We tried to tune our systems but often saw that the resulting translations were of poorer quality and thus the evaluations presented later are on our non-tuned systems. All phrase tables were binarized and provided as services using the Moses webserver daemon.

2.3 Marathi-Hindi Systems

Below are details of the development of the various systems for Marathi to Hindi translation. For each system we describe the processing steps, if any, of the corpora and give assumptions and reasons for doing so. We also indicate the pros and cons of performing these steps, most of which will be indicated by examples in the evaluation section. For factored systems we mention factors as <Factor-1 | Factor-2 | ... | Factor-n>, decoding steps as <Source Factor combinations → Target Factor Combinations> and generation

steps as <Target Factors → Target Surface Form>.

2.3.1 Baseline system

We trained a basic phrase based system using the full parallel corpus for training and the Hindi monolingual corpus for language modeling. This did not have substantial coverage of all word forms for Marathi and motivated us to utilize the Marathi morphological analyzer.

2.3.2 Suffix Split system

We performed morphological splitting on the Marathi corpus and replaced the surface word with its root form followed by suffixes with spaces in between. The original source sentence to target sentence length ratio was quite low (Marathi having lesser words per sentence due to agglutination) which was observed to become almost equal to 1 after morphological splitting. Keeping the words in the root form led to the loss of gender (G), number (N) and person (P) in many cases. Also in case of tense determining, auxiliary verb forms of "असणे" {asne} {to be} the root word form loses the tense information. Despite this, the morphological splitting resulted in a massive increase in translation quality (see Evaluation section). Words that were not translated in their agglutinative form get properly translated due to reduction in data sparsity.

2.3.3 Factored system – Suffixes as factors

As an initial experiment into factored models we processed the Marathi side of the corpus to have 4 factors: **<Surface Form | Root Word | Suffixes | POS Tag>**. The agglutinative suffixes for a word were grouped (separated by an underscore) and treated as a single factor. Not all suffix combinations exist in a small corpus and this grouping does not lower data sparsity much. The Hindi side is also processed to have 7 factors: **< Surface Form | Root Word | Gender | Number | Person | POS Tag | Case>**. Here Case means direct or oblique to indicate whether an inflection exists or not.

Initially we tried training a simple model in which our decoding step was: **<Marathi Factors → Hindi Factors>** which is followed by a generation step: **<Hindi Factors → Hindi Surface Word>**. But this ended up being the same as the baseline system. Since both root words and suffixes in Marathi map to words in Hindi we specified 2 additional decoding steps: **<Root Word + POS → Root Word + POS + Gender + Num-**

---

[4] http://sivareddy.in/downloads

ber + **Person** + **Case**> and <**Suffix** → **Root Word** + **POS** + **Gender** + **Number** + **Person** + **Case**>. The previous step we kept as a back-off. We assumed that the aligner would map Marathi root words and suffixes to Hindi root words and postpositions respectively. Since existence of suffixes are indicative of inflection in Marathi. We did not consider GNP and case information as factors. But on investigation of the phrase tables we saw that the phrase pairs recorded were of poor quality. The decoder effectively disregarded the new decoding steps and hence we refrained from pursuing this way of treating suffixes as factors.

2.3.4 Factored system – Suffixes separated from root

We realized that separating the suffixes from the roots was the best approach and thus augmented the Marathi corpus with GNP and case information. We first separated the suffixes from the root words by spaces and then added factors to the root word. The factored representation was <**Root Word** | **Gender** | **Number** | **Person** | **POS Tag** | **Case**>. The split suffixes were represented as <**Suffix** | **Gender** | **Number** | **Person** | **PSP** | **Case**>. The GNP's were copied over from the root word they were attached to and the POS was kept as PSP (postposition). The case was kept as 'd' (direct) if it was the last suffix and 'o' (oblique) otherwise. For verbs that indicated the tense (which don't have many morphological variations) of the sentence we kept them in their surface form. Finally we used our large monolingual corpora to train a generation model which would combine all factors on the Hindi side to generate the surface form.

2.3.5 Hybridized Rule based System (Sampark) – Injecting SMT into an RBMT system

The architecture of Sampark is given in Nair et al. (2013) and Bhosale et al. (2011). It is a transfer based rule based MT system and works in 3 phases: Analysis, Lexical transfer, Generation. The analysis phases generate the morphological analyses which our SMT systems can use. The original lexical transfer algorithm performed lookup in dictionaries to get root word and suffix translations. We modified the lexical transfer algorithm such that the verb groups would be translated by our best SMT system (2.3.2 in this case) by making translation requests to a Moses server daemon via a system call. This helped improve Verb Group translation quality (see Evaluation). The flow of translation is:

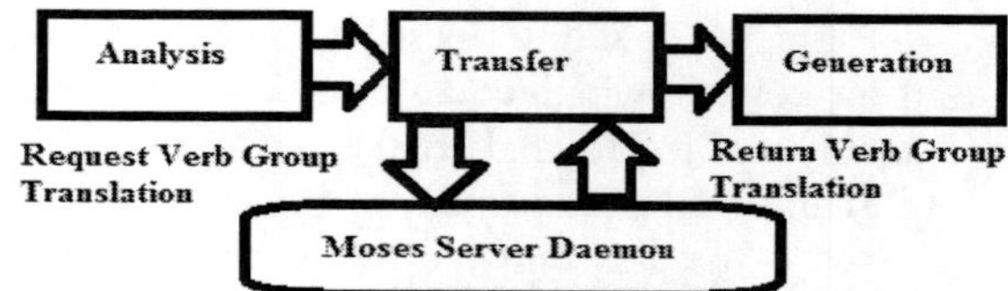

Figure 1: Modified Sampark

2.4 Hindi-Marathi Systems

The translation systems for Hindi to Marathi are given below. The terminology used is the same as before.

2.4.1 Baseline System

As before, we trained a baseline system by using the Marathi monolingual corpus for the language model. An interesting observation was that the quality of translation from Hindi to Marathi was better than the quality of translation in the reverse direction on the same corpus which furthers the belief that translation is not a bidirectional phenomenon.

2.4.2 Factored System

The factored corpus used in section 2.3.3 was reused for training this system. The decoding steps involved: <**Hindi lemma to Marathi Lemma**> and <**Hindi POS Tag** + **Suffix** → **Marathi POS Tag** + **suffix**>. An additional back-off decoding step was: <**Hindi Surface Word** → **Marathi Lemma** + **POS Tag** + **Suffix**>. Thereafter the generation step combines the Marathi factors to the surface form. However the quality of translations was not much better than the baseline system and upon investigation we observed that the decoder effectively used the back-off translation step. Once again we were faced with the same situation as in section 2.3.3. We realized that SMT should only take care of morpheme transfer as in sections 2.3.2 and 2.3.4. This led to the system below.

2.4.3 Marathi Suffix splitting + Generation

We used the processed corpus mentioned in section 2.3.2 with the modification in section 2.3.4, namely, keeping the tense determining verbs in their surface form. It is quite evident that there would be a loss of GNP but our objective at that time was to achieve morphological generation correctly. The resultant phrase based system translates a Hindi sentence into a suffix split Marathi sentence. We then wrote a simple module which would combine the morphemes into a surface form. With this in mind we turned to our Marathi monolingual corpus, morphologically analyzed it and generated a HashMap which contained morphemes and surface forms as key value pairs. One such entry would be: "घर समोर" {ghar samor} → "घरासमोर" {gharaa-samor} {in front of the house}. Since the monolingual corpus was quite large (89.6 k unique words) we assumed that all commonly used morphological forms would be contained in it. The suffix combination method used is:

1. Consider that the morphemes of the translated sentence are in an array **"split_morph"**. Let the hashmap containing morphemes to surface word mapping be called **"morpheme_to_word_map"**
2. For index = 1 to length(**split_morph**):
   a. Check the longest sequence of morphemes from current position which is present as a key in **morpheme_to_word_map**.
   a. Retrieve the surface form for this morpheme sequence.
   b. If no longest sequence can be found from current position then continue from next position.

It will be seen later that this method is quite naïve and quite drastically lowers the quality of translations.

3   Evaluation and Results

3.1   Evaluation methodology

We considered BLEU (Papineni et al.,2002) as the standard evaluation criteria which morphologically rich and free word order languages like Marathi and Hindi are not best evaluated by and hence we also performed Adequacy (meaning transfer) and Fluency (grammatical correctness) analysis as mentioned in Bhosale et al. (2011). A total of 100 sentences were translated and scores were calculated. A number of these were survival sentences. For adequacy (Ad) and fluency (Fl) the sentences were given scores from 1 to 5 (5 for best). Sentences of score 3 and above are considered acceptable. S_i is (#sentences with score i).

$$\text{Adequacy / Fluency} = 100 * (S_5 + 0.8 * S_4 + 0.6 * S_3) / (\text{#Total sentences})$$

This gives the percentage of total sentences that the user understands and has acceptable grammar.

3.2   Results

Table 2 below gives the scores for the various systems. The best results are highlighted. In case of Marathi to Hindi translation the suffix split systems perform the best. For Hindi-Marathi the baseline and factored system do reasonably well. The suffix split + generation system was the worst.

In order to check the improvement of Krudanta (Verb Group) translation by SMT injection into the RBMT system (Sampark) we constructed a set of 52 sentences (some of which were present in the above set of 100 sentences) which contained a variety of Krudanta types. Since Krudantas can have multiple translations (see Section 1.2) BLEU is not reliable and hence we evaluated them using Adequacy and Fluency only (Table 3). It was observed that there was a substantial increment in translation quality of Sampark especially due to high quality Krudanta translations.

System	BLEU	Adequacy	Fluency
Marathi-Hindi (Baseline)	24.46	44.6	55.8
Marathi-Hindi (Suffix split)	**29.68**	**63.2**	**59.4**
Marathi-Hindi (Suffix as factor)	18.42	47.0	47.6
Marathi-Hindi (Suffix split + factored)	**30.35**	**61.8**	**66.0**
Hindi-Marathi (Baseline)	**23.93**	**77.0**	**74.4**
Hindi-Marathi (Factored)	20.06	72.6	72.2
Hindi-Marathi (Suffix split + Marathi generation)	8.4	45.0	37.8

Table 3: Results of Evaluation

System	Adequacy	Fluency
Hindi-Marathi (Sampark)	46.0	40.0
Hindi-Marathi (Hybrid Sampark – SMT injection)	**61.0**	**62.0**

Table 2: Improvement in translation quality by SMT injection

3.3 Example translations and Analysis

Consider the following examples of translations which serve to indicate that the scores above are indeed valid.

3.3.1 Marathi to Hindi (SMT systems only)

- **Input:** राज्यांतील शहरांलगत बेकायदा बांधकामांचा प्रश्न गंभीर होत चालला आहे .

  {rajyan-til shahran-lagat bekayda baandhkaaman-cha prashna gambhir hot challa ahe}

  Meaning: The situation of illegal constructions near the cities in the states is becoming severe.

- **Expected translation:** राज्यों में/के शहरों के पास अवैध/बेकायदा निर्माणों की समस्या गंभीर होती जा रही है ।

  {rajya mein/ke shaharon ke paas avaidh/bekayda nirman ki samasya gambhir hoti jaa rahi hai}

- **Baseline translation:** राज्य में शहरांलगत बेकायदा बांधकामांचा समस्या गंभीर होती जा रही हैं ।

  {rajya mein shaharan-lagat bekayda baandhkaaman-cha samasya gambhir hoti jaa rahi hai}

- **Suffix split translation:** राज्य के शहर से सटे बेकायदा निर्माण की समस्या गंभीर होती जा रही है ।

  {rajya ke shahar se sate bekayda nirman ki samasya gambhir hoti jaa rahi hai}

- **Suffix as factor translation:** शहरांलगत बेकायदा राज्यों के निर्माण का मसला गंभीर होती जा रही हैं ।

  {shaharan-lagat bekayda rajyon ke nirman ka masla gambhir hoti jaa rahi hai}

- **Suffix split + factored translation:** राज्यों के शहरों से बेकायदा निर्माण की समस्या गंभीर होती जा रहा है ।

  {rajyon ke shaharon ke bekayda nirman ki samasya gambhir hoti jaa rahi hai}

- **RBMT system Sampark (Non Hybrid version):** राज्यों के शहरों के पास गैरकानूनी बनावटों की समस्या गंभीर <u>गुजरते गया है</u> ।

  {rajyon ke shaharon ke paas gairkanuni banavaton ki samasya gambhir gujarte gaya hai}

- **RBMT system Sampark (Hybrid version):** राज्यों के शहरों के पास गैरकानूनी बनावटों की समस्या गंभीर <u>होता जा रहा है</u> ।

  {rajyon ke shaharon ke paas gairkanuni banavaton ki samasya gambhir hota jaa raha hai}

Analysis: As expected, the baseline translation is quite bad because words like "शहरांलगत" {adjoining cities} and "बांधकामांचा" {of constructions} are not translated. But the suffix split translation is almost correct except that it does not generate the plural forms "राज्यों" {states}, "शहरों" {cities} and "निर्माणों" {constructions}. This was due to the loss of GNP information due to root forms. Here "राज्यातील" {in/of the state} has 2 translations of its suffix "तील" which can be "में" {in} (generated by baseline) के {of} (generated by suffix split). Also "शहरांलगत" which was translated as "शहर से सटे" (by suffix split system) which means "clinging to the city" is also acceptable but not as natural sounding as "शहरों के पास" {near the cities}. The factored system which had the suffix as a factor, fared rather poorly; as we had anticipated. But the suffix split factored system gave a near about perfect translation except for the plural form "निर्माणों". It only missed a word "सटे" {clinging}. Also one must note that the verb group "होत चालला आहे" {is becoming} is perfectly translated in all cases. In general, however, the suffix split systems gave better translations than others.

Comparing these to the RBMT systems translations, one must note that both the Hybrid and Non-Hybrid versions of Sampark do well in handling GNP inflections since all the morphological information is retained. Moreover it can be seen that the translations of nouns and their suffixes, "शहरांलगत" as "शहरों के पास", are much more natural than those of the SMT systems.

However, the translation of the verb group "होत चालला आहे" is translated as "गुजरते गया है" which is incorrect in the non-hybrid version. This is because sense of "होत" in this sentence is that of "happening" or "becoming", but "गुजरते" is a translation of another sense of that word which is indicative of "passage of time". "होत" whose root word is "होणे" is an extremely polysemous word having more than 10 senses. RBMT systems typically make mistakes in translating the proper sense of the word unless they have very high quality WSD (word sense disambiguation) modules which in the case of Sampark are not that good when disambiguating verbs. The hybrid version gives a near about perfect translation of "होत चालला आहे" as "होता जा रहा है" (masculine inflection) instead of "होती जा रही है" (feminine inflecion). This is because the inflection of the verb group depends on the gender of the word "समस्या". But when performing SMT injection, only the phrase "होत चालला आहे" is translated and without the context "प्रश्न" the SMT system is unable to perform gender agreement thereby affecting the fluency of the translation.

3.3.2 Hindi to Marathi

- **Input:** राज्यों के शहरों के पास बेकायदा निर्माणों की समस्या गंभीर होती जा रही है ।

  {rajyon ke shaharon ke paas bekayda nirmanno ki samasya gambhir hoti jaa rahi hai}

- **Baseline translation:** राज्याच्या शहराला लागून असलेल्या बेकायदा निर्माणों समस्या गंभीर होत चालली आहे.

  {rajya-chya shahara-la laga-un aslelya bekayda nirmanon samasya gambhir hoat chala-li ahe}

- **Factored translation:** राज्यातील शहरांमध्ये जवळ बेकायदा निर्माणों समस्या गंभीर होत चालली आहे.

  {rajya-til shaharan-madhye javal bekayda nirmanon samasya gambhir hoat chala-li ahe}

- **Suffix Split Translation:** राज्य च्या शहर च्या जवळ बेकायदा निर्माणों ची समस्या गंभीर हो त आहे.

  {rajya chya shahar chya javal bekayda nirmanon chi samasya gambhir ho ta ahe}

- **Marathi Generation:** राज्यांच्या शहराच्या जवळ बेकायदा निर्माणों ची समस्या गंभीर होत आहे.

  {rajyan-chya shahara-chya javal bekayda nirmanon chi samasya gambhir hoat ahe}

Analysis: "निर्माणों" {constructions} was not translated by any of the systems. The factored system managed to handle some inflections. In the suffix split translation the Marathi morphemes were translated properly and the required surface forms were generated. The suffix split + generation system dropped the word "चालली" {going} which is acceptable. In this case the baseline translation was better than the others.

3.4 Discussion

It is quite evident that translation from Marathi to Hindi is rather easier than the reverse which involves morphological generation. Although the suffix split + factored Marathi-Hindi system did pretty well on the overall test sentences, it suffered from factor data sparsity (Tamchyna et al. 2013) and missed on generating proper inflected forms. This prevented it from outperforming the non-factored suffix split system by a large margin. More study is needed, on properly utilizing factors, to get high quality translation.

The impact of SMT injection into the RBMT system Sampark is quite interesting from the point of view of translating Krudantas. It is clear that SMT manages to capture the structure of verb group translations along with translating proper senses of the verbs. The lexical transfer algorithm of the non-hybrid Sampark would translate the words in the verb group independently, only relying on the word sense indicated by the WSD module. Since SMT works at the phrasal level the translations are better. Another interesting observation is that short distance agreements are very good for SMT and Sampark. The lack of a dependency parser leads to problems in long distance agreements. At the current moment, the injection is very naïve and further study into performing intelligent injection needs to be done. In general, Sampark translates non-verbal class words better than the SMT systems do.

The case of Hindi-Marathi is the major challenge. The performance of the suffix split + generation method was very disappointing. But upon doing analysis we saw that the Hindi to Marathi morphemes translations were quite correct in many cases. There were some things wrong with our generation methodology. Firstly, on studying the morphemes to surface from mapping table we saw that there were many erroneous entries due to unknown lexicon words incorrectly morphologically analyzed. Secondly, sometimes suffix morphemes and root word morphemes are similar and get incorrectly joined to other words. This along with our decision to do longest morpheme sequence matching resulted in incorrect (over) generation.

"क्यों जा रहा हैं?" {kyo jaa raha hai} {why are you going} is translated as "काजा त आहे?" instead of "का जात आहे?" {kaa jaa-ta ahe}. The morpheme translation is "का जा त आहे?" which is correct. Here "काजा" is a village in India, not in the morph lexicon and incorrectly split as "का जा" and recorded in the mapping table leading to poor translation. The naïve algorithm resembles the morpheme concatenation method in Durgar et al. (2006). A proper morphological generator needs to be used.

4   Conclusion and Future work

We have presented our work and experiences in developing SMT systems for Marathi and Hindi. We have described the corpora used and the details of training the systems in necessary detail. We also have evaluated the systems and given analyses of sample translations. The Marathi to Hindi translation by SMT is more or less at a high quality owing to suffix splitting of Marathi whose morphemes map to appropriate words/post positions in Hindi. Further study into proper utilization of factors will be undertaken to improve quality. The improvement of the translation quality of the RBMT system, Sampark, by performing SMT injection of Krudanta translations is another testimony to the qualitative performance of the SMT systems. The reverse translation direction is rather difficult due to morphological generation for Marathi. Our current method is quite weak and relying on lookup is clearly not good. Currently we are working on developing a good morphological generator by reverse engineering the analyzer of Dabre et al. (2012). Their morphology grammar rules will be used. Indian Languages are all close cousins and Dravidian languages are similar to Marathi in respect to morphology. Our experiences should be applicable in the development of high quality SMT systems for these languages thereby ensuring effective sharing of knowledge written in any Indian language.

Reference

Sreelekha Nair, Raj Dabre, Pushpak Bhattacharyya. 2013. *Comparison of SMT and RBMT: The requirement of Hybridization for Marathi – Hindi MT*. ICON 2013, New Delhi, December, 2013.

Ganesh Bhosale, Subodh Kembhavi, Archana Amberkar, Supriya Mhatre, Lata Popale and Pushpak Bhattacharyya. 2011. *Processing of Participle (Krudanta) in Marathi*. ICON 2011, Chennai, December, 2011.

M.K. Damale. 1970. *Shastriya Marathii Vyaakarana*. Deshmukh and Company, Pune, India.

Dhongde and Wali. 2009. *Marathi*. John Benjamins Publishing Company, Amsterdam, Netherlands.

Peter E Brown, Stephen A. Della Pietra. Vincent J. Della Pietra, and Robert L. Mercer. 1993. *The Mathematics of Statistical Machine Translation: Parameter Estimationn*. Association for Computational Linguistics.

Philipp Koehn, Hieu Hoang, Alexandra Birch, Chris Callison-Burch, Marcello Federico, Nicola Bertoldi, Brooke Cowan, Wade Shen, Christine Moran, Richard Zens, Chris Dyer, Ondrej Bojar, Alexandra Constantin, Evan Herbst. 2007. *Moses: Open Source Toolkit for Statistical Machine Translation*, Annual Meeting of the Association for Computational Linguistics (ACL), demonstration session, Prague, Czech Republic, June 2007.

Raj Dabre, Archana Amberkar and Pushpak Bhattacharyya. 2012. *Morphological Analyzer forAffix Stacking Languages: A Case Study of Marathi*, COLING 2012.

Mugdha Bapat, Harshada Gune and Pushpak Bhattacharyya. 2010. *A Paradigm-Based Finite State Morphological Analyzer for Marathi*. Proceedings of the 1st Workshop on South and Southeast Asian Natural Language Processing (WSSANLP), pages 26–34, the 23rd International Conference on Computational Linguistics (COLING), Beijing, August 2010

Philipp Koehn, Franz Josef Och and Daniel Marcu. 2003. *Statistical phrase-based translation*. Association for Computational Linguistics 2003.

Philipp Koehn and Hieu Hoang. 2007. *Factored translation models*. In Proceedings of the 2007 Joint Conference on Empirical Methods in Natural Language Processing and Computational Natural Language Learning (EMNLP-CoNLL), pages 868-876, Prague, Czech Republic, June 2007. Association for Computational Linguistics.

Kishore Papineni, Salim Roukos, Todd Ward and Wei-Jing Zhu. 2002. *BLEU: a Method for Automatic Evaluation of Machine Translation*, Proceedings of the 40th Annual Meeting of the Association for Computational Linguistics (ACL), Philadelphia, July 2002, pp. 311-318.

İlknur Durgar El-Kahlout and Kemal Oflazer. 2006. Initial explorations in English to Turkish statistical machine translation. In *Proceedings of the Workshop on Statistical Machine Translation* (StatMT '06). Association for Computational Linguistics, Stroudsburg, PA, USA, 7-14.

Aleš Tamchyna and Ondřej Bojar. 2013. No free lunch in factored phrase-based machine translation. In Proceedings *of the 14th international conference on Computational Linguistics and Intelligent Text Processing - Volume 2* (CICLing'13), Alexander Gelbukh (Ed.), Vol. 2. Springer-Verlag, Berlin, Heidelberg, 210-223. DOI=10.1007/978-3-642-37256-8_18

Correlating decoding events with errors in Statistical Machine Translation

Eleftherios Avramidis   **Maja Popović**

German Research Center for Artificial Intelligence (DFKI GmbH)
Language Technology Lab
Alt Moabit 91c, 10559 Berlin
`eleftherios.avramidis@dfki.de`   `maja.popovic@dfki.de`

Abstract

This work investigates situations in the decoding process of Phrase-based SMT that cause particular errors on the output of the translation. A set of translations post-edited by professional translators is used to automatically identify errors based on edit distance. Binary classifiers predicting the sentence-level existence of an error are fitted with Logistic Regression, based on features from the decoding search graph. Models are fitted for 3 common error types and 6 language pairs. The statistically significant coefficients of the logistic function are used to analyze parts of the decoding process that are related to the particular errors.

1 Introduction

Evaluating the output of Machine Translation (MT) has been in the focus since the first developments of the field. There have been several efforts to measure the translation performance, or to identify errors by defining manual and automatic metrics.

Advanced automatic metrics and Quality Estimation methods have introduced machine learning (ML) techniques in order to predict indications about the quality of the produced translations (Lavie and Agarwal, 2007; Stanojevic and Sima'an, 2014). When compared to traditional automatic metrics, ML techniques allow acquiring knowledge about the quality of the translation out of a big amount of features. Such features are typically *black-box* features, generated by automatic analysis over the text of the source or the translations, or less often *glass-box* features, derived from the internal functioning of the translation mechanism.

In this work, we focus on the glass-box features. However, instead of focusing on the performance of a quality assessment mechanism, we look backwards into what happened during the decoding process and led into known errors in the translation output.

2 Problem definition

This work uses ML in order to fit a statistical model, associating properties and events of the decoding process with the existence of particular errors of a phrase-based statistical MT system. Such a model optimizes a function f:

$$Y = f(X) = \beta \circ X \qquad (1)$$

where:

- X is the independent variable, i.e. a feature vector representing properties and events of the decoding process and has been extracted from the decoding search graph

- Y is the dependent variable, i.e a value predicting the existence of errors

- β is a weight vector estimated by ML to minimize the error of the function $\circ$, given samples of X and Y. This vector contains coefficients for each one of the features. Given a well-fit model and a relevant statistical function, these coefficients can indicate the importance of each feature.

Our aim is to use the β coefficients in order to explain several behaviours of the decoding process, relevant to the errors. The exact formulation of the statistical function $\circ$ is given in Section 4.3.

Our intention is to not train the model using as a dependent variable a complex quality metric such as BLEU (Papineni et al., 2002) or WER, since this would increase complexity by capturing many issues in just one number. Instead, we choose a more fine-grained approach, by focusing onto specific type of errors that occur often in machine translation output (Section 4.1).

D S Sharma, R Sangal and J D Pawar. Proc. of the 11th Intl. Conference on Natural Language Processing, pages 20–29,
Goa, India. December 2014. ©2014 NLP Association of India (NLPAI)

3 Related Work

Error detection for MT and Quality Estimation is an important component of post-editing approaches. Our work focuses solely on features derived from the decoding process.

The first experiments on "Confidence Estimation" make use of a small number of Statistical Machine Translation (SMT) features in order to train a supervised model for predicting the quality of the Translation (Blatz et al., 2004). Later work, identified as "Quality Estimation", defines such features as "glass-box" features (Specia et al., 2009). 54 glass-box features are shown to be very informative, when fitted in a regression model, along with other black-box features.

Avramidis (2011) uses decoding features in a sentence-level pairwise classification approach for Hybrid MT in order to select the best translations out of outputs produced by statistical and rule-based systems, whereas a corpus of machine translation outputs with internal meta-data was released at that time (Avramidis et al., 2012). Later works use glass-box features in order to predict numerical indications of translation quality, such as post-editing effort (Rubino et al., 2013; Hildebrand and Vogel, 2013) or post-editing time (Avramidis et al., 2013). Contrary to these works, we only predict specific error types, with the focus on understanding the contribution of the features.

Prediction of specific error types was included in the shared tasks of the 8th and 9th Workshop on Statistical Machine Translation (Bojar et al., 2013; Bojar et al., 2014). Several participants contributed systems that predict error types (Besacier and Lecouteux, 2013; Bicici and Way, 2014; de Souza et al., 2014). In that case, prediction was done on the word level and contrary to our experiments, no glass-box features were used, therefore there was no connection of the ML with the decoding process.

Guzmán and Vogel (2012), in the work that is most related to ours, aim to identify the contribution of the features. Similar to several previously mentioned works, a multivariate linear regression model is trained in order to predict continuous quality values of complex metrics. Although the aim of this work is similar to ours, we work in a more fine-grained way: instead of modelling metrics, we try to explain the contribution of the decoding features on the occurrence of specific error types.

4 Methods

4.1 Error detection

The errors on the target output are used as a training material for the supervised ML algorithm. They are identified as a subset of commonly observed error categories (Vilar et al., 2006). For our purpose we focus on *missing words*, *extra words* and *re-ordering errors*, since our data give sufficient amounts for training a statistical model on these error categories.[1].

In order to detect the errors on the translation output, we follow the automatic method by Popović and Ney (2011), which has shown to correlate well with human error annotation. This method automatically detects errors based on the edit distance of the produced translation against a reference human translation. An example of how errors are detected can be seen in Figure 1.

4.2 Phrase-based SMT search graph

The glass-box features are extracted from the decoding process of a phrase-based SMT system (Koehn et al., 2003) with cube-pruning (Huang and Chiang, 2007). The decoding process performs a search in various dimensions, calculating scores for many phrases and hypothesis expansions. Most scores are difficult to be interpreted as glass-box features in their initial form. The amount of scores calculated per sentence is not fixed, whereas the basic requirement for each feature is to have only one value that is valid on a sentence level, so that it can be used in the sentence error prediction model.

For this purpose, we process the verbose output of the decoder and derive scores, counts and other statistics that can have this sentence-level interpretation. When decoding steps contain a number of scores which is not fixed for every sentence, we extract features out of their statistics, such as the mean and the standard deviation, the minimum/maximum value and their position in the sentence. An example of how some of these features are extracted is illustrated in Table 1. On the upper part of the table, one can see the log-probability and the future cost estimate for each one of the phrases in the sentences. On the lower part we demonstrate some statistics that are derived from the scores and the positions of the words in the upper part.

---

[1]Although previous work defines 5 error types, not all of them could be sufficiently modelled given this amount of data

source:	Überraschenderweise zeigte sich, dass die neuen Räte in Bezug auf diese neuen Begriffe etwas im Dunkeln tappen.
translation:	Surprisingly, showed that the new councils in relation to these new concepts slightly in the dark.
post-editing:	Surprisingly, [miss:it] [lex:seems] that the new [lex:councillors] [miss:are] [reorder: slightly in the dark] in relation to these new concepts.

Figure 1: Example of the results found with the automatic error detection process. One can see missing words, reordering of 4 words and some lexical errors, which are not discussed in this work

Similar practice is applied to extract the entire set of 104 glass-box features, which includes:

Phrase counts and positions: The produced translation consists of sets of phrases that are chosen as the most probable hypothesis. On this hypothesis we count the number of phrases, words, the length of the phrases, the length difference between source and aligned target phrases and also the position of the shortest and the longest phrase in the sentence.

Unknown tokens are words or phrases that are not found in the phrase table. Their count, their ratio and their position in the translated sentence (average position, standard deviation of their positions, position of first and last unknown word) are included as features.

Translation probabilities: *Log probability* (pC) and *future cost estimate* (c) are available for each phrase of the chosen hypothesis. We extract their average, standard deviation and also their minimum and maximum values and their position in the sentence. Additionally, we count phrases whose pC or c is too low or too high. This is done by checking whether their values are out of the standard deviation of all phrases in the sentence.

Time: The decoder reports the time required for the entire translation process, the search, the language model calculation, the generation of hypotheses other than the ones chosen and for collecting translation options. We use these as features, also averaged over the entire translation time.

Decoding graph: These features come from the entire set of alternative phrase hypotheses generated during the search. From the entire set of alternative hypotheses he derive statistics for their log probability, the future estimate (average, standard deviation, count of alternative phrase hypotheses lower and higher than the standard deviation).

4.3 Machine Learning

The existence of an error (binary classification) is modelled with **logistic regression**. It is a widely-used ML method that optimizes a logistic function to predict values Y in the range between zero and one (Cameron, 1998), given a feature set X:

$$Y = \beta \circ X = \frac{1}{1 + e^{-1(a + \beta X)}} \qquad (2)$$

For fitting the model we use the Newton-Raphson algorithm, which minimises iteratively the least-squares error given the training data (Miller, 2002). The regression fitting included *Stepwise Feature Set Selection* (Hosmer, 1989).

In order to assess the contribution of individual predictors in a given model, we examine the significance by calculating a p-value for each of them. This is the probability that the beta coefficient differs from 0.0. The probability is computed based on Wald statistic of each co-efficient, following the χ^2 distribution. The Wald statistic is the ratio of the square of the regression coefficient to the square of the standard error of the coefficient (Menard, 2002; Harrell, 2001).

5 Experiment

5.1 Data and models

For the purpose of our analysis we train one logistic regression model per error category and language pair, practically resulting into 21 models. We include a set of models trained on the data from all the language pairs, in order to model cases that are independent of the languages involved in the translation, or that are not statistically significant in single language pairs, due to data sparsity.

The experiment is based on data from WMT11 (Callison-Burch et al., 2011), augmented with a small amount of data of WMT10 (Callison-Burch et al., 2010) and technical documentation of mechanical engineering equipment, as provided

source: [überraschenderweise] [zeigte sich] [, dass die neuen] [Räte] [in Bezug auf] [diese neuen] [Begriffe] [etwas] [im Dunkeln tappen .]

translation: [surprisingly ,] [showed] [that the new] [councils] [in relation to] [these new] [concepts] [slightly] [in the dark .]

position	phrase	pC	c
[0..0]	surprisingly ,	−0·770335	−2·69341
[1..2]	showed	−1·54184	−2·81277
[3..6]	that the new	−0·563381	−2·65923
[7..7]	councils	−0·386571	−1·98291
[8..11]	in relation to	−1·29663	−2·85591
[12..13]	these new	−0·332607	−2·17422
[14..14]	concepts	−0·540415	−2·01213
[15..15]	slightly	−0·585549	−2·00382
[16..19]	in the dark .	−1·48327	−3·90992
minimum		−1·54184	−3·90992
maximum		−0·332607	−1·98291
average (avg)		−0·83334	−2·56715
standard deviation (std)		0·448	0·5862
no of phrases with score lower than avg-std		3	1
no of phrases with score higher than avg+std		1	0
averaged position of phrase with lowest score		0·11111	0·88889
averaged position of phrase with highest score		0·55556	0·33333

Table 1: Example glass-box feature extraction from the decoding result. Decoding scores such as phrase *log probability* (pC) and *future cost estimate* (c), whose number is not the same for every sentence (upper part of the table), are reduced to a fixed feature vector based on basic statistics (shown on the lower part of the table)

by a translation agency. The amount of sentences originating from each data source per language pair is shown in Table 2. Almost half of these sentences are given to professional translators, with the instructions to perform as few changes as possible in order to correct the translations. The size of the corpus and the number of post-edited (p.e) sentences can be seen in Table 3.

Minimal post-editing is considered to be ideal for automatic error detection. In contrast, reference translations may contain severe alterations to the structure of the sentence, misleading the automatic error detection. Nevertheless, as it can be seen in 3, the amount of sentences for certain error types and language pairs may be too small, leading to a severely sparse set of training data and therefore weak models. Consequently, as it was not technically possible to acquire post-editing on a bigger amount of data, we perform error-detection on a mixture of post-editions and reference translations, in case this increases the

quality of the statistical models. Preliminary experiments confirmed the positive effect, as the precision and recall was increased on most models (even up to 29%) when adding errors detected on reference translations to the ones detected on post-editing. Despite some obvious drawbacks, this move is also motivated by the fact that the original experiments that showed the accuracy of the automatic error detection (Popović, 2011a) were also performed against reference translations.

5.2 Experiment set-up

As a statistical phrase-based system we trained one Moses (Koehn et al., 2007) system per language direction, using Europarl (Koehn, 2005) and News Commentary corpora[2]. Its settings follow the WMT11 baseline, including a compound splitter for German-English and a truecaser for all language pairs. The system was tuned

---

[2]News Commentary was used only for German-English due to lack of alignments for the other languages

	de-en	de-fr	de-es	en-de	fr-de	es-de
wmt10	118	30	33	14	74	0
wmt11	952	952	80	1087	977	101
customer	741	0	430	0	0	830
total	1811	982	543	1101	1051	931

Table 2: Amount of senteces from various sources per language pair

lang	sentences		reordering err.		missing words		extra words	
	total	p.e	total	p.e	total	p.e	total	p.e
de-en	1811	1139	1043	474	1079	570	869	454
en-de	1101	315	891	232	671	151	722	208
de-fr	982	198	819	157	597	80	630	147
fr-de	1051	122	851	88	691	76	621	66
de-es	543	543	288	288	322	322	186	186
es-de	931	931	345	345	333	333	339	339
all	6419	3248	4237	1584	3693	1532	3367	1400

Table 3: The size of the corpus per error category and language pair. p.e. indicates the number of sentences that were minimally post-edited by professional translators

with MERT using the news corpus test set from WMT07 (Callison-Burch et al., 2007). The decoding features are extracted from Moses' verbose output of level 2. Our target language model with an order of 5 is trained with SRILM toolkit (Stolcke, 2002), based on the respective monolingual training material. The Orange toolkit (Demšar et al., 2004) is used for processing and running the Logistic Regression algorithms. The Hjerson tool (Popović, 2011b) was used in order to detect errors on the translation.

6 Results

6.1 Model performance

A necessary step is to check how well each model fits the data, since a well-fit model is required for drawing conclusions. For this purpose we perform cross-fold validation with 10 folds. The precision and recall scores are shown in Table 4. Precision indicates the ratio of the predicted sentences that contain an error, whereas recall indicates the ratio of the sentences that have an error and are successfully predicted.

The model predicting the existence of reordering errors has the highest precision and recall on all individual language pairs and achieves a generally high precision of about 83-87% (apart from Spanish-German). The model of predicting missing words seems most successful on the dataset combining all language pairs. Extraneous words have models with much lower scores, which means that it is more difficult to draw conclusions.

6.2 Analysing coefficients

We proceed to the analysis by considering the β coefficient of the fitted logistic function (function 2) for each feature. Additionally, the confidence p-value indicates the evidence that the respective feature contributes to the prediction of the outcome.

The feature coefficients given by the fitted logistic function vary per error category and language pair. This is understandable, given the fact that the translation systems and the test sentences are quite heterogeneous among language pairs.

Interpretation of the feature coefficients may vary. The most clear indication is the positive or negative sign of each coefficient. Additionally, one has to note that several features result as a mathematical function of other features; thus, when they all occur in the logistic function, explaining the coefficients of a feature should not neglect the existence of the features that are mathematically related to it.

In order to lead to useful conclusions, we show the feature coefficients who seem to have a statistically significant relation to known functionality of the decoding process for several language pairs. Conclusions are detailed per error category, based on Tables 5, 6 and 7 which include the beta co-

	all		de-en		de-fr		de-es		en-de		fr-de		es-de	
	prec	rec	prec	rec	prec	rec	prec	rec	prec	rec	prec	rec	prec	rec
ext	.70	.70	.68	.59	.72	.82	.61	.52	.73	.85	.67	.76	.62	.53
miss	.85	.88	.75	.76	.67	.79	.80	.82	.67	.78	.70	.86	.64	.52
reord	.70	.79	.83	.81	.88	.96	.85	.82	.85	.93	.87	.92	.77	.70

Table 4: Precision (prec) and recall (rec) of the logistic regression model, measure with cross-validation. There is one model per combination of language pair and error category; plus one model trained on data from all language pairs per error category. High precision and recall indicate that the model is well-fit.

efficient and the respective p-value for statistical significance. Coefficients not appearing in specific cells of the table have been eliminated by the stepwise feature set selection. For a few language pairs we also include coefficients with p-values higher than our confidence level, when the same coefficient is statistically significant for some other language pairs.

6.2.1 Reordering errors

The coefficients for the reordering errors are shown in Table 5. First, the sentence-level ratio of unknown words (unk-per-tokens) the standard deviation of the **position of an unknown token** in the translated sentence (unk-pos-std) has a positive effect towards the creation of a reordering error. A high standard deviation means that unknown tokens are scattered in distant places along the sentence; being "unknown" they cannot be captured by the lexical reordering model and it is therefore likely that they cause an erroneous phrase order in the parts of the sentence where they occur. This is confirmed for 3 of our models (Table 5) with p-value p <0.10, including the model trained on all language pairs.

Calculating the **length difference between the source phrases and the aligned target phrases** chosen for the translation output provides a useful feature too. The maximum difference of all source-phrase lengths minus the respective chosen target-phrase lengths (src-tgt-diff-max) has a positive effect into creating a reordering error. This effectively occurs for cases when the decoder chooses to translate a source phrase with a much shorter target phrase. Invertedly, the smallest difference between source and target phrase (src-tgt-diff-min) has a negative effect on creating reordering errors. The two indications are confirmed with a positive statistically significant coefficient for 6 cases in our models.

All of our translation systems into German in-

crease their reordering errors due to a big **length of the longest source phrase** chosen by the decoder (src-phrase-len-max). This may be due to the fact that German language has significantly different word order than the other languages and this results into a common error for SMT systems.

6.2.2 Missing words

For the language pairs indicated in Table 6, there is a positive effect on having missing words by the **standard deviation of the phrase log probability** (pC-std) and the **position of the phrase with the lowest log probability** (pC-min-pos) towards the end of the sentence, confirmed by our logistic regression models for 4 language pairs. Similar are the conclusions for the **future cost estimate** (c-avg) averaged to the number of phrases, and the **number of phrases with low future cost estimate**, i.e. when it is lower than the mean of all phrases minus the standard deviation. These features reflect situations during the decoding when dropping a phrase results to a higher overall probability. This may occur due to the low probability and the high future cost estimate of all the possible translations of the phrase.

In other cases, there may be words missing when the phrase alignments chosen for translating the source sentences are longer, namely when **the average source length** (src-phrase-len-avg) is higher and the **length of the shortest source phrase** (src-phrase-len-min) is lower. A positive impact to having words missing is also given by the **standard deviation of the length difference between respective source and target phrases** (src-tgt-diff-std), i.e. when the length between aligned source and target phrases varies a lot.

6.2.3 Extra words

The coefficients from the models on extra words are not so conclusive, due to their low precision and recall. One can note that the **time for calculating the language model** and the **total time**

	all		de-en		de-fr		de-es		en-de		fr-de		es-de	
	β	p	β	p	β	p	β	p	β	p	β	p	β	p
unk-per-tokens	2.08	.00									5.98	.07	3.03	.19
unk-pos-std	0.19	.00	0.22	.00					0.17	.15	0.25	.09		
pC-var	-1.42	.06	-0.70	.37	-10.66	.00					-9.95	.01		
src-phrase-len-max									-0.50	.04	-0.36	.17	-1.45	.02
src-tgt-diff-min	-0.26	.02					-0.60	.00	-0.50	.06	-0.84	.01		
src-tgt-diff-max	0.27	.02	0.14	.30	0.24	.21			0.83	.01	0.47	.13		

Table 5: Indicative beta coefficients and their respective p-values for the features affecting the existence of reordering errors.

	all		de-en		de-fr		de-es		en-de		fr-de		es-de	
	β	p	β	p	β	p	β	p	β	p	β	p	β	p
pC-min-pos	0.40	.00	0.57	.02			1.06	.03					1.15	.01
pC-std	2.11	.00	1.14	.50	3.82	.13	9.46	.00					7.05	.02
c-avg	0.52	.02	0.66	.08					1.44	.17	2.66	.07	2.14	.00
c-low			.11	.20	.19	.04	0.28	.18						
src-phrase-len-avg	0.70	.00	1.23	.00	1.56	.01							1.74	.01
src-phrase-len-min	-0.48	.08	-0.88	.13	-0.86	.30					-1.10	.09	-0.95	.38
src-tgt-diff-std	0.41	.02	0.87	.04	0.91	.08					1.06	.02	0.57	.16

Table 6: Indicative beta coefficients and their respective p-values for the features related to the error of missing words.

of the translation (time-translation) get increased when extra words occur, for some language pairs. The effect of the **standard deviation of the unknown tokens** (unk-pos-std) is opposite to what it causes to the reordering errors: the closer the unknown tokens are to each other, the more extra words occur.

For some models, including the model built on all language pairs, extra words correlate with the **length of the source sentence** (total-source-words), particularly when translating from English and French into German. Three models also indicate small but highly significant contribution by a feature from the search graph: the count of **alternative hypothesized phrases, whose log probability is lower** than the standard deviation of the log probability in their respective sentence (alt-pC-low).

7 Conclusions and further work

We have provided statistical evidence for how the functioning of the phrase-based SMT decoding process affects the existence of three frequently occurring error types. The existence of the errors in a sentence is modelled over some decoding process features with logistic regression, which resulted into several models with satisfactory precision and recall values.

By grouping the observations by error type, we managed to show important features (representing stages of the decoding process) that are common for several language pairs at the same time. Most of the indications observed are based on statistically significant coefficients.

One observation is that the chosen method is traditionally employed to examine feature contributions in a specific model, which is seldom generalized across different models. Moreover, although the features in the decoding procedure do affect the translation performance, there are concerns that the logistic relationship between decoding features and specific translation errors is very large, so that the statistical relationship is hard to be captured by simple binary classification approaches. Our next efforts will therefore look on other machine learning methods, also considering the possibility to model the amount and/or the exact location of errors.

Further work could extend this effort by including a wider range of error categories that describe better the requirements for a translation correct output. Instead of automatically detecting errors on post-edited output, a possible extension could consider modelling error types assigned by humans. Additionally, the analysis of features can be extended in order to cover other types of machine translation, such as hierarchical phrase-based translation and rule-based translation.

An obvious application of this analysis would be incorporating the findings into the decoding

	all		de-en		de-fr		de-es		en-de		fr-de		es-de	
	β	p	β	p	β	p	β	p	β	p	β	p	β	p
pC-std	1.55	.09	2.06	.17									7.03	.03
pC-max-pos	0.38	.00	0.46	.04			1.29	.01						
time-calculate-lm	0.89	.02												
time-translation	0.52	.34			2.35	.06	0.27	.37	2.07	.10				
unk-pos-std	-0.02	.16					-0.11	.11			-0.21	.01		
total-source-words	0.22	.01							0.18	.00	0.27	.01		
alt-pC-low	0.01	.03	0.02	.06	0.04	.00								

Table 7: Indicative beta coefficients and their respective p-values for the features affecting the existence of erroneous extra words.

process, in order to improve it, e.g. by introducing features to the decoding engine that directly indicates the factors that cause errors.

Acknowledgment

This work has received support by the EC's FP7 (FP7/2007-2013) under grant agreement number 610516: "QTLeap: Quality Translation by Deep Language Engineering Approaches".

References

Eleftherios Avramidis, Marta R Costa-Jussà, Christian Federmann, Josef van Genabith, Maite Melero, and Pavel Pecina. 2012. A Richly Annotated, Multilingual Parallel Corpus for Hybrid Machine Translation. In *Proceedings of the Eight International Conference on Language Resources and Evaluation (LREC'12)*, pages 2189–2193, Istanbul, Turkey, May. European Language Resources Association (ELRA).

Eleftherios Avramidis, Maja Popović, and Maja Popovic. 2013. Machine learning methods for comparative and time-oriented Quality Estimation of Machine Translation output. In *Proceedings of the Eighth Workshop on Statistical Machine Translation*, pages 329–336, Sofia, Bulgaria, August. Association for Computational Linguistics.

Eleftherios Avramidis. 2011. DFKI System Combination with Sentence Ranking at ML4HMT-2011. In *Proceedings of the International Workshop on Using Linguistic Information for Hybrid Machine Translation and of the Shared Task on Applying Machine Learning Techniques to Optimising the Division of Labour in Hybrid Machine Translation*, pages 99–103, Barcelona, Spain. Center for Language and Speech Technologies and Applications (TALP), Technical University of Catalonia.

Laurent Besacier and Benjamin Lecouteux. 2013. LIG System for WMT13 QE Task : Investigating the Usefulness of Features in Word Confidence Estimation for MT. In *Proceedings of the Eighth Workshop on Statistical Machine Translation*.

Ergun Bicici and Andy Way. 2014. Referential Translation Machines for Predicting Translation Quality. In *Proceedings of the Ninth Workshop on Statistical Machine Translation*, pages 313–321, Baltimore, Maryland, USA, June. Association for Computational Linguistics.

John Blatz, Erin Fitzgerald, George Foster, Simona Gandrabur, Cyril Goutte, Alex Kulesza, Alberto Sanchis, and Nicola Ueffing. 2004. Confidence estimation for machine translation. In *Proceedings of the 20th international conference on Computational Linguistics*, COLING '04, Stroudsburg, PA, USA. Association for Computational Linguistics.

Ondřej Bojar, Christian Buck, Chris Callison-Burch, Christian Federmann, Barry Haddow, Philipp Koehn, Christof Monz, Matt Post, Radu Soricut, and Lucia Specia. 2013. Findings of the 2013 Workshop on Statistical Machine Translation. In *8th Workshop on Statistical Machine Translation*, Sofia, Bulgaria, August. Association for Computational Linguistics.

Ondrej Bojar, Christian Buck, Christian Federmann, Barry Haddow, Philipp Koehn, Johannes Leveling, Christof Monz, Pavel Pecina, Matt Post, Herve Saint-Amand, Radu Soricut, Lucia Specia, and Aleš Tamchyna. 2014. Findings of the 2014 Workshop on Statistical Machine Translation. In *Proceedings of the Ninth Workshop on Statistical Machine Translation*, pages 12–58, Baltimore, Maryland, USA, June. Association for Computational Linguistics.

Chris Callison-Burch, Cameron Fordyce, Philipp Koehn, Christof Monz, and Josh Schroeder. 2007. (Meta-) Evaluation of Machine Translation. In *Proceedings of the Second Workshop on Statistical Machine Translation*, pages 136–158, Prague, Czech Republic, June. Association for Computational Linguistics.

Chris Callison-Burch, Philipp Koehn, Christof Monz, Kay Peterson, Mark Przybocki, and Omar Zaidan. 2010. Findings of the 2010 Joint Workshop on Statistical Machine Translation and Metrics for Machine Translation. In *Proceedings of the Joint Fifth Workshop on Statistical Machine Translation and Metrics*, pages 17–53, Uppsala, Sweden, July. Association for Computational Linguistics.

Chris Callison-Burch, Philipp Koehn, Christof Monz, and Omar Zaidan. 2011. Findings of the 2011 Workshop on Statistical Machine Translation. In *Proceedings of the Sixth Workshop on Statistical Machine Translation*, pages 22–64, Edinburgh, Scotland, July. Association for Computational Linguistics.

Adrian Cameron. 1998. *Regression analysis of count data*. Cambridge University Press, Cambridge UK; New York NY USA.

José Guilherme de Souza, Jesús González-Rubio, Christian Buck, Marco Turchi, and Matteo Negri. 2014. FBK-UPV-UEdin participation in the WMT14 Quality Estimation shared-task. In *Proceedings of the Ninth Workshop on Statistical Machine Translation*, pages 322–328, Baltimore, Maryland, USA, June. Association for Computational Linguistics.

Janez Demšar, Blaž Zupan, Gregor Leban, and Tomaz Curk. 2004. Orange: From Experimental Machine Learning to Interactive Data Mining. In *Principles of Data Mining and Knowledge Discovery*, pages 537–539.

Francisco Guzmán and Stephan Vogel. 2012. Understanding the Performance of Statistical MT Systems: A Linear Regression Framework. In *Proceedings of COLING 2012*, pages 1029–1044, Mumbai, India, December. The COLING 2012 Organizing Committee.

Frank E Harrell. 2001. *Regression modeling strategies: with applications to linear models, logistic regression, and survival analysis*. Springer.

Silja Hildebrand and Stephan Vogel. 2013. MT Quality Estimation: The CMU System for WMT'13. In *Proceedings of the Eighth Workshop on Statistical Machine Translation*, pages 373–379, Sofia, Bulgaria, August. Association for Computational Linguistics.

David Hosmer. 1989. *Applied logistic regression*. Wiley, New York [u.a.], 8th edition.

Liang Huang and David Chiang. 2007. Forest rescoring: Faster decoding with integrated language models. In *Annual Meeting-Association For Computational Linguistics*, volume 45, page 144.

Philipp Koehn, Franz Josef Och, and Daniel Marcu. 2003. Statistical phrase-based translation. In *Proceedings of the 2003 Conference of the North American Chapter of the Association for Computational Linguistics on Human Language Technology*, pages 48–54.

Philipp Koehn, Hieu Hoang, Alexandra Birch, Chris Callison-Burch, Marcello Federico, Nicola Bertoldi, Brooke Cowan, Wade Shen, Christine Moran, Richard Zens, Chris Dyer, Ondřej Bojar, Alexandra Constantin, and Evan Herbst. 2007. Moses: Open Source Toolkit for Statistical Machine Translation. In *Proceedings of the Annual Meeting of the Association for Computational Linguistics (ACL)*, pages 177–180, Prague, Czech Republic, June.

Philipp Koehn. 2005. Europarl: A parallel corpus for statistical machine translation. *Proceedings of the tenth Machine Translation Summit*, 5:79–86.

Alon Lavie and Abhaya Agarwal. 2007. METEOR: An Automatic Metric for MT Evaluation with High Levels of Correlation with Human Judgments. In *Proceedings of the Second Workshop on Statistical Machine Translation*, pages 228–231, Prague, Czech Republic, June. Association for Computational Linguistics.

Scott Menard. 2002. *Applied logistic regression analysis*, volume 106. Sage.

Alan Miller. 2002. *Subset Selection in Regression*. Chapman & Hall, London, 2nd edition.

Kishore Papineni, Salim Roukos, Todd Ward, and Wei-Jing Zhu. 2002. BLEU: a Method for Automatic Evaluation of Machine Translation. In *Proceedings of the 40th Annual Meeting of the Association for Computational Linguistics*, pages 311–318, Philadelphia, Pennsylvania, USA, July. Association for Computational Linguistics.

Maja Popović and Hermann Ney. 2011. Towards Automatic Error Analysis of Machine Translation Output. *Computational Linguistics*, 37(4), December.

Maja Popović. 2011a. From human to automatic error classification for machine translation output. In *15th International Conference of the European Association for Machine Translation*, Leuven, Belgium. European Association for Machine Translation.

Maja Popović. 2011b. Hjerson: An Open Source Tool for Automatic Error Classification of Machine Translation Output. *The Prague Bulletin of Mathematical Linguistics*, 96(-1):59–68.

Raphaël Rubino, Antonio Toral, Santiago Cortés Va\'illo, Jun Xie, Xiaofeng Wu, Stephen Doherty, Qun Liu, and Santiago Cortés Vaíllo. 2013. The CNGL-DCU-Prompsit Translation Systems for WMT13. In *Proceedings of the Eighth Workshop on Statistical Machine Translation*, pages 213–218, Sofia, Bulgaria, August. Association for Computational Linguistics.

Lucia Specia, M. Turchi, N. Cancedda, M. Dymetman, and N. Cristianini. 2009. Estimating the Sentence-Level Quality of Machine Translation Systems. In *13th Annual Meeting of the European Association for Machine Translation*, pages 28–35, Barcelona, Spain.

Milos Stanojevic and Khalil Sima'an. 2014. BEER: BEtter Evaluation as Ranking. In *Proceedings of the Ninth Workshop on Statistical Machine Translation*, pages 414–419, Baltimore, Maryland, USA, June. Association for Computational Linguistics.

Andreas Stolcke. 2002. SRILM – An Extensible Language Modeling Toolkit. In *Proceedings of the Seventh International Conference on Spoken Language Processing*, pages 901–904. ISCA, September.

David Vilar, Jia Xu, Luis Fernando D'Haro, and Hermann Ney. 2006. Error Analysis of Machine Translation Output. In *International Conference on Language Resources and Evaluation*, pages 697–702, Genoa, Italy, May.

Supertag Based Pre-ordering in Machine Translation

Rajen Chatterjee, Anoop Kunchukuttan, Pushpak Bhattacharyya
Department of Computer Science and Engineering
Indian Institute of Technology, Bombay
{rajen,anoopk,pb}@cse.iitb.ac.in

Abstract

This paper presents a novel approach to integrate *mildly context sensitive grammar* in the context of pre-ordering for machine translation. We discuss the linguistic insights available in this grammar formalism and use it to develop a pre-ordering system. We show that mildly context sensitive grammar proves to be beneficial over context free grammar, which facilitates better reordering rules. For English to Hindi, we see significant improvement of 1.8 BLEU and error reduction of 4.46 TER score over CFG based pre-ordering system, on the WMT14 data set. We also show that our approach improves translation quality for English to Indian languages machine translation over standard phrase based systems.

1 Introduction

India is a multilingual country with 22 official languages, spanning four language families (Indo-Aryan,Dravidian, Tibeto-Burman and Austro-Asiatic)[1]. In such a liguistically diverse country there is always a great need for translation services to serve government, business and overall social communication needs. Hindi and English act as *link languages* across the country and languages of official communication for the Union Government. Thus, the importance of English to Hindi translation is obvious.

Languages can be differentiated in terms of structural divergences and morphological usage. English is structurally classified as a Subject-Verb-Object (SVO) language as opposed to Hindi which follows Subject-Object-Verb (SOV) word order. Largely, these divergences are responsible for the difficulties

---

[1] http://en.wikipedia.org/wiki/Languages_of_India

in standard statistical machine translation (SMT) systems.

Our objective is to reduce the structural divergence by reordering words in the source language (English) to conform to the target language (Hindi) word order and then provide this data to train a pharse based SMT system. This approach is known as *pre-ordering* in SMT research. The novelty of our work is the inclusion of linguistic context obtained from higher level of grammar formalism known as *mildly context sensitive grammar*. To the best of our knowledge, this is the first approach to bring such a formalism for pre-ordering in machine translation.

To begin with, Section 2 discusses work related to pre-ordering. We then provide an introduction to TAG and Supertag, in Section 3. Section 4 describes our approach for pre-ordering. In Section 5, we provide the methodology for pre-ordering. Experimental setup is explained in Section 6, while corresponding results are shown in Section 7. We conclude our work in Section 8 providing acknowledgement in Section 9.

2 Related Work

Word order has direct impact on the fluency of transaltion obtained using SMT systems. There are basically two paradigms for generating correct word order. The first paradigm deals with developing a reordering model which is used during decoding. Different solutions such as syntax-based models (Chiang, 2005), lexicalized reordering (Och et al., 2004), and tree-to-string methods (Zhang et al., 2006) have been proposed. Most of these approaches use statistical models to learn reordering rules, but all of them have different methods to solve the reordering problem. The next paradigm deals with developing a reordering model which is used as pre-processing step (also known as pre-ordering) in SMT systems. In pre-ordering, the objective is to re-

D S Sharma, R Sangal and J D Pawar. Proc. of the 11th Intl. Conference on Natural Language Processing, pages 30–38,
Goa, India. December 2014. ©2014 NLP Association of India (NLPAI)

order source language words to conform to the target language word order.

Xia and McCord (2004) describe an approach for translation from French to English, where reordering rules are acquired automatically using source and target parses and word alignment. The reordering rules in their approach operate at the level of context-free rules in the parse tree. Collins et al. (2005), describe clause restructuring for German to English machine translation. They use six transformations that are applied on German parsed text to reorder it before training with a phrase based system. Popovic and Ney (2006) use hand-made rules to reorder the source side based on POS information. Zhang et al. (2007) propose chunk level reordering, where reordering rules are automatically learned from source-side chunks and word alignments. They allow all possible reorderings to be used to create a lattice that is input to the decoder. Genzel (2010), shows automatic rule extraction for 8 language pairs. They first extract a dependency tree and then converts it to a shallow constituent tree. The trees are annotated by both POS tags and by Stanford dependency types, then they learn reordering rules given a set of features. This paper discusses about creating manual reordering rules with the help of Tree Adjoining Grammar (TAG), a mildly context sensitive formalism as discussed in Section 3.

3 Introduction to TAG/Supertag

Tree Adjoining Grammar (TAG) was introduced by Joshi et al. (1975). Tree Adjoining Languages (TALs) generate some strictly context-sensitive languages and fall in the class of the so-called *mildly context-sensitive* languages. Lexicalized Tree Adjoining Grammar (LTAG) (Joshi and Schabes, 1991) is the TAG formalism where each lexical item is associated with atleast one elementary structure. This elementary structure of LTAG is known as *Supertag*. The concept of *Supertag* was first proposed by Joshi and Srinivas (1994). Supertag localize dependencies, including long-distance dependencies, by requiring that all and only the dependent elements be present within the same structure. They provide syntactic as well as dependency information at the

word level by imposing complex constraints in a local context. Supertags provide information like POS tag, subcategorization and other syntactic constraints at the level of agreement feature. Supertag can also be viewed as fragments of parse tree associated with each lexical item. An example of supertag is shown in Figure 1. This supertag is used for transitive verbs. Subcategorization information is

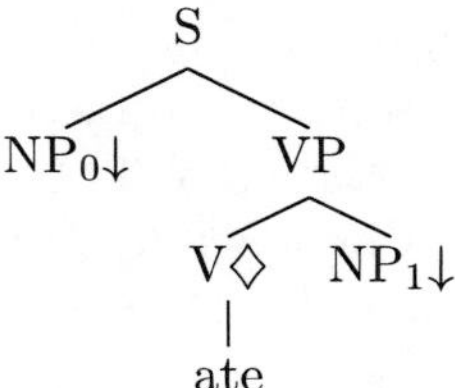

Figure 1: Supertag for transitive verb *ate*

clearly visible in the verb, which takes a subject to its left and an object to its right.

3.1 Structural description of supertag

Each supertag, at its frontier, has exactly one anchor node marked by ◇, to which a lexical item gets anchored. Apart from anchor node at its frontier, it may have an optional *substitution* node marked by ↓ or an *adjunction* node marked by *. *Substitution* and *adjunction* are those nodes which can be replaced by another supertag. For an adjunction node, it is necessary for its label to match the label of root node of supertag. A supertag can have atmost one adjunction node but can have more than one substitution node.

3.2 Supertagging

Supertagging refers to tagging each word of a sentence with a supertag. An example of a supertagged sentence is shown in figure 2.

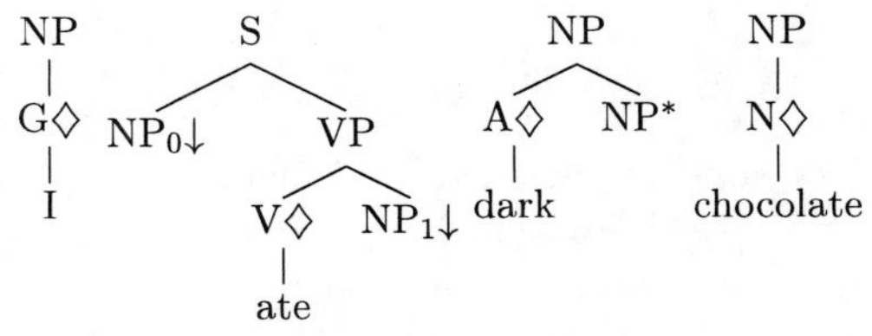

Figure 2: Supertagged sentence *"I ate dark chocolate"*

We use MICA Parser (Bangalore et al.,

2009)[2] to obtain rich linguistic information like POS tag, supertag, voice, the presence of empty subjects (PRO), wh-movement, deep syntactic argument (deep subject, deep direct object, deepindirect object), whether a verb heads a relative clause and also dependency relation, for each word. From this rich set of features, for each word, we extract word ID (essentially word position in a sentence), supertag, dependency relation and deep syntactic argument. Given a dependency relation, these supertags can be assembled using composition operation of TAG to form a constituent tree. Composition operation includes substitution and adjunction:

- **Substitution:** It deals with substituting a non-terminal node at the frontier of supertag with another supertag. An example of substitution operation is shown in Figure 3. When substitution occurs at a node, the node is replaced by the supertag to be substituted.

- **Adjunction:** It deals with inserting a supertag within another supertag satisfying adjunction constraints (Joshi, 1987). An example of adjoining operation is shown in Figure 4. One of the key contraint is the root label of supertag to be adjoined should match label of the node where adjunction occurs.

Figure 3: Example illustraing *Substitution* operation

4 Supertag Based Reordering

Each supertag encapsulates rich linguistic context, based on which, we reorder supertag nodes to preserve same context in target language. We first highlight linguistic relevance of supertag followed by showing why supertag facilitates reordering and finally illustrate reordering with supertag.

[2]http://mica.lif.univ-mrs.fr/

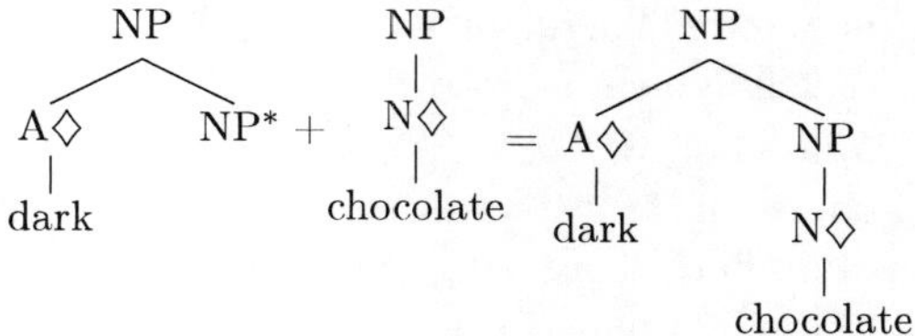

Figure 4: Example illustraing *Adjunction* operation

4.1 Linguistic Relevance

In this section, we show the linguistic relevance of supertag. Each Supertag falls in a specific syntactic environment, a few examples of supertag along with their syntactic environment are shown in Table 1. For each supertag ID, Table 1 gives the linguistic context (syntactic environment) in which a supertag appears along with an example sentence. The lexical item attached to the anchor node of supertag is written in *italic*, in the example sentence. Table 2 shows supertag ID and their corresponding tree structure.

Supertag ID	Linguistic Context	Example
t3	Noun Phrase	the *man*
t87	Topicalization	Those dogs, I am *terrified* of
t68	Imperative	Please *tidy* your room.
t36	Adjectival Modifier	*red* hat
t27	Transitive Verb	I *brought* dark chocolates.

Table 1: Example showing syntactic environment of different supertag

Syntactic environment of a supertag gives us the liberty to control reordering at a finer granularity. Thus, supertags of tree adjoining grammar prove to be advantageous over context free grammar (CFG) for reordering.

4.2 Why Supertag facilitates Reordering

In this section, we discuss key properties of LTAG which facilitates reordering, such as lexicalization, followed by Extended Domain of Locality (EDL) and finally Factoring of Recursion from the Domain of dependency (FRD)

Supertag ID	Supertag Structure
t3	NP → N◇
t87	NP → [NP*, S]; S → [NP_1 → -NONE-, S]; S → [NP_0↓, VP]; VP → [V◇, NP → -NONE-]
t68	S → [NP_0 → -NONE-, VP]; VP → [V◇, NP_1↓]
t36	NP → [A◇, NP*]
t27	S → [NP_0↓, VP]; VP → [V◇, NP_1↓]

Table 2: Figure showing supertag structure for each supertag ID

- **Lexicalization:**
  Lexicalization ensures that each supertag is anchored by a lexical item. This property prove to be linguistically crucial since it establishes a direct connection between the lexicon and the syntactic structures defined in the grammar. Reordering syntactic structure at word level for every word in a sentence helps us to obtain word order that conforms to target language word order.

- **Extended Domain of Locality (EDL):**
  This property of LTAG states that for each lexical item, the grammar must contain an elementary structure for each syntactic environment, the lexical item might appear in. This means that for each lexical item there can be multiple supertags representing different syntactic environment. Another part of EDL states that every supertag must contain all and only the argument of anchor in the same structure. This allows the anchor to impose syntactic and semantic constraints on its arguments directly since they appear in the same elementary structure that it anchors. This ensures, to reorder we deal only with primary features of lexical item on which the reordering primarily depends on.

- **Factoring of Recursion from the Domain of dependency (FRD):** This property ensures that supertags are *minimal* in nature; i.e. there is no recursion present within the given elementary structure of supertag. Recursive constructs are carried out with the help of adjunction operation. Auxiliary supertag, by adjunction to other supertag, accounts for long distance behavior of these dependencies. Due to this property the feature space of supertag is simplified without any recursive feature involved. This helps to build simple but strong reordering rules by just considering few but most important features of the supertag.

4.3 Detecting Linguistic Patterns for Reordering

In this section, we show that linguistic patterns can be detected with the help of supertag. English is structurally classified as a Subject-Verb-Object (SVO) language whereas Hindi is Subject-Object-Verb (SOV) language. However, this is not true for all verbs, specially in case of raising verb. We compare control verb v/s raising verb, where the former requires reordering as opposed to the later. An example has been shown in Table 3. It can be seen that supertag provides finer granularity to control reordering based on linguistic features. Studying supertag in-depth and associating it with linguistic context will help to discover various pattern useful for building better reordering system.

5 Methodology for Reordering

Listed below are the sequence of modules of our reordering system:

- **Reorder Supertags**
  We begin with reordering supertags, for

33

Control Verb		Raising Verb	
Sentence	Supertag	Sentence	Supertag
E: I <u>told</u> him. **H:** मैंने उसे <u>बोला</u> | **T:** mainne use <u>bola</u> **G:** I him <u>told</u>	S NP$_0$↓ VP V◇ NP$_1$↓	It <u>seems</u> you are busy. <u>लगता</u> है कि तुम व्यस्त हो | <u>lagta</u> hai ki tum vyast ho <u>seems</u> is that you busy are	S NP$_0$↓ VP V◇ S$_1$↓

Table 3: Table showing comparision of control verb v/s raising verb
E:English; H:Hindi; T:Transliteration; G:Gloss

which we are provided with 4725 supertags [3] in all, but seldom all of them are seen in action. Therefore, we supertag 50,000 sentences from health and tourism domain of ILCI corpus (Jha, 2010), from which we filter out spurious supertags which occur less than 10 times, leaving 600 supertags with us, for analysis. Our manual analysis shows that out of 600 supertags, 200 required reordering transformations to be applied.

Example of supertag, representing transitive verb, before and after reordering in shown in Table 4

Before Reordering	After Reordering
S NP$_0$↓ VP V◇ NP$_1$↓	S NP$_0$↓ VP NP$_1$↓ V◇

Table 4: Example showing transitive verb before and after reordering

An example of reordering prepositional phrase which gets adjunct to a noun phrase is shown in Table 5.

Before Reordering	After Reordering
NP NP* PP IN◇ NP$_1$↓	NP PP NP* NP$_1$↓ IN◇

Table 5: Example of prepositional phrase before and after reordering

---

³http://mica.lif.univ-mrs.fr/

- **Extract Linguistic Information**
  As stated in Section 3.2, we use MICA Parser to obtain linguistic information along with superatg at word level. For example, consider the input sentence "I told him", for which we extract essential information and append it with respective words as shown "I|1|2|PRP|t29|0   told|2|2|VBD|t27|. him|3|2|PRP|t29|1". Here, each word contains "lexical-item|ID|parent-ID|POStag|Supertag|deep-argument-position". We carry this example sentence in further modules of reordering.

- **Construct Derivation Tree**
  Once linguistic information is extracted, we proceed with construction of derivation tree. The process of combining the elementary trees (supertags) to yield a parse of the sentence is represented by the derivation tree. Derivation tree for the example sentence is shown in Figure 5.

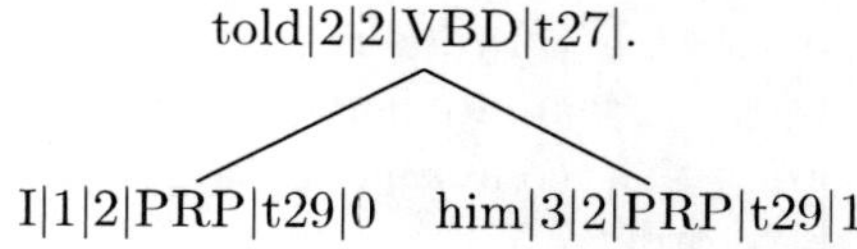

Figure 5: Example of Derivation Tree

- **Construct Derived Tree**
  We have implemented the composition operation (adjunction and substitution), which, given a derivation tree would build a derived/parse tree. Derived tree for the example sentence is shown in Figure 6. To build this derived tree we use reordered version of supertag (for eg. t27 for transitive verb from Table 4).

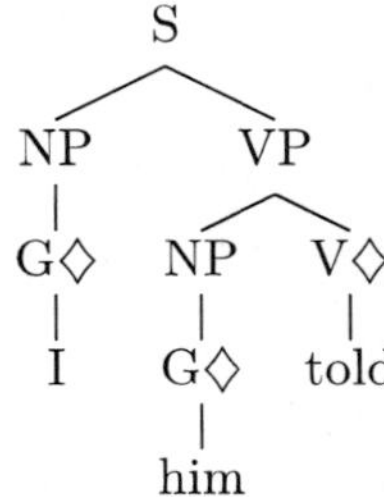

Figure 6: Example of Derived Tree

- **Extract leaf nodes** Finally, we extract leaf nodes from the derived tree, which gives us reordered English sentence. In our case, the input sentence is "I told him" for which, we get "I him told " as output. We now use these reordered English sentences along with their parallel Hindi translation to train English to Hindi machine translation system.

6 Experiment Setup

In this section, we discuss different data set used and various experiments that we have performed.

6.1 Data Sets

We use the shared task data set provided in *Workshop on Statistical Machine Translation, 2014* (WMT14)[4] to train English to Hindi translation system. WMT14 training set contains data from general domain, obtained from multiple sources, whereas test set belongs to news domain. The training set consist of 275K parallel segments, while test set contains 2.5K. We train a 5 gram language model using SRILM[5] on 1.5M monolingual Hindi corpus provided in WMT14 shared task.

For translation from English to multiple Indian languages we use *Indian Language Corpora Initiative* (ILCI) (Jha, 2010) corpus. ILCI data belongs to the health and tourism domain. The training set consist of 40K parallel sentences while test set contains 1.1K. We train a 5 gram language model using SRILM on a 50K monolingual Hindi corpus from the same domain.

---

[4]WMT14 resources:-http://ufallab.ms.mff. cuni.cz/~bojar/hindencorp/

[5]http://www.speech.sri.com/projects/srilm

The English data was tokenized using the Stanford tokenizer and then true-cased using truecase.perl provided in MOSES toolkit. We normalize Hindi corpus using NLP Indic Library (Kunchukuttan et. al.,2014)[6]. Normalization is followed by tokenization, wherein we make use of the trivtokenizer.pl provided with WMT14 shared task.

6.2 List of Experiments

We use the MOSES toolkit (Koehn et al., 2007) to train various statistical machine translation systems. For English to Hindi we train three systems, on each data set (WMT14 and ILCI), as follows:

- **Phrase Based Systems:** We train phrase based model without pre-ordering.

- **Context Free Grammar based pre-ordering:** In this model, we reorder both train and test set using Patel et al. (2013)'s source side reordering rules which is refinement of Ramanathan et al. (2008)'s rule-based reordering system.

- **Supertag based pre-ordering:** In this model, we reorder both train and test set using our supertag based pre-ordering method as discussed in Section 5.

We provide systematic comparision among these systems in Section 7. As the reordering rules are developed to conform Hindi word order, we were interested to see how does it affect other Indian languages which have the same word order as Hindi. So, we developed various translation systems from English to other Indian languages using ILCI corpus and compare it with standard pharse based systems.

7 Results

In this section, we also provide quantitative results for various systems and provide systematic comparision among them. We also provide couple of translations from English to Hindi, showing improvement in translation quality with our approach.

---

[6]https://bitbucket.org/anoopk/indic_nlp_ library

Data Set	Phrase Based		CFG based reordering		Supertag based reordering	
	BLEU	TER	BLEU	TER	BLEU	TER
WMT14	8.00	84.00	8.6	86.66	**10.40**	**82.20**
ILCI	23.77	58.36	**26.45**	56.24	25.75	**56.14**

Table 6: Result of English to Hindi SMT System
Higher BLEU Score and Lower TER Score indicate better system

Language Pair	Baseline Phrase Based		Supertag based reordering		Improvement over Baseline (BLEU %)
	BLEU	TER	BLEU	TER	
English-Punjabi	20.71	62.94	22.60	60.64	+9.12
English-Urdu	16.20	69.12	17.43	67.38	+7.59
English-Konkani	10.18	79.35	11.18	78.83	+9.82
English-Telugu	4.8	95.41	5.44	95.46	+13.33
English-Gujarati	14.76	70.42	15.40	69.34	+4.33
English-Bengali	12.73	75.49	13.26	74.48	+4.16
English-Malayalam	3.49	100.23	3.78	100.39	+8.31

Table 7: Result of English to Indian Language SMT System

7.1 Quantitative Evaluation

We use two standard evaluation metrics BLEU (Papineni et al., 2002) and TER (Snover et al., 2006), for comparing translation quality of various systems. Table 6 compares phrase based, CFG based reordering and supertag based reordering systems built using WMT14 and ILCI data set, for English to Hindi language pair. We see TER score of our system is best for both data sets. For WMT14 data set, our approach shows improvement of 1.8 BLEU score and error reduction of 4.46 TER score over CFG based reordering system.

For the ILCI data set, our approach shows significant improvement over both evaluation metrics over phrase based SMT sytem but shows slight degradation in BLEU score when compared with CFG based reordering system. However, TER score remains almost same. On an average, over both data sets, we see that TAG based reordering performs better than PB and CFG based systems.

Also from Table 7, we see our approch of reordering English data set proves to give significant improvement in translation quality over phrase based, for most of the English to Indian language machine translation systems. The result is statistically significant at the p <= 0.07 level.

7.2 Qualitative Evaluation

We provide two source (English) sentences (Example 1 and Example 2) along with their actual translation (AT) and machine translations obtained from phrase based system (PB), CFG based reordered system (CFG) and TAG based reordered system (TAG), as shown in Table 8. Transliteration of all Hindi sentences have been shown in corresponding column. We see that translations of TAG is much closer to the actual translation. Example 1 shows improvement in reordering which is the main focus of our work, whereas, Example 2 shows morphological improvement inherently achieved with reordering.

8 Conclusion

We presented a novel method of using mildly context sensitive grammar formalism in the context of pre-ordering in SMT systems. We show that the rich linguistic information embedded in supertags provides finer granularity for framing reordering rules over Context Free Grammar (CFG). We also showed that supertag can be used for detecting linguistic pattern based on which specific reordering rules can be written. We also discuss the linguistic relevance of Supertag and bridging it with machine translation. Finally our approach has shown significant improvement over CFG based reordered systems. In future

Example 1	One may wear clothes in many folds on body .	
AT	शरीर पर कई तह में कपड़े पहनें ।	sharir par kai taha mein kapade pahane .
PB	सकती है पर कई तह में कपड़े पहनें ।	sakti hai par kai taha mein kapade pahane .
CFG	एक कई तह में कपड़े शरीर पर पहन सकते हैं ।	ek kai taha mein kapade sharir par pahan sakte hain .
STAG	एक शरीर पर कई तह में कपड़े पहनें ।	ek sharir par kai taha mein kapde pahane .
Example 2	The symptoms of which are as follows :	
AT	जिसके लक्षण इस प्रकार हैं :	jisake lakshan is prakar hain :
PB	जो के लक्षण इस प्रकार हैं :	jo ke lakshan is prakar hain :
CFG	जो के लक्षण इस प्रकार हैं :	jo ke lakshan is prakar hain :
STAG	जिसके लक्षण इस प्रकार हैं :	jisake lakshan is prakar hain :

Table 8: Comparision of translation among various systems for English to Hindi

work, we would like to classify supertag based on their linguistic relevance and try to generalize reordering rules for each class.

9 Acknowledgement

We thank Owen Rambow and Srinivas Bangalore to help us in understanding supertags and also making the grammar file of supertags available to us. We would like to thank the Technology Development for Indian Languages (TDIL) Programme and the Department of Electronics Information Technology, Govt. of India for providing the ILCI corpus. Also we would like to thank all members of the Centre for Indian Language Technology (CFILT) for their valuable feedback and comments.

References

Srinivas Bangalore, Pierre Boulllier, Alexis Nasr, Owen Rambow, and Benoît Sagot. 2009. Mica: a probabilistic dependency parser based on tree insertion grammars application note. In *Proceedings of HLT-NAACL*, pages 185–188.

David Chiang. 2005. A hierarchical phrase-based model for statistical machine translation. In *Proceedings of the 43rd Annual Meeting on ACL*, pages 263–270.

Michael Collins, Philipp Koehn, and Ivona Kučerová. 2005. Clause restructuring for statistical machine translation. In *Proceedings of the ACL*, pages 531–540.

Dmitriy Genzel. 2010. Automatically learning source-side reordering rules for large scale machine translation. In *Proceedings of the COLING*, pages 376–384.

Girish Nath Jha. 2010. The tdil program and the indian language corpora initiative (ilci). In *Proceedings of the LREC*.

Aravind K Joshi and Yves Schabes. 1991. Tree-adjoining grammars and lexicalized grammars.

Aravind K Joshi and Bangalore Srinivas. 1994. Disambiguation of super parts of speech (or supertags): Almost parsing. In *Proceedings of the COLING*, pages 154–160.

Aravind K Joshi, Leon S Levy, and Masako Takahashi. 1975. Tree adjunct grammars. *Journal of computer and system sciences*, 10(1):136–163.

Aravind K Joshi. 1987. An introduction to tree adjoining grammars. *Mathematics of language*, 1:87–115.

Philipp Koehn, Hieu Hoang, Alexandra Birch, Chris Callison-Burch, Marcello Federico, Nicola Bertoldi, Brooke Cowan, Wade Shen, Christine Moran, Richard Zens, et al. 2007. Moses: Open source toolkit for statistical machine translation. In *Proceedings of the ACL*, pages 177–180.

Franz Josef Och, Daniel Gildea, Sanjeev Khudanpur, Anoop Sarkar, Kenji Yamada, Alexander Fraser, Shankar Kumar, Libin Shen, David Smith, Katherine Eng, et al. 2004. A smorgasbord of features for statistical machine translation. In *Proceedings of the HLT-NAACL*, pages 161–168.

Kishore Papineni, Salim Roukos, Todd Ward, and Wei-Jing Zhu. 2002. Bleu: a method for automatic evaluation of machine translation. In *Proceedings of the ACL*, pages 311–318.

Raj Patel, Rohit Gupta, Prakash Pimpale, and M. Sasikumar. 2013. Reordering rules for English-Hindi SMT. In *Proceedings of the Second Workshop on Hybrid Approaches to Translation*.

Maja Popovic and Hermann Ney. 2006. Pos-based word reorderings for statistical machine translation. In *Proceedings of the LREC*, pages 1278–1283.

Ananthakrishnan Ramanathan, Jayprasad Hegde, Ritesh M Shah, Pushpak Bhattacharyya, and M Sasikumar. 2008. Simple syntactic and morphological processing can help english-hindi statistical machine translation. In *Proceedings of the IJCNLP*, pages 513–520.

Matthew Snover, Bonnie Dorr, Richard Schwartz, Linnea Micciulla, and John Makhoul. 2006. A study of translation edit rate with targeted human annotation. In *Proceedings of the AMTA*, pages 223–231.

Fei Xia and Michael McCord. 2004. Improving a statistical mt system with automatically learned rewrite patterns. In *Proceedings of the COLING*, page 508.

Hao Zhang, Liang Huang, Daniel Gildea, and Kevin Knight. 2006. Synchronous binarization for machine translation. In *Proceedings of the HLT-NAACL*, pages 256–263.

Yuqi Zhang, Richard Zens, and Hermann Ney. 2007. Chunk-level reordering of source language sentences with automatically learned rules for statistical machine translation. In *Proceedings of the HLT-NAACL*, pages 1–8.

Duration Modeling by Multi-Models based on Vowel Production characteristics

V Ramu Reddy
TCS, Innovation Labs,
Kolkata - 700156, West Bengal, India
`ramu.vempada@tcs.com`

K Sreenivasa Rao and Parakrant Sarkar
Indian Institute of Technology Kharagpur,
Kharagpur - 721302, West Bengal, India
`ksrao@iitkgp.ac.in`
`parakrantsarkar@gmail.com`

Abstract

An accurate estimation of segmental durations is needed for natural sounding text-to-speech (TTS) synthesis. This paper propose multi-models based on production aspects of vowels. In this work four multi-models are developed based on vowel length, vowel height, vowel frontness and vowel roundness. In each multi-model, syllables are divided into groups based on specific vowel articulation characteristics. In this study, (i) linguistic constraints represented by positional, contextual and phonological features and (ii) production constraints represented by articulatory features are used for predicting duration patterns. Feed-forward Neural Networks are used for developing duration models. From the results, it was observed that the average prediction error is reduced by 23.21% and correlation coefficient is improved by 9.64% using multi-model developed based on vowel length production characteristics, compared to single duration model.

1 Introduction

Naturalness and intelligibility of the synthetic speech generated by the text-to-speech synthesis (TTS) systems can be improved by means of accurate prediction of prosodic parameters. Prosody refers to duration, intonation and intensity patterns of speech for the sequence of syllables, words and phrases. In this work, we focus on modeling or predicting one of the important prosodic parameters i.e., duration. Duration plays an important role in human speech communication. Duration patterns of an utterance is defined as the sequence of segmental (phone) or supra-segmental (syllable) durations. Variation in duration patterns provide naturalness to speech. Human hearing system is highly sensitive to variations in duration patterns. Hence, while developing speech synthesis systems, acquisition and incorporation of the duration knowledge is very much essential.

In this work, we are modeling the syllable durations for Indian language Bengali. In speech signal, the duration of each unit is dictated by the linguistic and production constraints of the unit (Reddy and Rao, 2012) (Rao and Yegnanarayana, 2007). In (Reddy and Rao, 2012), Ramu *et al* have developed single duration model using linguistic constraints represented by positional, contextual and phonological (PCP) features, and production constraints represented by articulatory (A) features (Reddy and Rao, 2012). From here onward it is referred as PCPA features in the rest of the paper. In most of the existing Indian context TTS works (Kumar and Yegnanarayana, 1989) (Kumar, 1990) (Kumar, 2002) (Krishna and Murthy, 2004) (Rao and Yegnanarayana, 2007) (Kumar et al., 2002) single duration models are developed by considering all the available syllables present in the training dataset irrespective of syllable position or articulation aspects of syllables. The distribution plot of duration of syllables present in our database is shown in Fig. 1. From Fig. 1, it is observed that duration values of syllables in the database vary from 50 to 560 ms with mean and standard deviations 212.9 ms and 80.6 ms, respectively. It is also observed that most of the duration values of syllables are concentrated between 110 ms and 350 ms, respectively. Therefore, the single duration model will be more prone to erroneous by classifying the low and high duration values to-

D S Sharma, R Sangal and J D Pawar. Proc. of the 11th Intl. Conference on Natural Language Processing, pages 39–47,
Goa, India. December 2014. ©2014 NLP Association of India (NLPAI)

wards mean values (central tendency) due to less frequency of low and high duration syllables in the training phase. This results in high average prediction error.

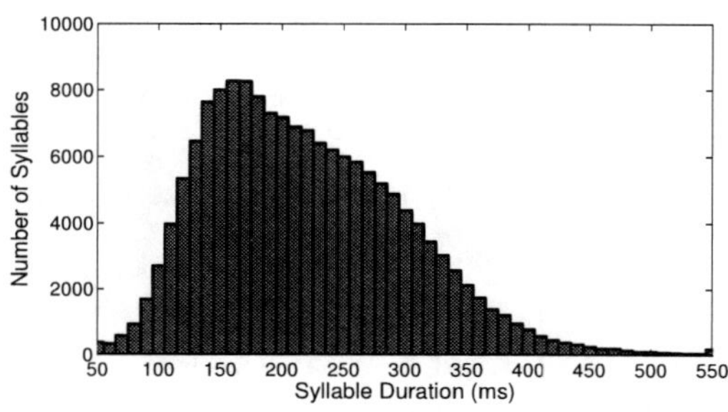

Figure 1: Distribution plot of Syllable durations

To improve the prediction accuracy by eliminating the biases of short durations of syllables towards long durations of syllables and vice-versa, Rao *et al* have developed two-stage duration model (Rao, 2005) (Rao and B.Yegnanarayana, 2004). However, the accuracy of second stage depends on the accuracy of first stage. Therefore, in this study, we have explored in a different way to improve the prediction accuracy of durations by separating or grouping the durations of syllables based on production aspects of vowel generation and thereby developing single stage multi-model based duration models rather than multi-stage duration model. The implicit knowledge of duration is usually captured by using modeling techniques. In this work, supervised learning is carried out using neural networks to capture the underlying interactions that exist between input and output features (Haykin, 1999). The main contributions of this paper are as follows:

1. Analysing the syllable durations based on the vowel production characteristics.

2. Separating the syllables based on production aspects of vowels and developing the duration models for each class of vowel articulations.

The paper is organized as follows: Section 2 presents an overview of the existing research on acquisition of duration knowledge using different models. Performance of single neural network model for predicting the duration values of syllables along with the details of database and feature is given in Section 3. Analysis of durations of syllables for different vowel production characteristics is discussed in section 4. Section 5 compares the performance results of the proposed multi-models with single duration model. Summary and conclusions of this paper is presented in Section 6.

2 Previous efforts

Different approaches have been proposed by many researchers for modeling durations of sound units in the development of TTS systems. Duration models range from rule-based methods to data-based methods (Mixdorff, 2002). In the rule-based models, some set of rules will be derived with the help of linguistic experts and phoneticians using limited amount of data. However, the state-of-art is dominated by data-based models which gain knowledge directly from the data. The data-based methods are generally dependent on the quality and quantity of available training data.

Rule-based models like Klatt model, which applies rules to lengthen or shorten the duration of the segments (Klatt, 1979). Umeda developed rule-based duration model (Umeda, 1976) which is distinctly different from Klatt's model. The Chinese and Japanese TTS systems emphasize more on pitch rather than durations, due to tonal nature of the languages. Lee *et al* have developed Chinese syllable based TTS system with simple rule-based duration model (Lee et al., 1989). Linear statistical model like sum-of-products models, which combine multiple features into single expression. Jan van Santen proposed sums-of-products (SoP) model (Santen, 1994). The model uses set of linear equations based on the prior phonetic and phonological information as well as the information obtained by analyzing the data. Due to availability of large speech corpora, many researchers have proposed non-linear statistical approaches for analyzing large data. The two major approaches follow under this category are Classification and Regression Trees (CART) and Artificial Neural Networks (ANN). The CART based models are typical data-based duration models that can be constructed automatically. The self-configuration capability of CART makes them very popular (Black and Lenzo, Beijing China 2000); for instance the Festival TTS system uses *'wagon'* tool to construct such trees from the existing databases. Riley used the CART based model for predicting the segmental durations (Riley, 1992). The prediction of syllable durations using neural networks is proposed by Campbell (Campbell, 1990). Neural network models also used by Barbosa and Bailly to predict the duration of unit, known as Inter Perceptual Center Group (IPCG) (Barbosa and Bailly, 1994). Neural network based duration models also exist for languages like Arabic (Hifny and Rashwan, 2002), Spanish (Cordoba et al., 1999), Portuguese (Teixeira and Freitas, 2003) and German (Sonntag et al., 1997).

In view of Indian context, the rule based duration model is developed by Kumar and Yegnanarayana for Hindi TTS system (Kumar and Yegnanarayana, 1989) (Kumar, 1990). The rules were derived by analyzing 500 sentences, considering contextual and positional information. About 31 rules were derived to predict the durations. Later the rules were upgraded by analysing the large broadcast news data in Hindi (Kumar, 2002) (Kumar et al., 2002). CART based duration models are developed for languages like Hindi and Telugu (Krishna and Murthy, 2004). Rao and Yegnanarayana have used statistical models such as neural networks and support vector machines for modeling the durations of syllables for Hindi, Telugu and Tamil (Rao and Yegnanarayana, 2007). The duration models were developed by using broadcast news data from the three languages. Linguistic constraints represented in the form of positional, contextual and phonological features were used to capture the durational phenomena. To improve the accuracy of prediction further, a two-stage duration model was developed. By using two-stage model prediction of short and long durations of syllables is better compared to single stage model.

3 Single duration model using feed-forward neural network

The details of experimental database, features, neural network and the evaluation results for single duration model is presented in the following subsections.

3.1 Experimental database

The text utterances of speech database used for this study are collected mainly from Anandabazar Patrika - a Bengali news paper. It consists of news from several domains like sports, politics, entertainment, and stories. The other sources include story and text books in various fields such as history, geography, travelogue, drama and science. The text corpus covers 7762 declarative sentences derived from 50,000 sentences through optimal text selection method (Narendra et al., 2011). The corpus covers 4372 unique syllables and 22382 unique words. The optimal text is recorded with a professional female artist in a noiseless chamber. The duration of total recorded speech is around 10 hrs. The speech signal was sampled at 16 kHz and represented as 16 bit numbers. The speech utterances are segmented and labeled into syllable-like units using ergodic hidden Markov models (EHMM) (Rabiner and Juang, 1993). For every utterance a label file is maintained, which consists of syllables of the utterance and their timing information. The percentage of different syllable structures present in the database are V(8.20%), VC(3.50%), VCC (0.20%), CV(50.41%), CVC(32.26%), CVCC(1.05%), CCV(2.50%), CCVC(1.77%) and CCCV(0.11%), where C is a consonant and V is a vowel.

3.2 Features

As we have developed syllable based TTS system, therefore we have used syllable specific features represented by linguistic and production constraints are represented by positional, contextual, phonological and articulatory (PCPA) features (Reddy and Rao, 2012)(Reddy and Rao, 2013). The features representing linguistic constraints are syllable position in the sentence, syllable position in the word, word position in the sentence, syllable identity, contextual information, syllable nucleus, whereas production constraints features are vowel length, vowel height, vowel frontness, vowel roundness, consonant type, consonant place, consonant voice, aspiration, nukta, first phone, last phone.

3.3 Feed-forward Neural Network

Feed-forward neural networks (FFNN) are used in this work for modeling the durations of sequence of syllables using PCPA features, since Ramu *et al* in (Reddy and Rao, 2012) had confirmed neural network model is outperformed compared to other models like classification and regression trees and linear regression trees. Therefore, in this work also a four layer feedforward neural network (FFNN) with the structure represented in Fig. 2 is used for predicting the duration values.

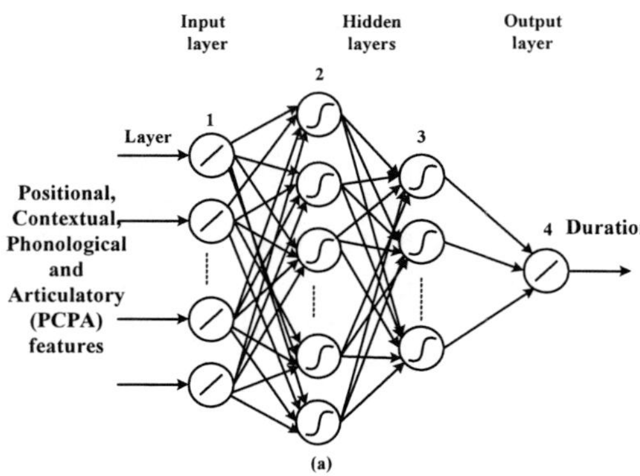

Figure 2: Architecture of four layer feedforward neural network for predicting the duration values of syllables.

In Fig. 2, the input layer which is the first layer consists of linear neuron units. The second and third layers are the hidden layers with non-linear neuron units. The last layer is the output layer with linear neuron units. The first hidden layer (second layer in Fig. 2) of the neural network consists of more units compared to the input layer (first layer in Fig. 2), so that network can capture local variations of features in the input space. The second hidden layer (third layer in Fig. 2) of the neural network has fewer units compared to the input layer, so that network can capture global variations of features in the input space (Haykin, 1999). The last layer (fourth layer in Fig. 2) is the output layer having one linear unit. The activation function for the units at the input and output layers is linear, whereas the activation function used at hidden layers is non-linear. The extracted PCPA feature vectors representing positional, contextual, phonological and articulatory features are presented as input, and the corresponding duration values are presented as desired outputs to the FFNN models.

The generalization by the network is basically influenced by three major factors : (1) the architecture of the network, (2) the amount of data used in the training phase of the network, and (3) the complexity of the problem. We have some control over the second factor but there is no control over the third factor. Different network structures were explored in this study to obtain the optimal performance, by incrementally varying the hidden layer neurons in between 5 and 100 as follows:

1. In the first iteration, the number of neurons in layer 2 (approximately 55) is considered to be greater than 1.5 times the number of neurons present in layer 1.

2. The number of neurons in layer 3 (approximately 25) considered in the first iteration is to be less than 0.75 times the number of neurons present in layer 1.

3. In this work, optimal structure is determined in 2 steps.the number of neurons in layer 2 are increased with an increment of 5 from 55 to 100, whereas in layer 3, the number of neurons are decreased with a decrement of 5 from 25 to 5. Based on the best performance (least training error) of all combinations (i.e., $10 \times 5 = 50$ combinations), layer 2 and layer 3 neurons are fixed.

4. In step 2, with the obtained neurons in step 1, fine tuning is carried out by incrementing the neurons of layer 2 and decrementing the neurons of layer 3 with the step count of 1.

5. For example in step 1, assume the best performance is obtained with h1 and h2 neurons in layer 2 and 3, respectively. In step 2, the neurons of layer 2 are varied from h1-4 to h1+4 excluding h1 (7 values) with step count of 1. Thus, in step 2, 49 possible combinations are tried out.

6. Overall, for finding the best optimal structure, we explored 99 possible combinations.

The structure of the network is represented by AL BN CN DL, where L denotes linear unit and N denotes non-linear unit. A, B, C and D are the integer values indicate the number of units used in different layers. The activation function used in the non-linear unit (N) is *tanh(s)* function, where 's' is activation value of that unit. The (*empirically arrived*) final optimal structures obtained with minimum generalization errors for predicting the durations is 35L 68N 17N 1L. The input and output features are normalized between [-1, 1], before giving to the neural network.

The training process of FFNN is carried out using Levenberg-Marquardt back-propagation algorithm to adjust the weights of the neural network, by back propagating the mean-squared error to the neural units and optimizes the free parameters (synaptic weights) to minimize the error (Yegnanarayana, 1999). The back-propagation network learns by examples. So, we use input-output examples to show the network what type of behaviour is expected, and the back propagation algorithm allows the network to adapt. The back propagation learning process works in small iterative steps as follows:

- One of the example cases is applied to the network.

- The network produces some output based on the current state of it's synaptic weights (initially, the output will be random).

- The network output is then compared to the desired output and a mean-squared error signal is calculated.

- The error value is then propagated backwards through the network, and weights are updated to decrease the error in each layer.

- The whole process is repeated for each of the examples.

For each syllable a 35 dimensional feature vector is formed, representing the positional, contextual, phonological and articulatory information. In this work, the data consists of 177820 syllables are used for modeling the duration. The data is divided into two parts namely design data and test data. The design data is used to determine the network topology. The design data in turn is divided into two parts namely training data and validation data. Training data is used to estimate the weights (includes biases) of the neural network and validation data is used to minimize the over-fitting of network, to verify the performance error and to stop training once the non-training validation error estimate stops decreasing. The test data is used once and only once on the best design, to obtain an unbiased estimate for the predicted error of unseen non-training data. The amount of data used for training, validation and testing the network are 70%, 15% and 15%, respectively. The motivation here is to validate the model on a data set from the one used for parameter estimation. As generalization is the goal of the neural network, hence we used cross validation.The early stopping method is used to avoid over-fitting of the neural network.

3.4 Objective and subjective evaluation

The performance of duration model is evaluated by using objective measures such as percentage of syllables predicted within different deviations from their actual duration values, average prediction error (μ), standard deviation (σ) and linear correlation coefficient ($\gamma_{X,Y}$) between actual and predicted duration values. The computation of objective measures are as follows:

$$D_i = \frac{|x_i - y_i|}{x_i} \times 100, \mu = \frac{\sum_i |x_i - y_i|}{N}, \quad (1)$$

$$\sigma = \sqrt{\frac{\sum_i d_i^2}{N}}, \text{ and } \gamma_{X,Y} = \frac{V_{X,Y}}{\sigma_X.\sigma_Y} \quad (2)$$

$$\text{where } d_i = e_i - \mu, e_i = x_i - y_i \quad (3)$$

$$\text{and } V_{X,Y} = \frac{\sum_i |x_i - \bar{x}|.|y_i - \bar{y}|}{N} \quad (4)$$

where x_i, y_i are the actual and predicted duration values respectively, and e_i is the error between the actual and predicted duration values. The deviation in error is d_i, and N is the number of observed duration values of the syllables. σ_X, σ_Y are the standard deviations for the actual and predicted duration values respectively, and $V_{X,Y}$ is the correlation between the actual and predicted duration values.

The performance of method is also evaluated by means of subjective analysis. Naturalness and intelligibility are two important key features to measure the quality of the synthesized speech. Naturalness can be defined as, how close the synthesized speech to human speech, whereas intelligibility is defined as how well the message is understood from the speech. The perceptual evaluation is conducted by incorporating FFNN based duration model developed into the TTS system. In this work, 20 subjects within the age group of 23-35 were considered for perceptual evaluation of synthesized speech. After giving appropriate training to the subjects, evaluation of TTS system is carried out in a laboratory environment. Randomly 10 sentences were selected, and played the synthesized speech signals through headphones to evaluate the quality. Subjects have to assess the quality on a 5-point scale (Reddy and Rao, 2012) for each of the synthesized sentences. The subjective listening tests are carried out for the synthesized sentences generated by FFNN duration model developed using the PCPA features. The mean opinion scores (MOS) are calculated for both naturalness and intelligibility of the synthesized speech.

The objective and subjective evaluation results of single duration model is given in Table 1.

Table 1: Performance of single duration model

% Predicted syllables within deviation			Objective measures			Subjective measures	
10%	15%	25%	μ (ms)	σ (ms)	γ	*Naturalness*	*Intelligibility*
35.14	50.63	72.56	39.04	35.09	0.83	3.53	2.86

4 Analysis of duration of syllables based on vowel articulation factors

Production aspect of speech segments (vowels and consonants) is one of the major factor influencing the variation in the duration of syllables. In syllables, major contribution of the duration values is mainly from the vowels compared to consonants. This can be verified from the example shown in Fig. 3. The phrase "sArodAdebI" contains two words("sArodA","debI"), 5 syllables("sA","ro","dA","de","bI") and 10 phones(s,A,r,o,d,A,d,e,b,I). The speech signal of the phrase "sArodAdebI" with its consonant and vowel portions (duration) shown in Fig. 3, indicates that major portion of duration of syllables is mainly from the vowel region.

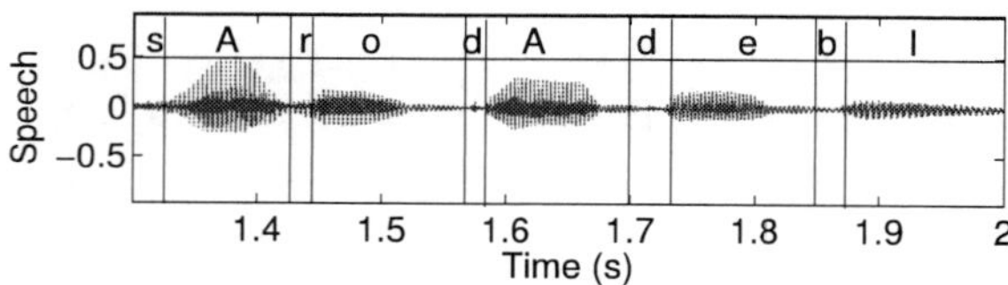

Figure 3: Durations of consonants and vowels of the syllables in the phrase "sArodAdebI"

Moreover, the duration values of vowels vary based on their place and manner of articulation while uttering. Therefore, in this study, analysis of duration is carried out based on production aspects of vowels. The features related to vowel are vowel length, vowel height, vowel frontness and vowel roundness. The distribution plot of syllables based on production characteristics of vowel is given in Fig. 4.

From Fig. 4, it is quite clear that there is a variations in the distributions of syllables of different vowel production characteristics. Therefore, if we separate the syllables based on these variations model and modeled each group separately, the prediction performance can be improved.

5 Proposed multi-model based approach

It was concluded that the durations of syllables depends on articulations of vowels from the analysis presented in Section 4. Therefore, in this study, multi-models are developed separately for each case to improve the prediction accuracy. The prediction performance of proposed FFNN multi-models is compared with the FFNN single duration model developed using PCPA features. The details of performance of multi-models are discussed in the following subsections.

In this study, multi-models are developed based on different vowel articulations described in the section 4. For the vowel length, durations of syllables are divided into 3 parts and hence 3 models are developed representing short, diphthongs and long vowels. For vowel height, syllables are divided into 3 parts such as high, mid and low vowels based on tongue height while articulating vowels, and hence 3 models are developed for vowel height. Similarly, based on tongue frontness, 3 models are developed representing front, mid and backness of tongue while articulating vowels. Lastly, 2 models based on vowel roundness is developed by categorizing syllables as lip roundness and no lip roundness while articulating vowels.

The input features used for developing multi-models is same as that of single model except the articulatory feature of the vowel type. For vowel length models, the articulatory feature vowel length is not used as it is redundant. This is applicable even for vowel height, vowel frontness and vowel roundness models. The performance of multi-models for each category of vowel articulations is given in Table 2. Column 1 of Table 2 indicate the vowel feature , column 2 indicate the models developed for each vowel feature, columns 3-5 indicates the percentage of syllables predicted within different deviations from their actual duration values and columns 6-8 indicates objective

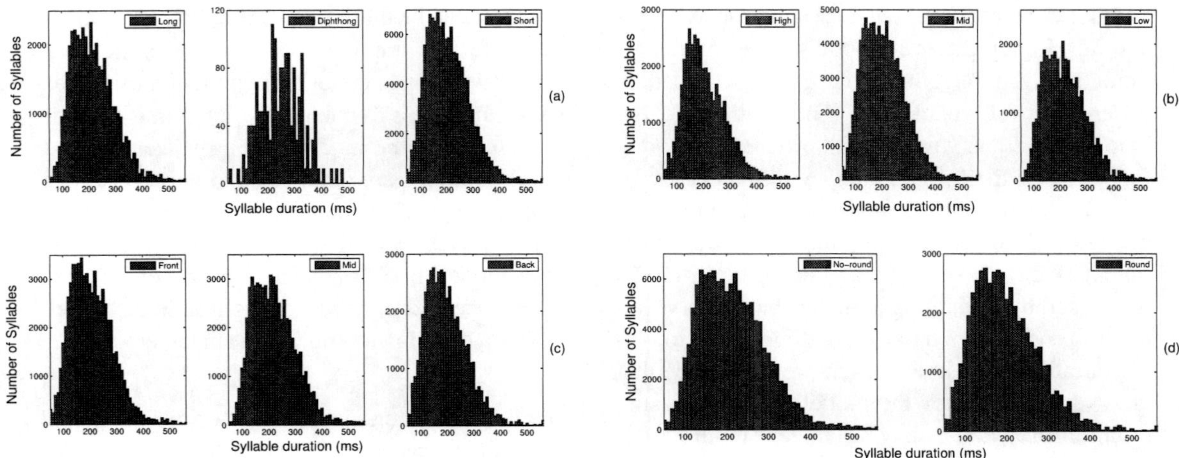

Figure 4: Distribution plots of the syllable durations based on different articulations of vowels related to (a) vowel length (b) vowel height, (c) vowel frontness, and (d) vowel roundness

Table 2: Performance of FFNN based multi-models based on vowel articulations for predicting the duration values of the syllables.

| Vowel features | Models | % Predicted syllables within deviation | | | Objective measures | | |
		10%	15%	25%	μ (ms)	σ (ms)	γ
Vowel Length	Long	36.82 (35.19)	54.87 (51.25)	73.08 (72.31)	36.50 (39.87)	29.09 (35.50)	0.86 (0.80)
	Dipthong	32.16 (48.39)	45.59 (63.40)	66.83 (88.56)	40.05 (33.63)	23.91 (30.66)	0.85 (0.78)
	Short	43.03 (34.99)	60.00 (50.30)	81.46 (72.47)	27.76 (38.83)	25.28 (35.00)	0.93 (0.84)
	AVERAGE	**41.44 (35.14)**	**58.64 (50.63)**	**79.31 (72.56)**	**29.98 (39.04)**	**26.20 (35.09)**	**0.91 (0.83)**
Vowel Height	High	40.63(35.11)	55.25(51.99)	77.30 (72.68)	31.33 (37.13)	28.72 (33.85)	0.84 (0.82)
	Mid	39.15 (34.77)	56.48 (49.61)	79.79 (72.61)	31.19 (39.66)	27.49 (35.34)	0.91 (0.85)
	Low	35.28 (36.11)	52.14 (51.75)	75.54 (72.29)	35.37 (39.54)	28.18 (35.78)	0.87 (0.80)
	AVERAGE	**38.66 (35.14)**	**55.25 (50.63)**	**78.29 (72.56)**	**32.13 (39.04)**	**27.93 (35.09)**	**0.89 (0.83)**
Vowel Frontness	Front	39.21 (34.61)	55.22 (51.01)	76.89 (73.64)	30.82 (38.36)	25.34 (32.89)	0.90 (0.83)
	Mid	41.13(37.01)	58.92 (53.23)	80.57 (74.70)	31.53 (39.12)	27.25 (35.57)	0.91 (0.83)
	Back	33.10 (33.52)	47.38 (46.89)	70.60 (68.47)	36.67 (39.84)	30.72 (37.41)	0.87 (0.83)
	AVERAGE	**38.17 (35.14)**	**54.31 (50.63)**	**76.41 (72.56)**	**32.71 (39.04)**	**27.51 (35.09)**	**0.90 (0.83)**
Vowel Roundness	No-round	33.50 (35.77)	50.14 (52.09)	72.43 (74.15)	37.88 (38.73)	30.53 (34.19)	0.85 (0.83)
	Round	34.71 (33.52)	51.02 (46.89)	74.68 (68.47)	33.24 (39.84)	28.61 (37.40)	0.89 (0.83)
	AVERAGE	**33.84 (35.14)**	**50.39 (50.63)**	**73.06 (72.56)**	**36.58 (39.04)**	**29.99 (35.09)**	**0.87 (0.83)**

measures.

Table 1 represents the average performance of all the syllables in the test set of the single duration model. The prediction performance of the syllables corresponding to different vowel production characteristics is also computed which is shown in brackets in Table 2 and the average performance of multi-models is shown in bold. From Table 2, it is quite clear that the performance of multi-models developed based on articulation of vowels is better compared to the performance of single duration model (the values in brackets). From this hypothesis, we concluded that the prediction accuracy of durations depends on the articulations of vowels, and it can be captured by separating the syllables and developing different models based on the articulations. Among all the multi-models based on different vowel articulations. The multi-model developed based on vowel length production characteristics is outperformed compared to other multi-models. It is found that the average prediction error is reduced by 23.21% and correlation coefficient is improved by 9.64% using multi-model developed by separating syllables based on vowel length production characteristic compared to single duration model. However, we can notice that the average error for the model developed using duration of syllables having vowel diphthongs is more compared to single duration model. This is expected because the amount of syllables having vowel diphthongs are quite less for training the neural network (0.89% in training set and 0.77% in test set). This error can be minimized by taking average duration value of diphthongs.

The subjective listening tests are also carried out for the synthesized sentences generated by FFNN multi-models as shown in Table 3. The mean opinion scores (MOS) are calculated for both naturalness and intelligibility of the synthesized speech. For comparing the quality of synthesized speech based on incorporation of specific duration models, we have also derived the mean opinion scores for the synthesized speech generated in the absence of duration model. From Table 3, it is observed that the MOS values for naturalness and intelligibility of FFNN multi-model developed based on vowel length production characteristics is better compared to other models. The scores indicate that the intelligibility of the synthesized speech is fairly acceptable, whereas the naturalness seems to be poor. Naturalness is mainly attributed to individual perception.

6 Summary and conclusions

In this work, novel multi-models are developed based on the articulation characteristics of vowels. Among all multi-models, the multi-model developed based on vowel length category is performed better compared to other multi-models developed based on vowel height, vowel frontness and vowel roundness. The prediction accuracy of multi-model is outperformed compared with single duration model. The prediction performance of diphthongs model in vowel length multi-model is dropped compared to single duration model.

The error can be minimized or prediction accuracy can be further improved by taking average duration of diphthongs rather than modeling using networks due to less frequency of diphthongs or it can be included in the model of long vowels as long vowel durations are quite close to duration values of diphthongs. The prediction accuracy can be further improved by analogizing and constructing the multi-models based on position aspect of syllables in sentence and in words, as well as multi-models based on consonant production characteristics.

Table 3: Mean opinion scores for the quality of synthesized speech of TTS after incorporating the multi-model based duration models

Models	Mean Opinion Scores	
	Intelligibility	*Naturalness*
Without Duration model	3.10	2.62
Single model	3.53	2.86
Vowel Length	3.70	3.01
Vowel Height	3.65	2.89
Vowel Frontness	3.62	2.88
Vowel Roundness	3.56	2.87

References

P. A. Barbosa and G. Bailly. 1994. Characterization of rhythmic patterns for text-to-speech synthesis. *Speech Communication*, 15:127–137.

Alan W Black and Kevin A. Lenzo. Beijing, China, 2000. Limited domain synthesis. In *ICSLP*.

W. N. Campbell. 1990. Analog I/O nets for syllable timing. *Speech Communication*, 9(1):57–61, Feb.

R. Cordoba, J. A. Vallejo, J. M. Montero, J. Gutier-rezarriola, M. A. Lopez, and J. M. Pardo. 1999. Automatic modeling of duration in a Spanish text-to-speech system using neural networks. In *Proc. European Conf. Speech Communication and Technology*, pages 1619–1622, Budapest, Hungary, Sept.

Simon Haykin, 1999. *Neural Networks: A Comprehensive Foundation*. Pearson Education Aisa, Inc., New Delhi, India.

Y. Hifny and M. Rashwan. 2002. Duration modeling of Arabic text-to-speech synthesis. In *Proc. Int. Conf. Spoken Language Processing*, pages 1773–1776, Denver, Colorado, USA, Sept.

D. H. Klatt. 1979. Synthesis by rule of segmental durations in English sentences. In B. Lindblom and S. Ohman, editors, *Frontiers of Speech Communication Research*, pages 287–300. Academic Press, New York.

N. Sridhar Krishna and Hema A. Murthy. 2004. Duration modeling of Indian languages Hindi and Telugu. In *5th ISCA Speech Synthesis Workshop*, pages 197–202, Pittsburgh, USA, May.

S. R. Rajesh Kumar and B. Yegnanarayana. 1989. Significance of durational knowledge for speech synthesis in Indian languages. In *Proc. IEEE Region 10 Conf. Convergent Technologies for the Asia-Pacific*, pages 486–489, Bombay, India, Nov.

K. Kiran Kumar, K. Sreenivasa Rao, and B. Yegnanarayana. 2002. Duration knowledge for text-to-speech system for Telugu. In *Proc. Int. Conf. Knowledge Based Computer Systems*, pages 563–571, Mumbai, India, Dec.

S. R. Rajesh Kumar. 1990. Significance of durational knowledge for a text-to-speech system in an Indian language. Master's thesis, Dept. of Computer science and Engineering, Indian Institute of Technology Madras, Mar.

K. Kiran Kumar. 2002. Duration and intonation knowledge for text-to-speech conversion system for Telugu and Hindi. Master's thesis, Dept. of Computer science and Engineering, Indian Institute of Technology Madras, May.

L. Lee, C. Tseng, and M. Ouh-Young. 1989. The synthesis rules in a Chinese text-to-speech system. *IEEE Trans. Acoustics, Speech, and Signal Processing*, 9(4):1309–1320.

Hansjorg Mixdorff. 2002. *An integrated approach to modeling German prosody*. Ph.D. thesis, Technical University, Dresden, Germany, July.

N. P. Narendra, K. Sreenivasa Rao, Krishnendu Ghosh, Vempada Ramu Reddy, and Sudhamay Maity. 2011. Development of syllable-based text to speech synthesis system in Bengali. *Int. J. of Speech Technology, Springer*, 14(3):167–181.

L. Rabiner and B. H. Juang. 1993. *Fundamentals of Speech Recognition*. Englewood Cliffs, NJ.

K. Sreenivasa Rao and B.Yegnanarayana. 2004. Two-stage duration model for Indian languages using neural networks. *Lecture Notes in Computer Science : Neural Information Processing, Springer*, 3316:1179–1185.

K. Sreenivasa Rao and B. Yegnanarayana. 2007. Modeling durations of syllables using neural networks. *Computer Speech and Language*, 21:282–295, Apr.

K. Sreenivasa Rao. 2005. *Acquisition and incorporation prosody knowledge for speech systems in Indian languages*. Ph.D. thesis, Dept. of Computer Science and Engineering, Indian Institute of Technology Madras, Chennai, India, May.

V. Ramu Reddy and K. Sreenivasa Rao. 2012. Better human computer interaction by enhancing the quality of text-to-speech synthesis. In *Proc. Int. Conf. Intelligent Human Computer Interaction (IHCI)*, pages 1–6, IIT Kharagpur, India, Dec.

V. Ramu Reddy and K. Sreenivasa Rao. 2013. Two-Stage Intonation Modeling Using Feedforward Neural Networks for Syllable based Text-to-Speech Synthesis. *Computer Speech and Language*, 27(5):1105–1126, Aug.

M. Riley. 1992. Tree-based modeling for speech synthesis. *in G. Bailly, C. Benoit, and T. Sawallis (Eds.), Talking machines: Theories, models and designs*, pages 265–273.

J. P. H. Van Santen. 1994. Assignment of segment duration in text-to-speech synthesis. *Computer Speech and Language*, 8:95–128, Apr.

G. P. Sonntag, Thomas Portele, and Barbara Heuft. 1997. Prosody generation with a neural network: Weighing the importance of input parameters. In *Proc. IEEE Int. Conf. Acoust., Speech, Signal Processing*, pages 931–934, Munich, Germany, Apr.

Joao Paulo Teixeira and Diamantino Freitas. 2003. Segmental durations predicted with a neural network. In *Proc. European Conf. Speech Communication and Technology*, pages 169–172, Geneva, Switzerland, Sept.

Noriko Umeda. 1976. Linguistic rules for text-to-speech synthesis. *Proc. IEEE*, 64:443–451, April.

B. Yegnanarayana, 1999. *Artificial Neural Networks*. Prentice-Hall, New Delhi, India.

Voice Activity Detection using Temporal Characteristics of Autocorrelation Lag and Maximum Spectral Amplitude in Sub-bands

Sivanand Achanta[1], Nivedita Chennupati[1], Vishala Pannala[1], Mansi Rankawat[2], Kishore Prahallad[1]

[1]Speech and Vision Lab, Language Technologies Research Center,IIIT - Hyderabad, India.
[2]Dhirubhai Ambani Institute of Information and Communication Technology, Gandhinagar, India
{sivanand.a,nivedita.chennupati,p.viahala}@research.iiit.ac.in,
mansirankawat19@gmail.com, kishore@iiit.ac.in

Abstract

A robust voice activity detection (VAD) is a prerequisite for many speech based applications like speech recognition. We investigated two VAD techniques that use time domain and frequency domain characteristics of speech signal. The temporal characteristic of the autocorrelation lag is able to discriminate speech and nonspeech regions. In the frequency domain, peak value of the magnitude spectrum in different sub-bands is used for VAD.

Performance of the proposed methods are evaluated on TIMIT database with noises from NOISEX-92 database at various signal-to-noise ratio (SNR) levels. From the experimental results, it is observed that VAD based on autocorrelation lag is working consistently better than the maximum peak value of the autocorrelation function based method. However, it performs inferior compared to our second approach and AMR-VAD2. Our second approach i.e., VAD based on maximum spectral amplitude in sub-bands outperforms AMR-VAD2 and Sohn VAD for some noise conditions. Moreover, it is shown that a threshold independent of noises and their levels can be selected in the proposed method.

1 Introduction

Voice activity detection (VAD) aims at separating the background noise and speech. VAD plays an important preprocessing role in applications like automatic speech recognition (Karray and Martin, 2003), speaker verification (Kinnunen and Rajan, 2013), wireless communications (Beritelli et al., 1998), speech enhancement for hearing aids (Itoh and Mizushima, 1997), etc. So, there has been growing interest for developing a robust VAD in low signal-to-noise ratio (SNR) conditions.

Approaches to VAD can be broadly classified as model-based and non-model based (signal processing) methods. One of the recent model-based approaches is based on using non-negative sparse coding (Teng and Jia, 2013). In this, a dictionary is trained for speech and noise separately and are concatenated to form a global dictionary. The noisy signals are represented as linear combination of elements of global dictionary. One inherent drawback of this technique is that it assumes noise during the test time to be known apriori.

In addition, there are also statistical model-based VADs (Sohn et al., 1999) (Ramirez et al., 2005) (Tan et al., 2010). Here, typically the noisy speech complex spectrum is assumed to follow a distribution like Gaussian and the parameters are estimated using various methods. This is followed by a likelihood ratio test on each frame to declare the signal frame to be speech absent or speech present. Improvements to incorporate continuity (Ramirez et al., 2005) and robustness (Tan et al., 2010) have also been proposed. Most of these techniques assume the noise statistics like variance to be known apriori. In general, these techniques perform poorly in low SNR conditions (You et al., 2012).

On the other hand, there are signal processing based approaches like using long-term signal variability (Ghosh et al., 2011), spectral flux (Sadjadi and Hansen, 2013), time-domain autocorrelation function (Ghaemmaghami et al., 2010), sub-band order statistic filters (Ramirez et al., 2004) to the VAD problem. These primarily involve ex-

D S Sharma, R Sangal and J D Pawar. Proc. of the 11th Intl. Conference on Natural Language Processing, pages 48–55,
Goa, India. December 2014. ©2014 NLP Association of India (NLPAI)

tracting a feature which is specific to speech and robust to various noises. For example, method based on time autocorrelation function proposed in (Ghaemmaghami et al., 2010), uses maximum peak of autocorrelation function (at non-zero lag) as the feature along with quasi periodicity property of speech to improve the robustness of VAD. In our time domain approach, we compare the performance of VAD using maximum peak of autocorrelation function (at non-zero lag) as a feature against the corresponding lag of autocorrelation function. The method using maximum peak of autocorrelation function (at non-zero lag) is referred to as ACF-MAX and that using corresponding lag is referred to as ACF-LAG hereafter. In frequency domain, the maximum amplitude of magnitude spectrum in sub-bands is used as a feature for VAD, we refer to this method as MSA-SB. While ACF-LAG method can be looked upon as an excitation based method, the MSA-SB can be accounted as a system based technique. Our techniques use speech production based features and are expected to be robust to a wide variety of noise conditions.

Our contributions in this paper are, investigating robustness of autocorrelation lag over peak method, proposing the use of maximum spectral amplitudes in speech specific sub-bands and combining these contours along with mean, variance normalizations to get a threshold independent of noises and their dBs.

Rest of the paper is organized as follows. The database and evaluation metrics used are described in Section 2. The detailed description of time domain approach is given in Section 3. Section 4 discusses the frequency domain technique. Conclusions follow in Section 5.

2 Database and Evaluation Metrics

The test signals are created by taking clean speech signals from TIMIT (tim, 1993) corpus and synthetically adding noise from the NOISEX-92 (Varga and Steeneken, 1993) corpus. Around 80 signals from TIMIT corpus sampled at 16000 Hz are taken. 10 signals from each of eight dialects with 7 male and 3 female sentences are randomly selected. Every signal is appended with approximately 2 sec silence before and after the speech signal and then noise is added to it at desired SNR. Seven different noises are used from NOISEX-92 database and SNRs at -10dB, -5dB, 0dB and 5dB

are considered. Approximately, each test signal has 40 % of noisy speech part and 60 % of noise part. The ground truth is generated by considering the appended silence along with labels of ' h# ', ' pau ' and ' epi ' in the TIMIT phone file as nonspeech and the other regions as speech. False alarm rate (% FAR) and miss rate (% MR) are used as evaluation metrics, and are given by,

$$\%FAR = \left(\frac{\text{nonspeech samples detected as speech}}{\text{total number of nonspeech samples}} \right) \times 100$$

$$\%MR = \left(\frac{\text{speech samples detected as nonspeech}}{\text{total number of speech samples}} \right) \times 100$$

The half total error rate (HTER) (Ghaemmaghami et al., 2010) is computed as the mean of FAR and MR. For a good VAD algorithm, FAR, MR and HTER must be as low as possible.

3 The Time Domain Method

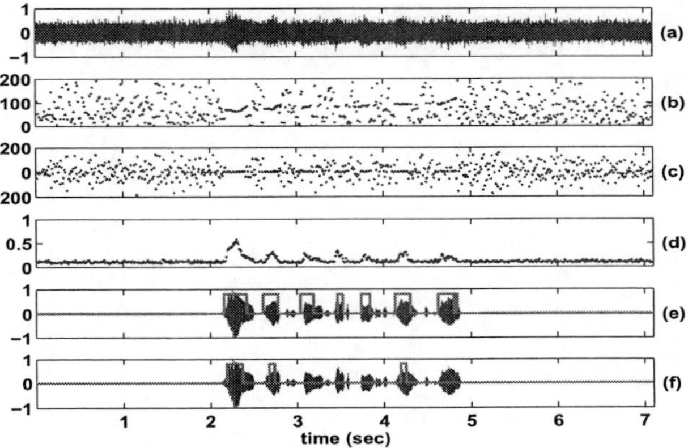

Figure 1: *Illustration of ACF-LAG and ACF-MAX methods; (a) Noisy speech signal (white noise at -10 dB), (b) Lag at the maximum in ACF plot, (c) Difference of (b), (d) Maximum peak of normalized ACF, (e) VAD from ACF-LAG method (displayed on clean speech signal for reference), (f) VAD from ACF-MAX method (displayed on clean speech signal for reference)*

The time domain autocorrelation function has been used in the past for many basic speech processing tasks like pitch extraction (de Cheveign and Kawahara, 2002). These methods exploit two key features associated with the autocorrelation function, one is the lag of the maximum peak which is usually used to compute F_0 and the other is the amplitude of maximum peak which is used to decide whether a speech frame is voiced or unvoiced. The maximum amplitude of autocorrelation function (ACF-MAX) is not a robust feature in low SNR conditions. So, in (Ghaemmaghami et al., 2010), along with ACF-MAX, the quasi periodicity property of speech is incorporated as a feature by using the cross-correlation to take the VAD decision. To exploit quasi-periodicity of speech, we propose to use the lag of the autocorrelation function (ACF-LAG) as a feature for VAD. The basis for our method comes from the observation that the pitch period of speech signals is locally stationary and varies smoothly in voiced regions (e.g., Fig. 1(b) region around 2-2.5 sec) where as in noise or unvoiced regions the lag varies erratically (e.g., Fig. 1(b) region around 0-1 sec). It is this speech specific feature which is exploited here to detect speech and noisy regions in a given signal. To the best of authors knowledge, pitch period or lag has not been solely used for VAD previously. Hence, ACF-LAG performance is analysed for VAD in this section.

In our method, the input speech is segmented into frames with frame size of 20 ms and shift of 10 ms. Let $x_p[n]$ be the pth signal frame, the normalised autocorrelation function for the frame is computed as,

$$R_p[l] = \frac{\sum_{n=0}^{L-l-1} x_p[n]x_p[n+l]}{\sum_{n=0}^{L-1} x_p[n]x_p[n]} \qquad (1)$$

where l is the autocorrelation lag and L is the length of the signal frame. Usually l is limited between 2 ms and 20 ms because any value of pitch outside this range is considered to be spurious.

$$V(p) = \max_{l} R_p(l) \qquad (2)$$

$$I(p) = \underset{l}{\operatorname{argmax}} R_p(l) \qquad (3)$$

where $V(p)$ is the peak of autocorrelation function at non-zero lag and $I(p)$ is the corresponding lag at which the peak occurs per frame.

In ACF-MAX method, peak of autocorrelation function (eq. 2) is thresholded to get the VAD decision. In ACF-LAG method, VAD decision is made using the lag (eq. 3) corresponding to maximum of autocorrelation function. $I(p)$ is plotted in Fig. 1(b). From the plot, it can be seen that for unvoiced/noise regions the values of index vary randomly where as in voiced regions, it varies smoothly. This characteristic of the contour is used to detect voiced and unvoiced/noise regions in speech. The difference operation on contour, will give its slope and slope should be minimal when the contour is slowly varying. VAD decision is taken by setting a threshold on differenced vector. Fig. 1 (e) and (f), shows VAD decisions from ACF-LAG and ACF-MAX methods respectively. It can be seen that ACF-LAG method performs better than ACF-MAX method.

Table 1: *FAR and MR for various noises in different SNRs for ACF-LAG and ACF-MAX methods*

White Noise	5 dB		0 dB		-5 dB		-10 dB	
	MR %	FAR %	MR %	FAR %	MR %	FAR %	MR %	FAR %
ACF-LAG	**52.90**	0.05	**58.61**	0.04	**67.64**	0.04	**81.96**	0.01
ACF-MAX	71.21	0.00	82.82	0.00	93.79	0.00	99.24	0.00

Pink Noise	5 dB		0 dB		-5 dB		-10 dB	
	MR %	FAR %	MR %	FAR %	MR %	FAR %	MR %	FAR %
ACF-LAG	**57.90**	0.07	**65.64**	0.04	**78.22**	0.04	**91.95**	0.09
ACF-MAX	69.71	0.00	81.44	0.00	92.62	0.00	98.89	0.00

HFchannel Noise	5 dB		0 dB		-5 dB		-10 dB	
	MR %	FAR %	MR %	FAR %	MR %	FAR %	MR %	FAR %
ACF-LAG	**55.49**	0.09	**63.38**	0.09	**75.44**	0.16	**89.96**	0.09
ACF-MAX	70.40	0.00	82.01	0.00	93.70	0.00	98.94	0.00

Factory1 Noise	5 dB		0 dB		-5 dB		-10 dB	
	MR %	FAR %	MR %	FAR %	MR %	FAR %	MR %	FAR %
ACF-LAG	**55.52**	3.29	**63.46**	4.70	**76.03**	3.83	**88.07**	3.62
ACF-MAX	69.96	0.02	81.25	0.01	92.03	0.00	98.00	0.00

Buccaneer1 Noise	5 dB		0 dB		-5 dB		-10 dB	
	MR %	FAR %	MR %	FAR %	MR %	FAR %	MR %	FAR %
ACF-LAG	**57.17**	0.21	**65.16**	0.26	**78.23**	0.19	**90.99**	0.28
ACF-MAX	70.73	0.00	83.04	0.00	94.25	0.00	99.29	0.00

Volvo Noise	5 dB		0 dB		-5 dB		-10 dB	
	MR %	FAR %	MR %	FAR %	MR %	FAR %	MR %	FAR %
ACF-LAG	**56.61**	0.07	**63.99**	0.04	**75.32**	0.01	**87.07**	0.00
ACF-MAX	63.70	0.01	72.07	0.01	83.25	0.00	92.36	0.00

Babble Noise	5 dB		0 dB		-5 dB		-10 dB	
	MR %	FAR %	MR %	FAR %	MR %	FAR %	MR %	FAR %
ACF-LAG	**51.25**	19.28	**59.45**	16.71	**70.41**	17.81	**77.93**	17.27
ACF-MAX	66.33	3.58	77.52	3.07	89.15	3.93	95.17	3.51

3.1 Results

Table 1 reports MR and FAR of ACF-LAG and ACF-MAX methods. FAR is low for both the methods across all the noises at different SNRs. This implies that rejection of nonspeech by both the algorithms is equally good. It can also be observed from the Table 1 that ACF-LAG method has relatively lower MR than the ACF-MAX method. Hence, our hypothesis that lag of the autocorrelation function at the maximum is a robust feature compared to the peak value itself is evident. The MR is high in both the methods indicating that actual speech is missed in most of the cases. This is due to the fact that proposed methods work only for voiced regions but ground truth includes both voiced and unvoiced regions as speech. Thus both the techniques are far from being useful as a practical VAD and hence we explore the frequency domain approach.

4 The Frequency Domain Method

The resonances of the vocal tract are high energy regions in the spectrum and are hence expected to be robust to noisy conditions. Due to inherent constraints in the human speech production mechanism, the variation of spectrum is slow as compared to noisy regions. This fact has been used in the literature for VAD, by utilizing feature such as spectral flux. However, our technique differs from all the previous techniques by making use of maximum of the magnitude spectrum alone as the feature. The maximum in magnitude spectrum corresponds to the strength of a resonance of vocal tract in speech regions and is used as a feature to distinguish speech from nonspeech.

The given noisy signal is first segmented into frames with frame size of 25 ms and hop of 5 ms. Each frame is windowed with a hamming window. The discrete Fourier transform (DFT) for p^{th} frame of the signal is computed as,

$$X_p[k] = \sum_{n=0}^{N-1} x_p[n]e^{-\frac{j2\pi kn}{N}} \qquad (4)$$

where N is the number of DFT points and k ranges from $0, \cdots, N-1$. N is set to 2048 in our experiments. Then the maximum of the magnitude part of the complex spectrum for each frame is the desired spectral feature.

$$M(p) = \max |X_p(k)|; \quad k = 0, 1, \cdots, N-1 \qquad (5)$$

In Fig. 2, noisy signal (signal corrupted with white noise at -5 dB) is shown in (a) and the corresponding maximum of the DFT spectrum extracted per frame is plotted in (b). It is observed that in the noise part, there is a high frequency ripple (e.g., Fig. 2(b) region around 0-1 sec) and in the speech region the variation of maximum over time is slow and smooth (e.g., Fig. 2(b) region around 2-3 sec). So, an FIR filter is used for low-pass filtering to remove the ripple. The low-pass filtered version of the maximum contour is plotted in (c) which is then thresholded to take the VAD decision.

While this method works for white noise, it fails for few noises like pink and volvo. As can be seen

from the Fig. 3 (b) and (c), for pink noise (at -5 dB SNR), passing the maximum contour through the low-pass filter, even the noisy region has a slowly varying maximum amplitude. This is because of the high concentration of low frequency energy in pink noise.

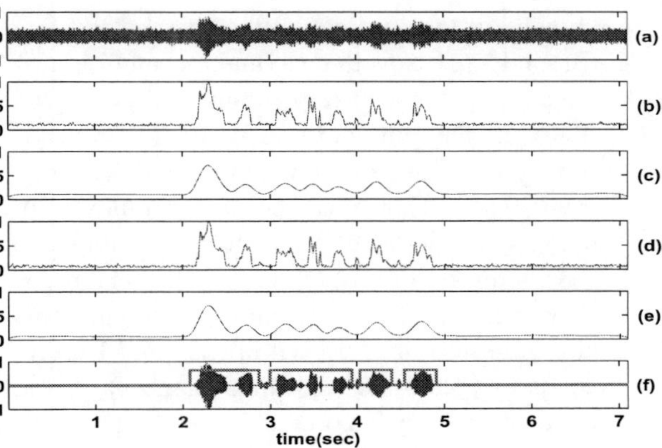

Figure 2: *The maximum contours of the DFT spectrum in white noise at -5 dB; (a) Noisy signal, (b) Maximum amplitude in the magnitude spectrum, (c) Low-pass filtered signal of (b), (d) Maximum amplitude in the resonance 1 sub-band of magnitude spectrum, (e) Low-pass filtered signal of (d), (f) VAD from MSA-SB method (displayed on clean speech signal for reference)*

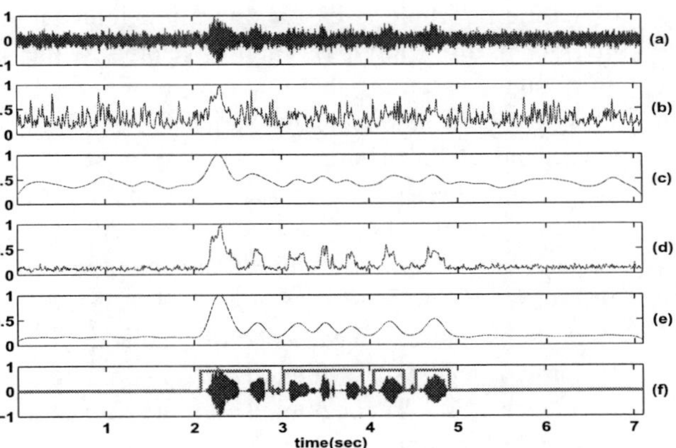

Figure 3: *The maximum contours of the DFT spectrum in pink noise at -5 dB; (a) Noisy signal, (b) Maximum amplitude in the magnitude spectrum, (c) Low-pass filtered signal of (b), (d) Maximum amplitude in the resonance 1 sub-band of magnitude spectrum, (e) Low-pass filtered signal of (d), (f) VAD from MSA-SB method (displayed on clean speech signal for reference)*

This motivated us to experiment with maximum contours in sub-bands that are specific to vocal tract resonances. The entire spectrum, is divided into three sub-bands, which were chosen to be 300-900Hz , 600-2800 Hz and 1400-3800 Hz corresponding to ranges of first three vocal tract resonances (Deng et al., 2006). The maximum in each sub-band of the spectrum is then computed. Fig. 2 (d) and 3 (d) show the maximum contour in resonance 1 sub-band corresponding to speech signal with white and pink noise at -5 dB. These maximum contours are then low-pass filtered (Figs. 2 (e) and 3 (e)). Thus, it can be seen that maximum contours in a sub-band specific to speech, is able to robustly discriminate speech and noise regions, as opposed to the full-band maximum contours. This is because maximum picked in sub-band 1 corresponds to vocal tract resonance in speech region and to an arbitrary maximum in noise regions. As transition of vocal tract is a continuum, the variation of maximum contour is smooth in speech regions and is otherwise in noise regions. And also in this sub-bands maximum of speech has higher amplitude than that of noise.

Experimental results show that maximum in sub-band 1 is sufficient for robust VAD. VAD decision is obtained by setting a threshold on the low-pass filtered version of maximum contour. Figs. 2 (f) and 3 (f) show the resulting VAD. One way of setting threshold is by picking a maximum in first 50 ms from low-pass filtered version of the noisy signal assuming that it is devoid of speech. This threshold automatically varies for different noises and SNRs. Though, it is the simplest way of selecting threshold, it might not be the appropriate way in all cases. Thus, for a more efficient thresholding operation, we used the combined decision of low-pass filtered versions of three bands. Mean subtraction and variance normalization is performed on low-pass filtered versions of three selected bands. The output is summed up and again mean subtraction and variance normalization is performed to get a final contour on which VAD decision is to be taken. The histogram for this final contour varies between -2 to 5. So, threshold is varied between -0.5 to 0.8 to decide upon a proper value for speech-nonspeech decision. ROC curves obtained are shown in fig. 4. We can observe that the same threshold that is independent of noise and SNR can be applied on final contour to get an appropriate VAD decision.

This is due to combination of three sub-bands, followed by mean and variance normalization that is canceling the effect of noise level through out the signal. Sohn method (Sohn et al., 1999) for VAD provides an option to vary thresholds. False alarm rate (FAR) and correct detection rate (CDR) varies according to threshold. ROCs are plotted by taking FAR on x-axis and CDR on y-axis for various thresholds. ROCs of our method are compared with VAD using Sohn (Sohn et al., 1999) method as shown in fig. 4. It is observed that our method outperforms Sohn for all the tested noises at different dBs. After selecting an appropriate threshold from ROC, our method is compared with AMR-VAD2 (AMR, 1998) in the results section.

Table 2: *FAR and MR for various noises in different SNRs for MSA-SB and AMR2 methods*

White Noise	5 dB		0 dB		-5 dB		-10 dB	
	MR %	FAR %	MR %	FAR %	MR %	FAR %	MR %	FAR %
MSA-SB	12.71	1.98	**15.79**	1.80	**20.62**	1.59	**28.50**	1.34
AMR2	6.92	2.39	20.83	1.49	47.80	0.63	83.38	0.32

Pink Noise	5 dB		0 dB		-5 dB		-10 dB	
	MR %	FAR %	MR %	FAR %	MR %	FAR %	MR %	FAR %
MSA-SB	14.70	**1.85**	**19.24**	**1.61**	**26.57**	1.46	**39.50**	2.28
AMR2	5.84	2.80	21.32	1.83	50.83	0.72	83.24	0.48

HFchannel Noise	5 dB		0 dB		-5 dB		-10 dB	
	MR %	FAR %	MR %	FAR %	MR %	FAR %	MR %	FAR %
MSA-SB	14.92	**1.87**	19.58	**1.67**	**26.24**	**1.51**	**37.19**	2.13
AMR2	3.89	3.95	17.04	2.66	42.69	2.05	73.95	1.40

Factory1 Noise	5 dB		0 dB		-5 dB		-10 dB	
	MR %	FAR %	MR %	FAR %	MR %	FAR %	MR %	FAR %
MSA-SB	16.73	**3.43**	23.00	**6.63**	32.32	**11.99**	39.39	**22.61**
AMR2	2.87	37.54	10.13	36.25	25.84	37.70	48.47	37.36

Buccaneer1 Noise	5 dB		0 dB		-5 dB		-10 dB	
	MR %	FAR %	MR %	FAR %	MR %	FAR %	MR %	FAR %
MSA-SB	15.46	**1.83**	**19.83**	**1.66**	**26.30**	1.63	**41.46**	3.73
AMR2	7.17	3.29	24.36	2.05	56.17	1.18	87.66	0.84

Volvo Noise	5 dB		0 dB		-5 dB		-10 dB	
	MR %	FAR %	MR %	FAR %	MR %	FAR %	MR %	FAR %
MSA-SB	9.59	**2.21**	10.36	**2.13**	11.54	**2.04**	13.64	**1.93**
AMR2	0.54	5.57	0.50	5.39	0.51	5.20	0.93	5.14

Babble Noise	5 dB		0 dB		-5 dB		-10 dB	
	MR %	FAR %	MR %	FAR %	MR %	FAR %	MR %	FAR %
MSA-SB	22.15	**6.16**	28.51	**14.84**	40.53	**20.44**	54.75	**24.30**
AMR2	0.93	36.78	4.57	34.05	14.58	31.98	29.80	30.42

4.1 Results

The proposed algorithms are compared against the standard ETSI AMR-VAD2 (AMR, 1998). The FAR and MR of our methods along with the baseline techniques in various noisy conditions in four different SNRs are reported in Table 2. The corresponding HTER is plotted in Fig. 5. The lower HTER indicates better performance of the algorithm. We can observe from the bar graph that for most of the noise conditions, MSA-SB method outperforms (3rd bar (light yellow) from the left in every noise) all other methods at low SNR levels. For volvo noise, we can see that MSA-SB method has lower FAR but higher MR compared

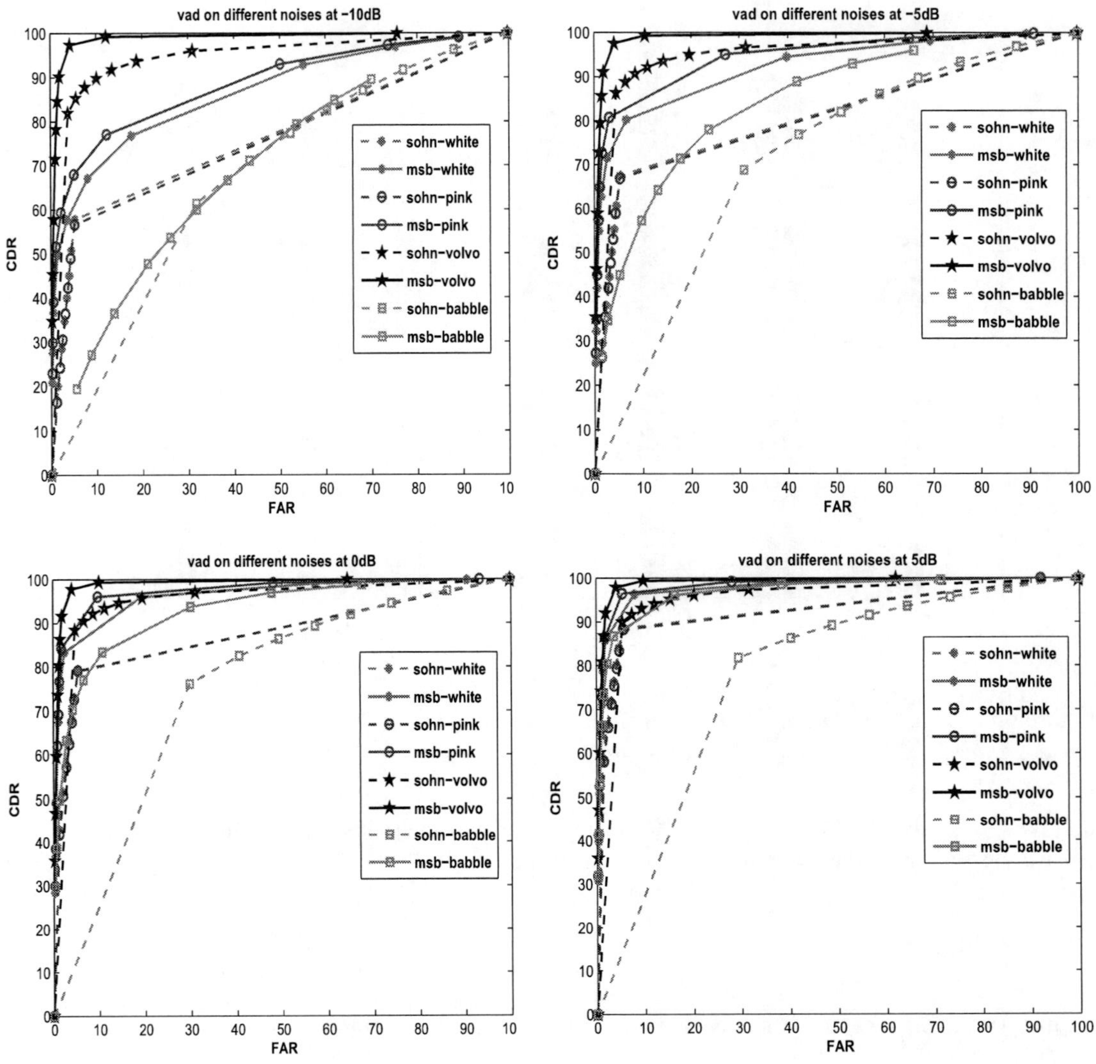

Figure 4: *ROC curves for different noises at -10, -5, 0 and 5 dB*

to AMR2. This is because of the threshold setting, some unvoiced and stop sounds might have been recognised as nonspeech in volvo. In babble noise, from the Table 2 one can observe that the FAR is consistently lower for MSA-SB than that of the AMR2 method. However in AMR2, MR is lower than all the methods for all SNRs in babble. This is attributed to the fact that our algorithms rely on speech specific features and babble being speech like noise, shows a drop in the performance. In summary, for most noises MSA-SB outperforms AMR2, while in some it performs comparable to it.

5 Conclusions and Future Work

In this paper, we investigated two methods for VAD in low SNR conditions. We experimented on seven noise conditions under four different SNRs. The time domain analysis revealed that lag of the autocorrelation function at peak (ACF-LAG) is more reliable than peak value (ACF-MAX) itself. The frequency domain MSA-SB method was found to be very robust even under very low SNR conditions and justifies our motivation for choosing sub-bands specific to vocal tract resonance ranges. The combination of sub-bands followed by mean and variance normalization has resulted in choosing a threshold independent of noise con-

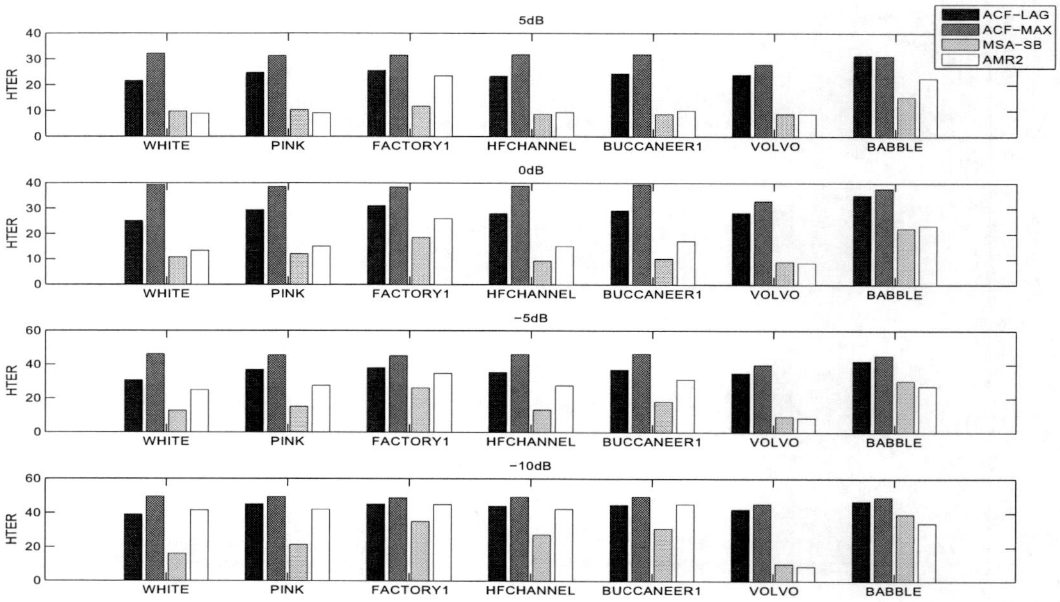

Figure 5: *% HTER performance of the proposed algorithms along with the baseline methods for each noise scenario at SNRs 5dB, 0 dB, -5dB, -10dB.*

ditions and levels. In future, we plan to do extensive evaluation of the technique on real world speech signals.

Acknowledgment

The authors would like to thank Sudarsana, Anand, Gautam, Vasanth, Bhargav and Santosh for their valuable feedback.

References

1998. Digital cellular telecommunications system (Phase 2+); Adaptive multi rate (AMR) speech; ANSI-C code for AMR speech codec.

F. Beritelli, S. Casale, and A. Cavallaero. 1998. A robust voice activity detector for wireless communications using soft computing. *IEEE Journal on Selected Areas in Communications*, 16(9):1818–1829, Dec.

Alain de Cheveign and Hideki Kawahara. 2002. Yin, a fundamental frequency estimator for speech and music. *The Journal of the Acoustical Society of America*, 111(4):1917–1930.

Li Deng, A. Acero, and I. Bazzi. 2006. Tracking vocal tract resonances using a quantized nonlinear function embedded in a temporal constraint. *IEEE Trans. Audio, Speech Lang. Process.*, 14(2):425–434, March.

Houman Ghaemmaghami, Brendan J Baker, Robert J Vogt, and Sridha Sridharan. 2010. Noise robust voice activity detection using features extracted from the time-domain autocorrelation function. *Proc., INTERSPEECH*.

P.K. Ghosh, A. Tsiartas, and S. Narayanan. 2011. Robust voice activity detection using long-term signal variability. *IEEE Trans. Audio, Speech Lang. Process.*, 19(3):600–613.

K. Itoh and M. Mizushima. 1997. Environmental noise reduction based on speech/non-speech identification for hearing aids. In *Proc., ICASSP*, volume 1, pages 419–422, Apr.

Lamia Karray and Arnaud Martin. 2003. Towards improving speech detection robustness for speech recognition in adverse conditions. *Speech Communication*, 40(3):261 – 276.

T. Kinnunen and P. Rajan. 2013. A practical, self-adaptive voice activity detector for speaker verification with noisy telephone and microphone data. In *Proc., ICASSP*, pages 7229–7233.

J. Ramirez, J.C. Segura, C. Benirez, A. de la Torre, and A. Rubio. 2004. A new voice activity detector using subband order-statistics filters for robust speech recognition. In *Proc., ICASSP*, volume 1, pages 849–52, May.

J. Ramirez, J.C. Segura, C. Benitez, L. Garcia, and A. Rubio. 2005. Statistical voice activity detection using a multiple observation likelihood ratio test. *IEEE Signal Process. Lett.*, 12(10):689–692, Oct.

S.O. Sadjadi and J.H.L. Hansen. 2013. Unsupervised speech activity detection using voicing measures and perceptual spectral flux. *IEEE Signal Process. Lett.*, 20(3):197–200, March.

Jongseo Sohn, Nam Soo Kim, and Wonyong Sung. 1999. A statistical model-based voice activity detection. *IEEE Signal Process. Lett.*, 6(1):1–3, Jan.

Lee Ngee Tan, B.J. Borgstrom, and Abeer Alwan. 2010. Voice activity detection using harmonic frequency components in likelihood ratio test. In *Proc., ICASSP*, pages 4466–4469, March.

Peng Teng and Yunde Jia. 2013. Voice activity detection using convolutive non-negative sparse coding. In *Proc., ICASSP*, pages 7373–7377, May.

1993. DARPA-TIMIT. *Acoustic-Phonetic Continuous Speech Corpus*.

Andrew Varga and Herman J. M. Steeneken. 1993. Assessment for automatic speech recognition: II. NOISEX-92: A database and an experiment to study the effect of additive noise on speech recognition systems. *Speech Communication*, 12(3):247–251.

Datao You, Jiqing Han, Guibin Zheng, and Tieran Zheng. 2012. Sparse power spectrum based robust voice activity detector. In *Proc., ICASSP*, pages 289–292, March.

Use of GPU and Feature Reduction for Fast Query-by-Example Spoken Term Detection

Gautam Mantena, Kishore Prahallad

International Institute of Information Technology - Hyderabad, India

`gautam.mantena@research.iiit.ac.in, kishore@iiit.ac.in`

Abstract

For query-by-example spoken term detection (QbE-STD) on low resource languages, variants of dynamic time warping techniques (DTW) are used. However, DTW-based techniques are slow and thus a limitation to search in large spoken audio databases. In order to enable fast search in large databases, we exploit the use of intensive parallel computations of the graphical processing units (GPUs). In this paper, we use a GPU to improve the search speed of a DTW variant by parallelizing the distance computation between the Gaussian posteriorgrams of spoken query and spoken audio. We also use a faster method of searching by averaging the successive Gaussian posteriorgrams to reduce the length of the spoken audio and the spoken query. The results indicate an improvement of about 100x with a marginal drop in search performance.

1 Introduction

Query by example spoken term detection (QbE-STD) task is to detect a spoken query within a spoken audio database. In a conventional approach, an automatic speech recognition (ASR) system is used to convert the speech signal to a sequence of symbols and then text-based search techniques are exploited for search (Szöke et al., 2008), (Saraclar and Sproat, 2004), (Miller et al., 2007). However, ASR-based techniques assume the availability of labelled data for training the acoustic and language models and thus a limitation for low resource languages. To overcome this issue, dynamic time warping (DTW) based techniques are

proposed for QbE-STD search (Zhang and Glass, 2009), (Anguera and Ferrarons, 2013), (Mantena et al., 2014), (Gupta et al., 2011), (Hazen et al., 2009).

Parameters extracted from the speech signal such as Mel-frequency cepstral coefficients and frequency domain linear prediction cepstral coefficients (Thomas et al., 2008), (Ganapathy et al., 2010) cannot be used directly as they also capture speaker information. To overcome this issue, Gaussian (Zhang and Glass, 2009), (Anguera and Ferrarons, 2013), (Mantena et al., 2014) and phone (Gupta et al., 2011), (Hazen et al., 2009) posteriorgrams are used as feature representations for DTW-based search. Gaussian posteriorgrams are a popular feature representation in low resource scenarios as they do not require any prior labelled data to compute them. In (Zhang and Glass, 2009), (Mantena et al., 2014), (Anguera, 2012), Gaussian posteriorgrams are shown to be a good feature representation to suppress speaker characteristics and to perform search across multilingual data.

Segmental DTW (S-DTW) is a popular technique for searching a spoken query within a spoken audio data (Zhang and Glass, 2009). In (Zhang and Glass, 2011), it is shown that the computational upper bound of S-DTW is of the order $O(mn^2)$, where m, n are the lengths of the spoken audio and spoken query respectively. To improve the search time, variants of DTW-based techniques with a computational upper bound of $O(mn)$ such as sub-sequence DTW (Anguera and Ferrarons, 2013) and non-segmental DTW (NS-DTW) (Mantena et al., 2014) are used for QbE-STD. However, DTW-based search techniques are still slow as compared to other model based approaches (Szöke et al., 2008), (Saraclar and

D S Sharma, R Sangal and J D Pawar. Proc. of the 11th Intl. Conference on Natural Language Processing, pages 56–62,
Goa, India. December 2014. ©2014 NLP Association of India (NLPAI)

Sproat, 2004), (Miller et al., 2007) and thus a limitation for searching large databases.

An approach to improve the search speed is to use hardware solutions such as graphical processing units (GPUs). GPU is a computing device that are designed for intensive, highly parallel computations that are often needed in real time speech applications. In ASR, GPUs have been used to compute the acoustic likelihoods for large mixture models (Shi et al., 2008), (Cardinal et al., 2008), and in building computation intensive machine learning algorithms such as deep neural networks (Povey et al., 2011), (Bergstra et al., 2010). In (Zhang et al., 2012), GPUs were used to perform constraint based search to prune out the spoken audio references to perform the QbE-STD search. The pruning process was implemented by computing a lower bound estimate for DTW.

In this paper, we use a GPU to improve the search speed of NS-DTW using Gaussian posteriorgrams as feature representation of speech. The contributions of this paper are as follows: (a) Experimental results to show the effect of the Gaussian posteriorgram dimension on the QbE-STD search using NS-DTW algorithm, (b) GPU implementation of NS-DTW. The results indicate that by using a GPU, NS-DTW search speed can be made independent (an approximation) of the dimension of the Gaussian posteriorgram, and (c) We also use a faster method of searching by averaging the successive Gaussian posteriorgrams to reduce the length of the spoken audio and the spoken query. The results indicate an improvement of about 100x with a marginal drop in search performance.

The organization of the paper is as follows: Section 2 describes the database used in this work. In Section 3, we describe the DTW-based algorithm used to perform the search. Section 4 and Section 4.1 describes the computation of Gaussian posteriorgrams and its effect on the search speed. Section 5 describes the GPU implementation of NS-DTW and followed by conclusions in Section 6.

2 Database and Evaluation

In this work, we use MediaEval 2012 data for evaluation which consists of audio recorded via telephone in 4 South African languages (Barnard et al., 2009). We consider two data sets, development (dev) and evaluation (eval) which contain spoken audio (reference) and spoken query data.

The statistics of the audio data is shown in Table 1.

Table 1: Statistics of MediaEval 2012 data.

Data	Utts	Total(mins)	Average(sec)
dev reference	1580	221.863	8.42
dev query	100	2.372	1.42
eval reference	1660	232.541	8.40
eval query	100	2.537	1.52

All the evaluations are performed using 2006 NIST evaluation criteria (Fiscus et al., 2007), (Metze et al., 2012) and the corresponding maximum term weighted values (MTWV), average miss probability (MP) and false alarm probability (FAP) are reported.

3 QbE-STD using NS-DTW

In this paper, a variant of DTW-based technique referred to as non-segmental DTW (NS-DTW) is used for QbE-STD search (Mantena et al., 2014). Let Q and R be a spoken query and a spoken audio (or reference) containing n and m feature vectors respectively and are given as follows:

$$Q = [\mathbf{q_1}, \mathbf{q_2}, \ldots, \mathbf{q_i}, \ldots, \mathbf{q_n}]_{d \times n} \qquad (1)$$
$$R = [\mathbf{u_1}, \mathbf{u_2}, \ldots, \mathbf{u_j}, \ldots, \mathbf{u_m}]_{d \times m} \qquad (2)$$

Each of these feature vectors represent a d dimensional Gaussian posteriorgrams (as described in Section 4). The distance measure between a query vector $\mathbf{q_i}$ and a reference vector $\mathbf{u_j}$ is the negative logarithm of the cosine similarity of the two vectors and is given by:

$$d(i, j) = -log\left(\hat{\mathbf{q}}_\mathbf{i}^T \hat{\mathbf{u}}_\mathbf{j}\right), \qquad (3)$$

where $\hat{\mathbf{q}}_\mathbf{i} = \frac{\mathbf{q_i}}{||\mathbf{q_i}||}$ and $\hat{\mathbf{u}}_\mathbf{j} = \frac{\mathbf{u_j}}{||\mathbf{u_j}||}$.

A similarity matrix S of size $m \times n$ is computed to align the reference and query feature vectors. Let i, j represent a column and a row of a matrix. For DTW search, the start and end time stamps are approximated by allowing the query to start from any point in the reference and is given by $S(1, j) = d(1, j)$. Once the matrix S is initialized the update equations for alignment are given by Eq. 4.

$$S(i,j) = min \left\{ \begin{array}{c} \dfrac{d(i,j) + S(i-1, j-2)}{T(i-1, j-2) + 1} \\ \dfrac{d(i,j) + S(i-1, j-1)}{T(i-1, j-1) + 2} \\ \dfrac{d(i,j) + S(i-1, j)}{T(i-1, j) + 1} \end{array} \right\},$$

$$(4)$$

where $T(i,j)$ is a transition matrix which represents the number of transitions required to reach i, j from a start point. On computing the similarity matrix, the end point of the query within a reference is given by $\min_j \{S(n,j)\}$ and followed by a path traceback to obtain the start time stamp.

In segmental-DTW the reference is partitioned based on the length of the query and a DTW is performed for each partition resulting in a computational upper bound of $O(mn^2)$ for search. However, in NS-DTW, the reference is not partitioned and a similarity matrix of size $m \times n$ is computed resulting in a computational upper bound of $O(mn)$ (Mantena et al., 2014).

During the QbE-STD search, there is a possibility of the query to be present in the reference more than once. Hence, 5 best alignment scoring indices are considered from the similarity matrix (Mantena et al., 2014).

4   Feature Representation using Gaussian Posteriorgrams

In general, Gaussian posteriorgrams are obtained by a two step process (Anguera, 2012), (Mantena et al., 2014). In the first step, acoustic parameters such as frequency domain linear prediction cepstral coefficients (FDLP) are extracted from the speech signal (Mantena et al., 2014). A 25 ms window length with 10 ms shift is considered to extract 13 dimensional features along with delta and acceleration coefficients for FDLP. An all-pole model of order 160 poles/sec and 37 filter banks are considered to extract FDLP.

In general, spectral features such as Mel-frequency cepstral coefficients (MFCC) are used to compute Gaussian posteriorgrams. However, in (Mantena et al., 2014), we have shown that the FDLP parameters were working better than the conventional features such as MFCC.

In the second step, Gaussian posteriorgrams are computed by training a Gaussian mixture model (GMM) with d number of Gaussians using the spoken audio data and the posterior probability obtained from each Gaussian is used to represent the

acoustic parameter. Thus, 39 dimensional FDLP parameters are mapped to d dimensional Gaussian posteriorgrams. In Section 4.1 we provide experimental results to show the effect of d on the search speed in the context of QbE-STD.

4.1   Effect of Gaussian Posteriorgram Dimension on the Search Time

In this Section, we compute the search performance and search time on dev dataset by varying the number of Gaussians (d). We consider the search time as the time required to search all the queries within a reference dataset. Table 2 show the miss probability (MP), false alarm probability (FAP), maximum term weighted value (MTWV), and search time (in minutes) obtained using the Gaussian posteriorgrams of FDLP for various values of d.

Table 2: Miss probability (MP), false alarm probability (FAP), maximum term weighted value (MTWV) and search time on dev dataset for various Gaussian posteriorgram dimensions (d) (Mantena et al., 2014).

d	MP	FAP (10^{-2})	MTWV	Search Time (mins)
8	0.824	0.595	0.084	18.39
16	0.652	0.917	0.207	22.57
32	0.540	1.098	0.292	30.60
64	0.465	1.207	0.349	47.53
128	0.426	1.136	0.399	80.24
256	0.400	1.241	0.410	145.07
512	0.476	0.658	0.422	274.98
1024	0.413	1.009	0.432	534.15

From Table 2, it can be seen that MTWV increases with an increase in d. However, with an increase in d there is increase in search time and thus resulting a slower QbE-STD search. In (Mantena et al., 2014), $d = 128$ is considered as an optimum value of the Gaussian posteriorgram dimension based on the MTWV and the search time. A more detailed description of the performance of NS-DTW by varying the dimensions of the Gaussian posteriorgrams is given in (Mantena et al., 2014).

To better understand the computation intensive components in NS-DTW, we calculate the time required for distance computation (as given by Eq. (3)) and to perform the update equations (as given by Eq. (4)) along with the path traceback for $d = 128$ (as shown in Table 3). It is to be noted that the path traceback includes the selection of 5 best alignment scoring indices from each of the reference file and thereby obtaining the start and end time stamps.

Table 3: Time taken for distance computation, $d(i, j)$, and for update equations, $S(i, j)$, along with the alignment path traceback. It is to be noted that we use $d = 128$ as the dimension of the Gaussian posteriorgrams.

	Time (mins)
$d(i, j)$	66.15
$S(i, j)$ + Path traceback	14.08

From Table 3, it can be seen that the distance computation occupies 82.44% of the total search time. Thus, we are motivated to use GPUs for fast distance computation. A more detailed description of GPU implementation of NS-DTW is provided in Section 5.

5   GPU Accelerated NS-DTW

In this Section, we use NVIDIA CUDA framework to exploit parallel processing for fast QbE-STD search. CUDA follows a single instruction multiple data (SIMD) paradigm where the GPU cores executes the same instruction on different portions of the data (Nickolls et al., 2008). DTW-based variants perform the update equations in a sequential manner and thus an issue for GPU implementations (Zhang et al., 2012), (Sart et al., 2010). A solution to overcome the problem is to parallelize a part of the computation such as the distance calculation for a search speedup. In this paper, we use NVIDIA GT 610 graphic card with 48 cores and a GPU memory of 2048 MB.

CUDA is known for fast matrix operations such as multiplication and thus we exploit its use for distance computation. To exploit the computing power of the GPU, we use matrix multiplication of the complete reference (R) and query (Q) feature vectors. Let $\hat{S}$ represent an $m \times n$ matrix such that $\hat{S}(i, j) = d(i, j)$. $\hat{S}$ can be obtained as follows: $\hat{S} = -log(R^T Q)$, where R and Q are the reference and query feature vectors (as described in Eq. (1) and Eq. (2)). It is to be noted that $R^T Q$ represents an $m \times n$ matrix and $log(R^T Q)$ performs a logarithmic operation on all the $m \times n$ elements in the matrix.

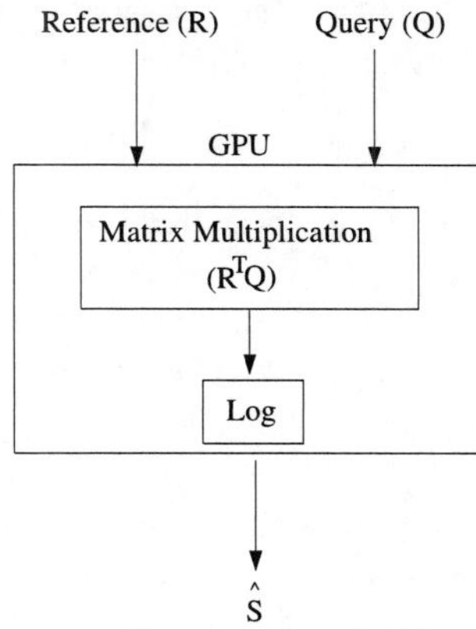

Figure 1: A general block diagram of the distance computation in a GPU for NS-DTW.

The GPU implementation of the NS-DTW is as follows:

1. CPU copies the reference and query Gaussian posteriorgrams into the GPU memory.

2. To initialize $\hat{S}$, CUDA kernels (or functions) are used and is obtained in a two step process: (a) Firstly, the dot product is performed using matrix multiplication given by $R^T Q$, and (b) Then the log operation is performed. Fig. 1 shows a general block diagram of the operations performed using GPU to obtain $\hat{S}$.

3. The CPU, then copies the $\hat{S}$ into the system memory (RAM) and then performs the update equations as described in Eq. (4). It is to be noted that the distance of each of the query and reference Gaussian posteriorgrams have been computed in *Step 2* and thus we use $\hat{S}(i, j)$ instead of $d(i, j)$ in the update equations given by Eq. (4).

5.1   Use of Batch Processing for Search

To maximize the number of parallel computations on the GPU we use batch processing wherein NS-DTW is performed on a query Q and the entire database of references pooled to a single sequence of Gaussian posteriorgrams. This single sequence of Gaussian posteriorgrams is referred to as a reference batch (R_b) and is given as follows:

$$R_b = [R^1_{d \times m_1}, R^2_{d \times m_2}, \ldots,$$
$$\ldots, R^k_{d \times m_k}, \ldots, R^L_{d \times m_L}]_{d \times M}, \quad (5)$$

where $R^k_{d \times m_k}$ is a matrix of size $d \times m_k$ which represents the kth reference containing m_k sequence of Gaussian posteriorgrams of dimension d. The size of R_b is $d \times M$, where $M = \sum_{k=1}^{L} m_k$.

On obtaining R_b, $\hat{S}$ is then computed as follows: $\hat{S} = -log(R_b^T Q)$. If R_b is very large we split the data into a smaller batches and processes a single batch at a time. On computing the similarity matrix S, we select 500 best alignment score indices and perform a path trace back to obtain the start time stamps of the possible search hits. From the dev dataset, we have observed that there were no queries which are present in more than 500 spoken audio and thus we select 500 best alignment score indices for detection.

5.2 Comparison of Search Time: GPU vs CPU

Fig. 2 shows the search speed of NS-DTW using CPU and GPU cores. It is to be noted that we use batch processing on the GPU for QbE-STD search. From Fig. 2, it can be seen that the GPU implementation is faster than that of the CPU and the search speed is independent (an approximation) of the dimension (d).

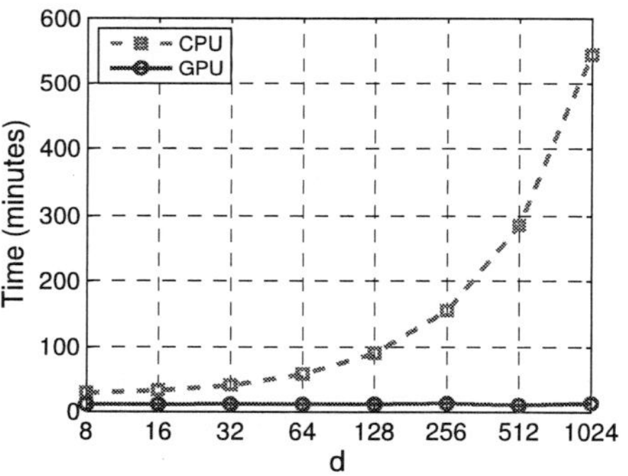

Figure 2: NS-DTW search time on dev data by varying the dimensions of the Gaussian posteriorgrams using CPU and GPU cores.

To summarize the search performance and speed of NS-DTW, in Table 4 we show MP, FAP, MTWV and speedup of QbE-STD search for $d \geq$ 128 using a GPU. We define speedup as the ratio of NS-DTW search time on CPU and to that of the search time obtained using a GPU.

From Table 4, it can be seen that there is an improvement in the search performance (MTWV) for $d = 128, 256, 512, 1024$ as compared to the

Table 4: Miss probability (MP), false alarm probability (FAP), maximum term weighted value (MTWV) and search speed on dev dataset using a GPU for $d = 128, 256, 512, 1024$.

d	MP	FAP (10^{-2})	MTWV	Speedup
128	0.363	1.214	0.450	6.91x
256	0.393	1.010	0.452	11.48x
512	0.359	1.078	0.475	27.06x
1024	0.334	1.149	0.489	40.80x

MTWVs as shown in Table 2. It is to be noted that, to compute the values in Table 2 we have selected 5 best alignment scores from each reference R (as described in Section 3) and to compute the values in Table 4, we have selected 500 best alignment scores from the reference batch R_b (as described in Section 5.1). The results indicate a decrease in the miss probability in Table 4 as compared to that of Table 2 for $d = 128, 256, 512, 1024$ and thus an improvement in the search performance (MTWV).

5.3 Use of Feature Reduction for Search

In this Section, we intend to further improve the search time by modifying the NS-DTW. In this paper, we reduce the query and reference Gaussian posteriorgram vectors before performing search. In this method, we average the successive Gaussian posteriorgrams to reduce the length of the spoken audio and the spoken query.

Consider a reduction factor $\alpha \in \mathbb{N}$. Let $\hat{Q}$, $\hat{R}$ be the sequence of reduced set of feature vectors representing the query and reference. $\hat{Q}$ and $\hat{R}$ are obtained as follows:

$$\hat{Q} = [\hat{q}_1, \hat{q}_2, \ldots, \hat{q}_i, \ldots, \hat{q}_{\hat{n}}]_{d \times \hat{n}}$$
$$\hat{R} = [\hat{u}_1, \hat{u}_2, \ldots, \hat{u}_j, \ldots, \hat{u}_{\hat{m}}]_{d \times \hat{m}},$$

where $\hat{n} = \frac{n}{\alpha}, \hat{m} = \frac{m}{\alpha}$ and

$$\hat{q}_i = \frac{1}{\alpha} \sum_{k=1}^{\alpha} q_{(i-1)\alpha+k}$$

$$\hat{u}_j = \frac{1}{\alpha} \sum_{j=1}^{\alpha} u_{(j-1)\alpha+k}$$

Given a reduction factor $\alpha \in \mathbb{N}$, a window of size α is considered over the posteriorgram features and a mean is computed. The window is then shifted by α and another mean vector is computed.

Table 5: Maximum term weighted value (MTWV), speedup and memory usage (%) obtained on dev and eval datasets for $\alpha = 1, 2, 3$ and $d = 1024$ using a GPU. It is to be noted that for $\alpha = 1$, the GPU memory is not sufficient to load the whole reference dev and eval database. Thus, for $\alpha = 1$, the reference dev and eval datasets are partitioned into 2 and 3 smaller batches respectively.

α	dev			eval		
	MTWV	Speedup	Memory	MTWV	Speedup	Memory
1	0.489	40.80x	83.15%	0.469	41.37x	63.46%
2	0.474	116.37x	88.63%	0.453	117.34	91.03%
3	0.462	211.12x	61.73%	0.4353	217.60x	63.31%

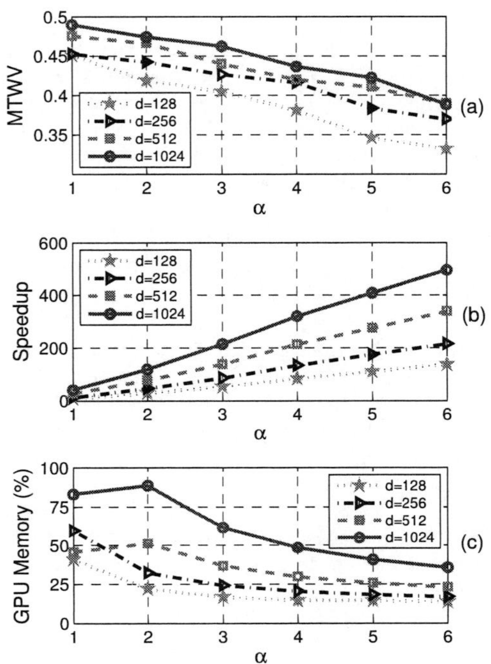

Figure 3: (a) MTWV, (b) Speedup, and (c) GPU memory usage (in percentage) obtained using $d = 128, 256, 512, 1024$ for various values of α on dev dataset. It is to be noted that $\alpha = 1$ represents the NS-DTW without feature reduction.

A more detailed description about the algorithm is provided in (Mantena et al., 2014).

In Fig. 3, we show the MTWV, speedup, and GPU memory usage (in percentage) obtained using $d = 128, 256, 512, 1024$ for $\alpha = 1, 2, 3, 4, 5, 6$ on dev dataset. It is to be noted that $\alpha = 1$ represents the NS-DTW without feature reduction. From Fig. 3, it can be seen that the search performance decreases with an increase in α but there is

an improvement in speedup and GPU memory usage. For $d = 512, 1024$, GPU memory is not sufficient to load the whole reference batch and so it is partitioned to 2 smaller batches for search. Thus, for $d = 512, 1024$, the memory usage is lower for $\alpha = 1$ as compared to that of $\alpha = 2$. From Fig. 3, it can be also be seen that by using feature reduction one can use higher dimensions of Gaussian posteriorgrams such as $d = 1024$ and thus enable searching a query in large reference files.

To summarize the QbE-STD performance, in Table 5, we show the MTWV, speedup and memory usage (%) on dev and eval datasets for $\alpha = 1, 2, 3$ and $d = 1024$. It is to be noted that on increasing the α the MTWV decreases and thus resulting in a poor search performance (as shown in Fig. 3). From Table 5, it can be seen that there is a good improvement in the speedup for $\alpha = 2$ resulting in a marginal drop in search performance. Thus, with the use of a GPU and feature reduction for $\alpha = 2$ we could attain a speedup of about 100x and thereby enable QbE-STD search in real time.

6   Conclusions

In this paper, we used a graphical processing unit (GPU) and improved the computation time of the distance calculation of non-segmental dynamic time warping (NS-DTW) algorithm in the context query-by-example spoken term detection (QbE-STD) search. We have shown with experimental results that the NS-DTW search speed can be made independent (an approximation) of the dimension of the Gaussian posteriorgram using a GPU. We have also used a faster method of searching by reducing the length of the spoken audio and the spoken query. The reduction of the feature vectors was done via arithmetic mean and it is shown that for a reduction factor of $\alpha = 2$, there is an improvement in the search speed of about 100x with a marginal drop in search performance using 1024 dimensional Gaussian posteriorgrams.

7 Acknowledgements

We would like to thank P. J. Narayanan, Kishore Kothapalli, Manoj Maramreddy and Sivanand Achanta from IIIT-H, India for their feedback on the GPU implementations of NS-DTW. We would also like to thank TCS, India for partially supporting Gautam's PhD fellowship.

References

X. Anguera and M. Ferrarons. 2013. Memory efficient subsequence DTW for query-by-example spoken term detection. In *Proc. of ICME*.

X. Anguera. 2012. Speaker independent discriminant feature extraction for acoustic pattern-matching. In *Proc. of ICASSP*, pages 485–488.

E. Barnard, M. H. Davel, and C. J. V. Heerden. 2009. ASR corpus design for resource-scarce languages. In *Proc. of INTERSPEECH*, pages 2847–2850.

J. Bergstra, O. Breuleux, F. Bastien, P. Lamblin, R. Pascanu, G. Desjardins, J. Turian, D. Warde-Farley, and Y. Bengio. 2010. Theano: a CPU and GPU math expression compiler. In *in Proc. of the Python for Scientific Computing Conference*, June. Oral Presentation.

P. Cardinal, P. Dumouchel, G. Boulianne, and M. Comeau. 2008. GPU accelerated acoustic likelihood computations. In *Proc. of INTERSPEECH*, pages 964–967.

J. G. Fiscus, J. Ajot, J. S. Garofolo, and G. Doddington. 2007. Results of the 2006 spoken term detection evaluation. In *Proc. of Workshop on Searching Spontaneous Conversational Speech*, pages 45–50.

S. Ganapathy, S. Thomas, and H. Hermansky. 2010. Temporal envelope compensation for robust phoneme recognition using modulation spectrum. *Journal of Acoustical Society of America*, 128:3769–3780.

V. Gupta, J. Ajmera, A., and A. Verma. 2011. A language independent approach to audio search. In *Proc. of INTERSPEECH*, pages 1125–1128.

T. J. Hazen, W. Shen, and C. White. 2009. Query-by-example spoken term detection using phonetic posteriorgram templates. In *Proc. of ASRU*, pages 421–426.

G. Mantena, S. Achanta, and K. Prahallad. 2014. Query-by-example spoken term detection using frequency domain linear prediction and non-segmental dynamic time warping. *IEEE/ACM Trans. on Audio, Speech and Lang. Processing*, 22(5):946–955, May.

F. Metze, E. Barnard, M. H. Davel, C. J. V. Heerden, X. Anguera, G. Gravier, and N. Rajput. 2012. The spoken web search task. In *MediaEval*.

D. R. H. Miller, M. Kleber, C.-L. Kao, O. Kimball, T. Colthurst, S. A. Lowe, R. M. Schwartz, and H. Gish. 2007. Rapid and accurate spoken term detection. In *Proc. of INTERSPEECH*, pages 314–317.

J. Nickolls, I. Buck, M. Garland, and K. Skadron. 2008. Scalable parallel programming with cuda. *Queue*, 6(2):40–53, March.

D. Povey, A. Ghoshal, G. Boulianne, L. Burget, O. Glembek, N. Goel, M. Hannemann, P. Motlicek, Y. Qian, P. Schwarz, J. Silovsky, G. Stemmer, and K. Vesely. 2011. The Kaldi speech recognition toolkit. In *in Proc. of ASRU*. IEEE Signal Processing Society, December.

M. Saraclar and R. Sproat. 2004. Lattice-based search for spoken utterance retrieval. In *Proc. of HLT-NAACL*, pages 129–136.

D. Sart, A. Mueen, W. Najjar, E. Keogh, and V. Niennattrakul. 2010. Accelerating dynamic time warping subsequence search with GPUs and FPGAs. In *in Proc. of International Conference on Data Mining (ICDM)*, pages 1001–1006, Dec.

Y. Shi, F. Seide, and F. K. Soong. 2008. GPU-accelerated gaussian clustering for fMPE discriminative training. In *Proc. of INTERSPEECH*, pages 944–947.

I. Szöke, M. Fapso, L. Burget, and J. Cernocky. 2008. Hybrid word-subword decoding for spoken term detection. In *Workshop on Searching Spontaneous Conversational Speech*, pages 4–11.

S. Thomas, S. Ganapathy, and H. Hermansky. 2008. Recognition of reverberant speech using frequency domain linear prediction. *IEEE Signal Processing Letters*, 15:681 –684.

Y. Zhang and J. R. Glass. 2009. Unsupervised spoken keyword spotting via segmental DTW on Gaussian posteriorgrams. In *Proc. of ASRU*, pages 398–403.

Y. Zhang and J. Glass. 2011. An inner-product lower-bound estimate for dynamic time warping. In *Proc. of ICASSP*, pages 5660–5663.

Y. Zhang, K. Adl, and J. Glass. 2012. Fast spoken query detection using lower-bound dynamic time warping on graphical processing units. In *in Proc. of ICASSP*, pages 5173–5176, March.

NATIVE LANGUAGE IDENTIFICATION BASED ON ENGLISH ACCENT

G. Radha Krishna
Electronics & Communication Engineering
VNRVJIET
Hyderabad, Telengana, India
guntur_radhakrishna@yahoo.co.in

R. Krishnan
Adjunct Faculty
Amritha University
Coimbatore, India
drrkdrrk@gmail.com

Abstract

Present work is aimed at investigating the influence of mother tongue (L1) of a South Indian speaker on a second language (L2). Second language can be a dominant local language, national language in India i.e., Hindi or a connecting language English. In the current study, L2 is a short discourse in English. Cepstral and prosodic features were used as in Language Identification (LID) to distinguish languages. Both perceptual features and acoustic prosodic features were employed to train Gaussian Mixture Models (GMMs). Studies are carried out with each of the South Indian languages Telugu, Tamil and Kannada as L1. Results showed accuracies upto 85%. Difference in prosodic features of non-native speech is found to be a useful tool for identifying the native state of a polyglot.

1 Introduction

A method of finding the mother tongue adds flexibility to a Text Independent Automatic Speaker Recognition (ASR) system [1] [2]. A possible implementation of this task can be an estimation of the influence of speaker's native language (L1) on a foreign Language (L2). In general, multilingual speakers do not acquire a second language (L2) thoroughly and speech by a particular group of non-native speakers has a distinct 'foreign accent', since they resort to similar type of pronunciation errors. Speaker nativeness or ethnicity can be identified by studying the acoustic and prosodic aspects that remain native like or become most prominent during a discourse [3]. It is observed that non-native speakers inadvertently carry phonemic details from L1 to L2. Studies indicate that Phonetic correlates of accent in Indian English are found in Indian languages [4]. The application areas of mother tongue identification ranges from Intelligence to adaptation in ASR and Automatic Speaker Verification System (ASV), which may require compensation for accent mismatch [5]. A user friendly ASV system for establishing speaker nativeness by establishing the Mother Tongue Influence (MTI) is attempted in this work.

For text-independent nativity recognition, it is possible to create models, which captures the sequential statistics of more basic units in each of the languages. For example, the phonemes or broad categories of phonemes. Modeling approaches can be on the lines of two well-known tasks: Language Identification (LID) and Automatic Speaker Verification/Identification [6]. Some of the successful approaches in this direction include LID using MFCC for Text Independent speaker recognition in multilingual environment and Regional and Ethnic group recognition using telephone speech in Birmingham.

Indian languages are among the less researched languages. ASR Systems are not yet launched into the Indian market at full level. In most of the Indian states, at least two languages are spoken apart from the local official language. This includes English, and a language of the neighbouring province. Popular languages from three South Indian states which are Telugu (ISO 639-3 tel), Tamil (ISO 639-3 tam), and Kannada (ISO 639-3 kan) are chosen for this study. Previous work on

D S Sharma, R Sangal and J D Pawar. Proc. of the 11th Intl. Conference on Natural Language Processing, pages 63–67, Goa, India. December 2014. ©2014 NLP Association of India (NLPAI)

Nativity identification involved in using both native and non-native acoustic phone models where mapping of phone set from non-native to native language were investigated [4]. In present work, detection of L1 has been attempted by estimating Mother Tongue Influence (MTI) on L2. Language models based on GMM technique were built for each language with a total duration of around 60 minutes per language. The procedure detailed in [7] is followed for this purpose. These models represent the vocal tract at the instance of articulation and will be able to distinguish phonetic features. This can help to identify the speaker's mother tongue which in turn gives the origin of the speaker. A series of experiments are conducted to prove the above approach. Test utterances used were English utterances from Speakers, belonging to the three South Indian regions with above languages as mother tongue. The results for establishing the nativity are promising.

The organization of the paper is as follows: In Section 2, Corpus collection is described. The Modelling technics employed in our experiments are given in Section 3. Results and discussion are contained in Section 4. Finally, Conclusion and scope for future work is given in Section 5.

2 Corpus Description

The speech corpus is collected based on the availability of native speakers of the particular language. Building up of the home grown corpus is described below. The speakers are separated into two groups: training and testing set. Speech samples are collected from native Speakers belonging to the states of Andhra Pradesh, Tamil Nadu or Karnataka whose mother tongue are respectively Telugu [TEL], Tamil [TAM] or Kannada [KAN]. This constituted the training set. The speakers are so chosen that they are not from places bordering other states. This ensures that dialectal variation is avoided in the training set. A total of 3600 seconds of speech corpus is developed for each of the three languages. The details are given in Tables 1 and 2.

Recording is carried out with text material from general topics related to Personality development and with the speakers under unstressed conditions. A different subsets of speakers who are capable of speaking English in addition to the above mentioned mother tongues are chosen as the testing set. Thus the testing database consisted of English utterance of the speakers with one of the three languages Telugu, Tamil or Kannada as mother tongue. It is ensured that Gender weightages are almost equally distributed in both the training and testing sets. The test utterances, which are English samples are recorded under similar conditions as training speech samples. The details of speakers of test set are detailed in Section 4. Each of the test sample is recorded for a duration of 90 Seconds. These details are shown in following Table 3

Table 1: Distribution of Training Set

Language		TEL	TAM	KAN
No. of speakers	M	5	3	4
	F	4	3	4
No. of minutes	M	30	35	25
	F	30	25	35

Table 2: Speaker Proficiency in other languages

Language	Male	Female
TEL	HINDI	NIL
TAM	NIL	ENGLISH
KAN	HINDI,ENGLIH	HINDI,ENGLISH

Table 3: Distribution of Testing Set

Language		TEL	TAM	KAN
No. of speakers	M	7	7	4
	F	7	5	8
No. of Seconds	M	30-90	30-90	30-90
	F	30-90	30-90	30-90

3. Experiments

3.1 System building: According to [6], Language identification is related to speaker-independent speech recognition and speaker identification. It is practically easy to train phoneme models than training models of entire language. Though they are found to outperform those based on stochastic models, the phonemic approach has the following drawback. It needs phonemically labeled data in each of the target languages for use during the training. The difference among languages, apart from their prosody lies in their short-term acoustic characteristics. Indian languages share many phones among themselves. Since there are many variants of the same phoneme, we need to consider the acoustic similarities of these phones. Combination of phonetic and acoustic similarities can decide a particular mother tongue [3]. For text-independent language recognition, it is generally not feasible to construct word models in each of the target languages [8]. So, models based on the sequential statistics of fundamental units in each of the languages are employed. Text independent recognizers use Gaussian mixture models (GMMs) to model the language dependent information. The modeling technic deciding the acoustic vectors should be multimodal, to represent the pronunciation variations of the similar phonemes in various languages. The language model used in this particular study is a GMM model of Mel Frequency Cepstral Coefficients MFCCs [9]. Following block diagram (Fig. 1) illustrates the implementation of above steps in the frame work of a Speaker Recognition system. The system is an acoustic information based LID system for which the proposed Foreign Accent Identification system is a special case.

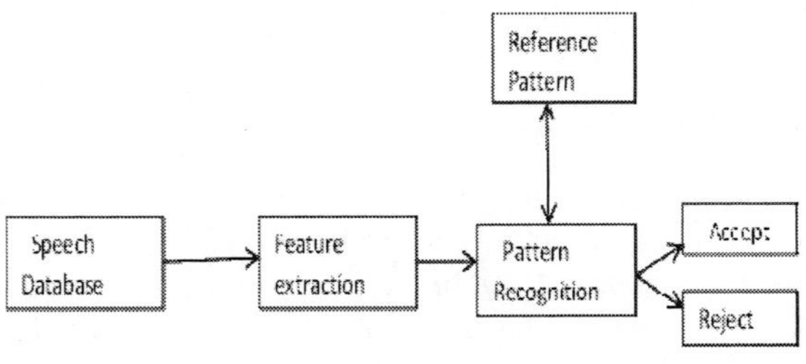

Figure 1: Speaker Recognition system for nativity identification

3.2 Spectral features for Language Identification:

Present day Speaker recognition systems rely on low-level acoustic information [10]. Studies indicate that a cohesive representation of the acoustic signal is possible by using a set of mel-frequency cepstral coefficients (MFCCs) which emulates the functioning of human perception. MFCCs are cepstral domain representation of the production system. MFCCs are 13 dimensional vectors which help in several speech engineering applications. The speech signal is converted into a set of perceptual coefficients represented by a 13 dimensional MFCC feature vector. After collecting the multilingual speech set, acoustic model parameters are estimated from the training data in each language. The extraction and selection of the parametric representation of acoustic signals is critical in developing any speaker recognition system. Cepstral features capture the underlying acoustic characteristics of the signal. They characterize not only the vocal tract of a Speaker but also the prevailing characteristics of the vocal tract system of a phoneme. In conclusion, MFCCs provide information about the phonetic content of the language. Hence, we used MFCC coefficients as feature vectors to model the phonetic information.

3.3 Experiments based on stochastic models:

GMMs are famous classification technique which helps to cluster the input data into a predetermined specifications about clusters. GMMs are a supervised technique which is efficient in classifying multi-dimensional data. The main purpose of using the Gaussian mixture models (GMM) in pattern recognition stage is because of its computational efficiency. Moreover, the model is well understood, and is most suitable for text-independent applications. It is robust against the temporal variations of the speech, and can model distribution of acoustic variations from a speech sample [7][9]. The GMM technique lies midway between a parametric and non-parametric density model. Similar to a parametric model it has structure and parameters that control the behavior of the density in known ways. It also has no constraints about the type of data distribution [7]. The GMM has the freedom to allow arbitrary density modeling, like a non-parametric model. In the present investigation, the Gaussian components can be considered to be modeling the broad phonetic sounds that characterize a person's voice. The proposed Mother Tongue Identification system is based on the statistical modeling of Gaussian mixtures [11].

4. Results and Discussion

In the testing phase, speech samples from a set of speakers with wide ranging geographical distribution within a state are collected. The speakers in test set are all educated, with at least graduation. Teachers of English language, convent educated are avoided in the test set. Most of the speakers have the ability to speak one or more local languages apart from English, representing a truly multilingual scenario. These speakers are fluent in English as well as in their mother tongue. The test samples are modeled similarly as training samples and compared with three baseline Language models developed in the earlier training phase. Distance measures are computed between the GMM mean of each language model and that of the test utterances of MFCCs parameters derived from the test utterance. Confusion matrix of pair-wise mother tongue identification task is performed and the results are presented in Table 4.

Table 4. Confusion matrix of pair-wise MTI task.
(a) Between Telugu and Tamil

(i) Cepstral features   (ii) Acoustic-prosodic features

30 Sec	TEL	KAN
TEL	80%	20%
TAM	20%	80%

60Sec	TEL	KAN
TEL	85%	15%
TAM	20%	80%

(b) Between Telugu and Kannada

(i) Cepstral features   (ii) Acoustic-prosodic features

30 Sec	TEL	KAN
TEL	80%	20%
KAN	20%	80%

6 0 Sec	TEL	KAN
TEL	80%	20%
KAN	20%	80%

(c) Between Tamil and Kannada

(i) Cepstral features   (ii) Acoustic-prosodic features

30 Sec	TEL	KAN
TEL	80%	20%
TAM	20%	80%

6 0 Sec	TEL	KAN
TEL	80%	20%
KAN	20%	80%

5. Conclusions and Future scope

An Automatic Speaker Recognition system for identification of mother tongue and thus the native state of the speaker is implemented successfully. Confusion is observed between Kannada and Tamil speakers. This confusion is found to be less when Acoustic prosodic features are introduced. We have proposed an effective approach to identify MTI in multilingual scenario by following the techniques available in Language and Speaker Identification. A general purpose solution is proposed with a multilingual acoustic model. Further improvements can be made by including prosodic features and also covering techniques such as inclusion of SDC features and also the i-vector paradigm. Most important advances in future systems will be in the study of acoustic-phonetics, speech perception, linguistics, and psychoacoustics [7]. Next generation systems need to have a way of representing, storing, and retrieving various knowledge resources required for natural conversation particularly for countries like India. With the same training and testing procedures, apart from English and other regional languages, national language Hindi can be modeled and influence of any particular language on it can also be studied.

Acknowledgments

The authors would like to acknowledge the cooperation of the staff and students of VNRVJIET, who co-operated readily by providing their voice samples. We profusely thank all these speakers for their kind co-operation towards carrying out this research. Special thanks are due to the Scientists of Speech and Vision Laboratory of IIIT, Hyderabad for their timely and invaluable advice.

References

[1] G. Doddington, P. Dalsgaard, B. Lindberg, H. Benner, and Z. Tan, "Speaker recognition based on idiolectal differences between speakers", in Proc. EUROSPEECH, pp. 2521–2524, Aalborg, Denmark, Sep. 2001.

[2] A. Maier et.al., "Combined Acoustic and Pronunciation Modeling for Non-Native Speech Recognition" Interspeech 2007, pp1449-1452.

[3] R.Todd, "On Non-Native Speaker Prosody: Identifying 'Just-Noticeable-Differences' of Speaker-Ethnicity", Proceedings of the 1st International Conference on Speech Prosody, 2002

[4] E. Shriberg, L. Ferrer, S. Kajarekar, N. Scheffer, A. Stolcke, and M. Akbacak, "Detecting non-native speech using speaker recognition approaches", in Proceedings IEEE Odyssey-08 Speaker and Language Recognition Workshop, Stellenbosch, South Africa, Jan. 2008.

[5] Sethserey et.al. Speech Modulation Features for Robust Nonnative Speech Accent Detection, Interspeech-2011

[6] "Multi Level Implicit features for Language and Speaker Recognition", Ph.D. Thesis, Leena Mary, Department of Computer Science, Indian Institute of Technology Madras, India ,June 2006.

[7] D. A. Reynolds, " Robust Text-Independent Speaker Identification Using Gaussian Mixture Speaker Models", IEEE Transactions on Speech and Audio Processing Vol.3,No.1,1995,72-83.

[8] A. Maier et.al "A Language Independent Feature Set for the Automatic Evaluation of Prosody " Interspeech 2009.

[9] N. Scheffer, L. Ferrer, Martin Graciarena, S. Kajarekar, E. S. Stolcke, " The SRI NIST 2010 Speaker Recognition Evaluation System ".

[10] D.A. Reynolds, T.F. Quatieri and R.B.Dunn, "Speaker Verification using adapted Gaussian mixture models", Digital Signal Processing vol 10, pp19-41, 2000.

[11] J. Cheng, N. Bojja, X. Chen " Automatic Accent Quantification of Indian Speakers of English" Interspeech 2011, pp2574-2578.

Keynote Lecture-2

Text Analysis for Identifying Entities and their Mentions in Indian Languages

Sobha L
AU-KBC Research Centre, Chennai, India
sobha@au-kbc.org

The talk deals with the analysis of text at syntactic-semantic level to identify a common feature set which can work across various Indian languages for recognizing named entities and their mentions. The development of corpora and the method adopted to develop each module is discussed. The talk includes the evaluation of the common feature set using a statistical method which gives acceptable levels of recall and precision.

D S Sharma, R Sangal and J D Pawar. Proc. of the 11th Intl. Conference on Natural Language Processing, page 68,
Goa, India. December 2014. ©2014 NLP Association of India (NLPAI)

HinMA: Distributed Morphology based Hindi Morphological Analyzer

Ankit Bahuguna
TU Munich
ankitbahuguna@outlook.com

Lavita Talukdar
IIT Bombay
lavita.talukdar@gmail.com

Pushpak Bhattacharyya
IIT Bombay
pushpakbh@gmail.com

Smriti Singh
IIT Bombay
smritismriti@gmail.com

Abstract

Morphology plays a crucial role in the working of various NLP applications. Whenever we run a spell checker, provide a query term to a web search engine, explore translation or transliteration tools, use online dictionaries or thesauri, or try using text-to-speech or speech recognition applications, morphology works at the back of these applications. We present here a novel computational tool *HinMA*, or the Hindi Morphological Analyzer, based on the framework of Distributed Morphology (DM). We discuss the implementation of linguistically motivated analysis and later, we evaluate the accuracy of this tool. We find, that this rule based system exhibits extremely high accuracy and has a good overall coverage. The design of the tool is language independent and by changing few configuration files, one can use this framework for developing such a tool for other languages as well. The analysis of Hindi inflectional morphology based on the Distributed morphology framework, its implementation in the development of this tool and integration with NLP resources like Hindi Wordnet or Sense Marker Tool and possible development of a word generator are interesting aspects of this work.

1 Introduction

Natural Language Processing (NLP) systems aim to analyze and generate natural language sentences and are concerned with computational systems and their interaction with human language. Morphology accounts for the morphological properties of languages in a systematic manner, enabling us to understand how words are formed, what their constituents are, how they may be arranged to make larger units, what are the semantic and grammatical constraints involved and how morphological processes interact with syntactic and phonological ones. An analysis of the inflectional morphology of Hindi has been presented here in the theoretical framework of Distributed Morphology, as discussed by Halle and Marantz (1993, 1994); Harley and Noyer (1999). The theory has been used to develop the rules required to analyze and describe the various inflectional forms of Hindi words. Our tool takes an inflected word as input and outputs its set of roots along with its various morphological features using the output of the stemmer. The suffixes extracted by the stemmer are used to get the various morphological features of the word: *gender, number, person, case, tense, aspect and modality*. The tool consist of two parts – ***Stemmer***, which takes inflected word as input and stems it, to separate root and suffix and **Morphological Analyzer,** which takes <Root, Suffix> pair as input and outputs a set of features along with the set of roots.

Stemming aims to reduce morphologically related word forms to a single base form or stem. Stemmers use an affix-list and morphological rules that isolate the base form by stripping off possible affixes from a given word. The final stem is usually then looked up in the online language lexicon to verify its validity. **Morphological analysis** is provided by morphological analyzers that include morphological information for each morpheme – both stems and suffixes isolated by the stemmer. A Morphological Analyzer (MA), exploits only word level information and produces all possible roots and analyses for a given word. An MA should be able to produce all the possibilities if a word can be decomposed into two or more different ways to produce the roots of different Part of Speech (POS) categories. For such a word, the root and the morpheme analyses may be different in each case. For example, the Hindi word *khāte* in sentences **1** and

D S Sharma, R Sangal and J D Pawar. Proc. of the 11th Intl. Conference on Natural Language Processing, pages 69–75,
Goa, India. December 2014. ©2014 NLP Association of India (NLPAI)

2 has two possible analyses: *khātā* 'ledger' as the root with suffix */-e/* and *khā* 'eat' as the root with suffixes */-t-/* and */-e/*. In Ex. 1, the word *khāte* has a noun root '*khātā*' and the suffix */-e/* appears to mark the plural number and the direct case. In Ex. 2, on the other hand, the word has a verb root *khā* 'eat' and the suffixes */-t/* and */-e/* appear to mark the features 'habitual aspect' and 'masculine-plural'. A morphological analyzer should typically provide both analyses for the word *khāte* unless some contextual information is used to resolve the categorical ambiguity. Examples:

1. मेरे कई खाते हैं.
   mere kəī khāte haĩ
   I-Poss many (bank) accounts be-pres-pl
   (I have many bank accounts)
2. वे रोज़ चावल खाते हैं.
   ve roz cāvəl khā-t-e haĩ
   They everyday rice eat-hab-pl be-pres,pl
   (They eat rice everyday)

Similarly, a word may also have multiple roots and multiple analyzes within the same POS category as shown in 3 below. The word *nālõ* can be analyzed in two ways: with *nāl* as the root or with *nālā* as the root. The suffix in both cases is same, *i.e., -õ* which represents the 'plural-oblique' case feature. Both are valid roots for the input word. Since an analyzer does not consider the contextual information of words to resolve POS ambiguities, it should be able to produce both outputs.

3. Input word form: नालों (*nālõ*)
   a. POS Category: Noun; Root 1: *nāl* 'horse-shoe'; Suffix: *-õ;* Analysis: Plural, Oblique
   b. POS Category: Noun; Root 2: *nālā* 'water channel/trough';Suffix: *-õ;* Analysis: Plural, Oblique

An MA usually relies on its accompanying lexicon to match the extracted root and to provide the category information for a given word. However, the analyzer may fail to recognize certain word forms if the root formed by the stemmer after stripping off the suffix is absent in the lexicon. The analyzer may also fail to recognize spelling variants of the roots stored in the lexicon such as कैदियों–कैदियों (kædiyõ) 'prisoners', हफ़्ते-हफ़्ते (həpʰte) 'weeks', etc. In the absence of the rules to handle spelling variations, the MA may not be able to analyse the

spelling variants of a word. The remainder of this paper is organized as follows. We describe related work and background in section 2. Section 3 explains the concept of Distributed Morphology (DM). Implementation details are discussed in Section 4. Results are discussed in Section 5 and Error analysis in Section 6. Comparison with existing MA(s) is mentioned in Section 7. Section 8 discusses applications and Section 9 concludes the paper and points to future directions.

2   Related Work and Background

Several techniques have been utilized in building stemmers and morphological analyzers for Hindi. Some of them are morphology based, some statistical and some a hybrid of the two. The first ever reported work on Hindi stemming and morphological analysis was by Bharati *et al.* (2001). They present an algorithm that learns and predicts morphological patterns of Hindi using an existing Hindi morphological analyzer (MA). The paradigm-based MA uses a very low coverage lexicon. Roots are stored in a dictionary along with the paradigm information. Each paradigm stores information of the add-delete characters for a set of items for various inflectional categories (such as number and case for nouns). A representative root is chosen for each paradigm and is used as a label for paradigm assignment for the other roots in that paradigm. For each input word, the MA applies the add-delete strings and looks for a possible match in the root lexicon. If a match is found, it is considered to be the correct root and is the final output. If not, the next string is applied. Using this MA, Bharati *et al.* (2001) applied an automatic-learning algorithm to predict the stem of an inflected word using the frequency of occurrences of word forms in the raw (unannotated) corpus. The idea is to use the suffix to determine the set of possible stems and paradigms that may generate the input word form. Using the pairs of stems and paradigms, all possible word forms are generated. The frequency of these word forms is then obtained from the corpus and is stored in a vector. These vectors are compared for each 'guess' in order to select the most likely stem and the paradigm for the input word. This algorithm reportedly gave better coverage. Goyal and Lehal (2008) too developed a Hindi Morphological Analyzer that relies on a list of possible forms of the commonly used Hindi root words. Their approach promises to perform better than previous approaches, as the search time in a storage-based approach is very low. Another obvious advantage of storing all the forms in a list is that the system only needs to find a correct match in the system and output the corresponding root. In that sense, the user will always get accurate results. Ramanathan and Rao (2003) worked on 'light-weight stemming' for Hindi. They tried to build a computationally inexpensive and domain independent stemmer that extracts out the stem of a word by stripping off suffixes based on the 'longest match'. They created a list of 65 possible inflectional suffixes for Hindi nouns, adjectives, verbs and adverbs using McGregor's (1995) analysis of Hindi inflectional morphology. For an input word, the stemmer keeps stripping off suffixes using the suffix-list until it finds the longest match. But, the system may produce many incorrect stems since it has no way to identify whether or not a particular suffix is applicable to the identified stem. In addition, the stemmer does not output the root of the input word. Purely statistical methods were also tried out for Hindi stemming and morphological analysis. Larkey *et al.* (2003) worked on Hindi stemming, as it was needed in their Cross language information retrieval task. They used a list of 27 common suffixes supplied by a Hindi speaker that indicate nominalization, gender, number and tense features. In their system, the stemming was done to first extract out the longest possible suffix followed by smaller suffixes. But, the stemming process did not give them encouraging results. Since, the morphological analysis was not exhaustive, their system could not handle many word forms. They reported that stemming did not lead to any improvement in their retrieval task.

3   Distributed Morphology

Distributed Morphology, a recent theory of the architecture of grammar, was proposed by Halle and Marantz (1993, 1994). The theory proposes that 'words' are structurally not different from other constituents such as phrases or sentences, and are formed and manipulated using syntactic rules. This suggests that word formation is primarily a syntactic operation, *i.e.,* the morphological structure of a word or a word form is generated using

syntactic operations. It is syntax that provides features and the structures upon which morphology operates. This view is opposed to the one that believes that morphology operates in an entirely separate component that generates words or word forms outside syntax that later feed into syntactic structures. Unlike lexicalist approaches that assume all morphology to happen in the lexicon, DM believes that the constituent components of morphology are distributed among various levels in the architecture of grammar and work in close connection with syntax and phonology. Halle and Marantz postulate a separate level of representation called *Morphological Structure* (MS) that operates in between *Syntactic Structure* (SS) and *Phonological Form* (PF). This level receives hierarchical structures from syntax that contain 'abstract' morphemes as the terminal nodes; abstract, because at this level, these nodes only have morpho-syntactic and semantic features and lack any associated phonological features. The DM grammar is represented by Halle and Marantz (1993) as shown in Figure 1.

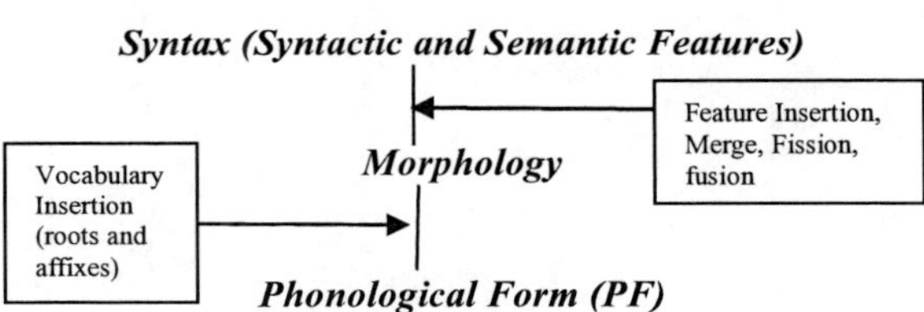

Figure 1. Architecture of grammar in DM.

4   Implementation of Distributed Morphology based Morphological Analyzer

The overall process can be summarised into *three distinct steps*: stemming, root formation and lexicon look-up and morphological analysis. For stemming, HinMA uses a set of ordered contextual rules to isolate and extract out suffixes from a given inflected word form. For implementation purposes, the vocabulary entries developed for nouns, adjectives, quantifiers, ordinals and verbs were converted into *if-then* rules arranged in order of specificity of inflectional and contextual features. The internal processes of HinMa is shown in Figure 2. The rules are applied from right to left iteratively until no suffixes remain and the base root is left. Readjustment rules apply wherever applicable to produce the correct root which is then matched with the incorporated root-list to determine match (es). Then, the root is validated by performing a lexicon lookup. On successful validation, root(s) is obtained and it completes the second step. The information associated with the various rules and the lexicon is combined and provided as output of morphological analysis. A number of rules Singh S. et al. (2011) were constructed over a period of one year and later another one year was taken to develop and test the system with the help of a dedicated team of 4 linguists and two computer scientists. Due to space limitation, we are unable to present the individual rules here.

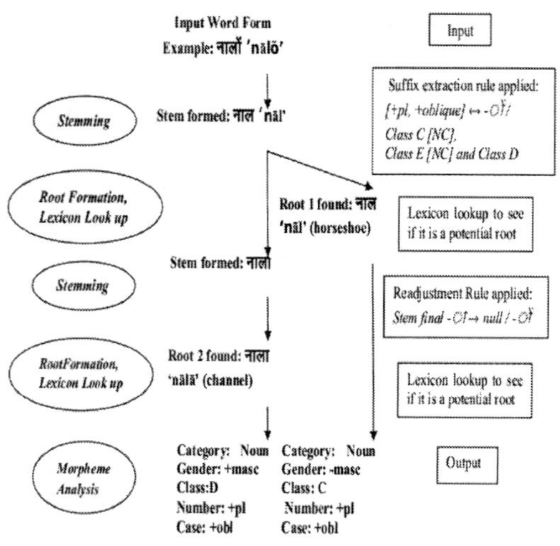

Figure 2. Steps show working of HinMa.

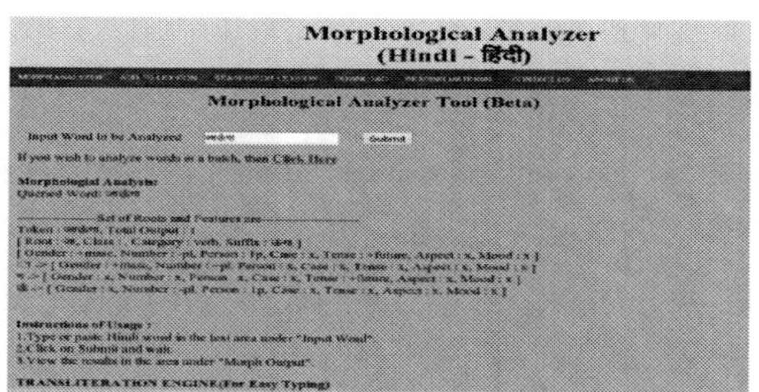

Figure 3: HinMA online implementation: Output of verb "जाऊंगा" (jAuMga ~ will go).

Output of the System: A detailed morpheme analysis is given as output for each word, with information such as root, grammatical category, inflection class and feature values. The system also produces a detailed morphological analysis for each morpheme that constitutes the word form. The output format is:

Input Token: XXXXX
Possible Root 1: class: category: suffix: morphemes (morpheme 1 … etc.): Morpheme Analysis (morpheme 1, morpheme 2, etc.)
Possible Root 2: …

The morpheme analysis of each suffix is produced in a seven field with values for the features *gender, number, person, case, tense, aspect,* and *mood.* Our system offers the analysis of words which could yield more than one root from with added capability of handling compound words. We provide demo output of online system[1] in Figure 3 and actual outputs categorised *w.r.t.,* various morphological phenomena below:

1. Multiple roots within the same category: The input word नालों 'nālõ' may have two possible noun roots which are नाल 'nāl' (horseshoe) and नाला 'nālā' (trough/channel). The two roots belong to different inflection classes. The system is able to output both analysis.

Token: नालों, Total Output: 2
Root: नाल, Class: C, Category: noun, Suffix: ओं
Gender: -masc, Number: +pl, Person: x, Case: +oblique, Tense: x, Aspect: x, Mood: x
Root: नाला, Class: D, Category: noun, Suffix: ओं
Gender: +masc, Number: +pl, Person: x, Case: +oblique, Tense: x, Aspect: x, Mood: x

2. Multiple roots across POS categories: The input word खाते 'khāte' may have two roots of different POS categories. It may be analyzed as a noun with the root खाता 'khātā' (ledger) and suffix -े 'e'. As a verb, its root is खा 'khā' (eat) with suffix -ते 'te'. Our MA is able to produce both outputs and their analysis, shown below:
Token: खाते, Total Output: 2
Root: खाता, Class: D, Category: noun, Suffix: े
Gender: +masc, Number: -pl, Person: x, Case: +oblique, Tense: x, Aspect: x, Mood: x
Root: खा, Class:, Category: verb, Suffix: ते
Gender: +masc, Number: +-pl, Person: x, Case: x, Tense: , Aspect: +conditional, Mood: x]
े -> [Gender: +masc, Number: +-pl, Person: x, Case: x, Tense: , Aspect: x, Mood: x
त -> [Gender: x, Number: x, Person: x, Case: x,

---

[1] http://www.cfilt.iitb.ac.in/~ankitb/ma/

Tense: x, Aspect: +conditional, Mood: x]
Gender: x, Number: x, Person: x, Case: x, Tense:
x, Aspect: (-perfect: +habitual), Mood: x

3. Multiple morphological analyzes for a word form: A word may have multiple analyzes possible for the same suffix and root. The token साए 'sāe' (shadows) may represent the features 'singular-oblique' or 'plural-direct'.
Token: साए, Total Output: 2

Root: सा, Class:, Category: particle, Suffix: ए
Gender: , Number: , Person: , Case: , Tense: , Aspect: , Mood: x

Root: साया, Class: D, Category: noun, Suffix: ए
Gender: +masc, Number: -pl, Person: x, Case: +oblique, Tense: x, Aspect: x, Mood: x

4. Irregular forms: The system is able to yield the roots of irregular forms using the set of rules specific to irregular verbs. Ex. For the inflected word "गए", we have:
Token: गए, Total Output: 1

Root: जा, Class:, Category: verb, Suffix: ए
Gender: +masc, Number: +pl, Person: x, Case: x, Tense: x, Aspect: +perfect, Mood: x

5. Stem modifications: The system is able to do phonological readjustment on the stem after affix stripping such as vowel lengthening (i-ī in ताइ-ताई 'tāi-tāī' and पि-पी 'pi-pī', u-ū in बहु-बहू 'bəhu-bəhū' and छु-छू 'chu-chu'), vowel addition at the end (द-दो 'd-do') etc. For Example, 'taiyan'
Token: ताइयाँ, Total Output: 1

Root: ताई, Class: B, Category: noun, Suffix: याँ
Gender: -masc, Number: +pl, Person: x, Case: -oblique, Tense: x, Aspect: x, Mood: x

6. Compound words: The system is able to yield the roots of compound words of the template [A-B] using the set of rules, which capture inflection on one or either both the words. We have introduced specific categories as compound-noun, compound-adj, compound-adv and compound-verb.
Example: For an inflected compound word "वर्ण-भेदों", 'varn-bhedon' we get the following output:
Token: वर्ण-भेदों, Total Output: 1

Root: वर्ण-भेद, Class: A, Category: noun, Suffix: ओं;
Gender: +masc, Number: +pl, Person: x, Case: +oblique, Tense: x, Aspect: x, Mood: x

5 Results

We tested HinMA on a corpus of around 66,000 words (annotated and manually cross-checked) to check its performance. We would like to emphasize that there was no instance of failure at analysis of an inflectional form as long as its root was available in the lexicon. In a few cases, the root of a given word is present in the root-list but under a different spelling. Since, the lexicon does not store variants of the same root word, many roots are left unidentified by the system. However, if we enrich the lexicon by adding more entries and include certain variations in spelling such as Urdu-Hindi letter alternations (क़ैदियों/कैदियों 'kædiyõ' (prisoners), हफ़्ते/हफ्ते 'həphte' (weeks)) and nasal vs. nasalization (क्रान्तिकारी/क्रांतिकारी 'krāntikārī' (revolutionists)), we ought to get better coverage. Below we discuss, results and error analysis for each POS category.
Nouns: We tested the Morphological Analyzer on 14475 Hindi noun forms extracted from the corpus and the results were verified manually. The system could correctly identify the roots and provide the morphological analysis for 13523 nouns (more than half of which require multiple analysis). A total of 1022 nouns remain unidentified, with 643 unique noun forms (rest repeated entries). **Verbs:** We tested the analyzer on 13160 Hindi verb forms and manually verified the results. The system was able to correctly analyze most of the regular and irregular forms. The system fails again with cases of incorrect spelling, hyphenated word forms, missing roots or where in the analyzed text there were extra/incorrect characters in the word form. The performance of the system on Hindi verbs is very impressive. The system fails to identify only 116 verbal forms.

6 Error Analysis

We performed error analysis based on a variety of different parameters with respect to the part of speech under consideration. The most error causing cases were that of Nouns and Verbs and hence we present their results here. We present them, specific to the observed parameter and the respective examples as follows:

- **Nouns:** Incorrect spelling: भैसों (correct spelling: भैंसों 'bhaĩsõ' (buffaloes)); Spelling Variations: क्रैदियों/कैदियों 'kædiyõ' (prisoners); Missing root entries in the lexicon: दोहराव 'dohrāv' (repetition); Borrowed nouns from foreign languages (foreign words): इंटरनेट 'intərnet (internet); Adjectives/qualifiers functioning as nouns: सैंकड़ों 'sænkədõ' (thousands).

- **Verbs:** With missing roots in the lexicon: पदा 'pədā' (make somebody run); Hyphenated verbs: आने-जाने 'āne-jāne'; Verbs with incorrect or variant spelling: रक्खा (correct spelling: रखा 'rəkhā' (kept)); Verbs with extra characters due to faulty tokenization: देखने 'dekhne'.

7   Evaluation

Currently, for Hindi, there is only one state of the art Morphological Analyzer which is under **active development** and provided **constant updates.** It is developed by IIIT Hyderabad[2]. Thus, to evaluate, we executed our system against 200 words chosen randomly from the BBC news corpus[3] and then manually checked the accuracy of results on both HinMa and IIITH-MA. This methodology was adopted, since there is no publicly available gold data for this task. The low number of the evaluation corpus was to provide ease to the verifying linguist. But, as the data is chosen in random order and only unique words are considered, this brings some integrity to the evaluation methodology.

MA Systems	*HinMa*	*IIITH - MA*
Correct Results	186	181
Wrong/Unknown Words	14	19
Accuracy (%)	93	90.5

Table 1: Accuracy figures for evaluation of HinMA results with that of IIIT-H MA.

8   Applications

We have integrated HinMa with Hindi Wordnet and Sense Marker tool, they are described below:
1. **Integration with Hindi Wordnet:** The work was inspired by English Wordnet[4] developed at Princeton, Miller (1995); Fellbaum (1998) which gives results based on the stem of the query words consisting of inflection. For example, if we search for the word "लड़कियाँ" (girls) in Hindi Wordnet integrated with HinMa, the result is same as for word "लड़की" (girl). "लड़की" (girl) is the root form of the inflected word "लड़कियाँ" (girls). Thus. such an integration increases the coverage of results.
2. **Integration with Sense Marker Tool:** The sense marker tool (Chatterjee et al.) is used for marking the correct sense of the word from a given set of senses. This allows one to create a corpora of manually tagged words and this is extremely useful in NLP problem areas like word sense disambiguation. We have integrated HinMa with the sense marker tool thereby providing a better coverage and accuracy in terms of returned result(s) whenever an inflected word needs to be sense marked.

9   Conclusion and Future Work

In our paper, we have described the Hindi Morphological Analyzer (*HinMA*) which handles the Inflectional Morphology in the framework of Distributed Morphology (DM). Our approach first analyses the formation of inflectional forms of Hindi through the application of suffix insertion rules and then apply phonological readjustment rules. It was found that it works quite well for the words that are present in the lexicon. Using the basic concepts of DM, our analysis of Hindi nouns and verbs is able to generate the inflectional forms using a very small set of rules and an inflection-based classification of nouns and adjectives. We showed that the DM-based Hindi morphological analyzer is quite accurate and reliable, capable of both analysis and generation. Future work involves developing a *Word Generator for Hindi*. The linguistic resources used in the DM-based MA namely, the vocabulary items (suffixal entries) and the readjustment rules need to be applied in the reverse direction to produce fully inflected words using the root entries from the root-list and combining them with the affixal entries to generate surface forms. We encourage using this framework to develop

---

[2] http://sampark.iiit.ac.in/hindimorph/web/restapi.php/indic/morphclient

[3] http://www.bbc.co.uk/hindi/

[4] http://wordnetweb.princeton.edu/perl/webwn

morphological analyzers for other languages as well.

Acknowledgements

The authors would like to thank our team of linguists, Mrs. Jaya Jha, Mrs. Laxmi Kashyap, Mrs. Nootan Verma and Mrs. Rajita Shukla for their valuable inputs and their work on manually developing lexicon for this task

10   References

A. Ramanathan, and D. D. Rao. 2003. *A Lightweight Stemmer for Hindi*, Proceedings of the 10th Conference of the European Chapter of the Association for Computational Linguistics, 2003.

Bharati, A., R. Sangal, S. M. Bendre, M. N. S. S. K. Pavan Kumar and K. R. Aishwarya. 2001. *Unsupervised Improvement of Morphological Analyzer for Inflectionally Rich Languages*. In the Proceedings of the 6th NLP Pacific Rim Symposium, 685-692. Tokyo, Japan, November.

Chatterjee Arindam, Joshi Salil Rajeev, Khapra Mitesh M. and Bhattacharyya Pushpak, 2010. *Introduction to Tools for IndoWordnet and Word Sense Disambiguation*, The 3rd IndoWordnet Workshop, Eighth International Conference on Natural Language Processing (ICON 2010), IIT Kharagpur, India.

Christiane Fellbaum (1998, edition) *WordNet: An Electronic Lexical Database*. Cambridge, MA: MIT Press.

Halle, M., and A. Marantz. 1993. *Distributed Morphology and the Pieces of Inflection*. In The View from Building 20: Essays in Linguistics in Honour of Sylvain Bromberger, eds. K.

Harley, H. and R. Noyer. 1999. *Distributed Morphology* In GLOT International 4.4:3-9.

George A. Miller (1995). WordNet: A Lexical Database for English. Communications of the ACM Vol. 38, No. 11: 39-41.

Goyal, V. and Lehal G. S. 2008. *Hindi Morphological Analyzer and Generator*. In the Proceedings of the First International Conference on Emerging Trends in Engineering and Technology, 1156-1159. Nagpur, IEEE Computer Society Press, California, USA.

Leah S. Larkey, Margaret E. Connell, Nasreen Abduljaleel. 2003 *Hindi CLIR in thirty days* ,ACM Transactions on Asian Language Information Processing (TALIP),Volume 2 Issue 2, pages 130 - 14, ACM New York, NY, USA, June 2003.

McGregor, R.S. 1995. *Outline of Hindi grammar*. Oxford: Oxford University Press.

Singh, Smriti 2011. *Hindi Inflectional Morphology and its implementation in Language Processing Tools: A distributed Morphology Approach,* PhD Thesis, IIT Bombay, Mumbai, India.

Roles of Nominals in Construing Meaning at the Level of Discourse

Soumya Sankar Ghosh
School of Languages and Linguistics
Jadavpur University
Kolkata-32, India
soumyaghosh73@gmail.com

Samir Karmakar
School of Languages and Linguistics
Jadavpur University
Kolkata-32, India
samir.krmkr@gmail.com

Abstract

Construction of meaning at the level of discourse involves complex procedures. Exploring this process reveals the hidden complexities of linguistic cognition. This paper mainly tries to unpack one such complexity in this paper. It attempts to answer the way complex and often metaphorical usages are construed in language with a special reference to the language data drawn from *Bangla* emphasizing the way nominals behave in language. In doing so, we have adopted a model proposed by Karmakar and Kasturirangan (2011) to explain the process of conceptual blending. We have also tried to push the boundary a little behind by incorporating few mathematical assumptions.

1 Introduction

As per the thesis of compositionality as is endorsed in the school of logical positivism, the meaning of a complex expression is the totality of its constituent parts and the way they are combined together into a structural whole. However, in contrary, it is often noticed that the meaning of whole is always more than the meaning of the totality of its constituents: This is primarily because of the reason that not all of the inferential tasks involved in meaning construction are realized explicitly in a communicative event. Therefore, the major challenge to interpret meaning construction at the level of discourse is to construct an account of implicit and explicit inferences and the way they are combined together into a coherent whole. In doing so, researchers have primarily tried to concentrate on the semantic-pragmatic behavior of the verbs; however it is hardly possible to come up with a theoretical solution to the problem of meaning construction simply by overlooking the roles of other syntactic categories (Pustejovsky, 1995).

1.1 Defining the research problem

Because of being motivated by the compositionality principle, most of the approaches in logical positivism tradition reduce the problem of meaning construction into the mere problem of combinatoriality under the assumption that semantic design is homomorphic to the syntactic design. Consider example (1):

1. The boy enters the house
   a.Syntactic Template:
   $[_{S}[_{NP}[_{art}\ ]\ [_{N}\ ]]\ [_{VP}[_{V}\ ]\ [_{NP}[_{art}\ ]\ [_{N}\ ]]]]$
   b. Semantic Template:
   $[_{Event}GO([_{Thing}\ ],\ [_{Path}TO([_{Place}IN([_{Thing}\ ])])])]$

Establishing one-to-one correspondence between the two templates stated in (1a) and (1b) above seems to be the most pressing problem in this stage of research. In comparison to (1a), (1b) contains several conceptual components which are not explicitly realized in the syntactic level, for example (1a) lacks syntactic equivalences for the semantic constituents like PATH and PLACE. Why is it so? – One probable answer to this kind of mismatch comes from the fact that unlike syntax conceptual representation involves different types of meaning relations. In fact the conceptual structure represented in (1b) is actually the semantic representation of 'the boy went into the house' – the sentence which is entailed by (1).

2. The boy enters the house
   → The boy goes into the house

However, this is not the end of the story. In reality, the comprehension of (1) presupposes a whole

D S Sharma, R Sangal and J D Pawar. Proc. of the 11th Intl. Conference on Natural Language Processing, pages 76–81,
Goa, India. December 2014. ©2014 NLP Association of India (NLPAI)

lot of information without which (1) will hardly make any sense. The semantics of *house*, as per our statement, stands in some congruity with the semantics of verb *enter* in virtue of having a sense of enclosure. More explicitly, the semantics of *enter* expects or presupposes a location which is enclosed.

These theoretical solutions are often considered as problematic primarily because of the reason that they have very little scope to incorporate various types of entailment and presupposition involved with a particular articulation. For example, (1) involved following types of inferences:

3. a. A living being enters into the room.
    b. A living being goes into an enclosed space.
    c. The enclosed space has an entrance.
    d. Entering-act ends inside the enclosed space.
    e. etc.

Syntactic and semantic representations of (1) fail to capture these detailing. Capturing these detailing seeks to develop a theoretical framework where linguistic expressions can control the inflow of common sense knowledge more efficiently. In doing so, one needs to put equal emphasis on all syntactic categories. Under this situation, present work seeks to model the functions of nominal at the level of discourse in construing meaning. To do so, we need to understand how nominal differs as well as resembles verb.

1.1.1 The Nature of Nominals

There are several remarkable differences between nominal and verbal predicates in the level of meaning construction. Firstly, a close analysis of a text will demonstrate that the number of nominal predicates is much larger than the number of verbs. For example in 1 we can see the number of nominals is two in contrast to the number of verbs which is one. Secondly, According to Geach (1962) and Gupta (1980) nominals are like intransitive verbs within the theoretical framework of predicate logic. This can even be noticed in the semantic interpretation 1, following Jackendoff's proposal (1995). The intransitive verb like behavior of nominals will become much clear in the following logical translation of 1:

4. $\exists x \exists y (BOY(x) \wedge HOUSE(y) \wedge ENTER(x,y)))$

From 4, it is possible to show that the nominals like *boy*, *house* etc. is behaving much like the one place predicates which can take single argument in contrast to the transitive predicate like *enter*. Finally, compared with a verb predicate, a nominal predicate tends to have fewer explicit and more implicit arguments that are not explicitly stated in the current sentence but can be recovered in a larger context (Gerber and Chai 2010). This claim is illustrated in 5.

5. a. ENTER:
$[X]_{\text{explicit-argument}}$ enters $[Y]_{\text{explicit-argument}}$ through $[Z]_{\text{implicit-argument}}$
b. BOY:
$[\text{living\_being, has\_the\_ability\_of\_moving, etc.}]_{\text{implicit-arguments}}$
c. HOUSE:
$[\text{enclosed\_space, has\_entrance, etc.}]_{\text{implicit-argumnet}}$

More the number of implicit arguments more informative the expression is. In fact, what amount of inferential task is involved in the unpacking of a particular utterance is largely determined by the fact how many implicit arguments the utterance has with it.

2 Theoretical Framework

Karmakar and Kasturirangan (2011) conceive a linguistic expression as a mental regulation consisting of intending function (= I_f) and contending function (= C_f). The intending function basically invokes the relevant conceptual category. A conceptual category indicates a systematic representation of interrelated knowledge systems (Laurence & Margolis, 1999; Aarts, 2006). For our study, a conceptual category is rather conceived as a cognitive capacitance, which stores all possible perspectives of a phenomenon (Merleau-Ponty, 1945/2002; Millikan, 2004). By definition we can say that a cognitive capacitance is a category, which is useful in presupposing and entailing large numbers of facts associated with it, because on activation it illuminates a cluster of other categories with which it is associated (Givon, 2005). However, intending alone is not enough to language a discourse, since linguistic communication is always context dependent. We need another cognitive function, whose role is to situate conceptual categories in that context (Zilberman,

1938/1988; Langacker, 2008). We call this act of relativization *contending*. The function of a linguistic expression, while contending, is to choose a particular perspective in a discourse context. For example if we consider the expression **'rose'**, we will see that the act of intending, associated with **'rose'** invokes the corresponding category which includes information about its structural aspects (like shape, size, constituencies etc.) and at the same time it also indicates the functional aspects (like symbol of love, friendship, peace etc.). From these two examples we can say that it is the communicative situation that will determine the selection of these structural and functional aspects.

In addition to this, we also want to argue that meaning construction can at best be conceived as the composition of intending and contending functions as is illustrated in 6 below with a provision for an intermediating domain essential for meaning transference:

6. $C_f \circ I_f =_{def} \{(x, z)$: for some y, $(x,y) \in I_f$ & $(y,z) \in C_f$; where $x \in$ Domain(I_f) & $z \in$ Range$(C_f)\}$

What seems to be of most interesting is the fact that composition of two functions leading towards the emergence of a third meaning presupposes the provision for an intermediating value commonly shared by both functions for successful meaning transference. While observing the similar phenomenon, Goguen (2006) suggests that this type of shared underlying substrates are significant since they do allow the cognizer to predict what else is being inherited in due course of forming the composition. The provision for intermediating value in construing the underlying substrate constitutes that frame of reference with respect to which the composed-meaning-space is interpreted.

So having discussed about these functions, we can say that meanings of the expressions (here, it is nominals) are not always the prepared items stored in a context; rather it is a product that we built and rebuilt on each time. The meaning construing capacities of nominals, as Karmakar and Kasturirangan (2010a,b) argues, in a discourse is determined by the way underlying domains of our cognition are grounded and situated by the respective functions associated with an expression – i.e. intending and contending. This way of grounding

and situating is what we call the *conceptual route* that a cognizer follows - though intuitively - in order to access the communicative intent. In fact, study of the conceptual route is an effort to explore the way conceptualization processes are structured.

3 Text Analysis

The claims that we have made till now, will further be justified through an analysis of a text. The following report is randomly selected from a Bengali news paper, Ananda Bazar Patrika, (dated 3rd February 2014):

7.

a.   *joRa*   *baunsar*
      double   bouncer
      Double bouncer.

b.   *ete*   *OboSSo*   *bharotio*   *krikeT*   *dOl-er*
      in this   however   Indian   cricket   team-of
      moto   *Sue*   *pOReni*   *bharotio*   *Orthoniti*
      like   lay down   fall-past-neg   Indian   economics
      tOtha   *deS-er*   *dui*   *prodhan*   *Sear SuchOk*
      means   country-of   two   main   share index
      However, like the Indian cricket team, Indian Economy – means two main share indices of the country – has not laid down.

The close analysis of the text indicates two different conceptual routes: (1) the *addresser*'s perspective and (2) the *addressee*'s perspective. From the beginning of this report it is quite clear that *addressee*, as *addresser*'s target, is not the economic scholars rather the common people of this country. By using the nominal word 'baunsar' (bouncer) the addresser is basically arresting reader's attention. The conceptual category 'baunsar' (bouncer) has an inbuilt orientation.

With the incorporation of the words like *baunsar* (= bouncer), *krikeT dOl* (= cricket team) in the above mentioned narrative, the speaker establishes the domain knowledge of game (here, cricket) as the pretext for the better performance of Indian economy during a particular point of time. More importantly, picturing the better performance of Indian economy as against the poor performance of Indian Cricket team attributes a sense of prominence to this story, in spite of the fact that domain knowledge of game shares very few information about the domain knowledge of economy. However, superimposition of these two domains of knowledge switches on various connections which remain nascent in this articulation. One such network of connections results into a kind of convolution (in a mathematical sense, if permitted), creating a third sense of 'competition' which may or may not have any connections with either of the domains of knowledge as is mentioned above.

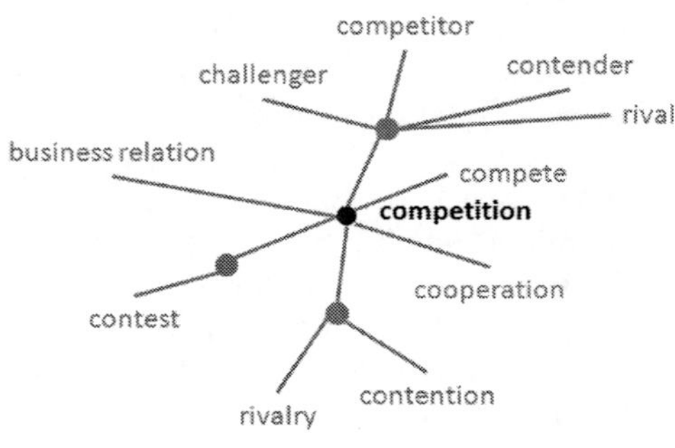

Figure 1

This convoluted sense of competition which is not apparent in 6, again, brings with it a baggage of information which definitely increases the richness of the information. The term convolution is used here in the following sense:

8.   a. A convolution is an integral that expresses the amount of overlap of one function I_f as it is shifted over another function C_f. It, therefore, "blends" one function to another. A more formal representation is given below:

    b. $(C_f*I_f)(D) =_{def} \int C_f(\tau)I_f(D-\tau)d\tau$, where τ is the time dependent variables and D is domain emerges due to the convolution

Significance of 8 lies with the terms like 'overlap' and 'blends': In continuation of our discussion on 6, we can further argue that τ as the contingent element constitute the frame of reference with respect to which the interpretation of newly evolved D is being done. More specifically, construction of D is dependent primarily on the integration of time dependent τ-contention and time independent intention represented as $(D - \tau)$.

Clearly, certain aspects of the background knowledge involved in increasing the richness of the information is taken care of by the semantics of the word which is time independent and some other aspect is taken care of by the time dependent pragmatics. Taken together these two aspects explains the meaning construction process of 6; or, in other word, determines the emergence of D.

A time dependent construal, here in this case the performance of Indian Cricket Team, is often picked up by the speaker not only to make the information rich but also to convey the message more effectively and efficiently. The time dependent aspect of D, then, should fall within the scope of contending; whereas the time independent aspect is taken care of by the intending function.

4. Discussion

The concept of blending, here, seems to be the most important one. Though in 7, we have shown blending of two major domains of knowledge, (namely the domain of cricket game and the domain of Indian economics,) a little attention will reveal the fact that the interpretation of 7 requires other instances of blending also. One such instance is *dOl* which corresponds with the concept of team, party etc. However, when it appears in the vicinity of cricket its intended sense is being coerced by the concept of cricket game. Similarly, cricket in isolation may intend several things but in conjunction with *dOl*, it results into a particular sense. Same situation can also be noticed in case of *sear* 'share' and *suchOk* 'index'. Therefore, what can at most be suggested that meaning in a discourse is a consequence of both invoking the default schemes of our thoughts and also combined them into some integral domain which may further transformed into a newer integral domain depending on the fact if newer information is being brought into the discussion. However what needs to be emphasized is the fact that the emerged meaning coexist with the original meaning relations out of which the former one arises under the direct influence of the context. A similar claim is also made in Guhe *et al.* (2011).

One way to deal with the formation of integral domain is to employ the concept of Cartesian product over a non-empty set of typed-concepts with restrictions. Under this assertion, then a blended type will be considered as the ordered pair. Lets unpack this assertion with a special reference a phrase *share index* whose Bangla correspondence is *sear suchOk*. Concept of *share* is connected with several other concepts as is shown in the following diagram:

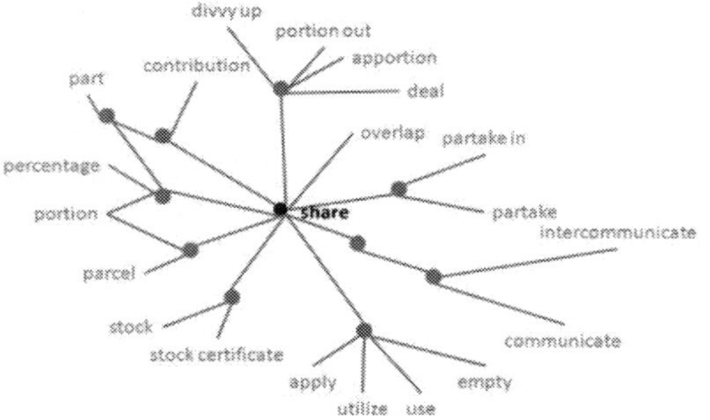

Figure 2

Same is also the case with the concept of *index*:

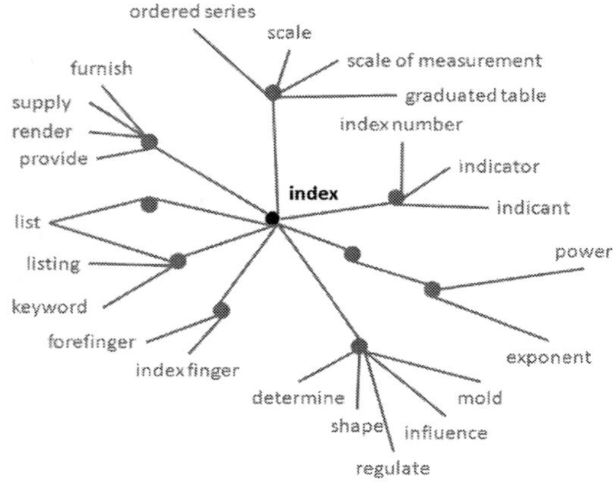

Figure 3

However, when they are combined together through the act of intending and contending, they results into a third domain of conceptual connections. Here, in this context, an indicative representation of *share index* is given in Figure 4.

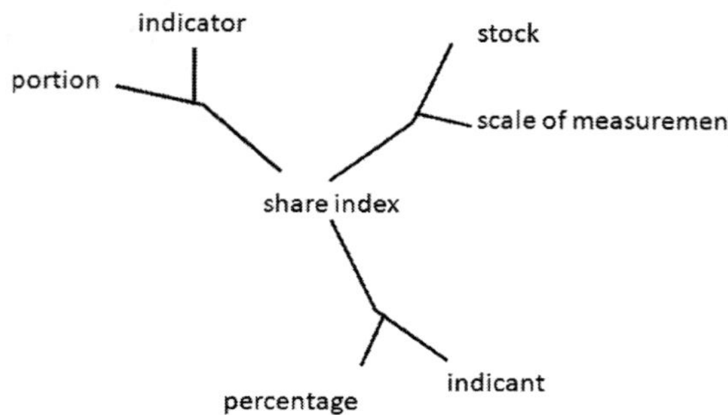

Figure 4

But, how does this fit into the theoretical framework which we have discussed above? – What remains common to both *share* and *index* is a *sense of measure*, however with some difference: When *index* is directly connected with the sense of measurement, *share* is indirectly connected to the sense of measuring. More specifically, *share* is connected to the sense of measurement only in virtue of being connected with the concepts like *portion*, *percentage* etc. Under this situation, sense of measurement is picked up as the τ-component to blend the conceptual spaces of *share* (= I_f(share)) and *index* (= I_f(index)) into the blended-space of *share index* (= D) where the sense of measurement is the dominant one. Picking up of τ-component to blend the conceptual spaces is what we have named as contending in our proposal.

Within the broader theoretical scope, then, a concept (both, simple and the complex, like *share*, *index*, and *share index*) can be visualized as a integral domain consisting of (i) a non-empty set of concepts it is associated with, and (ii) two binary operations called intending and contending.

5 Conclusion

This paper deals with the way concepts are integrated in a text. In dealing with this issue, we have concentrated on the nominals primarily. While developing our previous position on this issue, we have argued further that the issues in metaphorical meaning can be successfully explained with the help of some mathematical notions like convolution, integral domain etc.

References

Geach, P. 1962. *Reference and Generality*. Cornell University Press, Ithaca, NY.

Gerber, M., and J. Chai. 2010. Beyond nombank: A study of implicit arguments for nominal predicates. In *Proceedings of the 48th Annual Meeting of the Association for Computational Linguistics*, 1583–1592. Association for Computational Linguistics, Uppsala, Sweden.

Givón, T. 2005. *Context as other Minds: The Pragmatics of Sociality, Cognition, and Communication*. John Benjamins, Amsterdam.

Goguen, J. 2006. Mathematical models of cognitive space and time. In D. Andler, Y. Ogawa, M. Okada, & S. Watanabe (Eds.), *Reasoning and cognition:*

Proceedings of the interdisciplinary conference on reasoning and cognition, 125–128. Keio University Press, Japan.

Guhe, M. *et al.* 2011. A computational account of conceptual blending in basic mathematics. *Cognitive System Research*, 12: 249-265.

Gupta, A. 1980. *The logic of common nouns: an investigation of quantified modal logic*. Yale University Press, New Haven, CT.

Jackendoff, R. 1995. *Semantic Structure*. MIT Press, Massachusetts.

Karmakar, S. and R. Kasturirangan. 2011. Structural and Structuring: Issues in Designing an Expression. *Jadavpur Journal of Philosophy*, Vol. 21(1): 87-102.

Karmakar, S. and R. Kasturirangan. 2010a. "Perspectivizing Space in Bāŋlā Discourse." In *Proceedings of the 32nd Annual Conference of the Cognitive Science Society* (826-830). Cognitive Science Society, CSS. Austin, TX.

Karmakar, S. and R. Kasturirangan. 2010b. "Cognitive processes underlying the meaning of complex predicates and serial verbs from the perspective of individuating and ordering of situations in Bangla." In *Proceedings of the First International Conference on Intelligent Interactive Technologies and Multimedia*, (81-87). ACMIIIT Allahabad Professional Chapter & North India ACM-SIGCHI, ACM. Allahabad, India.

Langacker, R.W. 2008. *Cognitive Grammar: A Basic Introduction*. Oxford University Press, Oxford Oxford:.

Laurence, S. & Margolis, E. 1999. Concepts and Cognitive Science, in E. Margolis & S. Laurence (eds.), *Concepts: Core Readings* (3-81), Cambridge, MA: MIT Press.

M. Merleau-Ponty 1995/2002. *Phenomenology of Perception*. New York: Routledge.

R.G. Millikan. 2004. *Varieties of Meaning*, Massachussetts: The MIT Press.

Pustejovsky, J. 1995. *The Generative Lexicon*. Cambridge, MA: MIT Press.

Zilberman, David B. 1988. *The Birth of Meaning in Hindu Thought* (Boston Studies in the Philosophy of Science), Dordrecht, Boston: D. Reidel Publishing Company.

Anou Tradir: Experiences In Building Statistical Machine Translation Systems For Mauritian Languages – Creole, English, French

Raj Dabre
CFILT
IIT Bombay
prajdabre
@gmail.com

Aneerav Sukhoo
Central Informatics Bureau
Quatre Bornes, Mauritius
aneeravsukhoo
@yahoo.com

Pushpak Bhattacharyya
CFILT
IIT Bombay
pushpakbh
@gmail.com

Abstract

We present, in this paper, our experiences in developing Statistical Machine Translation (SMT) systems involving English, French and Mauritian Creole, the languages most spoken in Mauritius. We give a brief overview of the peculiarities of the language phenomena in Mauritian Creole and indicate the differences between it and English and French. We then give descriptions of the developed corpora used for the various MT systems where we also explore the possibility of using French as a bridge language when translating from English to Creole. We evaluate these systems using the standard objective evaluation measure, BLEU. We postulate and through an error analysis, indicated by examples, verify that when English to French translations are perfect, the subsequent translation of French to Creole results in better quality translations than direct English to Creole translation.

1 Introduction

Mauritius[1] is an island nation in the Indian Ocean about 2000 km off the south-east coast of the African continent. The population of Mauritius is approximately 1.3 million and it is the 151st most populated country in the world. While English language is the official language, French language is spoken to a greater extent and the Mauritian Creole (henceforth called creole) is the most common language used by the majority of the population. In addition, since the people of Mauritius have Indian ancestors, Indian languages such as Marathi, Hindi and Bhojpuri (a Bihari language) are also spoken amongst the populace. Mauritius is an extremely popular tourist spot and attracts many thousands of people every year and has such involves interaction with the local inhabitants. Although English is the main language, lack of knowledge of the Mauritian Creole (which is based on French) does lead to a gap in communication.

Various organisations have been actively involved in give the Mauritian Creole a new dimension, whereby a trilingual dictionary has been prepared by the University of Mauritius and a bilingual dictionary has also been provided online by Ledikasyon pu Travayer[2] on its website. There is room for further research in the area to come up with a dictionary for technical terms. Computational Linguistics can help to take the Mauritian Creole language to greater heights.

Google provides translation services between many languages but Mauritian Creole is not one of them which prompted us to begin the development of machine translation systems to achieve this end. To the best of our knowledge this is the first of its kind work involving translation to and from Mauritian Creole on such a large scale. We hope that this work will attract and help researchers in the development of machine translation systems involving a variety of Creole languages.

---

[1] http://en.wikipedia.org/wiki/Mauritius

[2] http://www.lalitmauritius.org/dictionary.php

D S Sharma, R Sangal and J D Pawar. Proc. of the 11th Intl. Conference on Natural Language Processing, pages 82–88,
Goa, India. December 2014. ©2014 NLP Association of India (NLPAI)

1.1 Related Work

Sukhoo et al. (2014) had developed a basic English Creole SMT system with a very small amount of parallel corpus (10000-13000 lines including many dictionary words). They manage to get simple sentences translated with reasonable quality but fail when longer sentences (more than five words) are tested. This corpus, after considerable augmentation was used in our experiments. Significant work has been done in using bridge languages (Bertoldi et al. (2008), Utiyama et al. (2007)) to improve translation quality. In many of these works, they develop translation systems from languages A to C using B, where A-B and B-C are resource rich, by either synthesizing new phrase tables or modifying existing corpora. In our case, we had a huge English French corpus but a very small French Creole corpus. Moreover no linguistic processing modules for Creole exist, which would help in reducing data sparsity. Thus we decided to adopt the "transfer method" described by Wu et al. (2009). The remainder of the paper involves a chapter on Linguistic phenomena in Mauritian Creole; describing peculiarities and how it is different from English and French; followed by a chapter describing the corpora used, the systems developed, the results and error analyses via examples finally leading to the conclusion and future works.

1.2 Purpose of the work

The outcome of our work is a set of online translation systems aiming to:

1. Assist young students to learn English as a second language.
2. Help tourists to learn the basics of the Creole language so as to enhance communication with the local community. This can provide better enjoyment during their stay.
3. Assist expatriates and foreign business people to interact with the people of Mauritius.
4. Assist the local people, who do not master the English language to be able to translate and understand English texts, which are available in huge amount online as well as from other sources.

2 Mauritian Creole

The Mauritian Creole is spoken in Mauritius and Rodrigues islands. A variation of the language is also spoken in Seychelles. Mauritius was colonized successively by the Dutch, French and English. Even though the English took over the island from the French in the early 1800, French remained as a dominant language and as such Creole language shares many features with French.

2.1 Similarities with French

The same alphabets are used in both cases and they are pronounced in a similar manner. In addition, some words are written and pronounced in the same way. These include words as per the table below (the English translation is also shown in the 3rd column):

French	Creole	English
avion	avion	aeroplane
bon	bon	good
gaz	gaz	gas
bref	bref	brief
pion	pion	pawn

Table 1: Words with similar orthography in French and Creole

One must note that, in French there is a heavy usage of accents while writing which is absent in Creole. Many words are pronounced similarly in French and Creole, but the grapheme is different. These include:

French (Fr)	Creole (Cr)	English (En)
mauvais	move	move
confort	konfor	comfort
méditation	meditasion	meditation
insecte	insekt	insect
condition	kondision	State, terms or provision

Table 2: Words with same pronunciation but different orthography

2.2 Creole Grammar

The grammar of Creole has been published in 2011 (Police-Michel, Carpooran and Florigny, 2011). The Mauritian Creole language has sentences with structure of Subject-Verb-Object as in the case of English and French language. Some differences with English language can be noted as follows:

1. Adjectives are sometimes moved after the object:

    "The brown bird" is translated as: **Zwazo maron-la**

    Here: "maron" for "brown" is moved after the object (Zwazo). "The" is moved at the end ("la"). However, the French translation follows the same pattern as Creole, e.g. "L'oiseau maron"

2. Difference between singular and plural: "There are many birds" is translated as:

Ena boukou zwazo laba

Here: The plural form does not take "s".

The word "boukou" indicates "many" and therefore, it can be deduced that there are many birds. In French, the translated sentence is "Il y a beaucoup d'oiseaux là-bas"

3. Dropping of verb: "He is bad" is translated as:

Li move

Here: "He" is translated to "Li" and "bad" to "méchant". The verb "is" is dropped. In French, the translated sentence becomes "Il est méchant", where the verb is retained.

This concludes the explanation of Creole linguistics. Due to the similar SVO syntax and limited morphological complexity of English, French and Creole, translation between them becomes tractable even which working without linguistic processing and small corpora. We now describe our experiments and systems developed.

3 Experiments

We begin by listing the various SMT systems developed. We have used only phrase-based methods due to the lack of linguistic processing modules for Creole.

3.1 Systems developed

All the systems developed and hosted are given below:

1. Direct English to Creole
2. Direct Creole to English
3. Direct French to Creole
4. Direct Creole to French
5. English to Creole using French as bridge

The front-end of our system was developed using a combination of HTML and DJANGO (Python). The SMT models, at the back end, are provided as services accessible by XMLRPC.

3.2 Corpora details

Plenty of parallel corpus is available for English-French however we had to manually, from scratch, create parallel corpus for Creole-French and Creole-English. These sets of corpora were developed by the sole Creole speaker in our group over a period of six months. A significant part of the corpora consists of dictionary words which ensure basic word substitution. Table 3 gives the details of the corpora used.

Language pair	#lines	#words (L1-L2)	Source
En-Fr	2000000	127405-147812	Europarl
En-Cr	25010	16294-17389	Manually created
Fr-Cr	18354	13769-13725	Manually created

Table 3: Corpora Details

In the French-Creole corpus 11,208 entries were just dictionary words and thus the number of parallel sentences was just around 7146. Similarly for the English-Creole corpus 11,423 entries were dictionary words making the number of parallel sentences around 13,795. For creole we had a monolingual corpus of around 100k lines.

3.3 Training and development

For purposes of training we used IBM models (Brown et al., 1993) implemented in GIZA++ for alignment and Moses (Koehn et al., 2007, 2003) for phrase extraction and decoding. Standard parameters were used. Training procedure following which the phrase tables and reordering tables were binarized in order to ensure on demand memory loading thereby reducing the requirement of RAM. The services for each language pair are hosted using mosesserver. The English-French system took the maximum training time; a total of 24 hours, including the time for tuning. All the other systems took around 5 minutes of training. Due to lack of corpora we did not perform tuning for these systems. For each system the target side corpus was used for generating the language model. For creole we used the monolingual corpus for language modelling. Tuning was done using MERT.

3.4 Using French as a bridge language

We used the "transfer method" or "sentence translation strategy", proposed by Utiyama and Isahara (2007) and described by Wu and Wang (2009), to translate from English to Creole using French; wherein the first translated from English to French using the En-Fr system and then from French to Creole using the Fr-Cr system. This method is only applicable when either both the En-Fr and Fr-Cr systems or only the En-Fr system is of high quality. The main idea is that French is close to Creole and thus an SMT system built on a small corpus would suffice for good translations. As long as the English-French

SMT system gives good translations the resulting Creole translations can be expected to be good.

The Moses decoder allows for n-best translations to be generated as outputs which we exploit to obtain improvements in translations. When Moses translates a sentence it uses 8 main features for decoding. These are: n-gram language model probability of the target language (1 feature), two phrase translation probabilities (both directions, 2 features), two lexical translation probabilities (both directions, 2 features), a word penalty (1 feature), a phrase penalty (1 feature), a linear reordering penalty (1 feature). Each of above is a feature for decoding procedure (Hoang et al., 2007; Koehn et al., 2003). The decoder gives values for each feature for a translation candidate. The final score of the translation is a weighted sum of the values of the above mentioned features. The weights are obtained using MERT.

Let "**f**" denote the source language, "**p**" the pivot language and "**e**" the target language. Let L_1-P denote the system that translates from source to pivot and P-L_2 the system that translates from pivot to target. In our case L_1 is English, P is French and L_2 is Creole. The sentence translation strategy is:

1. Translate source language sentence "f" into "N" intermediate sentences using L_1-P system.
   a. $f \rightarrow p_1, p_2, p_3 \ldots p_N$
   b. 8 values of feature functions per p_i: $h^p{}_{i1}, h^p{}_{i2}, \ldots, h^p{}_{i8}$
2. Translate each candidate into "N" target language sentences (e) using P-L_2 system
   a. $p_i \rightarrow e_{i1}, e_{i2}, e_{i3}, \ldots e_{iN}$
   b. 8 values of feature functions per e_{ij}: $h^e{}_{ij1}, h^e{}_{ij2}, \ldots, h^e{}_{ij8}$
3. Score $N*N$ target translations using feature values and Moses tuning parameters
   a. Each feature has a weight
   b. Weights obtained by tuning via MERT
   c. $\lambda^p{}_m$ (m=1 to 8): Parameter of L_1-P system
   d. $\lambda^e{}_m$ (m=1 to 8): Parameter of P-L_2 system
4. Select the sentence e_{ij} with the highest score.

The formula for scoring is:

$$S(e_{ij}) = \sum_{m=1}^{8} (\lambda^p{}_m * h^p{}_{im} + \lambda^e{}_m * h^e{}_{ijm})$$

We experimented with 2 values of "N" where N=1 and N=10. The above method has a time complexity of $O(N*N)$ and hence we refrained from going for any higher values of "N". Using this mechanism we tested sentences to validate the following hypothesis: "For simple sentences the translation of English to Creole using French as a bridge is much better than direct English to Creole translation". Although the Fr-Cr system is built from a relatively small corpus, we believe in the validity of this hypothesis because French is much closer to Creole than English.

3.5 Testing and Results

For the purpose of testing an additional 142 sentence triplets were created, one each for English, French and Creole. These are sentences with more than 10 words per sentence on an average. The number of OOV's was more in these sentences. Extra 142 simple (short) sentence pairs for English and Creole were created to verify our hypothesis mentioned above. These contained an average of 5 words per sentence with relatively lesser number of OOV's compared to the earlier sentences. We evaluated the quality using BLEU (Papineni et al. 2002). The scores are given in Table 4 below. In the table "easy" indicates that the simple (short) sentence pairs were used for testing whereas "hard" indicates that the longer ones were used for testing. For the Creole to English, Creole to French and French to Creole systems the pivot language mechanism was not applicable since effective pivot languages were not available.

Language Pair	BLEU
En-Cr (direct, hard)	12.90
En-Cr (direct, easy)	25.31
En-Cr (bridge (N=1), hard)	**9.44**
En-Cr (bridge (N=10), hard)	**10.96 (increase compared to N=1)**
En-Cr (bridge (N=1), easy)	**26.12 (increase)**
En-Cr (bridge (N=10), easy)	**29.77 (increase)**
Cr-En (direct, hard)	17.58
Cr-En (direct, easy)	22.58
Fr-Cr (direct, hard)	15.97
Cr-Fr (direct, hard)	14.54

Table 4: BLEU scores of systems

As expected, the English to creole translation using French as bridge yields a BLEU score higher than the direct translation for simple (short) sentences. This improvement is higher when the number of intermediate translations is increased from N=1 to N=10 (from 25.31 (direct) to 26.12 to 29.77). This is because when N=10 we may have a better intermediate French translation as compared to when N=1. The limitation is that when N=10 the time taken is 100 times more than when N=1. The increase is not observed for "hard" sentences. This is because their translations from English to French (as intermediates) were not of good quality and this led to a multiplicative degradation when translating the intermediate French sentence to Creole. However there is an improvement in BLEU from 9.44 to 10.96 when N is increased from 1 to 10.

We did significance testing using bootstrapping sampling and also performed subjective analysis for the bridge translations to verify that the increase in BLEU was not coincidental. We also observed the effects of the change in BLEU with increase in corpus size used for training for En-Cr and Cr-En which is given in the table 5 below. The BLEU scores are different here because the test set used was different from the 142 sentences mentioned before. The main difference between the corpus at 20000 size and 25000 is the increase in the number of non-dictionary sentences which indicates that even with small but good corpus size increments we can achieve tremendous improvement in quality.

No of training sentences	En-Cr (direct)	Cr-En
5,000	5.36	7.47
10,000	6.17	8.57
15,000	6.07	9.16
20,000	6.25	9.69
25,000 (full)	7.71	11.64

Table 5: Change in BLEU with corpus size

3.6 Example Translations and Error Analysis

For each language pair we give below examples of good and bad translations.

3.6.1 En-Cr

1. **Input:** They all had big ears and long legs.
   Direct Creole: zot tu ti ena gran zorey e longay mole.
   French (Bridge): ils avaient tous grandes oreilles et long jambes.
   Resulting Creole: zot ti ena tou gran zorey e long lazam.
   Evaluation: In this case, the French translation is of high quality and the Creole through bridge language is equally of high quality and is preferred as compared to the direct Creole translation.

2. **Input:** My name is John.
   Direct Creole: mo apel li.
   French (Bridge): mon nom est john.
   Resulting Creole: mo apel zan.
   Evaluation: Because the French translation is correct the Creole translation as compared to the direct Creole translation, whereby the name "John" has not been translated.

3. **Input:** There are birds like no other birds because they are not real.
   Direct Creole: ena bann zwazo kuma okenn lezot zwazo parski zot pa vre.
   French (Bridge): il y a des oiseaux comme aucun autre oiseaux car ils ne sont pas vraies.
   Resulting Creole: ena bann zwazo kuma okenn lot zwazo parski zot pa vraies.
   Evaluation: The direct Creole translation is correct. The French translation is correct, but the only issue in the Creole through bridge translation is the word "vraies" in French, that was left as it is given that it is not a stem word. The small size of the French-Creole parallel corpora has been a limitation to this translation. The translation of the other words, including the order, is also correct.

3.6.2 Cr-En

1. **Input:** mo pa kontan fason to koz ar mwa
   English: i don't like the way you talk with me
   Evaluation: Correct translation.

2. **Input:** boukou touris pou vizit Moris sa lane la
   English: many tourist to visit to mauritius this year
   Evaluation: The correct tense of the verb "to visit" is "will visit", otherwise the rest of the sentence is correct.

3. **Input:** alor li ti dir sa grenouy la , "si to pou donn mwa enn zafer , mo pou fer tou seki to dimande"
   English: so he said to the frog, if you will give me a thing, i will do what you ask
   Evaluation: Almost correct translation, apart from the elimination of the quotes. "a thing" should have been "something".

3.6.3 Fr-Cr

1. **French:** je voudrais regarder un film (I want to watch a movie)
   Creole: mo anvi get enn fim

Evaluation: This translation is perfect.

2. **French:** il y a des tigres et des lions dans la forêt (There are tigers and lions in the forest)
   Creole: ena bann tigres ek bann lions dan afore
   Evaluation: Here the Creole sentence sounds like "There are the tigers and the lions in the forest". The word "bann" (the) should be absent.

3. **French:** pourquoi êtes-vous en colère contre moi? (Why are you angry with me?)
   Creole: kifer eski zot ankoler kont mwa?
   Evaluation: This translation is particularly bad. The correct is: "kifer to ankoler ar mwa". The system was unable to correctly translate "êtes-vous" (are you). This we believe is a major limitation of small corpus size.

3.6.4 Cr-Fr

1. **Creole:** mo anvi manz enn dipin (I want to eat bread)
   French: je veux manger un pain
   Evaluation: This translation is perfect.

2. **Creole:** kifer to ankoler ar mwa (Why are you angry with me?)
   French: pourquoi vous en colère avec moi.
   Evaluation: The translation is almost perfect except that it sounds like "Why you angry with me?". "are" is missing as "vous" should have had "êtes" with it.

3. **Creole:** sa lane la Moris finn gagn boukou touris (This year Mauritius had a lot of tourists.)
   French: cette année de l'île maurice a eu beaucoup de tourists
   Evaluation: Here the French translation sounds like: "this year's maurice island had a lot of tourists". Here "la Moris" is a named Entity which actually means Mauritius and its translation as "l'île maurice" is acceptable. The "de" after "année" is incorrect.

3.7 Discussion

The examples given above should indicate that survival sentences are translated with a very high quality in most cases. Common mistakes are those involving incorrect tenses, dropping of words although they are present in the corpus, adding articles like "bann" (the) for each noun and the inability to handle named entities. The main reason for this we narrow down to the following:

1. Poor language model for creole due to relatively small corpus. The creole monolingual corpus was around 100k lines but not clean since it was collected from a variety of sources. Also it is common knowledge that a corpus of atleast 1 million lines is good for language modelling.
2. Insufficient decoding options due to lack of evidence in corpora (small corpus size) and hence phrase table.
3. Lack of factors (linguistic cues) leading to surface forms being un-translated.
4. Lack of lower/upper case information which can help recognize named entities; which is again due to small corpus size. (We lower-case then translating from/to Creole as true-casing is ineffective due to a small corpus.)
5. If a pivot language is used then the final quality depends on the quality of the intermediate translations which, if bad, lead to poorer target translations.

This gives sufficient reason for us to look deeper into the decoding procedure and perhaps fine tune it for our purposes. Also the development of a larger corpus is a necessary activity. Finally more linguistic phenomena have to be studied and uncovered which would eventually lead to analysis modules for Creole.

4   Conclusion and Future Work

We have presented our experiences in developing statistical machine translation systems for Mauritian languages. As can be seen, even with small amount of corpus, we are able to get reasonable quality translations which we believe will gradually improve as the dictionary and corpora size increases. We also validated our hypotheses that French, being closer to Mauritian Creole, is a good bridge language and translation from English to Creole via French, rather than directly, gives better translations when the English to French translation is near about perfect. In the future we plan to experiment with factored models (Koehn et al., 2007), which we were not able to use due to the lack of linguistic processing modules for Creole. We also plan to experiment on translating Creole to English using French as a bridge language when our Creole French corpora size becomes large. Naturally this would lead to work on the lesser spoken languages in Mauritius as also on other Creoles.

Reference

Aneerav Sukhoo, 2014. *Translation between English and Mauritian Creole: A Statistical Machine Translation Approach.* IST-2104, Mauritius, May, 2014.

Peter E Brown, Stephen A. Della Pietra. Vincent J. Della Pietra, and Robert L. Mercer. 1993. *The Mathematics of Statistical Machine Translation: Parameter Estimationn.* Association for Computational Linguistics.

Philipp Koehn, Hieu Hoang, Alexandra Birch, Chris Callison-Burch, Marcello Federico, Nicola Bertoldi, Brooke Cowan, Wade Shen, Christine Moran, Richard Zens, Chris Dyer, Ondrej Bojar, Alexandra Constantin, Evan Herbst. 2007. *Moses: Open Source Toolkit for Statistical Machine Translation,* Annual Meeting of the Association for Computational Linguistics (ACL), demonstration session, Prague, Czech Republic, June 2007.

Philipp Koehn, Franz Josef Och, and Daniel Marcu. 2003. *Statistical phrase-based translation.* Association for Computational Linguistics 2003.

Philipp Koehn and Hieu Hoang. 2007. *Factored translation models.* In Proceedings of the 2007 Joint Conference on Empirical Methods in Natural Language Processing and Computational Natural Language Learning (EMNLP-CoNLL), pages 868-876, Prague, Czech Republic, June 2007. Association for Computational Linguistics.

Kishore Papineni, Salim Roukos, Todd Ward and Wei-Jing Zhu. 2002. *BLEU: a Method for Automatic Evaluation of Machine Translation,* Proceedings of the 40th Annual Meeting of the Association for Computational Linguistics (ACL), Philadelphia, July 2002, pp. 311-318.

Nicola Bertoldi, Madalina Barbaiani, Marcello Federico, and Roldano Cattoni. 2008. Phrase-based statistical machine translation with pivot languages. Proceeding of IWSLT, pages 143–149.

Masao Utiyama and Hitoshi Isahara. 2007. *A comparison of pivot methods for phrase-based statistical machine translation.* In Human Language Technologies 2007: The Conference of the North American Chapter of the Association for Computational Linguistics; Proceedings of the Main Conference, pages 484–491, Rochester, New York, April. Association for Computational Linguistics.

Hua Wu and Haifeng Wang. 2009. *Revisiting pivot language approach for machine translation.* In Proceedings of the Joint Conference of the 47th Annual Meeting of the ACL and the 4th International Joint Conference on Natural Language Processing of the AFNLP, pages 154–162, Suntec, Singapore, August. Association for Computational Linguistics.

How Sentiment Analysis Can Help Machine Translation

**Santanu Pal[*], Braja Gopal Patra[†], Dipankar Das[†], Sudip Kumar Naskar[†],
Sivaji Bandyopadhyay[†] and Josef van Genabith[*]**
[*]Universität des Saarlandes, Saarbrücken, Germany
[†]Jadavpur University, Kolkata, India
[*]{santanu.pal, josef.vangenabith}@uni-saarland.de
[†]{brajagopal.cse, dipankar.dipnil2005}@gmail.com
[†]{sudip.naskar, sbandyopadhyay}@cse.jdvu.ac.in

Abstract

State-of-the-art Machine Translation (MT) does not perform well while translating sentiment components from source to target language. The components such as the sentiment holders, sentiment expressions and their corresponding objects and relations are not maintained during translation. In this paper, we described, how sentiment analysis can improve the translation quality by incorporating the roles of such components. We also demonstrated how a simple baseline phrase-based statistical MT (PB-SMT) system based on the sentiment components can achieve 33.88% relative improvement in BLEU for the under-resourced language pair English-Bengali.

1 Introduction

The Statistical machine translation (SMT) systems are considered as one of the most popular approaches to machine translation (MT). However, SMT can suffer from grammatically incorrect output with erroneous syntactic and semantic structure for the language pair on which it is being applied. It is observed that the grammatical errors not only weaken the fluency, but in some cases it may even completely change the meaning of a sentence. In morphologically rich languages, grammatical accuracy is of particular importance, as the interpretation of syntactic relations depends heavily on the morphological agreement within sentences. Morphological errors create serious problems in context of translating the sentiment related components from source to target language. In this paper, we handle these errors by focusing on the roles of sentiment-holder, sentiment expression,

corresponding objects and their relations with each other at the clause level.

A common error that occurs during translation using SMT is the relations among the holders, associated sentiment expressions and their corresponding objects in a sentence (in case of complex and compound sentences) may interchange. In the following example, the position of the sentiment expression has been changed in target language while translated. Similar instances are found if any interchange occurs in case of other sentiment components such as holder or object.

Example 1: Source: In 1905, *<holder>*Calcutta*</holder>* *<expression_1>*protested *</expression_1>* *<object_1>*the partition of Bengal*</object_1>* and *<expression_2>*boycotted *</expression_2>* *<object_2>*all the British Goods *</object_2>*.

Target: 1905 sale, *<holder>*Calcutta *</holder>* *<object_1>*bongo vongo-r*</object_1>* *<expression_2>*boykot korechilo *</expression_2 >* ebong *<object_2>*ssmosto british samogri *</object_2>* *<expression_1>* protibad janiyechilo *</expression_1>*.

Thus, the entire semantics of the sentence has been changed even the sentence is considered as grammatically correct. Another major challenge is to develop a sentiment phrase aligned system between a resource-rich language English and a resource-constrained language Bengali.

The scarcity in state of the art sentiment aligned translation system motivates us to perform this task. To the best of our knowledge, no previous work has been done for the English-Bengali language pair translation by considering the sentiment-aligned approach.

In our approach, sentiment expressions, sentiment holder and the corresponding objects of the holders are used to improve the phrase alignment

D S Sharma, R Sangal and J D Pawar. Proc. of the 11th Intl. Conference on Natural Language Processing, pages 89–94,
Goa, India. December 2014. ©2014 NLP Association of India (NLPAI)

of the SMT system during training stage. Sentiment information is also used in the automatic post-editing of the SMT output after the decoding phase. SMT is based on a mathematical model, is most reliable and cost effective in many applications. This is one of the main reasons to choose SMT for our English-Bengali translation task. For automatic post-editing, we marked the phrases that contain sentiment expression, holders and their corresponding object. After translating the marked-up sentences, we then restructure the restructure the output according to the sentiment relations between the sentiment holder and the sentiment expression. Our approach involves the following steps:

- We first identify phrases, which contain sentiment holder, sentiment expressions and their corresponding objects.
- We aligned these phrases using word alignment provided by GIZA++.
- The aligned phrases are incorporated with the PB-SMT phrase table.
- Finally, the automatic post-editing has been carried out using the positional information of sentiment components.

The rest of the paper is organized in the following manner. Section 2 briefly elaborates the related work. Section 3 provides an overview of the dataset used in our experiments. The proposed system is described in Section 4 while Section 5 provides the system setup for the various experiments. Section 6 includes the experiments and results obtained. Finally, Section 7 concludes and provides avenues for further work.

2   Related Work

SMT systems have undergone considerable improvements over the years. Moreover, PB-SMT models (Koehn et al., 2003) outperform word-based models. The alignment template approach for PB-SMT (Och et al., 2004) allows many-to-many relations between words. A model that uses hierarchical phrases based on synchronous grammars is presented in (Chiang et al., 2005). To date there is little research on English-Bengali SMT: PB-SMT systems can be improved (Pal et al., 2011; 2013) by single tokenizing Multiword Expressions (MWEs) on both sides of the parallel corpus. Researches on alignment were mostly developed for MT tasks (Brown, 1991; Gale and

Church, 1993). A Maximum Entropy model based approach for English-Chinese NE alignment has been proposed in Feng et al. (2004), which significantly outperforms IBM Model 4 and HMM. Fung (1994) presented K-vec, an alternative alignment strategy that starts by estimating the lexicon.

Sentiment detection is the task of determining positive or negative sentiment of words, phrases, sentences and documents. The computational approach to sentiment analysis in textual data requires annotated lexicons with polarity tags (Patra et al., 2013). Research has been carried out on building sentiment or emotional corpora in English (Strapparava and Valitutti, 2004; Baccianella et al., 2010; Patra et al., 2013) and Bengali (Das and Bandyopadhyay, 2010; Das and Bandyopadhyay, 2010a). Identifying the sentiment holder is another task closely related to subjectivity detection (Kim and Hovy, 2004). Several methods have been implemented to identify the sentiment holders such as rule based methods (using dependency information) (Kolya et al., 2012) and supervised machine learning methods (Kim and Hovy, 2004; Kolya et al., 2012).

To the best of our knowledge, no prior work on improving SMT systems using aligned sentiment expressions, holders and their corresponding objects have been developed yet. There is research on creating sentiment lexica and cross-lingual sentiment identification. Automatic translation is a viable alternative for the construction of resources and tools for subjectivity or sentiment analysis in a new resource-constrained language using a resource-rich language as a starting point (Banea et al., 2008). Banea et al., (2008) generated resources for subjectivity annotation in Spanish and Romanian using English corpora. In context of Indian languages, Das et al., 2010 have developed a sentiment lexicon for Bengali Languages using an English to Bengali MT system. Similarly, a Hindi sentiment corpus has been developed using English to Hindi MT system (Balamurali et al., 2010). Hiroshi et al., (2004) developed a high-precision sentiment analysis system with low development cost, by making use of an existing transfer-based MT engine.

3   Dataset

In our experiment, an English-Bengali parallel corpus containing 23,492 parallel sentences comprising of 488,026 word tokens from the travel and tourism domain has been used. We randomly selected 500 sentences each for the development set and the test set from the initial parallel corpus. The rest of the sentences were used as the training corpus. The training corpus was filtered with the maximum allowable sentence length of 100 words and sentence length ratio of 1:2 (either way). The corpus has been collected from the "Development of English to Indian Languages Machine Translation (EILMT) System[1]" project.

4 System Description

Initially, we identify the sentiment expressions, holders and objects from English-Bengali parallel sentences. Sentiment phrase alignment model has been developed using our existing baseline table provided by GIZA++. These aligned sentiment phrases are integrated with the state-of-the-art PB-SMT system. Finally, an automatic post editing system has been developed to correct the translation output using the textual clues identified from the sentiment components.

4.1 Sentiment expression, holder and object identification from Parallel corpus

Sentiment: Initially, sentiment expressions were not tagged with sentiment polarity. Therefore, we developed a bootstrapping method to tag the words with sentiment polarity. We have tagged the English sentiment words using the SentiWordNet 3.0 (Baccianella et al., 2010). The raw English sentences were parsed and the stems of the words were extracted using the Stanford parser[2]. SentiWordNet examines stemmed words along with their part of speech and provides a sentiment score for each stemmed word. The sentiment of the word is judged positive, negative or neutral according to its sentiment scores. We have manually created a stop word list of around 300 words that helps us to remove the stop words from the sentences. But the words 'not', 'neither' etc. are not removed as they are valence shifters and can change the sentiment of the whole sentence. We identified 76924 and

36125 number of positive and negative words respectively.

Holder (Subject Based): Sentiment analysis involves identifying its associated holder and the event or topic. A sentiment holder is the person or organization that expresses the positive or negative sentiment towards a specific event or topic. English input sentences are parsed by the Stanford Parser to extract the dependency relations. The output is checked to identify the predicates (i.e., "*nsubj*" and "*xsubj*"), so that the *subject* related information in the "*nsubj*" and "*xsubj*" predicates are considered as probable candidates of sentiment holders.

We correlate our sentiment words with the holder using the dependency tree. For example, the sentence "*I hate chocolate but he loves it.*" has two sentiment expressions, "hate" and "love". Here the root word and the sentiment expression is the same, i.e. "hate". We identify that the sentiment expression, "*hate*" and subject "*I*" are related with "*nsubj*" relation. We conclude that "*I*" is the sentiment holder of the word "*hate*". Similarly, we identify that "*he*" is the sentiment holder of word "*loves*".

Example 2: **nsubj**(hate-2, **I**-1), root(ROOT-0, hate-2), **dobj**(hate-2, **chocolate**-3), nsubj(loves-6, **he**-5), conj_but(hate-2, loves-6), **dobj**(loves-6, **it**-7).

We have identified only 22992 number of sentiment holders, in comparison to a total of 113049 sentiment expressions.

Object: The parsed data were analyzed to identify the object of a sentence. It is found that the relations, "*dobj*" and "*obj*" are considered as the probable candidates for the object. The above example sentence along with parsed output and dependency relations (example 2), the "*dobj*" dependency relation includes the object. Here, "*chocolate*" and "*it*" are identified and tagged as the "*object*".

4.2 Sentiment Phrase Alignment

In case of low-resource languages, chunking the parallel sentences (both source and target) adds more complexity in building any system. POS taggers or Chunkers might not be available for some low-resource languages. In such cases, the methodology we present below can help chunk sentences. In this paper, we propose a simple but effective

---

1 The EILMT project is funded by the Department of Electronics and Information Technology (DEITY), Ministry of Communications and Information Technology (MCIT), Government of India.

[2] http://nlp.stanford.edu/software/lex-parser.shtml

chunking technique. The sentence fragments are very similar with grammatical phrases or chunks. We collected the stop word lists for English as well as Bengali to implement this method (Groves and Way, 2005). We chop a sentence into several fragments whenever a stop word is encountered.

Example 3: English sentence fragmentation

"In 1905, <holder>Calcutta</holder> <expression_1>protested</expression_1> the <object_1>partition</object_1> of Bengal and <expression_2>boycotted</expression_2> all the <object_2>British Goods</object_2>."

1. (In 1905) (, Calcutta protested) 2. (the partition) 3. (of Bengal) 4. (and boycotted) 5. (all) 6. (the British Goods)

Sentiment relation	Phrasal sentiment relation

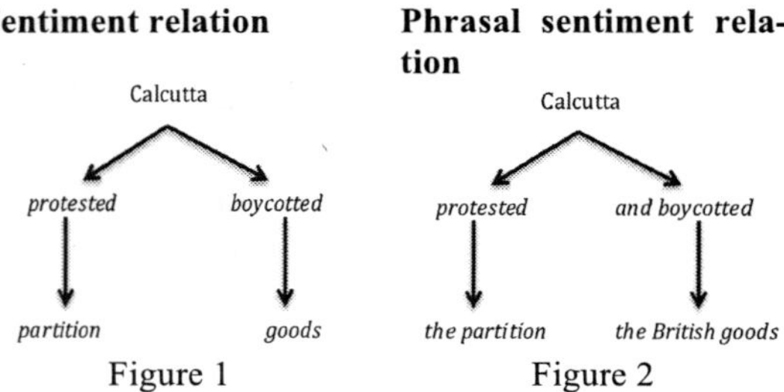

Figure 1   Figure 2

Bengali sentence fragmentation:

"1905 sale, Kolkata bongo vongo-r protibad janiyechilo ebong ssmosto british samogri boykot korechilo."

Pre-processing: *1905 sale , Kolkata bongo vongo -r protibad janiyechilo ebong ssmosto british samogri boykot korechilo.*

1. (1905 sale) 2. (, Kolkata bongo vongo) 3. (-r protibad janiyechilo) 4. (ebong ssmosto british samogri boykot korechilo.)

Initially, we built an English-Bengali word alignment model, which was trained with the same EILMT tourism domain parallel corpus of 22,492 sentences. Using this word alignment knowledge we aligned bilingual sentiment phrases. For establishing the alignment, we use the same phrase alignment algorithm which is used in existing state-of-the-art PB-SMT system Moses. The rest of the processes, such as scoring and phrase table creation also follow the state-of-the-art system.

4.3 Automatic Post Editing using Sentiment Knowledge

Begin The decoding process is carried out with the Moses decoder and the PB-SMT model is comput-ed with Moses. Recall our previous example, and that after translation, the sentiment relation may interchange, so that the semantic meaning of the sentence may be the opposite of what was stated in the source. For example:

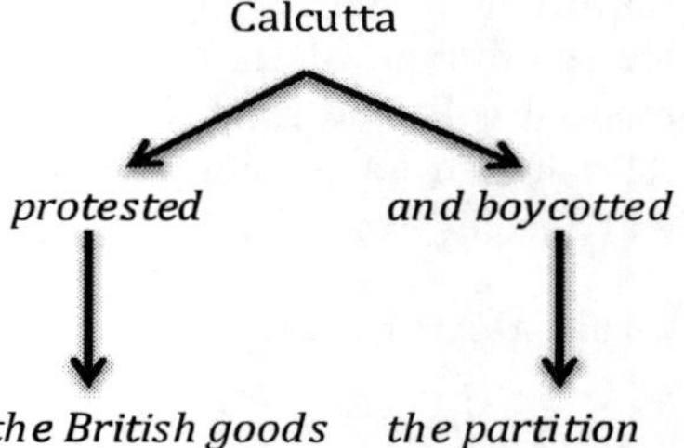

Figure 3

To correct this error in translation, we repositioned the words using our source sentiment relation knowledge obtained on the English side of the data. First, we marked the input source sentence with sentiment holder, sentiment word and their corresponding objects and measured the distance between them. The distance is then also measured on the translated sentence. If they maintained the similar distance, i.e. it ensures that they did not exchange their positions. Otherwise, we have to exchange the position of sentiment expression with their corresponding holder and object according to the distance measure. In this way, we automatically post-edited the entire translated sentences, if required.

5 System Setup

The effectiveness of the present work is demonstrated by using the standard log-linear PB-SMT model as our baseline system. For building baseline system, we use the maximum phrase length of 7 and a 5-gram language model. The other experimental settings were: GIZA++ implementation of IBM word alignment model 4 with grow-diagonal-final-and heuristics for performing word alignment and phrase-extraction (Koehn et al., 2003). The reordering model was trained msd-bidirectional (i.e. using both forward and backward models) and conditioned on both source and target languages. The reordering model is built by calculating the probabilities of the phrase pair associated with the given orientation such as monotone (m), swap(s) and discontinuous (d). We use Minimum Error Rate Training (MERT) (Och, 2003) on a held-out development set of 500 sentences, and a target language model with Kneser-Ney smoothing (Kneser and Ney, 1995) trained with SRILM (Stolcke, 2002).

6 Experiments and Results

Our experiments have been carried out in two directions. First we improved the baseline model using the aligned sentiment phrases. Then, we automatically post-edited the translation output by using the sentiment knowledge of the source input test sentence.

The evaluation results are reported in Table 1. The evaluation was carried out using well-known automatic MT evaluation metrics: BLEU (Papineni et al., 2002, NIST (Doddington, 2002), METEOR (Banerjee and Lavie, 2005), and TER (Snover et al., 2006). In experiment 2, the extracted parallel sentiment phrase alignments are incorporated with the existing baseline phrase table and the resulting model performs better than the baseline system. Experiment 3 shows how post-editing the output of experiment 2 brings about further improvements.

7 Conclusions and Future Research

In this paper, we successfully illustrated how sentiment analysis can improve the translation of an English-Bengali PB-SMT system. We have also shown how sentiment knowledge is useful for automatic post-editing the MT output. In either case, we were able to improve the performance over the baseline system. Using sentiment phrase alignment we obtained a 25.73% relative improvement in BLEU over the baseline system. The automatic post-editing method results in a 33.88% relative improvement in BLEU over the baseline system. On manual inspection of the output translation we found that after incorporating sentiment phrase alignment with the baseline PB-SMT system, the output delivers better lexical selection. The post-editing method also ensures better word ordering to some extent. In the near future, we will extend the post-editing process and improve our sentiment

alignment strategies by using machine learning algorithms.

Acknowledgments

The research leading to these results has received funding from the EU FP7 Project EXPERT the People Programme (Marie Curie Actions) (Grant No. 317471) and the "Development of English to Indian Languages Machine Translation (EILMT) System - Phase II" project funded by Department of Information Technology, Government of India.

References

Aditya Joshi, A. R. Balamurali and Pushpak Bhattacharyya. 2010. A fall-back strategy for sentiment analysis in Hindi: a case study. In *Proceedings of the 8th International Conference on Natural Language Processing*.

Amitava Das and Sivaji Bandyopadhyay. 2010. SentiWordNet for Indian Languages. In *Proceedings of the 8th Workshop on Asian Language Resources (ALR)*, August, pp. 56-63.

Andreas Stolcke. 2002. SRILM-An Extensible Language Modeling Toolkit. In *Proceedings of the Intl. Conf. on Spoken Language Processing*, pp. 901–904.

Anup K. Kolya, Dipankar Das, Asif Ekbal and Sivaji Bandyopadhyay. 2012. Roles of event actors and sentiment holders in identifying event-sentiment association. In *Proceedings of CICLing-2012*, pp. 513-525.

Arthur P. Dempster, Nan M. Laird and Donald B. Rubin. 1977. Maximum Likelihood from Incomplete Data via the EM Algorithm. *Journal of the Royal Statistical Society*, 39 (1): 1–38.

Braja G. Patra, Hiroya Takamura, Dipankar Das, Manabu Okumura and Sivaji Bandyopadhyay. 2013. Construction of Emotional Lexicon Using Potts Model. In *Proceedings of the 6th IJCNLP-2013*, Nagoya, Japan, pp. 674-679.

Carlo Strapparava and Alessandro Valitutti. 2004. Wordnet-affect: an affective extension of wordnet. In *Proceedings of the 4th LRE*, Lisbon, pp. 1083-1086.

Carmen Banea, Rada Mihalcea, Janyce Wiebe and Samer Hassan. 2008. Multilingual subjectivity analysis using machine translation. In *Proceedings of the EMNLP*, pp. 127-135.

Exp. No.	Experiments	BLEU	NIST	METEOR	TER
1	Baseline (B)	10.92	4.16	0.3073	75.34
2	B + Sentiment Phrase Alignment (SPA)	13.73	4.44	0.3307	72.93
3	B + SPA + Post Editing	14.62	4.44	0.3416	71.83

Table 1: Evaluation Result

David Chiang. 2005. A Hierarchical Phrase-Based Model for Statistical Machine Translation. In *Proceedings of 43rd Annual Meeting on Association for Computational Linguistics*, pp. 263-270.

Declan Groves and Andy Way. 2005. Hybrid data-driven models of machine translation. *Machine Translation* 19(3-4): 301-323.

Dipankar Das and Sivaji Bandyopadhyay. 2010. Developing Bengali WordNet Affect for Analyzing Emotion. In *International Conference on the Computer Processing of Oriental Languages*, pp. 35-40.

Donghui Feng, Yajuan Lü and Ming Zhou. 2004. A New Approach for English-Chinese Named Entity Alignment. In Proc. of the *EMNLP*, pp. 372-379.

Franz Josef Och and Hermann Ney. (2004). The Alignment Template Approach to Statistical Machine Translation. *Computational linguistics* 30(4): 417-449.

George Doddington. 2002. Automatic evaluation of machine translation quality using n-gram co-occurrence statistics. In *Proc. of the 2nd Human Language Technology Research*, pp. 138-145.

Hua Wu, Haifeng Wang and Chengqing Zong. 2008. Domain adaptation for statistical machine translation with domain dictionary and monolingual corpora. In *Proc. of the 22nd International Conference on Computational Linguistics (COLING 2008)*, Manchester, UK, pp. 993-1000.

Jaehyung Yang. 2004. Phrase chunking for efficient parsing in machine translation system. In *MICAI 2004: Advances in Artificial Intelligence*, pp. 478-487.

Kanayama Hiroshi, Nasukawa Tetsuya and Watanabe Hideo. 2004. Deeper sentiment analysis using machine translation technology. In *Proceedings of the 20th international conference on Computational Linguistics*.

Kneser, Reinhard, and Hermann Ney. 1995. Improved backing-off for m-gram language modeling. In Proc. of the IEEE International Conference on Acoustics, Speech, and Signal Processing (ICASSP), pp. 181–184.

Kishore Papineni, Salim Roukos, Todd Ward and Wei-Jing Zhu. 2002. BLEU: a method for automatic evaluation of machine translation. In *Proc. of the 40th Annual Meeting of the Association for Computational Linguistics*, Philadelphia, PA, pp. 311-318.

Marine Carpuat and Mona Diab. 2010. Task-based Evaluation of Multiword Expressions: a Pilot Study in Statistical Machine Translation. In *Proc. of HLT-NAACL*, Los Angeles, CA, pp. 242-245.

Pascale Fung and Kenneth Ward Church. 1994. K-vec: A new approach for aligning parallel texts. In *Proceedings of the 15th Association for Computational linguistics*.

Peter F. Brown, Vincent J. D. Pietra, Stephen A. D. Pietra and Robert L. Mercer. 1993. The mathematics of statistical machine translation: parameter estimation. *Computational Linguistics*, 19(2):263-311.

Philipp Koehn, Franz Josef Och and Daniel Marcu. 2003. Statistical phrase-based translation. In *Proc. of HLT-NAACL*, Edmonton, Canada, pp. 48-54.

Philipp Koehn. 2004. Statistical significance tests for machine translation evaluation. In *Proceedings of the EMNLP*, pp. 388-395.

Philipp Koehn, Hieu Hoang, Alexandra Birch, Chris Callison-Burch, Marcello Federico, Nicola Bertoldi, Brooke Cowan, Wade Shen, Christine Mo- ran, Richard Zens, Chris Dyer, Ondřej Bojar, Alexandra Constantin, and Evan Herbst. 2007. Moses: open source toolkit for statistical machine translation. In *Proc. of the 45th Annual meeting of the Association for Computational Linguistics (ACL 2007)*, pp. 177-180.

Santanu Pal, Sudip Kumar Naskar and Sivaji Bandyopadhyay. 2013. MWE Alignment in Phrase Based Statistical Machine Translation. In *Proceedings of the Machine Translation Summit XIV*, Nice, France. pp. 61-68

Santanu Pal, Tanmoy Chkraborty and Sivaji Bandyopadhyay. 2011. Handling Multiword Expressions in Phrase-Based Statistical Machine Translation. In *Proceedings of the Machine Translation Summit XIII*, Xiamen, China. pp. 215-224.

Satanjeev Banerjee and Alon Lavie. 2005. An Automatic Metric for MT Evaluation with Improved Correlation with Human Judgments. In *proceedings of the ACL Workshop on Intrinsic and Extrinsic Evaluation Measures for MT and/or Summarization*, pp. 65-72. Ann Arbor, Michigan.

Soo-Min Kim and Eduard Hovy. 2004. Determining the sentiment of opinions. In *Proceedings of the 20th international conference on Computational Linguistics*, pp. 1-8.

Soo-Min Kim and Eduard Hovy. 2006. Extracting opinions, opinion holders, and topics expressed in online news media text. In *Proceedings of the Workshop on Sentiment and Subjectivity in Text*. pp. 1-8. ACL.

Stefano Baccianella, Andrea Esuli and Fabrizio Sebastiani. 2010. Sentiwordnet 3.0: An enhanced lexical resource for sentiment analysis and opinion mining. In *Proceedings of the 7th conference on International Language Resources and Evaluation (LREC'10)*, Valletta, Malta.

Ted Dunning. 1993. Accurate methods for the statistics of surprise and coincidence. *Computational Linguistics*, 19:61–74.

William A. Gale and Kenneth W. Church. 1993. A program for aligning sentences in bilingual corpora. *Computational linguistics* 19(1): 75-102.

Introduction to Synskarta: An Online Interface for Synset Creation with Special Reference to Sanskrit

Hanumant Redkar, Jai Paranjape, Nilesh Joshi,
Irawati Kulkarni, Malhar Kulkarni, Pushpak Bhattacharyya
Center for Indian Language Technology,
Indian Institute of Technology Bombay, India.
hanumantredkar@gmail.com, jai.para20@gmail.com, joshinilesh60@gmail.com,
irawatikulkarni@gmail.com, malhar@iitb.ac.in, pb@cse.iitb.ac.in

Abstract

WordNet is a large lexical resource expressing distinct concepts in a language. Synset is a basic building block of the WordNet. In this paper, we introduce a web based lexicographer's interface 'Synskarta' which is developed to create synsets from source language to target language with special reference to Sanskrit WordNet. We focus on introduction and implementation of Synskarta and how it can help to overcome the limitations of the existing system. Further, we highlight the features, advantages, limitations and user evaluations of the same. Finally, we mention the scope and enhancements to the Synskarta and its usefulness in the entire IndoWordNet community.

1 Introduction

WordNet is a lexical resource composed of synsets and semantic relations. Synsets are sets of synonyms. They are linked by semantic relations like hypernymy (*is-a*), meronymy (*part-of*), troponymy, etc. IndoWordNet[1] is a linked structure of WordNets of major Indian languages from Indo-Aryan, Dravidian and Sino-Tibetan families (Bhattacharyya, 2010). WordNets are constructed by following the merge approach or the expansion approach (Vossen, 1998). IndoWordNet is constructed using expansion approach wherein Hindi is used as the source language; however, the Hindi WordNet[2] is constructed using merge approach (Narayan et al., 2002).

In this paper, we have taken reference of Sanskrit WordNet[3]. Sanskrit is an Indo-Aryan language and is one of the ancient languages. It has vast literature and a rich tradition of creating léxica. The roots of all languages in the Indo European family in India can be traced to Sanskrit (Kulkarni et al., 2010). Sanskrit WordNet is constructed using expansion approach where Hindi WordNet is used as a source (Kulkarni et al., 2010).

While developing Sanskrit WordNet, lexicographers create Sanskrit synsets by referring to Hindi synsets and by following the three principles of synset creation (Bhattacharyya, 2010). Since Sanskrit came into existence much before Hindi, it has many words which are not present in Hindi WordNet. These words are frequently used in the Sanskrit texts; hence, there was a need to create new Sanskrit synsets. In this case, the lexicographer creates new Sanskrit synsets by referring to electronic lexical resources such as Monier-Williams Dictionary, Apte's Dictionary, Spoken Sanskrit Dictionary, etc. and linguistic resources such as *Shabdakalpadruma and Vaacaspatyam*, etc. (Kulkarni et al., 2010).

The IndoWordNet community uses the IL-Multidict tool to create synsets. This tool is designed and developed by researchers at IIT Bombay (Bhattacharyya, 2010; Kulkarni et al., 2010). Though this existing lexicographer's interface is popular and widely used, it has major limitations. Some of them are – it uses flat files, has chances of data redundancy, inconsistency, etc. To overcome these limitations, we developed a new web based synset creation tool – 'Synskarta'. The features, advantages, limitations and user evaluations of Synskarta are detailed in this paper.

---

[1] http://www.cfilt.iitb.ac.in/indowordnet/
[2] http://www.cfilt.iitb.ac.in/wordnet/webhwn/wn.php

[3] http://www.cfilt.iitb.ac.in/wordnet/webswn/wn.php

D S Sharma, R Sangal and J D Pawar. Proc. of the 11th Intl. Conference on Natural Language Processing, pages 95–100,
Goa, India. December 2014. ©2014 NLP Association of India (NLPAI)

The rest of the paper is organized as follows: Section 2 describes the existing system – its advantages and disadvantages, section 3 describes Synskarta – its features, advantages, limitations and the user evaluations. Subsequently, the conclusion, scope and enhancements to the tool are presented.

2 Existing System

2.1 IL Multidic Development Tool

IL Multidict (Indian Language Multidict development tool) or the Offline Synset Creation tool is developed using Java and works with flat files. This tool, popularly known as the 'Lexicographer's Interface' is an offline tool which helps in creating synsets using the expansion approach.

The interface is vertically divided into the source language panel and the target language panel. At any given time, only the current source synset is displayed in the source language panel and its corresponding target synset is displayed in the target language panel. The source panel displays the details of the current synset of the source language such as number of records in source file, current synset id, its part-of-speech (POS) category, gloss or the concept definition, example(s) and synonym(s).

Similarly, the target panel displays the target synset details such as total number of synsets in the target file, number of complete synsets, number of incomplete synsets and the current synset id (which is the same as source synset id). These fields are non-editable. There are also editable fields which allow editing of target synset details such as gloss, example(s) and synonym(s). The lexicographer translates the source language synset into the target language synset, while the validator uses same tool to validate these translated synsets.

There is a navigation panel which allows a lexicographer to navigate between synsets. The button 'Save & Next' saves the current synset and moves to the next synset. The source and target synset data is extracted from source and target synset files respectively. These files are in Dictionary Standard Format (DSF) with extension '.syns'. Some of the features of the existing system are: search by

synset id, search by word, generate synset count, generate word count, reference to quotations, commenting on a current synset and linkage to the corresponding English synset, etc.

2.2 Advantages and Disadvantages of the Existing System

Some of the major advantages of the existing tool are: Firstly, it is a standalone tool. Hence it can be installed easily. Secondly, it is portable, i.e. the tool can be installed and used over different operating systems.

Though the existing Lexicographer's Interface has its own advantages and it is widely accepted by the IndoWordNet community, we can find several limitations with the system. Some of them are mentioned below:

- Tool works with flat files hence there is a high possibility of data redundancy, data inconsistency, etc.
- As the number of synsets increases, the processing time to perform various operations like searching, counting, synchronization, etc. increases.
- Being a standalone tool, the installation and configuration time increases with increase in number of machines.
- Merging data from different systems may lead to data loss, data redundancy as well as data inconsistency.
- Synset data is not rendered properly in the interface if there is any formatting mistake in the source or target file. Also, if any special character is added in a file then the synsets are not loaded in the system.

3 Developed System

3.1 Synskarta

The developed system, 'Synskarta' is an online interface for creating synsets by following the expansion approach. This web based tool is developed using PHP and MySQL which uses relational database management system to store and maintain the synset and related data. The IndoWordNet database structure (Prabhu et al., 2012) is used for storing and maintaining the synset data while

IndoWordNet APIs (Prabhugaonkar et al., 2012) are used for accessing and manipulating this data.

Synskarta overcomes the limitations of the standalone offline tool. The look and feel of the interface is kept similar to that of the existing system for ease of user adaptability. Most of the basic features of the existing system are incorporated in this developed system. Figure 1 shows the Lexicographer's Interface of the developed system.

3.2 Features of Synskarta

3.2.1 Features of Synskarta incorporated from the Existing System

The features of the existing system which are implemented with some improvements in Synskarta are as follows –

- *User Registration Module* - This module allows the system administrator to create user profiles and provide necessary access privileges to user. The user can login using the access privileges provided to him and accordingly the user interface is displayed to that particular user.
- *Configuration Module* – This module sets all the necessary parameters such as source language, target language and enables or disables certain features such as Source, Domain, Linking, Comment, References, etc.
- *Main Module* – This module allows the user to enter data in the target language panel by referring to data in the source language panel. The source panel and the target panel vertically divide the main module into two equal sized panels. Following are the major components of this module:
  - Source language panel – This panel is placed on the left of the screen which has fields for synset id, POS category, gloss, example(s) and synonyms of the source language synset.
  - Target language panel – This panel is placed on the right of the screen. This panel has non-editable fields such as synset id, POS category and editable fields such as gloss, example(s) and synonym(s) of the target language synset. The user is expected to enter the data in these editable

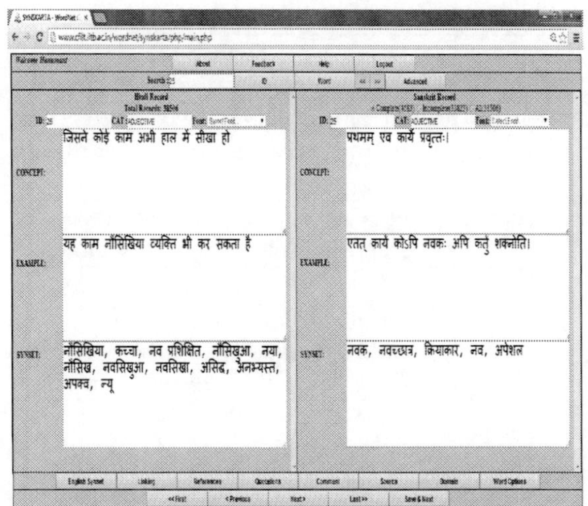

Figure 1. The Developed System – Synskarta

fields.

- Search – User can search a synset either by entering 'synset id' or a 'word' in a synset.
- Advanced Search – Here user is allowed to search synset data by entering various parameters such as POS category, words appearing in gloss or in example, etc.
- Comment – User can comment on a particular synset being translated.
- English Synset – User can check the corresponding English synset for better clarity in translation process.
- Navigation Panel – This panel allows the user to navigate between synsets. Button 'Save & Next' allows inserting or updating a current target synset and the data is directly stored in the IndoWordNet database.

3.2.2 Features of Synskarta specific to Sanskrit Language

Apart from the features of the existing system, there are features which are specific to the Sanskrit language. Some of these features can also be applicable to other languages.

As far as Sanskrit is concerned, some of the features can be specific to a particular word in the synset. These are given in table 1. To capture these word specific features, the 'Word Options' button is provided. This window has various features which users can set or unset for a selected word.

Feature	Details
Word Types	Word can have *vaidika* or *laukika* word types. *vaidika* words are from vedic literature and *laukika* words are from post-vedic literature.
Accent	Accent is an appropriate tone for utterance of any particular syllable.
Class	There are 10 classes of verbs in Sanskrit. They are *bhvādi*, *adādi*, *juhotyādi*, *divādi*, *svādi*, *tudādi*, *rudhādi*, *tanādi*, *kryādi* and *curādi*.
Etymology	It is the study of the origin of a word and historical development of its meaning.
Pada	There are *padas* for suffixes of a verb such as *parasmaipada*, *ātmanepada* or *ubhayapada*.
Ittva	Verb can be *aniṭ*, *seṭ* or *veṭ*.

Table 1. Special Features of Synskarta specific to Sanskrit

3.2.2.1 Noun Specific Features

Noun specific features are displayed only if the POS category of the synset is NOUN. Figure 2 shows a screenshot of the 'Word Options' window for noun synsets. Following are some of the noun specific features of a word in Sanskrit language –

- Indication of Word Type (शब्द प्रकार, *śabda prakāra*) – In Sanskrit, words can have वैदिक (*vaidika*) or लौकिक (*laukika*) word types.

- Indication of Accent (स्वर, *swara*) – In Sanskrit, if a word has *vaidika* word type then it can have accents such as उदात्त (*udaatta*), अनुदात्त (*anudaatta*) or स्वरित (*svarita*). Again, *udaata* has sub-accents such as आद्युदात्त (*aadyudaatta*), मध्योदात्त (*madhyodātta*) or अन्तोदात्त (*antodaatta*). It is needed particularly in Sanskrit because the meaning of a word changes according to the place of accent.

- Identification of Gender (लिङ्ग, *liṅga*) – In Sanskrit, a gender can be masculine (पुंल्लिङ्ग, *pumlliṅga*), feminine (स्त्रीलिङ्ग, *strīliṅga*) or neutral (नपुंसकलिङ्ग, *napuṃsakaliṅga*). For example, a word तट *(taṭa)* has two genders, mas-

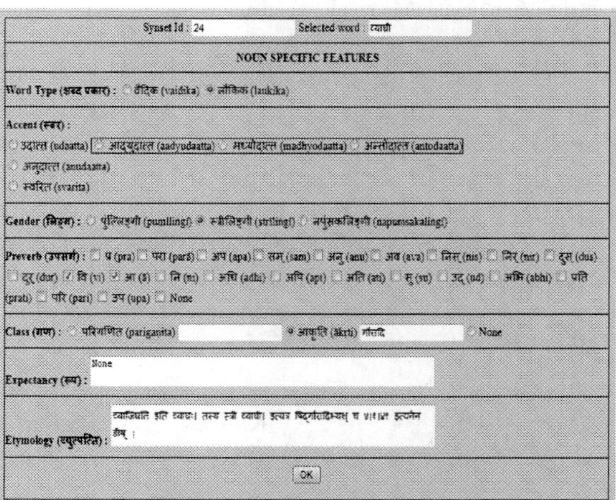

Figure 2. Word Options - Noun Specific Features

culine for तटः (*taṭaḥ*) and neuter for तटम् (*taṭam*). Hence, there is a need to store gender information for such type of words.

- Indication of Preverbs (उपसर्ग, *upasarga*) – In Sanskrit, there are 22 preverbs. Some of them are प्र (*pra*), परा (*parā*), अप (*apa*), etc. (Papke, 2005; Ajotikar et al. 2012). For example, for a word गन्ध (*gandha*), if we add preverbs सु (*su*), दुस् (*dus*) and उप (*upa*) we get words सुगन्ध (*sugandha*), दुर्गन्ध (*durgandha*) and उपगन्ध (*upagandha*) respectively.

- Indication of Class (गण, *gaṇa*) – Certain words in Sanskrit language belong to परिगणित (*pariganita*) or आकृति (*ākṛti*) class type. Each of this class type has class names. For example, a word शिव (*śiva*) belongs to *pariganita* class type having class name शिवादि (*śivādi*) and a word शौण्ड (*śauṇḍa*) belongs to *ākṛti* class type having class name शौण्डादि (*śauṇḍādi*).

- Expectancy (रूप, *rūpa*) – Certain words expect its related word to be in specific case(s). For example, a word अलम् (*alam*, 'enough') expects its related word to be in तृतीया (tṛtīyā, 'instrumental case') as अलं रोदनेन। (*alaṃ rōdanēna*, 'enough of crying').

- Etymology (व्युत्पत्ति, *vyutpatti*) – Most of the words in Sanskrit have etymology. For example, a word कूलङ्कषः (*kūlaṅkaṣaḥ,* 'the sea'), कूलं कषति इति। (*kūlaṁ kaṣati iti,* 'one who cuts the shore').

3.2.2.2 Verb Specific Features

Verb specific feature list is displayed only if the POS category of the synset is VERB. Figure 3 shows the 'Word Options' window for verb synsets. Following are some of the verb specific features of a word in Sanskrit language –

- Indication of Word Type (शब्द प्रकार, *śabda prakāra*) – Verbs can have वैदिक (*vaidika*) or लौकिक (*laukika*) word types.

- Indication of Accent (स्वर, *swara*).

- Indication of Transitivity (कर्मकत्व, *karmakatva*) – A verb can be सकर्मक (*sakarmaka,* 'active') or अकर्मक (*akarmaka,* 'passive').

- Indication of Iṭtva (इट्त्व, *iṭtva*) - A verb can be अनिट् (*aniṭ*), सेट् (*seṭ*) or वेट् (*veṭ*).

- Indication of Class (गण, *gaṇa*) – In Sanskrit, there are 10 classes of verbs. Some of them are भ्वादि (*bhvādi*), अदादि (*adādi*), जुहोत्यादि (*juhotyādi*), etc.

- Indication of Pada (पद, *pada*) – In Sanskrit, there are padas for suffixes of a verb such as परस्मैपद (*parasmaipada*), आत्मनेपद (*ātmanepada*) or उभयपद (*ubhayapada*).

- Indication of Preverbs (उपसर्ग, *upasarga,*) – For verbs also there are 22 preverbs in Sanskrit. For example, when preverbs are attached to a root गम् (*gam,* 'to go'), we get verb forms such as आ√गम् (*ā√gam,* 'to come'), अनु√गम् (*anu√gam,* 'to follow'), निर्√गम् (*nir√gam,* 'to go out'), वि√गम् (*vi√gam,* 'to go away').

- Indication of Verbal Root Types (धातु प्रकार, *dhātu prakāra*) – A verbal root can have types such as धातु (*dhātu*), साधितधातु (*sādhitadhātu*), वैदिकधातु (*vaidikadhātu*) and सौत्रधातु (*sautradhātu*).

- Expectancy (रूप, *rūpa*) – Certain verbs expect its related word to be in specific case(s). For example, a root भी (*bhī,* 'to fear') expects its related word in पञ्चमी (*pañcamī,* 'ablative case') such as व्याघ्रात् भीतः (*vyāghrāt bhītaḥ,* 'feared of tiger').

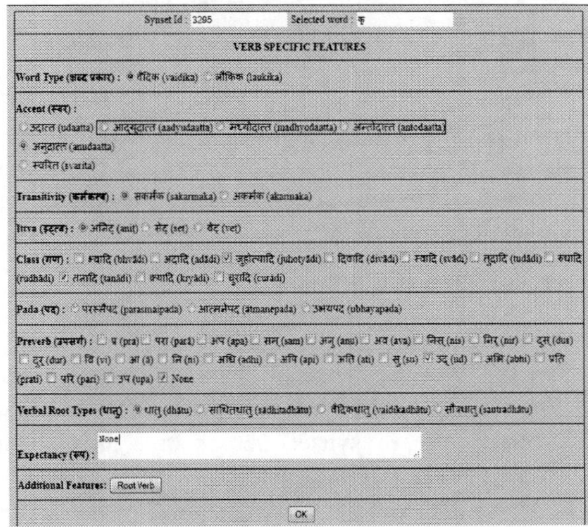

Figure 3. Word Options – Verb Specific Features

3.2.3 General Features not specific to any Language

Some of the general features which are not specific to any particular language are also provided in Synskarta, they are as follows:

- Vindication – This feature allows the user to record the special feature of a particular word in a current synset.

- Source – This feature allows the user to record the information about source of the synset.

- Domain – This feature allows the user to record the information about domain of the synset.

- Linking – Many-to-Many linking of words is supported in this feature.

- Quotations – The feature to add quotations as additional examples are supported.

- Root Verb – This feature allows the user to enter the root verb of a given word.

- Feedback – Feedback related to the tool and its features are captured here.

3.3 Advantages and Limitations of Synskarta

Major advantages of Synskarta are as follows:
- Centralized system
- No data redundancy and inconsistency.

- Online access from anywhere in the world
- No text files to maintain data
- Faster processing and updating
- Multiple users can work at the same time
- Can be used by all the language WordNets

Synskarta has a few limitations. The major limitation is that, it is heavily dependent on internet access or networking. Another limitation is that currently there are rendering issues depending on the device being used.

3.4   User Evaluation

The beta version of Synskarta was released to the Sanskrit WordNet creation team to capture users' experiences and the feedback which are as follows:

- Searching of synset from source as well as target language is faster.
- User does not have to maintain files for source and target language.
- Separate synchronization is not required. Everything is handled by the tool itself.
- The system always shows the updated synsets.
- User has to depend on the internet while using the system.

4   Conclusion

It has been observed that the existing system for synset creation activity is not up to the expectations of the user, as it uses text files for storage and processing. This may lead in creation of redundant synset data and hence, data maintenance becomes difficult. A web based tool 'Synskarta' is developed to overcome the limitations of the existing system. This is a centralized system which uses relational database to store and maintain data. The difficulty of maintaining data in flat files is taken care of. User feedback is found to be positive and this tool may prove essential for the IndoWordNet community.

5   Future Scope and Enhancements

In future, the tool can be expanded to link to the other Indian languages. This tool can have additional features such as capturing appropriate pronunciation of the synset, features to capture video, images or documents related to the synset. Features such as automatic translation, transliteration, transcription can also be implemented over the time. Further, there can be a feature to link IndoWordNet synsets to the foreign language WordNets. A feature to generate produced words can also be implemented. Link to FrameNet of Sanskrit verbs is an important work that will be undertaken in future. This will be useful in the light of development of dependency tree banks.

Acknowledgements

We sincerely thank the members of the CFILT lab – IIT Bombay and IndoWordNet community.

References

Malhar Kulkarni, Chaitali Dangarikar, Irawati Kulkarni, Abhishek Nanda and Pushpak Bhattacharyya. 2010. *Introducing Sanskrit Wordnet.* In Principles, Construction and Application of Multilingual WordNets, Proceedings of the 5th GWC, edited by Pushpak Bhattacharyya, Christiane Fellbaum and Piek Vossen, Narosa Publishing House, New Delhi, 2010, pp 257 – 294.

Malhar Kulkarni, Irawati Kulkarni, Chaitali Dangarikar and Pushpak Bhattacharyya. 2010. *Gloss in Sanskrit Wordnet.* In Proceedings of Sanskrit Computational Linguistics. Jha. G. Berlin: Springer-Verlag / Heidelberg. pp 190-197.

Tanuja Ajotikar Malhar Kulkarni, and Pushpak Bhattacharyya. 2012. *Verbs in Sanskrit Wordnet.* Proceeding of 6th Global WordNet Conference, Matsue, Japan. pp 30 – 35.

Narayan D., Chakrabarty D., Pande P. and Bhattacharyya P. 2002. *An Experience in Building the Indo WordNet - a WordNet for Hindi.* 1st Global WordNet Conference, Mysore, India.

Neha R Prabhugaonkar, Apurva S Nagvenkar, Ramdas N Karmali. 2012. *IndoWordNet Application Programming Interfaces.* COLING2012, Mumbai, India.

Papke Julia. 2005. *Order and Meaning in Sanskrit Preverbs.* 17th International Conference on Historical Linguistics, Madison, Wisconsin.

Pushpak Bhattacharyya. 2010. *IndoWordNet.* In the Proceedings of Lexical Resources Engineering Conference (LREC), Malta.

Venkatesh Prabhu, Shilpa Desai, Hanumant Redkar, Neha Prabhugaonkar, Apurva Nagvenkar, Ramdas, Karmali. 2012. *An Efficient Database Design for IndoWordNet Development Using Hybrid Approach.* COLING 2012, Mumbai, India. p 229.

Vossen Piek (ed.). 1998. *EuroWordNet: A Multilingual Database with Lexical Semantic Networks,* Kluwer, Dordrecht, Netherlands.

LMSim : Computing Domain-specific Semantic Word Similarities Using a Language Modeling Approach

Sachin Pawar[1,2]　　　Swapnil Hingmire[1,3]　　　Girish K. Palshikar[1]

{sachin7.p, swapnil.hingmire, gk.palshikar}@tcs.com
[1]Systems Research Lab, Tata Consultancy Services Ltd., Pune, India
[2]Department of CSE, IIT Bombay, Mumbai, India
[3]Department of CSE, IIT Madras, Chennai, India

Abstract

We propose a method to compute domain-specific semantic similarity between words. Prior approaches for finding word similarity that use linguistic resources (like WordNet) are not suitable because words may have very specific and rare sense in some particular domain. For example, in customer support domain, the word `escalation` is used in the sense of "problem raised by a customer" and therefore in this domain, the words `escalation` and `complaint` are semantically related. In our approach, domain-specific word similarity is captured through language modeling. We represent context of a word in the form of a set of word sequences containing the word in the domain corpus. We define a similarity function which computes weighted Jaccard similarity between the set representations of two words and propose a dynamic programming based approach to compute it efficiently. We demonstrate effectiveness of our approach on domain-specific corpora of Software Engineering and Agriculture domains.

1 Introduction

In text clustering, we expect to cluster these two sentences together - `Ricestar HT is a good product for sprangletop control.` and `Barnyardgrass can be controlled by usage of Clincher.` We observe that though these two sentences do not share any content word, still they are semantically similar to each other. The similarity between these two sentences will not be high unless the clustering algorithm takes into account that the words within the pairs `Ricestar-Clincher`[1] and `sprangletop-Barnyardgrass`[2] are semantically similar. In addition to text clustering, discovering semantically similar words has rich applications in the fields of Information Retrieval, Question Answering, Machine Translation, Spelling correction, etc.

We propose an algorithm which assigns high similarity for words, which are highly *replaceable* by each other in their context without affecting its syntax and "meaning". In above example, the words `sprangletop` and `Barnyardgrass` can be safely replaced by each other while preserving the syntax and "meaning" of the original sentences.

Approaches for computing similarity between words can be broadly classified into two types - i) Approaches using linguistic resources like WordNet (Miller, 1995) or thesaurus (Budanitsky and Hirst, 2006) and ii) Approaches using statistical properties of words in a corpus (Blei et al., 2003; Halawi et al., 2012; Brown et al., 1992).

In this paper, our focus is to develop a word similarity algorithm which discovers similar words for a specific domain. We mainly focus on two domains - Software Engineering (SE) and Agriculture. Our motivation behind choosing these domains is that these are relatively unexplored and as per our knowledge they lack domain-specific lexical resources.

WordNet-based approaches are not suitable for some domains because words may have very specific and rare sense in those domains. Moreover, creating lexical resources like WordNet for a certain domain is a quite challenging task as it requires extensive human efforts, expertise, time and cost. In SE domain, we can say that the words `Oracle` and `DB2` are simi-

---

[1]both are names of herbicides
[2]both are names of weeds

101

D S Sharma, R Sangal and J D Pawar. Proc. of the 11th Intl. Conference on Natural Language Processing, pages 101–106,
Goa, India. December 2014. ©2014 NLP Association of India (NLPAI)

lar because they both are Database Management Softwares. However, the word DB2 is not present in WordNet and the sense of the word Oracle as a "database management software" is not covered in WordNet.

Corpus-based approaches for finding word similarity using topic models (Blei et al., 2003) or Distributional Similarity (Lee, 1999) make use of word context to capture its meaning. Though these approaches use higher order word co-occurrence, they do not consider order of other words within the context of a word. Our hypothesis is that considering word order results in better word similarities and this is evident from our experimental results. Brown Word clustering algorithm (Brown et al., 1992) considers order of words and learns a language model based on word clusters. However, this algorithm is sensitive to number of clusters. In this paper, we use word-based Language Model to capture the context of words in the form of word sequences (preserving word order) and to assign weights for each of the word sequences by computing their probabilities. The major contributions of this paper are - i) a new algorithm (LMSim) to compute domain-specific word similarity and ii) an efficient dynamic programming based algorithm for fast computation of LMSim.

2   Related Work

Various WordNet-based approaches are proposed for computing similarity between two words which are surveyed by Budanitsky and Hirst (2006). Pedersen et al. (2007) adapted WordNet-based word similarity measures to the biomedical domain using SNOMED-CT, which is an ontology of medical concepts.

In order to overcome several limitations of WordNet, Gabrilovich and Markovitch (2007) proposed Explicit Semantic Analysis (ESA), that represents and compares the meaning of texts in a high-dimensional space of concepts derived from Wikipedia.

Halawi et al. (2012) proposed an approach for learning word-word relatedness, where known pairs of related words can be provided as an input to impose constraints on the learning process. For both the domains that we are focusing on - SE and Agriculture domain, we do not have any such prior knowledge about

Notation	Details
D	Domain-specific text corpus
K	Length of context window
$C(w_i, K)$	Set of context words for the word w_i
ws_i^j	j^{th} sequence of context words for w_i
$\lambda(ws_i^j)$	Weight of the word sequence ws_i^j
$n(w_i, w_j)$	Frequency of bigram $\langle w_i, w_j \rangle$ in D
$n(w_i)$	Frequency of word w_i in D
$P_f(w_i|w_j)$	Prob. of observing w_i after w_j
$P_b(w_i|w_j)$	Prob. of observing w_i before w_j
$C_{seq}(w_i, K)$	Set of all possible K length word sequences (formed using words in $C(w_i, K)$) that start or end in w_i

Table 1: Details of notations used in this paper

related word pairs.

3   Computing Word Similarity

We take help of a *statistical language model* to represent the context of each of the words.

3.1   Language Model

A statistical language model (Jurafsky and Martin, 2000) assigns a probability to a sequence of words using n-gram statistics estimated from a text corpus. Using bigram statistics, the probability of the word sequence w_1, w_2, w_3, w_4 is computed as follows,

$$P(w_1, w_2, w_3, w_4) = P(w_1)P(w_2|w_1)P(w_3|w_2)P(w_4|w_3)$$

The main motivation behind using a Language Model is that it not only provides a way to capture the context information for words but also retains the word order information of context words. Moreover, using a Language Model, we can weigh each word sequence in the context of a particular word by computing its probability as explained above.

In our work, we have used a bigram ($L_0 = 2$) Language Model along with Laplace smoothing. Our algorithm is currently designed for bigram model and in future we plan to extend it to higher order ($L_0 > 2$) models.

3.2   LMSim : Algorithm to Compute Language Model based Similarity

For finding semantic similarity between two any words w_1 and w_2 (refer Table 1 for notations), sets of context words ($C(w_1, K)$ and $C(w_2, K)$) are created by collecting all the words falling in the window of $\pm K$ in the given text corpus. Let I be the set of words which appear in the context of both w_1 and w_2, i.e. $I = C(w_1, K) \cap C(w_2, K)$.

For w_1		For w_2	
Forward	Backward	Forward	Backward
w_1, c_1, c_2	c_1, c_2, w_1	w_2, c_1, c_2	c_1, c_2, w_2
w_1, c_1, c_3	c_1, c_3, w_1	w_2, c_1, c_3	c_1, c_3, w_2
w_1, c_2, c_1	c_2, c_1, w_1	w_2, c_2, c_1	c_2, c_1, w_2
w_1, c_2, c_3	c_2, c_3, w_1	w_2, c_2, c_3	c_2, c_3, w_2
w_1, c_3, c_1	c_3, c_1, w_1	w_2, c_3, c_1	c_3, c_1, w_2
w_1, c_3, c_2	c_3, c_2, w_1	w_2, c_3, c_2	c_3, c_2, w_2

Table 2: Example word sequences considered

The context of w_1 and w_2 is then defined as set of word sequences of length K starting at or ending at either w_1 or w_2. The word sequences are formed by considering all possible combinations of the words in the set I. If $|I| = M$, then M^K word sequences starting at w_1 or w_2 are considered and M^K word sequences ending at w_1 or w_2 are considered. If $I = \{c_1, c_2, c_3\}$ and $K = 2$, then the word sequences created for w_1 and w_2 are as shown in the table 2. Each word sequence is also associated with a weight which corresponds to its Language Model probability. For a forward sequence w_1, c_1, c_2, its weight is set as follows,

$$\lambda_{w_1, c_1, c_2} = P_{forward}(c_1, c_2 | w_1) = P_f(c_1 | w_1) P_f(c_2 | c_1)$$

$P_f(c_1 | w_1)$ is computed by using the bigram statistics learnt from the text corpus, i.e. it is the ratio of number of times the word c_1 succeeds w_1 in the corpus to the number of times w_1 occurs in the corpus.

$$P_f(c_1 | w_1) = \frac{n(w_1, c_1)}{n(w_1)}$$

Similarly, for a backward sequence c_1, c_2, w_1, we set its weight as,

$$\lambda_{c_1, c_2, w_1} = P_{backward}(c_1, c_2 | w_1) = P_b(c_2 | w_1) P_b(c_1 | c_2)$$

$P_b(c_2 | w_1)$ is computed as the ratio of number of times the word c_2 precedes w_1 in the corpus to the number of times w_1 occurs in the corpus.

$$P_b(c_2 | w_1) = \frac{n(c_2, w_1)}{n(w_1)}$$

The context of a word is a set of word sequences (ws's) and their corresponding weights (λ's) as follows,

$$C_{seq}(w_1, K) = \{\langle ws_1^1, \lambda(ws_1^1)\rangle, \cdots, \langle ws_N^1, \lambda(ws_N^1)\rangle\}$$

$$C_{seq}(w_2, K) = \{\langle ws_1^2, \lambda(ws_1^2)\rangle, \cdots, \langle ws_N^2, \lambda(ws_N^2)\rangle\}$$

It is to be noted that the word sequence ws_i^1 (in $C_{seq}(w_1, K)$) corresponds to ws_i^2 (in $C_{seq}(w_2, K)$) and they both are equal except that ws_i^1 starts or ends in w_1 whereas ws_i^2 starts or ends in w_2.

Word pair	sim$_{jaccard}$	sim$_{context}$	LMSim
client, complaint	0.1545	0.754	0.1165
succession, plan	0.2019	0.9651	0.1949
collaboration, realization	0.4259	0.2643	0.1126
mapping, publication	0.4672	0.2951	0.1379

Table 3: Word pairs having low LMSim

We define similarity based on Language Model between w_1 and w_2 as follows,

$$sim_{jaccard}(w_1, w_2) = \frac{\sum_{i=1}^N \min(\lambda(ws_i^1), \lambda(ws_i^2))}{\sum_{i=1}^N \max(\lambda(ws_i^1), \lambda(ws_i^2))} \quad (1)$$

The similarity $sim_{Jaccard}$ between w_1 and w_2 is nothing but the weighted Jaccard similarity (Surgey, 2010) between $C_{seq}(w_1, K)$ and $C_{seq}(w_2, K)$. Here, we treat ws_i^1 and ws_i^2 as equal while computing Jaccard similarity as noted earlier.

As we are constructing the word sequences by only using the words in the intersection of the contexts of the two words, we weigh down the similarity by multiplying it with the common context factor, $sim_{context}$ defined as,

$$sim_{context}(w_1, w_2) = \max\left(\frac{|I|}{|C(w_1, K)|}, \frac{|I|}{|C(w_2, K)|}\right)$$

LMSim, the similarity between two words w_1 and w_2 is computed as,

$$LMSim(w_1, w_2) = sim_{jaccard}(w_1, w_2) * sim_{context}(w_1, w_2)$$

3.2.1 Why Are Both $sim_{jaccard}$ and $sim_{context}$ Important?

Considering only $sim_{context}$ can be misleading, as many co-occurring word pairs will have a high $sim_{context}$. This is evident for the top 2 word pairs in Table 3 which have got high $sim_{context}$ even though they are not similar. As $sim_{jaccard}$ for these pairs is very low, LMSim is reduced as desired.

On the other hand, due to smaller common context, considering only $sim_{jaccard}$ can be misleading. In Table 3, we can observe that the bottom 2 word pairs have relatively high $sim_{jaccard}$, but due to their smaller common context, their $sim_{context}$ is low which results in low LMSim as desired.

3.3 Efficient Computation of LMSim

For computing $sim_{jaccard}$ (Eq. 1), the sum of N terms is required to be computed. Here,

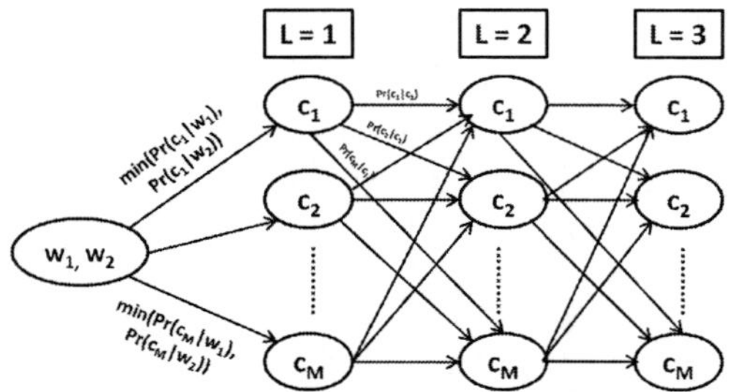

Figure 1: All possible forward word sequences (intersection scenario)

$N = 2 \cdot M^K$ where K is the context window considered and M is the number of words in the context of both the words in consideration for computing similarity. Even for a moderate size corpus, the value of M can be in thousands and even for a small window of size 3, N will be 1000^3 which is a huge number. Hence, it is infeasible to actually enumerate all the N distinct word sequences. We propose an efficient, dynamic programming based approach similar to Viterbi Algorithm (Forney, 1973) for fast computation of Language Model similarity.

Figure 1 shows all possible forward paths for words w_1 and w_2 formed using words in the set $I = \{c_1, c_2, \cdots c_M\}$. It depicts the scenario where the numerator (intersection of two sets with weighted members) of Eq. 1 is being computed. All possible backward paths can be constructed in similar way.

At each level (L in the figure 1 which varies from 1 to K), for each context word, we store sum of probabilities of all the word sequences ending in that particular word. This is similar to the Viterbi algorithm used for finding most probable state sequence for HMMs. The only difference is that, at each level for each state, Viterbi algorithm stores *maximum* of probabilities of all state sequences ending in that particular state whereas our algorithm stores the sum of probabilities of all word sequences ending in a particular word. This algorithm to compute $sim_{jaccard}$ reduces the number of computations from $O(M^K)$ to $O(KM^2)$.

4 Experimental Analysis

In this section, we describe details about experimental evaluation of our algorithm.

4.1 Datasets

We use text corpora from following domains:
1. SE domain: A collection of 138159 task descriptions/expectations for various roles performed in Software services industry containing 1276514 words.
2. Agriculture domain: A set of 30533 documents in English containing 999168 sentences and approximately 19 million words. It was collected using crawler4j[3] by crawling various agriculture news sites.

There are no publicly available datasets of similar words for the SE and Agriculture domains. We selected some domain-specific word pairs for these domains and obtained human assigned similarity scores for these pairs. For the SE domain, we had 500 word pairs annotated for similarity scores (0:No similarity, 1:Weak, 2:High) by 4 human annotators familiar with the domain terminologies. The average of the similarity scores assigned by all the annotators is then considered as the gold-standard similarities for these word pairs. Similarly, we created a standard dataset[4] of 200 word pairs in Agriculture domain.

4.2 Comparison with Other Approaches

1. Distributional Similarity (DistSim): For each word, a TF-IDF vector is constructed which encodes how the other words co-occur with that particular word. The similarity between any two words is then computed as the cosine similarity between their corresponding TF-IDF vectors.
2. Latent Dirichlet Allocation (LDA): LDA (Blei et al., 2003) is a probabilistic generative model that can be used to uncover the underlying semantic structure of a document collection. LDA gives per-word per-document topic assignments that can be used to find a likely set of topics and represent each document in the collection in the form of topic proportions. We find probability distribution of a word over topics using the number of times the word is assigned to a topic. We compute similarity between words w_i and w_j as the Jensen-Shannon (JS) divergence between their respective probability distributions over

---

[3]`code.google.com/p/crawler4j/`
[4]contact authors for the datasets

topics. We experimented with different number of topics and reported the results of best performing number of topics.

3. WordNet and Wikipedia based similarities: We used WordNet-based approach "Lin similarity" (Lin, 1998) for computing word similarities. We used its NLTK implementation[5] with Brown corpus for IC statistics. This algorithm computes similarity between two synsets (senses). As we are not disambiguating sense of the words in a given word pair, we compute Lin similarity between all possible combinations of senses of the two words and consider the maximum of these similarities as overall similarity between words. We consider that the words not present in WordNet have similarity score of 0 with any other word. We also compare LMSim with Wikipedia based ESA[6].

4. Brown Word Clustering: We used the Brown word clustering implementation[7] by Percy Liang. Each word cluster is represented by a binary (0/1) string indicating the path taken from the root to the word in consideration in the hierarchical word clustering output. The algorithm does not explicitly compute the word similarities, hence for any two words w_1 and w_2 having binary string cluster representations s_1 and s_2, we compute similarity as,

$$sim_{brown}(w_1, w_2) = \frac{|CommonPrefix(s_1, s_2)|}{Average(|s_1|, |s_2|)}$$

Here, $|s_i|$ indicates the length of the binary string s_i. The only parameter required for Brown word clustering algorithm is the number of clusters to form. We got the best results with 1000 clusters for SE domain and 500 clusters for Agriculture domain.

4.3 Results

We use each algorithm discussed above to assign similarity scores to each word pair in our gold-standard dataset. Performance of each algorithm (see Table 4) is judged by computing correlation between an algorithm assigned word similarities with the gold-standard word similarities. We could not compare LMSim with LDA for Agriculture

[5]www.nltk.org
[6]http://treo.deri.ie/easyesa/
[7]http://github.com/percyliang/brown-cluster

Algorithm	Correlation with Gold-standard	
	SE	Agriculture
Lin Similarity	0.1675	0.2303
ESA	0.1527	0.3940
DistSim	0.3278	0.3645
LDA	0.4738	NA
Brown	0.479	0.5945
LMSim	**0.5639**	**0.6229**

Table 4: Relative performance of algorithms

dataset due to large size of the corpus. We can observe here that for both the datasets, LMSim performs better than WordNet and Wikipedia based approaches because of absence of many domain-specific words/senses in these resources. At the same time, LMSim performs better than DistSim, LDA and Brown word clustering algorithm, so we can say that LMSim encodes the context information in better way through forward and backward context word sequences. Table 5 and Table 6 show some of the highly similar word pairs discovered for both the domains. Following are some key observations of the experimental results.

1. Importance of Word Order : LMSim scores over other context based word similarity approaches like DistSim and LDA because it encodes word order of the context words using Language Model. For example, a word pair `asset - wiki` incorrectly assigned high similarity scores by both DistSim and LDA, because these two words co-occur quite frequently. Some example text fragments in which they usually co-occur are as follows:

`-Number of Assets to be logged into wiki ...`

`-No. of assets created in team Wiki..`

At least one word not present in WordNet	
Word Pair	**Comment**
`clarity, epm`	Clarity is a tool for EPM (Enterprise Project Management)
`sit ,uat`	SIT:System Integration Testing, UAT:User Acceptance Testing
`solution, POCs`	POC : "Proof of concept"
`.Net, Java`	Types of softwares
Both words present in WordNet	
Word Pair	**Comment**
`people, resource`	"person" sense of `resource` not present in WN
`complaint, escalation`	"complaint" sense of `escalation` absent in WN
`test, regression`	Regression is a kind of testing

Table 5: Examples from SE domain

At least one word not present in WordNet

Word Pair	Comment
`cruiser, gaucho`	Both are insecticides
`clincher, regiment`	Both are herbicides
`ethanol, biodiesel`	`ethanol` is used in producing `biodiesel`
`fusarium, verticillium`	Names of fungi
`glyphosate, herbicide`	Glyphosate is a herbicide

Both words present in WordNet

Word Pair	Comment
`farmer, producer`	"farmer" sense of producer is absent in WN
`subsoil, topsoil`	Different layers of soils

Table 6: Examples from Agriculture domain

`-Number of assets posted to Wiki..`
For this word pair, LMSim assigns a low similarity score as they do not tend to share similar context word sequences.

2.   Limitations of LMSim: We observed that LMSim assigns high similarity for synonyms (`client-customer`), antonyms (`dry-wet`) and siblings (`spring-summer`, `.Net-Java`), but for some hypernymy relations (like `consultant-associate`) it assigns a low similarity score because of strict replaceability constraint. In future, we will revise our algorithm to overcome this limitation.

5   Conclusions and Future Work

We proposed a new algorithm LMSim using a Language Modeling approach for computing domain-specific word similarities. We demonstrated the performance of LMSim on two different domains - Software Engineering (SE) domain and Agriculture domain. To the best of our knowledge this is the first attempt for discovering similar words in these domains.

The important advantages of LMSim over previous approaches are - i) it does not require any linguistic resources (like WordNet) hence it saves cost, time and human efforts involved in creating such resources, ii) LMSim incorporates the word order information within context of a word resulting in better estimates of word similarity compared to other corpus-based approaches that ignore word order. We proposed an efficient dynamic programming based algorithm for computing LMSim. Our experiments show that LMSim better correlates with human assigned word similarities as compared to other approaches.

In future, we plan to revise LMSim by extending it to higher order language models, trying better smoothing techniques and using other information like POS tags for having better estimates of word probabilities. We also plan to extend our algorithm to work for Indian languages as lexical resources for these languages are not widely available. We would like to experiment with other domains like Mechanical Engineering, Legal domain etc. We believe that our algorithm can facilitate construction of domain-specific ontologies.

References

D. M. Blei, A. Y. Ng, and M. I. Jordan. Latent Dirichlet Allocation. *The Journal of Machine Learning Research*, 3:993–1022, March 2003.

A. Budanitsky and G. Hirst. Evaluating wordnet-based measures of lexical semantic relatedness. *Computational Linguistics*, 32(1):13–47, 2006.

G. D. Forney Jr. The viterbi algorithm. *Proceedings of the IEEE*, 61(3):268–278, 1973.

E. Gabrilovich and S. Markovitch. Computing semantic relatedness using wikipedia-based explicit semantic analysis. In *IJCAI*, volume 7, pages 1606–1611, 2007.

G. Halawi, G. Dror, E. Gabrilovich, and Y. Koren. Large-scale learning of word relatedness with constraints. In *SIGKDD*, pages 1406–1414. ACM, 2012.

S. Ioffe. Improved consistent sampling, weighted minhash and l1 sketching. *Data Mining (ICDM), 2010 IEEE 10th International Conference on. IEEE, 2010*, pages 246–255, 2010.

D. Jurafsky and J. H. Martin. *Speech & Language Processing*. Pearson Education India, 2000.

L. Lee. Measures of distributional similarity. In *ACL* 1999, pages 25–32.

D. Lin. An information-theoretic definition of similarity. In *ICML*, vol. 98, pages 296–304, 1998.

G. A. Miller. Wordnet: a lexical database for english. *Communications of the ACM*, 38(11):39–41, 1995.

T. Pedersen, S.V. Pakhomov, S. Patwardhan and C.G. Chute. Measures of semantic similarity and relatedness in the biomedical domain. *Journal of biomedical informatics*, 40(3):288–299, 2007.

Brown, P. F., Desouza, P. V., Mercer, R. L., Pietra, V. J. D., & Lai, J. C. Class-based n-gram models of natural language. In *Computational linguistics*, 18(4), pages 467–479.

Multiobjective Optimization and Unsupervised Lexical Acquisition for Named Entity Recognition and Classification

Govind
IIT Patna, India
govind.mc12@iitp.ac.in

Asif Ekbal
IIT Patna, India
asif@iitp.ac.in

Chris Biemann
TU Darmstadt, Germany
biem@cs.tu-darmstadt.de

Abstract

In this paper, we investigate the utility of unsupervised lexical acquisition techniques to improve the quality of Named Entity Recognition and Classification (NERC) for the resource poor languages. As it is not *a priori* clear which unsupervised lexical acquisition techniques are useful for a particular task or language, careful feature selection is necessary. We treat feature selection as a multiobjective optimization (MOO) problem, and develop a suitable framework that fits well with the unsupervised lexical acquisition. Our experiments show performance improvements for two unsupervised features across three languages.

1 Introduction

Named Entity Recognition and Classification (NERC) (Nadeau and Sekine, 2007) is a subtask of information extraction that has great importance in many Natural Language Processing (NLP) application areas. The objective of NERC is to find and assign tokens in unstructured text to pre-defined classes such as the names of organizations, persons, locations, miscellaneous (e.g. date-times, quantities, monetary expression etc.); and other-than-NE.

There have been a good number of research works in NERC area but these are mostly limited to the resource-rich languages such as English, the majority of the European languages and a few Asian languages like Japanese, Chinese and Korean. Research in NLP relating to the resource-scarce languages like the Indian ones is still evolving and poses some interesting problems. Some of the problems outlined previously in (Ekbal and Saha, 2011b) with reference to a specific NERC task include the absence of capitalization information, appearance of named entities (NEs) in the dictionary with other word classes, and the non-availability of various NLP resources and processing technology for non-Latin resource-poor languages.

In present work, we propose some novel methods based on the concepts of unsupervised lexical acquisition and multiobjective optimization (MOO) (Deb, 2001) for solving the problems of NERC for several languages. While we evaluate the proposed method with only three languages, the technique is generic and language-independent, and thus should adapt well to other languages or domains.

1.1 Multiobjective Optimization

The multiobjective optimization problem (MOOP) can be stated as follows: find the vectors x of decision variables that simultaneously optimize the M objective values $f_1(x), f_2(x), ..., f_M(x)$, while satisfying the constraints, if any. An important concept of MOO is that of domination. In the context of a maximization problem, a solution x_i is said to dominate x_j if $\forall k \in 1, 2, \ldots, M, f_k(x_i) \geq f_k(x_j)$ and $\exists k \in 1, 2, \ldots, M$, such that $f_k(x_i) > f_k(x_j)$. In general, a MOO algorithm usually admits a set of solutions that are not dominated by any solution encountered by it.

Genetic algorithms (GAs) are known to be more effective than classical methods such as weighted metrics, goal programming (Deb, 2001), for solving multiobjective problems primarily because of their population-based nature. Evolutionary approaches have also been used to solve few NLP problems including NERC (Ekbal and Saha, 2011a; Sofianopoulos and Tambouratzis, 2010).

1.2 Unsupervised Lexical Acquisition

One of the major problems in applying machine learning algorithms for solving information extraction problems is the availability of large annotated corpora. We explore possibilities aris-

107

D S Sharma, R Sangal and J D Pawar. Proc. of the 11th Intl. Conference on Natural Language Processing, pages 107–112,
Goa, India. December 2014. ©2014 NLP Association of India (NLPAI)

ing from the use of unsupervised part-of-speech (PoS) induction (Biemann, 2009) and lexical expansion (Miller et al., 2012) with distributional thesauri (Riedl and Biemann, 2013). Unsupervised PoS induction is a technique that induces lexical-syntactic categories through the statistical analysis of large, raw text corpora. As shown in (Biemann et al., 2007a), using these induced categories as features results in improved accuracies for a variety of NLP tasks, including NERC.

Lexical expansion (Miller et al., 2012) is also an unsupervised technique that needs a large corpus for the induction, and is based on the computation of a distributional thesaurus (DT), see (Riedl and Biemann, 2013; Lin, 1998). While (Miller et al., 2012) used a DT for expanding lexical representations and showed performance gains in knowledge-based word sense disambiguation (WSD), the expansion technique can also be used in other text processing applications including NERC: especially for rare words and unseen instances, lexical expansion can provide a useful back-off technique as it performs a generalization of the training and test data.

2 Technical Background

Unlike supervised techniques, unsupervised PoS tagging (Christodoulopoulos et al., 2010) techniques require no pre-existing manually tagged corpus to build a tagging model and hence highly suitable for the resource poor languages.

There have been various approaches to unsupervised PoS induction. One such approach, reported in (Brown et al., 1992) is based on the class based n-gram models. In (Clark, 2003) distributional and morphological information is used for PoS induction. We use the unsupervised PoS tagging system of (Biemann, 2009) because of its availability as an open source software. We use web-based corpus of 34 million tokens for Bengali (Ekbal and Bandyopadhyay, 2008), and the datasets reported in (Biemann et al., 2007b) for Hindi and German. These datasets were used for unsupervised lexical acquisition.

A Distributional Thesaurus (DT) is an automatically computed resource that relates words according to their similarity. A DT contains, for every sufficiently frequent word, the most similar words as computed over the similarity of contexts these words appear in, which implements the distributional hypothesis (Harris, 1951). We use the scalable, open source implementation of (Riedl and Biemann, 2013), based on the MapReduce paradigm.

Feature selection is the vital task which involves selecting a subset of relevant features for building robust classifier by eliminating the redundant and irrelevant features. It therefore, reduces the time complexity of the learning algorithm and improves performance. Overall results as reported in (Biemann, 2009) suggest that unsupervised PoS tagging provides an additional word-level feature, which can be computed for any language and domain, and has been proven to be useful in domain adaptation and in situations where we have scarcity of labelled training data. In our work, we employ unsupervised PoS tags as one of the important language independent features which can benefit NERC task for various Indian languages and German.

We also investigate the use of features based on distributional similarity. We incorporate three most similar words to a particular token as three features in training and test datasets. As an example, Figure 1 shows the three most similar words for tokens in a Hindi language sentence.

Tokens from a Hindi sentence	Similar words from Distributional Thesaurus		
राम(rAma)	कृष्ण(kRRiShNa)	नारायण(nArAyaNa)	प्रसाद(parsAda)
लंका(lankA)	कोलकाता(kolakAtA)	तो(to)	घर(ghara)
में(men)	मे(me)	मंठ	मेठं
सुरक्षित(surakSita)	खतरनाक(khataranAka)	उचित(uchita)	बेहतर(behatara)
स्थान(sthAna)	मिनट(minata)	ओवर(ovara)	नंबर(nambara)
पर(para)	से(se)	को(ko)	तक(taka)
बन्दिनी(bandinI)	ND	ND	ND
सीता(sitA)	संतोष(santoSha)	रमेश(ramesha)	मुकेश(mukesha)
को(ko)	उन्हें(unhen)	उसे(use)	द्वारा(dwArA)
खोज(khoja)	तलाश(talAsha)	ढूंढ(DhUnDha)	निकाल(nikAla)
सके(sake)	सकते(sakate)	सकती(sakatI)	सकता(sakatA)

Figure 1: Lexical expansion of tokens in Hindi language with ITRANS transliteration to English. Here, ND denotes the "not defined".

3 Named Entity Features

Following features constitute the available feature set for building the various models based on a first order Conditional Random Field (CRF) (Lafferty et al., 2001) classifier. Most of the following features do not require any language and domain specific resources or rules for their computation.
Context words: These denote the local contexts surrounding the current token.
Word suffix and prefix: Fixed length character sequences stripped from the leftmost and right

most positions of words.

First word: A binary valued feature which takes the value 1 when the current word is the first token of the sentence and 0 for the other case.

Length of the word: This feature takes the value 1 when the number of characters in a token is greater than a predetermined threshold value (here, set to 5).

Infrequent word: A binary valued feature which checks whether frequency of current word in the training set exceeds a threshold value (here, set to 5).

Last word of sentence: This binary valued feature checks whether the word is the last word of a sentence or not and turn on/off accordingly.

Capitalization: This binary valued feature checks whether the word starts with a capital letter or not and takes values accordingly. This feature is used only for German.

Part-of-speech (POS) information: PoS tags of the current and/or the surrounding token(s).

Chunk information: Chunk of the current and/or surrounding tokens. This is used only for German.

Digit features: These features are defined based upon the presence and/or the number of digits and/or symbols in a token.

Unsupos: Unsupervised PoS tag as obtained from the system developed in (Biemann, 2009) is used as a feature.

Unsupervised DT features: Three most similar word from the DT for each token in training and test dataset.

4   Feature Selection using MOO

In this section we formulate feature selection as an optimization problem that involves choosing an relevant feature subset for NERC. Mutiobjective optimization (MOO) can be effective for solving the problem of feature selection. Here we develop a feature selection method based on a popular MOO based technique, namely non-dominated sorting genetic algorithm (NSGA-II) (Deb, 2001). In order to implement our MOO-based feature selection we make use of NSGA–II (Deb et al., 2002). As a supervised learner we used Conditional Random Field (CRF) (Lafferty et al., 2001), and carried out experiments using its CRF++[1] implementation.

---

[1] CRF++: Yet another CRF toolkit http://crfpp.googlecode. com/svn/trunk/doc/index.html

4.1   Formulation of feature selection problem

Let us denote the N number of available features by $f_1, f_2, \ldots, f_N$ and suppose that the set of all features be denoted by $F = f_i : i = 1, 2 \ldots N$. Then the problem of feature selection can be stated as follows: Find a set of features G that will optimize a function $O(F)$ such that: $G \subseteq F$. Here, O is a measure of classification efficiency for the classifier trained using the features set G. The feature selection problem can be formulated under the MOO framework as: Find a set of features G such that maximize $[O_1(G), O_2(G)]$, where $O_1, O_2 \in$ recall, precision, F-measure, $-$(feature count). Here, we choose $O_1 =$ F-measure and $O_2 = -$(feature count)

4.2   Problem Encoding

Let the total number of features is N and size of the population is P. The length of the chromosome is determined from the number of available features and hence its size is N. If the ith position of chromosome is 0, then it represents that i^{th} feature does not participate in feature template set for construction of CRF-based classifier and opposite in case of 1. All the P number of chromosomes of initial population are initialized with a random sequence of 0 and 1.

4.3   Fitness Computation

For the fitness computation, the following steps are executed.

- There are $|G|$ number of features present in a particular chromosome (i.e., total $|G|$ number of 1's are there in the chromosome).

- Build a CRF classifier with only these $|G|$ features. We perform 3-fold cross validation and compute the F-measure value.

- Our objective is to maximize F-measure and minimize the feature count. NSGA-II (Deb, 2001) is used for optimization process using these two objective functions.

4.4   Selecting a single solution

The MOO based feature selection technique produces a set of solutions on the Pareto front. All these are best in their own and incomparable on the basis of aforementioned two objectives collectively. But in order to report the final results we build a CRF classifier with that particular feature combination that yields the highest F_1 measure

Language	Set	#tokens
Bengali	Training	328,064
	Test	34,200
Hindi	Training	462,120
	Test	60,810
German	Training	220,187
	Test	54,711

Table 1: Statistics of annotated training and test datasets

value among all the solutions of the final population.

5 Datasets and Experimental Setup

We use the web-based Bengali news corpus for our NERC experiments (Ekbal and Bandyopadhyay, 2008) in Bengali. A part of this corpus was manually annotated with four MUC NE categories, namely PER (*Person name*), LOC (*Location name*), ORG (*Organization name*) and MISC (*Miscellaneous name*). The *Miscellaneous name* includes date, time, number, percentages, monetary expressions and measurement expressions (Ekbal and Bandyopadhyay, 2008). In addition we also use the NER on South and South East Asian Languages (NERSSEAL)[2] Shared Task datasets of Bengali after mapping the fine-grained tagset to our coarse-grained form. For German we use the datasets obtained from datasets from the CoNLL 2003 challenge (Tjong Kim Sang and De Meulder, 2003). Statistics of training and test datasets are reported in Table 5.

The feature selection algorithm is run three times with different set of available features. Specifically we design three experiments, one with only basic lexical features, the second with lexical features along with unsupervised PoS tag, and the third experiment with three features from DT in addition to unsupervised PoS tag and lexical features. In order to properly denote the boundaries of a NE, we follow the IOB2 encoding scheme of the CoNLL-2003 shared task[3].

6 Evaluation of NERC for the Indian Languages

In this section we present the results along with the analysis for NERC on two Indian languages, namely Hindi and Bengali. For each of the languages, we extracted the features as defined in Section 3 including the token itself. We also incorporate features from the immediate contextual

<hr>

[2]http://ltrc.iiit.ac.in/ner-ssea-08
[3]http://www.cnts.ua.ac.be/conll2003/ner/

tokens (i.e. preceding token and following token). So the available number of features becomes equal to 27*3=81, and our goal is to find the best feature subset from this available feature set which optimizes our objective functions.

In all the experiments, we set the following parameter values for NSGA-II algorithm: population size = 32, number of generations = 50, probability of crossover = 0.8 and probability of mutation = 0.0125. The values of these parameters were determined using a held-out dataset (created by taking a portion from the training dataset).

Table 2 depicts the detailed evaluation results for NERC task on Hindi dataset. Results show that without using any lexical acquisition feature, we obtain the best results with a set of 41 features represented in the final population of MOO based feature selection algorithm. These results are considered as baseline for our further experiments on NERC.

In the next experiment we incorporate unsupervised PoS tag in the available set of features and apply the algorithm. It is observed that including unsuporvised PoS, recall increases but at the cost of precision. However this causes a small improvement in F_1 measure. This improvement is attributed because of the incorporation of unsupervised PoS tags for training the classifier. Thus, unsupos features generalize over the vocabulary, and subsume part of the lower-level features. We observe that the presence of the unsupervised PoS tag reduces the optimized feature set from 41 down to 25 features while at the same time improving in F_1.

Features	Tag	Precision	Recall	F_1	FC
Syntactic features only(Baseline)	LOC	82.71%	47.97%	60.72	
	MISC	83.37%	74.22%	78.53	
	ORG	52.63%	29.85%	38.10	
	PER	70.72%	29.15%	41.29	
	Overall	80.15%	52.19%	63.22	41
Syntactic + Unsupos features	LOC	82.20%	49.24%	61.59	
	MISC	83.00%	76.78%	79.77	
	ORG	62.50%	29.85%	40.40	
	PER	67.42%	32.14%	43.53	
	Overall	79.22%	54.45%	64.54	25
Syntactic + Unsupos + DT features	LOC	72.88%	63.39%	67.81	
	MISC	80.08%	82.76%	81.40	
	ORG	55.13%	56.95%	56.03	
	PER	63.87%	43.96%	52.08	
	Overall	73.26%	66.44%	69.68	32

Table 2: NERC performance for Hindi data–set, No. of generations=50, Size of population=32, FC= Feature Count

Next, we explore DT features by adding them to the pool of features. Algorithm for feature selection is again run with these additional features, and the results are reported in Table 2. With these DT features, recall goes up rapidly, but at the cost of precision. Again, we see a drop in precision, yet a relative recall increase of approximately 12% causes the F-measure to increase approximately by 5 percentage points.

The feature selection algorithm determines 32 features to be most relevant for the task. This feature combination includes several lexical expansion features that include the first two expansions of the preceding token and all the three expansions of the current token. It seems that the CRF profits rather from the expansion of contexts than from the expansions themselves. These DT in combination with unsupervised PoS features improve a total of 6 points F-measure over the baseline.

Thereafter we experiment with the Bengali datasets and its results are shown in Table 3. It shows how the performance can be improved with the use of unsupervised PoS tag and DT features. Although there is not much difference in the scores between the results obtained in the first two experiments, there is substantial reduction in the feature count. Again, recall is increased at cost of precision, as unsupervised features add coverage, but also noise at subsuming lower-level features. The performance obtained using unsupervised features are quite encouraging and comparable to the existing works (for both Hindi and Bengali). This also open a new direction for performing similar kinds of works in the resource-poor languages.

Feature set	F1–measure	FC
No unsupervised PoS Tag and DT features	72.44	30
With unsupervised PoS Tag	72.72	14
With unsupervised PoS Tag and DT features	73.50	21

Table 3: NERC performance for Bengali data–set, No. of Generations=50, Size of population=52

7 Experiments for NERC on German

In this section we report on our experiments for NERC in German language. For each token we extract twelve features including lexical features, unsupervised PoS tag and three most similar words from DT. We compute the values of these features at the preceding and succeeding tokens. We use the default parameter values of CRF and set of the parameters of NSGA-II as mentioned in the previous section.

Table 4 depicts the performance for NERC task on German dataset for the baseline model, which is constructed without using any unsupervised lexical acquisition features. Table also presents the results of the models which are constructed after incorporation of lexical acquisition features. For the baseline model, feature selection algorithm selects the solution representing 20 features for training CRF classifier. We obtain precision, recall and F_1 measure of 80.43%, 64.11% and 71.35%, respectively.

Features	Tag	Precision	Recall	F_1	FC
Syntactic features only (Baseline)	LOC	77.36%	67.94%	72.34	
	MISC	80.52%	30.10%	43.82	
	ORG	73.47%	59.76%	65.91	
	PER	86.83%	68.68%	76.70	
	Overall	80.43%	64.11%	71.35	20
Syntactic + DT features	LOC	81.40%	69.93%	75.23	
	MISC	79.22%	29.61%	43.11	
	ORG	74.50%	57.02%	64.60	
	PER	88.31%	72.40%	79.56	
	Overall	82.89%	65.72%	73.31	19
Syntactic + DT + Unsupervised PoS features	LOC	84.87%	72.60%	78.26	
	MISC	79.75%	30.58%	44.21	
	ORG	74.64%	61.99%	67.73	
	PER	93.07%	82.15%	87.27	
	Overall	86.21%	71.52%	78.18	21

Table 4: NERC performance for German data–set, No. of Generations=50, Size of population=52

In the next experiment on German dataset with DT features incorporated, we obtain improvements in both precision and recall, which causes substantial improvement in F_1. Lexical expansion reduces the chances of unseen instances during testing, which results in higher F_1 measure with one less number of features. The third experiment includes three DT features as well as the unsupervised PoS tag in the available set of features for feature selection. It is evident that we obtain significant improvements for both recall and precision, which in turn causing higher F_1 measure. Over the baseline we obtain an improvement of 6.83 in F_1 measure with the 21 most relevant features. The best solution includes all the four unsupervised lexical acquisition features.

8 Conclusion

In this present work, we proposed a unsupervised lexical acquisition and MOO-based technique for building NERC systems. It has been consistently observed that incorporation of unsupervised lexical acquisition features and using MOO-based feature selection result in significant improvement in NERC performance for a variety of languages. The performance of our models compares favourably with other works in the literature (Tjong Kim Sang and De Meulder, 2003). Also, we present a framework that can easily be transferred to the other languages and applications.

In future we would like to include more language independent features. Rather than selecting a single best-fitting feature set from best population produced by MOO algorithm, we would like to combine an ensemble of several classification systems based on different feature sets and/or different classification techniques.

References

Chris Biemann, Claudio Giuliano, and Alfio Gliozzo. 2007a. Unsupervised part-of-speech tagging supporting supervised methods. In *Proceedings of RANLP*, volume 7.

Chris Biemann, Gerhard Heyer, Uwe Quasthoff, and Matthias Richter. 2007b. The Leipzig Corpora Collection - Monolingual corpora of standard size. In *Proceedings of Corpus Linguistics 2007*, Birmingham, UK.

Chris Biemann. 2009. Unsupervised part-of-speech tagging in the large. *Research on Language and Computation*, 7(2-4):101–135.

Peter F. Brown, Peter V. deSouza, Robert L. Mercer, Vincent J. Della Pietra, and Jenifer C. Lai. 1992. Class-based n-gram models of natural language. *Comput. Linguist.*, 18(4):467–479, December.

Christos Christodoulopoulos, Sharon Goldwater, and Mark Steedman. 2010. Two decades of unsupervised POS induction: How far have we come? In *Proceedings of EMNLP*, pages 575–584.

Alexander Clark. 2003. Combining distributional and morphological information for part of speech induction. In *In proceedings of European chapter of the Association for Computational Linguistics (EACL-03)*, pages 59–66.

Kalyanmoy Deb, Amrit Pratap, Sameer Agarwal, and T. Meyarivan. 2002. A fast and elitist multiobjective genetic algorithm: NSGA-II. *IEEE Transactions on Evolutionary Computation*, 6(2):181–197.

Kalyanmoy Deb. 2001. *Multi-objective Optimization Using Evolutionary Algorithms*. John Wiley and Sons, Ltd, England.

Asif Ekbal and Sivaji Bandyopadhyay. 2008. A web-based Bengali news corpus for named entity recognition. *Language Resources and Evaluation*, 42(2):173–182.

Asif Ekbal and Sriparna Saha. 2011a. Multiobjective Optimization for Classifier Ensemble and Feature Selection: An Application to Named Entity Recognition. *International Journal on Document Analysis and Recognition (IJDAR)*, 8.

Asif Ekbal and Sriparna Saha. 2011b. Weighted vote-based classifier ensemble for named entity recognition: A genetic algorithm-based approach. *ACM Trans. Asian Lang. Inf. Process.*, 10(2):9.

Zellig S. Harris. 1951. *Methods in Structural Linguistics*. University of Chicago Press, Chicago.

John D. Lafferty, Andrew McCallum, and Fernando C. N. Pereira. 2001. Conditional Random Fields: Probabilistic Models for Segmenting and Labeling Sequence Data. In *ICML*, pages 282–289.

Dekang Lin. 1998. Automatic retrieval and clustering of similar words. In *36th Annual Meeting of the Association for Computational Linguistics and the 17th International Conference on Computational Linguistics*, pages 768–774, Stroudsburg, USA. ACM Press.

Tristan Miller, Chris Biemann, Torsten Zesch, and Iryna Gurevych. 2012. Using distributional similarity for lexical expansion in knowledge-based word sense disambiguation. *Proceedings of COLING–12, Mumbai, India.*

David Nadeau and Satoshi Sekine. 2007. A survey of named entity recognition and classification. *Lingvisticae Investigationes*, 30(1):3–26.

Martin Riedl and Chris Biemann. 2013. Scaling to large3 data: An efficient and effective method to compute distributional thesauri. In *EMNLP*, pages 884–890.

Sokratis Sofianopoulos and George Tambouratzis. 2010. Multi-objective optimisation of real-valued parameters of a hybrid mt system using genetic algorithms. *Pattern Recognition Letters*, 31(12):1672–1682.

Erik F. Tjong Kim Sang and Fien De Meulder. 2003. Introduction to the CoNLL-2003 shared task: Language-independent named entity recognition. In Walter Daelemans and Miles Osborne, editors, *Proceedings of CoNLL-2003*, pages 142–147. Edmonton, Canada.

Improving the accuracy of pronunciation lexicon using Naive Bayes classifier with character n-gram as feature: for language classified pronunciation lexicon generation

Aswathy P V
Language Technology Section
CDAC-T
India
aswathypv@cdac.in

Arun Gopi
Language Technology Section
CDAC-T
India
arungopi@cdac.in

Sajini T
Language Technology Section
CDAC-T
India
sajini@cdac.in

Bhadran V K
Language Technology Section
CDAC-T
India
bhadran@cdac.in

Abstract

This paper looks at improving the accuracy of pronunciation lexicon for Malayalam by improving the quality of front end processing. Pronunciation lexicon is an in evitable component in speech research and speech applications like TTS and ASR. This paper details the work done to improve the accuracy of automatic pronunciation lexicon generator (APLG) with Naive Bayes classifier using character n-gram as feature. n-gram is used to classify Malayalam native words (MLN) and Malayalam English words (MLE). Phonotactics which is unique for Malayalam is used as the feature for classification of MLE and MLN words. Native and nonnative Malayalam words are used for generating models for the same. Testing is done on different text input collected from news domain, where MLE frequency is high.

1 Introduction

Automatic pronunciation generator is one of the main modules in speech application which determines the quality of the output. In speech applications, pronunciation is generated online from the given input using dictionary or rules. For a language like Malayalam which has agglutination, rule based approach is more suitable than look up. Since English is the official language, the influence is such that the usage of English words is very common in Indian language scripts and texts. So APLG must be able to handle the pronunciation of these English words.

The inputs given to TTS are normally bilingual with English words in Latin script and native language script. In most cases the pronunciation model for MLE is different and depends on explicit knowledge of the language. Hence, it must be identified by the system in order to enable the correct model. Language identification is often based on only written text, which creates an interesting problem. User intervention is always a possibility, but a completely automatic system would make this phase transparent and increase the usability of the system (William. B).

In this paper we brief about the language identification from text, which is typically a symbolic processing task. Language identification is done to classify MLN and MLE and apply LTS to generate Indian English pronunciation. We used Naive Bayes classifier with character n-grams as feature, to identify whether the given word belongs to native or non-native Malayalam.

2 Structure of Malayalam

Malayalam is an offshoot of the Proto-Tamil-Malayalam branch of the Proto Dravidian Language. Malayalam belongs to the southern group of Dravidian Language. There are approximately 37 million Malayalam speakers worldwide, with 33,066,392 speakers in India, as of the 2001 census of India. Basically Malayalam words are derived from Sanskrit and Tamil. Malayalam script contains 51 letters including 15 vowels and 36 consonants, which forms 576 syllabic characters, and contains two additional diacritic characters named anuswara and visarga.

In the writing system of syllabic alphabet, all consonants have an inherent vowel. Diacritics, which can appear above, below, before or after a consonant, are used to change the inherent vowel. When they appear at the beginning of a

D S Sharma, R Sangal and J D Pawar. Proc. of the 11th Intl. Conference on Natural Language Processing, pages 113–118,
Goa, India. December 2014. ©2014 NLP Association of India (NLPAI)

syllable, vowels are written as independent letters. When certain consonants occur together, special conjunct symbols are used which combine the essential parts of each letter (omniglot). Consonants with vowel omission are used to represent the 5 chillu, which occurs in around 25% of words.

Malayalam has a canonical word order of SOV (subject–object–verb) as do other Dravidian languages. Phonetically a syllable in Malayalam consists of an obligatory nucleus which is always characterized by a vowel or diphthongal articulation; preceded and followed optionally by a 'releasing' and an 'arresting 'consonant articulation respectively (Prabodachandran, 1967 pp 39-40).

Among the vowel phonemes in Malayalam, two fronts, two are back and one is a low central vowel. Front vowels are unrounded and back vowels are rounded ones (Prabodachandran, 1967 pp 39-40). All vowels both short and long except |o| occurs initially medially and finally. Short |o| does not occur word finally medially short |e| and short |o| occur only in the first syllable. Malayalam has also borrowed the Sanskrit diphthongs of /äu/ (represented in Malayalam as ഔ, au) and /ai/ (represented in Malayalam as ഐ, ai), although these mostly occur only in Sanskrit loanwords.

In a syllable there will be at least one consonant and a vowel. By the combination of a consonant and a vowel, Malayalam syllable structure may be expressed by the simple formula (c) v (c).

The syllable structure occurring in Malayalam corpus and its frequency is shown in figure 1: C*VC* patterns occur in English words.

Harmonic sequence of vowels is one of the main characteristics of the Dravidian family of languages (Prabodhachandran).That is one vowel can influence sound of other.

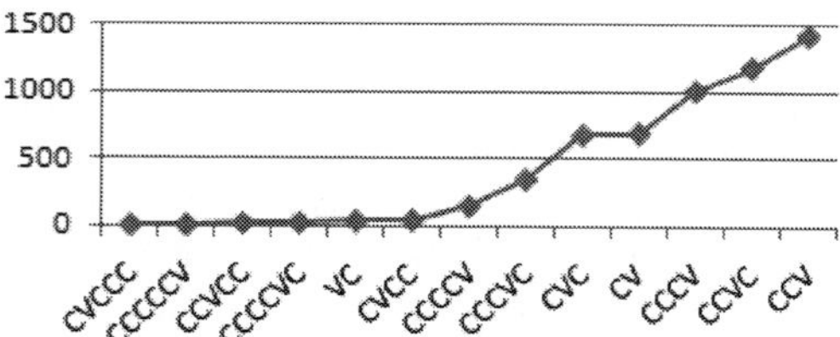

Figure 1. Syllable pattern and frequency

3 Malayalam corpus collection

The main input for speech research is a huge corpus, both text and speech properly annotated. For the major world languages, large corpora are publicly available. But for most other languages, they are not. But with the advent of the Web it can be highly automated and thereby fast and inexpensive (Adam and G V Reddy).

Malayalam corpus was created from online sources like newspapers, blogs and other sites, which is then used to extract data. Manual verification of the sites content is done to ensure that it contains good-enough-quality textual content. For domain coverage contents is manually prepared. 25GB of raw corpus is collected for extracting optimal text which covers the phonetic variations in the language. The collected corpus as such cannot be used for optimal text selection. The raw data contains junk characters, foreign words (frequent occurring of English words in Malayalam script) etc.

The optimal text selected for speech application like ASR and TTS, must be able to well represent the language. Optimal text (OT) must cover all phonemic variations occurring in the language. OT is the minimum text which covers the all/maximum possible units (variations) in the language.

Frequent occurrences of English words give higher rank for sentences containing more number of English words. This reduces the text with native content. If we have to select sentence with Malayalam words, these English words must not add to the unit count. Manually marking of these words is practically not possible. Post verification and cleaning of English words from OT is tedious and sometimes requires additional text selection.

Automatic language identification can be used in the text selection to improve the quality of OT.

4 Malayalam pronunciation and Letter to sound(LTS) rules

Malayalam is a phonetic language having a direct correspondence between symbols and sounds (Prabhodhachandran, 1997). The pronunciation lexicon generation is easy for phonetic languages when compared with English. But there exist few exceptions, in case of Malayalam.

Accurate pronunciation can be generated only by properly handling these exceptions. Pronunciation is one of the factors that determine the quality of TTS.

A detailed analysis on speech and text corpus is carried to identify the LTS rules for Malayalam. The identified rules are then verified and validated by language experts.

The Malayalam LTS rules can be categorized as below.

- Phonetic – direct correspondence between text and sounds

e.g.:
തിരുവനന്തപുരം   തി രു വ ന്ത പു രം
tiruvananthapuram   ti ru va na ntha pu ram

- Pronunciation different from orthography

e.g.: നനയുക   ന (ന) യു ക
"nanayuka   n a n@ a y u k a" (n represent dental and n@ represent the alveolar)

Dental and alveolar sounds for NA and its gemination

Influence of y in gemination of kk

Retroflex plosive and its allophone

Lexicons having multiple pronunciations – homonym/homophones

"ennaal"   e nn aa l
"nn" can be alveolar gemination or dental gemination. The occurrence of such cases is very less in Malayalam.

- Pronunciation by usage (Speaker specific pronunciation)

ഉത്സവം   ഉ ത്സ വം
"utsavam"   "u t s a v a m"
                    -Actual pronunciation
ഉ ത്സവം ഉ ത്സ വം
"utsavam"   "u l s a v a m"
                            - by usage
ദയ   ദ യ
"daya" "d a y a"
                  – Actual pronunciation
ദയ   ദെ യ
"daya" "d e y a"   – by usage

- Foreign word pronunciation (frequent usage of English words)

For generating proper pronunciation foreign words must be identified and separate rules or pronunciation lexicon must be applied for generating proper pronunciation. The influence or dominance of English has reached to an extent that the contents from few sources even contains more than 25% of foreign words.

For handling English pronunciation 3 additional phones are required.

"a" sound as in "bank"   (ബാങ്ക്)
"ph" sound as in "fan"   (ഫാന്)
"s" sound as in "zoo"   (സൂ)

In TTS application a standard pronunciation is used at synthesis time. Users can add user specific pronunciation dictionary to generate pronunciation in their own preference. In ASR, multiple pronunciation lexicons will be stored and pronunciation variations can be handled.

For generating accurate pronunciation, language identification is done and specific rules must be applied to handle the phone variations.

5   Pronunciation lexicon generation for Malayalam

Pronunciation lexicon for Malayalam is generated using LTS rules and exception list for handling the above listed cases.

Exception patterns for dental and alveolar NA gemination and allophonic variation of KK is extracted from corpus, and added to exception list. Pronunciation is generated based on these exception patterns. Other exceptions like pronunciation of nouns etc. are also included in this exception list.

5.1   Handling of English words pronunciation (English script)

For handling English word in latin script, encoding is checked to identify the language. Pronunciation is generated using a standard dictionary look up. CMU dictionary with 100K words is taken as the reference for English pronunciation.

A pattern based replacement is done to modify the pronunciation as Indian English (of native Malayalam speaker) pronunciation.

5.2 Handling of English word pronunciation (Native script)

The input text contains frequent occurrence of English words. Encoding based language identification is not applicable since both are in the same script.

All languages have a finite set of phonemic units on which the words are building and there are constraints on the way in which these phonemes can be arranged to form syllables. These constraints are called as phonotactics or phoneme sequence constraint. Phonotactics is language dependent.

In the process of recognition with respect to Spoken Languages it is observed that human are the best identifier of a language. However during automatic recognition we have to consider several factors like with respect to language identification one language differs from another language in one or more of the following: (M.A.Zissman, Navratil J, Mutusamy, Schultz, Mak).

- Phonology: Phone sets would be different for each of the languages

- Morphology: The word roots and the lexicons may be different for different category of languages

- Syntax: The sentence patterns with respect to grammar are different

- Prosody: Duration, pitch, and stress patterns vary from language to language

In this paper an attempt has been made to identify language using the phonology since we require word level identification. We use language specific phonotactics information to identify words that belong to native language.

5.3 Pattern based approach

Pattern based approach is a string matching method to classify words. A detailed analysis of corpus is done to extract 1200 patterns that do not occur in Malayalam. Pattern search is done on the input text and words with matching patterns were classified as English. Patterns that are common / noun patterns are not considered in the list. Only 70-75% of words are covered in this approach.

5.4 Naive Bayes classifier using character n-gram approach

Naive Bayes classifier begins by calculating the prior probability of each label, which is determined by checking the frequency of each label in the training set. The contribution from each feature is then combined with this prior probability, to arrive at a likelihood estimate for each label. The label whose likelihood estimate is the highest is then assigned to the input value.

Naive Bayes classifier with character n-gram as feature is used for categorizing MLN and MLE. In this approach two categories of texts are collected, one only with native c words (MLN) and the other with nonnative (MLE). From these texts n-gram model profile for MLN and MLE is generated. These profiles hold n-gram models up to order 3 and their individual frequencies. Generation of n-gram is shown in figure 2.

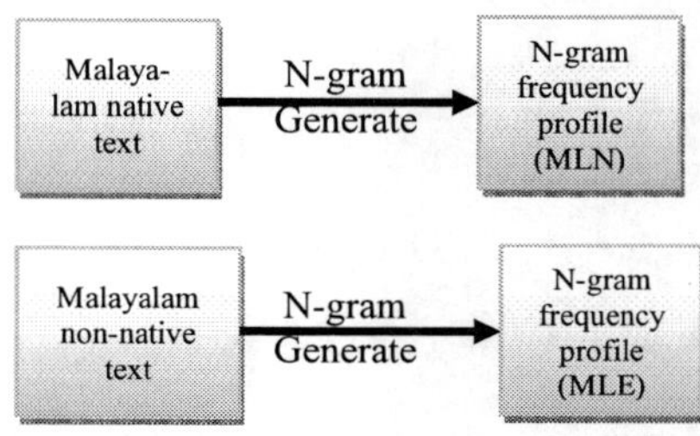

Figure 2. Generation of n-gram frequency profile for each word in the source

N-gram for Malayalam word മലയാളം

1-gram: മ ല യ ാ ള ം
            _ma la y aa lxa m _
2-gram: _മ മല ലയ യാ ാള ളം ം_
            ma mala lay yaa aalxa lxam m
3-gram: _മല മലയ ലയാ യാള ാളം ളം_
            ma malay layaa yaalx aalxam lxam

As n increases expressiveness of the model increases but ability to estimate accurate parameters from sparse data decreases, which is important in categorizing nonnative Malayalam words, so n-gram up to 3 servers the job.

N-gram decomposes every string into substrings, hence any errors that are present is limited to few n-grams (n-gram based text categorization, William B. Cavnar and John M. Trenkle).

5.4.1 Formulation of Naive Bayes

Given a word and the classes (C_{MLN} C_{MLE}) to which it may belong. Naïve Bayes classifier evaluates the posterior probability for which the word belongs to particular class. It then assigns the word to class with highest probability values(Jing Bai and Jian-Yun Nie. Using Language Model for Text Classification).

$$C_{MAP} = \text{argmax}_{c \in C} p(c|w)$$

MAP is Maximum a posteriori probability

$$= \text{argmax}_{c \in C} \frac{p(w|c)p(c)}{p(w)}$$

$$= \text{argmax}_{c \in C} p(w|c)p(c)$$

$$= \text{argmax}_{c \in C} p(x_1, x_2, .., x_n|c)p(c)$$
x represents feature

By Naive Bayes conditional independence assumption

$$p(x_1, x_2, .., x_n|c) = p(x_1|c) \times p(x_1|c) \times \\ .. \times p(x_n|c)$$

$$c_{NB} = \text{argmax}_{c_j \in C} p(c_j) \prod_{i \in positions} p(x_i|c_j)$$

5.4.2 Applying Naive with n-gram frequency as feature

1. Generate character based n-gram profiles for each category as discussed above

2. From training corpus extract vocabulary of model

3. Calculate $p(c_j)$ terms
   a. For each c_j in C do
      i. $w_j :=$ count of all words that belong to class C_j

$$p(c_j) = \frac{|w_j|}{W}$$

4. Calculate $p(x_i|c_j)$
   b. For each x_i
$$p(x_i|c_j) := \frac{n_{x_i} + \alpha}{n + \alpha |vocabulary|}$$
(Add 1 smoothing where $\alpha = 1$)

5. Return C_{NB} where
$$c_{NB} = \text{argmax}_{c_j \in C} P(c_j) \prod_{i \in positions} P(x_i|c_j)$$

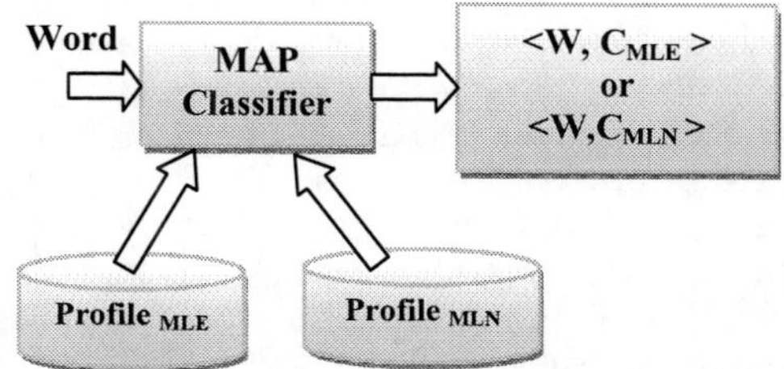

Figure 3: Categorization using Naïve Bayes

6 Experiment and results

We selected 200 sentences with 2000 unique words was taken as the input for verification of pattern based and Naive Bayes based classification. First we performed the words categorization based on the pattern list (for English words).391 words were identified and 97 were misclassified. We then used the Naive Bayes classifier to classify the words. The result is given in Table 1.0

Language identification	#Identified English word	#Miss classified
Pattern based	391	97
Naïve Bayes	782	47

Table 1.0 Category identified and misclassified

We also tested with random input collected from online sources. Naive Bayes with n-gram showed better word identification, than pattern. An average of 90% of word coverage was given by n-gram based language identification.

7 Conclusion

In this paper we brief about the effort for improving the accuracy of pronunciation lexicon for Malayalam. This method can be used to improve the quality of corpus, and speech applications like TTS and ASR. In text corpus selection, APLG using Naive Bayes classifier is used to identify foreign words in native script. This reduces the manual effort required for manual verification and cleaning of selected text corpus. For

TTS the pronunciation of words can be made accurate using Naive Bayes classifier. Depending on the domain this will increase the quality of synthetic speech.

In future we plan to improve the accuracy of Naive Bayes classifier by including the morphology rules to identify the root words. Using different smoothing technique can also improve performance(Sami Virpioja, Tommi Vatanen, Jaakko J. Vayrynen. Language Identification of Short Text Segments with N-gram Models).Naive Bayes classifier has wide range of applications which includes text categorization, development of multi-lingual speech recognizer etc.

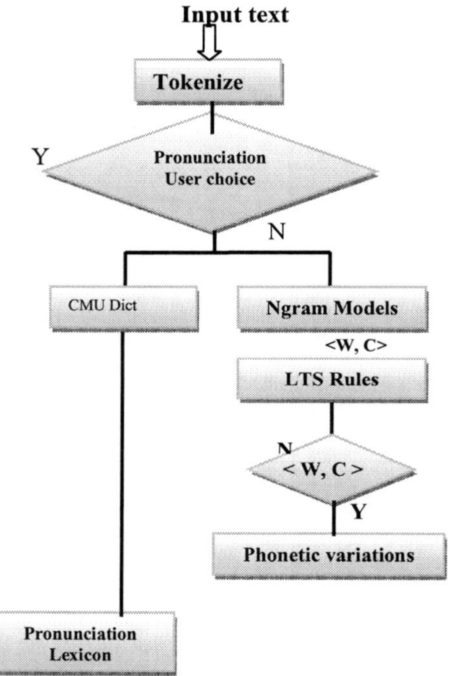

Figure 4: Implementation of APLG

Reference

Adam, G V Reddy Lexical Computing Ltd. IIIT Hyderabad, Masaryk University, IIIT Hyderabad United Kingdom, India, Czech Republic, India

M.A. Zissman, 1996 *Comparison of Four Approaches to Automatic Language Identification of Telephone speech*, IEEE Transactions on Speech and Audio Processing.

Milla Nizar, 2010, *Malayalam: Dative Subject Constructions in South-Dravidian Languages.*

Navratil. J, Sept. 2001 *Spoken Language Recognition - A Step toward Multilinguality in Speech Processing,* IEEE Transactions on Speech and Audio Processing.

T. Sajini, K. G. Sulochana, R. Ravindra Kumar, *Optimized Multi Unit Speech Database for High Quality FESTIVAL TTS*

Alan W. Black, Carolyn P. Rosé, Kishore Prahallad, Rohit Kumar, Rashmi Gangadharaiah, Sharath Rao, *Building a Better Indian English Voice using More Data*

Prabodachandran, 1967, *Malayalam structure* (Abercrombie 1 pp 39-40)

Sanghamitra Mohanty, April 2011 *Phonotactic Model for Spoken Language Identification in Indian Language Perspective,* International Journal of Computer Applications (0975 8887) Volume 19 No.9

Schultz.T, et al, 1999, *Language Independent and Language Adaptive Large Vocabulary Speech Recognition*, Proc. Euro Speech, Hungary.

Schultz. T and Kirchhoff. K, 2006, *Multilingual Speech Processing*, Academic Press

Mak. B, et al, 2002, *Multilingual Speech Recognition with Language Identification*, Proc. ICSLP.

William B. Cavnar and John M. *Trenkle N-Gram-Based Text Categorization.*

Jing Bai and Jian-Yun Nie, *Using Language Model for Text Classification*

Jaakko J. Vayrynen, Sami Virpioja, Tommi Vatanen, *Language Identification of Short Text Segments with N-gram Models*

Learning phrase-level vocabulary in second language using pictures/gestures and voice

Lavanya Prahallad
International Institute of Information Technology, Hyderabad
*lavanya.prahallad@resea
rch.iiiit.ac.in*

Prathyusha Danda
International Institute of Information Technology, Hyderabad
*danda.prathyusha@resea
rch.iiit.ac.in*

Radhika Mamidi
International Institute of Information Technology, Hyderabad
*radhika.mamidi@
iiit.ac.in*

Abstract

Earlier works has explored that a foreign language can be learnt from pictures than merely using native language word translations. These efforts on language learning using pictures were limited to colors, animals, birds, vehicles and common noun categories. In this paper, we present our research that learning of verbs is also possible by using right set of pictures and gestures, and we show that this is effective in second language learning. We report the acquisition of words in tourist domain in a second language by working with subjects who are between 14 and 48 years of age. From pre-learning and post-learning evaluations, we show that acquisition of vocabulary like nouns and verbs in a new language is better with the fusion of pictures and voice. We also show the subjects are able to generalize their learning towards phrase-level vocabulary without any additional training and efforts.

1. Introduction

Recalling the famous saying "A picture is worth thousand words", we explore whether a good enough vocabulary acquisition is possible using pictures as medium to learn an Indian language as a second language. India is a wide subcontinent broken down into states, where in each state has its own language; also many states or villages do not speak English. It is necessary for an Indian to learn another Indian language as second language. Typically a language deals with objects/persons and actions. We consider the fact that the actions exist for practical purposes are limited. Signs (gestures/pictures) used to express these actions appear same throughout the world, except the languages call the same action with different names depending on the spatial, cultural regions. For example, the sign or a picture depicting the action of eating would be same, however, has different names in different languages. Thus pictures supplement learning, helps to understand the words in a more meaningful method. This will indeed enable learners to learn, understand, and utilize that vocabulary in all aspects of their lives. With the recent advances made in education and technology language learning has been easier when voice is added with the picture and the learner hears the word in the second language and learns it by repeating any number of times. This combination enhances once language learning significantly.

Many researchers have explored this area of vocabulary acquisition and demonstrated that using pictures is better than just textual format in vocabulary acquisition while learning a foreign/second language. Experiments conducted by Carpenter and Olson (2011) shows that Swahili words were learned better from pictures than from translations. It appears, therefore, that pictures can facilitate learning of

D S Sharma, R Sangal and J D Pawar. Proc. of the 11th Intl. Conference on Natural Language Processing, pages 119–125,
Goa, India. December 2014. ©2014 NLP Association of India (NLPAI)

foreign language vocabulary. Taking the idea from the Dominance, Gentner and Boroditsky (2001) work, we exploit that words can be learnt by using pictures because of their concept-to-word mapping. Cognitive dominance prevails when concepts are simply named by language as in the case of nouns. Though the inspiration for this work is from earlier research, our approach differs in the following ways:

- This study is done for a set of Indian languages and can however easily be extended to other languages of the world.
- We show that even verbs can be learnt using right set of pictures in addition to nouns.
- Our study shows that the subjects can learn the phrase-level vocabulary as a generalization of their training on nouns and verbs.
- Use of voice with pictures aids in learning the second language and can relate that sound to the picture.

In our study we explore teaching a good enough way of learning verbs in Indian languages taken as second language. The medium is chosen to be pictures/signs, which are universal throughout the world; hence no first language influence is seen on the acquisition. This idea coupled with the voice has helped the learner to pronounce the word equivalent to a native language speaker. Even the illiterate folks can be benefitted with this research as objects he knows and sees everyday can be related to the audio being spoken out. This research is language independent and can be useful to learn any language as second language with the appropriate dataset. The idea is exploited from Chomsky's universal grammar that this theory suggests that linguistic ability manifests itself without being taught and that there are properties that all natural human languages share, the pictures of the actions will

immediately get related to a person's mental picture making him understand what that picture means, now with the help of voice he learns what the action is called in that second language.

2. Nouns and Verbs in second language learning

Nouns and Verbs form a pivotal part of learning a vocabulary in any language. Noun is an entity that denotes objects and Verb tells us about the action in a situation. There are several kinds of verbs. Though nouns and verbs exist universally in all languages of the world, the structure and the position of the verb and the object in a sentence varies. Unlike English, Indian languages have SOV word order where verb appears at the end of the sentence. The verbs in Indian languages are inflected gender and number and also for tense, aspect modality (TAM) where as in English they appear separately. In our work, we attempt to show that nouns and verbs can be learnt in a second language by using just pictures and there by one can achieve good enough vocabulary in a chosen domain.

3. Dataset

We have chosen 'tourist' domain to show that a related vocabulary in the domain can be acquired in a second language. As a pilot for our experiments and to present in this paper we have chosen the following Indian languages as second language: Kannada and Tamil. Any tourist or a visitor can benefit with this idea and can learn a good enough vocabulary when he/she visits a state where that particular language is spoken. The medium of learning is pictures, which prove to be more advantageous as a learner need not use first language to learn.

We carefully chose a set of pictures of nouns and a set of pictures of verbs that belong to tourist domain. Subjects of age 14-48 years participated in this experiment; a webpage is created with just pictures as shown in the Figure 1. These images are collected from Internet. When a learner clicks on the picture the corresponding audio of the picture is played in the second language. Learner can hear to this audio any number of times until he gets the word and learns the word in the second language.

4. Experimental Procedure

The experimental procedure consists of three phases: 1. Learning phase 2. Post-learning 3. Check for retention. Three experiments are conducted for this study dedicated for nouns, verbs and small phrases in the combination of already learnt nouns and verbs. Participants were informed at the beginning of the experiment that they would be learning Kannada/Tamil/Telugu words by viewing the picture and hearing the sound. All participants were instructed to try their best to learn the words in second language and that later their memory for these items would be tested. Once they complete the learning and proceed for test, participants cannot go back to the lesson. Participants would know their performance at the end of the test.

4.1 Experiment 1 – Nouns

A set of 25 images of Nouns is collected and shown to the learner. The images denote the names of the objects like transport, food, and professionals all are related to the tourist domain. Learner clicks on the each image to listen to the corresponding audio indeed to learn the word in the second language.

Learning phase: The web application was shown to the 10 subjects of age group (14-48years) and they were asked to go through the application if images of nouns for 20 minutes. Learners could hear the word by clicking on the image any number of times till they were

comfortable in remembering the word. (Shown in Figure 1)

Figure1: Demonstration of learning phase of experiment-one with nouns related to tourist domain using picture/gestures. Learner clicks on the word to hear the voice in second language

Post Learning: After 20 minutes, each person was given a test to evaluate the learning. Participants were then given a test with set of 10 questions in which they were asked to recall the word in the second language and chose the correct answer, given the picture and the four options. The performance of the test will be shown to the participant at the end of the test. We refer to this as error in retention. (Shown in Figure 2)

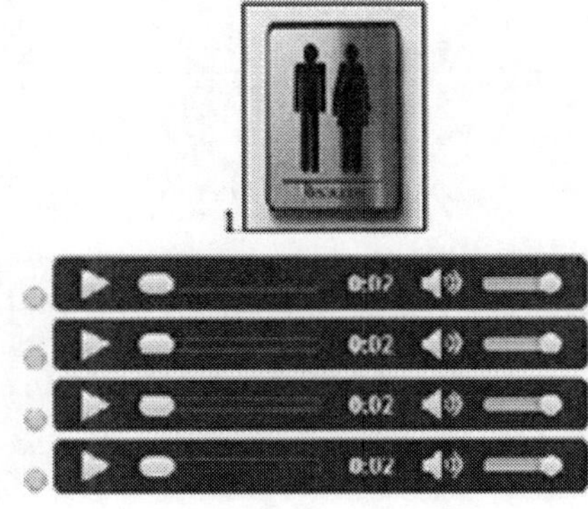

Figure2: Testing phase of nouns related to tourist domain using pictures. Learner has to listen to all four options of audio files and

Retention after 2 days: This post-learning phase
was conducted again after 2 days to check the
error in retention.

4.2 Experiment 2 – Verbs

In this experiment, a set of 25 images of verbs is
collected. The images denote the actions that are
carried by individuals as a tourist. These images
are selected as such it is performing an action.
The experimental procedure is same as
explained in section 4.1 with learning phase,
post learning phase and check for retention is
done for verbs. Figure 3 below shows the set of
images of verbs shown to user in learning phase.

*Figure 3: Demonstration of learning phase of
experiment-two with verbs related to tourist
domain using picture/gestures. Learner clicks on
the word to hear the voice in second language*

Figure 4 shows an evaluation test of post
learning for verbs.

*Figure 4: Testing phase of verbs related to
tourist domain using pictures. Learner has to
listen to all four options of audio files and
selects the voice option that is a match for the
given picture*

4.3 Experiment 3 – Small Phrases

This is the last experiment in the study. Please
note that this experiment does not have a
training test. A test is conducted by creating a
small parse in combination of noun and verb.
Learner uses their knowledge of already learnt
nouns and verbs Figure 5 shows the test in small
phrase-level.

This section which is an evaluation to test the
memory of the learner on how much he/she
remembers the experiment 1 and 2. A set of 10
combinations of verbs and nouns are displayed
for the learner, where he/she is required to listen
to the four options of the audio and select the
right audio combination of noun and verb.

Retention after 2 days: This process was
conducted again after 2 days to check the error
in retention.

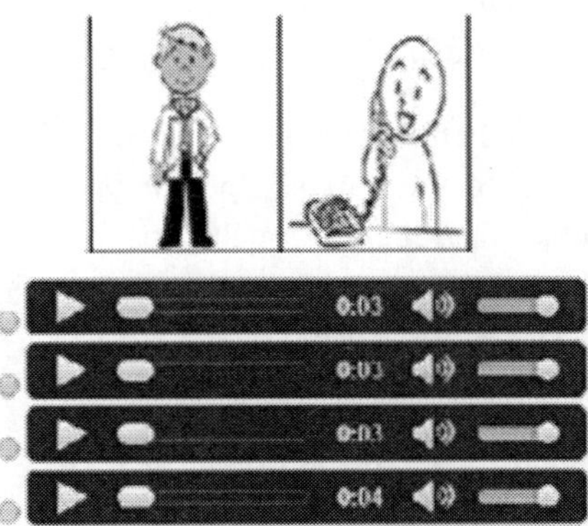

Figure5: Demonstration of testing phase of phrase-like sentences related to tourist domain using pictures. Learner has to listen to all four options of audio files and selects the voice that is a match for the given picture. There is no training for this phase. Learner has to create the right sentences with previous knowledge of already learnt nouns and verbs in second language.

5. Results

Table 1 and Table 2 show the results of the retention of nouns and verbs including small phrases immediately after learning-retention after 2 days. The average shows that performance of the participant is better in learning nouns and the retention percentage is also good when compared to verbs. It can be observed from the Table 1 and Table 2 that the retention after 2 days is also fairly well to indicate that learning through pictures helps in remembering the vocabulary learnt.

Participant number	Nouns	Verbs	Small Phrases
1	10-10	9-9	8-9
2	10-10	9-9	10-10
3	10-10	9-9	10-10
4	10-10	8-10	10-10
5	10-10	4-5	7-6
6	10-10	10-10	10-10
7	10-10	10-9	9-10
8	10-10	9-10	9-9
9	10-10	8-7	9-8
10	10-10	10-10	10-10
Average	10-10	8.3-8.8	9.2-9.2

Table1: Retention results of Kannada Nouns, Verbs and small phrases. Each entry indicates immediate retention-retention after 2 days.

Participant number	Nouns	Verbs	Small Phrases
1	10-10	8-9	9-9
2	10-10	10-10	8-10
3	8-7	7-6	9-7
4	10-10	10-10	10-10
5	10-10	10-10	10-10
6	8-7	8-6	9-7
7	10-10	9-8	9-8
8	10-10	9-8	9-8
9	8-7	7-8	8-9
10	10-10	9-9	10-9
Average	9.4-9.1	8.3-8.4	9.1-8.7

Table2: Retention results of Tamil Nouns, Verbs and small phrases. Each entry indicates immediate retention-retention after 2 days.

5.1 Observations

It is observed that a learner clicks 2 or more times to hear to the word in a second language and memorize the word and relate the picture to that sound. Also learners are able to relate to the language of same type. Though Tamil, Telugu, Kannada belongs to same language family of Dravidian there is more similarity between the structure, inflections between Kannada and Telugu. For learners whose first language is Telugu are able to perform better in Kannada but they are more time in understanding the accent, words, phones of Tamil. Learners of Telugu as first language feel that Tamil takes more time in learning even through pictures.

Another observation shows that nouns are easier to learn than verbs supporting previously done research. Another crucial observation is that the performance of the learner decreases or learners are taking more time in memorizing ambiguous words or similar sounding words. For example in Kannada "kudi – Drink", hidi – "catch".

For words, which are multi syllable or complex, learners find difficult to memorize it, they take more time in hearing these words again and again. Example in Kannada is "kaleduhoyitu – lost and karemadu – calling".

The performance of the learners while taking the test in constructing the small phrases is good compared to their performance in verbs as they are able to guess with their world knowledge and can relate the pictures of nouns with verbs. This shows that learning nouns and memorizing them is playing a crucial factor in constructing the small sentences. It's a time taking factor in learning verbs but they are able to memorize it and use it better as pictures are involved.

6. Conclusion

We conclude that our current study provides pivotal insight into the importance of pictures and gestures as educational tools in second language vocabulary learning. The novelty of this work is introducing a foreign word by means of a picture and no other medium of instruction. Learners are able to construct the small phrases by learning nouns and verbs and the score is around 9.2 in Kannada and 8.7 in Tamil. Our experiments explained in the section 4 are carried on 10 subjects of age group (14-48years). However, we plan to extend the scope of this experiment by extending to more languages as second language learning and conduct the experiments on more subjects of different age groups. This would also help us to analyze the learning capabilities of second language among the different age groups from younger to older.

This could be further extended in learning advanced features of second language such as grammar structure such as inflections, postpositions, tense aspect modality and sentence comprehension.

This application helps to learn a good enough vocabulary acquisition tailored to tourist domain. Traveling nationally and internationally has exponentially increased in today's world for various reasons like business or vacation. Learning a language of the visited places is always helpful to interact with localities, therefore as the part of phase one of this project; tourism domain is chosen as we see great potential of second language learning using pictures in this domain. However we plan to extend our project to different domains as medical, supermarkets etc.

Our idea of vocabulary learning using pictures can be easily ported to mobile phones. Moreover, the use of mobile phones and platforms could be effectively employed in acquiring a second language using contextual learning. This application is more helpful to tourists as adults are often busy and do not have the time to go through books which give an insight to a language that is spoken in other states if he/she visits a different place to cope up with transport, directions, food etc. This helps learning environment to be mobile and anytime anywhere.

7. Future Work

Our study for this paper paved a way to work further in this area of language learning using pictures and gestures. Important points to be addressed in future research include exploring more on the issue of showing expression, emotion, a short clip of an action captured as a video for verbs that are cognitive related to reduce ambiguity and bring clarity of the intended verb by showing action. The current limitation of our work is that we are not addressing to make them learn the inflections, grammar and the postpositions, which are pivotal in Indian languages; these issues need to be carefully worked out on to how to teach them using pictures. Also the issue of accuracy in recalling the pictures by the participants when checked after a week or a month should be taken care. This particular problem gave us an idea contextual learning by developing a mobile application on a smart phone where the learner can always use the app location and language based. We think that contextual learning using pictures and gestures (learning the words on the spot and using them with the native speakers) helps in learning the language better.

In keeping the view of learning a second language is a global requirement; we intend to extend our research for learning a second language that belongs to different language family with addition to add more languages to the list of same language family. Our work will be based on the idea that nouns and verbs of similar kind exist in all languages of the world; in this case pictures help to identify the words even they are of different language family. Voice coupled with the image helps the learner to build on their knowledge of language by making connections and comparisons between the home language and the target language.

8. Acknowledgements

We would like to thank all the participants for their participation in user studies.

9. References

Shana K. Carpenter and Kellie M. Olson. 2011. *Are Pictures Good for Learning New Vocabulary in a Foreign Language? Only If You Think They Are Not,* Journal of Experimental Psychology. Learning, Memory, and Cognition.

Dedre Gentner and Lera Boroditsky. *Early Acquisition of Nouns and Verbs Evidence from Navajo.*

K.G. Vijayakrishnan. 2007. *The "Noun Advantage" in English as a Second Language: A Study of the Natural Partitions Hypothesis'.* Dissertation in English and Foreign Languages University, Hyderabad, English Language Education.

Noam Chomsky. *Universal Grammar.* Retrieved from http://www.rit.edu/cla/philosophy/quine/universal_grammar.html and http://en.wikipedia.org/wiki/Universal_grammar

Handley Z. 2012. *Text-to-Speech Synthesis in Computer-Assisted Language Learning.* The Encyclopedia of Applied Linguistics.

Verbs in English Grammar. Retrieved from web https://www.tesol-direct.com/guide-to-english-grammar/verbs

Liz Stinson. 2014. *A Brilliant Way to Learn Chinese Through Pictures.* Retrieved from http://www.wired.com/2014/03/chineasy/

Timothy G. Collins. 2005. *English Class on the Air: Mobile Language Learning with Cell Phones.* Proceedings of the Fifth IEEE International Conference on Advanced Learning Technologies (ICALT'05).

Darren Edge, Elly Searle, Kevin Chiu, Jing Zhao, and James A. Landay. 2011. *MicroMandarin: mobile language learning in context.* In Proceedings of the SIGCHI Conference on Human Factors in Computing Systems (CHI '11). ACM, New York, NY, USA, 3169-3178.

Creating a PurposeNet Ontology: An insight into the issues encountered during ontology creation

Rishabh Srivastava
LTRC
IIIT Hyderabad
(rishabh.srivastava@research.,

Soma Paul
LTRC
IIIT Hyderabad
soma@)iiit.ac.in

Abstract

PurposeNet is an ontology based on the principle that all artifacts (man-made objects) exist for a purpose and all its features and relations with other entities are giverened by its purpose. We provide instances of ontology creation for two varied domains from scratch in the PurposeNet architecture. These domains include MMTS domain and recipe domain. The methodology of creation was totally different for the two domains. MMTS domain was more computaionally oriented ontology while recipe domain required a post-processing after manually entering the data. The post-processing step uses hierarchical clustering to cluster very close actions. MMTS ontology is further used to create a simple template based QA system and the results are compared with a database system for the same domain.

1 Introduction

This paper shows the procedure, advantages and disadvantages of enriching the datasets. The raw data we observed was different for the 2 domains. Once we decide the structure, the MMTS domain data was collected automatically. Although the integral actions had to be entered manually. On the other hand, for the recipe domain, after the initial manual population of data, post-processing for clubbing the nearest actions had to be carried out.

A question answering application in the domain of MMTS train timing has also been talked about in brief in this paper. The results are very satisfactory as they show a significant improvement over a similar RDBMS system. The prepared ontology can be put to use in several applications. Question answering, dialog systems, machine translation systems, etc.

1.1 Literature Review

Multiple attempts have been made in the past for populating data in PurposeNet. Some have tried automatic means while the others do it manually. (Singh and Srivastava, 2011a) have used surface text patterns (STPs) to extract information directly from Wikipedia text. They had tried populating only some of the descriptor features of the ontology. Other major works in automatic population for PurposeNet Ontology (Mayee et al., 2010a; Mayee et al., 2010b) have also tried to populate purpose of the artifact directly into PurposeNet using surface text pattern, typed dependency parser and neural networks. Although, the results of the dependency parser are quite convincing, the methodology by both the aforementioned techniques cannot be used to populate the complete ontology. (Singh and Srivastava, 2011b) give a deep insight into the various kinds of artifacts one can find in the real world. They also give a brief introduction to extract these into an ontology. None of the ontologies created in the PurposeNet architecture have been created completely using automatic methods.

One key thing to notice here is that both the domains chosen deal with abstract artifacts. When we talk of the MMTS timing domain, we talk about the artifact *journey* and MMTS train is just a medium to complete that journey, whereas when considering the recipe domain, we talk about an abstract artifact (a *knowledge* which can aid us in preparation of a physical artifact (Recipe is comparable to knowledge as mentioned by Singh and Srivastava (2011b)) . PurposeNet till now has only been populated for physical artifacts (vehicle and hotel (Rallapalli and Paul, 2012) artifacts).

Recently, a very active interest can be seen in the community for complex domains(Kambhatla et al., 2012). A very early work dealing with train-scheduling expert system has been reported

D S Sharma, R Sangal and J D Pawar. Proc. of the 11th Intl. Conference on Natural Language Processing, pages 126–132,
Goa, India. December 2014. ©2014 NLP Association of India (NLPAI)

in (Chang, 1988). They have made the system for
engineers to construct and schedule an AC elec-
trified railways. Chinese train ontology has been
created using UML has been presented in (Hu et
al., 2006).

Works of Kalem and Turhan (2005) try to explain how to create a recipe ontology in detail.
The difference however is that it captures only the
description part of the recipe and for the actual
recipe, redirects user to the url. It doesn't capture the series of steps and intermediates required
for a recipe. Our work is much influenced by ColibriCook (DeMiguel et al., 2008). Ontology defined in TAAABLE is also nearly the same as PurposeNet recipe ontology created by us (Badra et
al., 2008).

1.2 PuporseNet Architecture

The architecture of PurposeNet is described in details in (Sangal et al., 2013). There a few major
points we would like to emphasize here:

- All artifacts exist for a purpose, and all its components
  aid the artifact to satisfy its purpose.

- PurposeNet defines 3 kinds of relations, namely decrip-
  tor features, action features and action frames and relationships with other artifacts. They have listed a series
  of relations below these 3 categories. With a change of
  domain, one can change these listed relations, but one
  cannot change the 3 basic relations. PurposeNet by default allows:

  - 8 **artifact-artifact relation**
  - 25 **descriptor properties**
  - 3 **action features** (4 including maintenance)

  which totals to 37 relations.

- Similar is the claim for action frame. Precondition,
  subaction, outcome and semantic roles are enough to
  complete an action frame. Although one can increase
  the number of semantic roles according to a domain.
  PurposeNet by default allows:

  - 4 **action frames** (7 in nested)
  - 21 **semantic relations**

  which totals to 28 relations. Total default PurposeNet
  relations equals to 65 relations.

- Descriptor features can also be changed according to
  the domain.

Sanctity of these rules must be maintained, if
one wants to create a PurposeNet ontology. For
various domains, one needs to have a substantial
amount of data to understand all the possible variations.

1.3 Ontology reasoning

We emphasize on using OWL because firstly, it is
a W3C standard for ontologies and secondly, ontologies can help in inferencing of facts. Even a
proposition expressed in FOL (first order logic)
is more expressible than its sibling in relational
database. OWL supports description logic while
is a higher logic than FOL.

2 MMTS domain

Figure 1 shows the structure of the MMTS ontology.

2.1 Entities, Actions and Relations

In this section we explain the additional features
provided to the Ontology which contribute to the
real richness of the Ontology.

2.1.1 Entities

The prime entities featuring in the ontology include:

1. Day
2. Money
3. Coach
4. Place
   - Station
   - Non-Station
5. Route
6. Ticket
7. Train
   - AllDayTrain
   - AllPublicTrain
   - LadiesTrain
   - SundayTrain

2.1.2 Actions

1. Buy
2. Travel
3. StopAtStation

2.1.3 Relations

We had to include certain relations in the
MMTS ontology as PurposeNet architecture
doesn't completely clarify its support on timing,
duration, routes or stoppages. Apart from the relations declared by PurposeNet, we had to include:

1. atStation: to mark the stop of a train at a station.

2. comprisesOf (inverse belongsTo): to mark what a route
   comprises of.

3. forRoute: to mark the stop is for what route.

4. hasStopNo (inverse ofTrain): to mark the stops of a
   train.

---

[1]sr means semantic roles

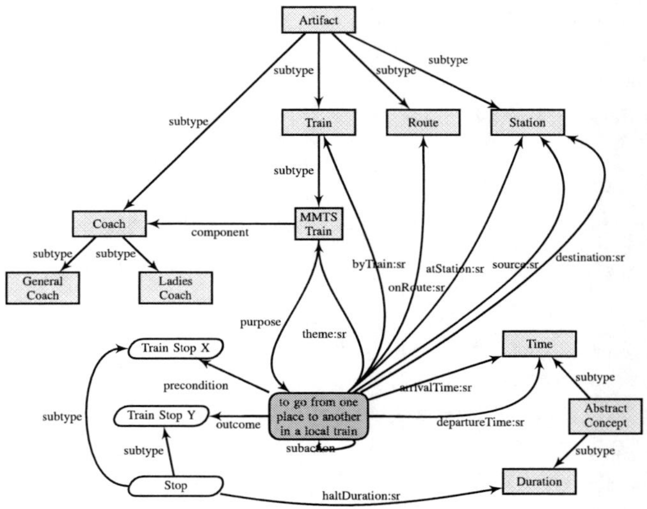

Figure 1: Figure shows the ontological structure of the MMTS train domain. Solid green boxes represent entities, blue rounded boxes represent actions and white trapeziums represent states. The upper ontology has not been shown for diagram clarity. [1]

5. isTravelledBy (inverse travelsThrough): to mark the trains which travel through a route.

6. reverseRouteOf (symmetric): to mark the route which is reverse of a route.

7. runs: to mark the days on which a train runs.

8. arrivesOn: to mark the arrival time of a train at a station.

9. departsAt: to mark the departure time of a train from a station.

10. stationHaltTime: to mark the halt time of a train at a station.

2.2 Algorithm for ontology population

The ontology population was primarily divided into 2 sections. One of them dealt with the train and stop information (Section 2.2.1), while ther other with the actions part of the ontology (Section 2.2.2).

2.2.1 Train Ontology

We start with the data from the MMTS website[2] and then apply the algorithm 1 for data population.

2.2.2 Action Ontology

The major actions in the MMTS train domain include:

1. Pick a route.

2. For all the trains that run in the route start.

3. Start from the train with the earliest starting time.

4. Start from the first stop and proceed towards the last and for each stop enter the following information.

- route
- train number
- station
- departing time

Algorithm 1: Algorithm shows the steps to be followed to populate MMTS ontology using MMTS online data.

1. buying a ticket
2. boarding a train at a stop
3. travelleing
4. alighting a train at another stop

They are basic actions and the information about them cannot be found in texts. We have tried to break these actions into more basic ones. eg. for buying a ticket, one has to pay money and receive ticket.

3 Recipe domain

We started populating this ontology from scratch, manually. All the information was filled in the PurposeNet framework. One of the interesting observations was that the recipe domain contained a lot of states which cannot be named. We called

---

[2]http://www.mmtstraintimings.in/

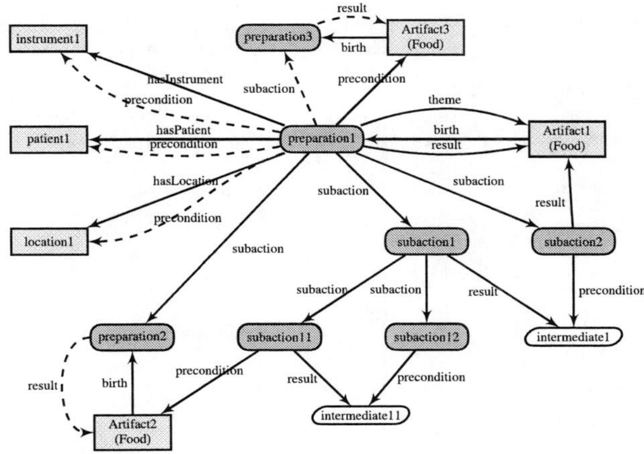

Figure 2: Figure shows the ontological structure of the recipe domain. Solid green boxes represent entities, blue rounded boxes represent actions and white trapeziums represent states. Dashed arrows represent the inferred relations.

them intermediates in our ontology. All the four action features including preconditions, subactions, semantic roles and outcomes, played a major roles in describing the ontological details. Location and themes were the two most prominent semantic roles in the action ontology. To describe an action or state, theme stated the artifacts. Figure 2 shows the structure of the recipe ontology.

3.1 Entities, Actions and Relations

3.1.1 Entities

A well structured list of Entities including the major classes of food so that hierarchy can later be explited has been included in the ontology. The upper hierarchy is enlisted below.

1. Natural artifacts
   - Spices
   - Vegetables

2. Physical artifacts
   - Food Artifact
     - Item Food Artifact
     - Prepared Food Artifact
     - Processed Food Artifact
   - Intermediate Artifact
   - Kitchen Artifact

3.1.2 Actions

This is a long list of basic actions which are used in the cooking domain. We have tried to build a hierarchy of actions here. Some part of this work is onfluenced by the work of Rajan (2013). The upper action hierarchy include:

1. Add
   - Apply
   - Fill
   - Sprinkle

2. Cool

3. Heat
   - Boil
   - Fry
   - Roast

4. Make
   - Prepare

5. Mix

   - Knead

6. Place
   - Cover

7. Press

8. Roll

9. Separate
   - Break
   - Chop
     - Grate
   - Cut
   - Mash
   - Peel
   - Scoop

3.1.3 Relations

No special relation has been added as the corePurposeNet architecture is sufficient for recipe ontology.

3.2 Algorithm for ontology population

For every dish, we seached for a legitimate recipe on the web and followed the algorithm 2.

3.3 Post-processing

Although the data populated by following algorithm 2 was quite correct, we identified 2 major areas where post processing was required.

1. We did not extract the components/ingredients required for making a dish. Section 3.3.1 talks about the solution of this problem.

2. There was a need for structuring the ontology. The identification of problem is discussed in section 3.3.2

- Continue from the first sentence. All the sentences will have an action.

- If the action is already existant, link it.

- else, create the action and find the thematic roles.

- Mostly, there will be 4 thematic roles, which include:

  - location
  - instrument
  - patient
  - theme

  There is a posibility of precondition also.

- if these are existing (or are raw material), add them, or create an entry.

- for the outcome, if it is existing add it, else
  - if the outcome is a named entity, i.e. it can be called something, create the named entity,
  - else, create an intermediate.

Algorithm 2: Algorithm shows the steps to populate recipe ontology using web recipes.

while section 3.3.3 talks about the solution of this problem.

3.3.1 Extracting raw materials and intermediates for a recipe

To identify the components of a dish, one information was to identify the preconditions. But as we have already seen, the subactions as well as the conditions can be recursive and so the identification of all the raw materials and intermediates becomes somewhat difficult[3]. To ease it, we have put in 4 set of rules in the ontology itself which are as follows:

1. If the birth of an artifact needs another as precondition, then the former requires latter.

2. Defines requires as a transitive entity.

3. If the requirement is a food artifact, then the food artifact is a component.

4. If the requirement is a natural thing, then the natural thing is a component.

3.3.2 Need for extraction of hierarchy

Although the process was quite straightforward, on studying recipes from various websites, we got a different picture altogether.

- Same subdish is prepared by Multiple dishes

  (aloo gobhi paratha: 1.5 cups mashed potatoes)

  (aloo paratha: 2 1/2 cups boiled , peeled and mashed potatoes)

---

[3]We have not differenciated core-coponents from other components as of now.

- different recipe documents of the same recipe have different text representation. In our ontology, we try to capture a generic version of those variation of dishes.

  (aloo paratha source 1: hierarchy)

  (aloo paratha source 2: flat)

- all the recipe documents consider different individuals as their starting point (ingredients)

  (3 medium potatoes or aloo)

  (2 1/2 cups boiled , peeled and mashed potatoes)

- some recipe documents give chunked information

  - for clarity
    (Masala dosa: Preparing the Dosa Batter, Preparing the potato filling-sabzi, Preparing the Masala Dosa)
  - sometimes chronology plays a part of subgrouping sub part of the dishes
    (Preparing the Dosa Batter: Cover and let the batter ferment for 8-9 hours.)

- similar/trivial activities are given together in recipe documents

  (chop the aloo and add all the spice powders, green chilies, salt.)

  (add the mashed potatoes. add chopped green chilies. mix well and keep aside.)

After the manual population of the PurposeNet data with the recipe information step by step, we got a rough data prepared. The next task at hand was to cluster the similar elements in an ontology so that the ontology can be properly structured. Section 3.3.3 explains how we post-process the ontology semi-automatically to create a structured ontology.

3.3.3 Extracting hierarchy of action in recipe domain

To begin with the experiments, we populated the ontology with our previous algorithm. We then apply agglomerative hierarchical clustering on this data to identify the sub-clusters/subgraphs which are very close. As the hierarchical clustering requires a metric, we chose the metrics as the frequency of edges required for making all the dishes (equations 1, 2 and 3).

$$FrequencySet(FS) = \nu(e),$$
$$\forall e \in all\_edges\_in\_the\_graph \quad (1)$$

$$max(FS) = argmax(FS) \quad (2)$$

$$merge(FS(i)), \forall n(i) = k,$$
$$where\ max(FS) \geq k \geq threshold \quad (3)$$

To identify the clusters in the recipes, we identified the edges which were most common in the various recipes. We fixed a certain threshhold and being above that threshhold the edges were selected. A subgraph of the selected edges is created and the outgoing edge of this subgraph is declared as the output of the subgraph. A subaction consisting all the actions and relations of tbis subgraph is entered into the ontology. The actions for which these subactions were a subaction is replaced with a higher subaction.

An example: Suppose we enter 5 dishes, 3 of which need a peeled boiled potato. So when we traverse the graph once to enquire the edges being traversed, we find the edges of boiling a potato, getting boiled potato as an outcome, peeling a potato and the outcome boiled peeled potato thrice. Now we create a subgraph of these 4 edges, with boiled peeled potato as outcome. We club these 4 into a single cluster.

Figure 3 represents the process of clubbing subactions in which Figure 3a shows 3 dishes all of which contain boiled and peeled potato either as a precondition or as a result of some subactions. Figure 3b shows the result of running the algorithm after which a new action *prepare peeled boiled potato* is introduced which has the subaction as boil potato and peel potato.

3.3.4 Algorithm

Algorithm 3 is used for extracting the subgraphs.

4   QA Application

To test the effectiveness of the MMTS ontology, we created a dummy QA application which answers questions related to the MMTS train timings. The input was html templates, which contained 20 different types of questions and these were internally mapped to sparql (PrudHommeaux et al., 2008) queries. The pellet reasoner was running over the MMTS ontology. The system is compared with a similar system created in mysql (RDBMS). Table 1 shows the results of the two system for same questions.

The results clearly show that by using an ontology one can answer a lot more questions by just inferring than answering by the information already provided. Traversal is not a very positive step, but at least one does not need to provide an extra information for the same. 14 questions out of 20 are

- For all the food artifacts, choose their preparation actions and for all such preparations, do the following,
    - Create a graph around the preparations.
    - create an indices of edges with the preparation.
    - While creating the dag keep an account of all the edges traversed.
    - Keep on incrimenting the edges as and when they are traversed.
- Sort the edges according to the frequency of their occurence.
- Set a threshhold below which the edges will not be considered.
- for all the frequqncies try to form a subgraph.
- The final state(s) will be taken as the outlet.
- Check in the index and in all the dishes where any one of the considered edges occurs, replace the subactions enlisted which occur in subgraph with a precondition of the final state in the obtained in the above step.

Algorithm 3: Algorithm shows the steps to post process the recipe domain ontology.

Table 1: Table shows the number of questions answered by both the system categorized by the type of answer required. The numbers in red indicate the strenghth of an ontology

Category	DB	OWL
Inference based answering	8	14
Information based answering	6	2
Traversal based answering	5	4
N.A.	1	0
Total	**20**	**20**

inference based and 4 are traversal based for an ontology. Only information for 2 questions needed to be specifically provided.

5   Summary

In this paper, we have explained the various data preparation techniques used in this work. A detailed explaination of the MMTS and recipe domain that follow with the structural changes and entity, action and relations is introduced. The methodology of creation was totally different for the two domains emphasizing on the point that a generic framework working for all domains and all resource types cannot be prepared. A small application for QA is also developed and comparison gives Ontology a clear upper hand over RDBMS system.

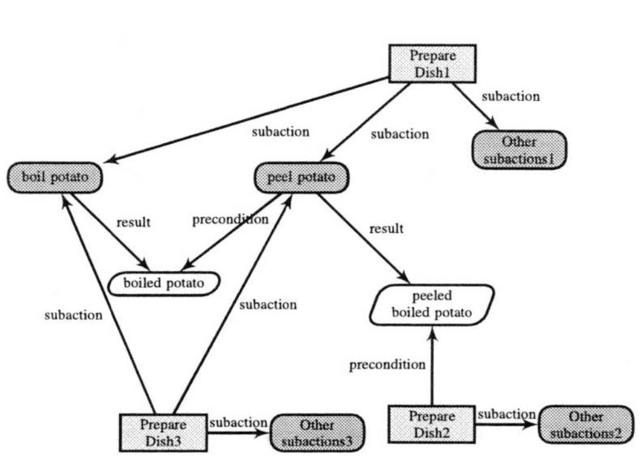

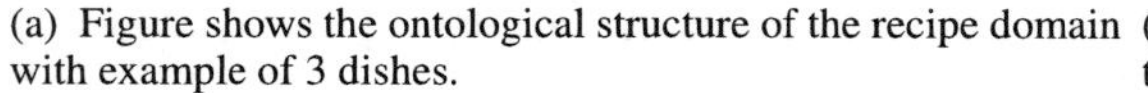

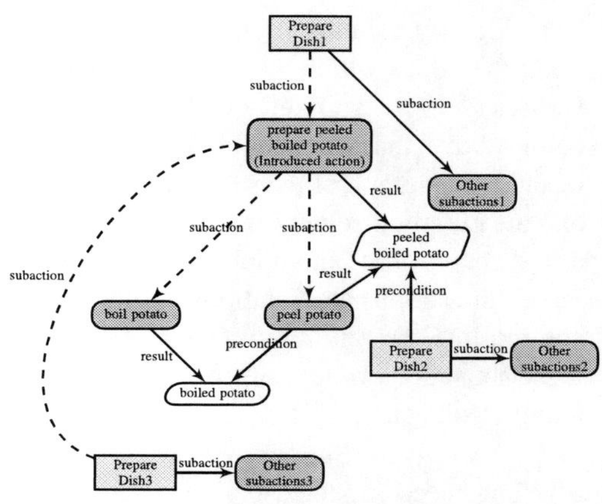

(a) Figure shows the ontological structure of the recipe domain with example of 3 dishes.

(b) Figure shows the change in the ontological structure after the grouping of identical actions. *boil potato* and *peel potato* form a cluster and *prepare boiled peeled potato* takes its place wherever possible. They become a subaction of the newly introduced action.

Figure 3: Figure shows the how the most frequently occuring action is combined to give a new information keeping the original information intact. Solid green boxes represent entities, rounded blue boxes represent actions and white trapeziums represent states. Dashed lines represent inferd infoormation.

References

Fadi Badra, Rokia Bendaoud, Rim Bentebibel, Pierre-Antoine Champin, Julien Cojan, Amélie Cordier, Sylvie Després, Stéphanie Jean-Daubias, Jean Lieber, Thomas Meilender, et al. 2008. Taaable: Text mining, ontology engineering, and hierarchical classification for textual case-based cooking. In *9th European Conference on Case-Based Reasoning-ECCBR 2008, Workshop Proceedings*.

C Chang. 1988. Development of a train-scheduling expert system for ac railway electrification. In *Control, 1988. CONTROL 88., International Conference on*, pages 259–264. IET.

Juan DeMiguel, Laura Plaza, and Belén Díaz-Agudo. 2008. Colibricook: A cbr system for ontology-based recipe retrieval and adaptation. In *ECCBR Workshops*, pages 199–208.

Xiao-Hui Hu, Xing-she Zhou, and Jian-Wu Dang. 2006. A designing method of simulation software for chinese train control system based on hybrid software agent model. In *Machine Learning and Cybernetics, 2006 International Conference on*, pages 148–153. IEEE.

Güler Kalem and Çiğdem Turhan. 2005. *Semantic web application: Ontology-driven recipe querying*. Atılım University.

Nanda Kambhatla, Sachindra Joshi, Ganesh Ramakrishnan, Kiran Kate, and Priyanka Agrawal, editors. 2012. *Proceedings of the Workshop on Question Answering for Complex Domains*. The COLING 2012 Organizing Committee, Mumbai, India, December.

P. Kiran Mayee, R Sangal, and S Paul. 2010a. Automatic extraction and incorporation of purpose data into purposenet. In *Computer Engineering and Technology (ICCET), 2010 2nd International Conference on*, volume 6, pages V6–154. IEEE.

P. Kiran Mayee, Rajeev Sangal, and Soma Paul. 2010b. Neural networks based detection of purpose data in text. In *ICT*, pages 606–609.

Eric PrudHommeaux, Andy Seaborne, et al. 2008. Sparql query language for rdf. *W3C recommendation*, 15.

Kavitha Rajan. 2013. Understanding verbs based on overlapping verbs senses. *ACL 2013*, page 59.

Sruti Rallapalli and Soma Paul. 2012. Evaluating scope for interpreting nominal compounds using ontology.

Rajeev Sangal, Soma Paul, and P Kiran Mayee. 2013. Purposenet: A knowledge base organized around purpose. In *Conceptual Structures for STEM Research and Education*, pages 29–30. Springer.

Chandni Singh and Rishabh Srivastava. 2011a. *PurposeNet: Knowledge Representation and Extraction*. PDPM-Indian Institute of Information Technology Design and Manufacturing Jabalpur.

Chandni Singh and Rishabh Srivastava. 2011b. Study and population of artifacts. *International Journal of Computer Technology and Electronics Engineering*, (NCETCSIT-Dec'2011):1–5.

Bundeli Folk-Song Genre Classification with kNN and SVM

Ayushi Pandey
Dept. of Computational Linguistics
The EFL University
ayuship.09@gmail.com

Indranil Dutta
Dept. of Computational Linguistics
The EFL University
indranil@efluniversity.ac.in

Abstract

While large data dependent techniques have made advances in between-genre classification, the identification of sub-types within a genre has largely been overlooked. In this paper, we approach automatic classification of within-genre Bundeli folk music into its subgenres; Gaari, Rai and Phag. Bundeli, which is a dominant dialect spoken in a large belt of Uttar Pradesh and Madhya Pradesh has a rich resource of folk songs and an attendant folk tradition. First, we successfully demonstrate that a set of common stopwords in Bundeli can be used to perform broad genre classification between standard Bundeli text (newspaper corpus) and lyrics. We then establish the problem of structural and lexical similarity in within-genre classification using n-grams. Finally, we classify the lyrics data into the three genres using popular machine-learning classifiers: Support Vector Machine (SVM) and kNN classifiers achieving 91.3% and 85% and accuracy respectively. We also use a Naïve Bayes classifier which returns an accuracy of 75%. Our results underscore the need to extend popular classification techniques to sparse and small corpora, so as to perform hitherto neglected within genre classification and also exhibit that well known classifiers can also be employed in classifying 'small' data.

1 Introduction

Bundeli is spoken in regions of Madhya Pradesh and Uttar Pradesh, in a region known as Bundelk-

hand, which encompasses several administrative districts in India. While the 2001 census identifies 3,070,000 Bundeli speakers, Ethnologue estimates 20,000,000 speakers[1]. Inspite of the large population, Bundeli, often considered a dialect of Western Hindi, would be considered an under-resourced language because of the lack of textual and literary resources that are available. Bundelkhand, however, is home to a rich tradition of lyrical styles and genres that are both performative and poetic. In addition to the major genres; Gaaris, Rais and Phags, several other genres can be found in this region, including Sora, Hori, and Limtera. With the exception of several Phags[2], Bundeli is a resource poor language, in that there are no available sources of textual material. Using a bag-of-words technique on the lyrics corpus, and Term Frequency-Inverse Document Frequency *tfidf* scores, we report on the performance of a k-Nearest Neighbour (kNN) classifier. We demonstrate that a 10-fold kNN cross validation exhibits an accuracy of nearly 85% in classifying within the Bundeli folk genres when a k of 2 neighbours is used. Using the SVM classification, we achieve an accuracy of over 90%. Following a brief description of related classification techniques applied to song genre classification within Indian and Western music, in general, in section 2 below, we provide a detailed account of methods used for creating news and folk song lyrics corpora in section 3. Following that, in section 4, we emphasize the need to use commonly-removed stopwords towards affecting a classification between news and song lyrics corpora. In this section, we also report on the feasibility of using probability density functions on word level

---

[1] http://www.ethnologue.com/language/bns
[2] http://www.kavitakosh.org

D S Sharma, R Sangal and J D Pawar. Proc. of the 11th Intl. Conference on Natural Language Processing, pages 133–138,
Goa, India. December 2014. ©2014 NLP Association of India (NLPAI)

n-grams to better understand lexical and structural similarity within-genres. In section 5, we present detailed classification analyses on the song lyrics corpus and show the extent of accuracy that can be achieved when popular machine learning techniques are employed to classify within folk genres, that exhibit a great deal of lexical and structural overlap. In Section 6, we present the conclusions our analysis and also future directions for further research.

2 Related Work

Song genre classification as one of the primary tasks of music information retrieval, has been approached from analysis and classification of audio signal features (Kini et al., 2011; Jothilakshmi and Kathiresan, 2012; Tzanetakis and Cook, 2002); retrieval of lyrics based features (Howard et al., 2011; Mayer et al., 2008) and approaches which use both audio and lyrics based features for genre classification (Mayer and Rauber, 2011; Neumayer and Rauber, 2007). Within the Western context, both popular, classical, and folk music genres have been classifed using common machine learning algorithms. The techniques used for classification include both stochastic and probabilistic methods; Hidden Markov Models (Chai and Vercoe, 2001), Machine-learning etc. However, within the Indian context most all work on song genre classification has been restricted to audio feature vector extraction and classification. More precisely, various classification techniques such as Gaussian Mixture Models (GMM), k-nearest neighbour (kNN) classifiers and Support Vector Machine classifiers (SVM) have been employed to classify between Hindustani, Carnatic, Ghazal, Folk and Indian Western genres (Kini et al., 2011) and north Indian devotional music (Jothilakshmi and Kathiresan, 2012). The only instance of lyrics based classification has been explored in the context of Bollywood music in an effort to identify specific features of Bollywood song lyrics using Complex Networks (Behl and Choudhury, 2011). However, classification of folk genres has not received any attention so far. In this paper, we propose a two-fold approach, first, we suggest that classification between broad text genres such as news and songs can be successfully accomplished using common stopwords in Bundeli. And second, we also demonstrate that big data based machine learning approaches could

be successfully used to classify, relatively small corpus of Bundeli folk songs into specific genres; namely, Gaari, Rai and Phag.

3 Corpus Creation

The three genres Gaari, Phag and Rai were chosen because they are commercially available in the form of analog audio tapes. These audio tapes were digitized and converted to MP3 format for transcription and future analyses. As far as stylistic register go, gaaris are marriage songs that are sung in repeated choruses. The chorus is periodically repeated after each verse. Phags are lyrical poems, showing rich lexical diversity and rhythmic meter. Rais are dance songs, sung to the beat of the increasing speed of the *Dholak* (local percussion instrument). In Rais, we see the usage of repeated lines more than any other genre. In Gaaris and Rais, a significant level of semantic overlap can be predicted. Both use simple, conversational terms, and owing to their content being repeated, they pose a challenge for classification. These patterns can be evinced from repetitive choruses as in Figure 1, below.

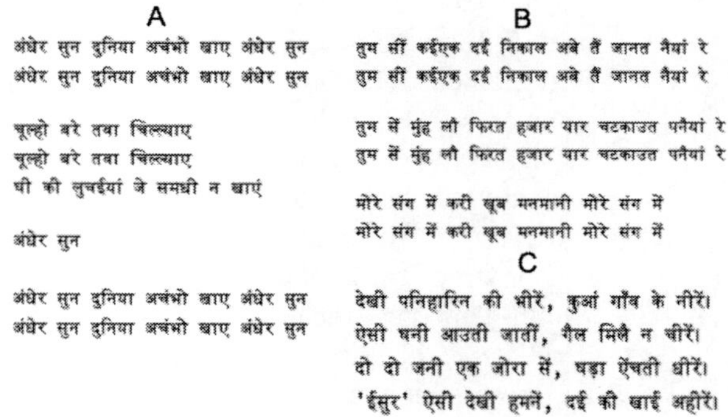

Figure 1: Panel A depicts Gaari with repeated chorus. Panel B shows Rais with repeated lines. Panel C shows the lyrical form of the Phag

Therefore, within-genre classification remains a problem at the textual level because there is significant lexical overlap between Gaaris and Rais.

3.1 Song Corpus

The songs come from various sources. Our first source was a collection from an oral tradition of singing from regions near Sagar, Madhya Pradesh. Online videos and audio cassestes from a Jhansi based casette company, Kanhaiya Casette, became our second source. Phags were mined from a web resource for poetry and prose which contains collections of the famous Bundeli poet Isuri [3]. Isuri's phags, however, are also available in a few textbooks on Bundeli folk culture. The lyrics were orthographically transcribed by listening to the song files in MP3 format in Devanagari. Owing to poor audio quality of the songs, they required a native Bundeli speaker for transcription, the first author being one. Orthographic normalisation was maintained for words that used non-contrastive phonemic or morphological features. For example, the function word "se" and "sein" meaning "from" was normalised to "sein". Similarly for "unhonein" and "unne", meaning third person ergative was normalised to "unne". Where necessary, similar normalization procedures were used to homogenize orthographic variation. Since there was no available list of stopwords, we adopted the corresponding stoplist from Hindi. We narrowed the scope of the exhaustive stopword list by selecting only the most frequent stopwords occurring in songs.

3.2 News corpus

Before analysing the songs within themselves, we needed to establish a differentiation between a generalised corpus and a song corpus. The only available online resource was the publication of a Delhi-based region specific newspaper[4]. Although the newspaper was published in Bundeli, there was no normalisation of dialectal variation. The articles featuring from Mahoba region alone were the ones that could be employed for comparison with our song corpus. This website was not properly designed using standardised web-designing techniques, and automatic web-scraping techniques. So the data was hand-mined by copy-pasting the relevant region-specific articles. Details of the song and news corpora are presented in Table 1. While 98 news articles formed the news corpus, the song corpus consisted of 37, 39 and 40 Gaaris, Rais, and Phags, respectively.

4 News and Song Corpus Classification

Most common text classification methods, including music genre classification, begin by removing common stopwords derived from a generalized corpus. Token frequencies of a set of 7 common stopwords was used for the purpose of

[3]http://www.kavitakosh.org
[4]http://www.khabarlahariya.org/?cat=64

Type of text	Number
News Articles	98
Gaaris (G)	37
Rais (R)	39
Phags (P)	40
Total songs (G+R+P)	116

Table 1: Details of the news and song corpora

this classification. One way ANOVA with Broad Genre as predictor shows a significant main effect F[1,26]=5.438;p<0.05. As the boxplot in Figure 2 shows, stopword token frequencies are significantly higher in news as compared to songs. Thus, stopwords when included in any corpus, can help classify news from songs, even though, more commonly, stopwords are excluded during the preprocessing stages of standard classification-based approaches.

We also performed a test of lexical diversity to classify between the news and song corpus. Using Python scripts we calculated the type-token ratio of the two broad genres. The news corpus had a lexical diversity of 0.028% while the song corpus had nearly half the lexical diversity of the news corpus, i.e., 0.014%.

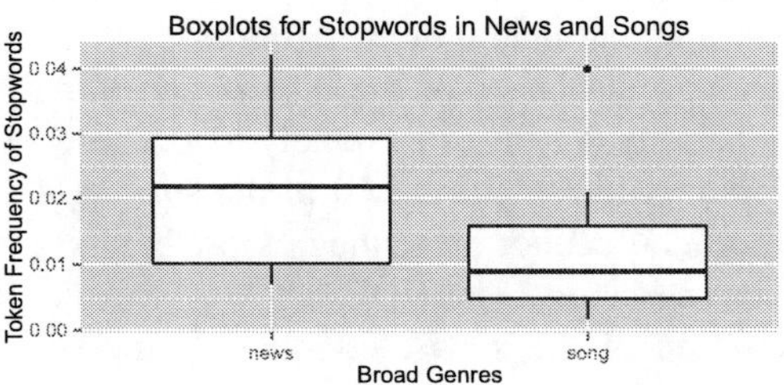

Figure 2: Higher stopword token frequencies in the Bundeli news corpus compared to the songs

4.1 Kernel Density Estimates

Kernel Density Estimates (KDEs) of ngram terms are generated using Equation 1 below. KDE is a non-parametric estimate of the probability density function of random variables, in this case the counts of the ngrams. KDEs allow for better inferences about the population, based on a real and finite data sample. KDEs make it possible for us to examine the probability density function of ngrams for the various genres. Based on the

KDEs we make inferences about the possible presence of categorical features in the sample based on smoothed bins and probability density. Equation 1 shows the KD function estimator. In our estimates, we use a normal kernel such that K(x) = ϕ(x), where ϕ is the standard normal density function.

$$\hat{f}_h(x) = \frac{1}{n}\sum_{i=1}^{n} K_h(x - x_i) = \frac{1}{nh}\sum_{i=1}^{n} K\frac{(x - x_i)}{h}$$

(1)

4.2 Structural Description using KDEs

After making a collection of the entire corpus, we employed n-gram methods to examine the structural distribution of the data with respect to the genres. Therefore, using Python scripts, we first generated unigrams, bigrams and trigrams for all the 3 genres. Then, we used R Studio to generate KDEs to identify the n-gram based structural description of Gaaris, Rais and Phags. A frequency range was used such that it captured the most frequent n-gram terms in Gaaris, Rais and Phags.

The figures show a representation of the n-gram structure of the songs. As can be seen in the three figures, unigrams and bigrams show a high degree of overlap between the three genres in the same frequency range. The genres cannot be differentiated using the structural description detailed by the unigrams and bigrams. In the case of trigrams, although the peaks of the distribution differ, the probability density is extremely low. These terms would easily be eliminated in the sparsity calculation and cannot be termed as predictors of the genre-variation. The KDEs show a structural description of the songs, establishing the existing overlap in the three genres.

5 Classification using Machine Learning Techniques

kNN, SVM and Naïve Bayes classifiers were the machine-learning techniques used for the purpose of this classification. The pre-processing techniques included collection and compilation of the corpus made of text files. The corpus was cleaned of stopwords, punctuation marks and white-spaces. The sparsity was set to 85%. A term-document matrix was created from the corpus where each song file is converted to a vector space where term frequency-inverse document frequencies (*tfidf*) are stored. The *tf* (term frequency)

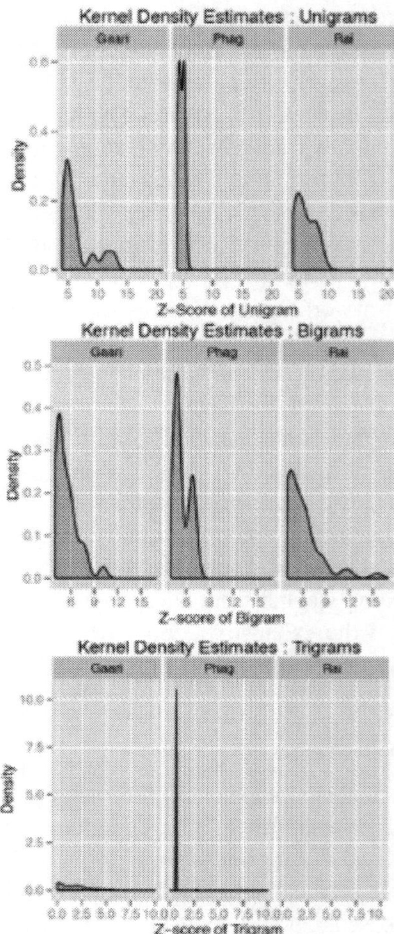

Figure 3: Kernel Density Estimates for Unigrams, Bigrams and Trigrams

scores were calculated with Equation 2 and the *inverse document document frequency (idf)* scores were calculated with equation 3. The product of the tf and idf scores are used to train a classifier with 10-fold cross-validation.

$$tf(t,d) = 0.5 + \frac{0.5 \times f(t,d)}{max\{f(w,d) : w\epsilon d\}}$$

(2)

$$idf(t,D) = log\frac{N}{|d\epsilon D : t\epsilon d|}$$

(3)

The tf-idf scores are a product of the tf and idf scores from equations 3 and 4.

$$tfidf(t,d,D) = tf(t,d) \times idf(t,D)$$

(4)

5.1 kNN Classification

A 10-fold kNN classifier is trained on a term document matrix where each song file is converted to

Test error	CV Mean error	CV Std.error	K
0.2173913	0.1588889	0.03085654	1
0.1739130	0.1600000	0.02772588	2
0.1739130	0.2155556	0.04641319	3
0.1739130	0.2588889	0.04930379	4
0.1739130	0.2733333	0.05612547	5
0.2173913	0.3322222	0.03668163	6
0.2173913	0.3322222	0.05670418	7
0.2173913	0.3322222	0.05772196	8
0.2173913	0.3444444	0.05062030	9
0.2608696	0.3688889	0.03988323	10

Table 2: 10-fold Cross-Validation results for a kNN classifier: Reported Test errors, Cross-Validation (CV) Mean errors, CV Standard errors and the associated k-neighbour

a vector space where term frequency-inverse document frequencies (*tfidf*) are stored.

For training, the rows and columns of the training set and the genre names for just the training set, and for testing, the rows and columns excluding that of genre names is passed to the kNN model. A sparsity of 85% is maintained for the training dataset.

kNN classification

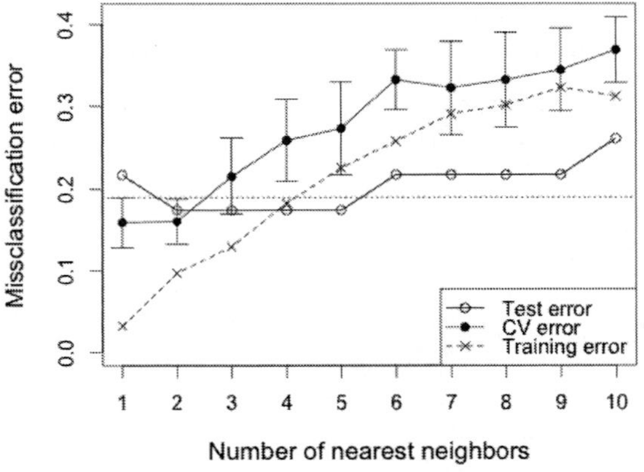

Figure 4: Misclassification errors from kNN training, testing and cross-validation

A first pass kNN classification yields an accuracy of 86.95% when k=2 nearest neighbours are used to measure the distance between the *tfidf* scores with a precision of 0.818 and an F-score of 0.9. A 10-fold cross-validation is then em-

ployed to choose the optimal k-neighbour, results of which are given in Table 2. Based on the lowest test, CV mean and CV Standard errors an optimal K=2 is found to be the best kNN classifier for our dataset. The results of the k=fold cross-validation can be seen in Figure 4.

5.2 SVM Classification

We use the e1071 package in R to perform a SVM classification on the songs dataset (Meyer et al., 2014). The term-document matrix used for kNN classification is passed to the SVM algorithm. We partition the corpus into training and test sets. An 80-20% partition is used for training and test, respectively. Thus, the training dataset contains 93 songs, and the test dataset has 23 songs. The training data contains the genre-labels but the test dataset does not. When a 5-fold cross-validated SVM is trained, the SVM performs classification with a diagonal accuracy of 91.3% and kappa accuracy of 85.7%. Table 3 shows the confusion matrix as predicted by the SVM Classifier.

	True		
Predictions	Gaari	Rai	Phag
Gaari	11	2	0
Rai	0	3	0
Phag	0	0	7

Table 3: True positives and false positives for Naïve Bayes Classification

5.3 Naïve Bayes Classification

We use the e1071 package in R to perform a Naïve Bayes classification on the songs dataset (Meyer et al., 2014). The term-document matrix used for kNN classification is passed to the Naïve Bayes algorithm. We partition the corpus into training and test sets. An 80-20% partition is used for training and test, respectively. Thus, the training dataset contains 93 songs, and the test dataset has 23 songs. The training data contains the genre-labels but the test dataset does not. When trained, the Naïve Bayes performs classification with a diagonal accuracy of 78.2% and kappa accuracy of 68.4%. Table 4 shows the confusion matrix as predicted by the Naïve Bayes Classifier.

6 Conclusions and Further Research

In this paper, we explored both statistical and machine-learning techniques to perform lyrics-

	True		
Predictions	Gaari	Rai	Phag
Gaari	6	0	0
Rai	5	5	0
Phag	0	0	7

Table 4: True positives and false positives for Naïve Bayes Classification

based classification within the genres of Bundeli folk music. Using different sources, we created a corpus of 116 Bundeli folk songs to perform classification. To separate lyrics from standard Bundeli texts, we performed a broad-genre classification using stopwords and lexical diversity measures. Finally, we extended existing machine-learning techniques to successfully classify the three genres. Our findings report that popular methods of classification that are employed on 'big data' can be used to perform within-genre classification. Our results indicate that the SVM and kNN Classifiers perform better than Naïve Bayes classifier.

The present research can be extended to classify more genres in Bundeli folk-music. The models can be further expanded to include genre-classification from other dialects of Western Hindi like Awadhi, Bagheli and Braj. The lyrics-based approach can be combined with an audio-feature vector analysis to build a multi-modal classfication system.

Acknowledgements

We are deeply thankful and appreciative of three anonymous reviewers for providing us with comments and suggestions that helped us better formulate our research initiative and reposition our efforts to apply 'big data' machine learning techniques to our 'small data' classification problem.

References

Aseem Behl and Monojit Choudhury. 2011. A corpus linguistic study of bollywood song lyrics in the framework of complex network theory. In *International Conference on Natural Language Processing*. Macmillan Publishers, India.

Wei Chai and Barry Vercoe. 2001. Folk music classification using hidden markov models. In *Proc. of International Conference on Artificial Intelligence*.

Sam Howard, Carlos N. Silla Jr., and Colin G. Johnson. 2011. Automatic lyrics-based music genre classification in a multilingual setting. In *Thirteenth Brazilian Symposium on Computer Music*, 31st August–3rd September 2011.

S. Jothilakshmi and N. Kathiresan. 2012. Automatic music genre classification for indian music. In *International Conference on Software and Computer Applications (ICSCA 2012)*.

S. Kini, S. Gulati, and P. Rao. 2011. Automatic genre classification of north indian devotional music. In *Proceedings of the National Conference on Communications (NCC)*, pages 1–5, Jan 2011, Bangalore, India.

Rudolf Mayer and Andreas Rauber. 2011. Music genre classification by ensembles of audio and lyrics features. In *Proceedings of the 12th International Society for Music Information Retrieval Conference*, pages 675–680, Miami (Florida), USA, October 24-28. http://ismir2011.ismir.net/papers/PS6-4.pdf.

Rudolf Mayer, Robert Neumayer, and Andreas Rauber. 2008. Rhyme and style features for musical genre classification by song lyrics. In *In Proceedings of the 9th International Conference on Music Information Retrieval (ISMIR'08*.

David Meyer, Evgenia Dimitriadou, Kurt Hornik, Andreas Weingessel, and Friedrich Leisch, 2014. *e1071: Misc Functions of the Department of Statistics (e1071), TU Wien.* R package version 1.6-3.

Robert Neumayer and Andreas Rauber. 2007. Integration of text and audio features for genre classification in music information retrieval (accepted for publication. In *Proceedings of the 29th European Conference on Information Retrieval (ECIR'07*, pages 724–727.

G. Tzanetakis and P. Cook. 2002. Musical genre classification of audio signals. *Speech and Audio Processing, IEEE Transactions on*, 10(5):293–302.

Word net based Method for Determining Semantic Sentence Similarity through various Word Senses

Madhuri A. Tayal

Research Scholar, G. H. Raisoni College of Engineering, Nagpur.

Asst. Prof. RCOEM, Nagpur, INDIA.

madhuri.tayal@gmail. com

M. M. Raghuwanshi

Principal, Rajiv Gandhi College of Engineering and Research Nagpur, INDIA.

m_raghuwanshi@rediffmail .com

Latesh Malik

HOD(CSE), G. H. Raisoni College of Engineering, Nagpur, INDIA.

latesh.malik@raisoni .net

Abstract

Semantic similarity is a confidence score that replicates semantic equivalence between the meanings of two sentences. Determining the similarity among sentences is one of the critical tasks which have a wide-ranging impact in recent NLP applications. This paper presents a method for identifying semantic sentence similarity among sentences using semantic relation of word senses across the different synsets using Wordnet for different part of speech of words. This method firstly detects all the semantic relations (hypernym, hyponym, holonym, meronymy etc.) considering the word as a noun and all the sense relations considering word as a verb from Wordnet respectively. Then it uses common senses between the two sets as Noun and Verb, for two input words for the calculation of semantic word similarity score. As sentence is made up of different words, these word similarity scores have been used for calculation of semantic sentence similarity among the sentences. It is difficult to achieve a high precision score because the exact semantic meanings will not be understood simply. However proposed method outperforms in comparison with existing methods. The evaluation is done for sentences using SemEval-12 Task 6 (Test-Gold-Set) with respect to human ratings.

1. Introduction

Now-a-days web is the largest and utmost useful knowledge base for users with bulky amount of information. The additional sources of information are newspapers, magazines, textbooks etc. Web consists of billions of text documents and daily many different documents are added to it. For understanding these types of documents/ texts many applications have been made such as Text Mining, Storytelling, Machine Translation, Deep Question and answering and Text Summarization etc. To develop and understand this kind of applications, there is a requirement of semantic similarity utility.

Various techniques for semantic similarity have been receiving escalating attention since their introduction by (Miller et al. 1997). Researchers have investigated that finding semantic similarity for the sentences is not an easy task as text document may contain complex sentences. Most of these techniques are based on statistics which indirectly use corpus. Some of them use multiple information sources, lexical chains etc. (Jiang et al., 1997; Li et al., 2009). Some of them are based on wordnet (Simpson et al., 2010; Pederson et al., 2004; Leacock et al., 1998; Budanitsky et al., 2006). WordNet is a lexical catalogue which is accessible online, and provides a large source of English lexical items. The proposed approach incorporates the various senses of the words and there relations from Wordnet.

This paper presents a method for identifying semantic sentence similarity among sentences using Wordnet. This method firstly identifies all the sense relations (hypernym, hyponym, holonym, meronymy etc.) considering the word as a noun and all the sense relations considering word as a verb from Wordnet respectively. Then it uses common senses between the two respective sets as Noun and Verb for two input words for the calculation of semantic word similarity score. The similar senses and their respective counts are useful for the calculation of semantic similarity among the words. Then these Word to Word values will be used for the calculation of semantic sentence similarity.

This paper is organized as follows: Section 2 comprises various methods which are available for

D S Sharma, R Sangal and J D Pawar. Proc. of the 11th Intl. Conference on Natural Language Processing, pages 139–145,
Goa, India. December 2014. ©2014 NLP Association of India (NLPAI)

determining Semantic sentence Similarity. Section 3 provides the motivation for this work. Section 4 proposes the method for the calculation of Semantic word similarity and sentence similarity. Section 5 contributes experimental results of proposed approach for identifying the semantic sentence Similarity and comparison with other method. The paper ends with parametric analysis, conclusion and work to be carried out in future.

2. Literature Survey

Based on the various ideas of computing similarity, the semantic similarity could use either the path distance between concepts or the information content of a concept as a quantifying measure (B. Plank et al., 2013; Veal et al., 2013; Simpson et al., 2010; Agirre et al., 2009; Turney et al., 2005; Dolan W. et al., 2004; Jiang et al., 1997;). In certain contexts, the combination of both the path distance and information content based methods has been tried out. Following section describes these measures.

2.1 Path Length based Measures

The similarity measurement between concepts is based on the path distance separating the concepts. In this method, the quantification of similarity is based on the taxonomy or ontology structure. In these taxonomical or ontology structure, it is assumed that major relations that connect different concepts is only is-a type relations. These measures compute similarity in terms of shortest path between the target synsets (group of synonyms) in the taxonomy. The different path length based similarity measures viz. Rada measure (Rada et al., 1989), Hirst Onge measure (Budanitsky and Hirst, 2006), Bulskov measure (Bulskov et al., 2002).

A. Rada Measure (1989):- The semantic distance is calculated by including the number of edges between concepts in the taxonomy. Let C1 and C2 be the two concepts in is-a semantic net. The conceptual Distance among C1 and C2 is specified by

Distance (C1, C2) = Minimum number of edges separating C1 and C2   (1)

B. Budanitsky and Hirst Measure (2006):- Similarity between concepts is described as a path distance between two concepts. The weight of the path linking the concepts C1, and C2 is given by

Weight= c – length (C1, C2) – k * turns (C1, C2)

        (2)

Where c and k are constants, length (C1, C2) is the distance of the shortest acceptable path connecting the synsets C1 and C2 and turns (C1, C2) is the number of changes in direction in the shortest allowable path.

C. Bulskov Measure (2002):- Similarity is based on the concept inclusion is-a relation for atomic and compound concepts of ontology. The quantification of similarity is based on the direction of concept inclusion.

D. Wu and Palmer Similarity Measure (Wu et al., 1998):-Wu and Palmer suggested a new method on semantic representation of verbs and investigated the influence on lexical selection problems in machine translation. Wu and Palmer describe semantic similarity measure amongst concepts C1 and C2 as

$$Sim_{WP}(C_1,C_2)=2\times\frac{N_3}{N_1+N_2+2\times N_3}$$

        (3)

Where N1 is the length given as number of nodes in the path from C1 to C3 which is the minimum collective super concept of C1 and C2 and N2 is the length given in number of nodes on a path from C2 to C3. N3 signifies the global depth of the hierarchy and it serves as the scaling factor. Wu and Palmer describe semantic similarity measure between concepts C1 and C2 as

Dist(C1,C2)=1-Sim(C1,C2)   (4)

(Leacock and Chodorow, 1998; Budanitsky and Hirst, 2006) advised an approach for measuring semantic similarity as the straight path using is-a hierarchy for nouns in the WordNet.

2.2 Information content based measures (corpus)

In the literature, the information content based approaches are also referred to as corpus based approaches or information theoretic based approaches. Some of them are listed here.

A. Resnik Measure (1995)

Similarity depends on the amount of information of two concepts have in common. This shared information is given by the Most Specific Common Abstraction (MSCA) concept that includes both the concepts.

B. Lin Similarity Measure (Lin et al., 1998)
Lin extended the Resnik(1995) method of the material content (Lin et al., 1998). He has defined three intuitions of similarity and the basic qualitative properties of similarity.
C. Jiang and Conrath measure (Jiang et al., 1997)
Semantic distance is derived from the edge-based view of distance. In order to reimburse for the unpredictability of edge distances, Jiang and Conrath weigh each edge by associating probabilities based on corpus data and also consider the link strength of each concept.

2.3 Hybrid approach

Hybrid approach combines the knowledge derived from different sources of information. The major advantage of these approaches is if the knowledge of an information source is insufficient then it may be derived from the alternate information sources. In this Direction, Li (Li et al. 2003) and Zuber and Faltings (Zuber and Faltings 2007) have been contributed. Li et al. overcomes the weakness of Rada edge counting method. Zuber and Faltings computed the similarity between two concepts using ontology structures.

The proposed method is based on Thanh Ngoc Dao, Troy Simpson's method (2010). This method uses Wordnet in background and Wu and Palmer distance measure for identifying sentence similarity. Given two sentences X and Y, indicate m to be length of X, n to be length of Y. The semantic similarity has been calculated as follows.

$$\text{Overall score} = 2 * \text{Match}(X, Y) / |X| + |Y| \qquad (4)$$

This method has following disadvantages.
1. It is likely for two synsets from the same part of speech to have no common sub-sumer. Since all the different top nodes of each part of the speech taxonomy did not joined, a path cannot continuously be found between the two synsets and that provides the incorrect results.
2. Multiple inheritances are allowed in Word Net, some synsets belongs to more than one taxonomy. So, if there is more than one way between two synsets, the direct such path is selected and that can give wrong value of semantic similarity.
3. Even it does not check the semantic similarity amongst positive and negative sentences.

These weaknesses tried to be removed in proposed approach, described in the next section.

3 Motivation for Proposed Work

Finding semantic sentence similarity is a very complex task in literature because, understanding will be done through interpreting the information from the sentence by a human brain. The task of replacing human brain with computer program is a challenging task. Following assumptions were taken into account while finding the similarity between the sentences.
1. Subject-Subject contains Noun/ Pronoun in the sentence. Nouns plays important role in the sentence, According to (Wren and Martin) noun entity is responsible for doing the actions. So Noun of sentence-1 and sentence-2 is important to check, as well as the similarity in between them.
2. Verb-Verb plays important role in the sentence; According to (Wren and Martin) this entity is responsible which actions are taking place in the sentence. So verb of sentence-1 and sentence-2 is important to check, as well as the similarity in between them.
3. Object-Object plays important role in the sentence, According to (Wren and Martin) object entity is responsible on whom the actions will be taken. So object of sentence-1 and sentence-2 is important to check, as well as the similarity in between them.
4. Similarity-To verify weather particular pairs of words are semantically related or not, human brain verifies the fact that for how much ways (Senses) they are identical.

For processing these observations, we have the whole process is structured for two types of sentences, simple and complex. Simple sentence comprises single Verb and complex sentence comprises of more than one verb. Example for simple sentence is "Stack uses arrays". Example for complex sentence is "Data structures arrange the required data properly for any application". Further two pairs (Noun-Noun, Verb-Verb pair) have been taken to find the identical senses wherever they are same using WORDNET. After this, average of mentioned pairs will be considered as a result of sentence similarity. Similarity for Simple and complex sentences is calculated as:
Similarity % (Simple sentence) = Average % [(Word-Similarity-Subject pair of sentence 1 and 2) + (Word-Similarity- Verb pair of sentence 1 and 2) + (Word-Similarity-Object pair of sentence 1 and 2)

Similarity % (Complex sentence) = Average % [(Word-Similarity-Subject pair of sentence 1 and 2) + (Word-Similarity- verb pair of sentence 1 and 2) + (Word-Similarity-Object pair of sentence 1 and 2) + (Word-Similarity-Additional pair of Verb Verb2)….n terms.

Above Presented Logic has been used throughout the procedure mentioned in the next section.

4. Proposed Method for Semantic Similarity between the Sentences

Semantic score is the key value to be used for numerous applications in the arena of Natural Language Processing. Following method is identified for the calculation of semantic similarity for the words and sentences.

4.1 Semantic Similarity for Words

Firstly the semantic similarity between words will be identified because sentence consists of words. The bottommost unit in a WordNet is synset, which indicates a sure meaning of a word. It contains the word, its description, and its synonyms. The exact meaning of one word under one type of POS is called a sense. At this time, all senses of the word (synonyms, hypernym, hyponym, holonym etc.) are utilized for the calculation of sentence similarity. In the wide sense the steps for word similarity are as follows.

Step-1 Find the Noun and Verb senses for the entered word from wordnet.
Step-2 For checking similarity between two words, Counts the noun and Verb senses, using

$$\text{Score} = A \cap B / \text{Min } (A, B) \qquad (5)$$

Consider word1 and word2 for which similarity is to be checked. Word1 having n1 as a count of all senses collected from different synsets through wordnet, considering as a Noun. And v1 as a count of all senses collected from different synsets through wordnet, considering as a Verb. Similarly, n2 and v2 for Word2. The common matches for word-1's and word-2's Noun and Verb senses are 'n' and 'v' respectively.   C is the overall count for the calculation of semantic similarity. The complete steps are as follows.

Word1's senses as (Noun sense/Verb sense) = n1 / v1, Word2's senses as (Noun sense/Verb sense) = n2 / v2, Common Matching word senses (Noun and Verb) among Word1 and Word2= as 'n' (for Noun) and 'v' (for Verb) calculated as n = n1∩n2 and v = v1∩v2. C = Final Similarity count, C1, C2, temporary Similarity counts.

1. If ((n1 ‖ n2 ‖ n) == 0) then C = C1 If (v1 < v2) C1 = v / v1 Else C1 = v / v2
2. If ((v1 ‖ v2 ‖ v) == 0) then C = C1 If (n1 < n2) C1 = n / n1 Else C1 = n / n2
3. Else if (n1<n2) C1 = n / n1 Else C1 = n / n2 If (v1 < v2) C2 = v / v1 else C2 = v / v2
Word Similarity = C = C1+C2

If word1 and word 2 has no noun senses then word similarity will be based on verb senses and vice versa, as indicated in step 1 and 2. Otherwise, it will be a summation of noun and verb senses. All senses of the word (synonym, hypernym, hyponym, holonym etc.) are taken into account while identifying different Verb and Noun senses for the words. If for both words, the noun senses and verb senses identified as nonzero then the summation of matching percentage for noun and Verb is taken into account for the calculation of word similarity.
Example-word similarity: For two words, "stack", "queue", n1=39, n2=77, v1=6, v2=18(counted from all the senses holonym, synonym, hypernym etc. using wordnet.) n=19 (common word senses of n1 and n2), v = 0, since n1 < n2:. C1=n/n1, 19/39=0.48= 0.5(rounding off)

4.2 Semantic similarity for Sentences

Sentence is a collection of words. Once the word to word similarity is known, this count has been used to calculate semantic similarity between the sentences, following steps to be followed for the calculation of sentence similarity.

Step-1 Tag entered two sentences using POS tagger.
Step-2 Identify the word similarity for all combinations of Noun-Noun pairs and Verb-Verb pairs.
Step-3 Calculate the final value of semantic similarity between the sentences by

averaging of all these pair's word similarity score from step-2.

Final Score =Average ($\sum_{i=1}^{n}$ NounScore +$\sum_{i=1}^{n}$ VerbScore).

Semantic similarity= $\sum_{i=1}^{n}$ (Subject, Verb, Object)

Consider, Sentence 1 and 2 for which the similarity is to be checked. Both the sentences get tagged using POS tagger. The Noun-Noun and Verb-Verb pairs will be identified between the sentences. Then there in between word similarity scores has been calculated. The total average of word similarities of all these pairs will be considered as the sentence similarity for two sentences.
Example-sentence similarity: - Consider, two sentences, 1. "Database keeps data.", 2. "Data is important.". N-N pairs are: Database-Data, data-Data. Their respective similarities are 0.3 and 1. Verb-Verb pair is "keeps" and "is" and its similarity is 0.2. So, the average of these three pair=0.5 and it is the sentence similarity for these two sentences. (50% matching). The experimental results for word and sentence similarity are presented in the next section.

5 Performance Evaluation and Comparison with other Methods

The accuracy of word similarity is tested through; Miller & Charles test set is used (Miller et al., 1997). This test set contains 353 word pairs with semantic similarities and their respective human ratings for pairs of words. Table 1 shows the word similarity results for some of the random words given in MC set. For this set, human ratings have been calculated from five language experts, and mean value is taken. Various scores for these pairs with Jiang and Conrath's method (Jiang et al.,1997), Wordnet based method based on Internet and knowledge by (Liu et al.), Wordnet based method by (Simpson et al., 2010), and also human ratings have been compared and presented. It is observed that proposed method's results closely matches with respect to human ratings compared to other methods. The minimum correlation value indicates the words are semantically closely related to human ratings.

MC-set	Jiang and Conrath's Method (1997)	WordNet-based internet knowledge (Liu et al.)	Wordnet-Wu /Palmer	**Proposed method**	Human ratings
car – automobile	0.341	0.347	1	1	0.894
gem – jewel	0.340	0.349	1	1	0.896
journey – voyage	0.306	0.330	0.5	1	0.929
boy – lad	0.289	0.325	0.5	0.6	0.883
asylum – madhouse	0.323	0.318	0.5	0.9	0.887
magician – wizard	0.343	0.344	1	0.8	0.902

Table 1. Semantic Similarity distance for various methods

From Table 1 it is found that the proposed method's results are closer to human ratings. The average semantic difference between proposed method and Wordnet based Simpsons's (Wu and Palmer Distance) method with respect to human ratings for hundred pairs of words of MC set is calculated and shown in Table 2 below.

Methods	Average Correlation for hundred pairs of words from MC set
For Proposed Method with respect to human ratings.	0.29
for Wordnet (Wu-Palmer)[Simpson et al., 2010] based Method with respect to human ratings.	0.34

Table 2. Average Correlation for hundred pairs of Words with respect to human ratings

Table 2 indicates that average difference for hundred pairs of word from MC set for proposed method with respect to human rating is found to be less as compared to Wordnet (Wu-Palmer) method. The motivation to take Wordnet-based (Wu and palmer) method for comparison, because it uses path length as a criteria for counting similarity from Wordnet. And in some cases the results are not precise. This method (Simpson et al., 2010), which uses Wordnet based (Wu-Palmer) distance is found to be challenging in comparison with proposed method and proposed method removes its disadvantages carefully. Comprehensive comparison clearly indicates that proposed method results are accurately similar to the human ratings.

Sentence-Evaluation is done for two hundred sentences from SemEval-12 Task 6 using Microsoft Research Paraphrase corpus i.e. Test-Gold-Set (Eneko Agirre et al., 2012) shown in Table 3. For Evaluation of these samples, two hundred sample sentences were given to five language experts. The mean of similarity score is calculated for the sentence similarities given by these experts. The results are compared and shown in Figure 1.

Methods	Average Correlation for 200 pairs for sentences from set
Proposed Method for SemEval-12 Task 6 Test-Gold-Set, with respect to human ratings	0.164
for Wordnet (Wu-Palmer)(Simpson et al., 2010)based Method with respect to human ratings	0.31

Table 3. Average Correlation for two hundred pairs of Sentences

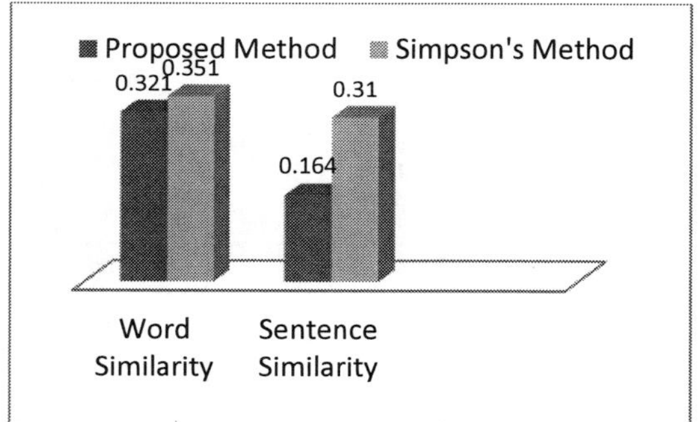

Figure 1. Comparative Chart for Average Correlation for two hundred pairs of words and sentences with respect to Human ratings.

Average correlation for two hundred pairs of sentences from SemEval-12 Task 6 for proposed method with respect to human rating is found to be less as compared to Wordnet based (Simpson et al. 2010) method. It indicates results are closer to human ratings.

Conclusion and Future Work

This paper presents semantic sentence similarity approach for language processing using various word senses of Wordnet, which removes the drawbacks of Simpson's Wordnet based method. This method does not rely on the path distances; between the synsets instead it depends upon all the semantic relation of word senses across the different synsets using Wordnet for different part of speech of words. In addition to this it correctly contributes the semantic similarity amongst positive and negative sentences too. After parametric analysis of Noun-Noun, Verb-Verb and averaging of both pairs, following conclusions have been drawn.

1. Sentence Similarity using averaging of Noun-Noun pair does not give appropriate results and it is less as compared to Verb-Verb pairs with respect to human ratings.
2. Sentence Similarity using averaging of Verb-Verb pair also does not give appropriate results and in comparison the average difference using Verb-Verb pairs is more than Noun-Noun pair with respect to human ratings. It indicates that Noun-Noun pair gives better results and are nearer to human ratings as compared to Verb-Verb pair results.
3. The combined score gives far better results than individual performance of Noun-Noun and Verb-Verb pair. It shows that the combined contribution of Noun and Verb in a sentence while finding the semantic similarity has major role. Because the combination of both, contributes for the meaning of a sentence and therefore it gives better results with respect to human ratings.

Some of the restrictions for this algorithm are as follows. In very few cases, it provides much underestimated results compared to human ratings. Due to which the results for sentence similarity becomes incorrect. This inadequacy is emerged from Wordnet utility which is capable to process available vocabulary. Proposed utility will be used in many NLP applications like question answering, text summarization, etc. and can be applied on Hindi, Marathi etc. languages. The performance can be further improved with more deep analysis of words with diverse mathematical parameters, domain corpora etc.

References

A.Budanitsky and G. Hirst. 2006. *Evaluating WordNet-based measures of semantic distance*, Computation Linguistics. 32(1): pp.13-47.

Barbara Plank, Alessandro Moschitti. 2013. *Embedding Semantic Similarity in Tree Kernels for Domain Adaptation of Relation Extraction*, Proceedings of the 51st Annual Meeting of the Association for Computational Linguistics: 1498–1507.

Claudia Leacock and Martin Chodorow. 1998. *Combining local context and WordNet similarity for word sense identification*. In Fellbaum, C. (ed.), WordNet: An Electronic Lexical Database: 265–283.

D.Lin. 1998. *An information-theoretic definition of similarity*, In Proc. of the Intl Conf. on Mach. Learn: pp: 296–304.

Dolan W, Quirk C. and Brockett C. 2004. *Unsupervised construction of large paraphrase corpora: Exploiting massively parallel new sources*. In Proceedings of the 20th International Conference on Computational Linguistics.

Eneko Agirre, Enrique Alfonseca, Keith Hall, Jana Kravalova, Marius Pasca and Aitor Soroa. 2009. *Study on Similarity and Relatedness Using Distributional and WordNet-based Approaches*. In Proceedings of NAACL '09, 2009 Annual Conference of the North American Chapter of the Association for Computational Linguistics: pp. 19-27.

Eneko Agirre, Daniel Cer, Mona Diab and Gonzalez-Agirre Aitore, 2012. SemEval-2012 task6: A pilot on Semantic textual Similarity. In Proc. 6th International Workshop on Semantic Evaluation (SemEval2012), First joint conference on Lexical and Computational Semantics, Montreal, Canada.

Gang Liu, Ruili Wang, Jeremy buckley, Helen Zhou. *A WordNet-based Semantic Similarity Measure Enhanced by Internet-based Knowledge*.

George A. Miller and Walter. G. Charles.1997. *Contextual correlates of semantic similarity*, Language and Cognitive Processes, 6(1):1-28.

H.Bulskov, R. Knappe, and T. Andreasen. 2002. *on Measuring Similarity for Conceptual Querying*. in T. Andreasen, A. Motro, H. Christiansen, H.L. Larsen (Eds.): Flexible Query Answering Systems, Lecture Notes in Artificial Intelligence 2522: pp. 100-111.

J.Jiang and D.W. Conrath.1997. *Semantic similarity based on corpus, statistics and lexical taxonomy*, In Proc. of the Intl Conf. on Research in Comput. Linguist: pp. 19–33.

P.Resnik. 1995. *Using information content to evaluate semantic similarity*, In Proc. of the 14th Intl Joint Conf. on Artificial Intelligence: pp. 448–453.

Peter Turney. 2005. *Measuring semantic similarity by latent relational analysis*. Proceedings of the 19th International Joint Conference on Artificial Intelligence: 1136-1141.

R.Rada, H. Mili, E. Bicknell, and M. Bletner. 1989. *Development and Application of a Metric on Semantic Nets*, IEEE Trans. Syst. Sci. Cybern, 19(1): pp. 17-30.

Troy Simpson, Thanh Dao. 2010. *Capturing the semantic similarity between two short sentences based on the WordNet dictionary*.

Ted Pederson, Siddarth Patwardhan and Jason Michelizzi. 2004. *WordNet-Similarity- measuring the relatedness of concepts*. In Proceedings of HLT-NAACL'04 Annual Conference of the North American Chapter of the Association for Computational Linguistics: pp. 38-41.

Vincent Schickel-Zuber, Boi Faltings. 2007. A Semantic Similarity Function based on hierarchical Ontologies, IJCAI.

Wren and martin, English grammar and composition. (Book) s. Chand & company ltd.

Yuhua LI, Zuhair A. andar, David McLean. 2003. *An Approach for Measuring Semantic Similarity between Words Using Multiple Information Sources*. IEEE Transactions on Knowledge and Data Engineering, Volume 15, Issue 4: 871-882.

Identification of Karaka relations in an English sentence

Sai Kiran Gorthi, Ashish Palakurthi, Radhika Mamidi, Dipti Misra Sharma
International Institute of Information Technology - Hyderabad
{saikiran.gorthi, ashish.palakurthi}@research.iiit.ac.in
{radhika.mamidi, dipti}@iiit.ac.in

Abstract

In this paper we explain the identification of karaka relations in an English sentence. We explain the genesis of the problem and present two different approaches, rule based and statistical. We briefly describe about rule based and focus more on statistical approach. We process a sentence through various stages and extract features at each stage. We train our data and identify Karaka relations using Support Vector Machines (SVM). We also explain the impact of our work on Natural Language Interfaces for Database systems.

1   Introduction

In any sentence, it is important that the relations between words are expressed properly in order to understand it. There are many widely used relations between words like subject and object relations, agent-patient of thematic relations. These are commonly used relations that we come across. The Computational Paninian Grammar (CPG) framework uses Karakas to express relations between words in a sentence. Karakas are classes with which relations between words in a sentence can be expressed. One of the key features of the karaka relations is that they are verb centric. All the relations are dependent on the main verb of the sentence. The advantage of using Karakas is that they provide proper mapping between verb and its relations using a very small set of tags. By providing a good understanding of the syntactic as well as the semantic relations, they help in resolving ambiguities posed by a sentence.

There are around 24 Karakas in total, but we generally take into consideration only 6 Karakas which are frequently occurring (75%) in most of the sentences. They are karta (k1), karma (k2),

karana (k3),sampradaan (k4), apadaan(k5) and adhikarana (k7). Karta is the doer of the action. It is independent of the other Karakas. Karma is the object of the action or verb. Karana helps in completing action. It acts as an instrument in the completion of the action. The beneficiary of the action is known as sampradana and the source of the action is called apadaan. There are three types of k7 Karakas namely k7t, k7p and k7. k7t denotes the time of action, whereas k7p denotes location of the doer or patient at the time of action. k7 represents location in topic. In the example, John gave the book to Clarke, we have John, who is the doer of the action as karta(k1), bag, which is the object of the action as karma(k2), Clarke, the beneficiary or sampradaan(k4) of the action. Let us take another example, He played cricket yesterday. Here yesterday is k7t. In this way, we can get different relations expressed for different sentences based on the verb.

NLIDB[1] system converts an input natural language query into an SQL query and then gets the answer from respective database by running the query on it. The NLIDB system proposed by (Gupta et al., 2012) requires two stages in the processing of the input query. The first stage is the syntactic stage and the second stage is the semantic stage.

In the syntactic stage, they give the input sentence to Stanford dependency parser. Once they get Stanford dependencies, they map them to karaka relations. These identified karakas are then used in the semantic stage to build semantic frames. This is where our work comes into effect. By identifying karaka relations in an English sentence, we address the issue of identifying karaka relations in the syntactic stage more effectively.

---

[1]Natural Language Interface for Databases

D S Sharma, R Sangal and J D Pawar. Proc. of the 11th Intl. Conference on Natural Language Processing, pages 146–149,
Goa, India. December 2014. ©2014 NLP Association of India (NLPAI)

2   Related work

Significant work happened in the identification of karaka relations in Indian languages. This is the first attempt to work on identifying karaka relations in English. (Bharati et al., 2008) demonstrated on constraint based parsing for free word order languages. (Vaidya et al., 2009) showed that it is possible to apply CPG to English. We propose a statistical method for identifying karaka relations from a given sentence using machine learning.

The remainder of this section is organized as follows. In section 3, we explain our different approaches. In section 4, we discuss about the experiments and results. In section 5, we discuss the impact of our system. In section 6, we conclude and discuss about future work.

3   Approach

3.1   Rule-based approach

The following are the steps we followed for identifying Karaka relations in English using rule based approach:

- As a first step, we analyzed the queries we made for the NLIDB system of our university courses portal.

- We generated the Stanford parse for each query and tried to map each dependency relation to a CPG relation.

- We then generated a rule set to to automate the mapping from Stanford dependencies to CPG relations.

- We developed a preference-based allotment system for the purpose of mapping.

- After parsing each query from the Stanford parse, we take the dependency relations from it and check them from the rules table in column2.

- If we find a relation, we map it to its corresponding CPG label. We continue this process for each Stanford dependency relation.

The overall performance of the system with the method above is 52%. We adopted a statistical approach for better results.

Karaka relation	Stanford dependency relation
k1	nsubj (subject)
k2	dobj (object)
k3	prep_with
k4	prep_to
k5	prep_from
r6	poss
k7	prep_at

Table 1: Basic rules for mapping

4   Statistical approach

4.1   Stage 1 $DataExtraction$

English Dependency Tree bank data is in SSF[2] format. We processed each sentence and extracted all of its relations(child node, parent node, karaka relation).We got 2557 such relations.

4.1.1   Example

4.1.1.1   SSF   Sentence id='2' $1((NP fsaf ='$ $'drel\ ='\ k1\ :\ VG'name\ ='$ $NP'\ 1.1 Bipasha NNP fsname\ ='$ $Bipasha'\ ))2((VG fsaf ='\ 'name\ ='$ $VG'\ 2.1 storms VM fsaf\ ='$ $storm, n, m, p, 3, 0\ 'name\ ='$ $storms'\ \|fsaf ='\ storm, v, m, s, 3, 0\ 'tense ='$ $PRES'\ ))3((PRT fsname ='\ PRT'drel ='$ $pof\_idiom\ :\ VG'\ 3.1 out RP fsaf\ ='$ $out, p, m, s, 3, 0\ 'name\ ='\ out'\ \|fsaf\ ='$ $out, n, m, s, 3, 0\ '\ \|fsaf\ ='$ $out, adj, m, s, 3, 0\ '\ \|fsaf\ ='$ $out, D, m, s, 3, 0\ '\ \|fsaf\ ='$ $out, v, m, s, 3, 0\ '\ |fsaf\ ='$ $out, p, m, s, 3, 0\ '\ ))4((PP fsname\ ='$ $PP'drel ='\ k5\ :\ VG'\ 4.1 of IN fsaf\ ='$ $of, p, m, s, 3, 0\ 'name\ ='$ $of'\ 4.2((NP fsname\ ='$ $NP2'\ 4.2.1 film NN fsaf\ ='$ $film, n, m, s, 3, 0\ 'name ='\ film'\ \|fsaf ='$ $film, v, m, s, 3, 0\ '\ 4.2.2 festival NN fsaf\ ='$ $festival, n, m, s, 3, 0\ 'name\ ='$ $festival'\ 4.2.3 Goa NN fsaf\ ='$ $goa, n, m, s, 3, 0\ 'name\ ='$ $Goa'\ ))))5.SYM fsaf\ ='$ $., punc, n, s, 3, 0\ 'name ='\ .'\ /Sentence$

4.1.1.2   Extracted data

4.1.1.2.1   Sentence   Bipasha storms out of film festival Goa.

---

[2] Shakti Standard Format

4.1.1.2.2   Relations   Bipasha, storms, k1
out of... , storms, pof_idiom
Goa, storms, k5

4.2   Stage 2   *DependencyParse*

Having extracted English sentence for each relation, we got the Stanford Dependency parse structure for the sentence. We then run a parallel check for the same sentence in the karaka relation we extracted in the first step. For a matching relation(child node, parent node), we add the corresponding verb of the relation(from Stanford Dependency Tree) and Stanford Dependency label to the relation and update as (verb of the relation, child node, parent node, Stanford dependency relation, karaka relation). Lets call it feature set.

4.2.1   Examples

storms, Bipasha, storms, nsubj, k1
storms, out of... , storms, prep_out_of, pof_idiom

4.3   Stage 3   *RootVerbExtraction*

We also extract the verb with respect to a relation in the format aforementioned. We take this verb from the feature set and replace with it's root verb using Morphadoner(Burns, 2013).

4.3.1   Example

declared - declare
said - say

4.4   Stage 4   *VerbClassification*

Beth Levin defined classes for verbs(Levin, 2011) based on their action. Each verb could fall into different categories depending on their varied action. Two verbs having the same set(list of different classes they belong to) could be considered as similar verbs. Using this classification, we built a dictionary (key : verb, value :class_number). Using this dictionary, we replace the root verb in the feature set with its class number.

4.4.1   Example

abandon - 1
abate - 3
desert - 1

4.5   Stage 5   *POSTagging*

The first two features we considered are the two words in the relation. The data is so sparse that the frequency of any noun in the entire dataset is frequently 1, very less, when we're dealing with a machine learning application which needs good density in the data point distribution. Since the data is very sparse and considerably less, we replaced the words in the relation with their POS tags. This step ensure that the features are more specific and suitable for training. We anyway get the stanford parse, so it's POS tags could also be used.

4.5.1   Example

Bipasha, storms : nsubj, VG

4.6   Stage 6   *FeatureEnumeration*

The feature set is ready. Now we need to make an appropriate format of the features. Machine Learning methods usually take features as numbers(each feature is a dimension).
From the annotated data, we've the result that these four features map to. We enumerate that too.

4.6.1   Example

Fx is Feature #x, OP is Output for the relation
{F1 F2 F3 F4 OP} is feature set
{685 VBD PRP nsubj k1} correspond to {1 1 1 1 1}.
685 is the verb class. It's given #1 because it comes first in the data. All other instances of 685, VBD, PRP, nsubj, k1 in the data also get the same numbers as these.

4.7   Stage 7   *Cross − Validation*

Using Support Vector Machines(Chang and Lin, 2011) and cross-validation method, we trained and tested on the enumerated feature set.

We experimented by dividing the data into 1:4, 3:7 and picked the best accuracy.

5   Experiments and results

Our training set consists of 18,345 tokens. Our dataset consisted of 1479 sentences. We divided our training sets into 4 equal subsets. One of the subsets is kept as a test set and we use the remaining three subsets for training. We repeated this process for 4 times to get an average result, which is called the 4-fold cross validation. After conducting many experiments and applying the grid-search method, we found that c=8.0 and g=0.125 were the values giving the best results. We experimented on the following kernels:

1. Polynomial Kernel.

2. Radial Basis Function kernel (RBF).

3. Linear Kernel.

Polynomial		RBF		Linear	
d	A	g	A	c	A
1	73.28%	0.125	74.14%	6.0	74.42%
2	74.26%	0.3	73.21%	8.0	74.14%
3	72.54%	0.6	73.23%	10.0	73.83%
4	67.10%	0.8	70.78%	12.0	73.75%

Table 2: Results

In the results table, d is the degree of the polynomial kernel.
g, c are the gamma and cost parameters respectively.

6 Impact

We used our module in the NLIDB system in the syntactic stage. We investigated our results over 213 natural language queries. Our module was found to be effective in improving the accuracy of the 'Stanford dependency to karaka mapping'. The error rate of the syntactic stage decreased by 4.79%, thus improving the overall performance of the NLIDB system.

7 Conclusions and Future work

This paper presents a statistical approach and a brief overview of rule based approach for identification of karaka relations in English. We would go further to explore more features and experiment with larger data-sets. We shall include many semantic features so that mapping becomes more compact.

Acknowledgements

We thank Yeka Jayendra Rakesh for his useful insights and Shalaka Vaidya for helping us with the extraction of data.

References

Akshar Bharati, Samar Husain, Dipti Misra Sharma, and Rajeev Sangal. 2008. A two-stage constraint based dependency parser for free word order languages. In *Proceedings of the COLIPS International Conference on Asian Language Processing 2008 (IALP)*.

Philip R Burns. 2013. Morphadorner v2: A java library for the morphological adornment of english language texts. *Northwestern University, Evanston, IL*.

Chih-Chung Chang and Chih-Jen Lin. 2011. Libsvm: a library for support vector machines. *ACM Transactions on Intelligent Systems and Technology (TIST)*, 2(3):27.

Abhijeet Gupta, Arjun Akula, Deepak Malladi, Puneeth Kukkadapu, Vinay Ainavolu, and Rajeev Sangal. 2012. A novel approach towards building a portable nlidb system using the computational paninian grammar framework. In *Asian Language Processing (IALP), 2012 International Conference on*, pages 93–96. IEEE.

Beth Levin. 2011. Verb classes within and across languages. *Handout, Leipzig, April*.

Ashwini Vaidya, Samar Husain, Prashanth Mannem, and Dipti Misra Sharma. 2009. A karaka based annotation scheme for english. In *Computational Linguistics and Intelligent Text Processing*, pages 41–52. Springer.

A Sentiment Analyzer for Hindi Using Hindi Senti Lexicon

Raksha Sharma, Pushpak Bhattacharyya
Dept. of Computer Science and Engineering
IIT Bombay, Mumbai, India
`{raksha,pb}@cse.iitb.ac.in`

Abstract

Supervised approaches have proved their significance in sentiment analysis task, but they are limited to the languages, which have sufficient amount of annotated corpus. Hindi is a language, which is spoken by 4.70% of the world population, but it lacks a sufficient amount of annotated corpus for natural language processing tasks such as Sentiment Analysis (SA). With the increase in demand and availability of Hindi review websites, an accurate sentiment analyzer for Hindi has become a need.

In this paper, we present a bootstrap approach to extract senti words from Hindi-WordNet. The approach is designed such that it minimizes the extraction of the words with the wrong polarity orientation, which is a crucial task, because a word can have positive and negative senses at the same time. The resultant set of 8061 polar words, we call it Hindi senti lexicon, is used for sentiment analysis in Hindi. We get an average accuracy of 87% for sentiment analysis in the movie and product domain.

1 Introduction

In the real world, people find themselves comfortable in their national language, both in case of reading and writing. Hindi is the national language of India, spoken and understood almost all over the country. Keeping this in mind, there is a tremendous growth in the Hindi review websites[1] on the Web. Besides this, a few Hindi lovers like to post their reviews in Hindi on English based e-commerce websites also, for example, we can find Hindi reviews on *www.flipkart.com* or *www.homeshop18.com* in a big number with English reviews. Therefore, an efficient sentiment analysis system for the Hindi language is the need of current e-commerce organizations and their customers.

The general approach of Sentiment Analysis (SA) is to summarize the semantic polarity (i.e., positive or negative) of sentences/documents by analysis of the orientation of the individual words (Riloff and Wiebe, 2003; Pang and Lee, 2004; Danescu-Niculescu-Mizil et al., 2009; Kim and Hovy, 2004; Takamura et al., 2005). In the absence of sufficient amount of corpora, the most efficient way of sentiment analysis is to rely on the words from sentiment lexicons as a key feature. There are many sentiment lexicons for English language, for example, subjectivity lexicon[2] by Wiebe and a list of positive and negative opinion words[3] by Liu, but there are not many instances of sentiment lexicons in Hindi that can build an efficient sentiment analysis system for Hindi. The main contributions of this paper are:

- A Hindi senti lexicon consisting polar words of four parts of speech: Adjective, Noun, Verb and Adverb, generated from extensive analysis of HindiWordNet[4].

- A multi module rule based sentiment analysis system for Hindi that uses words from Hindi senti lexicon as a polarity clue.

Our approach that generates Hindi senti lexicon is an improvement over the approach suggested by Bakliwal et al. (2012). They used the same source, that is, HindiWordNet for the polar words extraction, but their approach was not able to handle the instances, where a word has senses of both the orientations: positive and negative. A word can have

---

[1] hindi.webdunia.com/entertainment/film/review/

[2] http://mpqa.cs.pitt.edu/
[3] http://www.cs.uic.edu/liub/FBS/sentiment-analysis.html
[4] Available at: www.cfilt.com

D S Sharma, R Sangal and J D Pawar. Proc. of the 11th Intl. Conference on Natural Language Processing, pages 150–155,
Goa, India. December 2014. ©2014 NLP Association of India (NLPAI)

positive and negative senses at the same time. This combination is exemplified in figure 1. The approach of Bakliwal et al.(2012) assumes that all the senses (synsets) of a source word should receive the polarity same as the source word, consequently all the words in the synsets should bear the polarity same as the source word. This assumption will fetch the words with the wrong polarity orientation. Besides this, their approach considers that antonyms of a word should receive the opposite polarity of the source word, but it is not always true. There are the instances, where antonym and the word have the same polarity orientation. One such instance of this property is given in figure 2. In this paper, we present an approach that provides a very vigilant traversal of the HindiWordNet for the purpose of generation of senti lexicon. Our approach also implements that synonyms (words from a synset) must receive the same polarity, but it is able to distinguish among the positive and negative senses of the same word.

Index word = सस्ता with +ve polarity orientation	Synsets of सस्ता with actual Polarity orientations
Sense-1	+ve (सस्ता, अल्पमूल्य, सौघा, अनर्घ, सुहंग, अल्पक्रीत; जो कम मूल्य का हो)
Sense-2	-ve (घटिया, निकृष्ट, नीच, ओछा, छिछोरा, तुच्छ, कमीना etc; बिल्कुल निम्न या निकृष्ट कोटि का)

Figure 1: Synsets of the same word with opposite polarities

Results show that the sentiment analysis system based on sentiment lexicon generated by the proposed bootstrap approach outperforms the Hindi sentiment analysis system presented by Bakliwal et al.(2012) for the same data set. By considering four parts of speech as a source of polar words, our sentiment lexicon covers more range of polar words. We achieve an accuracy of 89.45% in the product domain and 85% in the movie domain.

Index word = सस्ता with +ve polarity orientation	Antonym of सस्ता with positive polarity orientation
+ve (सस्ता, अल्पमूल्य, सौघा, अनर्घ, सुहंग, अल्पक्रीत - जो कम मूल्य का हो)	+ve (बहुमूल्य, बेशकीमती, बेशकीमती, मूल्यवान, कीमती, कीमती, अनमोल - जिसका मूल्य बहुत अधिक हो)

Figure 2: Antonyms with the same polarity as the source/index word

Section 2 helps illustrate the generation of senti lexicon from HindiWordNet. Section 3 provides the statistics related to sentiment lexicon obtained as output. Section 4 expands on the the rule based classification algorithm that is used to find the overall polarity orientation of the document. Section 5 illustrates the results achieved for Sentiment analysis system. Sections 6 and 7 discuss related work and conclusion.

2 Identification of Polar Words from HindiWordNet

All the senses of a word may not necessarily be polar. In this section, we focus on the extraction of polar words from HindiWordNet.

2.1 Why HindiWordNet?

We find HindiWordNet the most efficient resource for generation of senti lexicon. HindiWordNet is the result of manual identification of all the senses of the word W, hence it is very accurate in terms of relations among the words. We give a formal characterization of HindiWordNet. A WordNet is a word sense network. A word-synset network N is a triple (W, S, ε), where W is a finite set of words, S is a finite set of synsets, ε is a set of undirected edges to link synsets of words, that is, $\varepsilon \subseteq W \times S$. Each synset in the Hindi WordNet is linked with other synsets through the well-known semantic relations of hypernymy, hyponymy, meronymy, troponymy, antonymy, entailment *etc*.

In HindiWordNet, the words are grouped in a synset according to a lexical concept, that is, synonymy. Two words that can be interchanged in a context are synonymous in that context. We observe that the synonymy relation is the most specific candidate for lexicon generation. The other semantic relations fetch the non polar words on expansion. This synonymy property assures that if we know the polarity orientation of a word in the synset, the same polarity orientation can be assigned to all the words in the synset. Figure 3 exemplified the inference of polarity orientation from a seed (index) word to the whole synset.

2.2 A Bootstrap Approach for Polar Words Identification

The process is based on the phenomenon that if we know the polarity orientation of a word, the same polarity orientation can be assigned to a synonymous word. Therefore, we start with two seed sets: positive (Each word has polarity value: +1) and negative (Each word has polarity value: -1). The

Index word with polarity orientation	Synset with inferred polarity orientation from the index word
−ve (घटिया)	−ve (घटिया, निकृष्ट, नीच, ओछा, छिछोरा, तुच्छ, कमीना, बाज़ारू, बाज़ारी, बज़ारू, बाजारू, बाजारी *etc.*)
+ve (विनम्र)	+ve (विनम्र, विनयी, विनीत, नम्र, विनयशील, विनययुक्त, आनत, निभृत, अनुनीत, प्रवण, अवाग्र, आजिज़, आजिज)

Figure 3: Polarity identification from a seed word to the whole synset

seed (index) words are manually identified polar words.

For each index word from seed set, we extract all the senses, considering they all will have the same polarity orientation as the index word, but there are instances where a word can have both positive and negative senses. To assure the rejection of opposite polarity sense, we extract all the words that belong to the sense and check the presence of any word in the opposite polarity seed-set or lexicon. For example, for a positive index word, we look into the negative seed-set or lexicon. For the first iteration, only seed-set is available for this check, in further iterations it becomes lexicon. If any word from the extracted sense is found in the opposite polarity lexicon, discard the sense and repeat the process for the next sense of the index word, else insert the words into the lexicon having polarity orientation of index word.

The decision about the discarded sense will remain pending till the word from the sense, which is found in the opposite polarity lexicon encounters as an index word. The whole process will be repeated for the newly added words till no new word is added in the lexicons. Once the process stops, it results into two separate lexicons: positive and negative lexicons. We combine these two as *Hindi senti lexicon*. The whole process is depicted in figure 4.

Objective Sense (synset): A polar index word may also have objective sense. To minimize the extraction of objective synsets, we analyzed the behavior of the words in a synset comprehensively. The words in a synset in HindiWordNet are arranged in the order of their frequency of usage. The words, which are at the head of the synset (most frequently used) fetch the polar synsets on further expansions, but the words which are at the tail of the synset (less frequently used) are prone to fetch objective synsets on further expansion. The

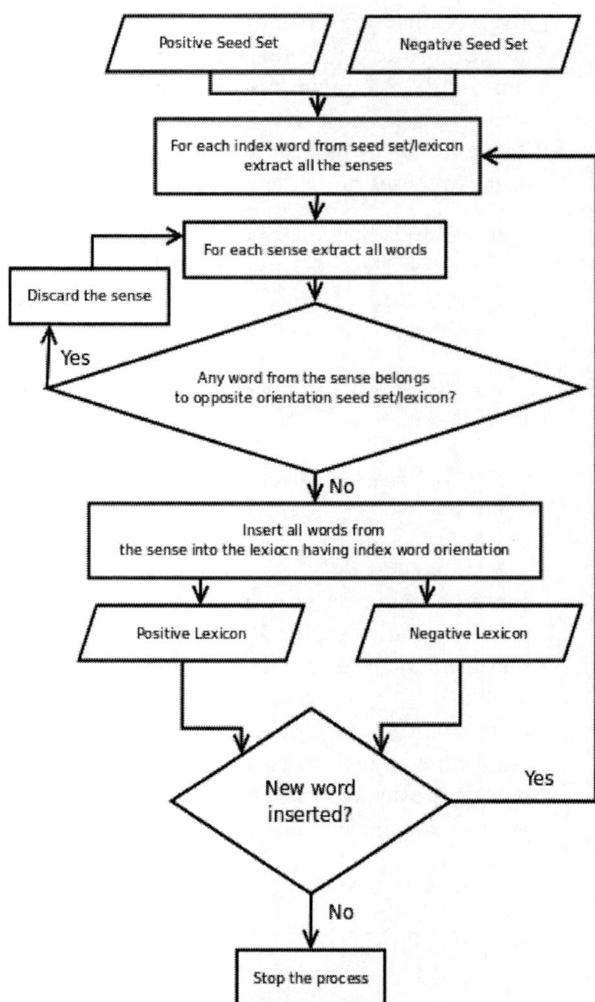

Figure 4: A bootstrap approach for polar words identification

152

head words are tightly coupled with polar synsets, while tail words fetch the polar synsets that can be extracted from head words, besides this they extract non polar synsets. To hinder the extraction of non polar words, we add a restriction that only the first seven (head) words of a synset will take part as index word in the next iteration, and the rest will remain the part of lexicon only. This constant 7 is selected after experimenting with a range of constants 2 to 10, such that it minimizes the extraction of the non polar words as well as keeps the lexicon compact.

3　Hindi Senti Lexicon Statistics

Most of the sentiment lexicons are limited to adjectives and adverbs, but there are many instances where a noun and verb can bear the polarity. We apply the same bootstrap approach discussed in section 2.2 on all four parts of speech, which are prone to bear polarity. The proposed constrained approach minimizes the possibility of extraction of wrong word as polar word. We extracted a comprehensive list of total 8061 true polar words, which we name as Hindi senti lexicon. The efficacy of this lexicon is evaluated by implementing Hindi sentiment analysis system (section 4) in the movie and product domains.

	Number
Adjective	Pos:2256 & Neg:2232
Noun	Pos:1551 & Neg:1558
Adverb	Pos:132 & Neg:94
Verb	Pos:83 & Neg:155
Total	8061

Table 1: Number of polar words obtained in different parts of speech

4　A Multi-module Sentiment Analysis System for Hindi Using Hindi Senti Lexicon

The Hindi senti lexicon generated by the proposed bootstrap approach contains polar words from the four parts of speech. Hence, identification of correct part of speech of the words in the input document, whose polarity has to be determined is the foremost step. We use Hindi POS tagger tool provided by CDAC[1] to tag the input documents with part of speech. The implemented rule based system is depicted in figure 5.

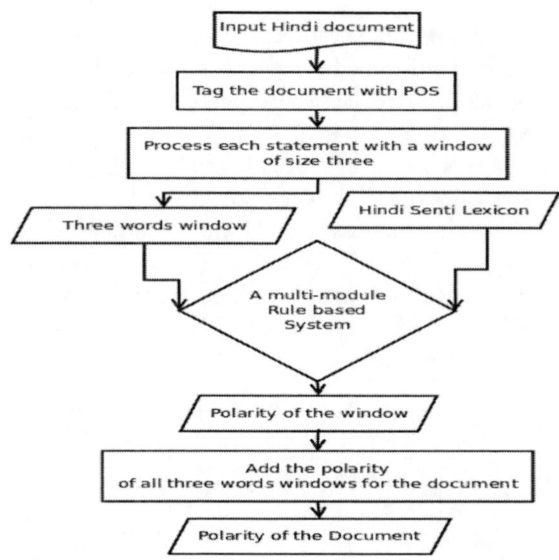

Figure 5: A multi-module sentiment analysis system for Hindi using Hindi senti lexicon

The designed SA system provides polarity of the review document as output. The system processes each sentence/line separately, because sentences are the basic units that determine the polarity of the document. The polarity of a sentence is determined by the analysis of words present in the sentence. The words in a sentence are observed in a window of 3 words to include the effect of several semantic relations among words, for example, the phrase "not so comfortable" has negation before a positive adjective.

The multi-module rule based system decides the polarity of the window of three words such that if there is a word from lexicon with matched part of speech, then the word gets the polarity orientation as given in senti lexicon. The complete polarity of window depends on the neighbor words. For this, the three words window is passed from multiple modules, depending on the part of speech of the words.

Module 1: The presence of negation after a polar word in Hindi reverses the orientation of polarity of the word. This module handles the presence of negation by assigning the reverse polarity of the polar word to the whole window.

Module 2: The presence of two same polarity words in a window enhances the polarity of the posterior polar word. The polarity of the window is determined by adding the individual polarity of each word present in the window.

Module 3: The presence of two opposite polarity words together enhances the polarity of the posterior word (semantic property). If such pattern is observed in the window of three words, this module assigns double polarity of the posterior word to the whole window.

A few instances from all three modules are depicted in figure 6. The ultimate polarity of the document is determined by adding up the polarity of all three words windows of the sentences of the document.

	Semantic Relation	Example Phrase	Polarity of Phrase
Module-1	Polar word + Negation	अभाव (-1) बिल्कुल नहीं	1
Module-2	PosAdj + PosAdj	जबरदस्त (+1) लाजवाब (+1)	2
Module-3	PosAdj + NegNoun	वास्तविक (+1) समस्याएं (-1)	-2
	PosAdj + NegVerb	आसानी (+1) से टूटना (-1)	-2
	PosAdv + NegAdj	अच्छी तरह (+1) अनुपयोगी (-1)	-2
	NegAdj + PosAdj	भयंकर (-1) पसंदीदा (+1)	2
	NegAdj + PosNoun	हद (-1) सिफारिश (+1)	2
	PosAdj + NegAdj	जबर्दस्त (+1) बदसूरत (-1)	-2

Figure 6: Modules of the rule based sentiment analysis system

5 Results of Sentiment Analysis

We validate the efficiency of Hindi senti lexicon generated from the proposed bootstrap approach through the implementation of sentiment analysis (SA) system. We did an extensive validation using two domains: movie and product. Providing sentiment in movie and product domain is a very useful service in current scenario. Its proof is the popularity of Hindi review websites and an umpteen number of Hindi reviews on Web in these two domains.

5.1 Dataset

The movie reviews are manually collected from: *hindi.webdunia.com/entertainment/film/review/.*
These reviews are posted by well known critics. If a reviewer has given below 2.5 (below average) star then the review is tagged as negative else the review is tagged as positive. Movie domain dataset contains 100 positive reviews and 100 negative reviews. The average length of the

review is 50 words. For product domain, we use the same dataset used by Bakliwal et al. (2012). The dataset contains 350 negative documents and 350 positive documents.

5.2 Accuracy Obtained

Domain	No. of Reviews	Accuracy
Movie	200	**85**
Movie+POS	200	**89.5**
Product	700	**81.4**
Product+POS	700	**85**

Table 2: Average sentiment classification accuracies in percentage

Accuracy is calculated as a fraction of correctly classified documents and total number of documents. The classification accuracies are depicted in table 2 . Presence of polar words in the lexicon from four parts of speech makes it a rich resource for sentiment analysis task. Improvement in accuracy with POS tagging indicates that identification of correct POS tag helps sentiment analysis system. We observe the best accuracy in the movie domain with POS tagging. We compare the results obtained using our sentiment lexicon with the results obtained using graph traversal based subjective lexicon of 8936 words (adjectives and adverbs), presented by Bakliwal et al. (2012) in figure 7. We observe a significant improvement in accuracy in both the domains.

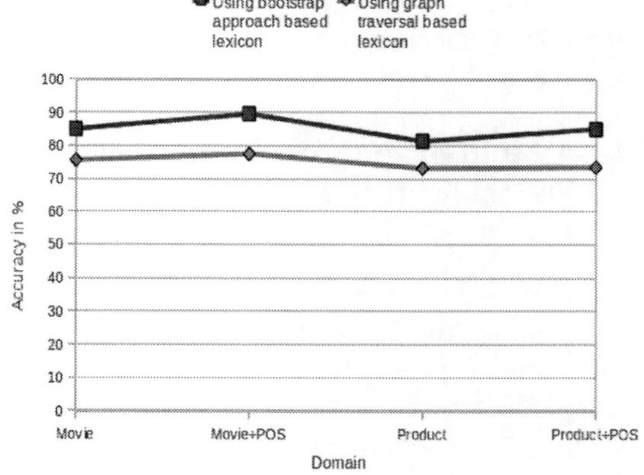

Figure 7: Accuracy obtained with our lexicon and graph traversal based lexicon provided by Bakliwal et al.

6   Related Work

There are many examples, where a lexical resource is used for sentiment analysis in English, but there are a very few instances of sentiment analysis in Hindi. Das and Bandyopadhyay (2009) are the first who report the sentiment analysis in one of the Indian language, that is, Bengali. Since, there is a lack of annotated corpus in Bengali also, their approach was based on sentiment analysis using subjectivity lexicon. Using the lexicon and a few other syntactic features , they achieved a precision of 74.6% and recall of 80.4%.

In case of Hindi, the first work was reported by Joshi et al. (2010). They created a Hindi SentiWordNet using English SentiWordNet and linking between English-HindiWordNet. Using their Hindi SentiWordNet as a lexical resource, they achieved an accuracy of 60.31% for sentiment analysis in Hindi. The reason behind the low accuracy is the distribution of polarity value among the senses of a word in Hindi SentiWordNet, while the testing corpus was not sense tagged. Getting a sense tagged corpora is more expensive than getting the corpora. Joshi et al. reported that a supervised sentiment classification is better than resource based sentiment classification. They got an accuracy of 78.14% using unigram based supervised classification in Hindi.

In our paper, we get an accuracy which is significantly higher than the results reported by Joshi et al. (2010), which indicates that an efficient lexical resource is a better choice than supervised classification in case of lack of corpora. Our work has a close resemblance with the work presented by Bakliwal et al. (2012). The subjectivity lexicon reported by them is used to compare the results (shown in figure 7).

7   Conclusion

In this paper, we present a sentiment lexicon for Hindi, which is a milestone for sentiment analysis in a language lacking in annotated corpus. The proposed bootstrap approach for generation of sentiment lexicon form HindiWordNet is able to extract polar words for all four parts of speech: adjective, noun, adverb and verb.

The senti lexicon obtained from the bootstrap approach is used to build a multi-module rule based sentiment analysis system in Hindi. Multiple modules are embedded to handle the effects of semantic relations among words on polarity of a

sentence. The resultant sentiment analysis system is able to produce an average accuracy of 87% for sentiment analysis in the movie and product domain. Besides the betterment of sentiment analysis, the research can be useful for corpora generation, for creating writing aids for authors and in natural language generation.

References

Akshat Bakliwal, Piyush Arora, and Vasudeva Varma. 2012. Hindi subjective lexicon: A lexical resource for hindi polarity classification. In *Proceedings of the Eight International Conference on Language Resources and Evaluation (LREC)*.

Cristian Danescu-Niculescu-Mizil, Gueorgi Kossinets, Jon Kleinberg, and Lillian Lee. 2009. How opinions are received by online communities: A case study on amazon.com helpfulness votes. In *Proceedings of the 18th International Conference on World Wide Web*, WWW '09, pages 141–150, New York, NY, USA. ACM.

Amitava Das and Sivaji Bandyopadhyay. 2009. Subjectivity detection in english and bengali: A crf-based approach. *Proceeding of ICON*.

Aditya Joshi, AR Balamurali, and Pushpak Bhattacharyya. 2010. A fall-back strategy for sentiment analysis in hindi: a case study. *Proceedings of the 8th ICON*.

Soo-Min Kim and Eduard Hovy. 2004. Determining the sentiment of opinions. In *Proceedings of the 20th international conference on Computational Linguistics*, page 1367. Association for Computational Linguistics.

Bo Pang and Lillian Lee. 2004. A sentimental education: Sentiment analysis using subjectivity summarization based on minimum cuts. In *Proceedings of the 42Nd Annual Meeting on Association for Computational Linguistics*, ACL '04, Stroudsburg, PA, USA. Association for Computational Linguistics.

Ellen Riloff and Janyce Wiebe. 2003. Learning extraction patterns for subjective expressions. In *Proceedings of the 2003 conference on Empirical methods in natural language processing*, EMNLP '03, pages 105–112, Stroudsburg, PA, USA. Association for Computational Linguistics.

Hiroya Takamura, Takashi Inui, and Manabu Okumura. 2005. Extracting semantic orientations of words using spin model. In *Proceedings of the 43rd Annual Meeting on Association for Computational Linguistics*, ACL '05, pages 133–140, Stroudsburg, PA, USA. Association for Computational Linguistics.

A Sandhi Splitter for Malayalam

Devadath V V   **Litton J Kurisinkel**   **Dipti Misra Sharma**   **Vasudeva Varma**
Language Technology Research Centre
International Institute of Information Technology - Hyderabad, India.
{devadathv.v,litton.jkurisinkel}@research.iiit.ac.in,{dipti,vasu}@iiit.ac.in

Abstract

Sandhi splitting is the primary task for computational processing of text in Sanskrit and Dravidian languages. In these languages, words can join together with morpho-phonemic changes at the point of joining. This phenomenon is known as Sandhi. Sandhi splitter splits the string of conjoined words into individual words. Accurate execution of sandhi splitting is crucial for text processing tasks such as POS tagging, topic modelling and document indexing. We have tried different approaches to address the challenges of sandhi splitting in Malayalam, and finally, we have thought of exploiting the phonological changes that take place in the words while joining. This resulted in a hybrid method which statistically identifies the split points and splits using predefined character level linguistic rules. Currently, our system gives an accuracy of 91.1% .

1 Introduction

Malayalam is one among the four main Dravidian languages and 22 official languages of India. It is spoken in the State of Kerala, which is situated in the south west coast of India . This language is believed to be originated from old Tamil, having a strong influence of Sanskrit in its vocabulary. Malayalam is an inflectionally rich and agglutinative language like any other Dravidian language. The property of agglutination eventually leads to the process of sandhi.

Sandhi is the process of joining two words or characters, where morphophonemic changes occur at the point of joining. The presence of Sandhi is abundant in Sanskrit and all Dravidian languages. When compared to other Dravidian languages, the presence of Sandhi is relatively high in Malayalam. Even a full sentence may exist as a single string due to the process of Sandhi. For example, അവനാരാണ്‌(avanaaraaN) is a sentence in Malayalam which means *"Who is he ?"*. It is composed of 3 independent words, namely അവൻ(avan (*he*)), ആര്‌(aar(*who*)) and ആണ്‌ (aaN(*is*)). However, ambiguous splits for a word is very less in Malayalam. Sandhis are of two types, Internal and External. *Internal Sandhi* exists between a root or a stem with a suffix or a morpheme. In the example given below,

$$പറ(para) + ഉന്നു(unnu) = പറയുന്നു(parayunnu)$$

Here പറ(para) is a verb root with the meaning "to say" and ഉന്നു(unnu) is an inflectional suffix for marking present tense. They join together to form പറയുന്നു(para**yu**nnu), meaning "say"(PRES). *External sandhi* is between words. Two or more words join to form a single string of conjoined words.

$$ചെയ്യും(ceyyu\mathbf{M}) + എങ്കില്‍(enkil) = ചെയ്യുമെങ്കില്‍$$
(ceyyu**m**enkil)

ചെയ്യും(ceyyu**M**) is a finite verb with the meaning "will do" and എങ്കില്‍(enkil) is a connective with meaning "if". They join together to form a single string ചെയ്യുമെങ്കില്‍(ceyyu**m**enkil).

For most of the text processing tasks such as POS tagging, topic modelling and document indexing, External Sandhi is a matter of concern. All these tasks require individual words in the text to

D S Sharma, R Sangal and J D Pawar. Proc. of the 11th Intl. Conference on Natural Language Processing, pages 156–161,
Goa, India. December 2014. ©2014 NLP Association of India (NLPAI)

be identified. The identification of words becomes complex when words are joined to form a single string with morpho-phonemic changes at the point of joining. More over, the sandhi can happen between any linguistic classes like, a noun and a verb, or a verb and a connective etc. This leads to misidentification of classes of words by POS tagger which eventually affects parsing. Sandhi acts as a bottle-neck for all term distribution based approaches for any NLP and IR task.

Sandhi splitting is the process of splitting a string of conjoined words into a sequence of individual words, where each word in the sequence has the capacity to stand alone as a single word. To be precise, Sandhi splitting facilitates the task of individual word identification within such a string of conjoined words.

Sandhi splitting is a different type of word segmentation problem. Languages like Chinese (Badino, 2004), Vietnamese (Dinh et al., 2008) Japanese, do not mark the word boundaries explicitly. Highly agglutinative language like Turkish(Oflazer et al., 1994) also need word segmentation for text processing. In these languages, words are just concatenated without any kind of morpho-phonemic change at the point of joining, whereas morpho-phonemic changes occur in Sanskrit and Dravidian languages at the point of joining (Mittal, 2010).

2   Related works

Mittal (2010) adopted a method for Sandhi splitting in Sanskrit using the concept of *optimality theory*(Prince and Smolensky, 2008), in such a way that it generates all possible splits and validates each split using a morph analyser. In another work, statistical methods like Gibbs Sampling and Dirichlet Process are adopted for Sanskrit Sandhi splitting (Natarajan and Charniak, 2011).

To the best of our knowledge, only two related works are reported for the task of Sandhi splitting in Malayalam. Rule based compound word splitter for Malayalam (Nair and Peter, 2011), goes in the direction of identifying morphemes using rules and trie data structure. They adopted a general approach to split both external and internal sandhi which includes compound words. But splitting a compound word which is conceptually united will lead to the loss of linguistic meaning. In an other work (Das et al., 2012), which is a hybrid approach for sandhi splitting in Malayalam, employs a TnT tagger to tag whether the input string to be split or not and splits according to a predefined set of rules. But this particular work does not report any empirical results. In our approach, we identify precisely the point to be split in the string using statistical methods and then applies predefined set of character level rules to split the string.

3   Our Approach

We have tried various approaches for sandhi splitting and finally arrived at a hybrid approach which decides the split points statistically and then splits the string in to words by applying pre-defined character level sandhi rules.

Sandhi rules for external sandhi, are identified from a corpus of 400 sentences from Malayalam literature, which includes text from old literature(texts before 1990) as well as modern literature. In comparison with text from old literatures, modern literature have very less use of sandhi. By analysing the text, we were able to identify 5 unambiguous character level rules which can be used to split the word, once the split point is statistically identified. Sandhi rules identified are listed in the **Table 1**.

R	Rule	Example
1	$(CSC)V_s =$ $(CSC)S + V$	വാക്കില്ല $=$ വാക്ക് $+$ ഇല്ല word(Noun)+no(verb)
2	$(യ/വ)V_s = V$	പേടിയാണ് $=$ പേടി $+$ ആണ് fear(Noun) + is(verb)
3	$മV_s = ം + V$	പണമില്ല $=$ പണം $+$ ഇല്ല money(Noun) + no(verb)
4	$(ര/ല/ള/ന/ണ)V_s =$ $(ര്/ൽ/ൾ/ൻ/ൺ) + V$	മുകളിലാണ് $=$ മുകളിൽ $+$ ആണ് above(Loc)+is(verb)
5	$CV_s =$ $(CS) + V$	ആണെന്ന് $=$ ആണ് $+$ എന്ന് is(verb)+that(quotative)
6	just split	അവൻവന്നു $=$ അവൻ $+$ വന്നു He(Noun)+Came(verb)

C=Consonant, V=Vowel, V_s=Vowel symbol, S=Schwa

Table 1: Sandhi rules

Rules in **Table 1** are given in a particular order corresponding to their inherent priority which avoids any clash between them. Every character level Sandhi rule is based on a consonant and a vowel. *Rule 5* is the most general rule for Sandhi that we could identify in Malayalam which states that a group of a consonant and a vowel can be split into a consonant and a vowel. *Rule* **1** is a special case of *Rule* **5**, which is framed in order to treat the special case of compound of consonants with a schwa in between. This rule is being introduced , because the consonants specified in rules **2, 3** *and* **4** can come as the last consonant in the case of a compound of consonants. This will lead to an improper split of the string by any of the rules **2, 3** *or* **4**. So every word, with an identified split point should be primarily checked against rule 1 to avoid wrong split by other rules in the case of a sandhi containing a compound of consonants. *Rule* **2** is to handle the process of phonemic insertion came after the process of Sandhi. In Malayalam, these extra characters യ/വ can be inserted between words after sandhi in certain context. *Rule* **3** and *Rule* **4** are to handle the case of phonemic variation caused due to the process of Sandhi. *Rule* **3** enforces that, the letter 'മ' with a vowel symbol becomes 'ം' and a vowel, while *Rule* **4** enforces that, the characters, 'ര/ല/ള/ന/ണ' with a vowel symbol becomes *chillu*[1], 'ർ/ൽ/ൾ/ൻ/ൺ' and a vowel.

The hybrid approach utilises the phonological changes (Klein et al., 2003) due to the presence of sandhi. The remaining part of the paper explains this approach in detail, with theoretical formulation, Experimental Results and Error analysis.

When the words are conjoined, they undergo phonological changes at the point of joining. These phonological changes can be evidential in identifying the split point in the given string of conjoined words. For example, words Wx and yZ are conjoined to form a new string $Wx^{'}y^{'}Z$. As a part of this process, substring x in the original string Wx has undergone a phonological change to become $x^{'}$ and the substring y in the original string yZ has undergone a phonological change to become $y^{'}$. We try to identify the split point between $x^{'}$ and $y^{'}$ in $Wx^{'}y^{'}Z$ using $x^{'}$ and $y^{'}$ as the evidence. Going forward, we use "S_p" to denote Split Point and "N_{sp}" to denote Non Split Point. $P(S_p|x^{'},y^{'})$ will give the probability of a character point between $x^{'}$ and $y^{'}$ within a conjoined string to be a split point. A character point will be classified as split point if,

$$P(S_p|x^{'},y^{'}) > P(N_{sp}|x^{'},y^{'}) \quad (1)$$

[1]A *chillu* is a pure consonant which can stand alone independently without the help of vowels

As per our observation, the phonological changes of x to $x^{'}$ and of y to $y^{'}$ are independent of each other. So,

$$P(S_p|x^{'},y^{'}) = P(S_p|x^{'}) * P(S_p|y^{'}) \quad (2)$$

To produce the values of $x^{'}$ and $y^{'}$ for each character point, we take k character points backwards and k character points forward from that particular point. For example, the probability of the marked point $PointX$ in the string given in the **Figure 1** below to be a split point is given by **equation (3)**

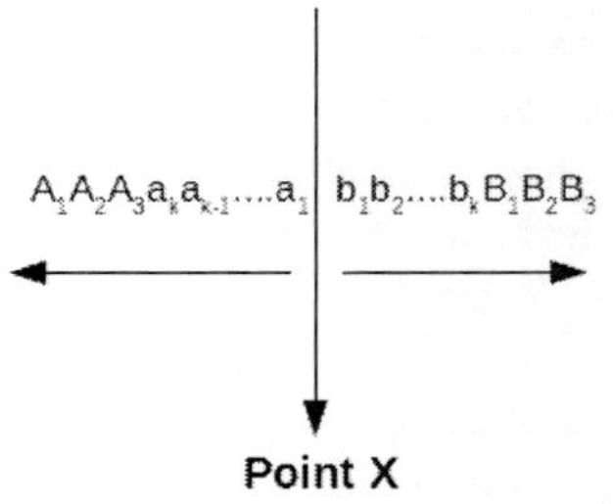

Figure 1: Split point

$$P(S_p|a_1a_2...a_k) * P(S_p|b_1b_2...b_k) \quad (3)$$

Where $a_1a_2...a_k$ is $x^{'}$ and $b_1b_2...b_k$ is $y^{'}$. The value of k is experimentally optimized.

The split points of different agglutinated strings in training data are annotated in the following format.

$$WordN = i_1, i_2, i_3, ...i_z$$

This indicates that the string $WordN$ needs to be splitted at "z" character indexes $i_1, i_2, i_3, ...i_z$ within the string.

We employ two Orthographic Tries (Whitelaw and Patrick, 2003) to statistically capture the phonological differences in $x^{'}$ and $y^{'}$ for split points and non-split points. A mould of orthographic tries used is given in **Figure 2**. The trie in **Figure 2** is trained with character sequences $c_1c_2c_3$, $c_1c_2c_4$, $c_1c_3c_4$, $c_1c_3c_5$. In the first trie, the path from root to k nodes represents the string $a_1a_2...a_k$. Each node $i(1 \leq i \leq k)$ in the path stores the number of occurrences of split points and non-split points in the entire training data which are preceded by $a_ia_{i-1}...a_1$. In the second trie, a path from root to k nodes represent

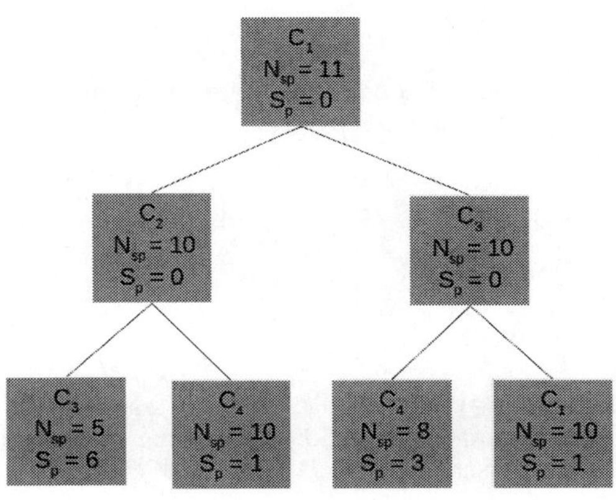

Figure 2: Word trie

the string $b_1b_2...b_k$. Each node $i(1 \leq i \leq k)$ in the path stores the number of occurrences of split-points and non-split points which are succeeded by $b_1b_2...b_i$. The frequencies stored in these trie nodes are used to calculate $P(C|a_1a_2...a_k)$ and $P(C|b_1b_2...b_k)$ where C is S_p or N_{sp}.

As split points are rare within a string $P(C|a_1a_2...a_k)$ and $P(C|b_1b_2...b_k)$ needs to be smoothed. For this purpose, we use the information stored along the depth of the tries for the strings $a_1a_2...a_k$ and $b_1b_2...b_k$ as follows

$$P(C|a_1a_2...a_k) = \sum_{i=initial\ skip}^{k} P(C|a_ia_{i+1}...a_k) \quad (4)$$

$$P(C|b_1b_2...b_k) = \sum_{i=initial\ skip}^{k} P(C|b_ib_{i+1}...b_k) \quad (5)$$

Here the initial-skip decides optimum 'smoothing range' within the string.The value of initial-skip decides the threshold phonological similarity that needs to be considered while smoothing. The experimental optimisation of initial-skip is done. The identified split points are splitted using the applicable sandhi rules.

4   Data and Results

Data Set

We created a dataset which contained 2000 Sandhi bound words for training. Each of the split point

within the word are annotated with the within-word index of the corresponding character point. The test data contains 1000 random words, out of which 260 are words with sandhi.

Results

In our experiments, we tried evaluating the accuracy of split point identification, split accuracy of different sandhi rules and overall accuracy of the system. By overall accuracy, we mean percentage of the words with sandhi in which the split is exactly as expected. We have conducted experiments on split point identification with different values of k and initial Skip.

k-S	P	R	F	Accuracy
3-1	85.37	75	79.85	89.6
3-2	84.73	73.26	78.58	88.7
4-1	86.56	76.04	80.96	90.1
4-2	85.48	73.61	79.10	89
5-1	88.37	79.16	83.51	90.9
5-2	85.94	74.30	79.30	88.7
6-1	88.50	80.20	84.15	91.1
6-2	85.59	76.38	80.88	89.2

Table 2: Results

Here P implies precision, R implies Recall, F implies F-measure and k-S implies k and Initial skip respectively. k=6 and initial Skip=1 have shown the better result. As per our observation, phonological changes as a part of sandhi would not happen beyond a range of six characters in each of the participating words. So the upper bound for k value is taken as 6.

5   Error Analysis

In Split point identification, most of the incorrectly identified split points are character points between a word and inflectional suffix attached to it. As the system evolve, this error can be rectified by the use of a post-processor which maintains the finite list of inflectional suffixes in the language. Wrong splits in the middle of an actual word are very few in number and will reduce as the size of the training data increases.

Most of the unidentified split points are due to the presence of certain rare patterns. These errors will be reduced with the incorporation of words from diverse texts in the training data.

When it comes to rules, we have used only character level rules for splitting the identified split points. Rule 1,4 and 5 go ambiguous at certain rare contexts. To resolve this, certain word level information like POS tags are required. But for an accurate POS tagging, particularly for this disambiguation purpose, a sandhi splitter with a good level of accuracy is inevitable. Our Sandhi splitter can contribute for a better POS tagger. Vice versa, a POS tagger can complement the Sandhi splitter.

Rule	Accuracy
1	92.10
2	96.29
3	100
4	80.64
5	87.71

Table 3: Rule accuracy when k=6 and S= 1

6 Conclusion & Future work

This experiment has given us a new insight that, there exists a character level pattern in the text where the sandhi can be splitted. When compared to a completely rule based approach which is effort intensive, a hybrid approach gives us a more fast and accurate performance with relatively lesser amount of training data. We expect that, this method can be successfully implemented in all other Dravidian languages for the Sandhi splitting. The only language dependent part will be to split the identified split points using language specific character level rules. The system component to split the identified split points can be decided at runtime based on the language on which it is operating on.

There is a possibility of improving the current system into a language independent and fully statistical system. Instead of totally depending on language specific Sandhi rules for splitting, phonological changes after split can be inferred from training data. For Example,

$$W x^{'} y^{'} Z \Rightarrow W x + y Z$$

$P(x|x^{'})$ and $P(y|y^{'})$ can be tabulated to predict the phonological changes after split. But an accurate tabulation demands a large amount of annotated training data.

Software

The source code of our Hybrid Sandhi splitter for Malayalam is available at `https://github.com/Devadath/Malayalam_Sandhi_Splitter`

References

[Badino2004] Leonardo Badino. 2004. Chinese text word-segmentation considering semantic links among sentences. In *INTERSPEECH*.

[Das et al.2012] Divya Das, Radhika K T, Rajeev R R, and Raghu Raj. 2012. Hybrid sandhi-splitter for malayalam using unicode. In *In proceedings of National Seminar on Relevance of Malayalam in Information Technology*.

[Dinh et al.2008] Quang Thang Dinh, Hong Phuong Le, Thi Minh Huyen Nguyen, Cam Tu Nguyen, Mathias Rossignol, Xuan Luong Vu, et al. 2008. Word segmentation of vietnamese texts: a comparison of approaches. In *6th international conference on Language Resources and Evaluation-LREC 2008*.

[Klein et al.2003] Dan Klein, Joseph Smarr, Huy Nguyen, and Christopher D Manning. 2003. Named entity recognition with character-level models. In *Proceedings of the seventh conference on Natural language learning at HLT-NAACL 2003-Volume 4*, pages 180–183. Association for Computational Linguistics.

[Mittal2010] Vipul Mittal. 2010. Automatic sanskrit segmentizer using finite state transducers. In *Proceedings of the ACL 2010 Student Research Workshop*, pages 85–90. Association for Computational Linguistics.

[Nair and Peter2011] Latha R Nair and S David Peter. 2011. Development of a rule based learning system for splitting compound words in malayalam language. In *Recent Advances in Intelligent Computational Systems (RAICS), 2011 IEEE*, pages 751–755. IEEE.

[Natarajan and Charniak2011] Abhiram Natarajan and Eugene Charniak. 2011. S3-statistical sam. dhi splitting.

[Oflazer et al.1994] Kemal Oflazer, Elvan Göçmen, Elvan Gocmen, and Cem Bozsahin. 1994. An outline of turkish morphology.

[Prince and Smolensky2008] Alan Prince and Paul Smolensky. 2008. *Optimality Theory: Constraint interaction in generative grammar*. John Wiley & Sons.

[Whitelaw and Patrick2003] Casey Whitelaw and Jon Patrick. 2003. Named entity recognition using a character-based probabilistic approach. In *Proceedings of the seventh conference on Natural language learning at HLT-NAACL 2003-Volume 4*, pages 196–199. Association for Computational Linguistics.

PaCMan : Parallel Corpus Management Workbench

Diptesh Kanojia
CSE, IIT Bombay
diptesh@cse.iitb.ac.in

Manish Shrivastava
CSE, IIIT Hyderabad
mani.shrivastava@gmail.com

Raj Dabre
GSI, Kyoto University
prajdabre@gmail.com

Pushpak Bhattacharyya
CSE, IIT Bombay
pb@cse.iitb.ac.in

Abstract

We present a Parallel Corpora Management tool that aides parallel corpora generation for the task of Machine Translation (MT). It takes source and target text of a corpus for any language pair in text file format, or zip archives containing multiple corresponding text files. Then, it provides with a helpful interface to lexicographers for manual translation / validation, and gives out the corrected text files as output. It provides various dictionary references as help within the interface which increase the productivity and efficiency of a lexicographer. It also provides automatic translation of the source sentence using an integrated MT system. The tool interface includes a corpora management system which facilitates maintenance of parallel corpora by assigning roles such as manager, lexicographer etc. We have designed a novel tool that provides aides like references to various dictionary sources such as Wordnets, Shabdkosh, Wikitionary etc. We also provide manual word alignment correction which is visualized in the tool and can lead to its gamification in the future, thus, providing a valuable source of word / phrase alignments.

1   Introduction

Statistical Machine Translation (SMT) depends primarily on parallel corpora. The quality of parallel corpora available can make or break a SMT system. The process of creating a parallel corpus is neither easy nor cheap. It is essential to produce good quality parallel corpus efficiently to ensure time and cost effectiveness of the process.

Traditional method of parallel corpus creation involves manual translation of every sentence by inputting a monolingual corpus and translating its each sentence. But, strict quality checks and skilled translators need to be employed to ensure correctness and, usually, the process of translation is followed by a validation phase to ensure quality and reliability.

The process of parallel corpora generation can be divided into the following phases: translation, validation and sentence alignment. Furthermore, to help SMT tools like Moses (Koehn et al., 2007), it would be desirable to manually correct word alignments generated by an automatic tool such as GIZA++ (Och and Ney, 2003).

We present a comprehensive workbench to streamline the process of corpora creation for SMT. This common workbench allows for corpora generation, validation, evaluation, alignment and management simultaneously. We aim to simplify the laborious manual task of corpora generation for all language pairs, and provide with aides at each step.

2   Related Work

There are a wide class of document management solutions and products which fall under the category of "corpora and text mining". We find that though a lot of effort has gone into creating tools to aid in corpora generation for lower level NLP tasks such as POS tagging and chunking, but not much work has gone in the direction of corpora generation aid for Machine Translation (MT). The few similar works that we did find are noted below.

PolyPhraZ (Hajlaoui and Boitet, 2004) is one such tool which helps in visualizing, editing and evaluating MT systems on parallel corpora. CasualConc (Imao, 2008) is a parallel concordancer which generates keyword in context concordance lines, word clusters, collocation analysis, and word counts.

MemoQ (Kilgray, 2006) and Trados (SDL, 2007) are also Computer Aided Translation (CAT)

D S Sharma, R Sangal and J D Pawar. Proc. of the 11th Intl. Conference on Natural Language Processing, pages 162–166,
Goa, India. December 2014. ©2014 NLP Association of India (NLPAI)

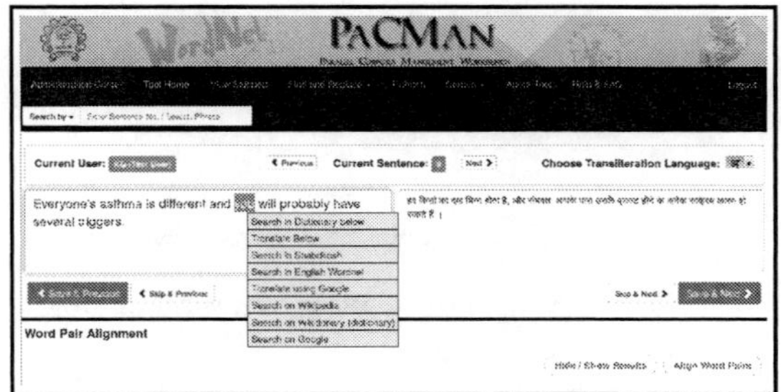

Figure 1: Snapshot of PaCMan on validation / translation screen

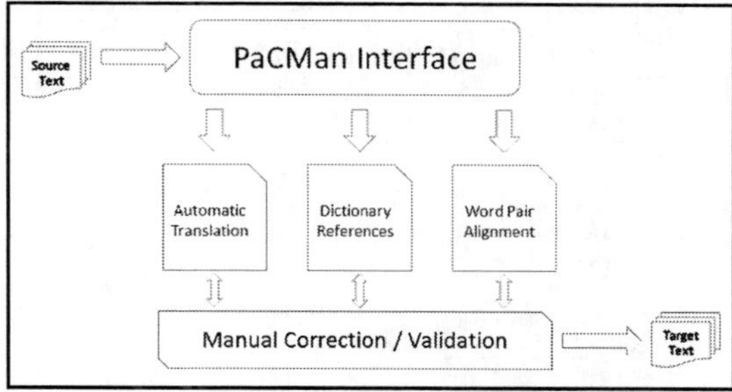

Figure 2: Workflow of the system

systems which are commercially available with features like Translation memory, and Term Extraction.

Wordfast is CAT system having just one free version "WordFast Anywhere". We studied and used the system, but found the interface less intuitive, and hard to use. "WordFast Anywhere" also has an integrated MT system which provides translations via Microsoft Bing and an integrated MT system.

Another system we came across is a web based text corpora development system (Yablonsky, 2003) that focuses on the development of UML-specifications, architecture and implementations of DBMS tools.

None of the above mentioned systems provide a word alignment visualization, which can be corrected manually, and saved to provide perfect phrase tables later.

3 Parallel Corpora Management System

Parallel Corpora Management System (PaCMan) (Figure: 1) is a platform-independent web-based workbench for managing all the processes involved in the generation of good quality parallel corpora. Along with covering the procedural / managerial aspects of the parallel corpora generation process, this tool also provides the means to track and manage the assignment and reporting of tasks in real-time.

As noted earlier, the tasks involved in the generation of a good quality parallel corpora can be broadly classified as follows:

- Translation

- Validation

- Sentence Alignment

- Word Alignment

Apart from these, there is also a need to manage the complete process. For an on-line tool such as the one we present, following activities need to be considered:

- User Registration for Superusers (Manager), translators / validators and aligners

- Task assignment and Tracking

- User session management

We have developed PaCMan to aid at every step of the process while ensuring high quality assistance. In the following sections we cover the various features that the tool provides.

3.1 Translation

Manual translation is the first step towards creating a parallel corpus. It is usually done by experienced translators who rely on their knowledge of source and target language to perform the task. But still, it proves a difficult task. From our experience in creating parallel corpus, we have learned that the task of manual translation can be made much easier if some assistances like dictionary aids, automated translations etc. are provided to the translators. We find that translators could do with some help on the following fronts:

- Translation of rare source language words

- Language input for non-standard scripts (Devanagari in case of Hindi and Marathi)

- Access to automatic translation of source text to speed up the translation process

- Access to previous translations of recurring phrases

In this tool, we have successfully addressed the above mentioned issues.

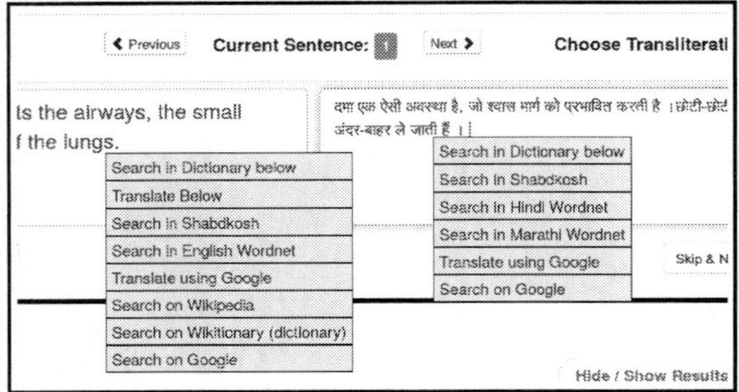

Figure 3: Snapshot of Right Click context menu

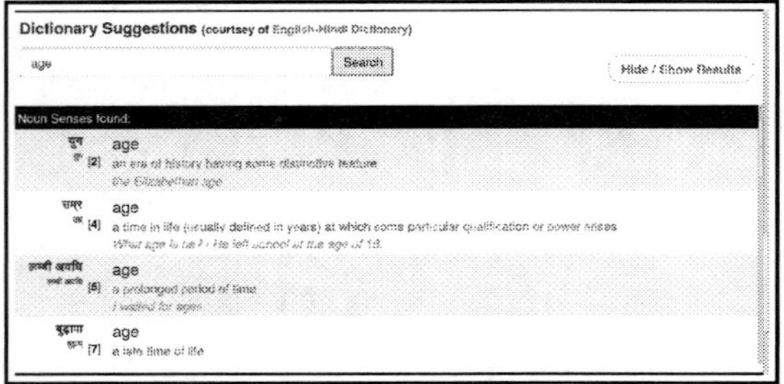

Figure 4: Snapshot of dictionary suggestions

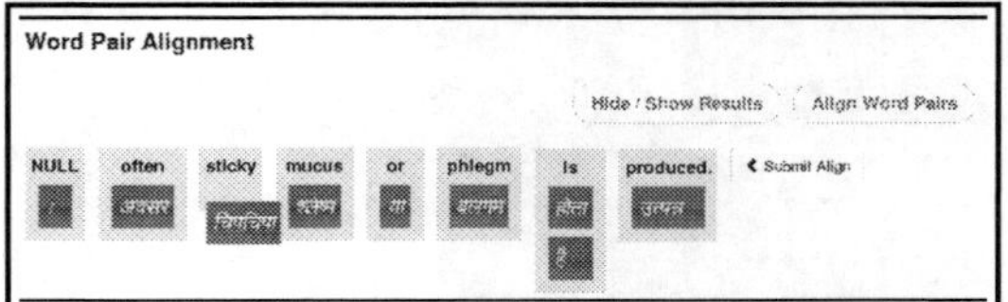

Figure 6: Snapshot of Word Alignment Box

3.1.1 Customized Context Menu Help

It is often the case that the translators, even with their substantial experience, find it hard to recall the meaning of some rare source language words. PaCMan helps overcome this difficulty by integrating various dictionary resources, and references. These dictionaries are provided on the translation screen as right-click menu items. Using these dictionaries the translator can get the meaning of a word simply by highlighting the word and choosing the preferred dictionary from the right-click menu (Figure: 3).

We have also integrated the corresponding UNL dictionary (Bhattacharyya, 2006) in the tool so that a user can select a word and can get its meaning on the same screen simply at the click of a button (Figure: 4). Further, we have integrated language specific Wordnets (Fellbaum, 1998) and (Dipak Narayan and Bhattacharyya, 2002), *ShabdKosh* (a Hindi-English dictionary) (Soni, 2003), Wikipedia and Wiktionary for these languages in the right-click menu. While these dictionaries provide the different meanings of a word, the user can also choose to translate a word or phrase directly by choosing "Google Translate" from the right-click context menu.

We found that the requirement of inputting data in Indian langugages can be easily overcome by integrating a transliteration API, using which the roman script should be converted to the chosed Indian script automatically. Thus, We integrated "Google Transliteration API" in our tool.

Further, if the user wants to see the word's use in contexts other than the given source language sentence, she can choose to fire a Google search query by choosing "Search in Google" option from the right-click menu.

3.1.2 Automatic Translation

It is sometimes easier and faster to correct a translation than to translate from scratch. Also, even if a machine generated translation is syntactically or semantically incorrect, it can give the translator a kernel around which the final correct translation may be built.

Thus, we have integrated Sata-Anuvadak (Anoop Kunchukuttan and Bhattacharyya, 2014), a Moses Decoder based SMT system for multiple Indic languages with our tool which can generate an automatic translation of a given English sentence at the click of a button. In the worst case, the translator would still need to manually translate but she would have gotten a fair idea of the possible translation, given some words get translated correctly.

3.1.3 Previous Translations

Parallel corpora generation very quickly becomes a repetitive task. A translator at times would like to find previously translated sentences. This has been made easy by introducing at ability to search for a word or a phrase and find the parallel sentences with the translations for that particular word or phrase (Figure: 5).

3.2 Validation

Validation or quality control of the translated sentences is the next logical step. Even the best translators can make mistakes, so it is imperative that we re-check the translations. Validation is very similar to translation except that the translations are already available. All the aids available to a

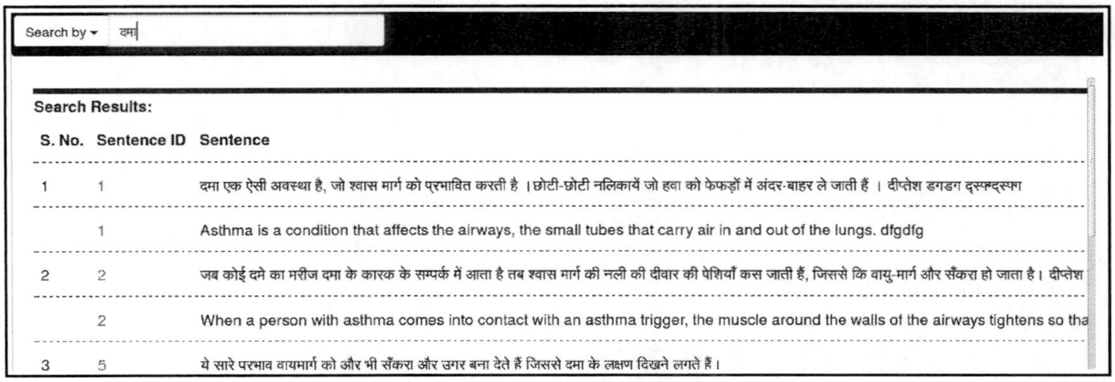

Figure 5: Snapshot of Search Results

translator are also available to a validator. A validator may change a sentence completely or make minor modifications as the need may be.

A validator can also be given fresh parallel corpus which is not generated on this work bench. Such corpus may be uploaded by any superuser responsible for a language pair.

3.3 Word Alignment Visualization and Gamification

The accuracy of a SMT system depends on the quality of word alignment produced by an aligner. For free word ordered languages and languages with rich morphology, aligners can often make many mistakes which eventually have dire effect on decoder accuracy. We aim to provide word level alignment for every sentence in the corpus (Figure: 6). It is expected that this will greatly enhance the performance of an SMT system trained on the alignment data provided by our tool. Currently, we have trained GIZA++ on nearly 48000 sentences.

We provide the means to augment the word alignments to eventually aid in higher accuracy for SMT. We have integrated GIZA++ aligner with our tool to allow a user to correct the alignments provided by it. A user might also choose to do the alignment completely manually using the visual drag and drop interface provided in the tool. Its rich interface lets you align words and phrases with a lot of ease. This can easily be pushed towards a crowd sourced word alignment collector with some gamification. We believe it can lead to a very high amount of perfect word / phrase alignments.

3.4 Administrative Tasks

Corpora Management System provides for various roles a user might need to play in the process of parallel corpus generation. The system is designed to work for multiple language pairs simultaneously. Each corpus can have its own superuser (manager). The superuser then distributes tasks among other users to work.

3.4.1 Corpora Upload and Download

Superusers can upload corpora to be translated, validated or aligned. Corpora upload is in the form of two plain text files in unicode encoding or two archives containing plain text files. For translation, only a single source file needs to be uploaded whereas for any other task two parallel files are needed. Once the assigned task has been performed the registered user can download complete or partial data or can commit the data which the superuser would finally commit to the master database.

3.4.2 Task Assignment

Superusers can assign tasks to different users. A superuser chooses complete or partial corpora and assigns it to a user who can perform the assigned task. At the time of corpora assignment a copy of the data is created specific to the user while the master database remains untouched. The master database can only be changed when the user finishes the task and sends the data back to the superuser. At which point the superuser commits the data back to the master database. A superuser can track the work done by any user who has been assigned a task by her.

3.4.3 Session Management

The system is equipped with both browser based and internal session management. When a user logs in, she is taken directly to the last sentence that was being validated / translated at the time of previous logout.

While navigating through the sentences a user can choose to skip sentences if she so desires. At any point of time she can choose to "View Skipped" sentences and work with them. When she is finished with the skipped sentences, she can go back to the normal view, landing on the last un-saved sentence.

4 Design

The system is developed in PHP and uses MySQL as backend. Various Javascript and jQuery snippets have b een developed along with AJAX to make sure the user stays on the same page. The system has been designed such that user would find every validation aid on the same screen, decreasing the shuffles between screens thus increasing productivity. The advantage of such a design is that the user would not have to change application for different tasks like referring to dictionaries etc.

5 Conclusion and Future Work

We have presented PaCMan, a web-based system that aids parallel corpora generation for the task of machine translation. The system provides an intuitive interface and many valuable features that increase the productivity at every stage of corpora generation process. It provides the user with dictionary references, and automatic translations during translation and validation of parallel corpus. The system also aids word pair alignments. It provides an authentication based corpora management system where multiple parallel corpora can be maintained. The system is open for use to everybody. We expect further extensions of our system will support the development of better parallel corpora and aid machine translation further.

We believe gamification of our word pair alignment feature will help in collecting perfect word / phrase pair alignments which can result in a better performing Moses decoder, and thus a higher accuracy of an SMT system. We aim at providing such an extension of our system soon.

References

Rajen Chatterjee Ritesh Shah Anoop Kunchukuttan, Abhijit Mishra and Pushpak Bhattacharyya. 2014. Shata-anuvadak: Tackling multiway translation of indian languages. In *Proceedings of the 9th Edition of its Language Resources and Evaluation Conference.*, LREC '14.

Pushpak Bhattacharyya. 2006. English - hindi dictionary. `http://www.cfilt.iitb.ac.in/~hdict/webinterface_user/`.

Prabhakar Pande Dipak Narayan, Debasri Chakrabarti and Pushpak Bhattacharyya. 2002. An experience in building the indo wordnet - a wordnet for hindi. In *Proceesdings of First International Conference on Global WordNet*, Mysore, India.

Christiane Fellbaum. 1998. *WordNet: An Electronic Lexical Database*. Bradford Books.

Najeh Hajlaoui and Christian Boitet. 2004. Polyphraz: A tool for the management of parallel corpora. In *Proceedings of the Workshop on Multilingual Linguistic Ressources*, MLR '04, pages 109–116, Stroudsburg, PA, USA. Association for Computational Linguistics.

Yasu Imao. 2008. Casualconc. `http://sites.google.com/site/casualconc/`.

Kilgray. 2006. memoq [computer software]. `http://kilgray.com/products/memoq`.

Philipp Koehn, Hieu Hoang, Alexandra Birch, Chris Callison-Burch, Marcello Federico, Nicola Bertoldi, Brooke Cowan, Wade Shen, Christine Moran, Richard Zens, Chris Dyer, Ondřej Bojar, Alexandra Constantin, and Evan Herbst. 2007. Moses: Open source toolkit for statistical machine translation. In *Proceedings of the 45th Annual Meeting of the ACL on Interactive Poster and Demonstration Sessions*, ACL '07, pages 177–180, Stroudsburg, PA, USA. Association for Computational Linguistics.

Franz Josef Och and Hermann Ney. 2003. A systematic comparison of various statistical alignment models. *Computational Linguistics*, 29(1):19–51.

SDL. 2007. Sdl trados studio [computer software]. `http://www.translationzone.com/products/sdl-trados-studio/`.

Manish Soni. 2003. Shabdkosh. `http://www.shabdkosh.com`.

Serge Yablonsky. 2003. The corpora management system based on java and oracle technologies. In *Proceedings of the Tenth Conference on European Chapter of the Association for Computational Linguistics - Volume 2*, EACL '03, pages 179–182, Stroudsburg, PA, USA. Association for Computational Linguistics.

How to Know the Best Machine Translation System in Advance before Translating a Sentence?

Bibekananda Kundu and Sanjay Kumar Choudhury
Language Technology, ICT and Services
Centre for Development of Advanced Computing, Kolkata
E-mail: {bibekananda.kundu,sanjay.choudhury}@cdac.in

Abstract

The aim of the paper is to identify a machine translation (MT) system from a set of multiple MT systems in *advance*, capable of producing most appropriate translation for a source sentence. *The prediction is done based on the analysis of a source sentence before translating it using these MT systems.* This selection procedure has been framed as a classification task. A machine learning based approach leveraging features extracting from analysis of a source sentence has been proposed here. *The main contribution of the paper is selection of source-side features.* These features help machine learning approaches to discriminate MT systems according to their translation quality though these approaches have no idea about working principle of these MT systems. The proposed approach is language independent and has shown promising result when applied on English-Bangla MT task.

1 Introduction

The question, *"Will machine translation ever replace human translation services?"*, is a long standing debate in the field of AI. Though state-of-the-art machine translation (MT) systems (Koehn, 2010; Koehn et al., 2007; Bach et al., 2007) often provide quite acceptable translations, but demand for producing high quality translations still requires professional human translators (HTs). In spite of debat-ing on selection of slow, expensive but effective human translations versus fast and acceptable machine translations, collaboration of human and machine is a preferable option towards producing fast and high quality translations (of Edinburgh, 2014). In this collaboration, MT systems are used as aids for HTs to craft their translations. Several studies (Specia, 2011; Skadiņš et al., 2011; Koehn and Germann, 2014; Koponen, 2013) have provided strong evidence for improvement of productivity by post-editing machine translated outputs instead of unassisted translations. These aids enabling HTs to translate faster by simply adding, deleting words or reordering a small portion of the machine translation. As a result more and more high quality translations are being produced in shorter time. This synergy also speeds up the parallel corpora creation process (Chaudary et al., 2008) which eventually boosts the performance of statistical MT systems.

In addition to this, these days more than one MT systems are also available for certain language pairs. For instance, to translate from English to Bangla we have three MT systems, namely, AnglaBharati[1] (Sinha et al., 1995), Anuvadaksh[2] and Google Translator.[3] However, qualities of translations produced by individual systems are not the same. One possible reason behind this is they follow different paradigms. These paradigms in-

---

[1] Online system is available at `http://tdil-dc.in/components/com_mtsystem/CommonUI/homeMT.php`

[2] Description is available at `http://tdil-dc.in/tdildcMain/IPR/Anuvaadaaksh.pdf`

[3] Online system and description are available at `https://translate.google.co.in/` and `http://translate.google.co.in/about/intl/en_ALL/`

D S Sharma, R Sangal and J D Pawar. Proc. of the 11th Intl. Conference on Natural Language Processing, pages 167–176,
Goa, India. December 2014. ©2014 NLP Association of India (NLPAI)

clude rule-based (Bharati et al., 2010; Sinha et al., 1995; Magnúsdóttir, 1993), example-based (Carl et al., 2004), statistical (Koehn, 2010; Kunchukuttan et al., 2014) and hybrid (Sánchez-Cartagena et al., 2014; Chatterji et al., 2009). Moreover, in case of statistical MT systems, acceptability of translations differs according to the training set on which they are trained. Now an obvious question can come to our mind, *"How does one can use more than one MT system for translating from a source to target language?"*. Answer to this question is twofold: using consensus translation (Macherey and Och, 2007; Bangalore et al., 2001) and selecting most appropriate one from a set of translations generated by different systems (Dara et al., 2013; Zwarts and Dras, 2008). However, both approaches require same source sentence to be translated multiple times which indeed is a time consuming task. The time required to translate is proportional to the number of available MT systems. However, the processing time is not a matter of big concern because of availability of high speed computers and parallel computing algorithms. The main challenge is manual selection of suitable translation from a set of auto generated translations. To address this issue, we have proposed a methodology that automatically predict the best MT system in advance that will produce most appropriate translation for a source sentence. The prior prediction of best MT system does not require translation of the source sentence. It is also unaware of the working principle of the underlying MT systems. We hope that this approach will speed up the manual translation even more by reducing the searching cost for the appropriate translation.

1.1 What is the Value of Another Approach?

Solution addressing this specific problem is already in place. In this context, work of Sánchez-Martínez (2011) is worth mentioning. He has proposed a methodology to select the best MT system by using only information extracted from the source sentence to be translated without knowing the inner working of the MT systems. He has experimented on two European language pairs viz. English-Spanish and French-Spanish. He has used five binary maximum entropy classifiers and used mainly two types of features, namely, phrase-structure features and probabilistic features. The features reported by him, have also been used for sentence-level confidence estimation of MT (Quirk, 2004; Blatz et al., 2004).

1.1.1 Contributions

In this paper, we have proposed a similar approach to leverage the features extracted from source sentences without considering inner working principle of the MT systems. However, *our work is different from the existing approach with respect to selection of features and machine learning algorithms*. Therefore, two main ingredients of our proposed approach are (a) rich feature set and (b) classification technique. In addition to using phrase-structure and probabilistic features, *we have introduced dependency based features extracted from dependency trees*. Dependency based features have already been proven to be a good parameter for measuring goodness of machine translation (Bach et al., 2011; Goldberg and Orwant, 2013). *Moreover, to the best of our knowledge this is the first work done on English to Indian language MT systems*.

1.2 Outline

With a aim to select best MT system for a given source sentence, we have formulated this problem as a classification task in Section 2. Types of features used for this classification task have been discussed here. Visualization technique along with feature selection methodologies also have been discussed in this section. In Section 3, we explain the experiments conducted on two English-Bangla MT systems from two different paradigms: one is rule-based and the other one is statistical. Preparation of training dataset has also been discussed here. Results are discussed in Section 4. Finally, we conclude the paper with future scope of actions in Section 5.

2 Brief Grounding for Our Approach

The selection of best MT system from a multiple MT systems can be seen as a multi-class classification problem where class labels are $C = \{MT_1, MT_2, \ldots, MT_n\}$, representing different MT systems. Our task is to discriminate the best class $MT_i \in C$ using a machine learning classifier that depends on the features $F = \{f_1, f_2, \ldots, f_n\}$ extracted from analysis of source sentences. For simplicity, in this paper, we have framed this problem as a binary classification having only two class labels. In any classification task features play an important role to disseminate among classes. Therefore, in the next subsection we will discuss on the types of features used in this classification task.

2.1 Feature Set for Selecting Best MT System

Identification of proper features is a vital task to address this classification problem. In our case, the problem is quite difficult because we are trying identify features from the analysis of a source sentence to predict the quality of MT system. The main assumption is that source side features will be able to capture the latent relationships with the translation quality for that sentence. Source side features are extracted from phrase-structure and dependency trees. Figure 1 and 2 show a phrase-structure tree and a dependency tree of an English sentence *"Was my camera repaired already?"*. Features extracted from phrase-structure tree represent structural complexity of a sentence. Similarly features extracted from a dependency tree represent how words in a sentence depend on each other even for long distances. As a result, long distance dependencies are good indicators of complexity of a sentence. Based on training data, probabilistic features represent complexity in term of out-of-vocabulary (OOV), likelihood of a sentence, likelihood of a dependency relation, mapping capability of a source word to multiple target words or vice versa. Complexity related to phrase-structure and dependency influences the translation quality of rule-based MT systems whereas statistical MT systems are influenced by probabilistic features. So for proper classification, we have considered three types of features viz. (a) **phrase-structure features**, (b) **dependency features** and (c) **probabilistic features**. Some of the phrase-structure and probabilistic features have already been considered in the work of Sánchez-Martínez (2011). However, *we have introduced new features like number of unique Parts of Speech (POS) tags, POS tag density etc. in our phrase-structure feature set*. Examples of phrase-structure features are as follows:

- Number of Unique POS Tags (NUPT)

- POS Tag Density (PTD): PTD is a measure of the ratio of the number of different POS tags to the total number of POS tags.

- Maximum Depth of the Phrase-Structure Tree (MDST)

- Mean Depth of the Phrase-Structure Tree (MeanDST) : MeanDST is a measure of the ratio of the sum of the individual depths of all leaf nodes to the total number of leaf nodes.

- Maximum Number of Child Nodes per Node Found in the Phrase-Structure Tree (MNCNNFST)

- Mean Number of Child Nodes per Node Found in the Phrase-Structure Tree (MeanNCNNFST)

- Number of Internal Nodes (NIN)

Examples of probabilistic features are

- Joint Probability of Input Sentence (JPIS): We have approximated JPIS using trigram sequences as shown in Equation 1.

$$
\begin{aligned}
P(S = w_1 w_2 w_3 \cdots w_n) = {} & P(w_1) \\
& \times P(w_2|w_1) \\
& \times P(w_3|w_1 w_2) \\
& \times \cdots \\
& \times P(w_n|w_{n-2} w_{n-1})
\end{aligned}
\tag{1}
$$

- Joint Probability Using N-gram Dependency (JPUND): We have used dependency based language model as reported in (Shen et al., 2008). JPUND for the dependency tree shown in Figure 2 is calculated using Equation 2.

$$
\begin{aligned}
JPUND = \; & P_T(repaired) \\
& \times P_L(camera \mid repaired_{head}) \\
& \times P_L(my \mid camera_{head}) \\
& \times P_L(was \mid my, camera_{head}) \\
& \times P_R(already \mid repaired_{head}) \\
& \times P_R(? \mid already, repaired_{head})
\end{aligned}
\tag{2}
$$

Here, $P_T(w)$ is the probability that word w is the root of a dependency tree. P_L and P_R are left and right side generative probabilities respectively.

- Maximum Fertility (MF) and Maximum Distortion (MD) : Fertility is defined as the number of target words generated from individual source words in a particular alignment of training data (Brown et al., 1990). Distortion is defined as the reordering distance of target words generated by a source word in a particular alignment (Brown et al., 1993). Depending on the target sentence alignment, each source word may have multiple fertilities and distortions. So maximum fertility and maximum distortion of a source sentence is defined as the highest fertility and distortion of individual constituent words of the source respectively. MF and MD of all vocabulary are pre-calculated during training. Later, these values are used to calculate the MF and MD of a source input sentence.

Features generated from dependency trees have already been used for measuring goodness of machine translation (Bach et al., 2011; Goldberg and Orwant, 2013). In this paper we have introduced dependency based features for selecting best translation system. Examples of some of our dependency based features are as follows:

- Number of Dependency Links (NDL)

- Maximum Dependency Distance (MDD): Dependency distance is the distance between head node and its dependent node. For example, in Figure 2 dependency distances between the head word *"repaired"*

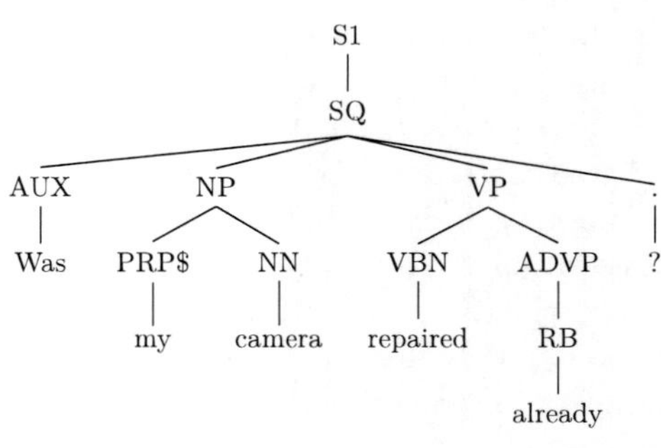

Figure 1: A phrase-structure tree.

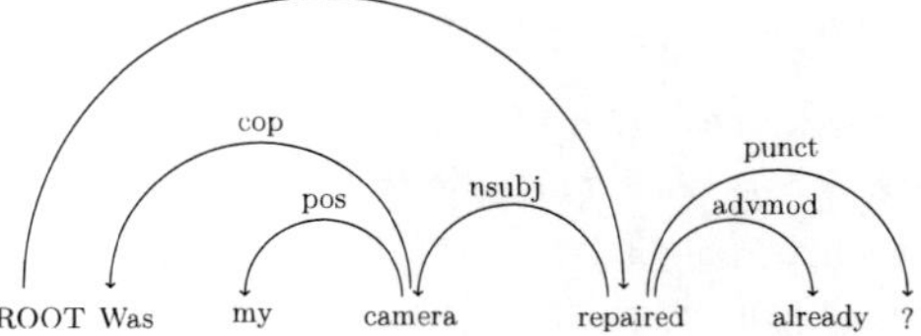

Figure 2: A dependency tree.

and its dependent words *"camera"*, *"already"* and *"?"* are 1, 1 and 2 respectively. MDD of the dependency tree shown in Figure 2 is 4 i.e. distance between *"ROOT"* and *"repaired"*.

- Mean Dependency Distance (MeanDD)

- Standard Deviation of Dependency Distances (SDDD)

- Maximum amongst the Number of Dependents of a Word (MNDW)

Now, using these three types of features we have extracted the feature values from the analysis of source sentences. An example of feature values extracted from the analysis of an English sentence, *"Was my camera repaired already?"*, has been shown in Table 1.

2.2 Feature Selection and Visualization

A large number of features have an adverse effect on efficiency and irrelevant features hamper the accurate prediction of class label. So, there is a requirement for reduction of dimensionality by filtering the irrelevant and redundant features. Manual identification of important features from a large number of features is practically not feasible. We have applied Information Gain (IG) (Lee and Lee, 2006)

Feature Attributes:	NDL	MDD	$\cdots$	MNDW	NUPT	PTD	MDST	NIN	JPIS
Feature Values:	6	4	$\cdots$	4	6	1.0	5	10	-14.4073

Table 1: An example of feature values extracted from the English sentence *"Was my camera repaired already?"*. Here, the joint probability value is shown in logarithm scale.

and Chi-square (χ^2) attribute evaluators (Jin et al., 2006) on our training data to find out features which are more relevant for this classification task. IG and χ^2 attribute evaluators evaluate the worth of an attribute by computing the value of the information grain and chi-squared statistic with respect to the class and rank features accordingly. IG and χ^2 attribute evaluators only provide rank of the features. Therefore, features having average merit value greater than a predefine threshold[4] are selected for the classification task. Impact of these features selected using different techniques, has been discussed in Subsection 3.2.3.

Visualization is important in the context of feature selection to visualize the underling representation and goodness of the training data (Feldman and Sanger, 2006). Visualization helps expert users to determine which features are important for their classification task. We have used a freely available visualization tool named as Hierarchical Clustering Explorer (HCE)[5]. Figure 3 shows mosaic view of the feature values in a representative sample of our training set[6]. In colour mosaic plot, graphical pattern of multidimensional data is represented using colourful tiles depending on the numerical value of data. High, low and medium values are represented using bright red, bright green and black colour respectively. As a value gets closer to the middle value from high to low or vice versa, the colour becomes darker. Here, each row represents individual feature values for all examples (training instances) whereas each column represents all feature values for individual instances.

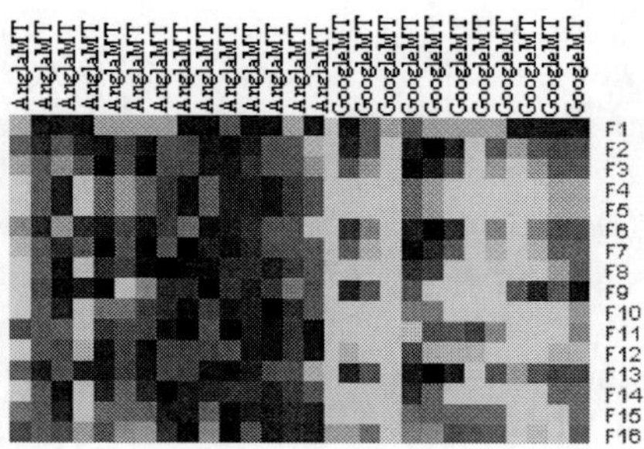

Figure 3: Visualization of multi dimensional features.

3 Experiments

3.1 Questions to Answer

Experiments in the current study are conducted to answer the following questions:

- Can features extracted from source sentences predict the quality of a MT system?

- Which machine learning algorithm is most appropriate for this classification task?

- How selection of different types of features influences the performances of classifiers?

In our work, the experiment has been conducted on English-Bangla MT systems.

3.2 Experiments on English-Bangla Machine Translation Systems

In our classification problem, we have two classes *"AnglaMT"* and *"GoogleMT"* representing AnglaBharati and Google MT system respectively. We have considered two MT systems belong to two different paradigms. The first one is a pseudo interlingua based (rule-based) MT approach and later one follows a statistical approach.

3.2.1 Data Preparation

We have collected 20k English sentences from Basic Travel Expression Corpus

---

[4]In our experiment we have manually selected the threshold values as 10±13 and 0.001±0.002 for χ^2 and IG attribute evaluators respectively

[5]HCE tool is available at http://www.cs.umd.edu/hcil/hce/

[6]Using HCE, interested readers can see the actual representation of the feature values in our training data which is available at http://14.139.223.131/download/

(BTEC) (Takezawa et al., 2007) and manually translated them into Bangla. At the time of translating these sentences, two machine translations generated from AnglaBharati and Google MT systems have been provided to manual translators for their assistance. We also have collected a corpus of 50k English-Bangla parallel sentences which has been prepared for Health and Tourism domain under the Indian Languages Corpora Initiative (ILCI) project initiated by the DEITY, Govt. of India[7] (Jha, 2010). The first corpus contains sentences from basic expression dialogues of Travel domain. The second corpus contains 25k sentences from Health and 25k sentences from Tourism domain. Thus, we have collected total 70k English-Bangla parallel aligned sentences. Then we randomly selected 7k English sentences out of 70k and automatically translated them using both rule-based and statistical MT systems. For the rule-based MT we selected English to Bangla AnglaBharati system and for statistical MT we used Google MT system. Thus, we have prepared a dataset of 7k sentences having three translations of each English sentence i.e. one manual translation, two machine translations from a rule-based and a statistical MT system. Both the systems provide multiple translations. In case of multiple translations, we have selected the translation having highest BLEU (Papineni et al., 2002) score with the reference manual translation, so that the translation closest to the reference translation gets selected. After preparing these raw data having English sentences with their respective translations, we have applied all the feature functions on the English sentences to extract the feature values. Phrase-structure features (Zhang et al., 2008) are extracted from phrase-structure trees generated using Charniak parser (`http://cs.brown.edu/~ec/`). We have extracted dependency based features from dependency trees. Dependency trees are extracted using malt parser (`http://www.maltparser.org/`). Probabilistic features are extracted using Moses toolkit (Koehn et al., 2007) (`http://www.statmt.org/moses/`). To

prepare the balanced dataset (Longadge and Dongre, 2013), we have selected 5906 instances[8] from 7k data, such that proportion of the classes become 50%. The final dataset has been prepared in *arff format* having 20 attributes, 2 classes and 5906 rows of instances. Each row contains 20 numerical feature values corresponding to 20 attributes. For the English sentence *"Was my camera repaired already?"*, an instance of the training data looks like $\{6, 4, \cdots, 4, 6, 1.0, 5, 10, -14.4073, AnglaMT\}$ (see Table 1). We assigned a class label *"AnglaMT"* if the BLEU score of the translation generated from AnglaBharati MT system is higher than translation generated from Google MT system otherwise, *"GoogleMT"* class label is assigned.

3.2.2 Experiment with Different Classifiers

We have used a WEKA data mining toolkit[9] (Witten and Frank, 2005) with default parameters for classifying MT systems based on the features extracted from the analysis of source sentences. Relevant features are extracted using an Information Gain Attribute Evaluator (IGAE) and a Chi-square Attribute Evaluator (CSAE) available in WEKA toolkit[10]. We have compared among different classifiers like WEKA implementation of Naïve Bayes, IBk (Aha et al., 1991) - a Lazy or Instance based learner that uses K-nearest neighbour algorithm, Multi Layer Perceptron (MLP) (Mitchell, 1997), LibSVM - a library for Support Vector Machines (Cristianini and Shawe-Taylor, 2000), Logistic - a class for building and using a multinomial logistic regression model with a ridge estimator (Le Cessie and Van Houwelingen, 1992) and Voted Perceptron (VP) (Freund and Schapire, 1999). These classifiers are trained on the dataset as discussed in Subsection 3.2.1. We have experimented using 10-fold cross validation on the same training

---

[7]The corpus is available at http://www.tdil-dc.in/

[8]Our dataset is available at `http://14.139.223.131/download/` so that researchers can experiment on it by applying their approaches.

[9]WEKA data mining toolkit is available at `http://www.cs.waikato.ac.nz/~ml/weka/`

[10]The class implementing IGAE and CSAE are `weka.attributeSelection.InfoGainAttributeEval` and `weka.attributeSelection.ChiSquaredAttributeEval`

data. To measure statistical significance of the performance of each of the classifiers, we have used the class implementing the Paired T-Tester (Mangal, 2012) which is `weka.experiment.PairedCorrectedTTester`.

3.2.3 Contributions of Feature Sets

We have designed our experiment to see the impact of individual types of features as well as combined effect on this classification task. We have conducted nine experiments using these WEKA implementations of classifiers on the same dataset. Each classifier is experimented using the following feature sets:

1. SF: a feature set contains only phrase-structure features.

2. DF: a feature set is prepared considering only dependency based features.

3. PF: a feature set having only probabilistic features.

4. SF + DF.

5. SF + PF: this is similar feature set used by Sánchez-Martínez (2011), except some extra phrase-structure features like NUPT, PTD etc.

6. DF + PF.

7. SF + DF + PF.

8. IGF: important features are extracted using IGAE.

9. χ^2F: relevant features are extracted using CSAE.

4 Results and Discussion

Figure 4 shows the performances of different classifiers using 10-fold cross validation and considering all feature values. These performances are measured in term of Percentage Correct. It has been seen that the nearest neighbour classifier i.e. IB1 outperforms any other classifier considered. It uses normalized Euclidean distance to find the training instance closest to the given test instance and predicts the same class according to this training instance. We have measured the contributions of different feature sets in terms of Percentage Correct obtained using 10-fold cross

validation of the same training data. The results of our experiments on different feature sets have been shown in Table 2. Standard deviations of Percentage Corrects of each of the classifiers are shown within brackets. Moreover, these values are statistically significant within 95% confidence intervals. From the experimental results, we can see that the performance constantly improves when we used combined feature sets. Moreover, performances of all the classifiers except IBk improve for the feature type SF+DF+PF. However, best performance has been achieved using IB1 for the feature type SF+PF. Though the introduction of DF does not substantially improve the performance of IB1, but it has been observed that this introduction helps to improve the performance of other classifiers. For instance, we can see from Table 2, an overall increment of 2.5 for LibSVM, 0.97 for MLP and 1.05 for VP has been achieved.

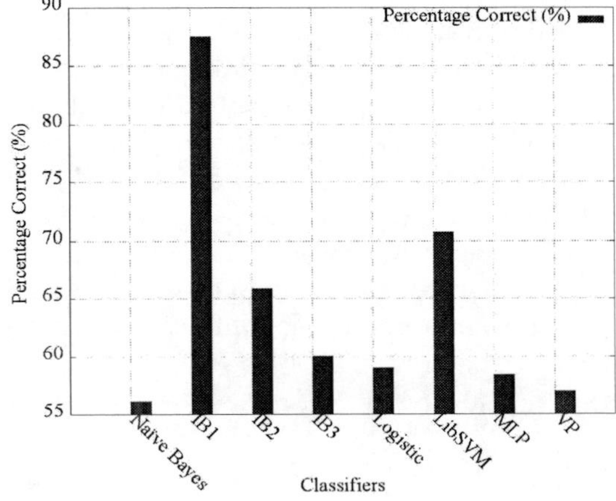

Figure 4: Comparison among performances of different classifiers for choosing best MT system.

5 Conclusions

In this paper, we have proposed a machine learning approach for selecting a MT system producing most appropriate translation before translating the input sentence. The prediction is done depending only on the features extracted from a source sentence without knowing the inner process of the MT system. Our approach uses phrase-structure, probabilistic and dependency features. Primarily, the proposed approached has been ap-

Feature Set	Classifiers							
	Naïve Bayes	IB1	IB2	IB3	Logistic	LibSVM	MLP	VP
SF	56.09	84.34	66.31	60.59	57.72	60.56	56.56	55.49
	(1.97)	(1.56)	(1.54)	(1.74)	(2.22)	(1.86)	(2.75)	(2.06)
DF	56.00	80.10	66.87	62.42	57.08	59.18	54.95	55.75
	(1.96)	(1.69)	(1.90)	(1.96)	(2.01)	(1.71)	(2.56)	(1.86)
PF	55.70	87.31	65.73	59.78	56.55	61.55	55.15	53.11
	(1.88)	(1.30)	(1.52)	(1.71)	(2.32)	(2.10)	(2.70)	(1.96)
SF+DF	**56.23**	86.14	66.20	60.19	58.27	66.44	57.69	57.13
	(1.98)	(1.70)	(2.07)	(2.05)	(2.00)	(2.07)	(2.47)	(1.91)
SF+PF	55.99	**87.77**	66.60	60.51	**59.09**	68.28	57.43	55.93
	(1.92)	**(1.36)**	(1.56)	(1.87)	**(2.22)**	(1.81)	(2.31)	(1.88)
SF+DF+PF	56.14	**87.55**	65.85	60.05	**59.02**	**70.78**	**58.40**	56.98
	(1.98)	**(1.38)**	(1.84)	(2.02)	**(2.56)**	**(2.10)**	**(2.56)**	(1.93)
IGF	55.78	87.03	65.11	59.82	58.86	69.86	57.64	**57.64**
	(1.94)	(1.47)	(1.82)	(2.08)	(2.26)	(2.07)	(2.64)	**(2.64)**
χ^2F	55.83	87.11	65.07	60.51	58.73	69.71	57.80	56.49
	(1.95)	(1.38)	(1.93)	(2.01)	(2.27)	(1.89)	(2.42)	(1.92)

Table 2: Contributions of different feature sets measure in Percentage Correct (%).

plied on English-Bangla MT systems. Experiment shows IB1 classifier provides statistically significant performance (with 95% confidence) considering all types of features. The proposed approach is language independent and can be applied on any language pair where multiple MT systems are available. Features used in this paper can also be applied on similar NLP tasks where measuring confidence of the system is required.

5.1 Where from Here?

We think the next step should be examining the human and machine translations in parallel to have insight into which features are more central in determining quality of MT systems. Given these features, we would like to employ an ensemble classifier (Dietterich, 2000) to combine the predictions of multiple classifiers. Because ensembles can often perform better than any single classifier. As a future work, we are also planing to use a development set to tune the trained classifiers. Moreover, we would also like to use different configuration of WEKA to see the changes in performances of individual classifiers. In this classification task, we have seen that the best performance is achieved by the IB1 which is basically an instance based classifier. The competence of instance based learners depends on several fac-

tors viz. size, position of instances in multidimensional feature space and inherent problem complexity due to decision boundary (Massie, 2006). Therefore, we are also planing to concentrate on these factors for further improvement of the performance of this classifier.

References

David W. Aha, Dennis Kibler, and Marc K. Albert. 1991. Instance-Based Learning Algorithms. *Machine Learning*, 6(1):37–66, January.

Nguyen Bach, Matthias Eck, Paisarn Charoenpornsawat, Thilo Khler, Sebastian Stker, ThuyLinh Nguyen, Roger Hsiao, Alex Waibel, Stephan Vogel, Tanja Schultz, and Alan Black. 2007. The CMU TransTac 2007 Eyes-free and Hands-free Two-way Speech-to-Speech Translation System. In *Proc. of the International Workshop on Spoken Language Translation*, Trento, Italy.

Nguyen Bach, Fei Huang, and Yaser Al-Onaizan. 2011. Goodness: A Method for Measuring Machine Translation Confidence. In *Proceedings of the 49th Annual Meeting of the Association for Computational Linguistics: Human Language Technologies - Volume 1*, HLT '11, pages 211–219, Stroudsburg, PA, USA.

Srinivas Bangalore, German Bordel, and Giuseppe Riccardi. 2001. Computing Consensus Translation from Multiple Machine Translation Systems. In *Automatic Speech Recognition and Un-*

derstanding, 2001. ASRU '01. IEEE Workshop on, pages 351–354.

Akshar Bharati, Vineet Chaitanya, and Rajeev Sangal. 2010. *Natural Language Processing: A Paninian Perspective.* PHI.

John Blatz, Erin Fitzgerald, George Foster, Simona Gandrabur, Cyril Goutte, Alex Kulesza, Alberto Sanchis, and Nicola Ueffing. 2004. Confidence Estimation for Machine Translation. In *Proceedings of the 20th International Conference on Computational Linguistics*, COLING '04, Stroudsburg, PA, USA.

Peter F. Brown, John Cocke, Stephen A. Della Pietra, Vincent J. Della Pietra, Fredrick Jelinek, John D. Lafferty, Robert L. Mercer, and Paul S. Roossin. 1990. A Statistical Approach to Machine Translation. *Comput. Linguist.*, 16(2):79–85, June.

Peter F. Brown, Vincent J. Della Pietra, Stephen A. Della Pietra, and Robert L. Mercer. 1993. The Mathematics of Statistical Machine Translation: Parameter Estimation. *Comput. Linguist.*, 19(2):263–311, June.

Michael Carl, Andy Way, and Walter Daelemans. 2004. Recent Advances in Example-Based Machine Translation. *Comput. Linguist.*, 30(4):516–520, December.

Sanjay Chatterji, Devshri Roy, Sudeshna Sarkar, and Anupam Basu. 2009. A Hybrid Approach for Bengali to Hindi Machine Translation. In *Proceedings of 7th International Conference on Natural Language Processing (ICON-2009)*, pages 83–91, India.

Sriram Chaudary, Kiran Pala, Lakshminarayana Kodavali, and Keshav Singhal. 2008. Enhancing Effectiveness of Sentence Alignment in Parallel Corpora: UsingMT & Heuristics. In *Proceedings of International Conference on Natural Language Processing (ICON-2008)*, India. Macmillan Publishers.

Nello Cristianini and John Shawe-Taylor. 2000. *An Introduction to Support Vector Machines and Other Kernel-base Learning Methods.* Cambridge University Press.

Aswarth Abhilash Dara, Sandipan Dandapat, Declan Groves, and Josef van Genabith. 2013. TMTprime: A Recommender System for MT and TM Integration. In *HLT-NAACL'13*, pages 10–13.

Thomas G. Dietterich. 2000. Ensemble Methods in Machine Learning. In *Proceedings of the First International Workshop on Multiple Classifier Systems*, MCS '00, pages 1–15, London, UK. Springer-Verlag.

Ronen Feldman and James Sanger. 2006. *Text Mining Handbook: Advanced Approaches in Analyzing Unstructured Data.* Cambridge University Press, New York, NY, USA.

Yoav Freund and Robert E. Schapire. 1999. Large Margin Classification Using the Perceptron Algorithm. *Machine Learning*, 37(3):277–296, December.

Yoav Goldberg and Jon Orwant. 2013. A Dataset of Syntactic-Ngrams over Time from a Very Large Corpus of English Books. In *Second Joint Conference on Lexical and Computational Semantics, Volume 1: Proceedings of the Main Conference and the Shared Task: Semantic Textual Similarity*, pages 241–247, Atlanta, Georgia, USA, June.

Girish Nath Jha. 2010. The TDIL Program and the Indian Langauge Corpora Intitiative (ILCI). In *Proceedings of the Seventh International Conference on Language Resources and Evaluation (LREC'10)*, Valletta, Malta, may.

Xin Jin, Anbang Xu, Rongfang Bie, and Ping Guo. 2006. Machine Learning Techniques and Chi-square Feature Selection for Cancer Classification Using SAGE Gene Expression Profiles. In *Proceedings of the 2006 International Conference on Data Mining for Biomedical Applications*, BioDM'06, pages 106–115, Berlin, Heidelberg. Springer-Verlag.

Philipp Koehn and Ulrich Germann. 2014. The Impact of Machine Translation Quality on Human Post-editing. In *Workshop on Humans and Computer-assisted Translation*, pages 38—46, Gothenburg, Sweden, April.

Philipp Koehn, Hieu Hoang, Alexandra Birch, Chris Callison-Burch, Marcello Federico, Nicola Bertoldi, Brooke Cowan, Wade Shen, Christine Moran, Richard Zens, Chris Dyer, Ondřej Bojar, Alexandra Constantin, and Evan Herbst. 2007. Moses: Open Source Toolkit for Statistical Machine Translation. In *Proceedings of the 45th Annual Meeting of the ACL on Interactive Poster and Demonstration Sessions*, ACL '07, pages 177–180, Stroudsburg, PA, USA.

Philipp Koehn. 2010. *Statistical Machine Translation.* Cambridge University Press, New York, USA, 1st edition.

Maarit Koponen. 2013. This Translation Is Not Too Bad: An Analysis of Post-editor Choices in a Machine-Translation Post-editing Task. In *Proceedings of Workshop on Post-editing Technology and Practice*, pages 1–9.

Anoop Kunchukuttan, Abhijit Mishra, Rajen Chatterjee, Ritesh Shah, and Pushpak Bhattacharyya. 2014. Shata-Anuvadak: Tackling Multiway Translation of Indian Languages. In

Proceedings of the Ninth International Conference on Language Resources and Evaluation (LREC-2014).

Saskia Le Cessie and JC Van Houwelingen. 1992. Ridge Estimators in Logistic Regression. *Applied Statistics*, 41(1):191–201.

Changki Lee and Gary Geunbae Lee. 2006. Information Gain and Divergence-based Feature Selection for Machine Learning-based Text Categorization. *Information Processing and Management*, 42(1):155–165, January.

Rushi Longadge and Snehalata Dongre. 2013. Class Imbalance Problem in Data Mining Review. *CoRR*, abs/1305.1707.

Wolfgang Macherey and Franz J. Och. 2007. An Empirical Study on Computing Consensus Translations from Multiple Machine Translation Systems. In *Proceedings of the 2007 Joint Conference on EMNLP-CoNLL*, pages 986–995, 209 N. Eighth Street, East Stroudsburg, PA, USA.

Guorñ Magnúsdóttir. 1993. Review of "An Introduction to Machine Translation" by W. John Hutchins and Harold L. Somers. Academic Press 1992. *Computational Linguistics*, 19(2):383–384, jun.

S. K. Mangal. 2012. *Statistic in Psychology and Education*. PHI, India.

Stewart Massie. 2006. *Complexity Modelling for Case Knowledge Maintenance in Case-based Reasoning*. Ph.D. thesis, The Robert Gordon University, December.

Tom Mitchell. 1997. *Machine Learning*.

University of Edinburgh. 2014. SMT Research Survey Wiki: a comprehensive survey of statistical machine translation research publications. http://www.statmt.org/survey/Topic/ComputerAidedTranslation. [Online; accessed 7-August-2014].

Kishore Papineni, Salim Roukos, Todd Ward, and Wei-Jing Zhu. 2002. BLEU: a method for automatic evaluation of machine translation. In *Proceedings of the 40th Annual Meeting on ACL*, pages 311–318, Stroudsburg, PA, USA.

Christopher B. Quirk. 2004. Training a Sentence-Level Machine Translation Confidence Measure. In *Proceedings of the Fourth International Conference on Language Resources and Evaluation*, pages 825–828, May.

Víctor M. Sánchez-Cartagena, Juan Antonio Pérez-Ortiz, and Felipe Sánchez-Martínez. 2014. The UA-Prompsit Hybrid Machine Translation System for the 2014 Workshop on Statistical Machine Translation. In *Proceedings of the Ninth Workshop on Statistical Machine Translation*, pages 178–185, Baltimore, Maryland, USA, June.

Felipe Sánchez-Martínez. 2011. Choosing the Best Machine Translation System to Translate a Sentence by Using only Source-Language Information. In *Proceedings of the 15th Annual Conference of the European Association for Machine Translation*, pages 97–104, Leuve, Belgium. European Association for Machine Translation.

Libin Shen, Jinxi Xu, and Ralph Weischedel. 2008. A New String-to-Dependency Machine Translation Algorithm with a Target Dependency Language Model. In *Proceedings of Association for Computational Linguistics*, pages 577–585.

RMK Sinha, K. Sivaraman, Aditi Agrawal, Renu Jain, Rakesh Srivastava, and Ajai Jain. 1995. ANGLABHARTI: a Multilingual Machine Aided Translation Project on Translation from English to Indian Languages. In *Systems, Man and Cybernetics Intelligent Systems for the 21st Century., IEEE International Conference*, volume 2, pages 1609–1614, October.

Raivis Skadiņš, Maris Puriņš, Inguna Skadiņa, and Andrejs Vasiljevs. 2011. Evaluation of SMT in Localization to Under-resourced Inflected Language. In *Proceedings of the 15th International Conference of the European Association for Machine Translation (EAMT 2011)*, pages 35–40, Leuven, Belgium.

Lucia Specia. 2011. Exploiting Objective Annotations for Measuring Translation Post-editing Effort. In *15th Conference of the European Association for Machine Translation*, EAMT, pages 73–80, Leuven, Belgium.

Toshiyuki Takezawa, Genichiro Kikui, Masahide Mizushima, and Eiichiro Sumita. 2007. Multilingual Spoken Language Corpus Development for Communication Research. *Computational Linguistics and Chinese Language Processing*, 12:303–324, September.

Ian H. Witten and Eibe Frank. 2005. *Data Mining: Practical Machine Learning Tools and Techniques, Second Edition*. Morgan Kaufmann Publishers Inc., San Francisco, CA, USA.

Min Zhang, GuoDong Zhou, and Aiti Aw. 2008. Exploring Syntactic Structured Features over Parse Trees for Relation Extraction Using Kernel Methods. *Information Processing and Management*, 44(2):687–701, march.

Simon Zwarts and Mark Dras. 2008. Choosing the Right Translation: A Syntactically Informed Classification Approach. In *Proceedings of the 22nd International Conference on Computational Linguistics (Coling 2008)*, pages 1153–1160.

A Domain-Restricted, Rule Based, English-Hindi Machine Translation System Based on Dependency Parsing

Pratik Desai, Amit Sangodkar, Om P. Damani
Department of Computer Science and Engineering
Indian Institute of Technology Bombay
`pratikdesai,amits,damani@cse.iitb.ac.in`

Abstract

We present a domain-restricted rule based machine translation system based on dependency parsing. We replace the transfer phase of the classical analysis, transfer, and generation strategy with a syntax planning algorithm that directly linearizes the dependency parse of the source sentence as per the syntax of the target language. While we have built the system for English to Hindi translation, the approach can be generalized to other source languages too where a dependency parser is available.

1 Introduction

We present the design of a domain-restricted rule based machine translation system based on dependency parsing (de Marneffe et al., 2006). In contrast with the classical Analysis-Transfer-Generation model (Boitet, 2003), we combine the Transfer and Generation phases in a single Generation phase based on the Descending Transfer. Figure 1 shows how our approach contrasts with the traditional approaches. Domain restriction comes in the form of use of a domain-specific dictionary with semantic properties. Other than restricting the vocabulary, no other restriction on the lnaguage is assumed.

We uses dependency parse of the source sentence as an intermediate representation from which the target language sentence can be directly generated. In contrast with the existing transfer-based, example-based, and statistics based English-Hindi translation systems (Bharati et al., 1997; Sinha and Jain, 2003; Ananthakrishnan et al., 2006; Ramanathan et al., 2009; Chaudhury et al., 2010; Venkatapathy, 2010), the key contribution of this work is an architecture (Figure 2) and a syntax planning algorithm(Algorithm 2) that directly linearizes the dependency parse tree of the source sentence as per the syntax of the target language. Both the architecture and the syntax planning algorithm are adapted from (Singh et al., 2007). We present the results for English to Hindi translation and evaluate several dependency parsers for this task. Our approach is generalizable and can easily be adapted for translation from English to several South-Asian languages. While our word reordering rules are based on dependency relations, we also make use of the phrase structure parse

to extract some of the information missing in a dependency parse.

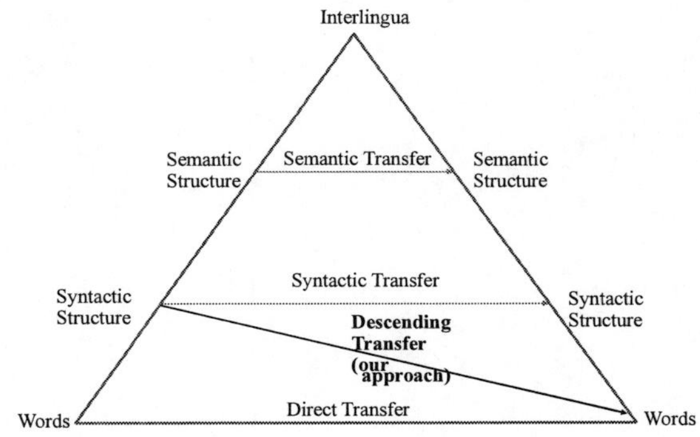

Figure 1: Situating our approach in the Vaquois Triangle

The rest of the paper is organized as follows. Section 2 gives an introduction to dependency parse representation used. Section 3 explains the architecture of our rule-based translation system using dependency parse, algorithms of various stages in language generation and the necessary resources. Section 4 presents the results of trying different dependency parsers and Section 5 contains the error analysis. Section 6 concludes the paper.

2 Dependency representation

Dependency parse represents semantic relations between words in a sentence. Dependencies are triplets containing name of the relation, parent and dependent like `relation(parent, child)`. They can be represented in the form of a graph with each edge representing the relation from a parent node to a child node. Our current system uses Stanford Dependencies Representation (de Marneffe et al., 2006) but our approach can be adapted for any dependency scheme like those used by Minipar (Lin, 1998) and Link parser (Sleator and Temperley, 1993). Consider the following example:

D S Sharma, R Sangal and J D Pawar. Proc. of the 11th Intl. Conference on Natural Language Processing, pages 177–185,
Goa, India. December 2014. ©2014 NLP Association of India (NLPAI)

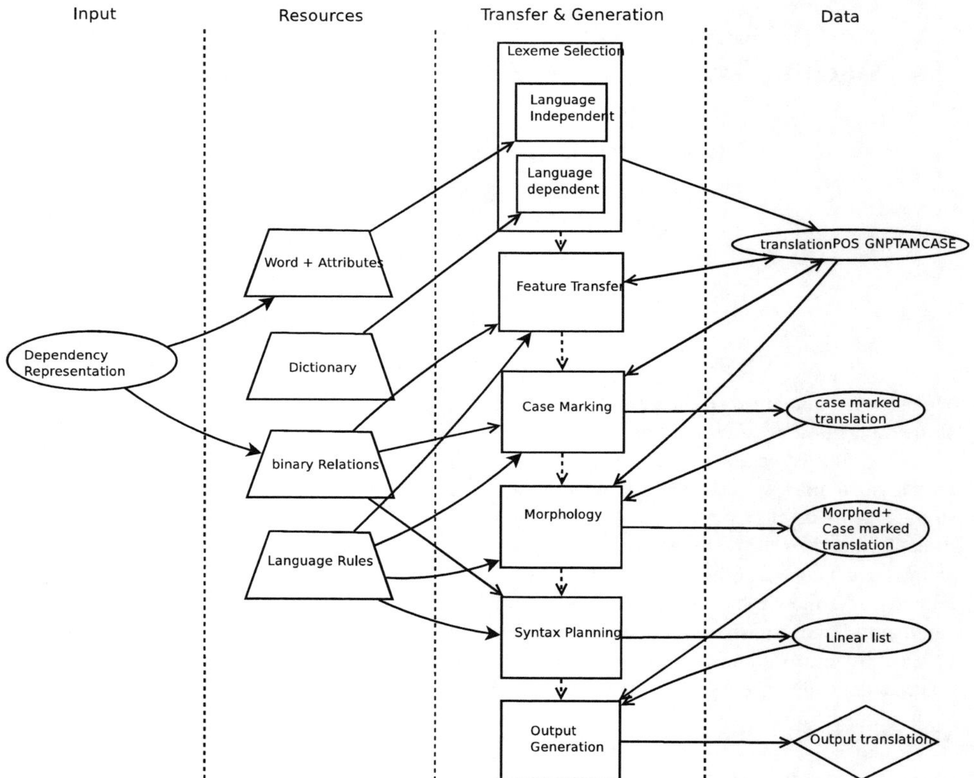

Figure 2: Generation Architecture

Sentence 1 *Many Bengali poets have sung songs in praise of this land.*

The dependency parse for the Sentence 1 given by the Stanford Parser is:

```
amod (poets-3, Many-1)
nn (poets-3, Bengali-2)
nsubj (sung-5, poets-3)
aux (sung-5, have-4)
dobj (sung-5, songs-6)
prep_in (sung-5, praise-8)
det (land-11, this-10)
prep_of (praise-8, land-11)
```

The parse can be represented in a tree form as shown in Figure 3. The words in the parse tree are numbered to distinguish between different occurrences of the same word in a sentence.

In Figure 3, edge labels like `nsubj` and `dobj` are dependency relations relating two words in the sentence. The first word is called a head/parent/governor and the second word is called a child/dependent. For the dependency `nsubj(sung-5, poets-3)`, *sung* is the head and *poets* is the dependent and the two are related by `nsubj` (subject) relation.

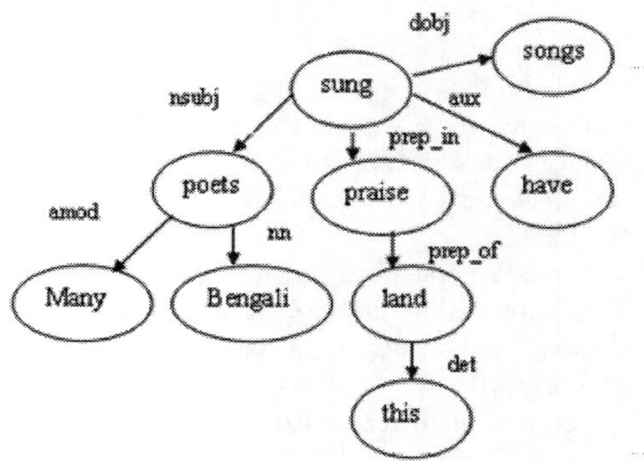

Figure 3: Dependency Tree for Sentence 1

2.1 Pre-processing the Dependency Tree

In our system, a dependency parse of the input sentence is obtained and the dependency tree is pre-processed before being fed to the generation sub-system. Following types of pre-processing are performed:

- All auxiliary verbs are removed from the tree and post-fixed to their respective main verbs. Relations *aux* and *auxpass* are removed from the tree as well. For example, in case of Sentence 1, rela-

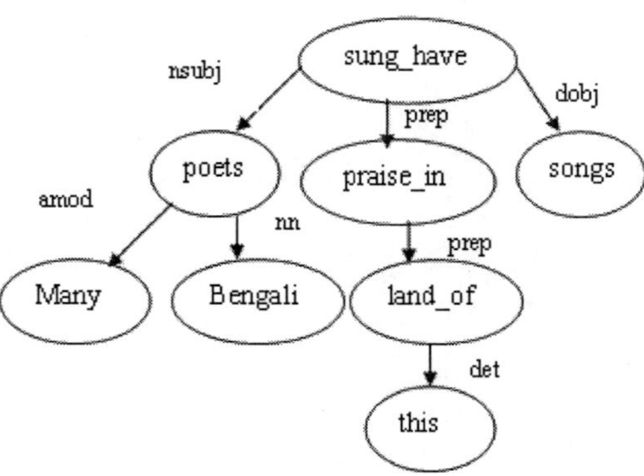

Figure 4: Modified Dependency Tree for Sentence 1

tion *aux (sung-5, have-4)*, is removed and *have* is attached to *sung* to form the combined unit *sung_have*.

- In Stanford dependency representation, prepositions are represented as *prep_xxx* dependency relations. During the pre-processing, prepositions are extracted from corresponding relations and re-inserted appropriately with the parent or the child word. In Sentence 1, preposition *in* and *of* are extracted from *prep_in* and *prep_of* and post-fixed to children *praise* and *land* respectively.

- part words (*prt* relation - e.g. shut down - *prt(shut,down)*) are post-fixed to the parent word to form a single word (*shut_down* in this case) and the *prt* relation is removed from the dependency tree. Similarly nn relation is removed and both child and parent nodes are combined to form a single node if both are proper nouns.

- For adverbial clauses, *mark* and *complm* relations are replaced with corresponding attributes. For example, in the sentence, `Forces engaged in fighting because insurgents attacked`, the dependency relations `advcl(enagaged, attacked)` and `mark(engaged, because)` are collapsed to a single relation `advcl(enagaged, attacked)` and the attribute `because` is added to parent `engaged`. This attribute helps in adding the correct function word *kyunki* during the case marking phase.

- *det* relation is removed and attribute `def` or `indef` is added to the parent node.

The modified tree for Sentence 1 is shown in Figure 4. Note that the preprocessing steps in our system are different from those in (Venkatapathy, 2010). In particular, our syntax planning algorithm (given in Section 3.5) does not require us to break cyclic dependencies.

3 Generation Architecture

Having explained the concept of dependency parsing, we now explain the the different subsystems of the generation system of Figure 2.

3.1 Lexeme selection and feature extraction

The dependency parse of the input sentence is a graphical data structure with the nodes representing the concepts and the arcs representing the dependency relations. The first stage of the translation process is the selection of the target word corresponding to each source word. Each word is looked up in the domain specific dictionary, and the corresponding lexeme is obtained. Since we are using a domain-specific dictionary, lexeme selection module is trivial in that most of the time there is only one target word for a source word. In the absence of a domain-specific dictionary, we will need a better lexeme selection module that incorporates word sense disambiguation.

We use three tools for feature extraction: Morpha (Minnen and Pearce, 2001), RelEx (Richardson et al., 2006), and Function Tagger (Blaheta and Charniak, 2000). All semantic and morphological properties of source words are not extracted by these tools and hence we assume the availability of a dictionary with various semantic and morphological attributes for each target word. Consider the following example:

Sentence 2 *This association gives training for emu-keeping and also supplies the birds.*

यह संघ इमूपालन के लिए प्रशिक्षण देता है और पक्षियों को भी उपलब्ध कराता है

```
yah sangh emu-paalan ke liye
prashikshan detaa hai aur pakshiyon
ko bhi uplabdh karata hai
```

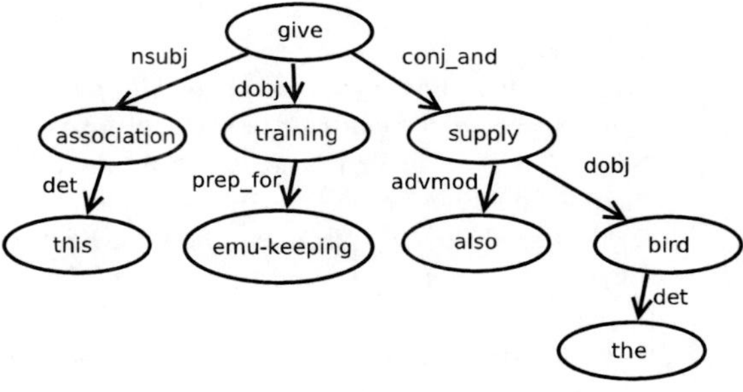

Figure 5: Dependency Tree for Sentence 2

The dependency parse for Sentence 2 is shown in Figure 5. Table 1 shows parts of the desired output of the lexeme selection and feature extraction stage for Sentence 2.

3.2 Feature transfer

This is one of the most important stage of the generation process. Attributes of the nodes are transferred

Word	Translation	Attributes/Features
give	द्	present, Verb,...
training	प्रशिक्षण	Noun, Male, Event,...
supply	उपलब्ध करा	present, Verb, Conjunct,...

Table 1: parts of the output of Lexeme Selection & Feature Extraction stage for Sentence 2

to each other in this stage. Most of the transferred attributes come from the nouns. The attributes are transferred to adjectives and verbs as follows:

- **Transferring features from nouns to adjectives**
  Adjectives need to take the number and gender information from the noun that it qualifies. This can be done by using the `amod` relation which has noun as parent node and adjective as child node. For example, `good boy` and `good girl` are translated to अच्छा लडका(*accha ladka*) and अच्छी लडकी(*acchi ladki*) respectively. Here, whether `good` gets translated to अच्छा(*accha*) or अच्छी(*acchi*) is dependent on the gender attribute that it gets from the noun *boy* or *girl*.

- **Transferring features from nouns to verbs**
  For verbs, gender and number information is obtained from the subject in case of active voice and object in the case of passive voice. For example, in Sentence 2 the gender attribute M is transferred from *association* to *give*.

A multi-phase algorithm is employed for transitive feature transfer. For example, for the dependency tree in Figure 5, after gender attribute M is transferred from *association* to *give*, in next phase, attribute M is transferred from *give* to *supply*.

For feature transfer, rules with the following format are used:

POS:Relation:with [p]arent or [c]hild:p+ve attr:p-ve attr:c+ve attr:c-ve attr:attr to be transferred

Here +ve/-ve attributes are those attributes which should/should not be possessed by the parent or child for the transfer to take place. For the same relation, the order of the rules application is important. For example, consider the following sequence of rules:

```
V:nsubj:c:null:null:null:null:morph
V:dobj:c:null:null:topic:null:passive
```

In the above rules, the first one checks whether a node with POS=V (verb) has the `nsubj` (subject) relation, and the second one checks for the `dobj` (object) relation. These rules are to be applied in the given order. The first rule in the above example refers to transfer of morphological attributes without any conditions. The second rule says that if the child node is the *topic* of the sentence, and has `passive` attribute, then transfer the `passive` attribute (and only this attribute) to the parent `verb`. Morphological attributes are not transferred in this case.

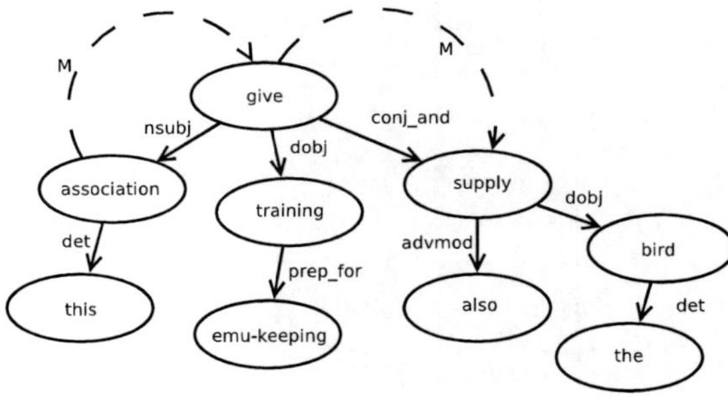

Figure 6: Feature Transfer in Dependency Parse

For Sentence 2, feature transfer is shown in Figure 6. As per the rules, child of `nsubj` relation (*association*) transfers its morphological features, 'M'(masculine) for instance, to the parent verb (*give*). Similarly, child of conjunction relation (*supply*), gets features ('M') from its parent (*give*), if the child is not governed by a subject, which is the case here.

3.3   Case marking

In this step, target language function words such as prepositions, conjunctions, clause markers e.t.c. are identified. Consider the following sentence

Sentence 3 *Ram ate rice with a spoon.*
राम ने चम्मच से खाना खाया
```
ram ne chammach se khanna khaaya
```

In the corresponding Hindi sentence, से/*se* is added to indicate the relation that चम्मच(*chammach/spoon*) has with the verb खाया(*khaaya/eat*) and ने/*ne* is added to indicate the relation between *Ram* and खाया(*khaaya/eat*). Case marker to be inserted is decided depending on the relation between two nodes and the lexical information present in dictionary entry of both child and parent node of the relation, and also some attributes that the parent node and child node should satisfy and some attributes that should not be satisfied. Therefore, an exhaustive list of rules is needed. Also, the rules must be ordered so that the most restrictive rule for a relation should be checked first and subsequently, lesser restrictive rules are checked.

The case (function words) depends on the dependency relation and the attributes of the two nodes involved in the relation. The case marking rules have the following format:

POS:p pre:p post:c pre:c post:p+ve attr:p-ve attr:c+ve attr:c-ve attr

`Pre/Post` are the case markers to be applied before/after the node (pre/post-positioning). +ve/-ve attributes are the attributes which a node should or should not have.

Example: For Sentence 2, function words (case markers) that are identified with dependency relations are given in Table 2.

180

Parent Node	Child Node	Relation	Case
give(present,V,M,sg)	*supply*(present,V,M,CJNCT)	conj_and	और
training(N,M,sg)	*emu-keeping*(N,M,oblique,sg)	prep_for	के लिए
supply(present,V,M,CJNCT)	*bird*(pl,def,N,M,oblique)	dobj	को

Table 2: Case Marking for Sentence 2

3.4 Morphology Generation

In this stage, words are inflected depending on the surrounding words. In the earlier stages, transitive feature transfer between words has already been done. Now all the inflection related information is available locally and all nouns, verbs, pronouns, and adjectives undergo inflections. Nouns and adjectives are inflected based on gender, number, and case marker information. For example, लडका(*ladka/boy*) in plural form becomes लडके(*ladke/boys*). In addition if it has a case marker like पे(*pe*), it becomes लडको(*ladko/on boys*). This case marker information is identified by the `oblique` attribute added to the noun *boy* during the case marking stage.

Verbs inflect depending on gender, number, person, tense, aspect and mood attributes and the voice in which it is used(active or passive). For example, *Vinod plays cricket* translates to विनोद क्रिकेट खेलता है(*Vinod kriket khelta hai*) and *Children play cricket* translates to बच्चे क्रिकेट खेलते है(*Bacche kriket khelte hai*). Here the different inflections of the verb खेल(*khel/play*) are due to the number information obtained in feature transfer stage from the qualifying noun *Vinod* or *children*.

Pronouns inflect purely based on case markers. For example, मे and case marker को are combined as मुझे.

Algorithm 1 is the Morphology generation algorithm. The procedure is recursive and the initial argument is the root of the dependency graph. Several morphology generation rules are required for each part of speech because the inflections differ dependning on the attributes.

Algorithm 1 Morphology(current)

1: **if** *current* is not marked **then**
2:     mark *current*
3:     **for** each unmarked parent p_i of *current* **do**
4:         Morphology(p_i)
5:     $pos \leftarrow$ POS of *current*
6:     $attrs \leftarrow$ attribute set of *current*
7:     **for** each rule r_i for pos **do**
8:         $ruleAttrs \leftarrow$ attribute set of r_i
9:         $match(r_i) = \frac{|attrs \cap ruleAttrs|}{|ruleAttrs|}$
10:     $r = argmax(match)$
11:     inflect *current* as per rules associated with r
12:     **for** each child c_i of *current* **do**
13:         Morphology(c_i)

Resources

Morphology of a word depends solely on the attributes of the word. The attributes obtained through dictionary look-up and during feature transfer (if any), decide the morphology on the word. For morphology of nouns, verbs and adjectives, the rule format is:

PenDel:UltDel:PenIns:UltIns:Attrs

In Hindi and many other South-Asian languages, morphological inflections apply to the last character and/or the last but one character of the word. In the above rules, <PenDel> is the character to be deleted from the penultimate position in the root word, while <UltDel> is the character to be deleted from the ultimate position. Similarly, <PenIns> and <UltIns> refer to the characters to be inserted in the penultimate and ultimate positions of the root word. <Attrs> is the attribute list. Since there are only small number of pronoun forms, the result of the combination of pronouns with case markers are pre-computed and stored. For example, pronoun मैं(*mein*), with case marker के(*ke*) gives morphed word as मेरे(*mere*).

Example: In Sentence 2, *bird* has attributes *pl*(plural) and *oblique*(the word takes case marker), which results in the morphed word पक्षियों(*pakshiyon*). Morphology example for several words are given in table 3.

Node	Attributes	Morphed Word
give	present,V,M,sg	देता है
supply	present,V,CJNCT,M	उपलब्ध कराता है
bird	pl,def,N,ANIMT,M,oblique	पक्षियों

Table 3: Results for morphology processing of Sentence 2

3.5 Syntax planning

This stage rearranges the words (nodes in the dependency tree) as per the syntax of the target language. It is this stage that determines the fluency of the obtained translation. For example, in the sentence I like apples, the words have to be reordered as I apples like, to finally get the translation मै सेब पसन्द करता हूं. Syntax planning algorithm works directly on the dependency parse of the sentence and is based on two parameters:

1. Parent-child precedence within a relation: Depending on the relation involved, parent has to be ordered before or after the child. Dependencies like conj(conjunction), appos(appos), advcl(adverbial clause) follow parent

181

before child order while `nsubj`, `dobj` follow child before parent order. For example, the dependencies for the sentence `I like apples` are:

```
dobj(like,apples)

nsubj(like,I)
```

For both these dependencies the child has to be ordered before parent to get `I apples like`.

2. Priority across relations: For a node with multiple children, left to right ordering of children nodes is done based on the priority given to their corresponding relations with the parent. For example, `nsubj` has a higher priority than `dobj`. Taking the previous example, `I` will be ordered before `apples` for the parent `like` which gives us the required word order `I apples like`.

Resources

For resolving parent-child precedence, all dependency relations are marked as parent-before-child or child-before-parent. For resolving the relation priority, a pair wise relation priority matrix is used. The order of the matrix equals the number of relations present. A part of the matrix for dependency relations is shown in the Table 4.

An 'L' in the ith row and j^{th} column means that the child of ith relation is ordered before the child of the jth relation in the final translation. From Table 4, it can be seen that `nsubj` (subject) has higher priority than `dobj` (object) and `prep` (preposition) has a lower priority than `nsubj` but higher priority than `dobj`, so `prep`'s child word is ordered between those of `nsubj` and `dobj`.

	nsubj	dobj	prep	amod	nn
nsubj	-	L	L	-	-
dobj	R	-	R	-	-
prep	R	L	-	L	L
amod	-	-	R	-	L
nn	-	-	R	R	-

Table 4: Relation Priority

The details of our syntax planning algorithm are given in Algorithm 2.

Example: For Sentence 2, syntax planning details are shown in Table 5. The output list at the end of the algorithm, gives the final ordering of the words in the target language syntax. For Sentence 2, the final output list is:

```
(this, association, emu-keeping,
training, give, bird, also, supply)
```

This word order is as per the expected translation and the final output sentence generated is:

यह संघ इमूपालन के लिए प्रशिक्षण देता है और पक्षियों को भी उपलब्ध कराता है

```
yah sangh emu-paalan ke liye
prashikshan detaa hai aur pakshiyon
ko bhi uplabdh karata hai
```

Algorithm 2 Syntax Planning

Require: 1. root node placed on Stack, and, 2. all nodes unmarked

1: **while** Stack is not empty **do**
2:     *current* ← POP node from Stack
3:     **if** *current* is not marked **then**
4:         mark *current*
5:         separate unmarked relatas of *current* into *beforeCurrent* and *afterCurrent* lists {depending on parent-child precedence, single and multiple rules }
6:         sort *beforeCurrent* and *afterCurrent* {depending on relation priority rules}
7:         push nodes on the Stack in the order, sorted *afterCurrent*, *current*, sorted *beforeCurrent* respectively
8:     **else**
9:         Output *current* node

This completes the description of our system.

4   Exploring other parsers

Parsing is the first and a very important stage of the rule based machine translation system discussed here. A wrong parse is bound to give a wrong translation and hence severely affects accuracy. It is important to have the most accurate dependency parser for the translation system for improving translation accuracy. The current system uses Stanford Parser for dependency parsing. A performance study of dependency parsers accuracies has been presented in (Cer et al., 2010). As per their results, the two parsers that rank higher than Stanford parser are CJ reranking parser (McClosky et al., 2006) and Berkley parser (Petrov and Klein, 2007). Both of these parsers can generate Stanford Typed Dependencies. Note that there are other dependencies schemes such as those used by Link parser (Sleator and Temperley, 1993) and Minipar (Lin, 1998). In (Popel et al., 2011), several dependency parsers were compared for a English-to-Czech dependency-based statistical translation system. Use of these other parsers will require rewriting of the rules in our system since they deploy different dependency schemes. Hence we restrict our comparison to CJ and Berkeley parsers since they employ Stanford Dependencies. The main difference between these three parsers is in their phrase structure parsing algorithm.

Stanford parser is an unlexicalized PCFG parser. CJ reranking parser consists of two components - a coarse-to-fine generative parser and a reranker for the parses generated from the parser. Berkeley parser uses a unlexicalized parsing with hierarchically split PCFG. All three use the same methodology for generating Stanford Dependencies from the phrase structure tree.

Step	State
1	Stack={give}
2	current={give} Stack={} output={}
5	before-current={training,association} after-current={supply}
6	sorted-before-current={association,training} after-current={supply}
7	Stack={supply,give,training,association}
2	current={association} Stack={supply,give,training}
5	before-current={this} after-current={}
7	Stack={supply,give,training,association,this}
2	current={this} Stack={supply,give,training,association}
9	output={this}
2	current={association} Stack={supply,give,training} output={this}
9	output={this, association}
2	current={training} Stack={supply,give} output={this, association}
5	before-current={emu-keeping} after-current={}
7	Stack={supply,give,training,emu-keeping}
2	current={emu-keeping} Stack={supply,give,training}
9	output={this, association, emu-keeping}
2	current={training} Stack={supply,give} output={this, association, emu-keeping}
9	output={this, association, emu-keeping, training}
2	current={give} Stack={supply} output={this, association, emu-keeping, training}
9	output={this, association, emu-keeping, training, give}
2	current={supply} Stack={} output={this, association, emu-keeping, training, give}
5	before-current={also,bird} after-current={}
6	sorted-before-current={bird,also}
7	Stack={supply,also,bird}
2	current={bird} Stack={supply,also}
9	output={this, association, emu-keeping, training, give, bird}
2	current={also} Stack={supply} output={this, association, emu-keeping, training, give, bird}
9	output={this, association, emu-keeping, training, give, bird, also}
2	current={supply} Stack={} output={this, association, emu-keeping, training, give, bird, also}
9	output={this, association, emu-keeping, training, give, bird, also, supply}
1	current={null} Stack={}
	output={this, association, emu-keeping, training, give, bird, also, supply}

Table 5: Syntax planning steps during the execution of Algorithm 2 for Sentence 2

4.1 Experimental Evaluation and Analysis

We use an 100 English sentences (1403 words) from agricultural domain for evaluation. The gold-standard Hindi translation contains 1231 words. These 100 sentences were chosen from 10 different discussion threads in an agricultural question-answer corpus. The average sentence length in words was 14. The input sentences were translated using Stanford typed dependencies from the three parsers. The output was evaluated against reference translations using BLEU (Papineni et al., 2002) score which ranges from 0 to 1. Despite the known limitations (Callison-Burch et al., 2006; Ananthakrishnan et al., 2007) we use BLEU, since it is the most popular translation evaluation metric. For completeness, we also evaluate *Google Translate* on the same test set.

Results in Table 6 show that for the task at hand, Stanford parser performs best and it is the only one that performs better than *Google Translate*. Note that we have used a domain-specific dictionary which also gives semantic properties of words. This plays an important part in improving the translation quality. In the absence of a domain-specific dictionary, we will need a better lexeme selection module that incorporates word sense disambiguation.

Based on the error analysis given next, we have identified several possible improvements to our system. In future, we plan to strengthen the rule base to the extent possible. We also need to strengthen the lexeme selection module by incorporating word sense disambiguation and multi-word expression identification modules. We have assumed the existence of a dictionary with various semantic attributes of target words. Automatic construction of such dictionaries from various parallel and monolingual sources is needed. We also plan to explore semantic parsers like Swirl (Surdeanu and Turmo, 2005) and Senna (Collobert et al., 2011) for determing source word attributes.

	Berkeley	CJ reranking	Stanford	Google Translate
BLEU	0.23	0.18	**0.27**	0.25

Table 6: Translation quality for different parsers and *Google Translate*

5 Error analysis

There are two types of errors in our system - those related to the parsers, and those related to the rest of the generation system. For parsers under considerations, dependency parse is derived from the phrase structure parse, hence parsing errors themselves can be divided into two categories:

- **Errors in the phrase structure parse** For example, in *What are its advantages?* the Stanford parser labels the phrase *are its advantages* accurately with `SQ` and gets the correct dependency `attr(are-2, what-1)`. Berkeley parser labels it inaccurately as `SINV` and hence generates the incorrect dependency `dep(are-2, what-1)`. CJ reranker gives wrong `POS` tag for *are* and hence generates `nsubj` instead of `attr`.

- **Errors in deriving the dependency parse** In the sentence *Also, remove all the rotten fruits and tips and destroy them*, all three parsers derive accurate phrase structure parses. But, CJ and Berkeley did not label *tip* as an NP and therefore they could not add label `predet` to the dependency between *fruit* and *all*.

Main errors in the rest of the system are:

1. **Limited rule base**: The current rule base of the system does not have enough coverage.

2. **Inaccurate phrase translations**: Dependency parsers give `prt`(*part of*) relation between words of some of the multi-word expressions. For rest of the phrases, system performs word by word translation. For example, phrases like *as soon as possible* end up getting translated word by word.

3. **Missing word properties**: Currently we depend on the parser and the dictionary for providing semantic properties of the words. Many semantic properties of the words are missing in the current system.

We use RelEx and Function Tagger for obtaining word attributes. In case of Relex, all the semantic attributes are not obtained for many words due to a incomplete and small rule base, while Function tagger provides a very limited set of attributes. Other semantic parsers like Swirl (Surdeanu and Turmo, 2005) and Senna (Collobert et al., 2011) need to be explored for this. Also, for Function tagger and Relex, better mapping of the attributes given by them to the attributes needed in the rule base(eg. `LOC` given by Function tagger is mapped to `PLACE` currently) needs to be done.

4. **Lack of sense disambiguation**: The current system does not take into account the sense of the word while selecting its translation from the dictionary.

5. **Imperfect syntax planning**: The syntax planning algorithm assumes fixed parent-child precedences. However, natural languages abound in exceptions. For example, `nsubj` generally has a higher priority than `advcl`. But for translating the sentence *the accident happened before he fell unconscious*, the priority of `advcl` should be greater than `nsubj`. The priority rules need to be extended and lexicalized.

6 Conclusions

In this work, we have shown that it is feasible to make a domain-retricted rule based machine translation system based on dependency parsing by directly linearizing the dependency parse tree of the source sentence as per the syntax of the target language. We experimented with three different parsers and found that the Stanford parser is the best among the three parsers for the task at hand. We have also identified a number of issues for improvement in our system.

References

R. Ananthakrishnan, M. Kavitha, J Hegde Jayprasad, Ritesh Shah Chandra Shekhar, and Sasikumar M. Sawani Bade. 2006. Matra: A practical approach to fully-automatic indicative english-hindi machine translation. In *Symposium on Modeling and Shallow Parsing of Indian Languages (MSPIL'06)*.

R. Ananthakrishnan, Pushpak Bhattacharyya, M. Sasikumar, and Ritesh M. Shah. 2007. Some issues in automatic evaluation of english-hindi mt: More blues for bleu. In *Intl. Conf. on Natural Language Processing (ICON)*.

A. Bharati, V. Chaitanya, A. P. Kulkarni, and R. Sangal. 1997. Anusaaraka: Machine translation in stages. *A Quarterly in Artificial Intelligence, NCST, Bombay (renamed as CDAC, Mumbai)*.

Don Blaheta and Eugene Charniak. 2000. Assigning function tags to parsed text. In *1st Annual Meeting of the North American Chapter of the Association for Computational Linguistics (NAACL)*.

C. Boitet. 2003. Revue franaise de linguistique applique. *Automated Translation* , VIII:99–121.

C. Callison-Burch, M. Osborne, and P. Koehn. 2006. Re-evaluating the role of bleu in machine translation research. In *EACL*.

Daniel Cer, Marie-Catherine de Marneffe, Daniel Jurafsky, and Christopher D. Manning. 2010. Parsing to stanford dependencies: Trade-offs between speed and accuracy. In *7th International Conference on Language Resources and Evaluation (LREC 2010)*.

S. Chaudhury, A. Rao, and D. M. Sharma. 2010. Anusaaraka: An expert system based machine translation system. In *Natural Language Processing and Knowledge Engineering (NLP-KE)*.

R. Collobert, J. Weston, L. Bottou, M. Karlen, K. Kavukcuoglu, and P. Kuksa. 2011. Natural language processing (almost) from scratch. *Journal of Machine Learning Research (JMLR)*.

Marie-Catherine de Marneffe, Bill MacCartney, and Christopher D. Manning. 2006. Generating typed dependency parses from phrase structure parses. In *5th International Conference on Language Resources and Evaluation (LREC 2006)*.

Dekang Lin. 1998. Dependency-based evaluation of minipar. In *Workshop on the Evaluation of Parsing Systems*.

D. McClosky, E. Charniak, and M. Johnson. 2006. Effective self-training for parsing. In *HLT/NAACL*.

J. Carroll Minnen, G. and D. Pearce. 2001. Applied morphological processing of english. *Natural Language Engineering*, 7(3):207–223.

K. Papineni, S. Roukos, T. Ward, and W. J. Zhu. 2002. Bleu: a method for automatic evaluation of machine translation. In *40th Annual meeting of the Association for Computational Linguistics (ACL)*.

S. Petrov and D. Klein. 2007. Improved inference for unlexicalized parsing. In *NAACL*.

Martin Popel, David Mareek, and Nathan Green. 2011. Influence of parser choice on dependency-based mt. In *EMNLP 6th Workshop on Statistical Machine Translation*.

A. Ramanathan, H. Choudhary, A. Ghosh, and P. Bhattacharyya. 2009. Case markers and morphology: Addressing the crux of the fluency problem in english-hindi smt. In *ACL-IJCNLP 2009*.

R. Richardson, B. Goertzel, H. Pinto, and E. A. Fox. 2006. Automatic creation and translation of concept maps for computer science-related theses and dissertations. In *Second Int. Conference on Concept Mapping*.

Smriti Singh, Mrugank Dalal, Vishal Vachhani, Pushpak Bhattacharyya, and Om P. Damani. 2007. Hindi generation from interlingua (unl). In *MT Summit XI*.

R. Sinha and A. Jain. 2003. Anglahindi: an english to hindi machine-aided translation system. In *MT Summit IX*.

Daniel D. Sleator and Davy Temperley. 1993. Parsing english with a link grammar. In *Third International Workshop on Parsing Technologies*.

M. Surdeanu and J. Turmo. 2005. Semantic role labeling using complete syntactic analysis. In *9th Conference on Computational Natural Language Learning (CoNLL)*.

Sriram Venkatapathy. 2010. *Statistical Models Suited for Machine Translation from English to Indian Languages*. Ph.D. thesis, Centre for Language Technologies Research Centre, IIIT, Hyderabad, India.

Translation of *TO infinitives* in Anusaaraka Platform: an English Hindi MT system

Akshar Bharati, Sukhada, Soma Paul
Language Technology Research Center
International Institute of Information Technology
Hyderabad, India
`sukhada@research.iiit.ac.in`
`soma@iiit.ac.in`

Abstract

In this paper, we study the *infinitive TO* constructions of English which can be variedly translated into Hindi. We observe that there can be different equivalents of *infinitive TO* into Hindi. Factors such as numerous semantic variants in translated equivalents and the syntactic complexity of corresponding English expressions of *infinitive TO* cause great difficulties in the English-Hindi translation. We systematically analyze and describe the phenomenon and propose translation rules for the conversion of English *infinitive TO* into Hindi. The rules have been implemented in the Anusaaraka Platform, an open source English-Hindi Machine Translation tool. The problem has been treated as translation disambiguation of the *infinitive TO*. We examine contexts of *infinitive TO* when it occurs as a dependent of various kinds of main verbs and attempt to discover clues for different translations into Hindi. We achieved a translation accuracy of over 80%. The experiments show that Anusaaraka gives significant improvement in translation quality of *infinitive TO* over Google Translator and Anuvad MT systems.

1 Introduction

We study the *infinitive TO* constructions of English which can be variedly translated into Hindi. The translation of *infinitive TO* in "TO verb" constructions is *-nā* form of the verb which is a *kṛdanta* (participial) form in Hindi, as illustrated in (1) and (2).

(1) I want **to go**.
  maiṃ cāha-tā[1] hūṃ **jā-nā**

maiṃ **jā-nā** cāha-tā hūṃ

(2) I prefer **to be** in the woods alone.
  maiṃ pasanda_karatā_hūṃ **raha-nā**
  jaṃgala_meṃ akelā
  maiṃ akelā jaṃgala meṃ **rahanā** pasanda karatā hūṃ

However we observe that there can be different equivalents of *infinitive TO* into Hindi. Factors such as numerous semantic variants in translated equivalents and the syntactic complexity of corresponding English expressions of *infinitive TO* cause great difficulties in English-Hindi translation. Therefore an English-Hindi translation software such as Google Translator[2] gives non-satisfactory translations and another MT system Anuvad[3] gives poor translations of *infinitive TO*.

We systematically analyze and describe the problem and propose translation rules for the conversion of English *infinitive TO* into Hindi. The rules have been implemented in Anusaaraka Platform[4], an open source English-Hindi Machine Translation tool. The problem has been treated as word translation disambiguation (WTD) of the *infinitive TO*.

This paper examines the behavior of the main verb on which the *infinitive TO* is a dependent and attempts to discover clues for translation variations in Hindi. We discover some interesting clues for translation as discussed below:

1. Structural Clue: The raising, exceptional case marking (ECM), control verbs license *infinitive TO* as their dependents. Translation of infinitives in the context of these type of verbs

---

[1]Following conventions for writing gloss are followed in this paper: '-' between morph boundary; '_' between word boundary in case of local word grouping. TO has been consistently glossed as *-nā*. In actual translation layer (3rd layer) the translation of *infinitive TO* construction has been given.

[2]`http://translate.google.com`
[3]`http://nlp.cdacmumbai.in:8081/anuvad/`
[4]`http://anusaaraka.iiit.ac.in/`

D S Sharma, R Sangal and J D Pawar. Proc. of the 11th Intl. Conference on Natural Language Processing, pages 186–195,
Goa, India. December 2014. ©2014 NLP Association of India (NLPAI)

systematically vary. English also uses periphrastic compounds with the verb 'get' in the causative sense when we want "to convince someone or trick someone into doing something" (Section 5 discusses all these verb types in detail).

2. Translation Clue: The translation of main verbs determines the translation of its TO infinitival dependent. This presents an important case that shows how the translation of the target language determines the information flow in that language. For example, the English verb *want* in *I want to go home* can have three translation equivalents: (i) *cāhanā*, (ii) *icchā karanā* and (iii) *icchā rakhanā*. If *want* is translated as *cāhanā* in Hindi then *infinitive TO* translates into *-nā*, with other two translations it translates into *-ne kā*[5], as shown in (3).

   (3)   I want **to go** home.
   maiṃ ghara **jā-nā** cāhatā hūṃ
   maiṃ ghara **jāne kī** icchā rakhatā hūṃ
   maiṃ ghara **jāne kī** icchā karatā hūṃ

3. Verb specific semantic Clue: The *-nā* form in Hindi takes different postpositions such as *-ne kā, -ne meṃ, -ne se* and so on. We consider that such variation is typically dependent on the semantics of source language verbs which might be sometimes difficult to formalize in terms of rules or conditions.

This paper explores the possibilities of identifying contexts that will help us predict the translation of *infinitive TO*. For the above mentioned cases we have created rules for translation disambiguation. We understand that there are cases where it is difficult to determine a specific rule for disambiguation because either we do not discover the context or it is difficult to translate the contextual clue into a rule that can be implemented. These cases can be handled through case-based reasoning where a deterministic rule is not available. Thus the WTD module proposed in this paper follows a hybrid approach. We have made an attempt to find out structural and semantic clues in the source language that can help us to predict translation variations. We have generated an output on the basis

---

[5]In case the following word is a feminine, the postposition *kā* takes feminine gender and becomes *kī*.

of the rules we framed. We manaually evaluated 100 such test sentences and achieved 80% accuracy. In comparision with Google Translator and Anuvad, we achieved significant improvement in translation.

The paper is organized as follows. Section 2 presents a brief review of word translation disambiguation. Section 3 gives an overview of the Anusaaraka system which has been used as a translation platform for implementing the translation rules. Section 4 briefly presents insights from Sanskrit grammar for the interpretation of *infinitive TO*. The insights have motivated the design of our rules. Section 5 illustrates different contexts where *TO* construction occur and also presents the translation equivalents in Hindi. Section 6 deliberates on our approach in handling *infinitive TO* Finally Section 7 presents the results.

2   Related Work

Earlier WSD based approaches like the one used in (Chan et al., 2007) assumed that different senses of a word in a source language may have different translations in the target language, depending on the particular meaning of the word in context. Hence, the assumption is that in resolving sense ambiguity on the source side, a WSD system will be able to help an MT system to determine the correct translation of an ambiguous word. However, in the context of translation, word sense disambiguation amounts to selecting the correct target translation which is termed as word translation disambiguation (WTD). This aims to select the best translation(s) given a source word in a context and from a set of target candidates.

In the current predominant paradigm for data driven phrase based statistical machine translation, the task of WTD is not explicitly addressed. Instead the influence of context on word translation probabilities is implicitly encoded in the model both in the phrasal translation pairs learned from parallel texts and stored in the phrase translation table and in the target language model (Bungum and Gambäck, 2011). The assumption is that both phrase table and n-gram language model in a way capture collocation and local dependencies and thus helps to disambiguate a possible translation candidate. (Chan et al., 2007) have made an effort to integrate a state-of-the-art WSD system into a state-of-the-art hierarchical phrase-based MT system, Hiero. They show that integrating a WSD system improves the performance of a state-of-the-art statistical MT system on an actual translation task. For their WSD classifier they select a window of three words (w_{-1}, w, w_{+1}), where w is the word to be disambiguated. One potential problem of such approach is that the amount of context taken into account is rather small. It is clear that WTD often depends on cues from a wider textual context, for instance, elsewhere in the same sentence, paragraph of the document as a whole. This is beyond the scope of most phrase-based MT approaches which work with relatively small phrases.

(Li and Li, 2004) propose a bilingual bootstrapping (BB) approach to disambiguate words to be translated. This approach does not require parallel corpora. Instead they make use of a small amount of classified data and a large amount of unclassified data in both the source and the target language in translation. It repeatedly constructs classifiers by classifying data in each of the languages and by exchanging information regarding the classified data between the two languages (Li and Li, 2004).

(Bharati et al., 2005) have made an attempt to disambiguate English *infinitive TO* from the MT perspective. They have devised rules for translating *infinitive TO* in Hindi. They analyze the phenomena which are discussed in Pāṇini's Aṣṭādhyaī for Sanskrit language. They missed the cases where a verb along with the dependent "TO VERB" translates into one verb unit in target language, such as causativization (see Section 5.4) and the cases where the "infinitive TO" marks subjunctive mood in TL as shown in "Rule 6" in Section 6.2.

3 Anusaaraka as an MT platform

Anusaaraka, a machine translation cum language accessor system, is a unique approach to develop machine translation system based on the insights of information dynamics from Paninian Grammar Formalism. The major goals of the system as stated in (Chaudhury et al., 2010) are the following:

- Reduce the language barrier by felicitating access from one language to others.

- Demonstrate the practical usability of the Indian traditional grammatical system in the modern context.

He	seems	to	be	intelligent.
वह{पु.}	प्रतीत~होना~{@s}	@to{->को[की~ओर]/ना}	होना{0}	बुद्धिमान^सुबोध[-].
वह	प्रतीत_हो{ता_है}	-	-	बुद्धिमान.
वह	प्रतीत होता है	-	-	बुद्धिमान.
वह	प्रतीत होता है	-	-	बुद्धिमान.

Figure 1: Anusaaraka interface showing output for the sentence *He seems to be intelligent.*

- Provide a free and open source machine translation platform for Indian language.

The Anusaaraka system prefers faithful representation of information to naturalness of translation because it aims at no loss of information. In order to achieve that it has designed a special graphical interface as shown in Fig. 1:

The layered output represented by this interface provides an access to all the stages of translation making the whole process transparent. For instance the output in Fig. 1 shows that the infinitival verb group *to be* can be translated as *honā* in isolation as it is clear in the initial layer. But it is dropped in the final Hindi output as shown in the final layers. Thus Anusaaraka provides a "Robust Fall Back Mechanism" which ensures a safety net by providing a "padasutra layer[6] ", which is a word to word translation represented in special formulatic form, representing various senses of the source language word. Users get opportunity to select one of the senses and continue reading the source text with better comprehension.

One of the unique ideas of Anusaaraka system is to utilize human intervention from the earlier stage of development of the system. It talks about a need for sharing the load between man and machine. Machines are equipped with large memory storage, they can "remember" large quantities of information. Humans are good at interpretation.

4 Insights from Sanskrit Grammar

Most of the *infinitive TO* verb constructions in English correspond to the *kṛt* (non-finite) suffix, *tumun* (*tum*) in Sanskrit. According to Sanskrit grammar, a word ending in a *kṛt* affix, where the *kṛt* affix ends in the letter *m*, is designated as an *avyaya* (indeclinable) (A. 1-1-39). Patanjali

---

[6]The concept of padasutra assumes that polysemous words have a "core meaning" and other meanings are natural extension of that meaning. In Anusaaraka, an attempt is made to relate all these meanings and show their relationship by means of a formula. This formula is termed as padasutra.

says the meaning of the affix *tumun* is *bhāva* (action)[7] (Patanjali, 1975).

Another law *avyayakṛto bhaāve* says that the *kṛt* affixes which are also *avyayas* denote *bhāva* (action). In English and Hindi *bhāva* is denoted by *to* and *-nā* affixes respectively. Ex.

Eng: 'to go', 'to read', 'to eat', 'to dance', 'to be', 'to feed' etc.

Hnd: *'jānā'*, *'padḥanā'*, *'khānā'*, *'nācanā'*, *'honā'*, *'khilānā'* etc.

The 'infinitive TO' forms of a verb in English seem to be indeclinable as these forms do not take any affixes further. In Hindi, though the affix denotes *bhāva*, it is not indeclinable. Hence the words ending in the affix *-nā* can take zero or some postposition like *'kā'*, *'ke liye'* etc. So, the 'to' in Hindi is translated as '*-nā* *' where '*' denotes zero or a postposition like *kā, se, mem, ke liye* etc.

5 Contexts of *infinitive TO* and their translation equivalents in Hindi

We have focused on the following constructions where *infinitive TO* occurs: the context of *raising*, *control* (subject control and object control) and ECM verbs in English. The examples of each case are illustrated below with their Hindi equivalents. We attempt to identify contexts that might account for the translation variations of these constructions into Hindi. Both raising and control verbs take an infinitival complement with 'TO', however they differ in what they take as their subject.

5.1 Raising verbs

Raising verbs are those verbs whose subject is not its logical subject. We notice that the *infinitive TO* is represented in Hindi in two different ways depending on what the infinitive verb is. If the infinitive verb is any verb other than copula, it occurs in its participial form as exemplified below in (4) and (5):

(4)   The girl appeared to enjoy the film.
      laṛakī{fem} laga{3,pt} **ānanda_uṭhā-nā**{fem} philma
      laṛakī philma kā **ānanda uṭhātī huī** lagī

(5)   The boy seems to know everything.
      laṛakā laga{3,pr} **jāna-nā**{masc} saba-kucha
      laṛakā saba-kucha **jānatā huā** lagatā hai

---

[7] *tumarthaśca kaḥ? bhāvaḥ.* What is the meaning of the words that end in *tumun* affix? It is *bhāvaḥ* (action) (3.4.26.2)

It is interesting to note that the Hindi equivalent expression corresponding to the *infinitive TO* (as ānanda_uṭhānā in (4) agrees with the subject (laṛakī) of the sentence. We consider this nonfinite form to be a *kṛdanta viśeṣaṇa* (adjectival participial) of the subject *laṛakī*. Given this observation, we propose to make a dependency representation of the above case as shown in Fig. 2:

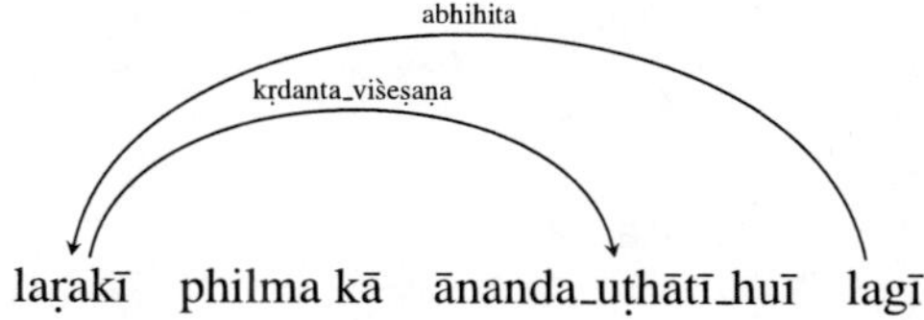

Figure 2: Dependency tree of example (4)

The tree in Fig. 2 represents information better than the one in Fig. 3, which does not account for the feminine marking on *kṛdanta viśeṣaṇa*:

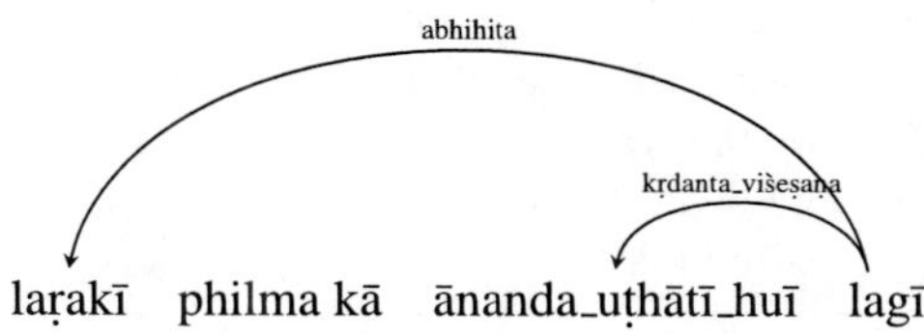

Figure 3: Dependency tree of example (4)

The analysis represented by Fig. 2 correctly predicts the translation equivalent in Hindi and thus can be used as a clue for determining the Hindi equivalents of the English raising verbs 'seem' and 'appear'.

When the *infinitive TO* takes the verb 'be', we note that the infinitives are consistently dropped in Hindi as shown below:

(6)   The car proved to be expensive.
      gāṛī nikala{3,pt} **ho-nā** mahangī
      gāṛī mahangī nikalī

(7)   Ram turned out to be a smart guy.
      rāma nikala{3,pt} **ho-nā** eka buddhimāna laṛakā
      rāma eka buddhimāna laṛakā nikalā

(8)   Higher floors tend **to be** hotter.
      jyādā umcī manjila{pl} jā{3,pr} **ho-nā** garama{comp_degree}
      jyādā umcī manjilem jyādā garama hotī haim

(9)   The boy seems **to be** intelligent.
laṛakā laga{3,pr} **ho-nā** buddhimāna
laṛakā buddhimāna lagatā hai

The syntactic analysis of these sentences are same as the one given in Fig. 4. For example, the translation equivalent of the sentences from (6)-(9) will have the following dependency analysis:

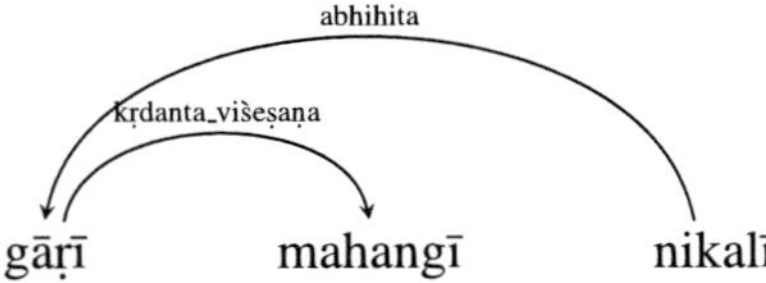

Figure 4: Dependency tree of example (6)

Aspectual and modal verbs of English have also been treated as raising verbs (Taylor, 2006). The verbs with *infinitive TO* are consistently translated into *-nā* form in Hindi as shown below:

(10)   Mohan began **to feel** useless.
mohana s̀uru kara{3,pt} **mahasusa kara-nā** bekāra
mohana ne bekāra **mahasūsa karanā** s̀uru kiyā

(11)   She will continue **to do** the work.
vaha jārī rakha{3,ft,fem} **kara-nā** kāma
vaha kāma **karanā** jārī rakhegī

(12)   This ought **to be** a very good moment for him.
yaha cāhiye **ho-nā** eka bahuta acchā kṣaṇa liye usake
yaha usake liye eka bahuta acchā kṣaṇa **honā** cāhiye

5.2   Control verbs

Control verbs are the verbs which share one of its arguments with that of the *infinitive TO* argument. When the subject is shared, those verbs are called subject control verbs. We note that the translation of *infinitive TO* in the context of subject control verb is always into *-nā kṛdanta* form. However, different postpositions can occur with the kṛdanta form depending on the semantics of the main verb of which the *infinitive TO* is an object:

(13)   He forgot **to tell** you something.
vaha bhūla jā{3,pt} **batā-nā** āpako kucha
vaha āpako kucha **batānā** bhūla gayā

(14)   I hate **to say** this.
maiṃ nāpasanda kara{3,pr} **kaha-nā** yaha
maiṃ yaha kahanā nāpasanda karatā hūṃ

(15)   He is presently attempting **to do** the translation work.
vaha rahā hai abhī prayāsa kara **kara-nā** anuvāda kārya
vaha abhī anuvāda kārya **karane kā** prayāsa kara rahā hai

(16)   He decided **to take** a nap on the sofa.
usane phaisalā kara{3,pt} **le-nā** jhapakī para sophā
usane sophe para jhapkī **lene kā** phaisalā kiyā

(17)   He managed **to get** home on Sunday
vaha kāmayāba raha{3,pt} **ā-nā** ghara para ravivāra
vaha ravivāra ko ghara **āne meṃ** kāmayāba rahā

(18)   They failed **to make** remarkable discoveries.
ve asaphala raha{3,pt,pl} **kara-nā** ullekhanīya khoja
ve ullekhanīya khoja **karane meṃ** asaphala rahe

The Hindi correspondence of the *infinitive TO* in (13) and (14) is kṛdanta form *-nā*; this form occurs in its ṣaṣṭhī (6th case maker) variant (-ne[8] kā) in (15) and (16) and saptamī (7th case marker) variant (-ne meṃ) in (17) and (18).

When the infinitive TO is not an argument of the subject control verbs, it conveys a sense of "purpose". In Hindi the postposition *ke liye* expresses the semantics of purpose.

(19)   She moved **to stand** behind Fiona.
vaha kadama badhā{3,pt} **khaḍā ho-nā** pīche Phionā
usane Phionā ke pīche **khaḍā hone ke liye** kadama baṛhāye

(20)   Dad is negotiating **to sell** his property.
pitā bātacīta kara{3,pr_cont} **beca-nā** vaha{gen,fem} sampatti
pitā usakī sampatti **becane ke liye** bātacīta kara rahe haiṃ

---

[8]"-ne" is the oblique form of the suffix *-nā* which appears when it is followed by postpositions.

(21) The staff bribed police **to get** information
on politicians.
karmacāri{pl} rishvata_de{3,pt}
pulisa_ko **prāpta_kara-nā** sūcanā
para rājanītijñoṃ
karmacāriyoṃ ne rājanītijñoṃ para
sūcanā **prāpta karane ke liye** pulisa ko
riśvata dī

In case of object control verb the object of the
main verb and the subject of the embedded *infinitive TO* verb are co-indexed. We note that the
Hindi equivalent of *infinitive TO* in the context of
object control verb is mainly *-ne ke liye* as exemplified below:

(22) We ask students **to write** something
about themselves.
hama kaha{3,pr} vidyārthiyoṃ **likha-nā**
kucha bāre meṃ khuda
hama vidyārthiyoṃ se khuda ke bāre
meṃ kucha **likha-ne_ke_liye** kaha-
te_haiṃ

(23) New rules push members to share more
information about themselves.
naye niyama{pl} bādhya_kara{3,pr,pl}
sadasya-pl **sāṃjhā_kara-nā** aura adhika
jānakārī bāre meṃ khuda
naye niyama sadasyoṃ ko khuda ke
bāre meṃ aura adhika jānakārī **sāṃjhā
karane ke liye** bādhya karate haiṃ

We understand from the aforementioned discussion that *infinitive TO* is translated into kṛdanta
form in Hindi. It appears that the selection of postpositions in different contexts depends on the semantics of the control verb. Similar observation is
made in (Bharati et al., 2005).

5.3 Exceptional Case Marking verbs

In English, there are verbs which assign accusative
case to nouns which are not its argument but
the argument of the embedded *infinitive TO* constructions. Such constructions are very differently
translated in Hindi as shown below:

(24) I want the students **to go**.
maiṃ cāha{1,pr} vidyārthī **jā-nā**
meṃ cāhatā huṃ ki vidyārthī **jāyeṃ**

(25) We need volunteers **to serve** as medical
assistants.
hama_ko jarurata_hai svayaṃsevaka

sevā_kara-nā ke_rūpa_me auṣadhīy
sahāyaka
hameṃ jarurata hai kī svayaṃsevaka
auṣadhīya sahāyaka ke rūpa me **sevā
kareṃ**.

In (24) and (25), the *infinitive TO* is translated as
a clause with subjunctive form of the verb. However we notice that ECM verbs can be variedly
translated in Hindi for which no immediate contextual clue is available.

5.4 Causative periphrastic compound

English causative construction is periphrastic in
nature where the grammatical meaning is distributed among more than one words. One
causative construction in English uses 'get' as exemplified below:

(26) They got me **to talk** to the police.
ve{nom} prāptā_kara{3,pt} maiṃ{acc}
bāta_kara-nā se - pulisa
unhoṃne merī pulisa se **bāta karavāyī**

(27) I got the mechanic **to check** the brakes of
my car.
meṃ prāpta_kara{3,pt} kārīgara
jāṃca_kara-nā breka kā merī kāra
maiṃne kārīgara se merī kāra ke breka kī
jāṃca karavāyī

This form of causative construction is used
when we want to convince someone or trick someone into doing something. Such construction is
systematically translated into causative form of the
embedded verb with the drop of equivalent of 'get'
in Hindi.

6 Our Approach to WTD

We have distributed the task of WTD in two
parts in consonance with the observation made
in (Kulkarni, 2003) in the context of design and
development of Anusaaraka system:

1. A need to share load between man and machine.

2. Distinguish reliable knowledge from heuristics.

We often come across ambiguous cases where
it is difficult to state the choice of a particular target translation for a word in terms of certain conditions from the context. This is so because the

information is not easily logically available in the context, but is rather distributed hence difficult to tap through certain conditions. Therefore, we propose to handle the WTD task of *infinitive TO* at two levels:

1. Rule based approach

2. Case based reasoning approach

1. Rule based approach: In order to handle logical type of cases, linguistic knowledge is represented in terms of rules. The discussion in Section 5 guides us to formulate rules and implement them. When number of rules increase, maintenance of rules becomes important in the sense that no rule should clash with any other rule and the syntactic format of the rules should be correct. The use of expert system CLIPS[9] for the rule writing makes the task simple. While making the rules, the developer is also requested to give at least one example English sentence with its translation for which the rule is written. Such an effort also helps in growing the parallel corpora.

2. Case based reasoning approach: We have identified cases where it is difficult to identify context which can be used as conditions in the rules. For example, the discussion in Section 5 illustrates that *-nā* kr̥danta form occurs with different postpositions such as *-ne kā, -ne mem̐, -ne ke liye* and so on while translating *infinitive TO* in the context of control verbs the semantics of individual verbs might give us clue for selecting the right postposition in a given case. But specifying that semantics in concrete fact is not easy. Also, we noted that the *infinitive TO* in the context of ECM verbs can be translated in various ways. For such cases, we have decided to adopt the case based reasoning option. We will develop translation copora for such cases and use machine learning technique for learning the correct translation automatically. However, further discussion on this approach is beyond the scope of this paper.

6.1 Data Preparation

We have taken the list of ECM, control and raising verbs from Treebank IIa Guidelines[10]. The

guidelines have 31 ECM, 34 raising verbs, 99 subject control verbs, 52 object control verbs and 34 raising verbs. We extracted sentences for these verbs from COCA[11] (Zhou and McKinley, 2005). Then the sentences were simplified as and when required and were manually translated into Hindi. We observed the patterns of translation from these translated pairs of sentences.

6.2 Formulation of Rules

Rule 1. The 'to' in 'infinitive TO' constructions translates into *nā* in Hindi if it occurs as an infinitival predicate of the following verbs when they have a PRO embedded subject, (with an embedded subject they will follow "Rule 6"): apt, begin, choose, continue, end, fail, figure, forget, happen, hate, keep, learn, like, love, need, ought, prefer, prove, quit, remain, start, stop, tend, want and wind. Ex.

(28)   a.   Jennifer began **to take** precautions.
       Jeniphar s̐uru_kara{3,pt} **barata-nā** sāvadhanī{fem}
       Jeniphar ne sāvadhanī **baratanā** *s̐uru kiyā*
   b.   He chose **to go** into teaching.
       vaha{masc} cuna{3,pt} **jā-nā** mem̐ s̐iksaṇa
       usane s̐iksaṇa mem̐ **jā-nā** cunā

Rule 2. If the 'infinitive TO' constructions are arguments of the verbs 'appear' or 'seem' then 'to' translates into 'verb + -tā huā' in Hindi. Ex.

(29)   a.   It appears **to move**.
       yaha laga{3,pr} **cala-nā**
       yaha **calatā huā** lagatā hai
   b.   She appeared **to enjoy** it.
       vaha{3,fem}   laga{3,pt,fem} **ānanda_uṭhā-nā** yaha{acc}
       vaha isakā **ānanda uṭhātī huī** lagī

Rule 3. If "infinitive TO" verb is an argument of a verb that translates into a conjunct verb and the first part of the verb is a noun as in *phaisalā kara,*

---

[9]http://clipsrules.sourceforge.net/
[10]Treebank IIa is the annotation style used in the English Treebank being created as part of the OntoNotes Project (DARPA GALE). It is based on the original Penn Treebank II Style (Taylor, 2006). http://www-users.york.ac.uk/~lang22/TB2a_Guidelines.htm
[11]COCA (Corpus of Contemporary American English) is the largest freely-available corpus of English. It contains more than 450 million words of text and is equally divided among spoken, fiction, popular magazines, newspapers, and academic texts. It allows limit searches by frequency and compare the frequency of words, phrases, and grammatical constructions. http://corpus.byu.edu/coca/

niścaya kara, ānanda uṭhā, āśā kara, paravāha kara, lakṣya rakha, anumati de etc. in Hindi then it is translated as '-ne kā'. Ex.

(30)   a.   I decided **to go** ahead.
maiṃ phaisalā_kara 3,pt{**jā-nā** āge
maiṃne āge **jāne kā** phaisalā kiyā

        b.   We have opted **to take** the research.
hama{1,pl}   phaisalā_le **le-nā** -
śodhakārya
hamane śodhakārya **lene kā** phaisalā liyā hai

Exception to this rule:

(31)   She declined **to comment**.
vaha{1,sg,fem} manā_kara **tippaṇī kara-nā**
usane **tippaṇī karane se** manā kiyā

Rule 4.: If the 'infinitive TO' constructions are 'to BE' where 'BE' occurs as a 'copula' verb then 'to BE' is dropped while translating it into Hindi. Ex.

(32)   a.   The car proved **to be** expensive.
- kāra   sābita_ho{3,pl}   *ho-nā*
mahaṃgā{fem}
kāra mahaṃgī sābita huī

        b.   The number of inputs is assumed **to be** two.
- saṃkhyā kā{fem} inaputa hai
māna{1,sg,passive} **ho-nā** do
inaputa kī saṃkhyā do mānī gayī hai

Rule 5.: English uses MAKE, HAVE and GET verbs for causativization, whereas Hindi uses *-ā* and *-vā* suffixes to the root to represent direct and indirect causation respectively (Ramchand, 2008). The pattern *GET + animate + to + Verb* marks causatives in English. For example in (33-a) the main verb 'got' and to-infinitive 'to paint' form a causative verb. Hence we group these verbs together and causativize them in Hindi.

(33)   a.   I **got** the boy **to paint** my house.
maiṃ{nom}   prāpta_kara{pt} -
ladakā **raṃga-nā** merā ghara
maine ladake se merā ghara **raṃgavāyā**

        b.   They **got** me **to talk** to the police.
ve{nom} prāpta_kara{pt} merī **bāta kara-nā** se - pulisa
unhoṃne pulisa se merī **bāta karavāī**

Rule 6. The 'TO infinitive dependent' of some verbs gets transferred into subjunctive clause in Hindi. Some verbs in this category are *command, demand, insist, order, recommend, suggest, want* and *wish*.

(34)   I want him **to go**.
*maiṃ usako **jānā** cāhatā hūṃ
*maiṃ usakā **jānā** cāhatā hūṃ
maiṃ cāhatā hūṃ ki vaha **jāye**

Rule 7. By default the 'infinitive TO' constructions translate into 'verb + *-ne ke liye*' in Hindi. Ex.

(35)   a.   7000 people turned out **to see** him.
7000 loga ā{3,pl,pt} - **dekha-nā** use
7000 loga use **dekhane ke liye** āye.

        b.   You were elected **to do** something.
āpa the cuna{2,pt} **kara-nā** kucha
āpa kucha **karane ke liye** cune gaye the

7   Results and Error Analysis

We randomly picked 100 sentences from COCA for testing the rules. We ran three translation systems Anusaaraka, Google and Anuvad on these 100 test sentences. Three evaluators evaluated the output of the systems for their accuracy. Accuracy was measured on a scale of 0-2; 0 being incomprehensible, 2 being comprehensible and 1 comprehensible with some effort. Generally when the output is not grammatical but the reader can comprehend the meaning from the output, the score 1 was given for such cases. Table 1 reports the results.

From Table 1, we observe that the performance of Anusaaraka is distinctly better than the two other systems.

	Anusaaraka	Google	Anuvad
Correct Translation	80	70	46
Incorrect Translation	20	30	54
Accuracy	**80%**	70%	46%

Table 1: Anusaaraka accuracy results compared with other MT systems.

We also compared the output of Anusaaraka with revised rules with the performance of the older version of Anusaaraka where the default translation of TO infinitive was given as *-ne ke liye*. We observed a distinct improvement of the system when we implemented our rules as shown in Table 2:

	Without Formulated Rules	With Formulated Rules
Correct Translation	50	80
Incorrect Translation	50	20
Accuracy	50%	**80%**

Table 2: Anusaaraka accuracy results before and after application of the *to-infinitive* rules.

We categorized the verbs which the TO infinitive is a dependent of into different verb types and examined the performance of Anusaaraka for each type of verb class.

Verb Type	Total	Correct	Accuracy
Aspectual	12	9	75%
Causative	4	4	100%
ECM	13	12	92%
Object control	25	20	80%
Raising	9	4	44%
Subject control	37	31	83%

Table 3: Accuracy results for various type of verbs present in the test set.

We observe from Table 3 that the TO infinitive with *Raising* type of verbs have mostly been incorrectly translated. The errors in various types of verb translations can be classified as follows:

1. Parser Error: Sometimes, the 'TO' is tagged as preposition and the parser inadvertently considers the *infinitive TO* as preposition and as a consequence the whole parse goes wrong. For example, infinitive TO (in bold characters) has been wrongly projected as a prepositional phrase (PP) for the following sentence: *I am going **to direct people** to read your writings at our website.*

2. For rule 3, it is important that our conjunct verb list be exhaustive. If a conjunct verb is not identified while translation, this rule will not fire and the translation of *TO infinitive* will be incorrect. For example, in (36), the

word 'advise' is translated as *sujhāva denā* in Hindi. Since we do not have that conjunct verb present in the list, hence, the *TO infinitive* "to pay" was translated as *dhyāna de-ne ke liye* while it should have been translated as *dhyāna de-ne kā*:

(36) I have advised them **to pay** attention to their intuition.
maiṃ sujhāva de{1,pt} unako dhyāna **de-nā** apane antarjñāna ko maiṃne unako apane antarjñāna kī ora dhyāna **dene kā** sujhāva diyā

3. Sometimes, a specific verb of a verb class has a very different behavior and therefore they cannot be handled with rules. For example the raising verb 'happen' with its dependent TO infinitive is translated into different constructions into Hindi such as:

(37) a. He **happened to see** the article.
vaha ho{pt} **dekh-nā** - lekha usakī lekha para **najara paḍī**
  b. I **happened to go** to the market one Saturday.
meiṃ ho{pt} **jā-nā** ko - bājāra eka šanivāra merā eka šanivāra ko bājāra **jānā huā**
  c. I **happen to disagree** with my husband on a lot of issues.
meiṃ **ho{1,pr}** **matabheda‿ho-nā** ke‿sātha mera pati para bahuta sāre viṣayoṃ para merā mere pati ke sātha bahuta sāre viṣayoṃ para **matabheda rahatā hai**

We observe that the word 'happen' is not a straightforward case to translate into Hindi. At present, our system does not handle 'happen to V' constructions.

8 Conclusion

In this paper, we presented the design and implementation of a resource namely WTD rules for disambiguating English *infinitive TO* in the context of English-Hindi machine translation. The results are promising and show that with the use of contextual knowledge, machine can produce satisfactory translation of English 'infinitive TO' in the context of raising, control, ECM and periphrastic causative constructions. Since availability of these constructions in parallel copora is not always possible, hence, we chose to utilize contextual translation and semantic clues for writing WTD rules. However, we also recognize cases where contextual clue is not available. Thus the method of WTD in this system respects the concept of sharing the work load between man and machine. As future work, we will create parallel corpora for such cases for case base reasoning.

Acknowledgments

The authors are grateful to Prof. Vineet Chaitanya, Dr. Dipti Misra Sharma and Dr. Aditi Mukherjee for having useful discussions on various aspects of the subject. We also thank Banasthali Vidyapith students, especially Ayushi Agarwal, Shivani Pathak, Anshika Sharma and Prajya Jha for evaluating the test output.

References

Akshar Bharati, R Vaishnavi Rao, and AP Tirupati. 2005. WSD of To-Infinitive into Hindi: An Information Based Approach.

Erwin Marsi André Lynum Lars Bungum and Björn Gambäck. 2011. Word Translation Disambiguation without Parallel Texts. *LIHMT 2011*, page 66.

Yee Seng Chan, Hwee Tou Ng, and David Chiang. 2007. Word sense disambiguation improves statistical machine translation. In *Annual Meeting-Association for Computational Linguistics*, volume 45, page 33. Citeseer.

Sriram Chaudhury, Ankitha Rao, and Dipti M Sharma. 2010. Anusaaraka: An expert system based machine translation system. In *Natural Language Processing and Knowledge Engineering (NLP-KE), 2010 International Conference on*, pages 1–6. IEEE.

Amba P Kulkarni. 2003. Design and Architecture of Anusaaraka-An Approach to Machine Translation. *Volume*, 1:Q4.

Hang Li and Cong Li. 2004. Word translation disambiguation using bilingual bootstrapping. *Computational Linguistics*, 30(1):1–22.

Patanjali. 1975. *Patanjali's Vyakarana mahabhasya : with English translation and notes*. Bhandarkar Oriental Research Institute.

Gillian Catriona Ramchand. 2008. *Verb meaning and the lexicon: A first phase syntax*, volume 116. Cambridge University Press.

Ann Taylor. 2006. Treebank 2a guidelines.

Zhinan Zhou and Philip K. McKinley. 2005. COCA: A Contract-Based Infrastructure for Collaborative Quality-of-Service Adaptation. Technical report, July.

Determing Trustworthiness in E-Commerce Customer Reviews

Dhruv Gupta
Department of Mathematics
and Computing
Indian Institute of Technology Patna
Patna, India
dhruv.mc12@iitp.ac.in

Asif Ekbal
Department of Computer Science
and Engineering
Indian Institute of Technology Patna
Patna, India
asif@iitp.ac.in

Abstract

In this paper, we delve into opinion mining and sentiment analysis of customer reviews posted on online e–Commerce portals such as *Amazon.com*. Specifically, we look at novel ways of automatic labelling of data for customer reviews by looking at the number of helpful votes and subsequently determine hidden factors that can explain why a customer review is more helpful or trustworthy in contrast to others. We further utilize the factors identified by Multiple Factor Analysis to training Logistic Regression and Support Vector Machine (SVM) models for classifying reviews into trustworthy and non-trustworthy. Experiments show the effectiveness of our proposed approach.

1 Introduction

As the e–Commerce business grows, more and more customer express their experience with the products bought online. There is no doubt about the ever growing number of customer reviews and the fact that the reviews can influence the potential buyer's decision. It has become exceedingly pertinent to develop algorithms that allow the e–Commerce industry to predict the potential trustworthiness of the customer reviews. In this direction, we attempt to utilize the concept of **Sentiment Analysis** to determine whether a customer review can be trusted or not.

Customer reviews on a online portal or social media platform such as Facebook[1], Twitter[2], Pinterest[3] etc. serve as advice for potential customers of service or products on whether the particular service suits their needs. Some statistics posed by

---

[1] www.facebook.com
[2] www.twitter.com
[3] www.pinterest.com

Pang et al. (Pang and Lee, 2007) puts the scope of importance of these customer reviews.

Following are some insights as quoted from (Pang and Lee, 2007):

- 81% of Internet users consult the web at least once before buying a product (Pang and Lee, 2007).
- 73% to 87% Internet users confirm that customer reviews about services relating to medical, travel etc have influenced their decision on availing the service (Pang and Lee, 2007).
- For a 5–star rated product customers are willing to shell out 20% to 99% more as compared to a 4–star rated product (Pang and Lee, 2007). The variability arises from the variety of services and products on offer (Pang and Lee, 2007)

As is evident from the above insights, we can conclude that customer reviews pay a pivotal role in a "strategic" customers decision to purchase high value products or services. However as the number of users entering the sphere of Web 2.0 grows, we see a surge in the amount of reviews that users are able to write across social media platforms'(Pang and Lee, 2007). In such a case, a customer can only look at a few customer reviews before s/he makes a final decision to purchase a product. Thus, there arises a need to automatize the process of identifying the sentiment, opinion and the subjectivity hidden amongst these reviews. So, that a crisp report on how a product or service fares amongst the online blogosphere and social media can be reported to the Internet user, allowing her to make informed decision on whether to purchase a particular service or product.

Due to growing number of online reviews for any product or service, a lot of attention has

D S Sharma, R Sangal and J D Pawar. Proc. of the 11th Intl. Conference on Natural Language Processing, pages 196–205,
Goa, India. December 2014. ©2014 NLP Association of India (NLPAI)

recently been focused on classifying the customer reviews based on their subjectivity of opinions (Jindal and Liu, 2008). Jindal et al. (Jindal and Liu, 2008) point out that little attention has been paid to classifying whether a customer review can be trusted or not. The motivation the authors point out is that fake reviews may be created to increase the popularity of a particular product in the market. This can create a illusion in the mind of the potential customer that a product s/he is about to purchase is worth amount to be paid. Hence, it becomes extremely important to check such kind of non–trustworthy reviews.

Our contribution to the detection of opinion spam analysis is two-fold. First, for labeling of the Amazon customer review dataset[4] (McAuley and Leskovec, 2013), we utilized the "helpfulness" votes as a measure to determine if a customer review was trustworthy or not. This method of labeling the corpora is akin to utilizing a crowd–sourcing platform to determine the trustworthiness of customer review. Unlike prior approaches such as (Lim et al., 2010), where the authors employ human evaluators for determining whether a customer review is trustworthy or not; we have taken a very simple yet intuitive approach to label a Web–scale web corpora.

Secondly, we hypothesize that by employing Multiple Factor Analysis (Abdi1 and Valentin, 2007) in generating principal components for the features identified for each customer review, we can enhance the performance of the machine learning algorithms. We hypothesize that this can be attributed to the fact that the data points are projected in a lower dimensional feature sub–space, where the data is scaled on the most pertinent dimensions.

2 Related Work

2.1 Detecting Opinion Spam

Jindal et al. (Jindal and Liu, 2008) utilize a logistic regression approach to identify Type 2 (reviews on brands only) and Type 3 (non-reviews) by utilizing a variety of features describing different aspects of the product, reviewer and the review itself. The authors' objective lies in training a supervised classifier that can tell whether a review posted is a spam or genuine. The authors also mention that the use of other supervised learning methods such as support vector machines (SVM)

(Cortes and Vapnik, 1995), naïve Bayes classifier etc. do not qualify to logistic regression in terms of quality of results obtained.

Jindal et al. (Jindal et al., 2010) study a constrained problem of identifying set of rules to predict whether a review is an anomaly with respect to the others. They mine these rules in a similar fashion to Association Rule mining, wherein they chalk out a separate definition of support and confidence to take into unexpectedness.

Lim et al. (Lim et al., 2010) present approaches to deal with review spammer behavior. They construct a linear regression model(Sharma, 1995) that takes into account features such as rating spamming, review text spamming, single product group multiple high ratings, single product group multiple low ratings etc. Their approach involves supervised machine learning algorithms, hence to acquire the labels for their dataset they took help of human evaluators.

Ghose et al. (Ghose and Ipeirotis, 2007) also train linear regression models to find whether a review is helpful or not. Also they extend their regression model to study the effect of various features on sales rank of products featured on Amazon.com. In addition to the features used by prior approaches (Jindal and Liu, 2008; Lim et al., 2010), the authors (Ghose and Ipeirotis, 2007) take into account review *subjectivity & objectivity* for the aforementioned objectives.

In our work we used Multiple Factor Analysis as a pre-processing step, and have been able to take into account the hierarchy and grouping of feature space whilst training machine learning algorithms. This can assist us in training of machine learning algorithms as learner do not take into consideration the grouping / hierarchy of features identified. Also, utilizing MFA as a preprocessing step we are able to scale continuous as well as nominal attributes on the most pertinent principal components identified by MFA. Having the feature vectors scaled, aids in improving the performance of the supervised machine learning algorithm. As we can see when comparing the AUC values of the baseline model and our proposed model (MFA used as pre-processing of SVM), we see that our proposed approach does better job in identifying the trustworthy reviews.

---

[4]https://snap.stanford.edu/data/web-Amazon.html

2.2 Multiple Factor Analysis

Pages et al. (Escofier and Pagès, 1994) in their work outline the Multiple Factor Analysis method for data containing groups of variables. They also outline methods for its application to sensory data. The authors outline solutions to solve the problem of introducing multiple groups of variables at once as active variables. This allows for weighing the groups of variables in a balanced manner and subsequently provides better insights into the data at hand. Abdi et al. (Abdi et al., 2013) work out a mathematical treatment behind Multiple Factor Analysis. The authors also outline several new algorithmic extensions of MFA. Some of the extensions at length they discuss are Hierarchical Multiple Factor Analysis (HMFA), Dual Multiple Factor Analysis, Procrustes Multiple Factor Analysis, Multiple Factor Analysis for Qualitative Data, and Multiple Factor Analysis Barycentric Discriminant Analysis (MUFABADA). HMFA entails hierarchically applying the MFA normalization; this assists in analysis of data sets that contain a hierarchical structure of variables (Abdi et al., 2013). Dual MFA is utilized in the cases where data contains in which the observations are partitioned (Abdi et al., 2013). Procrustes MFA is an extension that is useful for data in which we have several Euclidean distance matrices capturing the same observations (Abdi et al., 2013). MFA for qualitative data is an extension for qualitative data in the same vein as MFA is an extension of PCA for multi–block data (Abdi et al., 2013). A similar extension of PCA for qualitative data is Multiple Correspondence Analysis (MCA) (Abdi et al., 2013). MUFABADA is an approach of utilizing MFA in "multiblock barycentric discriminant analysis framework" (Abdi et al., 2013). MUFABADA addresses the problem of putting the observations in groups which have described these observations in different tables (Abdi et al., 2013).

3 Technical Background

In this section we familiarize the reader with the two pivotal approaches used for determing the trustworthiness of customer reviews on e–Commerce websites. We take the help of detailed literature available in the area of Factor Analysis (Escofier and Pagès, 1994), (Abdi et al., 2013), Logistic Regression (Sharma, 1995) and Support Vector Machine (Cortes and Vapnik, 1995).

3.1 Sentiment Analysis

Sentiment conveys humans emotions or opinions in a given piece of text. Sentiment Analysis as pointed out by Pang et al. (Pang and Lee, 2007) and Turney (Turney, 2002) is an attempt to identify the *subjectivity* or *sentiment polarity* of given piece of text. This is done by leveraging Natural Language Processing (NLP) techniques and trying to model a computation algorithm to identify the same automatically for a given piece of input text (Pang and Lee, 2007; Turney, 2002). Pang et al. (Pang and Lee, 2007) points out that the term "Sentiment Analysis" is more popular amongst the NLP community. "Opinion Mining" also conveys aggregating the subjectivity associated with the item (product) features being discussed in the text (Pang and Lee, 2007). For example, in the example below, "amazing" associates a certain opinion about the product camera, and the sentiment "really great" conveys the subjectivity about the "zoom" feature of the camera. Pang et al. (Pang and Lee, 2007) also point out that, the term opinion mining is favored amongst the information retrieval community.

> "Today I bought this *amazing* **camera** ! The *zoom* of this camera is **really great**."

In this work our proposed algorithm for sentiment analysis is based on logistic regression (Sharma, 1995) and support vector machine (Cortes and Vapnik, 1995). We make use of the implementations as available in Rinker et al. (Rinker, 2013).

3.2 Multiple Factor Analysis

Multiple Factor Analysis is one of the principal component methods that takes into account groupings of variables or attributes when describing the observations (Escofier and Pagès, 1994). MFA is multi–step process whereby in the intial step, a Principal Component Analysis (Jolliffe, 2005) is performed on each group of attributes followed by normalization of the data with eigenvalues (first singular value) found by PCA. Next, the normalized dataset is combined into a unique matrix to be further evaluated by doing a global PCA. MFA is most suitable to be applied to set of observations when the attributes describing it vary in nature i.e. they can be nominal and/or continuous in nature (Escofier and Pagès, 1994). The key distinguishing aspects of MFA (Abdi et al., 2013) are its ability (i). to consider groupings of different varia-bales describing the same set of observations, (ii). to determine "compromise factor scores" or "common factor scores" and (iii). to project the individuals (observations) onto these "compromise factor scores".

We shall adopt the notations used by Abdi et al. (Abdi et al., 2013) to illustrate the Multiple Factor Analysis algorithm. A matrix, $\mathbf{M}$, conveys, the dataset on which we wish to apply the MFA algorithm. The rows of $\mathbf{M}_{(i,)}$ conveys the vector of observations while the columns $\mathbf{M}_{(,j)}$ convey the value of a particular feature / attribute for all the observations. A single element of $\mathbf{M}$ is denoted by $\mathbf{M}_{(i,j)}$. Groupings of attributes in $\mathbf{M}$ are considered as *sub–matrices* $\mathbf{M}_{[i]}$. A congregation of sub–matrices is represented as $\mathbf{T} = [\mathbf{M}_{[1]}\mathbf{M}_{[2]} \ldots \mathbf{M}_{[i]}]$. The matrices, $\mathbf{M}^{\mathbf{T}}$ and $\mathbf{M}^{-1}$ denote the transpose and the inverse of $\mathbf{M}$ respectively. To obtain a column vector of the diagonal elements of matrix $\mathbf{M}$ we use the operator **diag**. The operator **diag** does the opposite in case it is applied to a vector i.e. it transforms the vector into a diagonal matrix. The identity matrix is denoted by $\mathbf{I}$. The vector $\mathbf{1}$ represents a vector of ones (Abdi et al., 2013). The dimension is specified by the index when referring to a vector of ones $\mathbf{1}$ (Abdi et al., 2013).

The procedure to carry out MFA can be decomposed into three steps (Abdi et al., 2013). The first steps entails performing a principal component analysis (PCA) of each individual grouping of attributes, and observing the eigenvalues (first singular value) obtained for each grouping of attributes (Abdi et al., 2013). The second step includes combining of all the groupings of attributes after they have been divided by their respective eigenvalues, and running a non–normalized PCA on this data set (Abdi et al., 2013). The final step involves projecting the groupings of attributes on the "common space" (Abdi et al., 2013).

The first step in Multiple Factor Analysis utilizes the Singular Value Decomposition of the data matrix to perform PCA (Abdi et al., 2013). Mathematically, it can be described as (Abdi et al., 2013)

$$\mathbf{X}_{[\mathbf{k}]} = \mathbf{U}_{[\mathbf{k}]}\boldsymbol{\Gamma}_{[\mathbf{k}]}\mathbf{V}_{[\mathbf{k}]}^{\mathbf{T}} \qquad (1)$$

with

$$\mathbf{U}_{[\mathbf{k}]}^{\mathbf{T}}\mathbf{U}_{[\mathbf{k}]} = \mathbf{V}_{[\mathbf{k}]}^{\mathbf{T}}\mathbf{V}_{[\mathbf{k}]} = \mathbf{I} \qquad (2)$$

Now we need to obtain the first singular values for each grouping of the attributes. For each grouping of attributes we get the first singular values by taking the inverse of the square of the first diagonal element of $\boldsymbol{\Gamma}_{[\mathbf{k}]}$ i.e. (Abdi et al., 2013)

$$\mathbf{diag}(\boldsymbol{\Gamma}_{[\mathbf{k}]}) = [\gamma_{(1,k)}, \gamma_{(2,k)}, \ldots \gamma_{(n,k)}] \qquad (3)$$

$$\alpha_k = \frac{1}{\gamma_{(1,k)}^2} = \gamma_{(1,k)}^{-2} \qquad (4)$$

All the singular values of each grouping of data are stored in a matrix $\mathbf{A}$ computed as follows (Abdi et al., 2013)

$$\mathbf{A} = \mathbf{diag}\left[\alpha_1\mathbf{1}_{[\mathbf{1}]}^{\mathbf{T}}, \alpha_2\mathbf{1}_{\mathbf{2}}^{\mathbf{T}}, \ldots, \alpha_K\mathbf{1}_{[\mathbf{K}]}^{\mathbf{T}}\right] \qquad (5)$$

Next, a Generalized SVD is performed on X (Abdi et al., 2013). Mathematically, it can be expressed as (Abdi et al., 2013)

$$\mathbf{X} = \mathbf{P}\boldsymbol{\Delta}\mathbf{Q}^{\mathbf{T}} \qquad (6)$$

with

$$\mathbf{P}^{\mathbf{T}}\mathbf{M}\mathbf{P} = \mathbf{Q}^{\mathbf{T}}\mathbf{A}\mathbf{Q} = \mathbf{I} \qquad (7)$$

In equation (6) the column vectors of matrix $\mathbf{P}$ and $\mathbf{Q}$ describe a principal component. The factor scores are stored in a matrix $\mathbf{F}$ and the loadings in $\mathbf{Q}$ by the following simple mathematical manipulation (Abdi et al., 2013)

$$\mathbf{X} = \mathbf{F}\mathbf{Q}^{\mathbf{T}} \qquad (8)$$

with

$$\mathbf{F} = \mathbf{P}\boldsymbol{\Delta} \qquad (9)$$

3.3 Logistic Regression

Suppose, we want to predict the outcome variable using k independent variables, X_i, we can leverage an *logistic regression model*. Mathematically, we can describe it as (Sharma, 1995)

$$ln\left(\frac{p}{1-p}\right) = \beta_0 + \beta_1 X_1 + \beta_2 X_2 + \ldots + \beta_k X_k \qquad (10)$$

Equivalently, the equation (10) can be re–written in the following form (Sharma, 1995)

$$ln\left(\frac{p}{1-p}\right) = \beta_0 + \sum_i \beta_i X_i \qquad (11)$$

$$p = \frac{1}{1 + e^{-\beta_0 + \sum_i \beta_i X_i}} \qquad (12)$$

3.4 Support Vector Machines

Support Vector Machines (SVM) illustrated by Cortes et al. (Cortes and Vapnik, 1995), are a class of large–margin classifier. Support Vector Machines as outlined earlier are a class of classifiers that determine a decision surface that is furtherest from any data–point (Manning et al., 2008), and *Support Vectors* are the subset of data–points that define the location of the decision surface. The SVM model for two-way classification problem is given in equation (13) (Manning et al., 2008). Where, $\vec{w}$, represents a weight vector and the intercept term b is used to define the decision hyperplane (Manning et al., 2008). A non–zero α_i points to the fact that the ith data–point viz. $\vec{x}_i$ is a support vector (Manning et al., 2008).

$$f(\vec{x}) = \text{sign}\left(\sum_i \alpha_i y_i \vec{x}_i^T \vec{x} + b \right) \qquad (13)$$

By utilizing a *kernel trick*, we can provide a mapping of data points from lower dimension to higher dimensions (Manning et al., 2008). In this work we analyze with different kernel functions including linear kernel and polynomial kernel. From, equation (13), the kernel function is a simple dot product of data point vectors ie. $K(\vec{x}_i, \vec{x}_J) = \vec{x}_i^T \vec{x}_j$ (Manning et al., 2008). This simple substitution transforms the equation into equation given below (Manning et al., 2008):

$$f(\vec{x}) = \text{sign}\left(\sum_i \alpha_i y_i K(\vec{x}_i, \vec{x}) + b \right) \qquad (14)$$

To transform the data points in lower dimensional space to a higher dimensional space, a transformation of the format $\Phi : \vec{x} \mapsto \phi(\vec{x})$ can be used (Manning et al., 2008). This then implies the simple dot product that becomes the following *Kernel Function* (Manning et al., 2008):

$$K(\vec{x}_i, \vec{x}_j) = \phi(\vec{x}_i)^T \phi(\vec{x}_j) \qquad (15)$$

A kernel function must satisfy *Mercer's condition* viz. it must be "continuous, symmetric and have a positive definite gram matrix" (Manning et al., 2008). If a kernel function does not satisfy such conditions then Quadratic Programming may not yield a answer for the optimization problem posed earlier for SVM's (Manning et al., 2008). Some kernel functions that satisfy Mercer's conditions and are popularly used are indicated below (Manning et al., 2008; Hornik et al., 2006):

- Linear Kernel Function

$$K(\vec{x}, \vec{z}) = (1 + \vec{x}^T \vec{z}) \qquad (16)$$

- Polynomial Kernel Function

$$K(\vec{x}, \vec{z}) = (1 + \vec{x}^T \vec{x})^d \qquad (17)$$

- Hyperbolic Tangent Kernel – where, C, is scaling constant and b, is a offset

$$K(\vec{x}, \vec{z}) = \tanh\left(C \cdot \vec{x}^T \vec{z} + b \right) \qquad (18)$$

- The Bessel function of the first kind kernel

$$K(\vec{x}, \vec{z}) = \frac{\text{Bessel}^n_{(\nu+1)}(\sigma \|\vec{x} - \vec{z}\|)}{(\|\vec{x} - \vec{z}\|)^{-n(\nu+1)}} \qquad (19)$$

- The Laplace Radial Basis Function (RBF) kernel

$$K(\vec{x}, \vec{z}) = exp\left(-\sigma \|\vec{x} - \vec{z}\| \right) \qquad (20)$$

- The ANOVA radial basis kernel

$$K(\vec{x}, \vec{z}) = \left(\sum_{k=1}^{n} exp\left(-\sigma(\vec{x}^k - \vec{z}^k)^2 \right) \right)^d \qquad (21)$$

- Gaussian Radial Basis Kernel Function

$$K(\vec{x}, \vec{z}) = exp\left(-\frac{(\vec{x} - \vec{z})^2}{2\sigma^2} \right) \qquad (22)$$

4 Identifying Trustworthy Customer Reviews

4.1 Approach

For identifying trustworthy customer reviews, we train a supervised machine learning algorithm in two steps. First we identify and implement the useful features keeping in view their effectiveness. In addition we also utilized features leveraged in prior approaches (Jindal and Liu, 2008). We classify these features as per (Jindal and Liu, 2008) into *Review Centric*, *Reviewer Centric*, and *Product Centric*. The features are tabulated in Table 1. Thereafter we perform Multiple Factor Analysis on the feature vectors that were generated by applying the features as described in Table 1. The result of MFA gives us with orthnormal independent dimensions (principal components) upon which we project the individuals (observations).

As a baseline model we omit MFA as a preprocessing step for the classifiers taken into consideration. Using this naïve approach we wanted to see to what degree MFA assists in the classification task of detecting trustworthy and non–trustworthy reviews. To label each individual observation as trustworthy or not we take up an intutive idea that takes into account the number of helpful feedbacks obtained for each of the customer reviews. We label a customer review as helpful if the total percentage of helpful feedbacks for that review is greater than equal to 75 %.

4.2 Feature Extraction

In this section we explain the various features that we take into account for the Amazon customer review data set[5] (McAuley and Leskovec, 2013). We leverage several features identified by prior approaches such as (Jindal and Liu, 2008) for the task of review spam analysis. We also augment them with several additional characteristics. The feature set utilized by us is tabulated in Table 1. We explain the intuition behind these features in the following subsections.

4.2.1 Review Centric Feature Group

Review centric features, as the name suggests are measures extracted from the review written by the online users. We have also taken into account the titles of the reviews that the users assign. Below we describe the explanations of the features listed in Table 1.

- **Length of the review title** and **length of review body** measure in the number of words captured in the body and title of the customer review. As indicated in (Jindal and Liu, 2008), Jindal et al. predict that long customer reviews tend to be more helpful; which we have also found in a case study we conducted utilizing MFA.

---

[5] https://snap.stanford.edu/data/web-Amazon.html

Feature Group	Feature
Review Centric	Length of Review Title
	Length of Review Body
	Contextual sentiment polarity of review body
	Contextual sentiment polarity of review summary
	Cosine similarity between review and the title
	Percentage of numericals
	Percentage of capitals
	Percentage of all capitals
	Rating of review
	Deviation of rating
	(Flag) Review is good
	(Flag) Review is average
	(Flag) Review is bad
	Time of postings of customer review
Reviewer Centric	Ratio of reviews written by the reviewer
	(Flag) Reviewer gives only good rating
	(Flag) Reviewer gives only average rating
	(Flag) Reviewer gives only bad rating
	(Flag) Reviewer gives both good and bad rating
	(Flag) Reviewer gives both good and average rating
	(Flag) Reviewer gives both bad and average rating
Product Centric	Price
	Average Rating

Table 1: Groupings of features used for MFA

- **Contextual sentiment polarity** is computed for both the customer review body and the review title. For the purpose of identifying the sentiment of given piece of text, the authors of (Rinker, 2013) utilize a "sentiment dictionary" (Hu and Liu, 2004) that is used to label the words carrying opinions. After identifying the "polarized" words (i.e. the words carrying sentiment), a "context cluster" is created by taking into account words surrounding the "polarized" cluster (Rinker, 2013). The "context cluster" is denoted by x_i^T and the words are considered as valence shifters (Rinker, 2013). The words in x_i^T are further labeled as –"neutral (x_i^0), negator (x_i^N), amplifier(x_i^a), or de–amplifier (x_i^d)" (Rinker, 2013). Each opinionated word is then assigned a weight, w, based on the amount of "valence shifters" as well as its position (Rinker, 2013). The final sentiment score is determined following the approach as described in Rinker et al. in (Rinker, 2013). It first adds the "context clusters" together. Next, the sum is divided by the square root of the number of words. $\delta = \frac{x_i^T}{\sqrt{n}}$

By capturing these feature we wanted to see if there was an agreement with the rating indicated by the user in the reviews. We also wanted to capture the true sentiment of the user writing the reviews and if this was predictor of whether a review was trustworthy or not.

- **Cosine similarity** between the review and the product title captures whether the reviewer has included a lot of technical details about the product or not. We wanted to see if a review, rich in technical description, is trustworthy or not. Also it is used to find the similarity between two reviews with the intuition that fake or genuine reviews have certain similarities in textual contents.

- **Percentage of numericals**, as outlined by Jindal et al. (Jindal and Liu, 2008) indicates a very technically oriented review. Percentage of capitalized letter, and all capitalized characters are indicators of not well crafted reviews (Jindal and Liu, 2008). We wanted to see if there was any relation between customer reviews containing a lot of technical details and a trustworthy review. Also, we wanted to see how not well drafted reviews correlate with trustworthy reviews.

- **Rating of review, deviation of rating, review is good, average, and bad** are all review rating related features. We wanted to see how the ratings and their associated flags correspond with trustworthy reviews. It may often be the case that rating which are exceptionally high do not necessarily correspond to trustworthy reviews or a thoughtful average rating may correspond to a helpful review.

- Further, we take into account the **time of postings of customer review** to see if the time a customer review was posted could be potentially linked to whether a customer review was trustworthy or not. For example, a review which was posted very late could potentially be of no help to the reader of the review.

4.2.2   Reviewer Centric Feature Group

Reviewer centric features were designed to capture various attributes related to the user writing the reviews, as the motivation given by Jindal et al. (Jindal and Liu, 2008). Given below are the detailed explanations of the features in this group :

- **Ratio of reviews written by reviewer** checks whether a user who is extremely vocal, writes trustworthy reviews or not.

- There are other features which are defined based on the observations such as reviewer gives only **good, average, and bad or a combination** of such ratings. These features try to capture if a variation in review rating given by the user is indicator of trustworthy

reviews (Jindal and Liu, 2008). Also these are the good indicators of the biased reviews that users write in favor of a particular brand.

4.2.3   Product Centric Feature Group

The last feature group is product centric feature group, which captures two features *price* and *average rating of the product*. Following set of features are included under this set of features :

- As mentioned by Jindal et al. (Jindal and Liu, 2008), we wanted see if **price** point of a product (cheap or expensive) could influence the reviewer in writing less trustworthy reviews.

- Similarly we wanted to see if the **average rating of the product** could evoke the same response.

5   Results and Analysis

We consider customer reviews from each of the product categories in the Amazon customer review data set[6] (McAuley and Leskovec, 2013). The training set was constructed by taking 80% customer reviews and holding out 20% as a test set. The datasets were generated using the sampling without replacement method. Please note that rather than manually labeling the reviews for supervised classification, we utilize the "helpfulness" votes as a measure to determine if a customer review was trustworthy or not. This method of labeling the corpora is akin to utilizing a crowd–sourcing platform to determine the trustworthiness of customer review. This seems to be very simple yet intuitive approach to label a Web–scale corpora.

We present results for the various classifiers considered for the task of determining trustworthy customer reviews. For training of the Logistic Regression (LR) model we utilize the R statistical computing programming language. The SVM models for the various kernel functions were created using the algorithmic implementation by Karatzoglou A. et al. (Karatzoglou et al., 2004) in the R statistical computing programming language. We performed MFA using the algorithmic implementation given by Husson et al. (Husson et al., 2014).

For the baselines we measure the performance of the classifiers trained without the MFA as a pre–processing step. Results for the LR model and

[6]`https://snap.stanford.edu/data/web-Amazon.html`

SVM models are presented in Table 2 and Table 3, respectively.

	AUC Value @ k			
Product Categories	2500	5000	7500	10000
Cell Phones & Accessories	0.72	0.74	0.75	0.77
Software	0.68	0.71	0.71	0.72
Clothing & Accessories	0.78	0.79	0.78	0.80
Amazon Instant Video	0.69	0.70	0.71	NA†
Video Games	0.74	0.73	0.76	0.77
Home & Kitchen	0.76	NA†	NA†	NA†
Electronics	0.72	0.75	0.75	0.77

†k number of customer reviews not available for this category

Table 2: AUC values for the ROC curves obtained from Liner Regression model trained for various product categories at *www.Amazon.com*

Thereafter we integrate MFA and LR model together (named as MFALR), and its results are reported in Table 4. We perform a similar exercise with MFA and SVM classifier (MFASVM) and obtain the AUC values for different kernel functions described in Section 3.4. The results are reported in Table 5.

5.1 Analysis

Comparing the baseline logistic regression model versus the MFARA, we see that the proposed approach attains performance increments for all the product categories. For some product categories such as *Clothing & Accessories* and *Software* our proposed approach encompassing MFA in the classification task along with LR model achieves impressive accuracies. Considering the baseline SVM model and the MFASVM model, we observe that for all the product categories, utilizing MFA as a pre-processing step aids in classification of trustworthy vs. non–trustworthy reviews.

We have shown that by utilizing an intuitive concept of using helpfulness scores in labeling a web–scale corpora we are able to achieve good classification accuracies in terms of AUC values. This is comparable to the prior approaches that utilized human evaluators (Jindal and Liu, 2008). However it is also to be noted that this direct comparison will not be fair as the experiments reported in (Jindal and Liu, 2008) were carried out in a different setting. Contrasting our approach of utilizing MFA as a pre-processing step for classification task and state-of-the-art approaches leveraging standard stand-alone classifiers, we see that

Product Categories	Kernel	AUC Value @ k			
		2500	5000	7500	10000
Cell Phones & Accessories	Polynomial	0.62	0.64	0.66	0.67
	"Gaussian" RBF	0.55	0.57	0.59	0.61
	Linear	0.64	0.66	0.67	0.69
	Hyperbolic Tangent	0.54	0.55	0.57	0.58
Electronics	Polynomial	0.65	0.67	0.68	0.68
	"Gaussian" RBF	0.50	0.50	0.52	0.53
	Linear	0.49	0.63	0.64	0.65
	Hyperbolic Tangent	0.50	0.50	0.50	0.50
Clothing & Accessories	Polynomial	0.81	0.86	0.86	0.89
	"Gaussian" RBF	0.72	0.73	0.73	0.75
	Linear	0.67	0.69	0.73	0.74
	Hyperbolic Tangent	0.59	0.61	0.62	0.64
Amazon Instant Video	Polynomial	0.49	0.50	0.51	NA†
	"Gaussian" RBF	0.54	0.55	0.56	NA†
	Linear	0.50	0.53	0.55	NA†
	Hyperbolic Tangent	0.47	0.48	0.51	NA†
Software	Polynomial	0.63	0.66	0.65	0.66
	"Gaussian" RBF	0.62	0.63	0.64	0.64
	Linear	0.64	0.67	0.69	0.70
	Hyperbolic Tangent	0.54	0.55	0.57	0.57
Video Games	Polynomial	0.59	0.62	0.64	0.65
	"Gaussian" RBF	0.54	0.54	0.55	0.57
	Linear	0.62	0.65	0.67	0.70
	Hyperbolic Tangent	0.48	0.49	0.55	0.57
Home & Kitchen	Polynomial	0.51	NA†	NA†	NA†
	"Gaussian" RBF	0.50	NA†	NA†	NA†
	Linear	0.63	NA†	NA†	NA†
	Hyperbolic tangent	0.50	NA†	NA†	NA†

†k number of customer reviews not available for this category

Table 3: AUC values for the ROC curves obtained from SVM model trained for various product categories at *www.Amazon.com*

our approach is promising with respect to the accuracy values as reported by Jindal et al. (Jindal and Liu, 2008). Ghose et al. (Ghose and Ipeirotis, 2007) reported the performance for regression model trained on data set comprising of a subset of electronic categories such as *Audio-Video* and *Digital Camera*. Our proposed approach encompassing MFA performs at an impressive rate in comparison to the approach presented by Ghose et al. (Ghose and Ipeirotis, 2007).

The key advantages of our proposed approach are as follows:

1. Using Multiple Factor Analysis as a pre-processing step we have been able to take into account the hierarchy and grouping of feature space whilst training machine learning algorithms. MFA is able to assign first singular value corresponding to each grouping of features. This can assist us in training of machine learning algorithms as learner do not take into consideration the grouping / hierarchy of features identified.

2. Also, utilizing MFA as a pre-processing step

Product Categories	AUC Value @ k			
	2500	5000	7500	10000
	2500	5000	7500	10000
Cell Phones & Accessories	0.73	0.74	0.77	0.79
Software	0.70	0.71	0.72	0.74
Clothing & Accessories	0.78	0.78	0.80	0.81
Amazon Instant Video	0.69	0.71	0.73	NA[†]
Video Games	0.76	0.73	0.78	0.78
Home & Kitchen	0.78	NA[†]	NA[†]	NA[†]
Electronics	0.74	0.75	0.77	0.79

[†] k number of customer reviews not available for this category

Table 4: AUC values for the ROC curves obtained from MFA + logistic regression model trained for various product categories at *www.Amazon.com*

Product Categories	Kernel	AUC Value @ k			
		2500	5000	7500	10000
Cell Phones & Accessories	Polynomial	0.66	0.67	0.69	0.69
	"Gaussian" RBF	0.56	0.56	0.58	0.59
	Linear	0.64	0.67	0.69	0.71
	Hyperbolic Tangent	0.56	0.56	0.58	0.59
Electronics	Polynomial	0.67	0.69	0.69	0.70
	"Gaussian" RBF	0.68	0.69	0.71	0.71
	Linear	0.65	0.69	0.72	0.73
	Hyperbolic Tangent	0.54	0.56	0.57	0.57
Clothing & Accessories	Polynomial	0.82	0.84	0.85	0.86
	"Gaussian" RBF	0.73	0.75	0.75	0.77
	Linear	0.71	0.73	0.75	0.77
	Hyperbolic Tangent	0.62	0.63	0.64	0.65
Amazon Instant Video	Polynomial	0.50	0.50	0.52	NA[†]
	"Gaussian" RBF	0.54	0.56	0.58	NA[†]
	Linear	0.52	0.55	0.57	NA[†]
	Hyperbolic Tangent	0.48	0.50	0.50	NA[†]
Software	Polynomial	0.68	0.69	0.69	0.71
	"Gaussian" RBF	0.64	0.65	0.66	0.68
	Linear	0.65	0.68	0.71	0.72
	Hyperbolic Tangent	0.54	0.56	0.56	0.57
Video Games	Polynomial	0.65	0.68	0.68	0.69
	"Gaussian" RBF	0.54	0.56	0.58	0.59
	Linear	0.64	0.66	0.68	0.71
	Hyperbolic Tangent	0.54	0.56	0.57	0.59
Home & Kitchen	Polynomial	0.60	NA[†]	NA[†]	NA[†]
	"Gaussian" RBF	0.70	NA[†]	NA[†]	NA[†]
	Linear	0.67	NA[†]	NA[†]	NA[†]
	Hyperbolic tangent	0.54	NA[†]	NA[†]	NA[†]

[†] k number of customer reviews not available for this category

Table 5: AUC values for the ROC curves obtained from MFA + SVM model trained for various product categories at *www.Amazon.com*

we are able to scale continuous as well as nominal attributes on the most pertinent principal components identified by MFA. Having the feature vectors scaled, aids in improving the performance of the supervised machine learning algorithms. As we can see when comparing the AUC values of the baseline model and our proposed MFASVM model (MFA used as pre-processing of SVM), we

see that our proposed approach does better job in identifying the trustworthy reviews.

6 Conclusions

In this paper we propose a novel method to classify a online review into trustworthy or non–trustworthy. Our results show that the proposed approach of taking into account MFA as pre-processing step for classification task increases the performance of the classifiers. We have also shown how the performance of classifier improves with the increment in the size of the training data. We additionally see that our proposed approach utilizing MFA achieves results comparable to the state–of–the–art–systems.

In the present work we utilize the concept of helpfullness votes to prepare the datasets for the experiments. This process contributes to false positive and false negative examples in the training data. Some amount of manual labeling could be useful to tackle this problem. As part of our future work we would like to see how the concept of classifier ensemble can help in classification of trustworthy reviews. Jindal et al. (Jindal and Liu, 2008), indicate that certain machine learning approaches such as SVM and Bayesian are not up to par in classification of review spam. We hypothesize that, by employing ensemble learning we can further improve the perofrmance. We also plan to use the concept of active learning method for creating the data automatically. We would also focus to identify more features for the target problem.

References

Hervé Abdi, Lynne J Williams, and Domininique Valentin. 2013. Multiple factor analysis: principal component analysis for multitable and multiblock data sets. *Wiley Interdisciplinary Reviews: Computational Statistics*, 5(2):149–179.

Herv Abdi1 and Dominique Valentin. 2007. *Multiple Factor Analysis*. Neil Salkind (Ed.), Encyclopedia of Measurement and Statistics.

Corinna Cortes and Vladimir Vapnik. 1995. Support-vector networks. *Machine Learning*, 20(3):273–297.

Brigitte Escofier and Jérôme Pagès. 1994. Multiple factor analysis (afmult package). *Computational statistics & data analysis*, 18(1):121–140.

Anindya Ghose and Panagiotis G. Ipeirotis. 2007. Designing novel review ranking systems: predicting the usefulness and impact of reviews. In *ICEC*, pages 303–310.

Kurt Hornik, David Meyer, and Alexandros Karatzoglou. 2006. Support vector machines in r. *Journal of statistical software*, 15(9):1–28.

Minqing Hu and Bing Liu. 2004. Mining opinion features in customer reviews. In Deborah L. McGuinness and George Ferguson, editors, *AAAI*, pages 755–760. AAAI Press / The MIT Press.

Francois Husson, Julie Josse, Sebastien Le, and Jeremy Mazet, 2014. *FactoMineR: Multivariate Exploratory Data Analysis and Data Mining with R*. R package version 1.26.

Nitin Jindal and Bing Liu. 2008. Opinion spam and analysis. In *WSDM*, pages 219–230.

Nitin Jindal, Bing Liu, and Ee-Peng Lim. 2010. Finding unusual review patterns using unexpected rules. In *CIKM*, pages 1549–1552.

Ian Jolliffe. 2005. *Principal component analysis*. Wiley Online Library.

Alexandros Karatzoglou, Alex Smola, Kurt Hornik, and Achim Zeileis. 2004. kernlab – an S4 package for kernel methods in R. *Journal of Statistical Software*, 11(9):1–20.

Ee-Peng Lim, Viet-An Nguyen, Nitin Jindal, Bing Liu, and Hady Wirawan Lauw. 2010. Detecting product review spammers using rating behaviors. In *CIKM*, pages 939–948.

Christopher D. Manning, Prabhakar Raghavan, and Hinrich Schütze. 2008. *Introduction to information retrieval*. Cambridge University Press.

Julian J. McAuley and Jure Leskovec. 2013. Hidden factors and hidden topics: understanding rating dimensions with review text. In Qiang Yang, Irwin King, Qing Li, Pearl Pu, and George Karypis, editors, *RecSys*, pages 165–172. ACM.

Bo Pang and Lillian Lee. 2007. Opinion mining and sentiment analysis. *Foundations and Trends in Information Retrieval*, 2(1-2):1–135.

Tyler W. Rinker, 2013. *qdap: Quantitative Discourse Analysis Package*. University at Buffalo/SUNY, Buffalo, New York. version 1.3.5.

Subhash Sharma. 1995. *Applied multivariate techniques*. John Wiley & Sons, Inc.

Peter D. Turney. 2002. Thumbs up or thumbs down? semantic orientation applied to unsupervised classification of reviews. In *ACL*, pages 417–424. ACL.

Naturalistic Audio-Visual Emotion Database

Sudarsana Reddy Kadiri[1], P. Gangamohan [2], V.K. Mittal [3] and B. Yegnanarayana [4]
Speech and Vision Laboratory,
Language Technologies Research Center,
International Institute of Information Technology-Hyderabad, India.
[1]sudarsanareddy.kadiri@research.iiit.ac.in, [2]gangamohan.p@students.iiit.ac.in,
[3]vinay.mittal@iiit.ac.in,[4]yegna@iiit.ac.in

Abstract

The progress in the areas of research like emotion recognition, identification, synthesis, etc., relies heavily on the development and structure of the database. This paper addresses some of the key issues in development of the emotion databases. A new audio-visual emotion (AVE) database is developed. The database consists of audio, video and audio-visual clips sourced from TV broadcast like movies and soap-operas in English language. The data clips are manually segregated in an emotion and speaker specific way. This database is developed to address the emotion recognition in actual human interaction. The database is structured in such a way that it might be useful in a variety of applications like emotion analysis based on speaker or gender, emotion identification in multiple emotive dialogue scenarios etc.

Keywords: Emotion analysis, Emotion recognition, Expressive synthesis, Simulated parallel database, Semi-natural database, Audio-visual data.

1 Introduction

Emotion databases provide an important experimental foundation for analysis when researchers aim at building emotion-aware speech systems (M. Gnjatovic et al., 2010). The basic requirement of database for studies in emotion analysis, identification, classification and synthesis is guided primarily by its suitability to the application chosen. Several emotion databases developed by different research groups can be categorized as simulated, semi-natural and natural databases (E. Douglas-Cowie et al., 2003; B. Schuller et al., 2011; D. Ververidis et al., 2003; S. G.Koolagudi, et al., 2012).

Simulated parallel emotion corpus are recorded from speakers (artists) by prompting them to enact emotions through specified text in a given language. The simulated parallel emotion corpus reported in (Zhihong Zeng et al., 2009; F. Burkhardt et al., 2005; I. S. Engberg et al., 1997; B. Schuller et al., 2010; S. G. Koolagudi et al., 2009), were collected from speakers by asking them to emote same text in different emotions. Their main disadvantage is that the deliberately enacted emotions are quite at variance from the natural 'spontaneous' emotions, and also at times they are out of context (D. Ververidis et al., 2003; D. Erickson et al., 2006).

Semi-natural is a kind of enacted corpus where the context is given to the speakers. The semi-natural emotion database in German language was developed by asking speakers to enact the scripted scenarios, eliciting each emotion (R. Banse et al., 1996; I. Sneddon et al., 2012). Similar semi-natural databases in English and Russian languages were reported in (E. Douglas-Cowie et al., 2000; N. Amir et al., 2000), respectively.

The third kind of emotion database is *natural database*, where recordings do not involve any prompting or the obvious eliciting of emotional responses. Sources for such natural situations could be like talk shows, interviews, panel discussions, and group interactions, etc., in TV broadcast. The Belfast natural database in English language was developed by segmenting 10-60 seconds long audio-visual clips from TV-talk shows (E. Douglas-Cowie et al., 2000). Similar kind of databases were developed in Korean (Zhihong Zeng et al., 2009), German and English languages such as, FAU Aibo (Steidl, S et al., 2009), USC-IEMOCAP (C. Busso et al., 2008), (S. Chung et al.,) etc. Geneva airport lost-luggage study database was developed by video-taping the interviews of passengers at lost-luggage counters (K. Scherer et al., 1997). The "Vera am

D S Sharma, R Sangal and J D Pawar. Proc. of the 11th Intl. Conference on Natural Language Processing, pages 206–213,
Goa, India. December 2014. ©2014 NLP Association of India (NLPAI)

Mittag" German audio-visual emotion database (M. Grimm et al., 2008), was developed by segmenting the audio-visual clips from the talk-show "Vera am Mittag". More details of the various types of databases, issues and important aspects of databases were given in (E. Douglas-Cowie et al., 2003; B. Schuller et al., 2011; D. Ververidis et al., 2003; Koelstra, S et al., 2012).

The simulated emotion parallel speech corpus are mainly used in the area of emotion conversion (M. Schroder et al., 2001; I. Murray et al., 1993; H. Kawanami et al., 2003). In these cases Gaussian Mixture Models (GMMs) and Artificial Neural Networks (ANNs) are used for developing these systems. The output speech from these systems is unnatural and has the constraints of parallel speech corpus. Also, the emotion recognition systems based on these parallel speech emotion corpus are not reliable in real life scenarios. The semi-natural emotion databases also have promptness, but they are useful for developing emotion recognition systems because the recorded utterances have context. The requirement is to have the sentences with context, and the artists to have good performance skills. For the collection of natural databases from TV talk shows and interactive sessions, the main difficulty is to label the emotion or expressive state of the dialogue. Also, it is possible that emotion states like extreme anger, sad, fear, etc., may not occur in such TV broadcasts. Therefore, in "Vera am Mittag" emotion corpus (M. Grimm et al., 2008), the annotation of the utterances was described by three basic primitives: Valence (positive or negative), Activation (calm or excited) and Dominance (weak or strong).

Speakers involved in TV broadcast like talk shows (M. Grimm et al., 2008), interviews, panel discussions, and group interactions, etc., control their emotions/expressive states, i.e., they cannot express the feelings that occur in natural communication among humans. There is always a trade-off between the controllability and naturalness of the interaction (M. Grimm et al., 2008).

In this paper, we describe an audio-visual emotion database named as *IIIT-H AVE*, developed at Speech and Vision Laboratory, IIIT Hyderabad. We have decided to use TV broadcast such as movies and soap-operas for data collection, because the emotions produced are more generic towards the natural communication, even though they are enacted.

The remaining part of the paper is organized as follows. Section II describes the challenges involved in the collection of emotion data for different applications. Section III describes data collection, recording parameters and various stages involved. In Section IV, the structure of the database and and in Section V, issues encountered, proposed solutions and limitations are reported. In Section VI, possible applications of the proposed database are discussed briefly. Finally, Section VII gives a summary and scope of future work.

2 Challenges involved in the collection of emotion data for different applications

In order to develop high quality text to emotion speech synthesis systems, large sized natural databases of each target emotion are required (M. Schroder et al., 2001). But it is impractical to develop a large sized natural emotion database with spontaneity (naturalness). Hence emotion conversion systems are adopted as a post-processing block for speech synthesis from neutral text. In this, a large database of neutral speech is used by text-to-speech (TTS) system to generate a neutral speech first, which is then fed to emotion conversion system where input neutral speech is converted to desired emotional speech. Since emotional speech is produced from emotion conversion systems, it is reasonable to use enacted parallel corpus (D. Erro et al., 2010).

Although it is practically reliable to use simulated parallel corpus for emotion synthesis systems, it does not serve the purpose of developing the emotion classification system because it consists of enacted speech. The original state of the speaker might be different as well. Most of the time, semi-natural and close to natural databases are used for developing emotion recognition systems.

The problem with semi-natural emotion type of databases is, whether the produced emotion is real or it is produced for the purpose of emotion data collection because the speakers know that they are being recorded.

Ideally, natural databases with multiple number of speakers, styles and contextual information are required to design emotion recognition systems for realistic applications. The collection of natural databases mostly from talk shows and interactive sessions in TV broadcast, call centers, interaction with robots, conversations in public places etc. The main difficulty is to identify and label the emotion or expressive state of the dialogue. The emotive states like extreme anger, sad, fear, etc., may not occur some times in such TV broadcasts because the expression of emotion is continuum in nature. Therefore, for natural emotion corpus the annotation of the utterances was described mostly by three basic primitives or dimensions: valence, activation and dominance because the labelling of the naturalistic emotions as highly subjective and categorization of emotions is always debatable (M. Grimm et al., 2008; K. P. Truong et al., 2012). The difficulties involved in natural databases are overlapping multiple speakers data in audio or video or both, background noise or music etc. The good ground truth for natural emotion databases is a difficult task as there are inconsistencies in the annotation. Databases with good emotion labels/annotation would be helpful for emotion recognition tasks.

There are some challenges involved in collection of audio-visual data of naturally occurring emotions. Different people annotate different emotions/expressive states for the same data (audio visual clips). Also, there is a possibility of inconsistency in annotation done by the same person. It is impossible to define strict boundaries for the occurrence of emotion, as presence of emotion is a continuum in speech. Also, emotion depends on the semantic and contextual information.

3 Data collection

The objective of this audio-visual emotion data collection is to have an emotion annotated database with adequate context and large number of speakers. We have chosen English movies and soap operas in TV broadcast as source for data collection.

3.1 Selection of sources

We began by watching a range of source videos over a period of time, and eventually identified a few sources that are potentially useful. For example, if the story of a source had some drama revolving around a group of characters then it was considered as useful source to yield good clips of emotional content. This collection of source videos is named as raw data.

3.2 Emotive and Expressive states

The emotive and expressive states are chosen based on the examples derived from the selected sources. It is also observed that the communication among people always exhibits expressions. The extreme cases of these expressions leads to different emotions. We have identified 7 basic emotions (anger, disgust, fear, happy, neutral, sad and surprise) and 6 expressive states (confusion, excited, interested, relaxed, sarcastic and worried) (K. Scherer et al., 2003; R. Cowie et al., 2003). The list of emotive and expressive states considered is shown in Table 1.

Table 1: *List of emotive and expressive states.*

Emotive states	Expressive states
1. Anger	1. Confusion
2. Disgust	2. Excited
3. Fear	3. Interested
4. Happy	4. Relaxed
5. Neutral	5. Sarcastic
6. Sad	6. Worried
7. Surprise	

3.3 Segregation of raw data

Segregation of audio-visual clip segments (or specific scene-selection) from the chosen source video is carried out on the basis of perceived significance of emotion/expressive state. The duration of such audio-visual clips ranges from 0.5-30 seconds, with average being around 5 seconds. The criteria adopted for selecting 'good source clip' are the following:

- *The audio-visual clips with no background music or noise*

- *Clips with only one actor speaking at a time*

There were 6 subjects, each a research scholar, involved in the segregation of source videos. The basic challenge was to annotate the segregated clips. Subjects were asked to label the clip with one of the emotion/expressive state, and also to specify the confidence level.

If a particular soap-opera has many episodes then during segregation of the clips, the prominent characters of that particular soap-opera are also labelled with speaker numbers.

3.4 Recording quality

From the segregated audio-visual clips, the audio and video streams are extracted. The video files are MPEG4 coded image sequences of frame sizes mostlt 1280×720 pixels, with frame rate of either 24 fps. Files are in *x.avi* and *x.wmv* formats. All the extracted audio wave files have sampling rates of 44.1/48 kHz and are in stereo/mono mode. The data is downsampled to 16 kHz.

4 Structure of database

This database consists of segregated emotion clips in three formats namely, audio, video, and audio-visual. It has 1176 clips in each format. For ease of usage, a consistent structure is maintained for labelling the database, which is explained as follows.

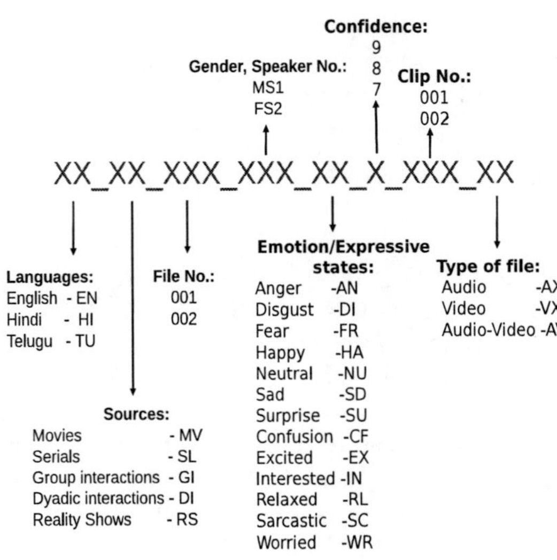

Figure 1: *Labelling structure of the segregated clips*

4.1 Labelling the raw data

The raw videos selected from the chosen source are labelled with a string of 9 characters as follows:
"XX_XX_XXX", where

- Characters 1-2 refer to *language code* [for example, the database collected in English language is coded as 'EN'].

- Characters 4-5 refer to the *kind of source* [for example code 'MV' specifies the source video as movie].

- Characters 7-9 refer to *source video number*.

Example: EN_MV_123

4.2 Labelling of segregated data

Each segregated clip of source video includes the raw label of source video along with labels specifying the gender, speaker, emotion category, confidence score and the type of file. The labelling scheme of segregated clips is as follows:
"XX_XX_XXX_XXX_XX_X_XXX_XX",
where

- Initial characters 1-9 are same as the *label of the raw source video*.

- Character 11 refers to the *gender* (M/F).

- Characters 12-13 refer to *speaker number*. Speaker numbering is kept consistent for all episodes of a particular soap-opera or movie [for example, code 'FS2' represents female speaker number 2].

- Characters 15-16 refer to *emotion category* [for example code 'AN' refers the particular clip to anger state].

- Character 18 refers to the *confidence score* [Range 2 to 9, 9 being highest].

- Characters 20-22 refer to the *clip number for a particular source video*.

- Characters 24-25 refer to the *type of clip* [for example codes 'AX', 'VX' and 'AV' specify the clip in audio, video and audio-visual formats, respectively].

Example: EN_MV_123_FS2_AN_9_106_AV

More details of labelling structure are given in Fig. 1.

The data can be sub-structured as per emotion, gender and speaker. It also has further levels of sub-structuring as per speaker-emotion and gender-emotion categories. The database consists of 1176 labelled clips, of which 741 clips are of male and 435 clips are of female speakers. The statistics of data as per emotion and per speaker is given in Tables II and III respectively.

Database also contains multiple emotions (one emotion followed by another) that occurred in a sentence continuously.

For example Anger followed by Frustration, Excitement followed by Anger or Happy etc.

Table 2: *Number of the clips per emotion/expressive state, with confidence score in each column (CX),(2 to 9, 9 being highest).*

Emotion	C9	C8	C7	C6	C5	C4	C3	C2	Total
1. Anger	5	24	60	44	27	7	2	2	171
2. Disgust	-	6	35	18	8	8	-	-	75
3. Fear	-	-	4	5	6	1	-	-	16
4. Happy	3	27	50	19	21	9	-	-	130
5. Sad	6	17	41	19	17	16	8	-	117
6. Surprise	5	11	28	27	8	12	2	-	93
7. Neutral	4	34	90	31	14	1	-	-	174
8. Confusion	-	1	2	4	4	-	-	-	11
9. Excited	5	19	77	28	11	8	1	-	149
10. Interested	-	4	46	11	5	4	1	-	71
11. Relaxed	-	-	5	2	4	3	-	-	14
12. Sarcastic	-	3	9	8	8	8	2	1	39
13. Worried	-	19	33	7	11	4	1	0	75

Table 3: *Number of the clips per speaker (SX).*

Speakers	S1	S2	S3	S4	S5	S6	S7	S8	S9
No. of clips	11	86	16	24	33	45	24	12	3
Speakers	S10	S11	S12	S13	S14	S15	S16	S17	S18
No. of clips	125	99	30	30	78	132	18	54	60

These are named as Multiple emotion Files (M-files). There are 41 such files obtained in this database. The labelling scheme of M_files is as follows:

"XX_XX_XXX_XXX_XXX_X_XXX_XX",

where

- Initial characters 1-13 are same as the *label of the segregated data.*

- Characters 15-17 refers to the *starting emotion clip number.*

- Character 19 as M, refer to *M-file.*

- Characters 21-23 refers to the *ending emotion clip number.*

- Characters 25-26 refer to the *type of clip* [for example codes 'AX', 'VX' and 'AV' specify the clip in audio, video and audio-visual formats, respectively].

Example: EN_MV_123_FS2_106_M_107_AV

To analyze the inter-evaluator agreement, Fleiss Kappa statistic was computed (Fleiss J et al., 1981). The result for the entire database is 0.31. Since the emotional content of the database mainly span the target emotions (see Table. 1), the Kappa statistic was calculated for the emotional states alone and it turns that 0.41. These levels of agreement, which are considered as fair agreement, are expected since people have different perception and interpretation of the emotions and these values are consistent with the agreement levels reported in previous work (Steidl, S et al., 2009; C. Busso et al., 2008; M. Grimm et al., 2008).

The database is also labelled in dimensional approach in two dimensions (primitives) namely arousal and valence. The labelling structure is same as described in Fig. 1. except the characters 15-16 refer to two dimensions. The codes using two primitives, arousal (active-A, passive-P) and valence (positive-P, negative-N), forms 4 combinations namely AP (active-positive), AN (active-negative), PP (passive-positive) and PN (passive-negative). The neutral samples are labelled as NN (neutral-neutral).

The statistics of the of data as per dimensions is shown in Table IV.

5   Issues in data collection

The ambiguity in annotating the emotion is indicated by specifying the confidence scores. There

Table 4: *Number of clips as per two dimensions - arousal (active/passive) and valence (positive/negative).*

	Positive	Negative
Active	309	245
Passive	198	209

are two reasons for ambiguity of annotating the emotions. One of them is occurrence of mixed emotions in a sentence. For example, there is a possibility of combinations like, surprise-happy, frustration-anger, anger-sad, etc., occurring in the dialogue at the same time. For these cases, the subjects were asked to annotate the clip with multiple emotions along with confidence score for each. If there exist two sub-dialogues in a dialogue, each corresponding to different emotions, then they are segregated separately as M-files. If there is only one dialogue which has mixed emotions, the emotion with maximum confidence is selected. These kind of clips with entire dialogue are considered as *special cases*.

The second reason for ambiguity is unsustainability of emotion throughout the dialogue. In the case of natural communication among human beings, emotion being non-normal (emotional) speech, may not be sustainable for the duration of entire dialogue. The emotion is mostly expressed in some segments of dialogue, like at the end or at the beginning of a dialogue, with the rest of the dialogue being neutral. Hence, the corresponding emotion is given in the annotation.

We have also given confidence score for each audio-visual clip. It indicates the degree of confidence in the labelled emotion actually being present in the clip. Since the confidence score is given by only one person, the clips with less confidence scores and ambiguities can be used better after performing the subjective evaluation. Some of the clips also have abrupt cut-off due to interruption made by other actors before completion of the dialogue. Although this database is more generic and is closer to the natural spontaneous communication, it is still from the enacted source.

6   Possible applications

Due to variety in this database, applications like emotion recognition based on speaker dependent and independent, gender dependent and independent cases can be studied in audio alone, video alone and audio-visual modes. Identification of non-sustainable regions in an entire dialogue will be an interesting research problem. The clips with multiple emotions can also be used to study how an individual can vary his/her emotive state in a dialogue. The perceptual evaluation of these clips with only audio, only video and audio-visual analysis can also be performed. The subjective scores with only audio can be used as ground truth for evaluation of emotion recognition system based on audio.

7   Summary

In this paper, we have described the audio-visual emotion data collection, segregation and labelling of audio-video clips from movies and soap-operas in TV broadcast. It is assumed that the generic and natural communication among the humans can be reflected closely in these sources. The data is collected in three modes: audio, video and audio-visual. The labelling of gender, speaker and emotion is described. Issues in special cases like multiple emotions and non-sustainability of emotions in a dialogue are addressed. The database is still limited in number of clips. Data with sufficient number of clips covering many other cases need to be developed. In order to standardize the data and to know the perception of emotions by human beings, subjective evaluation need to be carried out in all three modes (audio, video and audio-visual).

Acknowledgement

The authors would like to thank all the members of Speech and Vision Lab, especially to B. Rambabu, M. Vasudha, K. Anusha, Karthik, Sivanand and Ch. Nivedita, for spending their valuable time in collection of the IIIT-H AVE database.

References

M. Gnjatovic, D. Rosner, "Inducing Genuine Emotions in Simulated Speech-Based Human-Machine Interaction: The NIMITEK Corpus," *IEEE Transactions on Affective Computing*, vol.1, no.2, pp.132-144, July-Dec. 2010.

E. Douglas-Cowie, N. Campbell, R. Cowie, and P.Roach, "Emotional speech: Towards a new generation of databases," *Speech Communication*, vol. 40, pp. 33-60, 2003.

B. Schuller, A. Batliner, S. Steidl, and D. Seppi, "Recognising realisitic emotions and affect in speech: State of the art and lessions learnt from the first challenge," *Speech Communication*, vol. 53, pp. 1062-1087, 2011.

D. Ververidis, C. Kotropoulos, "A review of emotional speech database,". *In 9th Panhellenic Conf. on Informatics*, November 123, 2003, Thessaloniki, Greece, pp. 560-574.

S. G.Koolagudi, K. S. Rao, "Emotion recognition from speech: a review," *International Journal of Speech Technology*, Volume 15, Issue 2, pp 99117. 2012.

Zhihong Zeng, M. Pantic, G.I. Roisman, T.S. Huang, "A Survey of Affect Recognition Methods: Audio, Visual, and Spontaneous Expressions," *IEEE Transactions on Pattern Analysis and Machine Intelligence*, vol.31, no.1, pp.39-58, Jan. 2009.

F. Burkhardt, A. Paeschke, M. Rolfes, W. Sendlmeier, and B. Weiss, "A database of German emotional speech," *in Proc. Interspeech*, Lisbon, Portugal, pp. 1517-1520, 2005.

I. S. Engberg, A. V. Hansen, O. Andersen, and P. Dalsgaard, "Design, recording and verification of a Danish emotional speech database," *in Proc. Eurospeech*, Vol. 4, pp. 1695-1698, 1997.

B. Schuller, B. Vlasenko, F. Eyben, M. Wollmer, A. Stuhlsatz, A. Wendemuth, G. Rigoll , "Cross-Corpus Acoustic Emotion Recognition: Variances and Strategies," *IEEE Transactions on Affective Computing*, vol.1, no.2, pp.119-131, July-Dec. 2010.

S. G. Koolagudi, S. Maity, V. A. Kumar, S.Chakrabarti, K.S. Rao, "IITKGP-SESC: speech database for emotion analysis," *In LNCS Communications in computer and information science*, Berlin: Springer, August 2009.

D. Erickson, K. Yoshida, C. Menezes, A. Fujino, T. Mochida, and Y. Shibuya, "Exploratory study of some acoustic and articulatory characteristics of sad speech," *phonetica*, Volume 63, p. 1-5, 2006.

R. Banse, and K. Scherer, "Acoustic profiles in vocal emotion expression," *Journal of Personality and Social Psychology*, Vol. 70,no. 3, pp.614-636, 1996.

I. Sneddon, M. McRorie, G. McKeown, J. Hanratty, "The Belfast Induced Natural Emotion Database," *IEEE Transactions on Affective Computing*, vol.3, no.1, pp.32-41, Jan.-March 2012.

E. Douglas-Cowie, R. Cowie, and M. Schroeder, "A new emotion database: Considerations, sources and scope," *in proc. ISCA ITRW on Speech and Emotion*, Newcastle, pp. 39-44, Sep. 2000.

N. Amir, S. Ron, and N. Laor, "Analysis of an emotional speech corpus in Hebrew based on objective criteria," *in proc. ISCA ITRW on Speech and Emotion*, Newcastle, pp. 29-33, sep. 2000.

Steidl, S. Automatic classification of emotion-related user states in spontaneous childrens speech. Studien zur Mustererkennung, Bd. 28, ISBN 978-3-8325-2145-5, 1260 (January), 2009.

C. Busso, M. Bulut, C. Lee, A. Kazemzadeh, E. Mower, S. Kim, J. Chang, S. Lee, and S. Narayanan, IEMOCAP: Interactive emotional dyadic motion capture database, *J. Language Resour. Eval.*, vol. 42,pp. 335-359, 2008.

S. Chung, "Expression and perception of emotion extracted from the spontaneous speech in Korean and English," Ph.D. dissertation, Sorbonne Nouvelle University, Paris, France.

K. Scherer and G. Ceschi, "Lost luggage emotion: A field study of emotion-antecedent appraisal," *Motivation and Emotion*, Vol. 21, pp. 211-235, 1997.

M. Grimm, K. Kroschel, and S. Narayana, "The Vera am Mittag German audio-visual emotional speech database," *in proc. IEEE int. Conf. Multimedia and Expo (ICME)*, Hannover, Germany, pp. 865-868, Jun. 2008.

Koelstra, S.; Muhl, C.; Soleymani, M.; Jong-Seok Lee; Yazdani, A.; Ebrahimi, T.; Pun, T.; Nijholt, A.; Patras, I., "DEAP: A Database for Emotion Analysis ;Using Physiological Signals," *IEEE Tran. on Affective Computing*, vol.3, no.1, pp.18-31, Jan-Mar. 2012.

M. Schroder, "Emotional speech synthesis-a review," *in Proc. Eurospeech*, vol. 1, pp. 561-564, Aalborg, Denmark, 2001.

I. Murray and J. L. Arnott, "Toward the simulation of emotion in synthetic speech: A review of the literature on human vocal emotion," J. Acoust. Soc. Amer., pp. 1097-1108, 1993.

H. Kawanami, Y. Iwami, T. Toda, H. Saruwatari, and K. Shikano, "GMM-based voice conversion applied to emotional speech synthesis," *in Proc. Eurospeech*, pp. 2401-2404, Geneva, Switzerland, 2003.

D. Erro, E. Navas, I. Hernaez, and I. saratxaga, "Emotion conversion based on prosodic unit selection," *IEEE Trans. Audio. Speech, Lang. Process.*, vol. 18, no. 5, pp. 974-983, Jul. 2010.

C. M. Lee and S. S. Narayanan, "Toward detecting emotions in spoken dialogs," *IEEE Trans. Audio, Speech, Lang. Process.*, vol. 13, no. 2, pp. 293-303, Mar. 2005.

K. P. Truong, D. a. van Leeuwen, and F. M. G. de Jong, Speech-based recognition of self-reported and observed emotion in a dimensional space, *in Speech Communcation*, vol. 54, no. 9, pp. 1049-1063, Nov. 2012.

K. Scherer, "Vocal Communication of emotion: A review of research paradigms," *in Speech Communcation*, Vol. 40, pp. 227-256, 2003.

R. Cowie and R. R. Cornelius, "Describing the emotional states that are expressed in speech," *in Speech Communcation*, Vol. 40, pp. 2-32, 2003.

Fleiss J, "Statistical methods for rates and proportions". New York, NY, USA: John Wiley & Sons, 1981.

Discriminating Neutral and Emotional Speech using Neural Networks

Sudarsana Reddy Kadiri[1], P. Gangamohan [2] and B. Yegnanarayana [3]
Speech and Vision Laboratory,
Language Technologies Research Center,
International Institute of Information Technology-Hyderabad, India.
[1]sudarsanareddy.kadiri@research.iiit.ac.in, [2]gangamohan.p@students.iiit.ac.in,
[3]yegna@iiit.ac.in

Abstract

In this paper, we address the issue of speaker-specific emotion detection (neutral vs emotion) from speech signals with models for neutral speech as reference. As emotional speech is produced by the human speech production mechanism, the emotion information is expected to lie in the features of both excitation source and the vocal tract system. Linear Prediction residual is used as the excitation source component and Linear Prediction Coefficients as the vocal tract system component. A pitch synchronous analysis is performed. Separate Autoassociative Neural Network models are developed to capture the information specific to neutral speech, from the excitation and the vocal tract system components. Experimental results show that the excitation source carries more information than the vocal tract system. The accuracy neutral vs emotion classification using excitation source information is 91%, which is 8% higher than the accuracy obtained using vocal tract system information. The Berlin EMO-DB database is used in this study. It is observed that, the proposed emotion detection system provides an improvement of approximately 10% using excitation source features and 3% using vocal tract system features over the recently proposed emotion detection which uses the energy and pitch contour modeling with functional data analysis.

Keywords: Excitation Source, Vocal Tract System, Linear Prediction (LP) Analysis, Autoassociative Neural Network.

1 Introduction

Speech is produced by the human speech production mechanism, and it carries the signature of the speaker, message, language, dialect, age, gender, context, culture, and state of the speaker such as emotions or expressive states. Extraction of these elements of information from the speech signal depends on identification and extraction of relevant acoustic parameters. Information present in the speech signal, including emotional state of a speaker, has its impact on the performance of speech systems (Athanaselis et al., 2005).

In this study, emotion detection refers to, identification of whether the speech is neutral or emotional. Emotion recognition refers to determining the category of emotion, i.e., anger, happy, sad, etc. The focus in this study is on detection of presence of emotional state of a speaker with the use of reference models for neutral speech. Motivated by a broad range of commercial applications, automatic emotion recognition from speech has gained increasing research attention over the past few years. Some of the applications for emotion recognition system are in the fields of health care, call centre services and also for developing speech systems such as automatic speech recognizer (ASR) to improve the performance of dialogue systems (Athanaselis et al., 2005; Mehu and Scherer, 2012; Cowie et al., 2001; Morrison et al., 2007).

Extraction of features from speech signal that characterize the emotion content of speech, and at the same time do not depend on the lexical content is an important issue in emotion recognition (Schuller et al., 2010; Luengo et al., 2010; Scherer, 2003; Williams and Stevens, 1972; Murray and Arnott, 1993; Lee and Narayanan, 2005). From (Schuller et al., 2010; Hassan and Damper, 2012; Schuller et al., 2013; Schuller et al., 2011), it is observed that there is no clear understanding

D S Sharma, R Sangal and J D Pawar. Proc. of the 11th Intl. Conference on Natural Language Processing, pages 214–221,
Goa, India. December 2014. ©2014 NLP Association of India (NLPAI)

on what type of features can be used for emotion recognition task. Brute force approach involves extracting as many features as possible, and use these in the experiments, sometimes using feature selection mechanisms to choose appropriate subset of features (Schuller et al., 2013; Schuller et al., 2011; Schuller et al., 2009; Zeng et al., 2009). These features can be broadly classified as prosodic features (pitch, intensity, duration), voice quality features (jitter, shimmer, harmonic to noise ratio (HNR)), spectral features (Mel Frequency Cepstral Coefficients (MFCCs), Linear Prediction Cepstral Coefficients (LPCCs)), and their statistics such as mean, variance, minimum, maximum, range (Zeng et al., 2009; Schuller et al., 2011; Schuller et al., 2009; ?; Eyben et al., 2012). A limitation of this approach is the assumption that every segment in the utterance is equally important. Studies have shown that emotional information is not uniformly distributed in time (Jeon et al., 2011; Lee et al., 2011; Shami and Verhelst, 2007).

In (Busso et al., 2009; Bulut and Narayanan, 2008; Arias et al., 2014; Arias et al., 2013; Busso et al., 2007), authors observed that a robust neutral speech models can be useful in contrasting different emotions expressed in speech. Emotion detection study was made by creating acoustic spectral features of neutral speech with HMMs (Busso et al., 2007). In (Busso et al., 2009), authors used the pitch features of neutral speech to discriminate the emotions using the Kullback-Leibler distance. It was observed that gross pitch contour statistics such as mean, minimum, maximum and range are prominent than pitch shape. Recently, emotion detection is performed using functional data analysis (FDA) (Arias et al., 2014; Arias et al., 2013). In this approach, pitch and energy contours of neutral speech utterance are modeled using FDA. In testing, pitch and energy contours are projected onto the reference bases, and their projections are used to discriminate neutral and emotional speech. Similar studies were made to model the shape of pitch contour of emotional speech by analyzing the rising and falling movements (Astrid and Sendlmeier, 2010). One limitation with the studies (Arias et al., 2014; Arias et al., 2013) is that, all the utterances should be temporally aligned with the Dynamic Time Warping and it may not be realistic for most of the situations.

Here, we propose an approach based on AANN

(Yegnanarayana and Kishore, 2002) to detect whether a given utterance is neutral or emotional speech. The detection of emotional segments or emotion events may help the current approaches in automatic emotion recognition. This approach avoids the interrelations among the lexical content used, language and emotional state across varying acoustic features. The discrimination capabilities of AANN models are exploited in various areas of speech such as speaker identification, speaker verification, speaker recognition, language identification, throat microphone processing, audio clip classification etc (Reddy et al., 2010; Murty and Yegnanarayana, 2006; Yegnanarayana et al., 2001; Mary and Yegnanarayana, 2008; Bajpai and Yegnanarayana, 2008; Shahina and Yegnanarayana, 2007).

This present work is based on our previous work (Gangamohan et al., 2013) for capturing the deviations of emotional speech from neutral speech. In that paper (Gangamohan et al., 2013), it was shown that the excitation source features extracted in the high signal to noise ratio (SNR) regions of the speech signal (around the glottal closure) capture the deviations of emotional speech from neutral speech. This paper presents a framework to characterize the high SNR regions of the speech signal using the knowledge of speech production mechanism. In (Reddy et al., 2010; Murty and Yegnanarayana, 2006; B. Yegnanarayana and S. R. Mahadeva Prasanna and K. Sreenivasa Rao, 2002), the authors showed the importance of processing the high SNR regions of speech signal for various applications such as speaker recognition (Reddy et al., 2010; Murty and Yegnanarayana, 2006), speech enhancement (B. Yegnanarayana and S. R. Mahadeva Prasanna and K. Sreenivasa Rao, 2002), emotion analysis (Gangamohan et al., 2013), etc. Hence, in this study, our focus is on the processing of high SNR regions of speech.

The remaining part of the paper is organized as follows: Section 2 describes the basis for the present study. Databases used and feature extraction procedures are described in Section 3. In Sections 4 and 5, description of the AANN models for capturing the excitation source and vocal tract system information are given. Emotion detection experiments and discussion on results are given in Section 6. Finally, Section 7 gives a summary and scope for further study.

2 Basis for the Present Study

Speech production characteristics are changed while producing emotional speech, and the changes are mostly in the excitation component. The changes are not sustainable for longer periods, and hence are not likely to be present throughout. This is due to an extra effort needed to produce the emotional speech. The primary effect is on the source of excitation due to pressure from the lungs and the vibration of the vocal folds. Moreover, the changes in production can be affected only in some selected voiced sounds. Hence, some neutral speech segments are also present in emotional speech. While most changes from perception point of view take place at the suprasegmental level (pitch, intensity and duration), it is less likely that significant changes take place at the segmental level (vocal tract resonances). Changes at the suprasegmental level are mostly learnt features (acquired over a period of time). It is difficult to find consistent suprasegmental features which can form a separate group for each emotion. In this study, changes in the subsegmental features are examined for discriminating neutral and emotional speech of a speaker (speaker-specific) using AANN models. The features are referred to as subsegmental features, since we consider only 1-5 ms around the glottal closure of the voiced excitation for deriving these features.

3 Emotion Speech Databases and Feature Extraction

Two types of databases (semi-natural and simulated) are used for discrimination of neutral and emotional speech.

3.1 Emotion Speech Databases

Semi-natural database was collected from 2 female and 5 male speakers of Telugu language. They are uttered in 4 emotions (angry, happy, neutral and sad), and it was named as IIIT-H Telugu emotion database (Gangamohan et al., 2013). Speakers were asked to script the text themselves by remembering past memories and situations which make them emotional. The lexical content is different for each speaker and for each emotion. The data was collected in 2 or 3 sessions for each speaker, and consists of around 200 utterances. The complete database was evaluated in perceptual listening tests for recognizability of emotions by 10 listeners. A total of 130 utterances were se-

lected, in which anger, happy, neutral and sad are 35, 27, 34 and 34 utterances, respectively.

To test the effectiveness of language independent emotion detection, the Berlin emotion speech database (EMO-DB) (Burkhardt et al., 2005) is chosen. Ten professional native German actors (5 male and 5 female) were asked to speak 10 sentences (emotionally neutral sentences) in 7 different emotions, namely, anger, happy, neutral, sad, fear, disgust and boredom in one or more sessions. The total database was evaluated in a perception test by 20 listeners regarding the recognizability of emotions that had recognition rate better than 80% and naturalness better than 60% for analysis. A total of 535 good utterances were selected, in which anger, happy, neutral, sad, fear, disgust and boredom are 127, 71, 79, 62, 69, 46 and 81 utterances, respectively.

3.2 Feature Extraction

The features related to the excitation source and the vocal tract system components of speech signal are used in this study. The major source of excitation of the vocal tract system is due to vocal folds vibration at the glottis. The instant of significant excitation is due to sharp closure of the vocal folds, and it is almost like impulse. Hence, the high SNR of speech is present around Glottal Closure Instants (GCIs). By extracting the GCIs from the signal, it is possible to focus the analysis around the GCIs to further extract the information from both the excitation source and the vocal tract system. The features investigated for the detection of emotions are Linear Prediction (LP) residual for excitation source and weighted Linear Prediction Cepstral Coefficients (wLPCCs) for vocal tract system component extracted around the GCIs of speech signal. For this purpose, we use two signal processing methods, one is, a recently proposed method of Zero Frequency Filtering (ZFF) (Murty and Yegnanarayana, 2008) for extraction of GCIs, and another is LP analysis (Makhoul, 1975) for extraction of LP residual and wLPCCs.

3.2.1 Zero Frequency Filtering (ZFF) Method

The motivation behind this study was that, the effect of impulse-like excitation is reflected across all frequencies including zero frequency (0 Hz) of the speech signal. The method uses the zero frequency filtered signal obtained from the speech signal by filtering the signal through a cascade of two 0 Hz resonators to get the epoch locations. The instants of negative-to-positive zero crossings (NPZCs) of the ZFF signal correspond to the instants of significant excitation, i.e., epochs or Glottal closure instants (GCIs) in voiced speech (Murty and Yegnanarayana, 2008). This method is also useful for detecting voiced and unvoiced regions. Because of significant contribution by the impulse-like excitation, ZFF signal energy is high in voiced regions (Dhananjaya and Yegnanarayana, 2010). In this paper, we considered only voiced regions for analysis.

3.2.2 Linear Prediction (LP) Analysis

The production characteristics of speech has the role of both excitation source and the vocal tract system. LP analysis with proper LP order gives the excitation source (LP residual) component and vocal tract system component through LPCs. In the LP residual, the region around the GCI within each pitch period is used for processing the high SNR regions of speech (Reddy et al., 2010). For deriving the LP residual and LPCs, a 10th order LP analysis is used on the signal sampled at 8 kHz. Two pitch periods of signal are chosen for deriving the residual and a 4 ms segment (i.e, 32 samples) of the LP residual is chosen around each epoch to extract the information from the excitation source component. The vocal tract system characteristics around each GCI is represented by a 15 wLPCC vector derived from the 10 LPCs.

4 AANN Models for Capturing the Excitation Source Information

Autoassociative Neural Network (AANN) is a feedforward neural network model which performs identity mapping (Yegnanarayana and Kishore, 2002; Yegnanarayana, 1999). Once the AANN model is trained, it should be able to reproduce the input at the output with minimum error, if the input is from the same system. The AANN model consists of one input layer, one or more hidden layers and one output layer (Haykin, 1999). The units in the input and output layers are linear, whereas the units in the hidden layers are nonlinear. The AANN is expected to capture the information specific to the neutral speech present in the samples of LP residual. A five layer neural network architecture (Fig. 1) is considered for the study.

The structure of the network $33L\ 80N\ xN\ 80N\ 33L$, is chosen for ex-

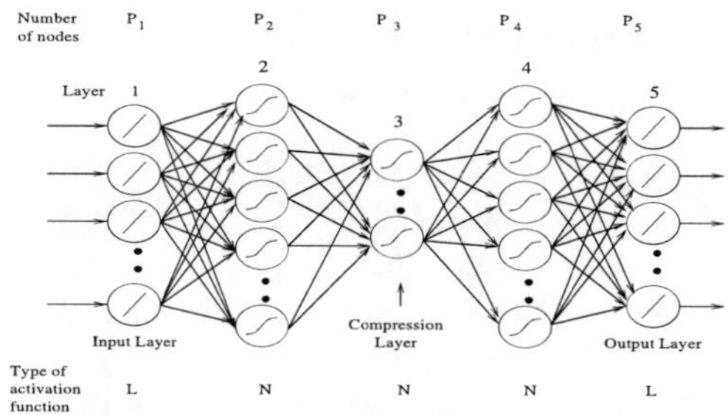

Figure 1: Structure of the AANN model

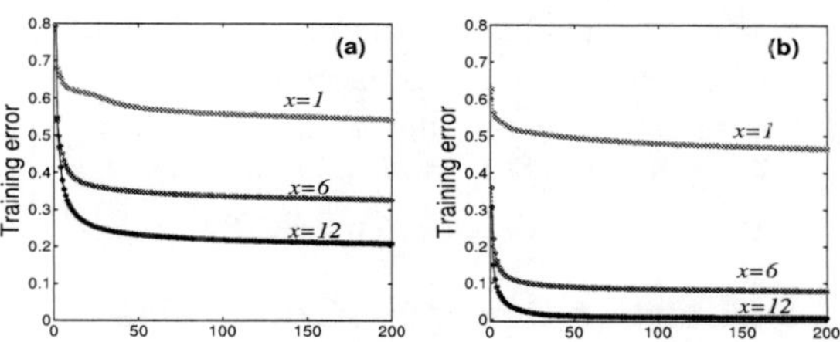

Figure 2: Training error as a function of iteration number, for (a) excitation source models and (b) vocal tract system models. Here x indicates number of nodes in the compression layer.

tracting the neutral speech information using the 4 ms LP residual around each GCI. Here L refers to linear units, and N refers to nonlinear ($tanh()$) output function of units. Here x refers to the number of units in the compression layer, which is varied to study its effect on the model's ability to capture the neutral speech specific information. The sizes of input and the output layer are fixed by the number of residual samples (around each GCI) used to train and test the models. The hidden layers provide flexibility for mapping and compression.

The network is trained for 200 iterations. The training error plots are shown in Fig. 2(a) for different values of the number of units (x) in the compression layer. From Fig. 2(a), it is observed that the error is decreasing with number of iterations, and hence the network is able to capture neutral speech information of a speaker in the residual. It can also be observed that the decrease in error is more as the number of units in the compression layers are increasing. Even if the error decreases, the generalizing ability may be poor beyond a certain limit on the number of units in the compression layer (Reddy et al., 2010).

5 AANN Models for Capturing the Vocal Tract System Information

A 5-layer AANN model with the structure $15L\ 40N\ xN\ 40N\ 15L$ is used for extracting the neutral speech specific information using 15 dimensional wLPCC vectors derived using LP analysis on two pitch period segment around each GCI. The model is expected to capture the distribution of the feature vectors of neutral speech of a speaker. The training error plots for a neutral speech of a speaker for x =1, 6 and 12 units in the compression layer are shown in Fig. 2(b). It is observed that the information in the distribution of the feature vectors is captured. The ability of the model to capture the neutral speech information can be determined through emotion detection experiments, as described in Sec. 6.

6 Emotion Detection Experiments

In order to know the capturing ability of AANN models for emotion detection, in the experiments we used all the speech samples from two types of databases described in Sec. 3.1. The speech samples are picked randomly while training and it is noted that the experiments are conducted in lexical independent way. For EMO-DB database, a universal background model (UBM) is built from 10 speakers (5 male and 5 female) using 15 s neutral speech data from each speaker. We have used all 10 speakers data for emotion detection experiments. Approximately 20 s of neutral speech data from a speaker is used to train over the UBM to build the speaker-specific neutral speech AANN models using 200 iterations. For testing, emotional speech utterance is presented to the neutral speech AANN model, and the mean squared error between the output and input, normalized with the magnitude of the input, is computed.

Fig. 3(a) shows the plots of the normalized errors obtained from the neutral speech AANN models using excitation source information (LP residual) of a speaker at each GCI. The solid ('—') line is the output from the model of the neutral speech of the same speaker. The emotional speech test utterance is fed to the neutral speech AANN models and the resulting error is shown by dotted ('···') lines. The plots correspond to three different cases, i.e., for 1, 6, 12 units in the middle compression layer. It can be seen that the solid line (neutral speech) has the lowest normalized error values for most of the frames (from GCI in-

dex 1 to 150). As the number of units in the middle layer increases, the error for the neutral speech is decreasing and the error for emotional speech is increasing. Similar observations can be made from Fig. 3(b) for the error plots for an emotional test utterance tested against neutral speech models using vocal tract system information (wLPCCs).

Since the neutral speech AANN models are built, it is expected that the error range should show discrimination for neutral and emotional speech. It is observed that the network is giving lower error values when the test utterance is neutral and higher error values when the test utterance is emotional. Using a threshold on the averaged normalized error value (averaged over all the frames of an utterance), emotion detection studies are performed. The averaged normalized error is given by

$$\frac{1}{l} \sum_{i=1}^{l} \frac{\|y_i - z_i\|^2}{\|y_i\|^2}. \tag{1}$$

where y_i is the input feature vector of the model, z_i is the output given by the model, and l is the number of frames of the test utterance.

The results of emotion detection (neutral vs emotion) using the excitation source information and the vocal tract system information for EMO-DB are shown in the Table 1. To test the effectiveness of language independent emotion detection, similar study is performed on IIIT-H Telugu emotion database, and the results are shown in Table 2. The accuracy for EMO-DB database using excitation source information is 91%, which is nearly 8% higher than that for the vocal tract system information. This is because, for the production of emotional speech, the primary effect is on the excitation source component such as pressure from the lungs and the changes in the vocal fold vibration. Similar observations can be made for the IIIT-H Telugu emotion database. For both the databases, it is indicative that the excitation source information carries more information than the vocal tract system information, and also the performance is consistent across the speakers. It is observed that, proposed excitation source and vocal tract system features with AANN models provides an improvement of approximately 10% and 3% over the recently proposed emotion detection method (Arias et al., 2014; Arias et al., 2013) which uses the energy and pitch contour modeling

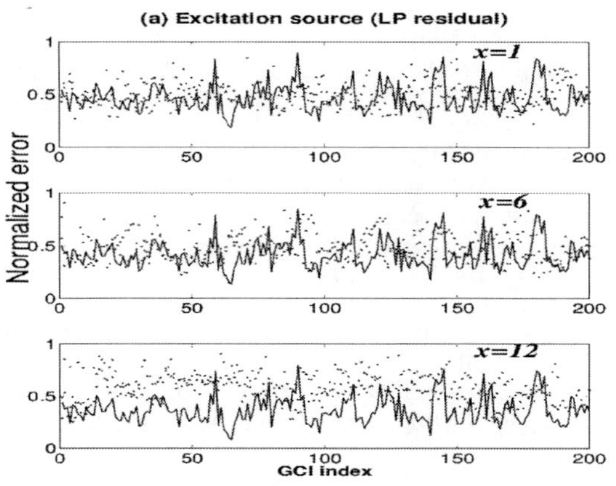
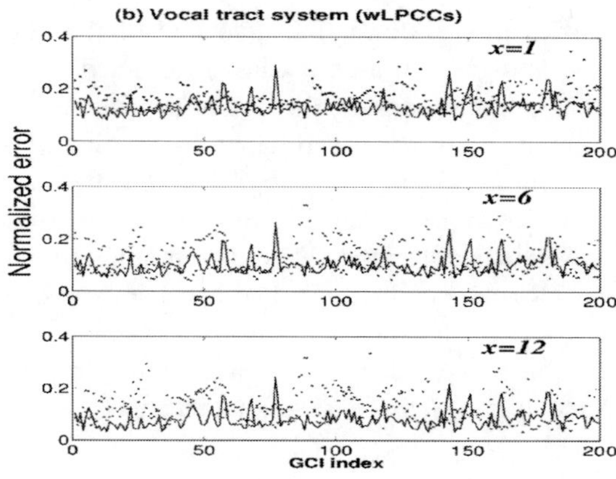

Figure 3: Normalized errors obtained from AANN models of various architectures, using (a) excitation source (b) vocal tract system information. In each plot, solid line ('—') and dotted line ('· · ·') correspond to neutral and emotion utterance normalized error curves, respectively.

with functional data analysis (accuracy is 80.4%) for EMO-DB database.

From Tables 1 and 2, it is observed that the higher activated emotion states (anger, happy, disgust and fear) are more discriminative compared to the lower activated emotion (sad and boredom) states. This is in conformity with the studies reported in (Jeon et al., 2011; Lee et al., 2011; Shami and Verhelst, 2007), where generally the acoustic features effectively discriminate between high activated emotions and low activated emotions. The accuracies for lower activation states is low, because some of the speech segments in these emotion signals are closer to neutral speech. Thus, AANN models are able to discriminate higher activated and lower activated states using neutral speech reference model. This study can be extended by training models with the lower activation states and testing with the higher states and vice versa. It is also noted that (from Fig. 3), all the frames of an utterance are not important in taking the decision, i.e., emotion information may not be uniformly distributed in time and hence, automatic usage of the high confidence frames may improve the accuracy. Also, the proposed emotion detection system can be evaluated using other spectral parameters such as variants of LPCs, MFCCs, MSFs (Schuller et al., 2013; Schuller et al., 2011; Schuller et al., 2009; Zeng et al., 2009; Ayadi et al., 2011; Eyben et al., 2012) etc. The advantages of the present study are, it is independent of lexical content used, language and channel.

Table 1: *Results for neutral vs emotion detection for Berlin EMO-DB database (in percentage).*

	Excitation Source	Vocal Tract System
Neutral vs Anger	100	100
Neutral vs Happy	100	100
Neutral vs Sad	73.50	62.93
Neutral vs Disgust	100	81.24
Neutral vs Fear	100	91.32
Neutral vs Boredom	72.72	64.02
Neutral vs Emotion	**91.03**	**83.25**

Table 2: *Results for neutral vs emotion detection for IIIT-H Telugu emotion database (in percentage).*

	Excitation Source	Vocal Tract System
Neutral vs Anger	100	92.86
Neutral vs Happy	100	96.43
Neutral vs Sad	82	75.4
Neutral vs Emotion	**94**	**88.23**

7 Summary

In this paper, we have demonstrated the significance of pitch synchronous analysis of speech data using AANN models for discriminating neutral and emotional speech. We have shown that the excitation source information of neutral speech is captured using 4 ms LP residual around the GCI, and the vocal tract system information of neutral speech is captured using 15 dimensional wLPCC vectors derived from 10 LPCs around each GCI. Emotion detection (neutral vs emotion) experiments were conducted using two databases one is IIIT-H Telugu emotion database, and the other is a well known emotion speech database EMO-DB. The results show that excitation source component carries more information than that of the vocal tract system. Further, it can be extended for the discrimination among the emotions, such as discrimination of anger and happy by training anger models and testing with happy emotion utterances, and vice versa. Also, it is important to develop speaker-specific models by determining suitable AANN models for individual speakers and emotions. It is also necessary to explore methods to combine the evidence from excitation source and vocal tract system for emotion detection.

References

J.P. Arias, C. Busso, and N.B. Yoma. 2013. Energy and F0 contour modeling with functional data analysis for emotional speech detection. In *INTERSPEECH*, pages 2871–2875, August.

Juan Pablo Arias, Carlos Busso, and Nestor Becerra Yoma. 2014. Shape-based modeling of the fundamental frequency contour for emotion detection in speech. *Computer Speech and Language*, 28(1):278 – 294.

Paeschke Astrid and W F Sendlmeier. 2010. Prosodic characteristics of emotional speech: Measurements of fundamental frequency movements. In *SpeechEmotion*, pages 75–80.

Theologos Athanaselis, Stelios Bakamidis, Ioannis Dologlou, Roddy Cowie, Ellen Douglas-Cowie, and Cate Cox. 2005. Asr for emotional speech: Clarifying the issues and enhancing performance. *Neural Networks*, 18(4):437–444.

Moataz El Ayadi, Mohamed S. Kamel, and Fakhri Karray. 2011. Survey on speech emotion recognition: Features, classification schemes, and databases. *Pattern Recognition*, 44(3):572 – 587.

B. Yegnanarayana and S. R. Mahadeva Prasanna and K. Sreenivasa Rao. 2002. Speech enhancement using excitation source information. In *ICASSP*, volume 1, pages 541–544.

A. Bajpai and B. Yegnanarayana. 2008. Combining evidence from subsegmental and segmental features for audio clip classification. In *TENCON IEEE Conference*, pages 1–5, Nov.

Murtaza Bulut and Shrikanth Narayanan. 2008. On the robustness of overall f0-only modifications to the perception of emotions in speech. *J. Acoust. Soc. Am.*, 123(6):4547–4558, June.

Felix Burkhardt, Astrid Paeschke, M. Rolfes, Walter F. Sendlmeier, and Benjamin Weiss. 2005. A database of german emotional speech. In *INTERSPEECH*, pages 1517–1520.

C. Busso, S. Lee, and S.S. Narayanan. 2007. Using neutral speech models for emotional speech analysis. In *INTERSPEECH*, pages 2225–2228, August.

Carlos Busso, Sungbok Lee, and Shrikanth Narayanan. 2009. Analysis of emotionally salient aspects of fundamental frequency for emotion detection. *IEEE Transactions on Audio, Speech & Language Processing*, 17(4):582–596.

R. Cowie, E. Douglas-Cowie, N. Tsapatsoulis, G. Votsis, S. Kollias, W. Fellenz, and J.G. Taylor. 2001. Emotion recognition in human-computer interaction. *Signal Processing Magazine, IEEE*, 18(1):32–80.

N. Dhananjaya and B. Yegnanarayana. 2010. Voiced/nonvoiced detection based on robustness of voiced epochs. *IEEE Signal Processing Letters*, 17(3):273–276, March.

Florian Eyben, Anton Batliner, and Björn Schuller. 2012. Towards a standard set of acoustic features for the processing of emotion in speech. *Proceedings of Meetings on Acoustics*, 16.

P Gangamohan, Sudarsana Reddy Kadiri, and B. Yegnanarayana. 2013. Analysis of emotional speech at subsegmental level. In *INTERSPEECH*, pages 1916–1920, August.

Ali Hassan and Robert I. Damper. 2012. Classification of emotional speech using 3dec hierarchical classifier. *Speech Communication*, 54(7):903–916.

Simon Haykin. 1999. *Neural networks: A Comprehensive Foundation*. Prentice-Hall International, New Jersey, USA.

Je Hun Jeon, Rui Xia, and Yang Liu. 2011. Sentence level emotion recognition based on decisions from subsentence segments. In *ICASSP*, pages 4940–4943.

Chul Min Lee and Shrikanth S. Narayanan. 2005. Toward detecting emotions in spoken dialogs. *IEEE Trans. Audio, Speech, and Language Processing*, 13(2):293–303.

Chi-Chun Lee, Emily Mower, Carlos Busso, Sungbok Lee, and Shrikanth Narayanan. 2011. Emotion recognition using a hierarchical binary decision tree approach. *Speech Communication*, 53(9-10):1162–1171.

Iker Luengo, Eva Navas, and Inmaculada Hernáez. 2010. Feature analysis and evaluation for automatic emotion identification in speech. *IEEE Transactions on Multimedia*, 12(6):490–501.

J. Makhoul. 1975. Linear prediction: A tutorial review. *Proc. IEEE*, 63:561–580, Apr.

Leena Mary and B. Yegnanarayana. 2008. Extraction and representation of prosodic features for language and speaker recognition. *Speech Communication*, 50(10):782–796.

Marc Mehu and Klaus R. Scherer. 2012. A psycho-ethological approach to social signal processing. *Cognitive Processing*, 13(2).

Donn Morrison, Ruili Wang, and Liyanage C. De Silva. 2007. Ensemble methods for spoken emotion recognition in call-centres. *Speech Communication*, 49(2):98–112.

Iain R. Murray and John L. Arnott. 1993. Toward the simulation of emotion in synthetic speech: A review of the literature on human vocal emotion. *J. Acoust. Soc. Am.*, 93(2):1097–1108.

K. Sri Rama Murty and B. Yegnanarayana. 2006. Combining evidence from residual phase and MFCC features for speaker recognition. *IEEE Signal Process. Letters*, 13(1):52–55, Jan.

K. Sri Rama Murty and B. Yegnanarayana. 2008. Epoch extraction from speech signals. *IEEE Trans. Audio, Speech, and Language Processing*, 16(8):1602–1613, Nov.

Sri Harish Reddy, Kishore Prahallad, Suryakanth V. Gangashetty, and B. Yegnanarayana. 2010. Significance of pitch synchronous analysis for speaker recognition using aann models. In *INTERSPEECH*, pages 669–672.

Klaus R. Scherer. 2003. Vocal communication of emotion: A review of research paradigms. *Speech Communication*, 40(1-2):227–256.

Björn Schuller, Stefan Steidl, and Anton Batliner. 2009. The interspeech 2009 emotion challenge. In *INTERSPEECH*, pages 312–315.

Björn Schuller, Bogdan Vlasenko, Florian Eyben, Martin Wöllmer, André Stuhlsatz, Andreas Wendemuth, and Gerhard Rigoll. 2010. Cross-corpus acoustic emotion recognition: Variances and strategies. *IEEE Tran. Affective Computing*, 1(2):119–131.

Björn Schuller, Anton Batliner, Stefan Steidl, and Dino Seppi. 2011. Recognising realistic emotions and affect in speech: State of the art and lessons learnt from the first challenge. *Speech Communication*, 53(9-10):1062–1087.

Björn Schuller, Stefan Steidl, Anton Batliner, Felix Burkhardt, Laurence Devillers, Christian A. Müller, and Shrikanth Narayanan. 2013. Paralinguistics in speech and language - state-of-the-art and the challenge. *Computer Speech & Language*, 27(1):4–39.

A. Shahina and B. Yegnanarayana. 2007. Mapping speech spectra from throat microphone to close-speaking microphone: A neural network approach. *EURASIP J. Adv. Sig. Proc.*, 2007.

Mohammad Shami and Werner Verhelst. 2007. An evaluation of the robustness of existing supervised machine learning approaches to the classification of emotions in speech. *Speech Communication*, 49(3):201–212.

Carl E. Williams and Kenneth N. Stevens. 1972. Emotions and speech: Some acoustical correlates. *J. Acoust. Soc. Am.*, 52(4B):1238–1250.

B. Yegnanarayana and S. P. Kishore. 2002. AANN - an alternative to GMM for pattern recognition. *Neural Networks*, 15:459–469, Apr.

B. Yegnanarayana, K. Sharat Reddy, and Kishore Prahallad. 2001. Source and system features for speaker recognition using AANN models. In *Proc. Int. Conf. Acoustics Speech and Signal Processing*, pages 491–494, Salt Lake City, Utah, USA, May.

B. Yegnanarayana. 1999. *Artificial Neural Networks*. Prentice-Hall of India, New Delhi.

Zhihong Zeng, Maja Pantic, Glenn I. Roisman, and Thomas S. Huang. 2009. A survey of affect recognition methods: Audio, visual, and spontaneous expressions. *IEEE Trans. Pattern Anal. Mach. Intell.*, 31(1):39–58.

Modeling Non-Propositional Semantics

Lori Levin
Carnegie Mellon University, USA
lsl@cs.cmu.edu

By non-propositional semantics, we mean things other than semantic roles that are expressed in a single sentence and tend to be grammaticalized. These include tense, aspect, modality, existence, possession, causality, conditionality, comparison, quantification, and definiteness. Non-propositional semantic categories evade definition because they are prototypes, not discrete categories. The centroids match across languages, but the extensions of the prototypes do not match. Furthermore, the grammaticalization of non-propositional semantics varies widely, including lexical items, affixes, and syntactic constructions, making cross-linguistic models difficult. In this talk we will focus on definiteness. Definiteness differs widely in grammaticalization across languages. We will present an annotation scheme that captures the semantic points that are relevant for definiteness across languages and logistic regression model of definiteness for English.

D S Sharma, R Sangal and J D Pawar. Proc. of the 11th Intl. Conference on Natural Language Processing, page 222,
Goa, India. December 2014. ©2014 NLP Association of India (NLPAI)

Text Readability in Hindi: A Comparative Study of Feature Performances Using Support Vectors

Manjira Sinha
Department of Computer
Science and Engineering
Indian Institute of Technology
Kharagpur
West Bengal, India
manjira@cse.iitkgp.e
rnet.in

Tirthankar Dasgupta
Department of Computer
Science and Engineering
Indian Institute of
Technology Kharagpur
West Bengal, India
tirtha@cse.iitkgp.e
rnet.in

Anupam Basu
Department of Computer
Science and Engineering
Indian Institute of
Technology Kharagpur
West Bengal, India
anupam@cse.iitkgp.e
rnet.in

Abstract

In this paper, we have presented support vector classification of Hindi text documents based on their reading difficulty. The study is based on diverse textual attributes over a broad spectrum to examine their extent of contribution in determining text readability. We have used support vector machines and support vector regressions to achieve our objective. At each step, the models are trained and tested on multiple combinations of text features. To achieve the goal, we have first built a novel readability annotated dataset of Hindi comprising of 100 documents ranked by 50 users. The outcomes of the models are discussed in context of text comprehensibility and are compared against each other. We have also provided a comparative analysis of our work with the existing literatures.

1 Introduction

Readability of a text indicates its reading or comprehension difficulty as perceived by a reader (Dale, 1949). Research on text readability has a vast and well developed literature; in the past century, numerous measures and approaches towards text readability has been developed (refer to (Benjamin, 2012) for a detailed survey). Consequently, it has been established that readability is subjective to the corresponding language of the text; for this reason different metrics of readability has been developed in different languages (Rabin et al., 1988). Languages of India such as Hindi have vast characteristics differences from the Indo-European counterparts like English. Therefore, the widely used readability metrics for English have been observed to be not appropriate for determining the same property of Hindi texts (Sinha et al., 2012). Yet, despite the large user pool, till now very little have been achieved in analyzing reading difficulty in Hindi (see section 2).

In this paper, we have modeled Hindi text readability with support vector machines (SVM) and support vector regression (SVR). Using both SVM and SVR view the problem of text readability from two perspectives: as a classification problem for SVM and as an estimation problem for SVR. By far, the only definitive model to predict readability of a Hindi text has been proposed by Sinha et al. (2012). Their work is based on six syntactic and lexical parameters of a text and they have used least square regression technique for modeling. We have used a vast range of text features (a total of 20) from lexical, syntactic to discourse

D S Sharma, R Sangal and J D Pawar. Proc. of the 11th Intl. Conference on Natural Language Processing, pages 223–231,
Goa, India. December 2014. ©2014 NLP Association of India (NLPAI)

perspective: among them, the six features from Sinha et al. (2012) have also been included. Therefore, our feature set consists of 14 'new' features and 6 'old' features (refer to section 3). We have explored the relative effect of the *new* and *old* features in the context of text readability in Hindi as well as the performances of regression and support vector techniques.

The rest of the paper is organized as follows: section 2 presents a brief background on text readability in general and Hindi in specific; section 3 presents the annotated corpus preparation and justification behind the selection of features; section 4 describes results and analysis and finally we conclude our work in section 5.

2   Related Works

The quantitative analysis of text readability started with L.A. Sherman in 1880 (Sherman, 1893). Till date, English and other languages have got over 200 readability metrics (DuBay, 2004; Rabin et al., 1988).The existing quantitative approaches towards predicting readability of a text can be broadly classified into three categories (Benjamin, 2012):

Classical methods: they analyze the syntactic features of a text like sentence length, paragraph length etc. The examples are Flesch Reading Ease Score (Flesch, 1948), FOG index (Gunning, 1968), Fry graph (Fry, 1968), SMOG (McLaughlin, 1969) etc. The formulae do not take into account the background of the reader and the semantic features of the text such as whether the actual contents are making sense or not. Despite their shortcomings, these simple metrics are easy to calculate and provide a rough estimation of reading difficulty of a text provided.

Cognitively motivated methods: texts are analyzed based on the cognitive features like, cohesion, organization and users' background. Proposition and inference model (Kintsch and Van Dijk, 1978), prototype theory (Rosch, 1978), latent semantic analysis (Landauer et al., 1998), Coh-metrix (Graesser et al., 2004) are some

prominent members of this group. This group of models moves beyond the surface features of a text and try to measure objectively the different cognitive indicators associated with text and the reader. However, it has been observed that, many situations, some traditional indicators perform as well as the newer and more difficult versions (Crossley et al., 2007).

Statistical language modeling: This class of approaches incorporates the power machine learning methods to the field of readability. They are particularly useful in determining readability of web texts (Collins-Thompson and Callan, 2005; Collins-Thompson and Callan, 2004; Si and Callan, 2003) (Liu et al., 2004). SVM has been used to identify grammatical patterns within a text and classification based on it (Schwarm and Ostendorf, 2005; Heilman et al., 2008; Petersen and Ostendorf, 2009). Although, these methods sound promising, the problem is that they cannot act as standalone measure as they need an amount of training data for classifiers appropriate to a particular user group.

In Hindi, Bhagoliwal (Bhagoliwal, 1961) applied the Johnson (Johnson and Bond, 1950), Flesch Reading Ease, Farr-Jenkins-Paterson (Farr et al., 1951), and Gunning FOG formulae to 31 short stories in Hindi. He used these formulae since they involve syllable counts, which are possible with a phonetic language like Hindi. He was not able to use wordlist-based formulae, by contrast, because comparable Hindi wordlists were not available. Bhagoliwal found the Farr-Jenkins-Paterson formula to be the best of the group. In 1965, he examined the features of Hindi typography affecting the legibility of Hindi texts (Bhagoliwal, 1965). In that paper a 'Reading Ease Index' has been applied to Hindi, but no definitive model to predict Hindi text readability was obtained in the literature. Agnihotri and Khanna (Agnihotri and Khanna, 1991) applied the classical English formulae to Hindi textbooks and studied the relative ordering of the predictions against user evaluations. They concluded that along with surface features, readability of a text depends on its linguistic and conceptual organisation. Sinha et al. (Sinha et al., 2012) have developed two readability formulae for Hindi texts using regression analysis. They have considered six structural or syntactic features of a text for the work. They have demonstrated that the English readability formulae such as Flesch Reading Ease Index, SMOG Index do not perform appropriately while being applied to Hindi documents. They have found the textual features like average word length, number of polysyllabic words and number of jukta-akshars (consonant conjuncts) in a text to be the most influential ones.

3 Annotated Corpus and Feature Selection

3.1 Data preparation

At present, by the best of our knowledge, there is no accessible resource pool of Hindi text documents that are annotated by multiple users according to their reading level, and are suitable for automatic processing. To address the issue, we have developed a corpus of 100 documents of length about 1000 words in Unicode encoding. The documents range from domain like literature to news and blogs. The distribution has been provided in table 1.

Source of text	Number
Literary corpora_classical	13
Literary corpora_contemporay	12
News corpora_general news	13
News corpora_interview	13
Blog corpora_personal	12
Blog corpora_official	12
Article corpora_ scholar	13
Article corpora_general	12

Table1: Text details

For the present study, we have selected 50 out of the 100 texts. The documents were annotated by a group of 25 native users of Hindi. The participants have mean age of 23 years (standard deviation = 1.74); they all have similar educational background pursuing undergraduate or graduate studies and represents medium to low socio-economic background. Each participant was asked 2 questions:

1. "How easy was it for you to understand/comprehend the text?"

2. "How interesting was the reading to you? (here interesting refers to the document specific interest not the topic specific, we have assumed that the participants did not have any previous bias towards a particular topic)

They were to answer on a 10 point scale (1=easy, 10=very hard). One point worth to be mentioned here is that although the blog data sometimes contains emoticons and other non text parts, we have considered only the pure text for our analysis. However, we have retained the punctuation symbols for the cause of sentence segmentation, but we have treated all of them as equal.

3.1.1. Normalization of user data

Perception of difficulty of a text is quite subjective in nature. Some annotators perform strict scrutiny than the others, consequently the range of ratings used by different annotators vary. Therefore, instead of considering the absolute user rating, we have performed a step of user data normalization. From this point onwards, reference to user ratings by default means normalized ratings unless stated otherwise. Gaussian normalization (Resnick et al., 1994) technique has been to map each user data in the range [-1, 1]. This method takes into account two variations that occur when feedbacks from different individuals are collected over a topic: shift of average ratings of different users and different rating scale by different users. The normalization method works as:

$$\hat{R}_y(x) = \frac{R_y(x) - \overline{R_y}}{\sqrt{\Sigma_x\left(R_y(x) - \overline{R_y}\right)^2}}$$

$\hat{R}_y(x)$ = normalized rating for item x by user y

$R_y(x)$ = actual rating for item x by user y

$\overline{R_y}$ = average of ratings for user y

Inter-annotator reliability was measured through Krippendorff's alpha[1] and $\alpha = 0.81$ was found. Therefore, we concluded that annotators agree more often than would have occurred by chance. We have measured the correlation between the outcomes of two questions corresponding to each of the fifty annotators; and found that in each case the correlation was greater than 0.8 ($p <$ 0.05). Therefore, the questions can be considered as equivalent, and subsequently we have considered the rating for the first question as user input for our readability models. Against each text, the median of the user ratings was taken as the central tendency for further processing.

3.2   Feature set

We have extracted 20 text features at different textual level (refer to table 2) to study their effect on reading difficulty. We have determined the textual features following the rationale:

Inferring form the cognitive load theory (Paas et al., 2003), we have assumed that the cognitive load exerted by a text on a reader depends on syntactic and lexical properties of a text like, average sentence length, average word length, number of polysyllabic words and as well as discourse features like the counts of the different parts of speeches and the number of co-references one has to resolve in order to comprehend the text. While processing a text a user has to parse the sentences in it and extract semantically relevant meaning from those sentences and the words. In order to process a sentence, one has to take into account the length of the sentence and types of words contained in it; it is also important to establish the connections or the nature of dependencies among the different words in a sentence. The role of a word is determined by its parts of speech and its way of use in that context; apart from it, the words can have varied complexity based on factors like their length, count of syllables. In the discourse level, a reader not only has to comprehend each sentence or paragraph, but also has to infer the

necessary co-references among them to understand the message conveyed by the text. The complexity of this task depends on the number of entities (noun, proper nouns) in the text and the way one entity is connected with other. To capture the effects of all these parameters in our readability models, we have considered text features over a broad range. The word features like average word length, average syllable per word, sentence features like average sentence length and discourse features like number of polysyllabic words, number of jukta-akshars (consonant conjuncts) have been calculated as stated by Sinha et al. (Sinha et al., 2012), as the features need customizations for Hindi. The calculations based on lexical chains have been followed from Galley and McKeown (Galley and McKeown, 2003).

4   Result and Analysis

4.1   Correlation coefficients (CC)

We have performed partial spearman rank correlation (Zar, 1998) between each of the features and user rating. The values are given in table 2 along with the feature descriptions. The values of correlation are divided in three groups: low ($r<0.35$), moderate ($0.35<r<0.65$), high ($r>0.65$); and test of significance by $p>0.05$ condition. Some observations that can be made from the results are:

- Average sentence length has been considered as a strong predictor of text difficulty (Crossley et al., 2007), however, in our case although it has a moderate correlation with the user rating, the value is insignificant.

- Average word length and number of consonant conjuncts have significant and high correlation with user data. This result is in tune with the study by Sinha et al. (2012).

- Discourse features have altogether high correlation coefficients than sentence level features.

- Except for $(entity), $(clauses), and $(verb phrase), all other sentence level features have insignificant correlation coefficient.

- Discourse features like #(noun phrase), #(unique entity), #(verb phrase) have significant correlation.

- Postpositions in both sentence and discourse contexts have insignificant effect on text comprehension.

- Properties like lexical chain, which require a reader to establish connections among different attributes of a concept and are indicators of text cohesion, have high and significant correlation.

4.2 Modeling the data

In the previous section, we have observed correlation of different text attributes with text features. But correlation does not provide a measure of causality. Therefore, to investigate

Feature	Description	CC (r)	p value
word features			
average word length	Standard Hindi uses the Devanagari script which is of the style abugida; the consonants have an inherent vowel or vowel diacritic[2], a consonant with the attached vowel, or an independent vowel is considered as a single visual unit. Average word length is total word length in terms of visual units divided by number of words.	0.75	0.01
average syllable per word	Total word length in terms of syllable divided by total number of words.	0.7	0.03
sentence features			
average sentence length	Total sentence length in terms of words divided by number of sentence.	0.63	0.14
$(noun phrase)	Average number of NP per sentence	0.46	
$(verb phrase)	Average number of VP per sentence	0.69	0.004
$(adjective)	Average number of adjectives per sentence		
$(postposition)	Average number of postpositions per sentence. Hindi grammar has postpositions, instead of prepositions present in English. Unlike English, postpositions in Hindi do not belong to separate part of speech. The postpositions require their object noun to take possessive, objective or locative case. Suffixes act as the case markers.	0.34	0.21
$(entity)	average number of named entity per sentence	0.73	0.007
$(unique entity)	Average number of unique entity per sentence	0.52	0.07
$(clauses)	Average number of clauses per sentence	0.73	0.003
discourse features			
Number of polysyllabic words and normalized measure for 30 sentences	Polysyllabic words are the words whose count of syllable exceeds 2.	0.71	0.004

---

[2] http://en.wikipedia.org/wiki/Hindustani_orthography

number of jukta-akshars (consonant conjuncts)	Total number of jukta-akshars in a text of 2000 words. It is an important feature for Hindi because each of the clusters has separate orthographic representation than the constituent consonants.	0.81	0.001
#(noun phrase)	Total number of NP in the document	0.65	0.005
#(verb phrase)	Total number of VP in the document	0.76	0.03
#(adjective)	Total number of adjective in the document.	0.43	0.07
#(postposition)	Total number of postpositions in the document.	0.36	0.12
#(entity)	Total number of named entity in the document	0.67	0.04
#(unique entity)	Total number of unique entity in the document	0.72	0.002
#(lexical chain)	Total number of lexical chain in the document	0.77	0.002
average lexical chain length	Computed over the document	0.79	0.002

Table 2: Details of the text features and their correlations with user rating.

how different features cause the comprehension difficulty of text to vary, we have used support vector machine (SVM) and support vector regression (SVR) modeling techniques. The reason behind using support vectors as tools of trade is to compare the outcomes with the regression analysis present in literature. The features have been used in three combinations. First they were divided in two categories i) comprising of only the six features used by Sinha et al. (2012) [they are termed as 'old'] and ii) second category consists of the rest 14 features and the group is termed 'new'; finally, third combination consists of all the features. Therefore, we have evaluated three different types of SVM and SVR models for each type of kernel.

We have employed a binary SVM classifier in this paper. Given a training set instance-class pairs $(\overline{x}_i, y_i)$, $i = 1...l$, where $\overline{x}_i \in R^n$ and $\overline{y} \in \{1, -1\}^l$, the general equation of a SVM is (Manning et al., 2008):

$$\frac{1}{2}\overline{w}^T\,\overline{w} + C \sum_i \xi_i \ \text{is minimized,}$$

$$\overline{w} = weight\ vector, C$$
$$= regularization\ term \qquad ...(1)$$

$$y_i\left(\overline{w}^T \Phi(\overline{x}_i) + b\right) \geq 1 - \xi_i,$$
$$\xi_i\,(slack\ variable)$$
$$\geq 0 \qquad ...(2)$$

The minimum, maximum and median of the rating distribution lie respectively at (-0.86), (+0.81) and (-0.053). To train and test the SVM models, we needed to spit the data in two classes (easy and hard), this has been done by assigning the ratings less than the median in to class easy (label '-1') and the rest to the class hard (label '1'). For support vector regression, the absolute values were used as it is. Among the 50 texts, 35 have been used as training data and 15 as test data. We have used two types of kernel functions on the data using LIBSVM (Chang and Lin, 2011) software, namely: linear and polynomial. To evaluate the quality of the classifications for SVM, multiple correlations (R) and percentage of texts accurately classified (Acc) have been used. R denotes the extent to which the predictions are close to the actual classes and its square (R^2: goodness of fit), indicates the percentage of dependent variable variation that can be explained by the model. Therefore, while percentage accuracy is an indicator to how well the model has performed to classify, R indicates the extent of explanatory power it posses. A better fit will have large R value as well as Accuracy. For SVR, root mean square error (RMSE) instead of accuracy and R^2 have been reported for the sake of comparison with the earlier models; a good fit will have less RMSE and greater R^2.

Features	Old		New		All	
SVM parameters	$C = 1; d = 2; \gamma = 1/6 = 0.1; \xi_i = 0.001$					
Kernel	**R**	**Acc.**	**R**	**Acc.**	**R**	**Acc.**
linear	0.67	70%	0.73	75.5%	0.81	79%
Polynomial	0.65	65%	0.69	67%	0.75	72%

Table 3: SVM results for different text features

Table 3 and 4 present the SVM and SVR classification results for different combination of features. The classifications were evaluated for a number of SVM and SVR parameter

combinations and only the result corresponding to the most efficient one is presented.

Feature	Old		New		All	
Kernel	**rmse**	**R^2**	**rmse**	**R^2**	**rmse**	**R^2**
linear	1.5	0.44	1.4	0.43	1.2	0.58
Polynomial	2.2	0.36	15.2	0.39	21.3	0.51

Table 4: SVR results for different text features

Table 5 provides a comparison between performances of three combinations of features. It can be seen that, both feature

Method	R^2	RMSE
First model proposed by Sinha et al. (2012): takes average word length and number of polysyllabic words	**0.44**	**1.04**
Second model proposed by Sinha et al. (2012): takes average word length and number of consonant conjuncts	**0.36**	**0.81**
Our models		
SVM with *three* features	**0.37**	-
SVM with *old* features	**0.44**	-
SVM with *all* features	**0.67**	-
SVR with *three* features	**0.28**	**1.3**
SVR with *old* features	**0.44**	**1.5**
SVR with *all* features	**0.58**	**1.2**

Table 5: Comparison of our model predictions with existing literature

combinations (old and new) are comparable in terms of their prediction accuracy and explanatory power if taken one set at a time; however, if all the old and new features are used together, the performance and accuracy improves significantly. This is true for in case of SVM as well as for SVR. This observation indicates that to develop an efficient model for text readability prediction in Hindi, we need to take into account various types of text attributes such as part of speech features, sentential features, text cohesion and lexical aspects. Moreover, from the above tables it can also be inferred that binary classification using support vector machines yields better results than estimation of text difficulty using support vector regression, in terms of the goodness of fit. In addition, linear kernel was found to do better in all cases than polynomial kernel.

Now, we will compare the outcomes of our models with the outcomes reported by Sinha et al.(2012). For this comparison, we have also evaluated SVM and SVR with only the three text features shortlisted by them as most influential in determining text difficulty. Table5 below presents the results (against SVM, only R^2 values are provided), only linear kernels are compared for SVM and SVR.

From table 5, it can be inferred that support vector classification and support vector regression performs better in terms of the goodness of fit than linear regression models reported by Sinha et al. (2012). In a close comparison of two types of regression reveals that support vector regression performs poorly than linear regression when only three features are considered; performs comparably when the *old* features are involved and do very well when all the features are incorporated. However, the root mean square errors of SVR are found to be slightly more than those by linear regression, for all the cases.

From the above results and discussions, we can state prediction of text readability in Hindi language can be done more efficiently and accurately if various text features at different textual levels are taken into account instead of taking a small subset. Moreover, model developed using support vectors to determine reading difficulty in Hindi performs better than models which use linear regression.

5 General Discussion and Conclusion

In this paper, we have studied and compared different text feature performances in the context of text readability in Hindi. Support vector classification and regression techniques are used to develop models for determining the reading difficulty of a text document in Hindi. During our work, we have built a novel readability annotated Hindi text resource pool. We have compared the performances of our models with that are present in the literature. According to our analysis, in contrast to applying only the *old* features or the *new* features, performance of the classifier improves if both types of features are used. This is true for classification as well as regression techniques. Overall, we have achieved 79% accuracy for binary text classification approach and root mean square error of 1.2 for regression approach. To the best of our knowledge, no such work on text readability has been recorded earlier in Hindi. In future, we are planning to develop for multi-class text readability models along with extending our user annotation database to incorporate better user perception in our studies. In addition, we will also explore the performances of SVM and SVR when applied separately to different genres of text.

The work will also be extended to model text comprehensibility for reading disabilities in Hindi.

Reference

Agnihotri, R. K. and Khanna, A. L. (1991). Evaluating the readability of school textbooks: An indian study. *Journal of Reading*, 35(4):pp. 282–288.

Benjamin, R. (2012). Reconstructing readability: Recent developments and recommendations in the analysis of text difficulty. *Educational Psychology Review*, 24:1–26.

Bhagoliwal, B. (1961). Readability formulae: Their reliability, validity and applicability in hindi. *Journal of Education and Psychology*, 19:13–26.

Bhagoliwal, B. (1965). Typographic dimensions affecting the legibility of hindi print: a factorial experiment. *Journal of Education and Psychology*.

Chang, C.-C. and Lin, C.-J. (2011). Libsvm: a library for support vector machines. *ACM Transactions on Intelligent Systems and Technology (TIST)*, 2(3):27.

Collins-Thompson, K. and Callan, J. (2004). A language modeling approach to predicting reading difficulty. In *Proceedings of HLT/NAACL*, volume 4.

Collins-Thompson, K. and Callan, J. (2005). Predicting reading difficulty with statistical language models. *Journal of the American Society for Information Science and Technology*, 56(13):1448–1462.

Crossley, S., Dufty, D., McCarthy, P., and McNamara, D. (2007). Toward a new readability: A mixed model approach. In *Proceedings of the 29th annual conference of the Cognitive Science Society*, pages 197–202.

Dale, E. (1949). Readability.

DuBay, W. (2004). The principles of readability. *Impact Information*, pages 1–76.

Farr, J., Jenkins, J., and Paterson, D. (1951). Simplification of flesch reading ease formula. *Journal of applied psychology*, 35(5):333.

Flesch, R. (1948). A new readability yardstick. *Journal of applied psychology*, 32(3):221.

Fry, E. (1968). A readability formula that saves time. *Journal of reading*, 11(7):513–578.

Galley, M. and McKeown, K. (2003). Improving word sense disambiguation in lexical chaining. In *IJCAI*, volume 3, pages 1486–1488.

Graesser, A., McNamara, D., Louwerse, M., and Cai, Z. (2004). Coh-metrix: Analysis of text on cohesion and language. *Behavior Research Methods*, 36(2):193–202.

Gunning, R. (1968). *The technique of clear writing*. McGraw-Hill NewYork, NY.

Heilman, M., Collins-Thompson, K., and Eskenazi, M. (2008). An analysis of statistical models and features for reading difficulty prediction. In *Proceedings of the Third Workshop on Innovative Use of NLP for Building Educational Applications*, pages 71–79. Association for Computational Linguistics.

Johnson, R. and Bond, G. (1950). Reading ease of commonly used tests. *Journal of Applied Psychology*, 34(5):319.

Kintsch, W. and Van Dijk, T. (1978). Toward a model of text comprehension and production. *Psychological review*, 85(5):363.

Landauer, T., Foltz, P., and Laham, D. (1998). An introduction to latent semantic analysis. *Discourse processes*, 25(2-3):259–284.

Liu, X., Croft, W., Oh, P., and Hart, D. (2004). Automatic recognition of reading levels from user queries. In *Proceedings of the 27th annual international ACM SIGIR conference on Research and development in information retrieval*, pages 548–549. ACM.

Manning, C. D., Raghavan, P., and Schütze, H. (2008). *Introduction to information retrieval*, volume 1. Cambridge University Press Cambridge.

McLaughlin, G. (1969). Smog grading: A new readability formula. *Journal of reading*, 12(8):639–646.

Paas, F., Renkl, A., and Sweller, J. (2003). Cognitive load theory and instructional design: Recent developments. *Educational psychologist*, 38(1):1–4.

Petersen, S. E. and Ostendorf, M. (2009). A machine learning approach to reading level assessment. *Computer Speech & Language*, 23(1):89–106.

Rabin, A., Zakaluk, B., and Samuels, S. (1988). Determining difficulty levels of text written in languages other than english. *Readability: Its past, present & future. Newark DE: International Reading Association*, pages 46–76.

Resnick, P., Iacovou, N., Suchak, M., Bergstrom, P., and Riedl, J. (1994). Grouplens: an open architecture for collaborative filtering of netnews. In *Proceedings of the 1994 ACM conference on Computer supported cooperative work*, pages 175–186. ACM.

Rosch, E. (1978). Principles of categorization. *Fuzzy grammar: a reader*, pages 91–108.

Schwarm, S. and Ostendorf, M. (2005). Reading level assessment using support vector machines and statistical language models. In *Proceedings of the 43rd Annual Meeting on Association for Computational Linguistics*, pages 523–530. Association for Computational Linguistics.

Sherman, L. (1893). Analytics of literature: A manual for the objective study of english poetry and prose. *Boston: Ginn*.

Si, L. and Callan, J. (2003). A semisupervised learning method to merge search engine results. *ACM Transactions on Information Systems (TOIS)*, 21(4):457–491.

Sinha, M., Sharma, S., Dasgupta, T., and Basu, A. (2012). New readability measures for Bangla and Hindi texts. In *Proceedings of COLING 2012: Posters*, pages 1141–1150, Mumbai, India. The COLING 2012 Organizing Committee.

Zar, J. (1998). Spearman rank correlation. *Encyclopedia of Biostatistics*.

Sangam: A Perso-Arabic to Indic Script Machine Transliteration Model

Gurpreet Singh Lehal
Department of Computer Science
Punjabi University, Patiala
147002 Punjab, India
gslehal@gmail.com

Tejinder Singh Saini
Advanced Center for Technical Development of
Punjabi Language Literature and Culture
Punjabi University, Patiala Punjab, India
tej@pbi.ac.in

Abstract

Indian sub-continent is one of those unique parts of the world where single languages are written in different scripts. This is the case for example with Punjabi, written in Indian East Punjab in Gurmukhi script (a Left to Right script based on Devnagri) and in Pakistani West Punjab, it is written in Shahmukhi (a Right to Left script based on Perso-Arabic). This is also the case with other languages like Urdu and Hindi (whilst having different names, they are the same language but written in mutually incomprehensible forms). Similarly, Sindhi and Kashmiri languages are written in both Persio-Arabic and Devanagri scripts. Thus there is a dire need for development transliteration tools for conversion between Perso-Arabic and Indic scripts. In this paper, we present Sangam, a Perso-Arabic to Indic script machine transliteration system, which can convert with high accuracy text written in Perso-Arabic script to one of the Indic script sharing the same language. Sangam is a hybrid system which combines rules as well as word and character level language models to transliterate the words. The system has been designed in such a fashion that the main code, algorithms and data structures remain unchanged and for a adding a new script pair only the databases, mapping rules and language models for the script pair need to be developed and plugged in. The system has been successfully tested on Punjabi, Urdu and Sindhi languages and can be easily extended for other languages like Kashmiri and Konkani.

1 Introduction

Indian sub-continent is one of those unique parts of the world where single languages are written in different scripts. This is the case for example with Punjabi, spoken by tens of millions of people, but written in Indian East Punjab (20 million) in Gurmukhi script (a Left to Right script based on Devnagri) and in Pakistani West Punjab (80 million), it is written in Shahmukhi (a Right to Left script based on Perso-Arabic). Whilst in speech, Punjabi spoken in the Eastern and the Western parts is mutually comprehensible in the written form it is not. This is also the case with other languages like Urdu and Hindi (whilst having different names, they are the same language but written, as with Punjabi, in mutually incomprehensible forms). Hindi is written in the Devnagri script from left to right, Urdu is written in a script derived from a Persian modification of Arabic script written from right to left. A similar problem resides with the Sindhi language, which is written in a Persio-Arabic script in Pakistan and both in Persio-Arabic and Devanagri in India. Similar is the case with Kashmiri language too. Konkani is probably the only language in India which is written in five scripts Roman, Devnagri, Kannada, Persian-Arabic and Malayalam (Carmen Brandt. 2014). The existence of multiple scripts has created communication barriers, as people can understand the spoken or verbal communication, however when it comes to scripts or written communication, the number diminishes, thus a need for transliteration tools which can convert text written in one language script to another script arises. A common feature of all these lan-

232

D S Sharma, R Sangal and J D Pawar. Proc. of the 11th Intl. Conference on Natural Language Processing, pages 232–239,
Goa, India. December 2014. ©2014 NLP Association of India (NLPAI)

guages is that, one of the script is Perso-Arabic (Urdu, Sindhi, Shahmukhi etc.), while other script is Indic (Devnagri, Gurmukhi, Kannada, Malayalam). Perso-Arabic script is a right to left script, while Indic scripts are left to right scripts and both the scripts are mutually incomprehensible forms. Thus is a dire need for development of automatic machine transliteration tools for conversion between Perso-Arabic and Indic scripts.

Machine Transliteration is an automatic method to generate characters or words in one alphabetical system for the corresponding characters in another alphabetical system. The transformation of text from one script to another is usually based on phonetic equivalencies. Transliteration is usually categorized as forward and backward transliteration. Forward transliteration refers to transliteration from the native language to foreign language, while the process of recalling a word in native language from a transliteration is defined as back-transliteration. Forward transliteration plays an important role in natural language applications such as information retrieval and machine translation, especially for handling proper nouns, technical terms and out of vocabulary words. While back transliteration is popularly used as an input mechanism for certain languages, where typing in the native script is not very popular. In such cases, the user types the native language words and sentences (usually) in Roman script, and a transliteration engine automatically converts the Roman input back to the native script. This input mechanism is popularly used for all Indian languages including Hindi, Punjabi, Tamil, Telugu, etc., and also, Arabic, Chinese etc.

In this paper, we present Sangam, a Perso-Arabic to Indic script machine transliteration system, which can convert with high accuracy text written in Perso-Arabic script to one of the Indic script sharing the same language. The system has been successfully tested on Punjabi (Shahmukhi-Gurmukhi) , Urdu (Urdu-Devnagri) and Sindhi(Sindhi Perso Arabic - Sindhi Devnagri) languages and can be easily extended for other languages like Kashmiri and Konkani. One should note that the transliteration model presented in this paper can neither be categorized as forward nor as backward since it is concerned with script conversion in same language, so the usual techniques for forward or backward transliteration cannot be applied here and we have to develop a special me-thodology to handle the transliteration issues related to conversion between scripts of same language.

2 Related Work

The first transliteration system for a Perso-Arabic to Indic script was presented by Malik (2006), where he described a Shahmukhi to Gurmukhi transliteration system with 98% accuracy. But the accuracy was achieved only when the input text had all necessary diacritical marks for removing ambiguities, even though the process of putting missing diacritical marks is not practically possible due to many reasons like large input size, manual intervention, person having knowledge of both the scripts and so on. Saini et al. (2008) developed a system, which could automatically insert the missing diacritical marks in the Shahmukhi text and convert the text to Gurmukhi. The system had been implemented with various research techniques based on corpus analysis of both scripts and an accuracy of 91.37% at word level had been reported.

Durrani et al. (2010) presented an approach to integrate transliteration into Hindi-to-Urdu statistical machine translation. They proposed two probabilistic models, based on conditional and joint probability formulations and have reported an accuracy of 81.4%. Lehal and Saini (2012) presented an Urdu to Hindi transliteration system and had claimed achieving an accuracy of 97.74% at word level. The various challenges such as multiple/zero character mappings, missing diacritic marks in Urdu, multiple Hindi words mapped to an Urdu word, word segmentation issues in Urdu text etc. have been handled by generating special rules and using various lexical resources such as n-gram language models at word and character level and Urdu-Hindi parallel corpus. Recently Malik et al. (2013) have analysed the application of statistical machine translation for solving the problem of Urdu-Hindi transliteration using a parallel lexicon. The authors reported a word level accuracy of 77.8% when the input Urdu text contained all necessary diacritical marks and 77% when the input Urdu text did not contain all necessary diacritical marks, which is much below the accuracy reported in earlier works.

A rule based converter for Kashmiri language from Persio-Arabic to Devanagari script has been developed by Kak et al. (2010) and authors have claimed 90% conversion accuracy.

Leghari and Rehman (2010) have discussed the different issues, complexities and problems of Sindhi transliteration and presented a model for transliteration between Perso-Arabic and Devanagari scripts of Sindhi language, which is based on an intermediate Roman script.

Malik et al. (2010) described a finite-state scriptural translation model based on Finite State Machines to convert the scripts for Urdu, Punjabi and Seraiki languages. But the transliteration results for Urdu-Hindi, Punjabi Shahmukhi-Gurmukhi and Seraiki Shahmukhi-Gurmukhi have not been very encouraging, with transliteration accuracy at word level ranging from 31.2% to 58.9% for Urdu-Devnagri script pair and 67.3% for Shahmukhi-Gurmukhi.

3 Challenges in Perso-Arabic to Indic Script Transliteration

Transliteration is not trivial to automate, but transliteration of Perso-Arabic script to Indic scripts is even more challenging problem. Since the language does not change, so it becomes important the correct spellings and context of the words is maintained in target script. The major challenges of transliteration of languages using Perso-Arabic script to Indic scripts are as follows:

3.1 Missing Diacritical marks and short Vowels

Diacritical marks are critical for correct pronunciation and sometimes even for disambiguation of certain words. The diacritical marks are also used for gemination (doubling of a consonant) and mark the absence of a vowel following a base consonant. But the diacritical marks and short vowels are sparingly used in Perso-Arabic script writings. These missing diacritical marks and short vowels create substantial difficulties for transliteration systems, as the missing diacritic marks and vowels have to be guessed by the system and added for correct transliteration. For example in Table 1, we see how the words in Perso-Arabic script, which are commonly written without diacritic marks, will be transliterated in Indic script, if we go in for character by character substitution and do not put the missing short vowels.

Perso-Arabic script	Word	Indic Script	Indic Transliteration	Actual transliteration
Urdu	دنیا	Devnagri	दनया	दुनिया
Shahmukhi	وچ	Gurmukhi	ਵਚ	ਵਿੱਚ
Sindhi	سنڌ	Devnagri	सनध	सिंधु

Table 1. Transliteration without diacritical marks

3.2 Filling the Missing Script Maps

There are many characters which are present in the Perso-Arabic script, corresponding to those having no character in Indic script, e.g. *Hamza* ء, *Do-Zabar* ٌ *Aen* ع, ٰ (*Khadi Zabar*) etc.

3.3 Multiple Mappings for Perso-Arabic Characters

It is observed that corresponding to many Perso-Arabic characters there are multiple mappings into Indic script as shown in Table 2. Additional information such as grammar rules and context are needed to select the appropriate Indic script character for such Perso-Arabic characters.

Perso-Arabic Script	Char	Indic script	Equivalent Mappings
Urdu	و	Devnagri	व, ो, ौ, ु, ू, ऊ, ओ, औ
Shahmukhi	ں	Gurmukhi	ੋ, ੌ, ਨ, ੲ

Table 2. Multiple Mappings of Perso-Arabic characters

3.4 Transliteration Ambiguity at Word level

Due to multiple character mappings and missing short vowels, many words in Perso-Arabic script get mapped to multiple Indic words as shown in Table 3. Higher level language information will be needed to choose the most relevant word in Indic script.

Perso-Arabic script	Word	Indic script	Equivalent words in Indic script
Urdu	کیا	Devnagri	क्या, किया
Shahmukhi	ہن	Gurmukhi	ਹਨ, ਹੁਣ
Sindhi	جان	Devnagri	जां, जान, जानि

Table 3. Multiple Mappings of Perso-Arabic words

3.5 Word-Segmentation Issues

Space is not consistently used in Perso-Arabic words, which makes word segmentation a non-trivial task. Many times the space is deleted resulting in many Perso-Arabic words being jumbled together and many other times extra space is put in word resulting in over segmentation of that word. This problem is more pronounced in Urdu and Shahmukhi scripts as compared to Sindhi script. We see in Table 4, samples of Urdu and Shahmukhi words containing multiple merged words and their transliterations if the words are transliterated as such without splitting them at proper positions.

Word Perso-Arabic	Transliteration without splitting	Actual translite- ration
انکار کردیاہے (Urdu script)	अनकारकरदयाहे (Devnagri script)	इन्कार कर दिया है (Devnagri script)
پہلاثکار (Shahmukhi script)	ਪਹਲਾਸ਼ਕਾਰ (Gurmukhi script)	ਪਹਿਲਾ ਸ਼ਿਕਾਰ (Gurmukhi script)

Table 4. Merged Perso-Arabic Words and their Transliterations without splitting words

4 System Architecture

The system architecture of the general Perso-Arabic - Indic transliteration model developed by us is shown in Figure 1. The system has been designed in such a fashion that the main code, algorithms and data structures remain unchanged while depending on the script pair, the databases, mapping rules and language models need to be plugged in. The source text is in S1 script while the target text is in script S2. For example if text in Urdu script has to be converted to Devnagri, then we need to plug in word frequency list of Urdu and Urdu-Devnagri dictionary along with n-gram language models at word and character level for Devnagri script and mapping tables for Urdu to Devnagri transliteration. The system has been successfully tested on three script pairs(Urdu-Hindi, Sindhi-Devnagri and Shahmukhi-Gurmukhi) and has been able to successfully handle most of the issues raised in the previous section. We have developed the lexical resources for all the scripts and depending on our need, the relevant data is used. In case a new script pair has to be added, only the lexical resources have to be created As can be seen in figure 1, the complete transliteration system is divided into three stages: pre-processing, processing and post-processing. In the pre-processing stage, the text in S1 script is cleaned and prepared for transliteration by normalizing and joining the broken Perso-Arabic words. In the processing stage, corresponding to each word in S1 script, one or several possible words in S2 are generated. If only one word is produced, then that word is finalised. Otherwise for multiple alternatives, the final decision is taken in the post processing stage.

In the post-processing stage, the final decision about choosing from multiple S2 alternatives is made using language models for S2. The three stages are discussed in detail in the following sections.

4.1 Pre-Processing

In the pre-processing stage, the Urdu words are cleaned and prepared for transliteration by normalizing the Urdu words as well as joining the broken Urdu words. The two main stages in pre-processing are:

4.1.1 Normalizing Perso-Arabic words

Two kinds of normalization are required for Perso-Arabic words. First, a letter may be represented by multiple Unicode points, and thus the redundancy in encoding has to be cleaned in raw text before further processing. As for example, from transliteration point of view, ی(0649), ي(064a) and ی(06cc) represent the same character in Perso-Arabic script. Secondly, a letter or a ligature is sometimes encoded in composed form as well as decomposed form. Thus, the two equivalent representations must also be reduced to same underlying form before further processing. For example, آ (0622) can be also be represented by the combination ا (0627) + ٓ (0653). All such forms are normalized to have only one representation.

4.1.2 Joining the broken Perso-Arabic words

The transliteration system faces many problems related to word segmentation of Perso-Arabic script, as in many cases space is not properly put between words. Sometimes it is deleted resulting in many Perso-Arabic words being jumbled together and many other times extra space is put in word resulting in over segmentation of that word. The space insertion problem is handled in pre-processing stage, while the space deletion problem is handled in the processing stage. The space insertion problem usually occurs due to conventional way of writing in Perso-Arabic script or due to extra space being inserted during typing. The typing related space insertion problems are handled by using the word frequency list of script S1 (Lehal, 2009). If the product of probability of occurrence of two adjacent words in S1 is lesser than the probability of occurrence of the word formed by joining the two, then the two words are joined together.

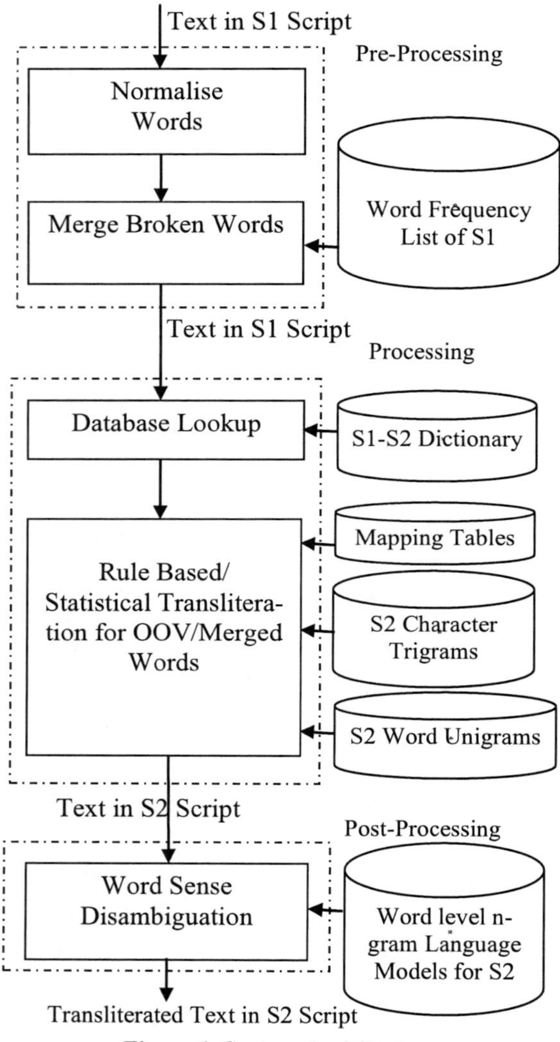

Figure 1. System Architecture

4.2   Processing Stage

This is the main stage and in this stage, corresponding to each word in S1 script, one or several possible words in S2 script are generated. For multiple alternatives, the final decision is taken in the post processing stage. First the word is searched in the S1-S2 dictionary and if it is found, then all its alternatives are passed onto post processing stage. In case the word is not found, then it is fed to a multi-stage transliteration engine. In the first stage a Hybrid-wordlist-generator (HWG) is used to convert the word. The HWG uses the mapping rules and a trigram character language model to generate a set of words in S2. A unigram word language model is then used to rank these words, after dropping words with zero probability. If there is no word with non-zero probability, then the word is inspected for presence of merged words which can be transliterated to non empty sets of words in S2 words. If no such sets can be generated then we use the simple character mapping rules to convert the word to S2.

We now discuss in detail, the main modules used in the multi-stage transliteration engine. These modules are:

4.2.1 Hybrid-wordlist-generator (HWG)

This is the major module in the transliteration engine. It generates multiple transliterations for a word in S1. The multiple outputs are produced due to ambiguity both at character and word level as already mentioned in above sections.

The sequence of probable Indic words is produced by a hybrid system, which uses rule based character mapping tables and a trigram character Language Model. The Perso-Arabic word is processed character by character, which are mapped directly to their corresponding similar sounding Indic characters based on their position in word and syntax rules (snippet shown in the Table 5). In most of the cases, there is a 1-1 mapping, but a few characters such as ن و, ی, which have multiple mappings and also some character combinations in Perso-Arabic script such as تھ (062A+06BE) have single representation in some of Indic scripts such as in Devnagri (थ) or Gurmukhi (ਥ), while in Sindhi(Devnagri) we have character combination तह. Similarly the character ۀ (U06FE) gets mapped to word में in Sindhi(Devnagri) script, while it has no equivalent mapping in Devnagri and Shahmukhi scripts. In some cases the mapping is dependent on the position of the character. As for example, the character ا (U0627) is mapped to character अ if it is in beginning of the word else it gets mapped to आ and ा in Devnagri script. Similarly, the character ن

(U0646) gets mapped to character न in Sindhi(Devnagari), if it is in the starting of the word, and gets mapped to न, ◌ and ◌ँ otherwise. The same character, ن (U0646), gets mapped to न and ण in Devnagri, if it comes in beginning or ending of a word, else it gets mapped to न, ण, ◌ and ◌ँ .

Char At	Perso Arabic	Devna-gri	Gurmukhi	Sindhi (Dev)
Any	ب	ब	ਬ	ब
	تھ	थ	ਥ	तह
	ہ	-	-	में
Start	و	व, ऊ, ओ, औ	ਵ, ਉ, ਓ, ਐ	व, ऊ, ओ, औ
Start	ن	न, ण	ਨ, ਣ	न
Start	ا	अ	ਅ	अ
Mid	ن	न, ण, ◌ं, ◌ँ	ਨ, ਣ, ◌ं, ◌ँ	न, ◌ं, ◌ँ
Mid/ end	ا	अ, ◌ा	ਅ, ◌ा	अ, ◌ा
Mid /end	و	व, ◌ो, ◌ौ, ◌ु, ◌ू, ऊ, ओ, औ	ਵ, ◌ੁ, ◌ੋ, ◌ੌ, ਉ, ਓ, ਐ	व, ◌ो, ◌ौ, ◌ु, ◌ू, ऊ, ओ, औ
End	ن	न, ण	ਨ, ਣ	न, ◌ं, ◌ँ

Table 5. Portion of Perso Arabic - Indic character mapping Tables

As already mentioned, the short vowels and diacritical marks are usually omitted in Perso-Arabic text and there are no half characters in Perso-Arabic script, so the result is that the resultant text in Indic script has poor accuracy. For example, the Urdu word in Perso-Arabic script, قسمت, gets transliterated to कसमत, while the actual word in Devnagri should be क़िस्मत. This is because the character स is written as half character in Devnagri while the short vowel ि which is missing in original Perso-Arabic word has to written in Devnagri to maintain proper spellings in Devnagri. To fill these missing diacritical marks and put half characters at appropriate locations in Indic word, we consider all its possible mappings in Indic which include the missing short vowels and half characters. So we modify our mapping table to include all such forms for all the Perso-Arabic characters resulting in multiple mappings. Thus for example the character combination تھ (062a+06be) and character و (0648) get mapped to as shown in in Table 6.

We form all possible combinations, which could be generated from these multiple mappings and the top N combinations are retained. The character based trigram language model for Indic script is used to select the top N combinations. To avoid processing exponential number of candidates, we process the input characters one at a time and use the character trigram probability for pruning the partially generated candidates at each step.

Char At	Perso Arabic	Devnagri	Gurmuk-hi	Sindhi (Dev)
Any	تھ	थ, थ्, थि, थु	ਥ, ਥਿ, ਥੁ	तह, तहि, तिहि, तिह, तुह, तुहु, तह
Start	و	व, व्, वु, वि, व्व, व्वु, व्वि, ऊ, ओ, औ	ਵ, ਵਿ, ਵੁ, ਉ, ਓ, ਐ	व, व्, वु, वि, व्व, व्वु, व्वि, ऊ, ओ, औ
Mid/ end	و	व, व्, वु, वि, व्व, व्वु, व्वि, ◌ौ, ◌ो, ◌ु, ◌ू, ऊ, ओ, औ	ਵ, ਵਿ, ਵੁ, ◌ं, ◌ँ, ◌ँ, ਉ, ਓ, ਐ	व, व्, वु, वि, व्व, व्वु, व्वि, ◌ौ, ◌ो, ◌ु, ◌ू, ऊ, ओ, औ

Table 6. Portion of Modified Perso Arabic - Indic character mapping Tables

It should be noted that not all the suggestions generated by the character language model are valid words in Indic script. To further rank these words, we use the Unigram Word Model for Indic script. Words with zero probability in the Unigram word model are ignored and rest of the words are ranked on their probabilities. It could also happen that all the top N alternatives suggested by the character level trigram may be having zero probabilities, in which case no alternative is returned by HWG.

4.2.2 Merged word segmentation

As already discussed above, space is not consistently used in Perso-Arabic, which gives rise to both space omission and space insertion errors. Due to the space deletion problem, a sequence of words is jumbled together as a single word and when the HWG tries to generate the equivalent Indic alternatives it fails. The sequence of Perso-Arabic words written together without space is still readable because of the character joining property in Perso-Arabic. We have used the space deletion algorithm presented by Lehal (Lehal, 2010) to split the Perso-Arabic words. The algorithm makes use of unigram wordlist of S2 and statistical word disambiguation techniques to first detect if the Perso-

Arabic word contains multiple words. And in case multiple words are present, the algorithm splits them at appropriate positions. The Indic Script alternatives for these individual Perso-Arabic words are then generated using the HWG module.

4.2.3 Handling Out of Vocabulary Words

For out of vocabulary words, no possible suggestions will be generated by the dictionary or HWG. So if after passing through all the modules, still no transliteration alternatives are generated, it implies that the word is out of vocabulary. For such words the Indic Script word is generated by using the mapping rules and trigram character language model and the top most alternative is selected for further processing.

4.3 Post Processing Stage

The main task of post processing is to select the best alternative amongst the various transliteration options. The HWG module presents a set of ranked transliterations instead of a single transliteration, due to multiple character mappings as shown in Table 5 and 6. Up to this point, we were only considering the Indic words in isolation, without any consideration to their neighbouring words. Now we consider the whole sentence instead of isolated words.

$$\Pr\left(w_i \mid w_{i-2}w_{i-1}\right) = \\ \lambda_3 \frac{c\left(w_{i-2}w_{i-1}w_i\right)}{c\left(w_{i-2}w_{i-1}\right)} + \lambda_2 \frac{c\left(w_{i-1}w_i\right)}{c\left(w_{i-1}\right)} + \\ \lambda_1 \frac{c\left(w_i\right)}{N} + \lambda_0 \frac{1}{V}$$

Where

N = Number of words in the training corpus,
V = Size of the vocabulary

To choose between the different alternatives we have used the word trigram probability. To take care of the sparseness in the trigram model, we have used deleted interpolation, which offers the solution of backing away from low count trigrams by augmenting the estimate using bigram and unigram counts. The deleted interpolation trigram model assigns a probability to each trigram which is the linear interpolation of the trigram, bigram, unigram and uniform models. The weights are set automatically using the Expectation-Maximization (EM) algorithm.

5. Experimental Results

We have tested our system on text in Perso-Arabic script in Urdu, Punjabi and Sindhi languages and converted it to respective Indic scripts. The transliterated text has been manually evaluated. The results are tabulated in Table 7. We can see from the table, that the transliteration accuracy for the three scripts ranges from 91.68% to 97.75%, which is the best accuracy reported so far in literature for script pairs in Perso-Arabic and Indic scripts. As can be observed the transliteration accuracy for Sindhi language is much lesser as compared to Urdu and Punjabi languages. The main reasons for this are:

a) Lack of linguistic resources and digital text in Sindhi(Devnagri).

b) High level of ambiguity at word level in Sindhi(Perso-Arabic) words, which is much more pronounced than Shahmukhi and Urdu words.

A sample of the output for the three scripts is shown in Figure 2.

Script Pair	Words	Transliteration Accuracy
Urdu-Devnagri	30,248	97.75%
Shahmukhi-Gurmukhi	26,141	97.02%
Sindhi (Perso Arabic) to Sindhi (Devnagri)	29,131	91.68%

Table 7. Word level Transliteration Accuracy of different script pairs

سب کام اپنے وقت پر ہی ہوتے ہیں۔ ہمیں کام کرنا چاہیے۔ پھل کی فکر نہیں کرنی چاہیے۔

सब काम अपने वक़्त पर ही होते हैं। हमें काम करना चाहिए।फल की फ़िक्र नहीं करनी चाहिए।

a) Urdu-Devnagri

سارے کم اپنے سمیں سر ہی ہندے ہن۔ سانوں کم کرنا چاہیدا ہے، پھل دی چنتا نہیں کرنی چاہیدی۔

ਸਾਰੇ ਕੰਮ ਆਪਣੇ ਸਮੇਂ ਸਿਰ ਹੀ ਹੁੰਦੇ ਹਨ। ਸਾਨੂੰ ਕੰਮ ਕਰਨਾ ਚਾਹੀਦਾ ਹੈ, ਫਲ ਦੀ ਚਿੰਤਾ ਨਹੀਂ ਕਰਨੀ ਚਾਹੀਦੀ।

b) Shahmukhi-Gurmukhi

سيڀ ڪم پنهنجي وقت تي ئي ٿيندا آهني۔ اسان کي ڪم ڪرڻ گھرجي، ڦل جي چنتا نہ ڪرڻ گھرجي ۔

सभु कम पंहिंजे वक़्त ते ई थींदा आहनी। असां खे कमु
करणु घुर्जे, फल जी चिंता न करणु घुर्जे ।

c) Sindhi (Perso-Arabic) - Sindhi (Devnagri)

Figure 2. Samples of Transliteration output of text
in three languages (Urdu, Punjabi and Sindhi) by
Sangam

Conclusion

In this paper, we have presented Sangam, a Perso-
Arabic to Indic script machine transliteration model, which can convert with high accuracy text written in Perso-Arabic script to one of the Indic script
sharing the same language. The system has been
successfully tested on Punjabi, Urdu and Sindhi
languages and can be easily extended for other
languages like Kashmiri and Konkani. The transliteration accuracy for the three languages ranges
from 91.68% to 97.75%, which is the best accuracy reported so far in literature for translateration
from Perso-Arabic to Indic script. The system has
been designed in such a fashion that the main code,
algorithms and data structures remain unchanged
and for a adding a new script pair only the databases, mapping rules and language models for the
script pair need to be developed and plugged in.

Acknowledgments

The authors would like to acknowledge the support
provided by PAN ASIA Grants Singapore and ISIF
grants Australia for carrying out this research. The
Sindhi language support provided by Dr. Bharat
Ratanpal and Ms. Madhuri Wardey, Faculty of
Technology & Engineering, MSU Baroda is also
duly acknowledged.

References

Aadil Amin Kak, Nazima Mehdi and Aadil Ahmad La-
waye. 2010. Building a Cross Script Kashmiri Converter: Issues and Solutions, In *Proceedings of
Oriental COCOSDA (The International Committee
for the Co-ordination and Standardization of Speech
Databases and Assessment Techniques)*. web access :
http://desceco.org/O-
COCOSDA2010/proceedings/paper_38.pdf

Carmen Brandt. 2014. Script as a Potential Demarcator
and Stabilizer of Languages in South Asia Language, *Documentation & Conservation Special Publication No. 7 in Language Endangerment and
Preservation in South Asia*, ed. by Hugo C. Cardoso,
pp. 78-99

Durrani, N., Sajjad, H., Fraser, A. and Schmid, H. 2010.
Hindi-to-Urdu Machine Translation through Transliteration. *In Proceedings of the 48th Annual Conference of the Association for Computational
Linguistics*, pp 465–474, Uppsala, Sweden.

G. S. Lehal, 2009. A Two Stage Word Segmentation
System For Handling Space Insertion Problem In Ur-
du Script, *Proceedings of World Academy of Science,
Engineering and Technology,* Bangkok, Thailand,
Vol. 60, pp 321-324.

G. S. Lehal, 2010. A Word Segmentation System for
Handling Space Omission Problem in Urdu Script,
*Proceedings of the 1st Workshop on South and
Southeast Asian Natural Language Processing
(WSSANLP)*, the 23rd International Conference on
Computational Linguistics (COLING), pp. 43–50,
Beijing.

Gurpreet S. Lehal and Tejinder S. Saini. 2012. Development of a complete Urdu-Hindi transliteration system. In *Proceedings of the 24th International
Conference on Computational Linguistics*, pp 643–
652, Mumbai, India.

Leghari, M., and Rahman, M. U. 2010. Towards Transliteration between Sindhi Scripts by using Roman
Script. *Conference on Language and Technology*. Is-
lamabad: National Language Authority, Pakistan.
http://www.cle.org.pk/clt10/papers/Towards%20Tran
sliteration%20between%20Sindhi%20Scripts%20
by%20using%20Roman%20Script.pdf

M. G. Abbas Malik, Christian Boitet, and Pushpak
Bhattacharyya. 2010. Finite-state scriptural transla-
tion. In *Proceedings of the 23rd International Confe-
rence on Computational Linguistics:
Posters* (COLING '10). ACL, pp 791-800,
Stroudsburg, PA, USA.

Malik, M. G. Abbas. 2006. Punjabi Machine
Transliteration. *Proceedings of the 21st International
Conference on Computational Linguistics and 44th
Annual Meeting of the ACL*, pp 1137-1144.

Malik. M. G. Abbas, Boitet. Christian, Besacier. Laurent, Bhattcharrya. Pushpak. 2013 Urdu Hindi Machine Transliteration using SMT, *The 4th Workshop
on South and Southeast Asian Natural Language
Processing (WSSANLP), a collocated event at International Joint Conference on Natural Language
Processing (IJCNLP)*, pp. 43-57, Nagoya, Japan.

T. S. Saini, G. S. Lehal and V. S. Kalra. 2008. Shahmukhi to Gurmukhi Transliteration System, *Coling:
Companion volume: Posters and Demonstrations*, pp.
177-180, Manchester, UK.

AutoParSe: An *Auto*matic *Paradigm Selector* For Nouns in Konkani

Shilpa Desai
Department of Computer Science and
Technology,
Goa University,
Goa - India
sndesai@gmail.com

Neenad Desai
N.D. Consultancy,
Cuncolim,
Goa - India
neenad@gmail.com

Jyoti Pawar
Department of Computer Science and
Technology,
Goa University,
Goa - India
jyotidpawar@gmail.com

Pushpak Bhattacharyya
Department of Computer Science and
Engineering,
IIT, Powai,
Mumbai - India
pb@cse.iitb.ac.in

Abstract

In this paper, we discuss a rule based method which automatically assigns paradigms to Konkani nouns using morphophonemic rules, stem formation rules and relevance score of the paradigms. The first contribution is computation of relevance score of a paradigm, which is computed using a corpus and paradigm differentiating measure assigned to inflectional suffixes in the paradigm. Relevance score helps assign multiple paradigms to the input word wherever appropriate. The other contribution is a method for computing paradigm differentiating measure for inflectional suffixes. We have proposed a pruning technique based on derivational suffixes to further improve the precision. The experimental study has been carried out using the Konkani WordNet and the Asmitai Corpus. The proposed method successfully assigned relevant paradigms to 10,068 nouns with F-Score of 0.93.

1   Introduction

A Morphological Analyzer for a language is a tool which is used to analyze a word into constituent morphemes. Morphological Analysis is required in NLP applications such as spell checkers and rule based machine translation. Various approaches have been used for morphology acquisition. Amongst all, finite state based approaches perform the best. Finite state approaches are based on paradigms[1]. These paradigms are defined by linguistic experts. Words in the language are then assigned to an appropriate paradigm. If this mapping of words to paradigms is done manually it requires linguistic experts and is time consuming. Based on the morphological richness of the language and level of expertise and availability of the linguists, it takes about 3 to 6 months to map words to paradigms.

Previous work which assign paradigms to words (Carlos et al., 2009) use POS tagged data to improve precision. Since we do not have a POS tagger tool for Konkani Language, our method attempts to improve precision of paradigm assignment by using morphophonemic rules and computing relevance score for paradigms.

The input to our system is as follows: a) raw text corpus, b) morphological rules and c) root word lexicon for Konkani. We output a noun paradigm repository, wherein a noun in the WordNet is assigned its inflectional paradigm. Our automatic paradigm selector method is implemented for Konkani nouns. We have defined our own paradigm structure for Konkani nouns which uses Finite State based sequencing of morphemes.

---

[1] Words which inflect similarly belong to the same paradigm. That is, these words follow the same stem formation rule and get attached to a common set of suffixes

240

D S Sharma, R Sangal and J D Pawar. Proc. of the 11th Intl. Conference on Natural Language Processing, pages 240–248,
Goa, India. December 2014. ©2014 NLP Association of India (NLPAI)

In this paper we present a detailed study of Konkani noun morphology and a technique which can be used to assign paradigms to Konkani nouns. The rest of the paper is organized as follows: section 2 is devoted to related work. A description of the Konkani noun morphology is discussed in section 3. Section 4 presents our AutoParSe system design and description. In Section 5, we discuss experimental results and evaluation. Section 6 concludes the paper.

2   Related Work

Automatic mapping of word to a paradigm have been done earlier for other languages. Rule based systems which map words to paradigms have been attempted (Sanchez, 2012). These systems use POS information or some additional user input from native language speakers to map words to paradigms, instead of a corpus alone. A corpus assisted approach (Desai et al., 2012) has been used to map Konkani verbs to a single paradigm.

Lexicon acquisition methods exist for many languages that map words to morphological paradigms. (Attia et al., 2012; Clement et al., 2004; Carlos et al., 2009; Forsberg, 2006) Functional Morphology has been used to define morphology for languages like Swedish and Finnish, and tools based on Functional Morphology, namely Extract (Forsberg, 2006) which suggest new words for a lexicon and map them to paradigms, have been developed. Functional Morphology based tools use constraint grammars to map words correctly to paradigms. To be able to use a tool like Extract, the morphology of the language has to be fitted into the Functional Morphology definition.

N-gram based model of lexical categories (Linden, 2009) and inflection information to select a single paradigm in cases where more than one paradigm generates the same set of word forms are available.

3   Konkani Noun Morphology

Noun forms are usually obtained by attaching prefix or suffix. In Konkani, prefixing is not very productive[2]. Suffixes could be derivational suffixes or inflectional suffixes. Mostly lexicons maintain the derivational forms of a word. Hence we do not need map derivational words to paradigms. Inflectional forms are not maintained in lexicons, hence there is a need to group all inflectional forms into paradigms. An inflectional paradigm for a noun in Konkani will be a set of suffixes which can be attached to a common stem.

3.1   Konkani Noun Inflectional Morphology

All nouns in Konkani are inflected for number and syntactic case. Number can be singular or plural. Konkani cases are nominative, accusative, dative, locative, instrumental, vocative and genitive. Besides nominatives, other cases show a suffix before the case marker which is referred to as oblique suffix. Thus Konkani cases are divided into two basic types, direct and oblique (Almeida, 1989). Cases which require oblique suffixes are called oblique case types.

Example 1: Consider the inflected form *ghodyakuch* (घोड्याकूच) of noun ghodo (घोडो). The inflectional segmentation can be given as: ghodyakuch = ghod+ya+k+uch (घोड्याकूच = घोड+ःया+क+ःूच) where:
Noun root[3]: ghodo (घोडो means horse)
Noun stem: ghod (घोड)
Oblique singular suffix: ya (ःया)
Case marker suffix: k (क)
Clitic: uch (ःूच emphatic particle)

Table 1 shows the different case-marker suffixes a Konkani noun can take.

Case Marker	Case Marker Suffix		Case type
	Singular	Plural	
Nominative	*Unmarked*		Direct
Dative	-k (क)	-k (क)	Oblique
Accusative	-k (क)	-k (क)	Oblique
Locative1	-˜t (ःत)	-ni (नी)	Oblique
Locative2	-r/cer (र/चेर)	-r/cer (र/चेर)	Oblique
Instrumental	-n (न)	-ni (नी)	Oblique
Vocative	NULL ( )	-no (नो)	Oblique
Genitive	-co …(चो…)	-co …(चो…)	Oblique

Table 1: Case Marker suffixes in Konkani

Konkani leaves the nominative case unmarked. The genitive case has many case marker suffixes

---

[2] Attaching a prefix to a Konkani word to get inflected word forms is rare.

[3] Here we refer to the citation form of the noun in the dictionary or WordNet as the root.

which are not listed in Table 1. To obtain the inflections of a given Konkani noun which is in root form, we need to first obtain the corresponding stem and oblique form. We can than attach case marker suffixes to obtain noun forms. Clitics (Walawalikar et al., 2010) can be appended to noun forms to obtain variants of the noun forms.

4 AutoParSe Design and Description

In order to map Konkani nouns in root form to corresponding paradigm, we use a rule-based approach.

4.1 AutoParSe Design

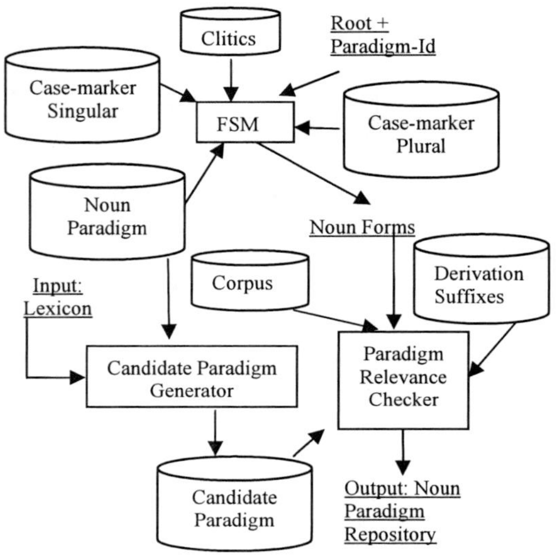

Figure 1: AutoParSe Design

AutoParSe, our noun paradigm selector has three modules listed below:
1. Finite State Machine (FSM).
2. Candidate Paradigm Generator (CPG)
3. Paradigm Relevance Checker (PRC)
Each of the modules is described in detail below.

4.2 FSM: Finite State Machine

FSM module is used to sequence morphemes in noun forms. It is called by the paradigm relevance checker module to obtain the inflectional word forms, for a given input root word and paradigm id. There will be an instance of the FSM for each noun paradigm. Figure 2 shows the general FSM for Konkani nouns. Sample input and output to FSM module is illustrated in Table 2

Sample Input	ghodo (घोडो) , P-19
Sample Output	**ghode, ghodyak, ghodyakch, ghodyan, ghodyacho** … घोडे, घोड्याक, घोड्याकच, घोड्यान, घोड्याचो ….

Table 2: Sample input and Output for FSM Module

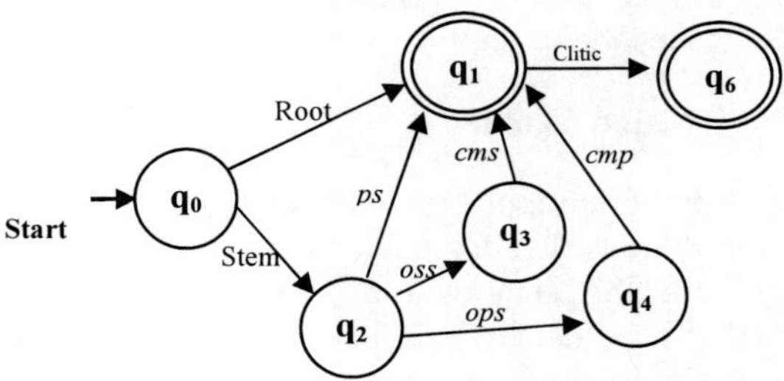

Figure 2: FSM for Konkani Noun Morphology

Input: Root noun and paradigm id
Output: Inflected noun forms with analysis
Resources used: The FSM module uses four resources namely
- Clitics : List of clitic suffixes for the language
- Case-marker Singular (CMS): List of case marker suffixes[4] which gets attached to singular noun oblique form with analysis.
- Case-marker Plural (CMP) : List of case marker suffixes which gets attached to plural noun oblique form with analysis
- Noun Paradigm: This resource is made of 5-tuple which consists of
  o Paradigm id: Unique identifier for paradigm
  o Stem Rule (SR)[5]: Rule to obtain stem from root.
  o Plural Suffix: Ordered pair (ps, pdm) where ps is the plural suffix and pdm[6] is corresponding paradigm differentiating measure assigned.
  o Oblique singular suffix: Ordered pair (oss,pdm) where oss is the oblique singular suffix and pdm is corresponding paradigm differentiating measure assigned.
  o Oblique plural suffix: Ordered pair (ops,pdm) where ops is the oblique plural suffix and pdm is corresponding paradigm differentiating measure assigned.

---

[4] CMS and CMP suffixes are listed in Table 1
[5] SR rule is discussed in subsection 4.2.1
[6] Computation of pdm is discussed in subsection 4.4.2

Constraint on noun paradigm design: The noun paradigms are designed in such a way that the tuple (SR, *ps, oss, ops*) is unique for a paradigm in Konkani.

Algorithm:
For input noun_root and paradigm id,

    NF = Empty Set
    Get corresponding noun paradigm
    stem = SR(noun_root)
    plural = stem+*ps*
    NF = NF U {plural}
    For each *cms* suffix in CMS
        nf = stem+*oss*+*cms*
        NF = NF U {nf}
    End For
    For each *cmp* suffix in CMP
        nf = stem+*ops*+*cmp*
        NF = NF U {nf}
    End For
    For each *c* suffix in Clitics
        nf = nf+*c*
        NF = NF U {nf}
    End For
End For
Output NF

4.2.1 Stem Rule (SR)

Most of the time a stem is obtained from the root by simply dropping the end letters as in case of example 1. Let us consider another example.

Example 2: Consider the word form *sorpak* (सोरपाक)
The inflectional segmentation can be given as:
sorpak = sorp+a+k (सोरपाक = सोरप+ाा+क)
where
Noun root: sorop (सोरोप means *snake*)
Noun stem: sorp (सोरप)
Oblique suffix: a (ाा)
Case marker suffix: k (क)

Here the stem is not obtained directly by dropping end characters, but also follows some morphophonemic rules. The following Table 3 lists some of the morphophonemic rules to be followed to obtain a stem. Note that the morphophonemic rule stated above will be applied to those root words which do not end in a vowel.

Type	Morphophonemic Rule	Example (root →stem)
Vowel Shortening	If syllable count equals two and penultimate character is i:/u: replace by i/u	ki:r →kir (कीर→किर)
Vowel Deletion	If syllable count greater than two and penultimate character is i:/u:/o delete penultimate character	hūdi:r → hūdr (हुंदीर→हूंदर)

Table 3: Morphophonemic Rules in Konkani

For noun roots which end in a vowel, the stem rule is of the form αβγ.
α → Delete (refers to the operation to be performed)
β → END (refers to position)
γ → ending vowel (refers to the ending vowel to be deleted to get stem)
The Delete operation converts root to stem by removing the end vowel. For noun roots which do not end in a vowel, the stem rule is the morphophonemic rule.

4.3 Candidate Paradigm Generator (CPG)

This module uses linguistic knowledge of the Konkani language to choose candidate paradigms. All paradigms which have compatible SR to the input root will be picked. In Konkani, a compatible paradigm will be based on the ending vowel of root word. Sample input and output to CPG module is illustrated in Table 4

Sample Input	man (मान)
Sample Output	P-1, P-2, P-6

Table 4: Sample input and output for CPG Module

Input: Word from lexicon
Output: List of candidate paradigm ids
Resources used: Noun Paradigm
Algorithm:
For paradigm id in Noun Paradigm,

    CP = Empty Set
    Get corresponding SR
    If SR compatible with root noun
    CP = CP U {paradigm id}
End For
Output CP

4.4 Paradigm Relevance Checker

This module computes relevance score for input paradigms and outputs those paradigms with relevance score greater than a set threshold. It makes use of paradigm differentiating measure and suffix evidence (Carlos et al.) to compute the relevance score for a paradigm. We first discuss a few terms which are used to compute relevance score of a paradigm.

4.4.1 Common Paradigm Group (CPG)

The paradigms in Candidate Paradigms (CP) are compatible with SR rule. We can further prune CP to get CPG. We prune paradigms in CP to whose stem either *ps*, *oss* or *ops* suffix cannot be attached. Such an attachment is not possible in cases where stem ends in vowel and any one of *ps*, *oss* or *ops* begins with a vowel.

4.4.2 Paradigm Differentiating Measure

We define suffix paradigm differentiating measure *pdm* for a suffix *s*, as the number of times a suffix *s* occurs in Common Paradigm Group (CPG). A *pdm* of one indicates that the presence of this suffix is a deciding factor to assign the corresponding paradigm. Table 5 illustrates the computation of *pdm* for a suffix.

CPG	P-1, P-2,P-5,P-6		
Suffix	*ps*	*oss*	*ops*
P-1	-a	-o	-yã
P-2	-i:	-ya	-yã
P-5	-a	-a	-yã
P-6	-e	-a	-ã
	$pdm(\text{-a}) = 2$ $pdm(\text{-i:}) = 1$ $pdm(\text{-e}) = 1$	$pdm(\text{-o}) = 1$ $pdm(\text{-ya}) = 1$ $pdm(\text{-a}) = 2$	$pdm(\text{-yã}) = 3$ $pdm(\text{-ã}) = 1$

Table 5: Paradigm differentiating measure (*pdm*) computation

From Table 5, we observe that the *oss* suffix *–o* is more useful to disambiguate the paradigm as compared to *oss* suffix *–a*. That is, if many words with *oss* suffix *–o* are obtained in the corpus, we give a high relevance score to paradigm P-1.

4.4.3 Suffix Evidence Value (SEV)

Suffix evidence value for a paradigm is the cardinality of intersection of two sets, namely word forms in the corpus with word forms the given paradigm generates. Table 6 illustrates the computation of suffix evidence value for a given paradigm.

Corpus	ghodo, ghode, ghodyacho, ghodekar, ghodegiri, **ghodyan**
P-1 **Generated**	**ghodo**, **ghode**, ghodyak, **ghodyan**, ghodyat, ghodyar, ghodyacer
SES for P-1	**ghodo, ghode, ghodyan**
SEV for P-1	3

Table 6: Suffix Evidence value computation

4.4.4 Suffix Evidence Set (SES)

Suffix evidence set for a paradigm is the intersection of two sets, namely word forms in the corpus with word forms the given paradigm generates.

4.4.5 Derivational cum Oblique Suffix (DOS)

Derivational cum oblique suffix set is the intersection of derivational suffix set for nouns and oblique suffix set for nouns. Table 7 illustrates an example of DOS set.

Derivation Suffix Set (DSS)	{ari, er, ist, vot, i, kar, pon, al, est, adik, vot, ik, e, si, li, ul}
oss	{a, i, e, ya, ye, va}
ops	{ã, ĩ, ĕ, yã, vã}
Oblique suffix set O = *oss* U *ops*	{ a, i, e, ya, ye, va, ã, ĩ, ĕ, yã, vã }
DOS = O ∩ DSS	{ i, e}

Table 7: DOS computation

Sample input and output to Paradigm Relevance Checker module is illustrated in Table 8

Sample Input	{raja, P-1, P-2,P-8,P-9} {ghodo, P-4, P-6} {man, P-1,P-2,P-3, P-7} {soso, P-15} {goru, P-17,P-18} ……… …
Sample Output	{raja = P-8} {ghodo = P-6} {man = P-1,P-3} {soso = P-15} {goru, P-17}

Table 8: Sample input and output for Paradigm Relevance Checker module

Note that in case of the word *man*, paradigm relevance checker outputs two paradigms for one word which is correct. If a word has more than one sense as a noun and the senses inflect differently two paradigms should be given to that word. In Konkani, the word *man* (मान) has two senses namely *respect* and *neck*.

Computation of relevance score: The relevance score for a paradigm is computed with respect to the CPG for the input root word. For each paradigm in a CPG, we compute paradigm differentiating measure for *ps*, *oss* and *ops* and compute SEV, using SES to check only for those having suffix with *pdm* one. We refer to the SEV computed in this manner as the relevance score for that paradigm.

Methodology: To assign a paradigm to a given input noun, we first get candidate paradigms CP. We prune the CP list to obtain CPG applicable to the input noun. We compute relevance score for each paradigm in CPG.

All paradigms in CPG with relevance score greater than a threshold are assigned to the input noun. We have set the threshold to two[7].

An important step of the relevance checker to increase precision, in case more than one paradigm is assigned to a noun, is to prune the derived word inflectional paradigm that is incorrectly assigned. To do this pruning, we prune the paradigm assigned to a noun if its corresponding SES can be generated by the derived form of the noun. We use DOS to get the derived form of the noun. We check if the derived form is present in the lexicon. We re-compute SES for the derived form and match it to the SES generated earlier. If SES matches, then the assigned paradigm has to be pruned.

Since there are oblique suffixes which can also act as derivational suffixes, we observed that a wrong paradigm was being assigned to the input noun in some cases where the derived word inflections present in the corpus resulted in a high SEV for the wrong paradigm. Example; for the noun *naukar* which means *servant*, two paradigms were being assigned. The other paradigm was in fact corresponding to the derived word *naukari* which means *job*. We use DOS to prune such erroneous paradigm assignments and improve the precision of the relevance checker.

The details for the paradigm relevance checker module are as follows:
Input: List of candidate paradigm CP for input root noun.
Output: Paradigm id corresponding to input root.
Resources used: Corpus, Word Forms

Algorithm:
FP = Empty set
For para_id in CP,
    Obtain CPG
End For
For para_id in CPG,
    Compute Suffix Evidence
    If Suffix Evidence = 0
        Delete paradigm id from CPG
    End If
End For
For para_id in CPG,
    If only one paradigm in CPG
        Found_Paradigm_id = para_id
    Else
        count = 0
        For wf in suffix evidence set
            If wf has suffix *pdm* 1
                and MBS > threshold
                count++
            End If
            If count > 2
                FP = FP U {para_id}
            End If
        End For
    End If
End For
Prune derivational paradigms assigned.
Output FP

5   Experimental Results and Evaluation

The goal of our experiment was to build a high accuracy paradigm selector for nouns and to be able to identify nouns from other part of speech categories. We selected 2000 words randomly from the input lexicon which were assigned paradigms manually, to obtain a gold standard data for comparison. These consisted of nouns for which paradigms were assigned, and other parts of speech for which paradigms were not assigned. The implementation of AutoParSe is done in Java using NetBeans IDE on Windows.

---

[7] If many paradigms find relevance score of more than two in the corpus, it indicates that the inflections are commonly used in the language for that word.

5.1 Results for AutoParSe

AutoParSe tool selects a paradigm for an input noun and generates Noun Paradigm Repository. Data sets used and the results obtained for Konkani nouns are as follows:

5.1.1 Data Sets

The following resources were used as input:
- Konkani WordNet, developed as part of the Indradhanush WordNet Project funded by DIT, New Delhi, India was used as an input resource to get the word lexicon for Konkani.
- Asmitai corpus consisting of approximately 268,000 unique word forms was used for selecting the appropriate paradigm.
- Noun Paradigm List was manually prepared with help from linguists and reference from Konkani grammar book and Konkani linguistic dissertation studies. (Almeida, 1989; Sardesai, 1986; Borkar, 1992)
- Case marker lists and clitic list were manually prepared.

To obtain the input word lexicon we had to undertake some pre-processing tasks which are covered in the following subsection.

Data Pre-processing

We extracted the words for our input lexicon from the synset in a WordNet (Bhattacharyya, 2010). We performed two pre-processing tasks discussed below.

Multiword removals: Words in the synset represented by multiword expression such as lhan_dongor (ल्हान_दोंगर means *hillock*) were pruned from the input. Such multiword expressions will inflect the same as its component last word namely dongor (दोंगर).

Unique word forms: Since in a WordNet, a word can appear in more than one synsets, we removed the duplicates and retained only unique word forms in our input lexicon.

5.1.2 Experimental Results

Total number of unique root words, which form the input lexicon, used for the study was 18301. Following results were obtained
- Total number of nouns identified by the program, for which noun paradigms were mapped: 10068
- Total number of words for which noun paradigms were not mapped by the program: 8233[8]

Comparison with gold standard data:
The output generated by the program was filtered to obtain those words which are present in our gold standard for comparison. The comparison is as follows:
- Total number of words in gold standard manually assigned to some noun paradigm: 1109
- Total number of words in gold standard unassigned to any noun paradigm: 891
- Total number of words AutoParSe assigns to some noun paradigm: 1101
- Total number of words AutoParSe does not assign any noun paradigm: 899
- Total number of words assigned to same noun paradigm in gold standard and AutoParSe (true positives): 1066
- Total number of words unassigned to any noun paradigm in gold standard and AutoParSe (true negatives): 774
- Total number of words unassigned to any noun paradigm in gold standard, but incorrectly assigned to a noun paradigm by AutoParSe (false positives): 26
- Total number of words assigned to noun paradigm by both gold standard and AutoParSe which mismatch (false positives): 9
- Total number of words assigned to noun paradigm by gold standard, but is incorrectly unassigned by AutoParSe (false negatives): 125

Precision = 1066 / (1066+26+9) = 0.968

Recall = 1066 / (1066+125) = 0.895

F-Score = 0.93

---

[8] Along with nouns, the input lexicon also contained verbs, adjectives and adverbs, which were correctly not mapped.

5.1.3   Analysis of Results

We analyzed the results from two perspectives namely
1. Precision of paradigm assignment
2. Recall of paradigm assignment

Precision of Paradigm Assignment

We observed a high precision of words assignment to noun paradigms. However we observed certain places where the assignment faltered. The cases are as below:

- Some verbs were incorrectly assigned to noun paradigms. This happens because a verb gerund in Konkani acts as a nominal and all suffixes that apply to nouns also apply to verbs. This cannot actually be termed as error but needs to be handled separately.
- In some rare cases, the inflected form of the noun obtained is not actually an inflection, but another word present in the corpus, which happens to have a word ending which matches the noun suffixes; for the word *kat* (कात means *skin*), a particular paradigm generates an inflected form *katar* (कातार means *Qatar country*) found in the corpus and hence adds a wrong paradigm to the word. Correct inflection for *kat* would be *katir* (कातीर means *on the skin*)

We prune derivational word inflections paradigms incorrectly assigned. This pruning increases precision. Table 9 illustrates the effect of pruning on precision.

Method	Precision
AutoParSe without pruning	0.932
AutoParSe with pruning	0.968

Table 9: Effect of pruning on precision

Recall of Paradigm Assignment

When we analyzed the results to check if we could further improve the recall, we realized that it was not absolutely necessary to do so. We looked into the factors which caused the recall to reduce and found that it was unassigned nouns. We refer to those nouns for which paradigms were not assigned as unassigned nouns. We studied these unassigned nouns to find possible reasons why they remained unassigned. We observed that the nouns which remained unassigned were not present in the corpus used. Table 10 shows the classification of the unassigned nouns. We can clearly see that these words are not natural to Konkani language. A natural question arises as how they appear in the input if they are not natural to the language. The answer lies in the resource used, namely, Konkani WordNet, to create the lexicon.

In a WordNet, a word is a part of a synset[9] which follows the principal of minimality, coverage and replacebility (Bhattacharyya, 2010). As a result, to comply with the principal of coverage, rarely used synonyms of the word are also present in the WordNet.

Unassigned Types	Examples
Named Entities	*Angola* (अंगोला, name of a country)
Foreign words or borrowed words	*Accordion* (अकार्डियन) *Infrastructure* (इंफ्रास्ट्रक्चर) *Attack* (अटॅक)
Coined words	*Aksharganit* (अक्षरगणीत means *algebra*)
Rare usage words	*Akrutya* (अकृत्य means *an action not to be performed*)

Table 10: Unassigned Nouns

The fall in recall is due such rare words, which would have to be manually assigned paradigms.

6   Conclusion

Selecting paradigms by giving priority to morphophonemic rules of the language helps improve the precision of paradigm selection. Overlap in inflectional and derivational suffixes in Konkani tend to reduce the precision and need to be handled appropriately.

By assigning *pdm* to paradigm differentiating suffixes, we get a new way to correctly map multiple paradigms to a noun root, which reflects the different senses in which the noun could occur. To the best of our belief, most automatic paradigm

---

[9] A synset stands for synonymous set, consists of a group of synonymous words which can be used interchangeably. Synset are used to represent a concept in the language.

selectors tend to produce a single mapping which does not capture multiple senses of words. Sometimes, linguists assigning paradigms to words could miss a word sense which is better captured by our automatic paradigm selector. Multiple paradigms also suggest multiple acceptable inflectional form uses for a word. For example, *nhayr* and *nhayer* (न्हंयर and न्हंयेर both mean *on the river*) inflectional forms used are both present in the corpus and should be captured by a good system. A corpus is bound to have spelling dialect variations of word form. AutoParSe is flexible enough to accommodate such inflectional form variations which a linguist may disagree with and stick to standard inflectional rules of the language. Thus, our AutoParSe method will be able cater better to a true real life corpus morphological analysis requirement.

References

Almeida Matthew, S.J. 1989. A Description of Konkani. Thomas Stephens Konknni Kendr, Miramar Panaji, Goa.

Attia Mohammed, Samih Younes, Khaled Shaalan Josef van Genabith. 2012. The Floating Arabic Dictionary: An Automatic Method for Updating a Lexical Database through the Detection and Lemmatization of Unknown Words. In Proceedings of COLING 2012, Mumbai.

Bhattacharyya Puskpak, IndoWordNet, Lexical Resources Engineering Conference 2010 (LREC 2010), Malta, May, 2010.

Borkar Suresh Jayvant, Konkani Vyakran, Konkani Bhasha Mandal, 1992.

Carlos Cohan Sujay, Manojit Choudhury and Sandipan Dandapat. 2009. Large-Coverage Root Lexicon Extraction for Hindi. In Proceedings of the 12th Conference of the European Chapter of the ACL, Athens, Greece.

Clement Lionel, Sagot Benoit and Lang Bernard. 2004. Morphology based automatic acquisition of large coverage lexica. In Proceedings of LREC 2004, Lisbon, Portugal.

Desai Shilpa, Pawar Jyoti, Bhattacharya Pushpak. 2012. Automated Paradigm Selection for FSA based Konkani Verb Morphological Analyzer. In Proceedings of COLING 2012: Demonstration Papers, Mumbai.

Forsberg Markus, Hammarstrom Harald and Ranta Aarne. 2006. Morphological Lexicon Extraction from Raw Text Data. In Proceedings of the 5th International Conference on Advances in Natural Language Processing, FinTAL, Finland.

Linden, K. and Tuovila, J. 2009. Corpus-based Paradigm Selection for Morphological Entries. In Proceedings of NODALIDA 2009, Odense, Denmark.

Sardesai Madhavi, Some Aspects of Konkani Grammar, M. Phil Thesis(1986).

V. M. Sanchez-Cartagena, M. Espla-Gomis, F. Sanchez-Martnez, J. A. and Perez-Ortiz 2012. Choosing the correct paradigm for unknown words in rule-based machine translation systems. In Proceedings of the Third International Workshop on Free/Open-Source Rule-Based Machine Translation, Gothenburg, Sweden.

Walawalikar Shantaram, Desai Shilpa, Karmali Ramdas, Naik Sushant, Ghanekar Damodar, D'Souza Chandralekha and Pawar Jyoti. 2010. Experiences In Building The Konkani WordNet Using The Expansion Approach. In Proceedings of the 5th Global WordNet Conference, Mumbai, Narosa Publishing House, India.

Continuum models of semantics for language discovery

Deepali Semwal, Sunakshi Gupta and Amitabha Mukerjee
Department of Computer Science and Engineering
Indian Institute of Technology, Kanpur
{deepalis,sunakshi,amit}@cse.iitk.ac.in

Abstract

What if we had to work in language with a semantic model that was shared with robotics and vision? We consider the question of bootstrapping NLP based on an unified continuum semantics for actions. We consider a scenario with contrastive concepts – objects (*ball, square*), actions (*throw, roll*), colours, and agents. We first acquire the semantics, then map these to crowd-sourced adult Hindi commentaries without any parse or POS knowledge. Despite wide variations across commentaries, a small subset of high-confidence labels is acquired with a simple contrastive association measure. This seed knowledge is used to iteratively bootstrap larger syntactic patterns, starting with the noun phrase and going on to the NP VP complex. Using a syllabic model of the input, we also discover morphological structure and agreement ("chaukor fenk-A", "ball fenk-I"). Since the approach is agnostic to language, we can work just as well with narratives in another language; results are shown for English. With this work, we are also releasing the action videos and the Hindi / English corpora, part of the planned multi-lingual *Videobabel* corpus.

1 Introduction

Do we use different models when we throw a ball, see a ball thrown, or talk about throwing a ball? Today each of these fields - robotics, vision, and NLP, use machine learning approaches with isolated training sets, separate models and differing paradigms (robotics and vision are continuous, NLP semantics is often discrete). As NLP gets integrated into the whole agent, one should try to consider if it may be more efficient if we could share some of the semantic structure across such related situations. This idea is also motivated by the discovery of motor neurons which seems to relate

Secondly, suppose we have a unified model such as this, would it be useful for learning language? Clearly infants have some conceptual priors before they come to language, and there is good reason to believe that these are not modeled as crisp, boolean predicates. Can we use such a model to learn words, morphology, and syntax?

We discuss these two main contributions next.

Mapping concepts multi-modally

Consider an AI agent which is in the following situations:

(a) The agent recognizes [Sam throwing a ball to Jane]

(b) The agent understands the sentence "Sam threw the ball to Jane"

(c) The agent executes [throwing the ball to Jane].

Classical AI divides up the problem of intelligence into aspects that can be distinguished based on the input and output. Thus the task (a) above would typically be handled by computer vision. Researchers would take a large class of videos labelled as [throw], and would build a classifier function, f_{vis} that would distinguish it from other actions. For the language input in task (b), one would use a pre-trained parser and a semantic analyzer trained on a very large set of POS-, parse-,

D S Sharma, R Sangal and J D Pawar. Proc. of the 11th Intl. Conference on Natural Language Processing, pages 249–257,
Goa, India. December 2014. ©2014 NLP Association of India (NLPAI)

and semantically- annotated sentences. Given these tools, it may be able to map the input to a formal structure such as `throw(agent:Sam, object: Ball, path: $p)∧goal($p, Sita)`. Let us call designate this mapping process as f_{nlp}. For task (c) a robotic agent would operate in a space where it can evaluate the result of a throwing action. It would do many trials of throwing along different 3D paths (or at goals), and come up with a function f_{rob} that can throw the ball effectively along any target path.

Now we observe that these three functions are completely disjoint, and there can be no synergy in terms of correlating knowledge between these modalities. For example, consider an expert throwing robot - after lots of training, it has a very fine f_{rob}, and can throw balls very well. However, its f_{vis} is just about average. Now, when the agent is looking at Sam's throw, it cannot use it's own f_{rob} to determine if the throw is good or bad, or make suggestions for Sam to improve his throw; for that, it would need to be trained on the image data all over again.

This separation is even more critical when it comes to language. Given a language statement it cannot relate it to the seen or executed throw. The area in NLP called grounded language learning attempts to provide mechanisms for learning the grounded meaning of a symbol, but these are limited to linking up a recognizing function f_{vis} as the semantic map of the word "throw". (Kwiatkowski et al., 2011) But the actual throw depends on what is being thrown, and who is throwing it, and how - so the actual f_{vis} will either fail for other objects, or it will have to have a potentially infinite set of arguments to handle all sorts of contextual variations. That is, it runs into the frame problem.

Now consider these two sentences:

(a) Sam threw a glance at Sita.

(b) Sam threw the flashlight beam into the cave.

Indeed, primate brains seem to be operating in a more integrated manner. Motor behaviour invokes visual simulation to enable rapid detection of anomalies, while visual recognition invokes motor responses to check

if they match. Linguistic meaning activates this wide range of modalities (Binder and Desai, 2011). Such a cross-modal model also permits affordance and intentionality judgments, which our system can also achieve.

The first part of this work (section 2) is inspired by the observation that each time the robot throws the ball for motor learning, it also generates a visual trajectory from which it can learn a visual model of the action. Further, the motion parameters are correlated with the visual feedback - both lie on matched low-dimensional curved manifolds which can be aligned.

We develop a unified approach for modeling actions, based on visual inputs (say trajectories or paths) resulting from given motor commands. The model constitutes a low-dimensional manifold that discovers the correlations between visual and motor inputs. The model can be applied to either visual recognition or to motor tasks.

Bootstrapping a lexicon and syntax

For the language task (section 3), we consider the system which already has a rudimentary model for [throw], being exposed to a set of narratives while observing different instances of throwing. The narratives are crowdsourced from speakers for a set of synthetic videos which have different actions (throw or roll), agents ("dome" or "daisy" - male/female), thrown object or trajector (ball or square), colour of trajector (red or blue) and path (on target, or short, or long). We work with transcribed text, and not with direct speech, so we are assuming that our agent is able to isolate words in the input.

An important aspect of working with crowdsourced data is that for the very beginning learner, we need a more coherent input where similar phrases are used for similar situations. This is difficult, given the diversity of our crowdsourced input, so we first identify a small coherent subset (called the *family lect*) on which initial learning is done. This is then extended to the remaining narratives (the *multilect*).

The system works on subsets of the narratives for each semantically distinct category. The joint word-semantics probabilities are computed. To learn the label for [ball], we contrast the frequency of a word being uttered when a [ball] is thrown or rolled, vs a [square]. Candidate labels are ranked based on the ratio of these joint probabilities - p(word,concept) / p(word,non-concept). The high-confidence matches - those significantly higher than the next match (abt 20%) are taken as the initial bootstrapping map (fig. 4). This partial lexicon is then used to learn a partial syntax, which is ploughed back to learn more lexemes (and also synonyms and alternations). When this interleaving stabilizes, we broaden the semantic context to learn other structures. Finally, we find that we are able to discover a good chunk of transitive verb syntax. The system is demonstrated on Hindi, where we are also able to discover some morphological agreement relations. Since we use no knowledge of langauge, the same approach also works for English.

This partial-analysis based approach is substantially different from other attempts at grounded modeling in NLP, which have focused on demonstrating the acquisition of syntax /morphosyntax (Madden et al., 2010), (Kwiatkowski et al., 2011), (Nayak and Mukerjee, 2012). One may call this approach *dynamic NLP*, since it keeps learning from every sentence, and does not generate a static model. Also, after an initial bootstrapping phase driven by this multi-modal corpus, learning can continue to be informed by text alone, a process well-known from the rapid vocabulary growth after the first phase of language acquisition in children (Bloom, 2000).

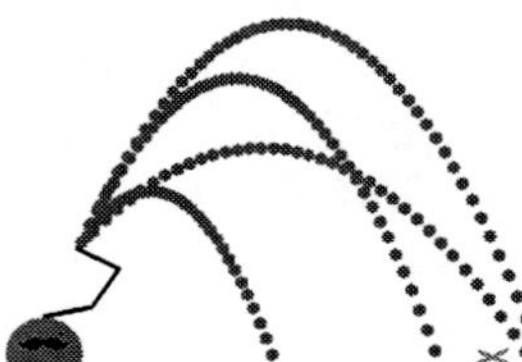

Figure 1: Set of trajectory images. Each trajectory is associated with the motor parameters of the throw.

2 Visuo-motor Pattern Discovery

Learning a few visuo-motor tasks are among our agent's very first achievements. Let us consider the act of throwing a ball. Our learner knows the motor parameters of the throw as it is being thrown - here we focus not on the sequence of motor torques, but just the angle and velocity at the point of release.

Each trajectory gives us an image (samples - fig. 1). We are given a large set of images (say, N=1080), each with $100{\times}100$ pixels. Each image can be thought of as a point in a 10^4-dimensional space. The set of possible images is enormous, but we note that if we assign pixels randomly, the probability that the resulting image will be a [throw] trajectory is practically zero. Thus, the subspace of [throw] images is very small.

Next we would like to ask what types of changes can we make to an image while keeping it within this subspace? In fact, since each throw varies only on the parameters (θ, v), there are only two ways in which we can modify the images while remaining locally within the subspace of throw images. This is the dimensionality of the local tangent space at any point, and by stitching up these tangent spaces we can model the entire subspace as a non-linear manifold of the same intrinsic dimensionality. The structure of this image manifold exactly mimics the structure of the motor parameters (the motor manifold). They can be mapped to a single joint manifold, which can be discovered using standard non-linear dimensionality reduction algorithms such as ISOMAP. In fig. 2, we show the resulting manifold obtained using a hausdorff distance metric (Huttenlocher et al., 1993): $(h(A, B) = max_{a \in A} min_{b \in B} \|a - b\|)$.

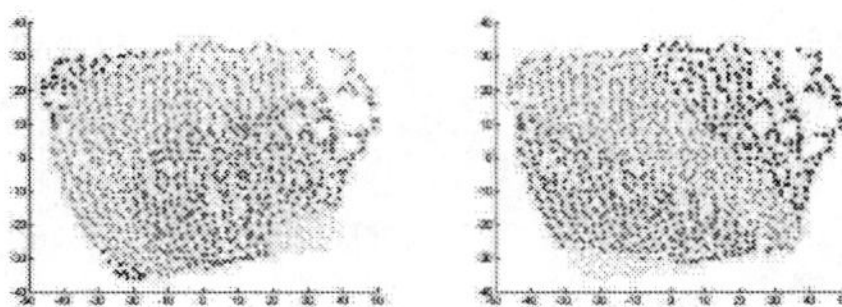

Figure 2: Variations in the manifold according to a) angle of projection, and b) velocity. (low values in yellow)

The same idea can be used to find correlations in any system involving a motion or a change of initial conditions, using this algorithm:

Algorithm 1   Visuo-motor law discovery Algorithm

No. of images	100	200	400	600	800	1000
SAE in velocity	3.69	3.57	3.85	2.71	2.38	1.93

Table 1: Sum Absolute Error (Velocity) falls as N increases

1: **Input:** Set of high dimensional images $\{I_1, I_2, I_3, ...I_N\}$, and corresponding control parameters.
2: **Step1:** Obtain a low dimensional embedding for the images using ISOMAP.
3: **Step2:** Train a regression model to acquire the mapping from the low dimensional (curved) coordinates to the control parameters.
4: **Step3:** For executing a new throw, use a (query) image with desired path. Find a linear interpolation J for this query image: $J = \sum_{j=1}^{k} w_j I_j$
5: **Step4:** Calculate the embedding points for the query image using the weights learnt in Step3. $\hat{Q} = \sum_{j=1}^{k} w_j \hat{q}_j$
6: **Step5:** Use the mapping learnt in Step2 to obtain the corresponding parameters for the query image J_i.

end

This is a generic algorithm for discovering patterns in visuo-motor activity. Initially, its estimate of how to achieve a throw are very bad, but they improve with experience. We model this process in table 1 - as the number of inputs N increases, the error in predicting a throw decreases - at N=100, the error is nearly twice that at N=1000.

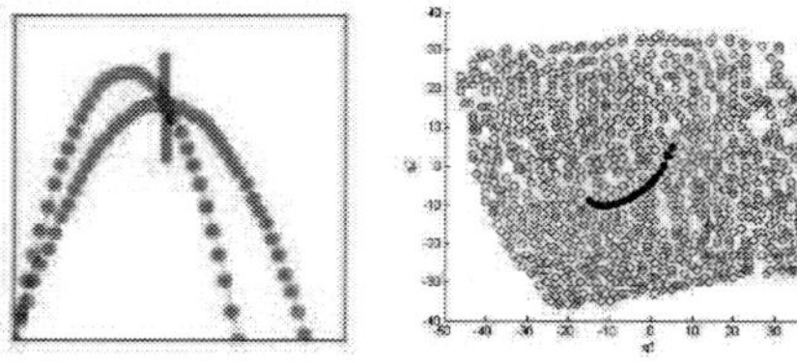

Figure 3: *Throwing darts.* a) Two trajectores that hit the board near the middle. b) 2D manifold of projectile images, showing band for "good throws", and interpolated curve for "best" throws.

The visuo-motor manifold model developed here is not task-specific, but can be applied for many tasks involving projectile motion, catching a ball, throwing at a basket, darts, tennis, etc. As an example we can consider darts - ignoring the lateral deviations, the successful trajectories are those that intersect the dartboard near its center (fig. 3a). This corresponds to a "good zone" in the latent space (central band in fig. 3b) Of these, one may wish to select those that are nearly orthogonal to the board at contact (short curved axis). Of course, actual task performance will improve with experience (more data points in the vicinity of the goal), resulting in better performance. This model only provides a starting point.

3   Bootstrapping Language

In order to learn language, we create a set of 15 situations involving the actions [throw] and [roll] (one of the agents is shown in fig. 1). The videos of these actions are then put up for commentary. Largely students on the campus network contributed; we obtain 18 transcribed narratives in Hindi. Later we also collected 11 English commentaries.

The compiled commentaries vary widely in lexical and constructional choices. An example description for of a video is "daisy throws a blue square". Another subject describes the same video as "now daisy threw the blue box which fell right on the mark". Both these narratives varies in terms of lexical units used as well as the details incorporated in description.

As described earlier, we first select a more coherent subset of narratives - those that have a more consistent vocabulary from - and identify these as the *family lect*.

Given the [throw] model, the system can identify the act of throwing, and also the agent who throws, the object thrown, and its path. Further, we assume similar capabilities (not implemented) for [roll], and also the ability to discriminate a square from a circle, red from blue, and the two agents - [Dome] with a moustache (fig. 1, male), and [Daisy] with a ponytail. Based on these distinctions, it tries to find words that differ in their usage between the two contrasting situations. (Note: we use square brackets to indicate a concept, the semantic pole of a linguistic symbol) This contrastive approach has been suggested as a possible strategy applied by child learners (Markman, 1990). Given two contrasting concepts c_1, c_2, we compute the empirical joint probabilities of word (or later, n-gram) ω_i and concept c_1, c_2, and compute their contrast score:

$$S_{\omega_i, c_1} = \frac{P(\omega_i, c_1)}{P(\omega_i, c_2)}$$

We also compare the corpus of narratives

Schema	Top Hindi Lexemes	Score	Freq	ratio
[circle]	बॉल (ball) [ball]	19.9	19	1.43
	गयी (gayi) [went]	13.9	13	
[square]	चौकोर (chaukor) [square]	25.1	24	5.00
	गिरा (giraa) [fell]	5.01	9	
[daisy]	डेज़ी (daisy)	27.5	29	10
	उछाली (uchaali) [toss]	2.75	3	
[dome]	डोम (dome)	13.5	36	1.76
	पहले (pehley) [before]	7.67	6	
[throw]	पहले (pehley) [before]	6.95	6	1.27
	फेंकी (phenki) [throw]	5.48	10	
[roll]	सरकाया (sarkaayaa) [roll]	16.2	15	2.01
	सरकायी (saraayi) [roll]	8.05	7	
[red]	लाल (laal) [red]	10.9	31	3.53
	रुकी (ruki) [stopped]	3.08	2	
[blue]	नीली (neeli) [blue]	14.6	14	1.37
	नीले (neeley) [blue]	10.7	10	

Figure 4: High confidence lexeme discovery : Contrastive scores and dominance ratio for top lexemes in. Highlighted squares show high-confidence lexemes (ratio more than twice)

here with that from a larger unannotated corpus CIIL/IITB Corpus for Hindi. We look for words that are more frequent in the input domain than in a general situation. This rules out many frequent words like है,के *(hai,ke)* [is, of]. The small set of high confidence words - whose contrastive probability is more than twice the next best match - are highlighted in Fig. 4.

3.1 Interleaving of Word / Syntax learning

Once the system has a few grounded lexemes, we proceed to discovering syntactic constructions. At the start, we try to learn the structure of small contiguous elements. One assumption we use here is that concepts that are very tightly bound (e.g. object and its colour) are also likely to appear in close proximity in the text (Markman, 1990). Another assumption (often called *syntactic bootstrapping*), is used for mapping new phrases and creating

| लाल चौकोर (laal chaukor) [red square] |
| लाल रंग का चौकोर |
| (laal rang ka chaukor) [red coloured-GEN square] |

Table 2: Initial constructions learned from the trajector delimited strings

| लाल बॉल (laal ball) [red ball] |
| नीले रंग का चौकोर |
| (blue coloured-GEN square) [blue square] |

Table 3: Syntax for trajector - iteration 1, Family-lec

equivalence classes or contextual synonyms. This says that given a syntactic pattern, if phrase $p1$ appears in place of a known phrase $p0$, and if this substitution is otherwise improbable (e.g. the phrase is quite long), then $p0, p1$ are synonyms (if in the same semantic class) or they are in the same syntactic lexical category.

We find that one type of trajector (e.g. "ball") and its colour attribute (e.g. "lAl", [red]) have been recognized. So the agent pays more attention to situations where these words appear. Computationally this is modelled by trying to find patterns among the strings starting and ending with (delimited by) one of these high-confidence labels (e.g. "red coloured ball"). This delimited corpus consistes of strings related to a known trajector-attribute complex. Within these tight fragments, we show that standard grammar induction procedures are able to discover preliminary word-order patterns which can be used to induce broader regularities. We compare two available unsupervised grammar induction systems - Fast unsupervised incremental parsing (Seginer, 2007) and ADIOS(Solan et al., 2005); results shown here adopt the latter because of a more explicit handling of discovered lexical classes.

The initial patterns learned for the trajector in this manner are shown in Table 2. These are generalized using the phrase substitution process to yield the new lexeme बॉल (ball), [ball] (Table. 3). This is done based on the family-lect (Figure 4), and the filtered sub-corpus is used to learn patterns and equivalence classes.

The system now knows patterns for [red square], say, and it now pays attention to situations where the pattern is almost present,

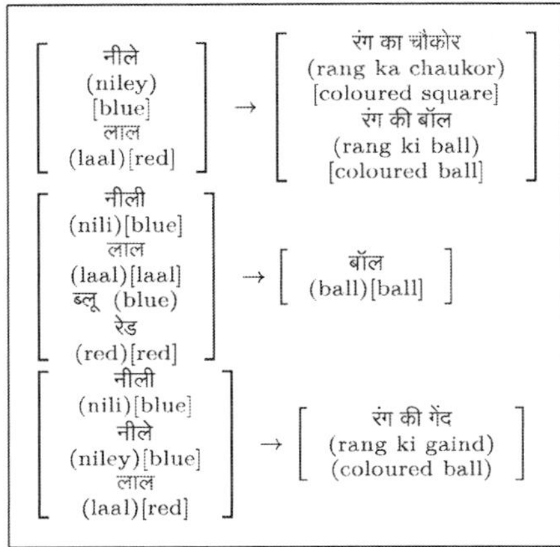

Table 4: Learned constructions pertaining to trajectors : The coloured units are the initially grounded lexemes

SCHEMA	Top scoring Hindi lexical units / cluster	score	ratio
[throw]	पहले (pehley) [before]	6.89	1.49
	गिरा, गिर, गिरी (gira, gir, giri) [fall]	4.6	
[roll]	सरकायी, सरकाया (sarkaaya, sarkaayi) [roll]	23.66	7.78
	वहीं (wahin) [there]	3.04	

Figure 5: *Verb learning.* Recomputed contrast scores after morphological clustering. Note that "threw" now appears as a high-confidence label.

$$[AGT] \text{ ने } [TRJ] \rightarrow \begin{bmatrix} \text{सरकाया (sarkAyA)} \\ \text{सरकायी (sarkAyI)} \end{bmatrix}$$
$$[AGT]\text{-NOM rolls }[TRJ]$$

Table 5: Initially acquired sentence constructions

except for a single substitution. It can look into other semantic classes as well, (e.g. [blue square], [red ball]). In most of these instances (Fig. 4) we already have partial evidence for these units from their contrastive scores. Now if we discover new substitution phrases $p1$ in the position of $p0$, referring to a concept in the same semantic class (e.g. [ball] for [square]), and if $p1$ is already partially acceptable for [ball] based on contrastive probability, then $p1$ becomes an acceptable label for this semantic concept. This process iterates - new lexemes are used to induce new patterns, and then further new lexemes, until the patterns stabilize. This is then extended to the entire corpus beyond the small family lect; results are shown in Table 4.

The table captures a reasonable diversity of Noun Phrase patterns describing coloured objects. Note that words like "red" and "ball" have also become conventionalized in Hindi. We also observe that the token *niley* appears in the 4-word pattern *niley rang kaa chaukor* and is highly confident even from a single occurrence; this reflects the *fast mapping* process observed in child language acquisition after the initial grounding phase (Bloom, 2000). As the iteration progresses, these patterns are used for further enhancing the learners inventory of partial grammar.

3.2 Verb phrases and sentence syntax

Having learned the syntax for a trajector, this part of the input is now known with some con-fidence, and the learner can venture out to relate the agent to the action and path. In this study, we failed to find any high-confidence lexemes related to path, hence we were not able to bootstrap that aspect. In the following we restrict ourselves to patterns for the semantic classes [agent], [action], [trajector].

At this stage, the agent notes that many of the words seem rather similar (e.g. "sarkAyA", "sarkAyI" (H); or "throwing", "thrown" (E)). A text-based morphological similarity analysis reveals several clusters with alterations at the end of words (Fig. 5). To quantify this aspect, we consider normalised Levenshtein distance and perform a morphological similarity analysis. Since our input is text, we limit ourselves to analysis based on the alphabetic patterns as opposed to phonemic maps. Similar words are clustered using a normalized similarity index .Thus we have twelve type instances of (◌ा -aa) - (◌ी ii), and seven types for *(◌ा -aa) - (◌ -e).* We find that these variants - e.g. "sarkaayaa", "sarkaayii" - appear in the same syntactic and semantic context. These clusters are now used to further strengthen the lexeme and action association.

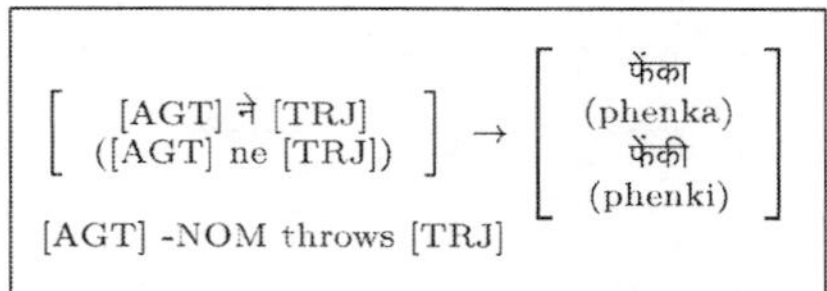

Table 6: Sentence syntax discovered - iteration 1 - FL

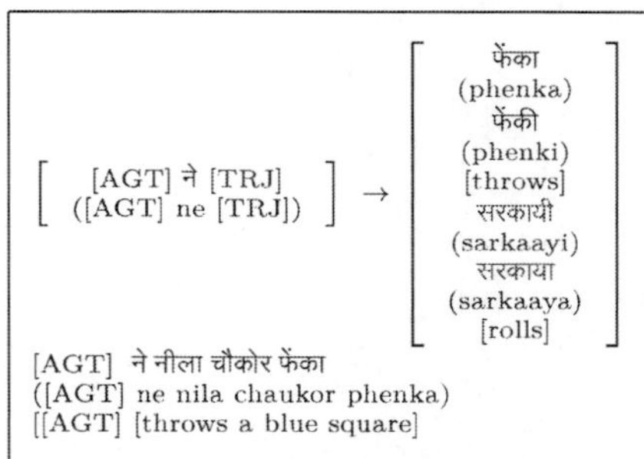

Table 7: Learned constructions over trajector phrases, The coloured units are the initially grounded lexemes

Again, we use an iterative process, starting with grounded unigrams, moving a level up to learn simple word-order patterns, learning alternations and lexical classes through phrase substitution, and so on to acquire a richer lexicon and syntax. The learner has the concept of agent and has associated the words "daisy" and "dome". One action word is known ("sarkaaya", roll) while the word for "throw" is not discovered due to lexical variations. (Fig. 5). We now filter the corpus with these known words and try to discover the verb phrase syntax. Here the known trajector syntax (table 4) is considered as a unit (denoted as **[TRJ]**, and the concept of agent ([daisy] or [dome]) is denoted **[AGT]**. Results of initial patterns, obtained based on the known action lexeme, are shown in Table 5.

Next, we interleave this syntactic discovery with lexical discovery, permitting also bigram substitutions. This gives us the more general results of Table 6. Again the system iterates over the corpus till the discovery of new patterns converges (Table 7). An interesting observation is that the Hindi data finds a phrase in the TRJ position - नीला चौकोर (nilaa chaukor) [blue square]. This had not been learned in the trajector iteration, since *nilaa* was less frequent.

Objects	Abstract	Fauna
बॉल, गेंद नाख़ूनों (naakhunon) *[nails]* बम *[bomb]* रस्सा (rassa) *[rope]*	दृष्टि (drishti) *[glance]*	नाग (naag) *[Cobra]*

Table 8: Trajector classes for Hindi

Thus we see that with this approach we are able to acquire several significant patterns. These patterns apply to only a single action input, and for a very limited set of other participants. But it would be reasonable to say that the agent may observe similar structures elsewhere - e.g. in a context involving hitting, say, if we have the sentence "Daisy hit Dome" then the agent may use the syntax of [AGT] [verb] [TRJ] to extend to this context and guess that "hit" may be a verb and "Dome" the object of this action (which it knows from the semantics). Thus, once a few patterns are known, it becomes easier to learn more and more patterns, which is the fast mapping stage we have commented upon earlier.

4 Expanding the selection set for the verbs classes

In the grounded phase, we discovered that objects like [ball] can be thrown or pushed. Thus, the verbs "फेंकी (phenki)" would select for trajectors such as "ball" or गेंद gaind.

As the learner matures, she acquires a richer ontology of actions and objects, and is of course exposed to large amounts of language, mostly without direct grounding. In the next phase, we consider how this process enables an expansion of the selection set for these verbs. For this purpose, we consider the already familiar syntactic patterns. We use Hindi word-Net as our knowledge base and analyse the new situations with already familiar verbs and syntaxes. We here consider the objects that our known verbs take as arguments in a bigger Hindi CIIL/IITB corpus.

A total of 29 sentences for Hindi are extracted by filtering for the verb forms learned for the actions in the grounded phase ("फेंकी" (phenki) etc .) While the syntax patterns for these new sentences are much more complex, we expect the trajector term to appear as the noun that is closest to the verb; based on the syntax learned we look at nouns before the verb for Hindi language.

$$\left[\begin{array}{c}\text{red}\\ \text{blue}\end{array}\right] \rightarrow \left[\begin{array}{c}\text{square}\\ \text{ball}\\ \text{box}\end{array}\right]$$

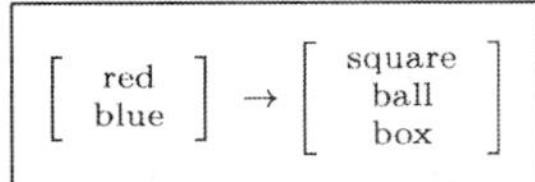

Table 9: Learned trajector constructions

$$[\text{AGT}] \rightarrow \left[\begin{array}{c}\text{threw}\\ \text{has thrown}\\ \text{is throwing}\\ \text{has slid}\\ \text{is throwing}\\ \text{throws}\\ \text{pushed}\\ \text{rolled}\end{array}\right] \rightarrow \text{E23 [TRJ]}$$

$$[\text{AGT}] \rightarrow \left[\begin{array}{c}\text{is throwing}\\ \text{pushed}\end{array}\right] \rightarrow [\text{TRJ}]$$

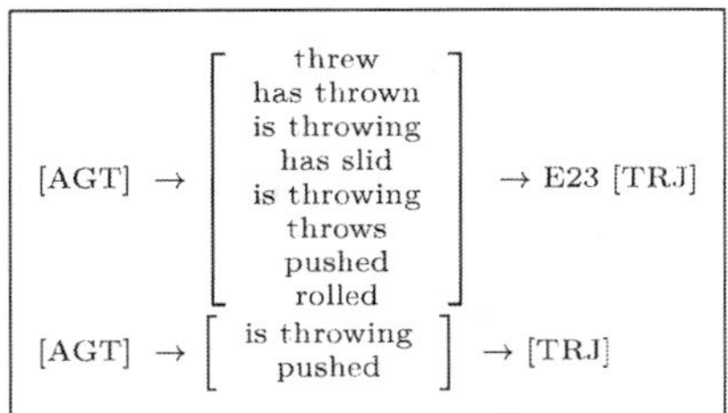

Table 10: Learned constructions over trajector phrases. E23 is the equivalence class learned for *a, the*

We discover sentences such as "स्टोव वाले बाबू ने मोतीभाई के चेहरे पर एक सहानुभूतिपूर्ण दृष्टि फेंकी" *[the stove man threw a sympathetic glance at Motibhai's face]*, where the token दृष्टि (drishti) *[glance]* appears in the place of [trajector]. Here it is as the object which belongs to *perception class* and hence an abstraction (see Table 8).

5 Acquiring another language: English

Here we collected 11 commentaries, which also vary widely. Again, starting with a "family" corpus, we obtain a small set of high-confidence labels (Figure 6, 7). At the bigram discovery stage, *"threw"* and *"rolled"* are found to be substitutable by *has thrown, is throwing*; and *has slid* respectively. Interestingly in expanding the corpus with wordnet knowledge, we find that words such as "glance", "flashlight" etc. also appear as throw-able in English, paralleling the Hindi usage.

Note that our lexical categories differ widely from syntactic categories, since they are influenced considerably by semantics. It is quite possible that human language users also use such mixed categories. At the same time, several traditional structures (e.g. Adj-N (red ball, laal chaukor),Art-N (E23 ball),

Top English lexemes	score	Freq	ratio
ball	28.7	27	3.99
near	7.19	6	
square	17.5	17	3.59
box	4.87	4	
daisy	23.6	22	7.63
right	3.09	2	
dome	29.3	29	6.00
before	4.88	4	
threw	14.8	14	1.91
throwing	7.72	7	
rolled	8.12	7	1.12
slid	7.28	6	
red	8.10	23	3.95
slightly	2.05	1	
blue	5.67	22	1.43
which	3.95	7	

Figure 6: High Confidence units

Top scoring English lexical units / cluster	score	ratio
threw	14.86	2.36
Throwing, thrown	6.29	
rolled	8.07	1.11
slid	7.27	

Figure 7: High Confidence clusters

etc are also discovered (Table 9, 10). It also discovers agreement between the unit "chaukor", [`square, M`] and verbs ending in -aa. However, following the usage-based approach (Tomasello and Tomasello, 2009), we would be inclined to view these constructions as reducing the description length needed to code for the strings arising in this context.

Thus the system has learned that the set of objects (and words) selected by an action such as "throw" may be broader than the initial set. This process actually broadens the semantics of throw itself, from the initial interpretation as a physical action, to something broader. This broader semantics is actually reflected in alternate word senses. One task which we do not attempt here is to discover this semantics as an extension of the original semantics in the physical sense; this would also be an important part of core NLP, but it is quite a challenging topic in itself.

This work however lies in the space of vision and action, and one may consider this process in terms of discovering similarities between different actions in videos, an area that is otherwise well-researched, but yet to reach this level of analysis (e.g. (Efros et al., 2003)).

6 Conclusion

The above analysis provides a proof-of-concept that a system starting with very few priors can, a) combine motor, visual (and possibly other modalities) into an integrated model, and b) use this rudimentary concept knowledge to bootstrap language. We also note that such a system can then learn further refinements to this concept space using language alone.

From here work needs to proceed in two directions. First would be to demonstrate scalability by including actions other than [throw]. One of our main claims is that neither the semantics nor the linguistic components had any kind of annotation, so the training data set needed for this should be relatively easy to generate compared to tree banks and semantically annotated data. The two linguistic corpora and the videos are being released as part of a multi-lingual, action centric corpus that we call *Videobabel*. It is plausible that with increasing availability of such unannotated multi-modal corpora, along with motor-enabled models of action, would permit the rapid scaling of conceptual and linguistic models.

References

Jeffrey R Binder and Rutvik H Desai. 2011. The neurobiology of semantic memory. *Trends in cognitive sciences*, 15(11):527–536.

Paul Bloom. 2000. *How Children Learn the Meaning of Words*. MIT Press.

Alexei A Efros, Alexander C Berg, Greg Mori, and Jitendra Malik. 2003. Recognizing action at a distance. In *Computer Vision, 2003. Proceedings. Ninth IEEE International Conference on*, pages 726–733. IEEE.

Daniel P. Huttenlocher, Gregory A. Klanderman, and William J Rucklidge. 1993. Comparing images using the hausdorff distance. *IEEE PAMI*, 15(9):850–863.

Tom Kwiatkowski, Luke Zettlemoyer, Sharon Goldwater, and Mark Steedman. 2011. Lexical generalization in ccg grammar induction for semantic parsing. In *Proc. EMNLP*, pages 1512–1523.

C. Madden, M. Hoen, and P.F. Dominey. 2010. A cognitive neuroscience perspective on embodied language for human-robot cooperation. *Brain and Language*, 112(3):180–188.

Ellen M Markman. 1990. Constraints children place on word meanings. *Cognitive Science*, 14(1):57–77.

Sushobhan Nayak and Amitabha Mukerjee. 2012. Grounded language acquisition: A minimal commitment approach. In *Proc. COLING 2012*, pages 2059–76.

Yoav Seginer. 2007. Fast unsupervised incremental parsing. In *ACL Ann. Meet*, volume 45, page 384.

Zach Solan, David Horn, Eytan Ruppin, and Shimon Edelman. 2005. Unsupervised learning of natural languages. *PNAS*, 102(33):11629–34.

Michael Tomasello and Michael Tomasello. 2009. *Constructing a language: A usage-based theory of language acquisition*. Harvard University Press.

Syllables as Linguistic Units?

Amitabha Mukerjee
Computer Science & Engineering
Indian Institute of Technology, Kanpur
`amit@cse.iitk.ac.in`

Prashant Jalan
Computer Science & Engineering
Indian Institute of Technology, Kanpur
`prasant@cse.iitk.ac.in`

Abstract

While there continues to be a debate in linguistics and speech processing as to the nature of an atomic unit, in computational approaches the atomic unit is universally taken to be the orthographic, space-demarcated "word". We argue that for many richly inflected languages such as Indo-European languages, syllable-based approaches together with semantic grounding may provide certain advantages. As a demonstration, we consider a language-acquisition system for Hindi, and propose a text syllabification technique, and show that syllable-based models perform somewhat better than the traditional word-based approach in building up a noun lexicon based on unannotated commentaries on video. We suggest further exploration of this potentially important idea in other domains.

1 Introduction

For resource-poor languages that are also morphologically complex - which applies to most of the languages in India - we suggest that instead of the orthographic word, the syllable may provide some advantages in terms of discovering structures in the language. This is motivated by the fact that the high number of morphological variants make it difficult to align verbs if we consider orthographic word boundaries. However, a syllabic approach is more likely to find overlaps with alternately inflected forms.

While a number of approaches seeking to discover morphological structure have worked with syllable-like structures (Creutz and Lagus, 2007;

Clark, 2001), these approaches, like the rest of NLP, assume that the linguistic input occurs isolated from the extra-linguistic situation of the utterance. Thus, while the term "morpheme" is usually defined based on semantics (the smallest meaning-bearing unit), past work in NLP at the syllabic level are almost invariably based solely on linguistic input.

The primary contribution of this work is that to our knowledge this may be among the early works on syllabic-unit approach to text analysis that also operates in a grounded manner for discovering semantic codes in NLP. The main difference with traditional parsing driven models is that here semantics, in the form of visual or non-textual inputs, is used to segment the input into maximal syllable-sequences. Thus, semantics is being invoked from the very earliest stages. Later interpretations can then fall back on such sensorimotor models of meaning for interpreting novel structures such as metaphor, etc. Here we consider the language acquisition problem, where we attempt to map a lexical item from a textual description stream to its referent in a visual input stream. The proposal involves three steps:

1. Syllabification from text input without the knowledge of word-boundary. This is known to be relatively simpler in most Indian languages (Kishore et al., 2002; Patil et al., 2013) than some others (e.g. English (Marchand et al., 2009)).

2. Association of syllables with concept structures that are learned independently, e.g. using contrasting concepts. (Nayak and Mukerjee, 2012; Semwal et al., 2014).

3. Attention to relations between patterns of syl-

258

D S Sharma, R Sangal and J D Pawar. Proc. of the 11th Intl. Conference on Natural Language Processing, pages 258–266,
Goa, India. December 2014. ©2014 NLP Association of India (NLPAI)

lables across different utterances (e.g. object verb agreement).

1.1 Problem with POS tags

We observe that while the semantics in this present approach is based on visual input, the same can also apply to formal semantic models for the data. However, annotating an input with such semantic labels is as difficult a problem as creating a treebank, and possibly subject to even greater ambiguities and disagreements. Also, a formal semantic tagger is based on some kind of a parse structure (typically a constituency tree or a dependency graph) - and the accuracy of such semantic models is dependent on the parse. The best POS taggers today perform at approx. 97%, but at a phrasal level, POS tags are accurate for only 50% of the sentences (Manning, 2011). Further, discrete, atomic word sense categories cannot diffuse into one another like a continuum model based on sensorimotor abstraction. Thus, the disjoint word senses often have conceptual overlaps which restrict accuracy severely (Jurgens and Stevens, 2011). Another difficulty is that standardizing on a single tag-set seems impossible, with each group suggesting its own set of tags; this is because all intermediate level tagsets constitute a compromise. Also, discrete partitions on the input space, hide the overlaps and similarities that actually exist across concepts, and are disambiguated by considering other information such as that from perception or other modalities (Fig. 1) (Pezzulo et al., 2011).

Just as continuum models of semantics provide a finer decomposition of the meaning space, so also a syllabic-unit model of the input itself provides a finer discrimination of the target map.

1.2 Grounded language models

The traditional ideas of formal semantics has also been applied to the notion of "grounding" linguistic structures. Grounding as used in computational modelling may define "meaning" in terms as an intermediate level of formal descriptions (Matuszek et al., 2012; Liang et al., 2009; Chen and Mooney, 2011), or it may attempt to relate the elements of language directly to clusters discovered on perceptual or motor data (Steels and Loetzsch, 2012). The former, in which good results have been obtained for sentential data, require rich training databases of sentence/meaning pairs, as well as supervised training datasets for learning classifiers

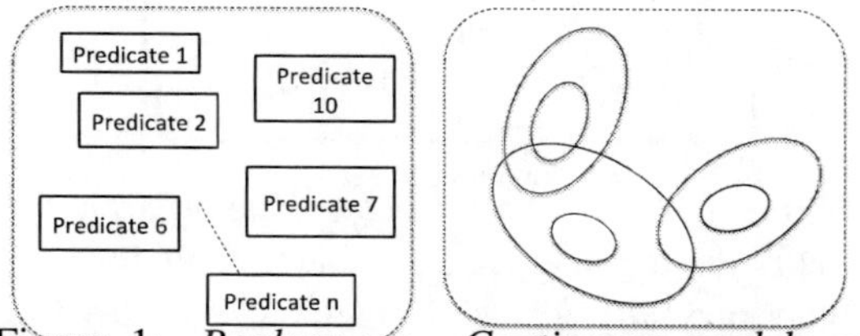

Figure 1: *Boolean vs. Continuous models of meaning.* Formal descriptions use boolean predicates to partition the world. Continuous models discover distributions in the input. The latter permits notions of similarity and conceptual overlap which are extremely difficult in boolean models.

that will work on visual input (Matuszek et al., 2012). The deeper problem with such systems is that the set of predicates used often have overlaps or gaps and just as with intermediate levels in other NLP situations, may not scale well to discourse modelling.

When mapping language directly to sensorimotor data, the scenes are often isolated for a particular concept, and the description may be short or even a single word (Stramandinoli et al., 2013; Steels and Loetzsch, 2012). At other times, the scenes may have many concepts marked already (Reckman et al., 2011). Unconstrained sentential commentary, together with dynamically changing scenes, make for considerable ambiguity in association, and have been investigated very little. Yet, this is the type of input that children learn language from.

In theory, approaches based on grounding should work with any language. However, in practice, many approaches use knowledge of parsers or other intermediate levels (Chen and Mooney, 2011). At the very least, most approaches use morphological knowledge in the form of stemmers; even this can be problematic for richly-inflected languages.

Drawing on ideas in developmental cognition which indicate that infants are aware of conceptual distinctions well before they come to language (Mandler, 2007), our goal in this paper is to investigate the present-day limits of what we call *Uninformed symbol grounding* for morphologically rich languages. The attempt is to discover grounded lexemes in a system that associates an unparsed video and a set of unconstrained raw commentaries (sentential text).

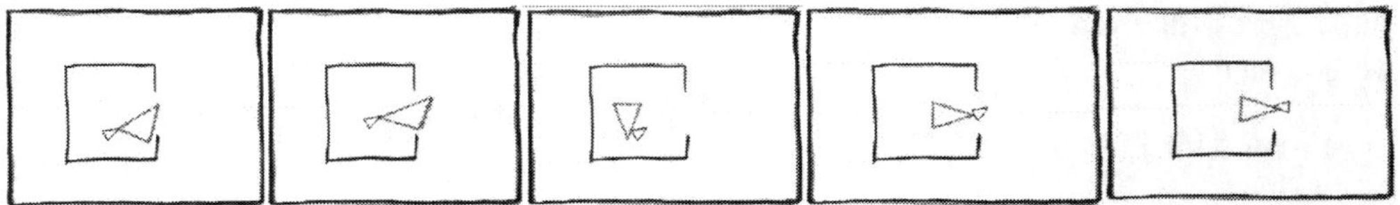

Figure 2: *Stills from the video.* The big triangle is pulling the little one, trying to get it outdoors. Eventually the big one pushes it out, and blocks it from coming back in. Finally, the two circle around each other playfully. The blocks are clustered by shape into C1(big red triangle) and C2(small blue triangle).

1.3 Grounding of syllable sequence

When using syllables, we search for maximal syllable sequences that associate strongly with a chunk of extra-linguistic context. Later, when the same syllable-gram occurs in a slightly different context, its semantics is broadened to include the new situation. Thus, the lexicon is a dynamic entity that changes with experience.

In this work, we attempt to ground syllable-grams from the input to structures in the video. Given the ambitious nature of the project, we chose a simple schematic video, one that has been developed for psychological experiments to detect autism (Sarah J. White and Frith, 2011)(Fig 2).

The only perceptual priors we assume are for identifying objects as coherently moving connected blobs. We use no other priors in either the visual or the linguistic processing. Thus, we use no knowledge of objects or shapes or actions, nor any language model. In order to be able to handle richly-inflected or agglutinative languages, we ignore word boundaries and start from syllable level and discover putative words that may be matched with the various concepts.

These perceptual priors are then mapped to syllable-clusters in the language stream. Hindi is a richly inflected language, with rich inflectional paradigms. We try to find descriptors for objects using a number of association measures.

Owing to lack of other experimentation in similar processes, we are not able to compare the results with other work. The commentaries are being made available at (Jalan, 2012).

The rest of the paper is organised as follows: in the next section we present the idea of using syllables as linguistic units followed by the explanation of the psychological video, the commentaries collected and the process of finding syllables in a sequence. Later, we present the noun discovery model followed by the results obtained.

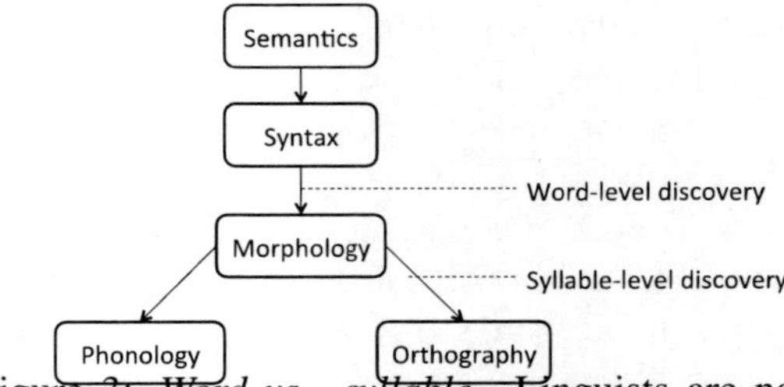

Figure 3: *Word vs. syllable.* Linguists are not sure if the morphology-syntax boundary can be defined clearly enough. Possibly a better place for starting the analysis may lie near the phonology-morphology boundary, where syllables occur.

2 Syllables as Units for NLP

A syllable is the segment of speech uttered in a single impulse of air. The nucleus of a syllable is usually the high-energy vowel sound, surrounded by co-articulations of lower energy occurring near the syllable boundary. As with all aspects of language, there is no single best mechanism for identifying syllables in text. However, for languages such as Hindi, syllabification is relatively easier than for other systems.

While linguists have been very careful in analyzing what is a "unit" for different levels of analysis, computational approaches have overwhelmingly gone with the orthographic word as its dominant unit. What some linguists (Cahill and Gazdar, 1997) said more than two decades ago - "morphemes also exist, but only as second class citizens" - holds even more strongly today. This word-focus obscures the structures hidden within words and makes it particularly difficult for highly inflected languages. However, as "word" is difficult to define for linguists, so also is "morpheme". A typical word in computational linguistics today (e.g. "boys" or किया (*kiyā*)) often has some structure hidden inside it.

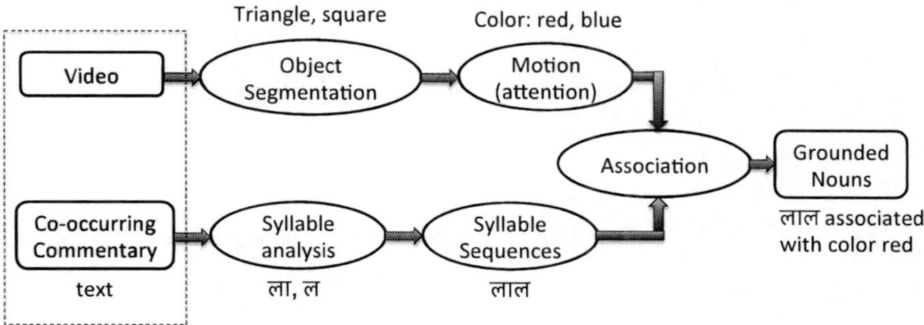

Figure 4: *Association approach for grounded noun learning.* The syllable sequences are potential words. Syllables ला (*lā*), ल (*la*) will form a syllable sequence लाल (*lāla*). All three of these would be strongly associated with the extra-linguistic context "color: red", but since लाल is a superset of the other two, we take this to be a word.

The morpheme-level syntax is hard to distinguish from word-level syntax (is "was clean" two words and "cleaned" only one?). Thus, linguists prefer to look at morphosyntax rather than word-level syntax (Fig 3). In lightly-inflected languages like English - only eight inflective variations, mostly at start or end of a "word" - one can get by with "stemmers" to identify a root. Some computational morphologists have pointed to the emphasis on English for the very poor development of morphological approaches in NLP (Clark, 2001). However, in Hindi, करवाया (*karavāyā*) is much harder to relate to किया (*kiyā*). The main idea here is that in such situations, syllables may be a better place to start than at word boundaries.

Morphemes arise at a level of segmentation that is smaller than the word, but larger than a letter (Goldsmith, 2010). This is also the space occupied by syllables. However, morpheme boundaries need not coincide with syllable boundaries, but in this work, our primary goal is not to discover morphemes per se, but words, so we assume an edge constraint, for which syllables are appropriate. Another model for this analysis could have been at the level of larger structures called feet, but since analysis of feet usually involves stress, and our work is based on text, we have kept it at the syllable level.

While syllables are not free from debate, they are certainly easier to identify than words, and also more useful as atomic constituents than phonemes (or in orthography, characters). Syllables are phonological clusters that may combine to make morphemes. While syllable boundaries are not

aligned with morpheme boundaries, the more detailed analysis is still useful for identifying familial relations between a group of words. Thus, inflectional variants may retain some core syllables while changing others, enabling a syllable-based n-gram approach to identify these core elements.

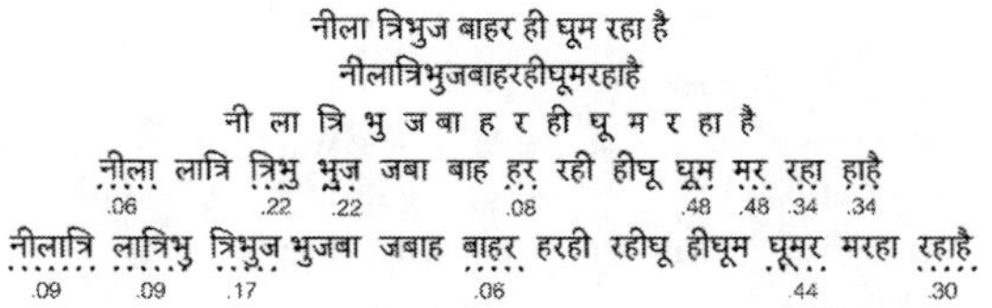

नीला त्रिभुज बाहर ही घूम रहा है
नीलात्रिभुजबाहरहीघूमरहाहै
नी ला त्रि भु ज बा ह र ही घू म र हा है

Figure 5: *Syllabic analysis of text.* The text is re-segmented based on meaning associations rather than on orthographic cues. The last two sentences show the two and three syllable grams. The numbers shown are the mutual information score evaluated only for the narration shown in fig: 6. The process discovers structures such as नी (*nī*) which can now be related to other forms such as नीले (*nīle*) and नीला (*nīlā*). 3-syllable-grams such as घमर (*ghūmara*) would have a strength almost same as the 5-syllable-gram घमरहा (*ghūmarahā*) and hence only the latter would be taken as an unit, not the shorter fragment.

In the following, we begin by removing all word boundaries in the text, (preserving gaps at punctuations) and describe the input as a sequence of syllables. This is similar to the analysis in Chinese or Thai, which do not use spaces in orthography. The linguistic units then emerge as meaning-mapped substrings on the syllable space. Because similarity in meaning is used to learn these syllable se-

0-13
14-46 एक चतुर्भुज में दो त्रिभुज हैं *"There are two triangles in one square."*
47-55
56-72 एक त्रिभुज लाल है *"One triangle is red"*
73-102 एक त्रिभुज नीले रंग का है *"One triangle is of blue colour'*
103-160 दोनों त्रिभुज एक दूसरे से लड़ने की कोशिश कर रहे हैं
"Both triangles are trying to fight each other"

161-201 और लाल त्रिभुज बाहर भाग गया है
"and red triangle has gone outside"

202-249 फिर चतुर्भुज में आने का प्रयास कर रहा है
(again trying to come back into the square)

250-311 नीला त्रिभुज और लाल त्रिभुज एक दूसरे से टकरा रहे हैं
"blue triangle and red triangle are hitting each other"

312-388 लाल त्रिभुज नीले त्रिभुज को बाहर धकेल रहा है
"red triangle is pushing the blue triangle outside"

389-466 नीला त्रिभुज लाल त्रिभुज से लड़ने के लिए तैयार हो रहा है
"blue triangle is getting ready to fight the red triangle"

467-500 नीला त्रिभुज बाहर ही घूम रहा है
"blue triangle is roaming outside'

501-552 लाल त्रिभुज उसके पीछे भागने की कोशिश कर रहा है
"red triangle is trying to run after it"

553-598 दोनों एक दूसरे से टकराकर घूम रहे हैं
("both are circling around by touching/hitting each other")

Figure 6: *Samples from narratives in Hindi.*

quences, they are closer in spirit to the definition of morpheme in linguistics. Fig 4 represents the model for grounded noun learning.

We demonstrate this process on a small example of lexeme acquisition from an unparsed unannotated corpus (fig. 5). Note that some forms such as रहाहै (*rahā-hai*) has a strong semantic relevance and is suggested as an unit, which is plausible, (and so are कररहाहै (*kar-rahā-hai*) and some larger strings). Also, syllable-grams such as त्रिभु (*tribhu*) which are appearing as frequently as the longer syllable-gram त्रिभुज (*tribhuj*) would be discarded as candidate units. On the other hand, लालत्रिभुज (*lāltribhuja*) is not an unit because लाल (*lāl*) and त्रिभुज (*tribhuj*) are independently associated with items "red" and "triangle" in the semantic inventory. Thus, लालत्रिभुज (*lāltribhuja*) is recognized as a compound of two words.

3 Video and Co-occurring Narrative Dataset

For the lexeme semantics acquisition task, extra-linguistic context is obtained from a short video (Fig 2). Language commentaries were recorded from university students (ages 21-24), by showing them the Frith-Happe video, in which two abstract

shapes (triangles) engage in what may be called *coaxing* (Sarah J. White and Frith, 2011)(Fig 2). The two agents are a big red triangle (बड़ा लाल त्रिभुज; *baṛā lāla tribhuja*) and a small blue triangle (छोटा नीला त्रिभुज; *chōṭā nīlā tribhuja*). A total of 21 commentaries were collected.

Each subject was given the following instructions:

You will be shown this 39 seconds video thrice.

For the first two times you can just see the video and gain an understanding of what is happening in the scene.

The third time you have to describe whatever is going on in the video in Hindi without involving yourself in the description.

You should not metaphorize the objects in the video.

A small, variable time lag between the action shown on screen and the subjects description can be introduced. Being familiar with the video (showing it thrice) reduced this time lag.

Three corrupt narratives with extensive English and Hindi code-mixing were removed from the dataset for instruction non-following. The last instruction was added after a subject metaphorized the triangles, describing the small one as चोर(thief) and the big as पुलिस (police).

The spoken narratives were manually transcribed as text, maintaining a standardised spelling. The sentences were manually time-stamped, and sentences were broken at pauses, roughly longer than 10 frames (0.67 seconds), or non-language sounds or breathing breaks.

Another difficulty was that the two main objects were a large red triangle (C1) and a small blue triangle (C2). Our speakers divided into three groups - one described the triangles predominantly in terms of size (six narratives), other in terms of colour (ten narratives) and few of them described in terms of both size and color or very vaguely without ample information (five narratives). Given the lack of prior knowledge of any kind, it is important that we have a coherent narrative for lexicon discovery. So the results are reported here only for the larger of these two sets - the colour distinguishing narratives.

3.1 Syllabic Analysis of Commentary corpus

The morphological root (lemma or stem) may be difficult to identify owing to variations. Associations are then diluted across a large number of

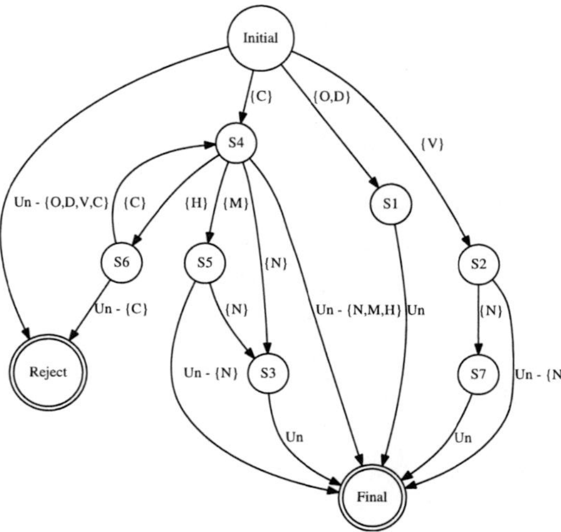

Figure 7: *FSM to identify syllables in Hindi.* Here $\{U_n\}$ = set of all unicode characters; $\{C\}$ = consonants (क, ख, ग,...); $\{V\}$ = set of all vowels (अ, आ, इ, ई, ...); $\{M\}$ = vowels on consonants (*mAtrAs*) (का, की, ...); $\{O\}$ = character ॐ ; $\{N\}$ = nasals (ः) ; $\{H\}$ = halant; $\{D\}$ = digits.

morphological variants. To avoid this, it may be useful to discover smaller units driven by the association itself.

A character in Indian language scripts is close to syllable and can be typically of the following form: C, V, CV, CCV and CVC, where C is a consonant and V is a vowel (Kishore et al., 2002).

In our **syllabic analysis**, we consider the narratives without any knowledge of the word boundaries, and discover syllable sequences with good correlation with the concepts. The syllables are based on the orthography and are defined as a unit of speech having one vowel sound, with or without surrounding consonants - implemented as a Finite State Machine (Fig. 7), based on the automata defined by Nikhil Joshi (Mukerjee and Joshi, 2011). We made a few modifications to include the nasal sounds and other characters such as digits and the character ॐ. S_1 to S_7 are the intermediate states with 'Reject' and 'Final' as two accept states. At the 'Reject' state the scanned input till now is rejected and the machine goes back to the 'Initial' state. At the 'Final' state, we declare the whole sequence of Unicode characters except the last one as a syllable and start searching for next syllable with the last character observed. Note that punctuation symbol, non recognised foreign characters and illegal Hindi characters are rejected ('Reject'

state).

Finally, the learning agent is not operating in a linguistic void. This enables it to identify the very common words that occur in a wide range of contexts. This is done by computing the frequencies on a large Hindi corpus (CFILT, 2010). The top 1000 words are considered frequent, and not analysed.

4 Object name association : Noun discovery

The object concepts being associated here are the two objects that are the primary agents in the scene. It is assumed that at any time, only the moving objects will be in attentive focus, and are more likely to be spoken about. Thus, the sentences that are spoken when the *big red triangle* (C1) is moving are associated with it, whereas those that are associated with the *small blue triangle* (C2) are considered as the contrastive set. We consider all lexical candidates occurring in sentences that overlap with the interval when either C1 or C2 is in motion as candidates for association with these concepts.

4.1 Association measures

For a label (lexeme) l, concept c, speaker s and time t, we define following probabilities.

Attention probability of the concept c for the speaker s at time t

$$P(c|s,t) = \begin{cases} 1 & \text{if } c \text{ is attended by speaker } s \\ & \text{at time } t \\ 0 & \text{otherwise} \end{cases}$$

$$P(l|s,t) = \begin{cases} 1 & \text{if } l \text{ is uttered by speaker } s \\ & \text{at time } t \\ 0 & \text{otherwise} \end{cases}$$

We define the Joint probability of a label l and an object category c as

$$J(l,c) = \frac{1}{T*|S|} * \sum_{t=1}^{T} \sum_{s \in S} P(c|s,t) * P(l|s,t)$$

Similarly, we define the concept probability of a concept c as

$$P(c) = \frac{1}{T*|S|} * \sum_{t=1}^{T} \sum_{s \in S} P(c|s,t)$$

263

	Contrastive Mutual Information (Syllabic)	Relative Frequency (Syllabic)	Contrastive Mutual Information (Word)	Relative Frequency (Word)
C1	लाल (*lāla*), "red" - 108.5 नीलात्रि (*nīlātri*) "'blue [frag]" - 28.9 नीलात्रिभुज (*nīlātribhuja*) "blue triangle" - 27.6	लाल (*lāla*) "red" - 9.5 त्रिभुज (*tribhuja*) "triangle" - 6.0 नीलात्रिभुज (*nīlātribhuja*) "blue triangle"- 4.5	अभी (*abhī*) "now" - 2.3 उसने (*usane*) "he/it" - 1.9 चतुर्भुज (*caturbhuja*) "square" - 1.4	लाल (*lāla*) "red" - 6.0 घूम (*ghūma*) "roam"- 5.0 त्रिभुज (*tribhuja*) "triangle" - 3.5
C2	नीला (*nīlā*) "blue" - 42.3 लालि (*lālatri*) "red+[frag]" - 25.9 लालत्रिभुज (*lālatribhuja*) "red triangle" - 25.2	नीला (*nīlā*) "blue" - 7.3 लालत्रिभुज (*lālatribhuja*) "red triangle"- 6.5 लाल (*lāla*) "red"- 6.0	अभी (*abhī*) "now" - 4.9 बक्से (*bakse*) "box(s)" - 2.9 रंग (*raṅga*) "color" - 2.8	त्रिभुज (*tribhuja*) "triangle" - 13.5 नीला (*nīlā*) "blue" - 10.0 अंदर (*andara*) "inside" - 2.5

Table 1: *Hindi lexeme association.* The top three associated lexemes (ranked based on the score obtained) for both the concepts (C1: big red triangle and C2: small blue triangle) are presented for syllabic analysis and word analysis. Word analysis makes use of the word boundary knowledge. Meaningful results are obtained in the syllabic analysis.

The label probability of a label l is given as

$$P(l) = \frac{f(l)}{\sum_l f(l)}$$

where $f(l)$ is the frequency of label l in the narrative corpus.

Based on the above, we used three association measures to identify the label maximally associated with a perceptual category.

1. *Conditional Probability* for a label l given a concept c is $P(l|c) = J(l, c)/P(c)$. However, this fails to penalise labels which co-occur with multiple categories; in practice it gave poor results and is not being reported in the results.

2. *Contrastive Mutual Information.* Mutual information is given as

$$MI(l, c) = J(l, c) * log(\frac{J(l, c)}{P(c) * P(l)})$$

It favours rare concepts and rare labels having sufficient degree of co-occurrence. Contrastive mutual information is the ratio of mutual information between label and concept for a binary contrastive situation.

3. *Relative Frequency*: This is a ratio of the label frequency when concept c is in focus (object is moving), versus the frequency (l) when c is not in focus.

4.2 Results

We report the top three associated lexemes for the concepts C1 (big red triangle) and C2 (small blue triangle) for both syllable analysis and for space demarcated orthographic words (Table 1). In syllable analysis, only k-grams occurring more than once are considered as candidate words, but for whole words, all words are candidates.

We observe that the key discriminants, "red" and "blue" are discovered as being more relevant for the large red triangle or the small blue triangle in the syllabic approach whereas such discovery is not made for the word analysis. Both Relative frequency and contrastive Mutual Information works reasonably well for syllabic analysis. Plain conditional probability results were poor and is not reported.

5 Conclusion

The main intent of this work was to investigate the possibility of computation with something smaller than orthographic words. This was motivated by the idea that in highly inflected languages such as Hindi, such structures may hold certain advantages, particularly for finding stems etc. It is certainly able to do this, but for our purposes, it also finds structures such as रहाहै (*rahA-hai*) which may be considered as an compound auxiliary unit. While the empirical demonstration here is very primitive and only scratches the surface of the problem, the results do suggest that this is an idea that deserves being investigated further as an alternative approach that shifts the boundaries at the very base of the model, and hence for the entire computational superstructure.

Here we have attempted to learn lexical associations with perceptual data, in an *Uninformed symbol grounding* approach. This implies that we discover any intermediate structures that arise, and minimize priors for the visual data. This is an ambitious task, and we have attempted this based on a meagre 39 second video, albeit a simple schematic one.

This work derives from cognitive ideas, but we do not consider many aspects such as shared attention, prosody and the simpler constructs in child-directed speech. It is possible that if one could collect corpora of this kind, we may obtain somewhat improved results. Nonetheless, it is surprising that even with such meagre input, many "correct" phrases emerge.

Once a few words are learned, the initial semantic models corresponding to these (often called *image schema*) become pivots around which other words can be learned (Kuhl, 2004). The lexeme learned serves as an index or a handle, so that future exposure to it invokes the same image schema, which is thereby defined more crisply and associated with a host of other concepts. Further, a few pivot words in an utterance helps the recovery of meaning for nearby elements.

This preliminary investigation suggests that the conviction that the orthographic word can be the only possible unit for computations in NLP may be worth revisiting. Many of the processes in language, particularly those involving acquisition without prior biases such as grammars and parse structures may be easier if we move down the scale from a word to a syllable. It is hoped that this preliminary exercise may induce others to take up this exploration so that such a process may expand and become an important part of NLP in times to come.

Acknowledgments

We would like to thank Dr. Uta Frith and Sarah White for providing and permitting us to use their psychological videos (Sarah J. White and Frith, 2011). We would like to thank Mr. Diwakar Chauhan for his help in collecting the narrations.

References

Lynne Cahill and Gerald Gazdar. 1997. The inflectional phonology of german adjectives, determiners, and pronouns. *Linguistics*, 35(2):211–246.

IIT Bombay CFILT. 2010. Ciil hindi corpus. http://www.cfilt.iitb.ac.in/Downloads.html.

David L. Chen and Ray J. Mooney. 2011. Learning to interpret natural language navigation instructions from observations. *Association for the Advancement of Artificial Intelligence (AAAI), Cambridge, MA.*

Alexander Simon Clark. 2001. *Unsupervised Language Acquisition: Theory and Practice.* Ph.D. thesis, September.

Mathias Creutz and Krista Lagus. 2007. Unsupervised models for morpheme segmentation and morphology learning. *ACM Transactions on Speech and Language Processing (TSLP)*, 4(1):3.

John A Goldsmith. 2010. Segmentation and morphology. *The Handbook of Computational Linguistics and Natural Language Processing*, 57:364.

Prashant Jalan. 2012. Dataset. http://www.cse.iitk.ac.in/users/grounded-lang/prashant/syllable/.

David Jurgens and Keith Stevens. 2011. Measuring the impact of sense similarity on word sense induction. In *Proceedings of the First Workshop on Unsupervised Learning in NLP*, pages 113–123.

SP Kishore, Rohit Kumar, and Rajeev Sangal. 2002. A data-driven synthesis approach for indian languages using syllable as basic unit. In *Proceedings of Intl. Conf. on NLP (ICON)*, pages 311–316.

P.K. Kuhl. 2004. Early language acquisition: cracking the speech code. *Nature reviews neuroscience*, 5(11):831–843.

Percy Liang, Michael I Jordan, and Dan Klein. 2009. Learning semantic correspondences with less supervision. In *Proceedings ACL '09 / IJCNLP Volume 1*, pages 91–99.

Jean M. Mandler. 2007. Actions organize the infant's world. In K. Hirsh-Pasek & R. M. Golinkoff, editor, *Action meets word: How children learn verbs*, pages 111–133. Oxford University Press, New York.

Christopher D Manning. 2011. Part-of-speech tagging from 97% to 100%: is it time for some linguistics? In *Computational Linguistics and Intelligent Text Processing*, pages 171–189.

Yannick Marchand, Connie R Adsett, and Robert I Damper. 2009. Automatic syllabification in english: A comparison of different algorithms. *Language and Speech*, 52(1):1–27.

Cynthia Matuszek, N. FitzGerald, L. Zettlemoyer, L. Bo, and D. Fox. 2012. A joint model of language and perception for grounded attribute learning. *Arxiv preprint arXiv:1206.6423*.

Amitabha Mukerjee and Nikhil Joshi. 2011. Word and phrase learning based on prior semantics. In *RANLP*, pages 616–621.

Sushobhan Nayak and Amitabha Mukerjee. 2012. Grounded language acquisition: A minimal commitment approach. In *COLING*, pages 2059–2076. Citeseer.

Hemant A Patil, Tanvina B Patel, Nirmesh J Shah, Hardik B Sailor, Raghava Krishnan, GR Kasthuri, T Nagarajan, Lilly Christina, Naresh Kumar, Veera Raghavendra, et al. 2013. A syllable-based framework for unit selection synthesis in 13 indian languages. In *Oriental COCOSDA held jointly with 2013 Conference on Asian Spoken Language Research and Evaluation (O-COCOSDA/CASLRE), 2013 International Conference*, pages 1–8. IEEE.

G. Pezzulo, L.W. Barsalou, A. Cangelosi, M.H. Fischer, K. McRae, and M.J. Spivey. 2011. The mechanics of embodiment: a dialog on embodiment and computational modeling. *Frontiers in psychology*, 2.

Hilke Reckman, Jeff Orkin, and Deb Roy. 2011. Extracting aspects of determiner meaning from dialogue in a virtual world environment.

Rosannagh Rogers Sarah J. White, Devorah Coniston and Uta Frith. 2011. Developing the frith-happe animations: A quick and objective test of theory of mind for adults with autism. Technical Report 149-154, Institute of Cognitive Neuroscience.

Deepali Semwal, Sunakshi Gupta, and Amitabha Mukerjee. 2014. Continuum models of semantics for language discovery. In *ICON*.

Luc Steels and Martin Loetzsch. 2012. The grounded naming game. *Experiments in Cultural Language Evolution. Amsterdam: John Benjamins*.

Francesca Stramandinoli, Davide Marocco, and Angelo Cangelosi. 2013. Grounding abstract action words through the hierarchical organization of motor primitives. In *Development and Learning and Epigenetic Robotics (ICDL), 2013 IEEE Third Joint International Conference on*, pages 1–2.

Accurate Identification of the Karta (Subject) Relation in Bangla

Arnab Dhar
Computer Science and Engineering
Indian Institute of Technology
Kharagpur, WB, India
arnab832007@gmail.com

Sudeshna Sarkar
Computer Science and Engineering
Indian Institute of Technology
Kharagpur, WB, India
shudeshna@gmail.com

Abstract

This paper presents an accurate identification of different types of *karta (subject)* in Bangla. Due to the limited amount of annotated data of dependency relations, we have built a baseline parser for Bangla using data driven method. Then a rule based post processor is applied on the output of baseline parser. As a result, average labeled attachment score improvement of *karta (subject)* based on F-measure on KGPBenTreeBank and ICON 2010 Treebank are 25.35% and 9.53%, respectively.

1 Introduction

Machine translation, anaphora resolution, question answering, etc., are the major application areas under natural language processing. While translating a source language to target language, the dependency structure of a sentence of source language plays a key role. Dependency grammar is a form of syntactic representation, where the syntactic structure consists of lexical elements linked by binary dependency relations. Dependency parsing involves syntactic analysis based on dependency representation (Nivre, 2005). The dependency structure is more suitable for handling highly inflected languages and the languages where word order is not very rigid.

The objective of our work is to build a high accuracy dependency parser for Bangla to facilitate Bangla to Hindi Machine Translation (BHMT) system. We have built a baseline dependency parser for Bangla using data driven method which implements inductive dependency parsing using the framework of Malt-Parser (Nivre et al., 2006; Nivre et al., 2007), in which we adapted the parameters and features for Bangla sentence parsing. We have analyzed different types of errors in the output of this baseline parser. We note that the correct identification of *karta (subject)* is a very important task for good quality BHMT system. We have analyzed different types of errors of *karta (subject)* and proposed some methods to rectify those errors by post processing the output of the baseline parser.

The rest of the paper is organized as follows. Section 2 describes the previous work related to dependency parsing. Section 3 describes the motivation and objective of our work. Section 4 describes the development of dependency parser for Bangla using data driven method. Section 5 presents rule based post processing. Section 6 presents the conclusion and the future directions of this research.

2 Literature Survey

Dependency parsing approaches can be broadly classified into three categories, namely, grammar driven, data driven and hybrid approaches. Grammar driven parsers have been developed based on context free dependency grammar (Hays, 1964) and constraint dependency grammar (Maruyama, 1990). Graph-based (McDonald et al., 2005) and transition-based parsing (Nivre et al., 2007) are some methods of data driven parsing. Marneffe et al. (2006) has proposed a system[1] which extracts dependency parses

---

[1] http://nlp.stanford.edu:8080/parser/

D S Sharma, R Sangal and J D Pawar. Proc. of the 11th Intl. Conference on Natural Language Processing, pages 267–276,
Goa, India. December 2014. ©2014 NLP Association of India (NLPAI)

from phrase structure parses of English sentences.

We now discuss work on parsing of Indian languages. Bharati et al. (1993) has described a constraint based Hindi parser by applying the Paninian framework (Bharati et al., 1995). Bharati et al. (2002) have also used the computational Paninian framework for parsing Hindi sentences (Bharati and Sangal, 1993) without using lakshan charts (discrimination nets) for nouns and verbs. Bharati et al. (2009) has described a two stage constraint based approach for parsing Hindi sentences. Dhar et al. (2012) has described a two-stage approach for parsing Bangla sentences.

The Tool Contests of ICON 2009 (Husain, 2009) and ICON 2010 (Husain et al., 2010) released three Indian language Treebanks for Hindi, Bengali and Telugu. The system of De et al. (2009b) had the best performance for Bangla. They used a grammar driven approach for parsing. They have used 500 demand frames in Bangla (De et al., 2009a) for parsing. A hybrid approach has been suggested by Chatterji et al. (2009) and Ghosh et al. (2010) where data driven parser used as a baseline system and followed by a rule based post processor. We have also followed a hybrid approach (Chatterji et al., 2009; Ghosh et al., 2010; Dhar et al., 2012), but in rule based post processing we mainly focus on correct identification of different types of *karta (subject)* in a sentence. Kolachina et al. (2010) and Kosaraju et al. (2010) have built a dependency parser for Indian languages using data driven method. For this, they have used the framework of MaltParser.

3 Motivation and Objective

The objective of our work is to build a high accuracy dependency parser for Bangla to facilitate BHMT system. The Bangla verb form does not depend on gender and number of *karta (subject)* of a sentence, but sometimes in Hindi the verb form depends on gender, number and person of the *karta (subject)* of a sentence. Bangla *karta (subject)* takes different types of vibhaktis (suffixes) such as কে (ke), র (ra), 0 (shUNya) [zero]. Identifying *karta (subject)* is a non-trivial task.

There is no one to one correspondence between Bangla sentence and its corresponding Hindi translation. Sometimes in Hindi, the *karta (subject)* is followed by post position markers but it is absent in corresponding Bangla sentence. For example, in Hindi, when the transitive verb is in the past tense a post position marker ने (ne) is added to the *karta (subject)*. So, correct identification of *karta (subject)* is very useful for good quality BHMT system.

4 Our Approach

In this section, we describe the development of our basic data driven parser for Bangla.

4.1 Development of Dependency Parser

In our work, we have developed a Bangla dependency parser using the framework of MaltParser. We follow the MaltParser settings for Bangla used in Kosaraju et al. (2010). They used Covington's algorithm and run this algorithm in a non-projective mode which allows crossing edges in dependency structure.

4.2 Feature Description for Data Driven Parser

Features are very important element of statistical modeling of data. We follow the basic features used in Kolachina et al. (2010), and we added two additional features, namely, named entity (NE) tag and semantic class (SC). Named entity tag indicates the class in which a proper noun belongs. Class here refers to person name, locations, organizations, times etc. Named entity tag also helps to identify that a proper noun is animate if that proper noun belongs to person name class. Semantic class contains semantic property of each word (mainly noun) i.e. it is either animate or inanimate. Sometimes, vibhakti (suffix) information fails to resolve the ambiguity in identifying *karta (subject)* and *karma (object)* in a sentence when both have same vibhakti (suffix). In this case, semantic property of the words help to resolve the ambiguity. Basic features refer to root (LEMMA), word (FORM), part-of-speech (POSTAG), chunk (CPOSTAG) and morphological (MORPH) features. Morphological features include lexical category, number, person, case and vibhakti (suffix). We have used some tools and resources, namely, Tokenizer, Morph Analyzer, Chunker, Head Computation, Named Entity Recognizer, Clause Boundary Identifier and Dictionary resource, for extracting the above features of word token in training and test data. We have used varying window length of basic features on LEFT, RIGHT, LEFTCONTEXT and RIGHTCONTEXT data structures which are used in MaltParser. The feature template for Bangla which is used in our experiments, is shown below.

1. A set of FORM features over LEFT and RIGHT of length 2.

2. A set of FORM features of dependent word and head word over LEFT and RIGHT of length 1.

3. A set of LEMMA features over LEFT and RIGHT of length 2.

4. A set of POSTAG features over LEFT and RIGHT of length 4.

5. A set of POSTAG features of dependent word and head word over LEFT and RIGHT of length 1.

6. A set of POSTAG features over LEFT-CONTEXT and RIGHTCONTEXT of length 1.

7. A set of CPOSTAG features over LEFT and RIGHT of length 1.

8. A set of CPOSTAG features of dependent word and head word over LEFT and RIGHT of length 1.

9. A set of combinations of the POSTAG and FORM features over LEFT and RIGHT of length 2.

10. A set of DEPREL (dependency relation) features over LEFT and RIGHT of length 1.

11. A set of DEPREL features of dependent word over LEFT and RIGHT of length 1.

12. A set of MORPH features over LEFT and RIGHT of length 3.

13. A set of NE features over LEFT and RIGHT of length 3.

14. A set of SC features over LEFT and RIGHT of length 3.

4.3 Data Set

We discuss the description of the data sets which are used in our experiments. The Treebanks used in our experiment are KGPBenTreeBank (Chatterji et al., 2013) and ICON 2010 Treebank (Husain et al., 2010). We follow the dependency relations used in Chatterji et al. (2013) and Husain et al. (2010). Dependency relations in KGPBenTreeBank are assigned between words in a sentence. Dependency relations in ICON 2010 Treebank are assigned between chunks in a sentence.

Chatterji et al. (2013) categorize these dependency relations in Bangla into three main types, namely, intrachunk relations, interchunk relations and interclause relations. Interchunk relations include *karta (subject)*, *karma (object)*, *karan (instrumental)*, *adhikaran (locative)* etc. *Karta (Subject)* is further subdivided into six categories, namely, *sadharan karta (general subject)*, *kriya sampadak karta (doer subject)*, *anubhav karta (experiencer subject)*, *paroksha karta (passive subject)*, *samanadhikaran (noun of proposition)* and *sahakari karta (associate subject)*. Data sets are shown in table 1.

	TB1	TB2
No of tags	55	37
No of training sentences	2905	1130
No of test sentences	322	150
Average sentence length	13.78	10.03

Table 1: Data sets
TB1: KGPBenTreeBank, TB2: ICON 2010 Treebank

4.4 Experimental Results

The metrics used to evaluate parser are labeled attachment score (LAS), unlabeled attachment score (UAS) and label accuracy (LA).

We have done experiments on KGPBenTreeBank using MaltParser settings and the features of Kolachina et al. (2010) and Kosaraju et al. (2010). The evaluation results are shown in the table 2. It is observed from the experiments that MaltParser settings and the features of Kosaraju et al. (2010) give the better result.

Experimental result of our data driven parser: We have done a set of experiments on KGPBenTreeBank and ICON 2010 Treebank using different combinations of basic features. The best experimental results on KGPBenTreeBank and ICON 2010 Treebank are shown in table 3. It is observed from

Systems	LAS	UAS	LA
S1	59.34	72.30	67.28
S2	61.19	72.97	69.36

Table 2: Evaluation results on KGPBenTree-Bank using settings of different systems
S1: Kolachina et al. (2010), S2: Kosaraju et al. (2010)

the experiments that the following feature combinations FORM, LEMMA, POSTAG, CPOSTAG, number, person, vibhakti, NE and SC give the best result. It is observed in table 3 that the above experiments give better result on ICON 2010 Treebank than KGPBen-TreeBank because sentences in KGPBenTree-Bank are very complex.

Corpus	LAS	UAS	LA
TB1	61.51	73.20	69.52
TB2	75.75	88.97	79.08

Table 3: Parser evaluation results for KGP-BenTreeBank and ICON 2010 Treebank

4.5 Analyzing the Mistakes of Data Driven Parser

We have analyzed the major errors that occur in the output of the baseline parser, and some of them are described below. The *sadharan karta (general subject)* is sometimes wrongly identified as *karma (object)*, the *vidheya karta (noun of proposition)* is wrongly identified as *sadharan karta (general subject)*, the *karma (object)* is wrongly identified as *sadharan karta (general subject)* or *kriya antargata bisheshya (part of relation)* and some *kriya antargata bisheshya (part of relation)* are wrongly identified as *sadharan karta (general subject)*.

Example sentence with mistake is shown below. In the following example, নগেন (nagena) [Nagen] is the *sadharan karta (general subject)* and নৃপতি (nRRipati) [king] is the *vidheya karta (noun of proposition)* of the verb ছিলেন (chhilena) [was]. But the data driven parser identifies both নগেন (nagena) [Nagen] and নৃপতি (nRRipati) [king] as *sadharan karta (general subject)*.

নগেন নামে এক নৃপতি ছিলেন. (nagena nAme eka nRRipati chhilena) [There was a king named Nagen.]

5 Rule Based Improvement

As discussed in previous section, the data driven approach has limited data. For this reason, the data driven approach fails to produce a good quality parser. Since it is time consuming to get a large annotated Treebank, can be improved the quality of the baseline parser in other way.

We used the parser with BHMT system and observed many errors related to adding incorrect vibhakti (suffix) to the noun phrases in the translated Hindi sentences. After analysis it is found that such errors occur because of incorrect identification of *karta (subject)* in the source Bangla sentences.

So, correct identification of *karta (subject)* is very useful for BHMT system. As an initial problem, we decided to work on accurate identification of *karta (subject)*. We have classified the major types of errors of *karta (subject)*. Some of them are discussed below. The relation between the noun phrase and an intransitive verb is often wrongly labeled as *karma (object)* instead of *karta (subject)*. We also observed several cases where two noun phrases related to the same verb, one of which is *sadharan karta (general subject)*, and the other is *vidheya karta (noun of proposition)*, are both wrongly identified as *karta (subject)*.

Some of these errors can be fixed if we have the argument structure and constraints associated with the different values. For these reasons, we have classified Bangla verbs based on valency, which is the number of arguments taken by a verb. The arguments of a verb include subject and all the objects of that verb. There are three basic classification of verbs based on valency, namely, intransitive, transitive and ditransitive. We have also classified the verbs based on action. The action of verbs indicates either physical action or mental action. We have created a list of mental verbs and a list of linking verbs, which are also known as copula verb, join the subject of a sentence with its complement.

We also created the karaka (case) frames of 29 common verbs with the help of Bangla corpus IL-POST (Baskaran et al., 2008). We study this corpus to know which verbs take which dependency relations and its relation with vibhakti (suffix), lexical type, named entity and semantic class. For Bangla, we follow the argument structure of karaka (case) frame for each verb entry used in Begum et al. (2008) and De et al.(2009a). We kept the following information in the karaka (case) frame for each verb entry, name of the verb, type of the verb i.e. transitive, intransitive, ditransitive, mental verb or linking verb, karaka (case) relations, necessity of the arguments which can be either mandatory (M) or desirable (D), vibhakti (suffix) information, lexical category, named entity tag and semantic class of each arguments. Table 4 shows the karaka (case) frame of the verb যা (yA) [go].

Dep rel	Necessity	Vibhakti	Lexical type	NET	Semantic class
k1d	M	0	NN |NNP |PRP	0 |PER-SON	Animate |Inani-mate
k7p	D	0|এ (e) |য় (Ya)	NN |NNP |PRP	0 |LO-CA-TION	0
k7t	D	0|এ (e) |য় (Ya) |পর (para)	PRP |NN	0 |TIMEX	0

Table 4: Karaka frame of the verb যা (yA) [go]
NN: Noun, NNP: Proper Noun, PRP: Pronoun, Dep rel: Dependency Relation, NET: Named Entity Tag, k1d: *kriya sampadak karta (doer subject)*, k7p: *sthanadhikaran (spatial locative)*, k7t: *kaladhikaran (temporal locative)*

In table 4, the features of three dependents, namely, *kriya sampadak karta (doer subject)*, *sthanadhikaran (spatial locative)*, and *kaladhikaran (Temporal Locative)* of the verb যা (yA) [go] are shown. The *karta (subject)* is mandatory (M) and the other two dependents are desirable (D) for this verb. The possible values of the features are separated by |(pipe) symbol. Zero (0) indicates that the corresponding value of the feature is either null or unknown.

We have proposed some methods to improve the accuracy of *karta (subject)* using karaka (case) frames and Bangla specific rules, which are discussed in the next sections.

5.1 Correction of Improper Relations using Karaka Frames

In this section, we discuss the methods for detection and correction of improper dependency relations in the output of the data driven parser using karaka (case) frame of the verbs.

Karaka (case) frame of a verb consists of mandatory karaka (case) relations and desirable karaka (case) relations. We first assign every mandatory karaka (case) relations in the karaka (case) frame of a verb to the noun phrases in a sentence. After assigning the mandatory karaka (case) relations to the noun phrases in a sentence, if there exists any noun phrases in a sentence that are not assigned by the mandatory karaka (case) relations then from these noun phrases in a sentence, some or all are assigned by the desirable karaka (case) relations in the karaka (case) frame. The detail study is discussed below.

Preprocessing steps of the Algorithm: A sentence in the output of the data driven parser is taken. We split up the sentence into n clauses using clause boundary identifier. We consider the karaka (case) frame of the verbs in each sentence.

Description of feature structure: Consider a noun phrase np with head $h(np)$ in the output of data driven parser is related to a verb vg with dependency relation dr. The relevant features of $h(np)$ refer to the root, person, number, vibhakti (suffix), lexical type, named entity tag and semantic class. The relevant features of vg refer to the root, person and vibhakti (suffix). The relevant features of dr in the karaka (case) frame refer to set of vibhakti (suffix), set of lexical type, set of named entity tag and set of semantic class.

Definition of Match: If *vibhakti*, *lexical_type*, *NET* and *semantic_class* of $h(np)$ belong to *vibhakti* list, *lexical_type* list, *NET* list and *semantic_class* list of dr in the karaka (case) frame of vg, respectively, then we say that this instance of the relation dr between $h(np)$ and vg are matched, else we call them unmatched. This procedure is outlined in Procedure Match.

This is explained in more detail below: Initially we mark each relation type ka_r_m in the karaka (case) frame $k\_f(vg_i)$ of each verb vg_i and each $h(np_j)$ in a sentence as unmatched. For each clause cl_i in a sentence s, we consider each $h(np_j)$ with dr_j and check whether the features of $h(np_j)$ and features of dr_j in $k\_f(vg_i)$ are matched. If it is matched then we mark both the $h(np_j)$ and dr_j in

Input: Features of $h(np)$ and features of dr in karaka (case) frame of vg.

let $fs(h(np))$ be the features of $h(np)$.
let $k\_f(vg)$ be the karaka (case) frame of verb vg.
let $fs(dr, k\_f(vg))$ be the features of dr in karaka (case) frame of vg.

if $fs(h(np)).vibhakti \in$
$fs(dr, k\_f(vg)).vibhakti$ *list* **and**
$fs(h(np)).lexical\_type \in$
$fs(dr, k\_f(vg)).lexical\_type$ *list* **and**
$fs(h(np)).NET \in fs(dr, k\_f(vg)).NET$
list **and** $fs(h(np)).semantic\_class \in$
$fs(dr, k\_f(vg)).semantic\_class$ *list* **then**
   return *Matched*
else
   return *Unmatched*

Procedure Match

$k\_f(vg_i)$ as matched. This method is shown in Algorithm 1.

Input: A sentence.
Resources used: Karaka (case) frame of verbs.
Step 1: Run data driven parser on the input sentence.
Step 2: Run clause boundary identifier on the input sentence.
Initialize: Mark each ka_r_m in the karaka frame and each $h(np_j)$ in a sentence as unmatched.

begin
   for *each* cl_i *in* s **do**
      for *each* np_j *in* cl_i **do**
         if dr_j *is in* $k\_f(vg_i)$ **then**
            if $fs(h(np_j))$ *matched with*
            $fs(dr_j, k\_f(vg_i))$ **then**
               mark both $h(np_j)$ and dr_j
               in $k\_f(vg_i)$ as matched .
      end
   end
end

Algorithm 1: Correction of Improper Relations using Karaka Frames- Part 1

If any unmatched ka_r_m exists in $k\_f(vg_i)$ then for each of unmatched ka_r_m in $k\_f(vg_i)$, first we consider mandatory karaka (case) relation Mr_j. Then we search for the np in a clause whose features of $h(np)$ are matched with the features of the unmatched Mr_j in $k\_f(vg_i)$. If multiple records are found, we pick up the first one f_np and assign that unmatched Mr_j to the dependency relation of $h(f\_np)$. We also assign vg_i to the parent of $h(f\_np)$. We mark both the $h(f\_np)$ and that unmatched Mr_j in $k\_f(vg_i)$ as matched.

Now we consider the desirable karaka (case) relation Dr_j. If Dr_j is found unmatched then, we search for the unmatched np in a clause whose features of $h(np)$ are matched with the features of the unmatched Dr_j in $k\_f(vg_i)$. If multiple records are found, we pick up the first one f_np and assign that unmatched Dr_j to the dependency relation of $h(f\_np)$. We also assign vg_i to the parent of $h(f\_np)$. We mark both the $h(f\_np)$ and that unmatched Dr_j in $k\_f(vg_i)$ as matched. This method is shown in Algorithm 2.

5.2 Correction of Improper Relations using Rules

In this section, we discuss the correction of improper *karta (subject)* relation in the output of baseline parser using Bangla specific rules. We observed and classified major types of errors and formulated 45 rules. Some of them are discussed below.

Observation 1: We observed that in several cases *anubhav karta (experiencer subject)* is incorrectly identified. We observed in the output of data driven parser is that some head of noun phrases with genitive marker (র) (ra), which is related to the noun of mental verbs with the relation *sambandha (genitive relation)*.

The *anubhav karta (experiencer subject)* takes genitive marker র (ra) and nominative marker. The *anubhav karta (experiencer subject)* is always animate entity. A noun phrase with genitive marker র (ra), it's semantic class is animate and it is followed by a mental verb, we say that this noun phrase is *anubhav karta (experiencer subject)*.

In the following example, আমার (AmAra) [my] with র (ra) vibhakti (suffix) is related to the mental verb শীত করছে (shIta karachhe) [getting cold] with the relation *anubhav karta (experiencer subject)*. Rule 1 takes care of this observation.

272

Input: Each token in the parsed sentence and each dependency types in the karaka (case) frame of verbs mark with matched or unmatched.

```
begin
    for each cl_i in s do
        /* Mandatory karakas         */
        for each Mr_j in k_f(vg_i) do
            if Mr_j is unmatched then
                Search for np in cl_i whose
                fs(h(np)) matched with
                fs(Mr_j, k_f(vg_i)).
                if one or more records are
                found then
                    pick up f_np.
                    assign Mr_j to dependency
                    relation of h(f_np) and
                    vg_i to parent of h(f_np).
                    mark h(f_np) and Mr_j
                    as matched.
        end

        /* Desirable karakas          */
        for each Dr_j in k_f(vg_i) do
            if Dr_j is unmatched then
                Search for unmatched np in
                cl_i whose fs(h(np)) matched
                with fs(Dr_j, k_f(vg_i)).
                if one or more records are
                found then
                    pick up f_np.
                    assign Dr_j to dependency
                    relation of h(f_np) and
                    vg_i to parent of h(f_np).
                    mark h(f_np) and Dr_j
                    as matched.
        end
    end
end
Output: Corrected output of the output
        of data driven parser.
```

Algorithm 2: Correction of Improper Relations using Karaka Frames- Part 2

আমার শীত করছে. (AmAra shIta karachhe) [I am getting cold.]

Observation 2: We observed several cases where two noun phrases related to the same linking verb, one of which is *sadharan karta (general subject)*, and the other is *vidheya karta (noun of proposition)*, are both wrongly

identified as *sadharan karta (general subject)*.

There are many sentences which have linking verbs. These sentences have different structures. We discuss one of them. A noun phrase with null marker is followed by a noun phrase with genitive marker র (ra) is followed by another noun phrase with null marker which is followed by a linking verb, we say that the first noun phrase is *sadharan karta (general subject)* and the third noun phrase is *vidheya karta (noun of proposition)*.

In the following example, এটাই (eTAi) [this] is *sadharan karta (general subject)* and বই (ba_i) [book] is *vidheya karta (noun of proposition)*. Both are related to the linking verb ছিল (chhila) [was]. Rule 2 takes care of this observation.

এটাই আমার বই ছিল. (eTAi AmAra ba_i chhila) [This was my book.]

Observation 3: We observed that a noun phrase is immediately followed by a verbal noun is identified as *karta (subject)* instead of *karma (object)* or *sthanadhikaran (place related locative)*.

Vibhakti (suffix) of the noun phrase is এ (e) or য় (Ya), type of the noun phrase is location and it is immediately followed by a verbal noun, we say that this noun phrase is *sthanadhikaran (place related locative)*.

In the following example, পাহাড়ে (pAhA.De) [hill] takes এ (e) vibhakti (suffix) and it is related to the verbal noun ওঠার (oThAra) [climbing] with relation *sthanadhikaran (place related locative)*. Rule 3 takes care of this observation.

পাহাড়ে ওঠার পর সে হাঁপিয়ে গেল. (pAhA.De oThAra para se hA.NpiYe gela) [He became tired after climbing the hill.]

Format of the rules: The rules have two parts, namely, LHS (left hand side) and RHS (right hand side), which are separated by ⇒ symbol. The format of the rule is shown below.

CNA1 < feature1: value1 /value2, feature2: value3, ... > CNA2 < feature1: value4, ... > CN CNB1 < feature1: value5, ... > ⇒ CNA1 < feature5: value6, ... > CNA2 < > CN* CNB1 < >*

LHS consists of chunks ids with features of the head of the chunk which are enclosed

within $< >$. Features are separated by ','
(comma). Multiple values of the features
are separated by '|'. Chunk id consists of
name of the chunk followed by number. Same
chunk names are distinguished by numbers i.e.
CNA1, CNA2. When new chunk name comes
it's number starts from 1 i.e. CNB1. '...' inside
the $< >$ indicates multiple combinations of different features with values can be included in
the rule. CN* indicates that there exists none
or more number of chunks in between CNA2
and CNB1. Those chunks have no significance
in the rule.

RHS consists of same number of chunk
ids as in LHS. If the features in LHS of the
rule are satisfied then the rule is fired and
the required modification of the value of the
features are done in RHS of the rule. Empty
$< >$ and features with values inside the $<
>$ after chunk id in the RHS indicate value
of the features remain same as the value of
the features of the corresponding chunk in
LHS and only value of those features of the
corresponding chunk in LHS are modified,
respectively.

Rule 1: *NP1 < pos: PRN |NN |NNP, vibhakti:* র *(ra), ner: 0 |PERSON, animacy: animate > VGF1 < class: mental verb > ⇒ NP1
< dep_rel: k1e, parent: VGF1 > VGF1 < >*
Rule 2: *NP1 < pos: PRN |NNP, vibhakti:
0 > NP2 < pos: PRN |NN |NNP, vibhakti:*
র *(ra) > NP3 < pos: NN |NNP, vibhakti: 0
> VGF1 < class: linking verb > ⇒ NP1 <
dep_rel: k1, parent: VGF1 > NP2 < > NP3
< dep_rel: k1s, parent: VGF1 > VGF1 < >*
Rule 3: *NP1 < pos: NN |NNP |PRP, vibhakti:* এ *(e) |য় (Ya), ner: 0 |LOCATION >
VGNN1 < pos: NN > ⇒ NP1 < dep_rel: k7p,
parent: VGNN1 > VGNN1 < >*

5.3 Experimental Results after Post Processing

We improved our results by post processing
the output of the data driven parser using
karaka (case) frames and Bangla specific rules.
Two different stages (baseline parser and after rule based post processing) of the overall
evaluation results are shown in table 5. LAS
and LA of different types of *karta (subject)*
are shown in table 6 and table 7, respectively.
Average LAS improvement of *karta (subject)*

based on F-measure on KGPBenTreeBank and
ICON 2010 Treebank are 25.35% and 9.53%,
respectively. Average LA improvement of
karta (subject) based on F-measure on KGP-
BenTreeBank and ICON 2010 Treebank are
25.5% and 9.79%, respectively.

6 Conclusion and Future Work

A hybrid approach of dependency parsing
for Bangla is presented in this paper. We
have combined two methods i.e. data driven
method and rule based post processing for development of dependency parser for Bangla.

In future, we may extend this work to other
dependency relations. We may analyze in
depth the errors of other dependency relations in order to get more effective features for
the development of more karaka (case) frames
and develop more Bangla specific rules. We
may improve dependency parser for Bangla
through unsupervised learning as manually
annotated data of dependency relations is very
limited.

Acknowledgment

This work is partially supported by the ILMT
project sponsored by TDIL program of MCIT,
Govt. of India. We would like to thank
all the members in Communication Empowerment Lab, IIT Kharagpur.

References

Sankaran Baskaran, Kalika Bali, Tanmoy Bhattacharya, Pushpak Bhattacharyya, Girish Nath
Jha, et al. 2008. A common parts-of-speech
tagset framework for indian languages. In *In
Proc. of LREC 2008*. Citeseer.

Rafiya Begum, Samar Husain, Lakshmi Bai, and
Dipti Misra Sharma. 2008. Developing verb
frames for hindi. In *LREC*.

Akshar Bharati and Rajeev Sangal. 1993. Parsing
free word order languages in the paninian framework. In *Proceedings of the 31st annual meeting
on Association for Computational Linguistics*,
pages 105–111. Association for Computational
Linguistics.

Akshar Bharati, Vineet Chaitanya, Rajeev Sangal,
and KV Ramakrishnamacharyulu. 1995. *Natural language processing: a Paninian perspective*.
Prentice-Hall of India New Delhi.

Akshar Bharati, Rajeev Sangal, and T Papi Reddy.
2002. A constraint based parser using integer
programming. *Proc. of ICON*.

	Baseline parser			After rule based post processing		
Corpus	LAS	UAS	LA	LAS	UAS	LA
TB1	61.51	73.20	69.52	65.38	74.64	73.22
TB2	75.75	88.97	79.08	80.35	89.63	84.20

Table 5: Evaluation results on KGPBenTreeBank and ICON 2010 Treebank

			Baseline parser			After rule based post processing		
corpus	deprel	#occ	recall	precision	F-measure	recall	precision	F-measure
TB1	k1	278	60.79	57.68	59.19	76.98	79.55	78.24
	k1a	5	20.00	100.00	33.33	100.00	83.33	90.91
	k1d	90	46.67	41.58	43.97	82.22	77.08	79.56
	k1e	10	20.00	28.57	23.53	100.00	66.67	80.00
	k1s	40	25.00	50.00	33.33	60.00	77.42	67.61
TB2	k1	166	76.85	72.51	74.62	86.06	81.61	83.78
	k1s	18	66.67	80.00	72.73	83.33	88.24	85.71

Table 6: Labeled attachment score of different types of *karta (subject)*

deprel: Dependency Relation, #occ: no of occurrences in the text, k1: *sadharan karta (general subject)*, k1a: *sahakari karta (associate subject)*, k1d: *kriya sampadak karta (doer subject)*, k1e: *anubhav karta (experiencer subject)*, k1s: *samanadhikaran (noun of proposition)*

		Baseline parser			After rule based post processing		
corpus	deprel	recall	precision	F-measure	recall	precision	F-measure
TB1	k1	62.95	59.73	61.29	80.22	82.90	81.54
	k1a	20.00	100.00	33.33	100.00	83.33	90.91
	k1d	56.67	50.50	53.41	88.89	83.33	86.02
	k1e	20.00	28.57	23.53	100.00	66.67	80.00
	k1s	25.00	50.00	33.33	60.00	77.42	67.61
TB2	k1	81.03	74.02	77.37	87.35	86.30	86.82
	k1s	66.67	80.00	72.73	83.33	88.24	85.71

Table 7: Label accuracy score of different types of *karta (subject)*

Akshar Bharati, Samar Husain, Meher Vijay, Kalyan Deepak, Dipti Misra Sharma, and Rajeev Sangal. 2009. Constraint based hybrid approach to parsing indian languages. In *PACLIC*, pages 614–621.

Sanjay Chatterji, Praveen Sonare, Sudeshna Sarkar, and Devshri Roy. 2009. Grammar driven rules for hybrid bengali dependency parsing. *Proceedings of ICON09 NLP Tools Contest: Indian Language Dependency Parsing, Hyderabad, India.*

Sanjay Chatterji, Tanaya Mukherjee Sarkar, Pragati Dhang, Samhita Deb, Sudeshna Sarkar, Jayashree Chakraborty, and Anupam Basu. 2013. A dependency annotation scheme for bangla treebank. In *Language Resources and Evaluation*.

Sankar De, Arnab Dhar, and Utpal Garain. 2009a. Karaka frames and their transformations for bangla verbs. In *31st All-India Conference of Linguists-2009 (to appear)*.

Sankar De, Arnab Dhar, and Utpal Garain. 2009b. Structure simplification and demand satisfaction approach to dependency parsing for bangla. In *Proc. of 6th Int. Conf. on Natural Language Processing (ICON) tool contest: Indian Language Dependency Parsing*, pages 25–31.

Marie-Catherine De Marneffe, Bill MacCartney, Christopher D Manning, et al. 2006. Generating typed dependency parses from phrase structure parses. In *Proceedings of LREC*, volume 6, pages 449–454.

Arnab Dhar, Sanjay Chatterji, Sudeshna Sarkar, and Anupam Basu. 2012. A hybrid dependency parser for bangla. In *10th Workshop on Asian Language Resources, COLING 2012*, page 55.

Aniruddha Ghosh, Amitava Das, Pinaki Bhaskar,

and Sivaji Bandyopadhyay. 2010. Bengali parsing system at icon nlp tool contest 2010. *ICON10 NLP TOOLS CONTEST: INDIAN LANGUAGE DEPENDENCY PARSING*, 960(7269):20.

David G Hays. 1964. Dependency theory: A formalism and some observations. *Language*, 40(4):511–525.

Samar Husain, Prashanth Mannem, Bharat Ram Ambati, and Phani Gadde. 2010. The icon-2010 tools contest on indian language dependency parsing. *Proceedings of ICON-2010 Tools Contest on Indian Language Dependency Parsing, ICON*, 10:1–8.

Samar Husain. 2009. Dependency parsers for indian languages. *Proceedings of ICON09 NLP Tools Contest: Indian Language Dependency Parsing*.

Sudheer Kolachina, Prasanth Kolachina, Manish Agarwal, and Samar Husain. 2010. Experiments with maltparser for parsing indian languages. *Proc of ICON-2010 tools contest on Indian language dependency parsing. Kharagpur, India*.

Prudhvi Kosaraju, Sruthilaya Reddy Kesidi, Vinay Bhargav Reddy Ainavolu, and Puneeth Kukkadapu. 2010. Experiments on indian language dependency parsing. *Proceedings of the ICON10 NLP Tools Contest: Indian Language Dependency Parsing*.

Hiroshi Maruyama. 1990. Structural disambiguation with constraint propagation. In *Proceedings of the 28th annual meeting on Association for Computational Linguistics*, pages 31–38. Association for Computational Linguistics.

Ryan McDonald, Fernando Pereira, Kiril Ribarov, and Jan Hajič. 2005. Non-projective dependency parsing using spanning tree algorithms. In *Proceedings of the conference on Human Language Technology and Empirical Methods in Natural Language Processing*, pages 523–530. Association for Computational Linguistics.

Joakim Nivre, Johan Hall, and Jens Nilsson. 2006. Maltparser: A data-driven parser-generator for dependency parsing. In *Proceedings of LREC*, volume 6, pages 2216–2219.

Joakim Nivre, Johan Hall, Jens Nilsson, Atanas Chanev, Gülsen Eryigit, Sandra Kübler, Svetoslav Marinov, and Erwin Marsi. 2007. Maltparser: A language-independent system for data-driven dependency parsing. *Natural Language Engineering*, 13(2):95–135.

Joakim Nivre. 2005. Dependency grammar and dependency parsing. Technical report, Växjö University.

Manipuri Chunking:
An Incremental Model with POS and RMWE

**Kishorjit Nongmeikapam[1],
Thiyam Ibungomacha Singh[2], Ngariyanbam Mayekleima Chanu[3],
Sivaji Bandyopadhyay[4]**

[1,2]Deptt. of Computer Science and Engg., MIT
Manipur University, Imphal, India
kishorjit.nongmeikapa@gmail.com
ibomcha.2007@rediffmail.com

[3]Deptt. of Education, Govt. of Manipur, India
mayekleima.ng@gmail.com

[4]Deptt. of Computer Science and Engg.
Jadavpur University, Kolkata, India
sivaji_cse_ju@yahoo.com

Abstract

This paper records the work of Manipuri Chunking by using the commonly use tool of Support Vector Machine (SVM). Manipur being a very highly agglutinative language have to be careful in selecting the features for running the SVM. An experiment is being performed with 35,000 words to check whether the POS tagged and the Reduplicated Multiword Expression (RMWE) can improve the Chunk identification. With a linguistic expert the Newspaper corpus is maintained to the Gold standard. The experimental system is designed as an incremental model with notation and identification in each stage. The Chunks are identified with a list of selected features. The chunks are very much related with the Part of Speech (POS) thus in the second stage POS tagging is done with the identified Chunks as one of the features which is again followed by the chunking. The third stage is with the RMWE. An experiment is again conducted with a list of carefully selected features for the SVM in order to find the Chunk with POS and RMWE as other features. Comparisons and evaluations are performed in each phase and the final output is drawn with completely tagged chunk Manipuri text. The experiment also identifies the POS tagging with a Recall (R) of 71.97%, Precision (P) of 87.16% and F-measure (F) of 78.84%. Apart from POS it also identifies the RMWE with a Recall (R) of 89.39%, Precision (P) of 98.33% and F-measure (F) of 93.65%. The system shows a final chunking with a Recall (R) of 70.45%, Precision (P) of 86.11% and F-measure (F) of 77.50%.

Keywords-SVM; POS; Chunk; RMWE; Manipuri

1. INTRODUCTION

Chunking is the process of identifying and labeling the simple phrases (it may be a Noun Phrase or a Verb Phrase) from the tagged output, of which the utterance of words for a given phrase forms as a chunk for this language [1]. The POS and RMWE might also play an important role in the SVM-based Manipuri chunking.

The present work of chunking is done in order to come up with a reliable chunking system for this under privilege Language. Manipuri language is a schedule Indian language widely spoken in the state Manipur, a North-Eastern part of India, and in the countries of Myanmar and Bangladesh. The Manipuri

D S Sharma, R Sangal and J D Pawar. Proc. of the 11th Intl. Conference on Natural Language Processing, pages 277–286,
Goa, India. December 2014. ©2014 NLP Association of India (NLPAI)

Language belongs to the Tibeto-Burman type of language and is a high agglutinative class of language.

The work reported here consists of a multi stage identification or incremental model of the Chunks. The first output is a chunk file which is followed by the POS then again a chunk tagged file. The RMWE is identified in the next incremental stage which is again followed by a Manipuri chunked file. The final output being the SVM based Manipuri chunk with POS and RMWE as one among the selected features.

The paper is arranged in such a way that the related works is listed in Section 2. Section 3 writes about the Reduplicated Multiword Expression (RMWE) which is followed by the Manipuri agglutinative explanation at Section 4. Section 5 describes the concept of Support Vector Machine (SVM) which is followed by the System design at 6. The experiment and evaluation is discussed at Section 7 and the conclusion is drawn at Section 8.

2. RELATED WORKS

Works on chunking are reported in [2] using Maximum Entropy Model. Apart from the above approaches, the CRF based chunking utilizes and gives the best of the generative and classification models. It resembles the classical model, in a way that they can accommodate many statistically correlated features of the inputs. And consecutively, it resembles the generative model, they have the ability to trade-off decisions at different sequence positions, and consequently it obtains a globally optimal labeling. It is shown in [3]-[4] that CRFs are better than related classification models. Parsing by chunks is discussed in [5]. Dynamic programming for parsing and estimation of stochastic unification-based grammars is mentioned in [6] and other related works are found in [7]-[9].

Manipuri Chunking using with CRF is reported in [1]. Until now, no works of SVM based chunking has ever been reported for the Manipuri language. Most of the previous works for other languages on this area make use of two machine-learning approaches for sequence labeling, namely CRF and the second approach as the sequence labeling problem as a sequence of a classification problem, one for each of the labels in the sequence.

The works on chunking can be observed applying both rule based and the probabilistic or statistical methods and for the Manipuri text chunking, the paper in [1] proposed a Conditional Random Field based approach.

3. REDUPLICATED MWE

Manipuri is a tonal language and Reduplicated Multiword Expressions are abundant. Work of RMWE identification Works for Manipuri is reported in [10] and using CRF in [11]. Reduplicated Multiword Expression is as defined in [12] as: 'reduplication is that repetition, the result of which constitutes a unit word'. The Classification for reduplicated MWEs in Manipuri mention in [12] is as follows: 1) Complete Reduplicated MWEs, 2) Mimic Reduplicated MWEs, 3) Echo Reduplicated MWEs and 4) Partial Reduplicated MWEs. Apart from these fours there are also cases of a) Double reduplicated MWEs and b) Semantic Reduplicated MWEs.

3.1 Complete Reduplicated MWEs

The single word or clause is repeated once forming a single unit regardless of phonological or morphological variations in the complete Reduplication MWEs. In the Manipuri Language these complete reduplication MWEs can occur as Noun, Adjective, Adverb, *Wh*-question type, Verbs, Command and Request. For example, মরিক মরিক (*'mərik mərik'*) which means *'drop by drop'*.

3.2 Partial Reduplicated MWEs

The second word carries some part of the first word as an affix to the second word, either as a suffix or a prefix for the partial reduplication. For example, চৎথোক চৎসিন (*'cət-thok cət-sin'*) means *'to go to and fro'*, শামী লানমী (*'sa-mi lan-mi'*) means *'army'*.

3.3 Echo Reduplicated MWEs

In the Echo RMWE the second word does not have a lexicon semantics and is basically an echo word of the first word. For example, *thk-si kha-si* means *'good manner'*. Here the first word has a dictionary meaning *'good manner´*

but the second word does not have a dictionary meaning and is an echo of the first word.

3.4 Mimic Reduplicated MWEs

The words are complete reduplication but the morphemes are onomatopoetic, usually emotional or natural sounds in the mimic RMWE. For example, করক করক ('khrək khrək') means *cracking sound of earth in drought*.

3.5 Double Reduplicated MWEs

The double Reduplicated MWE consists of three words, where the prefix or suffix of the first two words is reduplicated but in the third word the prefix or suffix is absent. An example of double prefix reduplication is ইমুন ইমুন মুনবা ('i-mun i-mun mun-ba') which means, *completely ripe*. It may be noted that the prefix is duplicated in the first two words while in the following example suffix reduplication take place, ঙৗশোক ঙৗশোক ঙৗবা ('ŋəω-srok ŋəω-srok ŋəω-ba') which means *shining white*.

3.6 Semantic Reduplicated MWEs

In the case of Semantic RMWE, both the reduplication words have the same meaning as well as the MWE. Such type of MWEs is very special to the Manipuri language. For example, পামবা কৈ ('pamba kəy') means *tiger* and each of the component words means *tiger*. Semantic reduplication exists in Manipuri in abundance as such words have been generated from similar words used by seven clans in Manipur during the evolution of the language.

4. MANIPURI AGGLUTINATIVENESS AND STEMMING

As in mention in [13] altogether 72 (seventy two) affixes are listed in Manipuri out of which 11 (eleven) are prefixes and 61 (sixty one) are suffixes. Table I shows the prefixes of 10 (ten number) because the prefix ম (mə) is used as formative and pronomial so only one is included and like the same way Table II shows the suffixes in Manipuri with only are 55 (fifty five) suffix in the table since some of the suffixes are used with different form of usage such as ওম

(gum) which is used as particle as well as proposal negative, দা (də) as particle as well as locative and না (nə) as nominative, adverbial, instrumental or reciprocal.

To prove with the point that Manipuri is highly agglutinative let us site an example word: "পুশিনহনজৱৰমগদবনিদকো" ("pusinhənjərəmgədəbənidəko"), which means "(I wish I) myself would have caused to bring in (the article)". Here there are 10 (ten) suffixes being used in a verbal root, they are "*pu*" is the verbal root which means "to carry", "*sin*" (in or inside), "*hən*" (causative), "*jə*" (reflexive), "*rəm*" (perfective), "*gə*" (associative), "*də*" (particle), "*bə*" (infinitive), "*ni*" (copula), "*də*" (particle) and "*ko*" (endearment or wish).

Prefixes used in Manipuri
অ, ই, ই, থু, চা, ত, থ, ন, ম and শে

TABLE I.   PREFIXES IN MANIPURI

Suffixes used in Manipuri
কন, কুম, কো, থরে, থৎ, থাই, খি, খোয়, গা, গনি, গী, গুম, ঙৈ, চা, চো, থ, থৎ, থেক, থোক, দা, দি, দুনা, দে, না, নতৈ, নি, নিং, নু নে, পী, ফাৎ, বা, বু মক, মল, মিন, মুক, লে, লা, লক, ল্ম, লি, লী, লু, লু লে, লো, লোয়, শনু, শি, শিং, শিন, শু, হৎ and হন

TABLE II.   SUFFIXES IN MANIPURI

The stemming of Manipuri words are stemmed by stripping the suffixes in an iterative manner as mention in [13]. As mention in above a Manipuri word is rich of suffixes and prefixes. In order to stem a word an iterative method of stripping is done by using the acceptable list of prefixes (11 numbers) and suffixes (61 numbers) as mention in table 1 and table 2 above.

5. CONCEPT OF SUPPORT VECTOR MACHINES (SVM)

The idea of Support vector machines (SVM) were first shared by Vapnik [14]. In the work of

[15] it is mention that Support Vector Machines is one of the new techniques for pattern classification which have been widely used in many application areas. The kernel parameters setting for SVM in training process impacts on the classification accuracy. Feature selection is another factor that impacts classification accuracy.

5.1 The optimal hyperplane (linear SVM)

SVM concepts for typical two-class classification problems can be discussed for explanation. Given a training set of instance-label pairs $(x_i, y_i), i = 1,2, \ldots, m$ where $x_i \in R^n$ and $y_i \in_i \{+1, -1\}$, for the linearly separable case, the data points will be correctly classified by,

$$\langle w.x_i \rangle + b \geq +1 \; for \; y_i = +1 \tag{1}$$

$$\langle w.x_i \rangle + b \leq +1 \; for \; y_i = -1 \tag{2}$$

Combining Eqs. (1) and (2) into one set of inequalities.

$$y_i(\langle w.x_i \rangle + b) - 1 \geq 0 \; \forall \; i = 1, \ldots m \tag{3}$$

The SVM finds an optimal separating hyperplane with the maximum margin by solving the following optimization problem:

$$Min_{w,b} \frac{1}{2} w^T w \tag{4}$$

$$subject \quad to: \qquad y_i(\langle w.x_i \rangle + b) - 1 \geq 0$$

It is known that to solve this quadratic optimization problem one must find the saddle point of the Lagrange function:

$$L_p(w, b, \alpha) = \frac{1}{2} w^T.w - \sum_{i=1}^m (\alpha_i \, y_i(\langle w.x_i \rangle + b) - 1) \tag{5}$$

Where, the α_i denotes Lagrange multipliers, hence $\alpha_i \geq 0$. The search for an optimal saddle point is necessary because the Lp must be minimized with respect to the primal variables w and b and maximized with respect to the non-negative dual variable α_i. By differentiating with respect to w and b, the following equations are obtained:

$$\frac{\partial}{\partial w} L_p = 0, \; w = \sum_{i=1}^m \alpha_i y_i x_i \tag{6}$$

$$\frac{\partial}{\partial w} L_p = 0, \; \sum_{i=1}^m \alpha_i y_i = 0 \tag{7}$$

The Karush Kuhn–Tucker (KTT) conditions for the optimum constrained function are necessary and sufficient for a maximum of Eq. (5). The corresponding KKT complementarity conditions are:

$$\alpha_i[y_i(\langle w.x_i \rangle + b) - 1] = 0 \; \forall \; i \tag{8}$$

Substitute Eqs. (6) and (7) into Eq. (5), then L_p is transformed to the dual Lagrangian $L_D(\alpha)$,

$$Max_\alpha L_D(\alpha) =$$

$$\sum_{i=1}^m \alpha_i - \frac{1}{2} \sum_{i,j=1}^m \alpha_i \alpha_j y_i y_j \langle x_i.x_j \rangle \tag{9}$$

$$subject \quad to \qquad \alpha_i \geq 0, i = 1, \ldots, m \quad and$$
$$\sum_{i=1}^m \alpha_i y_i = 0$$

To find the optimal hyperplane, a dual Lagrangian $L_D(\alpha)$ must be maximized with respect to non-negative α_i. This is a standard quadratic optimization problem that can be solved by using some standard optimization programs. The solution α_i for the dual optimization problem determines the parameters w^* and b^* of the optimal hyperplane. Thus, we obtain an optimal decision hyperplane $f(x, \alpha^*, b^*)$ (Eq. (10)) and an indicator decision function sign $[f(x, \alpha^*, b^*)]$.

$$f(x, \alpha^*, b^*) = \sum_{i=1}^m y_i \alpha_i^* \langle x_i, x \rangle + b^* - \sum_{i \in sv}^m y_i \alpha_i^* \langle x_i.x \rangle + b^* \tag{10}$$

In a typical classification task, only a small subset of the Lagrange multipliers α_i usually tends to be greater than zero. Geometrically, these vectors are the closest to the optimal hyperplane. The respective training vectors having nonzero α_i are called support vectors, as the optimal decision hyperplane $f(x, \alpha^*, b^*)$ depends on them exclusively.

5.2 The optimal hyper-plane for non-separable data (linear generalized SVM)

The above concepts can also be extended to the non separable case, i.e. when Eq. (3) there is no solution. The goal is to construct a hyperplane that makes the smallest number of errors. To get a formal setting of this problem we introduce the non-negative slack variables $\xi_i \geq 0, i = 1, \ldots, m$. Such that

$$\langle w.x_i \rangle + b \geq +1 - \xi_i \; for \; y_i = +1 \tag{11}$$

$$\langle w.x_i \rangle + b \leq -1 + \xi_i \; for \; y_i = -1 \tag{12}$$

In terms of these slack variables, the problem of finding the hyperplane that provides the minimum number of training errors, i.e. to keep the constraint violation as small as possible, has the formal expression:

$$\text{Min}_{w,b,\xi} \frac{1}{2} w^T w + C \sum_{i=1}^{m} \xi_i$$

$$(13)$$

subject to : $y_i(\langle w.x_i \rangle + b) + \xi_i - 1 \geq 0, \xi_i \geq 0$

This optimization model can be solved using the Lagrangian method, which is almost equivalent to the method for solving the optimization problem in the separable case. One must maximize the same dual variables Lagrangian $L_D(\alpha)$ (Eq. (14)) as in the separable case.

$$\text{Max}_\alpha L_D(\alpha) =$$
$$\sum_{i=1}^{m} \alpha_i - \frac{1}{2}\sum_{i,j=1}^{m} \alpha_i \alpha_j y_i y_j \langle x_i.x_j \rangle$$

$$(14)$$

subject to: $0 \leq \alpha_i \leq C, i, \dots, m$ and $\sum_{i=1}^{m} \alpha_i y_i = 0$

To find the optimal hyperplane, a dual Lagrangian $L_D(\alpha)$ must be maximized with respect to non-negative α_i under the constrains:

$$\sum \alpha_i y_i = 0 \ and \ 0 \leq \alpha_i \leq$$

$C, i = 1, \dots, m$. The penalty parameter C, which is now the upper bound on α_i, is determined by the user. Finally, the optimal decision hyperplane is the same as Eq. (10).

5.3 Non-linear SVM

The nonlinear SVM maps the training samples from the input space into a higher-dimensional feature space via a mapping function Φ, which are also called kernel function. In the dual Lagrange (9), the inner products are replaced by the kernel function (15), and the non-linear SVM dual Lagrangian $L_D(\alpha)$ (Eq. (16)) is similar with that in the linear generalized case.

$$\left(\Phi(x_i).\Phi(x_j) \right) \coloneqq k(x_i x_j)$$

$$(15)$$

$$L_D(\alpha) = \sum_{i=1}^{m} \alpha_i - \frac{1}{2}\sum_{i,j=1}^{m} \alpha_i \alpha_j y_i y_j k \langle x_i.x_j \rangle$$

$$(16)$$

subject to: $0 \leq \alpha_i \leq C, i = 1, \dots, m$ and $\sum_{i=1}^{m} \alpha_i y_i = 0$

This optimization model can be solved using the method for solving the optimization in the separable case. Therefore, the optimal hyperplane has the form Eq. (17). Depending upon the applied kernel, the bias b can be implicitly part of the kernel function. Therefore, if a bias term can be accommodated within the kernel function, the nonlinear SV classifier can be shown as Eq. (18).

$$f(x, \alpha^*, b^*) = \sum_{i=1}^{m} y_i \alpha_i^* \langle \Phi(x_i).\Phi(x_j) \rangle + b^*$$
$$= \sum_{i=1}^{m} y_i \alpha_i^* k(x_i, x) + b^*$$

$$(17)$$

$$f(x, \alpha^*, b^*) = \sum_{i \in sv} y_i \alpha_i^* \langle \Phi(x_i), \Phi(x_j) \rangle$$
$$= \sum_{i \in sv} y_i \alpha_i^* k(x_i, x)$$

$$(18)$$

Some kernel functions include polynomial, radial basis function (RBF) and sigmoid kernel, which are shown as functions (19), (20), and (21). In order to improve classification accuracy, these kernel parameters in the kernel functions should be properly set.

Polynomial kernel:

$$k(x_i, x_j) = \left(1 + x_i x_j \right)^d$$

$$(19)$$

Radial basis function kernel:

$$k(x_i, x_j) = exp\left(-\gamma \|x_i - x_j\|^2 \right)$$

$$(20)$$

Sigmoid kernel:

$$k(x_i, x_j) = tanh(kx_i.x_j - \delta)$$

$$(21)$$

6. WORKING OF THE SYSTEM

The experimental set up of the system uses SVM. The running of the training process has been carried out by YamCha[1] toolkit, an SVM based tool for detecting classes in documents and formulating the tagging task of Chunking, POS and RMWE as a sequential labelling problem. Here, the *pairwise* multi-class decision method and *polynomial kernel function* have been used. For classification, TinySVM-0.07[2] classifier is used which is readily available as open source for segmenting or labeling sequential data.

A list of possible features is prepared. The listed features are tried with different combinations in order to come up with the best possible Chunk. The best output Chunk is evaluated with the best features combinations. The features are again used for the SVM based POS tagging with the identified Chunk. The words are now tag with the POS. This POS is used as another feature for the chunking. This is

---

[1] http://chasen-org/~taku/software/yamcha/
[2] http://chasen-org/~taku/software/TinySVM/

done because chunking is very much related with POS.

Manipuri generally is a tonal language and is abundant with the RMWEs. RMWEs are identified using the SVM with features selected including POS and the identified Chunk. These identified RMWEs are used again for the identification of final Chunks in the text file. Fig.1 explains the System block diagram.

The Chunk tag is the I-O-B tagging as shown in Table III:

B-X	Beginning of the chunk word X
I-X	Intermediate or non beginning chunk word X
O	Word outside of the chunk text

TABLE III.   IOB CHUNK TAGGING

The processing and running of the SVM is shown on Fig. 2.

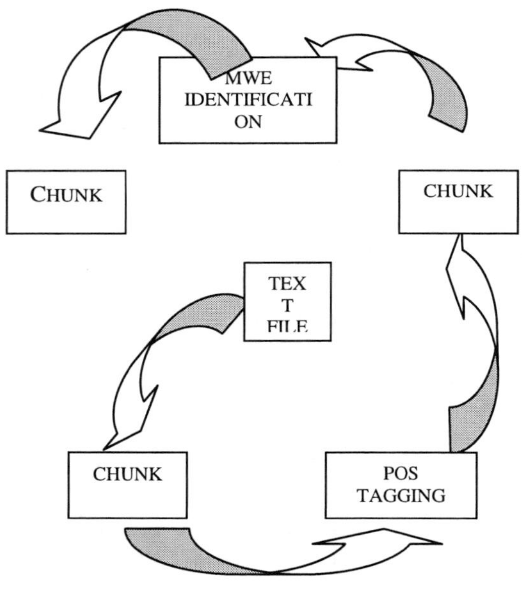

Figure 1.   System Block diagram

The input file for the first time is a training file which gives an output in the form of a model file and in the second run the input file is a testing file. The output file after running the SVM on the input testing file is a labeled file.

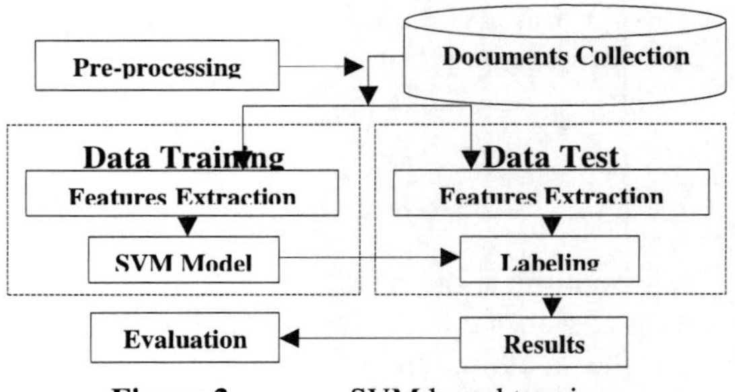

Figure 2.   SVM based tagging

The working of SVM is mainly based on the feature selection. The feature listed for the Chunk tagging is as follows:

$F= \{$ $W_{i-m}, \ldots, W_{i-1}, W_i, W_{i+1}, \ldots, W_{i+n},$ $SW_{i-m}, \ldots, SW_{i-1}, SW_i, SW_{i+1}, \ldots, SW_{i-n}$, **number of acceptable standard suffixes, number of acceptable standard prefixes, acceptable suffixes present in the word, acceptable prefixes present in the word, word length, word frequency, digit feature, symbol feature**$\}$

The details of the set of features that have been applied for Chunking in Manipuri text are as follows:

1. Surrounding words as feature: Preceeding word(s) or the successive word(s) are important in Chunking because these words play an important role in determining the Chunk of the present word.

2. Surrounding Stem words as feature: The Stemming algorithm mentioned in [13] is used. The preceding and the following stemmed words of a particular word can be used as features. It is because the preceding and the following words influence the present word Chunk.

3. Number of acceptable standard suffixes as feature: As mention in [13], Manipuri being an agglutinative language the suffixes plays an important in determining the Chunk of a word. For every word the number of suffixes are identified during stemming and the number of suffixes is used as a feature.

4. Number of acceptable standard prefixes as feature: Prefixes plays an important role for Manipuri language. Prefixes are identified during stemming and the prefixes are used as a feature.

5. Acceptable suffixes present as feature: The standard 61 suffixes of Manipuri which are identified is used as one feature. The maximum number of appended suffixes is reported as ten. So taking into account of such cases, for every word ten columns separated by a space are created for every suffix present in the word. A "0" notation is being used in those columns when the word consists of no acceptable suffixes.

6. Acceptable prefixes present as feature: 11 prefixes have been manually identified in Manipuri and the list of prefixes is used as one feature. For every word if the prefix is present then a column is created mentioning the prefix, otherwise the "0" notation is used.

7. Length of the word: Length of the word is set to 1 if it is greater than 3 otherwise, it is set to 0. Very short words are generally pronouns and rarely proper nouns.

8. Word frequency: A range of frequency for words in the training corpus is set: those words with frequency <100 occurrences are set the value 0, those words which occurs >=100 are set to 1. It is considered as one feature since occurrence of determiners, conjunctions and pronouns are abundant.

9. Digit features: Quantity measurement, date and monetary values are generally digits. Thus the digit feature is an important feature. A binary notation of '1' is used if the word consist of a digit else '0'.

10. Symbol feature: Symbols like $,% etc. are meaningful in textual use, so the feature is set to 1 if it is found in the token, otherwise 0. This helps to recognize Symbols and Quantifier number tags.

7. EXPERIMENT AND EVALUATION

The text document file collected from a Newspaper domain is cleaned for processing where the error and grammatical mistakes are minutely checked by a linguist. For the Chunking the expert also marks each word with the IOB format of Chunk. The marked Chunk texts are used for both training and testing.

Apart from the above IOB-Chunk marking the expert is asked to identify the POS and RMWE for the use in training and testing of the system.

The system used approximately 35000 words corpus for the training and testing. This corpus is considered as gold standard since an expert manually identifies the required Chunk, POS and RMWE words. Fig.3 shows the sample of POS and chunking which are marked by the expert.

....

....

চাওবনা NN B-X

অঙাংবা JJ B-X

লৈ NC I-X

অমা QT I-X

পায় VFC B-X

। SYM O

....

....

Figure 3. Sample of the words with POS and BOI chunking

Of the 35000 words 25000 words are considered for the training and the rest of the 10000 are used for the testing.

Evaluation is done with the parameter of Recall, Precision and F-score as follows:

$$\text{Recall, } R = \frac{\textit{No of correct ans given by the system}}{\textit{No of correct ans in the text}}$$

$$\text{Precision, } P = \frac{\textit{No of correct ans given by the system}}{\textit{No of ans given by the system}}$$

$$\text{F-score, } F = \frac{(\beta^2 + 1)\ PR}{\beta^2 P + R}$$

Where β is one, precision and recall are given equal weight.

7.1 Chunking using SVM

The first step of the identifying the chunks are performed using SVM. As mention in Section 6, the feature list is identified and performs the experiment with different combinations.

Notation	Meaning
W[-*i*,+*j*]	Words spanning from the ith left position to the jth right position
SW[-*i*, +*j*]	Stem words spanning from the ith left to the jth right positions
P[*i*]	The *i* is the number of acceptable prefixes considered
S[*i*]	The *i* is the number of acceptable suffixes considered
L	Word length
F	Word frequency
NS	Number of acceptable suffixes
NP	Number of acceptable prefixes
D	Digit feature (0 or 1)
SF	Symbol feature (0 or 1)

TABLE IV.   MEANING OF THE NOTATIONS

Feature	R(in %)	P(in %)	FS(in %)
W[-1,+1], SW[-1,+1], P[1], S[4], L, F, NS, NP, D, SF	**60.61**	**79.21**	**68.67**
W[-2,+1], SW[-2,+1], P[1], S[4], L, F, NS, NP, D, SF	60.61	79.21	68.67
W[-3,+1], SW[-3,+2], P[1], S[5], L, F, NS, NP, D	62.96	61.82	62.38
W[-1,+1], SW[-1,+1], P[1], S[4], L, F, NS, NP	50.00	82.50	62.26
W[-1,+2], SW[-2,+2], P[1], S[4], L, F, NS, NP, D, SF	41.67	73.33	53.14
W[-4,+4], SW[-4,+4], P[3], S[10], NS, NP	52.78	58.76	55.61
W[-1,+4], SW[-4,+1], P[2], S[6], L, NP, SF	39.39	69.33	50.24
W[-3,+3], SW[-2,+3], P[2], S[5], L, F, NS, SF	39.39	67.53	49.76
W[-1,+3], SW[-3,+3], P[3], S[9], L, F, D, SF	31.25	74.47	44.03

TABLE V.   SYSTEM PERFORMANCE WITH VARIOUS FEATURE COMBINATIONS FOR CHUNK IDENTIFICATION

The Table no V shows some of the best combinations of the results with Table no IV showing the explanations of the symbols used. The best combination for the chunking after performing the experiments is as follows:

F= { W $_{i-1}$, W $_i$, W $_{i+1}$, SW$_{i-1}$, SW$_i$, SW$_{i+1}$, **upto one acceptable prefixes present in the word, upto four acceptable suffixes present in the word, word length, word frequency, number of acceptable standard suffixes, number of acceptable standard prefixes, digit feature, symbol feature}**

The above feature combination shows the Recall (**R**) of **60.61%**, Precision (**P**) of **79.21%** and F-measure (**F**) of **68.67%**.

7.2 SVM based POS tagging with Chunks

Similar with the experiment mention in [16] is performed in order to identify the best suitable features. Same experimental set up is used for the SVM based POS tagging. The best F-measure among the results of the SVM based POS tagging is considered the best result. This happens with the following feature set:

F= {W$_{i-2}$, W $_{i-1}$, W $_i$, W $_{i+1}$, SW$_{i-1}$, SW$_i$, SW$_{i+1}$, **number of acceptable standard suffixes, number of acceptable standard prefixes, acceptable suffixes present in the word, acceptable prefixes present in the word, word length, word frequency, digit feature, symbol feature}**

The experimental result of the above feature combination shows the best result, which gives the Recall (**R**) of **71.43%**, Precision (**P**) of **83.11%** and F-measure (**F**) of **77.67%**.

Now with the identification of the Chunk as mention in the above Section 7.2, the SVM based POS tagging is added with an extra feature in the above mention feature set. This is done in order to compare with the new set of POS tagging.

The new experimental result shows a better Recall (**R**) of **71.97%**, Precision (**P**) of **87.16%** and F-measure (**F**) of **78.84%**.

7.3   SVM based Chunking with POS tag

The experiment is followed with the chunking of the system again. In this experiment the identified chunk by the SVM in the previous run is neglected instead replace with the gold standard Chunk data for training and testing. This is done so that a better result is yield. Also the previous chunking was done in order to make comparison and only to identify the POS. In the repeat of the experiment with the additional feature of POS tagging, the new feature combination becomes as follows:

F= {POS, W $_{i-1}$, W $_i$, W $_{i+1}$, SW$_{i-1}$, SW$_i$, SW$_{i+1}$, **upto one acceptable prefixes present in the word, upto four acceptable suffixes present in the word, word length, word frequency, number of acceptable standard suffixes, number of acceptable standard prefixes, digit feature, symbol feature}**

The new experimental result shows a better Recall (**R**) of **61.36%**, Precision (**P**) of **81.82%** and F-measure (**F**) of **70.13%**.

7.4 SVM based RMWE identification with Chunk and POS features

From the list of features listed in Section 6 the experiment of SVM based RMWE identification is performed. In this experimental run the Chunks and POSs are included as other features. The POS plays an important role in the identification of the RMWE also the Chunks. Like before different features combination are tried to identify the best possible combination.

Feature	R(in %)	P(in %)	FS(in %)
C*, POS**[-1,+1], W[-1,+1], SW[-1,+1], P[1], S[4], L, F, NS, NP, D, SF	**89.39**	**98.33**	**93.65**
C, POS[-1,+1], W[-2,+1], SW[-2,+1], P[1], S[4], L, F, NS, NP, D, SF	87.88	96.67	92.06
C, POS[-1,+1], W[-3,+1], SW[-3,+2], P[1], S[5], L, F, NS, NP, D	87.76	84.78	86.24
C, POS[-1,+1], W[-1,+1], SW[-1,+1], P[1], S[4], L, F, NS, NP	82.58	90.83	86.51
C, POS[-2,+2], W[-1,+2], SW[-2,+2], P[1], S[4], L, F, NS, NP, D, SF	78.87	76.87	77.86
C, POS[-3,+3], W[-4,+4], SW[-4,+4], P[3], S[10], NS, NP	64.78	63.99	64.38
POS[-1,+1], W[-1,+4], SW[-4,+1], P[2], S[6], L, NP, SF	56.82	66.96	61.48
C, W[-3,+3], SW[-2,+3], P[2], S[5], L, F, NS, SF	50.76	59.82	54.92
W[-1,+3], SW[-3,+3], P[3], S[9], L, F, D, SF	52.88	50.14	51.47

* C= Chunk and **POS[-*i*, +*j*]= POS spanning from the ith left position to the jth right position

TABLE VI.   SYSTEM PERFORMANCE WITH VARIOUS FEATURE COMBINATIONS FOR RMWE IDENTIFICATION

The best feature selection for SVM based RMWE identification is as follows:

F= { C, POS[-1,+1], W $_{i-1}$, W $_i$, W $_{i+1}$, SW$_{i-1}$, SW$_i$, SW$_{i+1}$, upto one acceptable suffixes present in the word, upto four acceptable prefixes present in the word, word length, word frequency, number of acceptable standard suffixes, number of acceptable standard prefixes, digit feature, symbol feature}

From the Table no VI we can observe that the best result is with the Recall (**R**) of **89.39%**,

Precision (**P**) of **98.33%** and F-measure (**F**) of **93.65%**.

7.5 SVM Based Chunking after POS tagging and RMWE identification

The best result of the experiment for chunking so far without the RMWE is Recall (**R**) of **61.36%**, Precision (**P**) of **81.82%** and F-measure (**F**) of **70.13%**.

The features combination was as follows:

F= {POS, W $_{i-1}$, W $_i$, W $_{i+1}$, SW$_{i-1}$, SW$_i$, SW$_{i+1}$, upto one acceptable prefixes present in the word, upto four acceptable suffixes present in the word, word length, word frequency, number of acceptable standard suffixes, number of acceptable standard prefixes, digit feature, symbol feature}

After the identification of RMWE the new feature set becomes the following:

F= {RMWE, POS, W $_{i-1}$, W $_i$, W $_{i+1}$, SW$_{i-1}$, SW$_i$, SW$_{i+1}$, upto one acceptable prefixes present in the word, upto four acceptable suffixes present in the word, word length, word frequency, number of acceptable standard suffixes, number of acceptable standard prefixes, digit feature, symbol feature}

The best result for chunking with POS tagging and the Reduplicated MWEs is shown in table 7.

Model	Recall	Precision	F-Score
SVM	**70.45**	**86.11**	**77.50**

TABLE VII.   CHUNKING RESULT WITH POS AND RMWE

8. CONCLUSION

So far, the SVM based chunking work on Manipuri is not reported. An incremental approach is designed where the Chunking is performed at the first stage which is followed by the POS tagging, which is again followed by Chunking. With Chunk and POS as features it tagged the RMWE and Chunking is followed to find the final result.

In this experiment the POS tagging with the identified Chunks shows a Recall (**R**) of **71.97%**, Precision (**P**) of **87.16%** and F-measure (**F**) of **78.84%**.

The RMWE identification also shows a Recall (**R**) of **89.39%**, Precision (**P**) of **98.33%** and F-measure (**F**) of **93.65%**.

Comparatively, from the initial stage Chunking with a Recall (**R**) of **60.61%**, Precision (**P**) of **79.21%** and F-measure (**F**) of **68.67%** the Chunking improves to a Recall (**R**) of **70.45%**, Precision (**P**) of **86.11%** and F-measure (**F**) of **77.50%** with the POS and RMWE in this incremental way of Chunking experiment.

The complexity still lies with the agglutinative nature of the language. Other algorithms for the improvement of the score can also be worked on for different domains.

REFERENCES

[1] Kishorjit N,Chiranjiv Ch, Nepoleon K,Biakchungnunga Varte and Sivaji B., "Chunking in Manipuri Using CRF", International Journal on Natural Language Computing (IJNLC) Vol. 3, No.3, June 2014, pp. 121-127.

[2] Rob Koeling, 2000, "Chunking with Maximum Entropy Models", Proceedings of CoNLL-2000 and LLL-2000, pp. 139-141, Lisbon, Portugal, 2000

[3] Fei Sha and Fernando Pereira,"Shallow Parsing with Conditional Random Fields".In the Proceedings of HLT-NAACL 2003.

[4] John Lafferty, Andrew McCallum and Fernando Pereira, Conditional Random Fields: Probabilistic Models for Segment-ing and Labeling Sequence Data.

[5] S. Abney. Parsing by chunks. In R. Berwick, S. Abney, and C. Tenny, editors, *Principle-based Parsing*. Kluwer Academic Publishers, 1991.

[6] S. Geman and M. Johnson. Dynamic programming for parsing and estimation of stochastic uni_cation-based grammars. In *Proc. 40th ACL*, 2002.

[7] A. Ratnaparkhi. A linear observed time statistical parser based on maximum entropy models. In C. Cardie and R. Weischedel, editors, *EMNLP-2*. ACL, 1997.

[8] E. F. T. K. Sang. Memory-based shallow parsing. *Journal of Machine Learning Research*, 2:559.594, 2002.

[9] T. Zhang, F. Damerau, and D. Johnson. Text chunking based on a generalization of winnow. *Journal of Machine Learning Research*, 2:615.637, 2002.

[10] Kishorjit, N., Bandyopadhyay, S.: Identification of Reduplicated MWEs in Manipuri: A Rule based Approached. In: Proceedings of 23rd International Conference on the Computer Processing of Oriental Languages (ICCPOL-2010), pp 49-54, Redwood City, San Francisco, USA(2010)

[11] Kishorjit, N., Dhiraj, L., Bikramjit Singh, N., Mayekleima Chanu, Ng. & Sivaji, B., (2011) *Identification of Reduplicated Multiword Expressions Using CRF*, A. Gelbukh (Ed.):CICLing 2011, LNCS vol.6608, Part I, Berlin, Germany: Springer-Verlag, pp. 41–51

[12] Singh, Ch. Y.:Manipuri Grammar, Rajesh Publications, pp.190-204, Delhi, India (2000)

[13] Kishorjit, N., Bishworjit, S., Romina, M., Mayekleima Chanu, Ng. & Sivaji, B., (2011) *A Light Weight Manipuri Stemmer*, In the Proceedings of Natioanal Conference on Indian Language Computing (NCILC), Chochin, India

[14] Vapnik, Vladimir N.:The Nature of Statistical Learning Theory. Springer (1995).

[15] Cheng-Lung Huang & Chieh-Jen Wang: A GA-based feature selection and parameters optimization for support vector machines, Expert Systems with Applications 31 (2006), doi:10.1016/j.eswa.2005.09.024, Elsevier Publication, pp. 231–240 (2006)

[16] Kishorjit, N. , Nonglenjaoba, L., Roshan, A., Shenson Singh, T., Naongo Singh T. and Sivaji Bandyopadhyay, „Transliterated SVM Based Manipuri POS Tagging", David C. Wylt et al (Ed): Advances in Intelligent and Soft Computing, Berlin, Germany: Springer-Verlag, pp.989-999, 2012

Segmentation of Navya-Nyāya Expressions

Arjuna S.R. & Amba Kulkarni
Department of Sanskrit Studies,
University of Hyderabad,
Hyderabad, India
arjunsr1987@gmail.com, apksh@uohyd.ernet.in

Abstract

Navya-Nyāya (NN), a school of Indian logic and philosophy, has evolved a sophisticated language to deal with verbal cognition, logic and epistemology. This language is known for its use of long compounds, productive use of secondary derivational suffixes, and a special technical vocabulary. In this paper we present a specially designed domain specific splitter to split the NN compounds into its components. The performance of this splitter is tested on a set of compounds from a Navya-Nyāya text. The result on the test data show a recall rate of 91%. While the average number of splits was around 50, in 75% cases the correct split was found to be the first one.

1 Introduction

Segmentation is an important task in NLP. Sanskrit being dominated by an oral tradition, most Sanskrit texts are written as a continuous stream of phonemes, without any explicit word or sentence boundaries. Moreover such a continuous stream of phonemes also undergoes phonetic changes at the juncture of word boundaries. This makes the task of splitting more complex.

There are noteworthy efforts in the field of Sanskrit segmentation in the past years. Hyman (2008) describes a Finite State Transducer (FST) for the Paninian sandhi rules. Huet (2009) has discussed the segmentation in Sanskrit in detail and has built an efficient Finite State Automata (FSA) based segmenter. Mittal (2010) describes two approaches; one using FST and the other one based on Optimality Theory, by defining the posterior probability function to choose among the valid splits. Kumar et al. (2010) used different posterior probability function and obtained better results. Natarajan and Charniak (2011) proposed sandhi splitting based on the Dirichlet process. Mittal, Kumar et al. and Natarajan and Charniak report the evaluation of their segmenters on a Sanskrit text corpus developed by the Sanskrit Consortium of India. This corpus does not contain very long sequences of characters. In the real corpus such as plays by Kālidāsa, strings containing more than hundred phonemes are very common. The possible segmentations of such strings run into millions. Huet and Goyal (2013) describe the design of a lean interface for displaying all such possible segmentation in a compact form.

Sandhi operation (phonological changes at the juncture of word boundaries) is just one reason behind the long strings of characters in Sanskrit. Rich derivational morphology that results due to possible recursion in the morphological process is another reason behind the long character sequences. This recursion is discussed in (Akshar Bharati, 2006) and (Kulkarni and Shukl, 2009). For quick reference, we produce the automaton showing the recursion in Sanskrit morphology in Figure 1.

As can be seen from this figure, theoretically the possible forms are infinite in number and owing to the finite size of the alphabet these forms can potentially be of infinite length. This figure does not show the compound formation in Sanskrit. Compound formation is typically binary where each component can in turn be a compound. The re-

D S Sharma, R Sangal and J D Pawar. Proc. of the 11th Intl. Conference on Natural Language Processing, pages 287–294,
Goa, India. December 2014. ©2014 NLP Association of India (NLPAI)

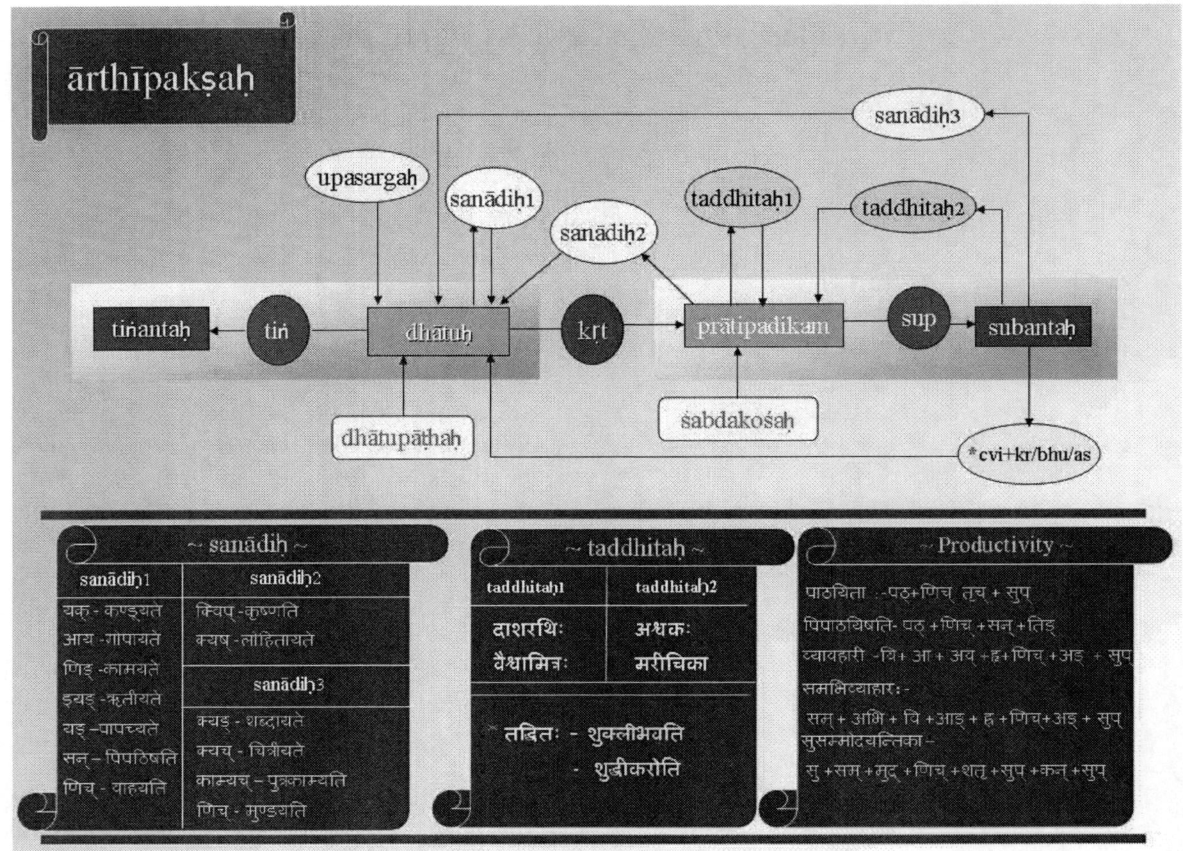

Figure 1: Recursion in Sanskrit Morphology

Table 1: Legends

dhātu (verbal root)	*dhātupāṭha*(list of verbal roots)	*kṛt*(non-finite verbal suffix)
samāsa(compound)	*sanādi*(derivational suffixes)	*śabdakoṣa*(lexicon)
subanta(noun)	*sup*(nominal suffix)	*taddhita*(secondary derivational suffix)
tiṅ(finite verbal suffix)	*tiṅanta*(finite verb form)	*upasarga*(verbal prefix)

cursion in the definition results in compounds of arbitrary long length. The Navya-Nyāya 'Neo-Logic' (NN) school of Indian tradition sees the culmination of productive compound formation in the form of compounds running through pages. The components of such compounds are typically formed with more than one *taddhita* (secondary derivational) suffixes. Such compounds also use the technical language of NN.[1]

Here is an example of linguistic expression in Navya-Nyāya (NNE) involving a compound with ten components:

samavāya-sambandha-avacchinna-gandhatva-avacchinna-gandha-niṣṭha-ādheyatā-nirūpita-adhikaraṇatāvatī.

For the sake of readability we have split the components, but in the printed texts this is written as a single word with underlying phonological changes as

samavāyasambandhāvacchinnagandhatvāva-cchinnagandhaniṣṭhādheyatānirūpitādhikara-ṇatāvatī.

In spite of a continuous stream of characters in-

---

[1]The technical language of NN consists of a few conceptual terms and it provides a mechanism to express the underlying cognitive structure corresponding to a linguistic expression in an unambiguous way.

volving arbitrarily long compounds, the cognitive structure being described by such an expression helps a human mind to understand them.

All the efforts related to segmentation described earlier had focused on general Sanskrit texts. But for much more complex and domain-specific inputs like NNE, which is known for long compounds, use of technical vocabulary, and productive use of secondary derivational suffixes (*taddhita*) a specially trained segmenter is needed.

In this work we present a segmenter specially designed for NNE taking into consideration the special vocabulary and secondary derivative suffixes NNE uses. In the next section we describe the earlier work on handling NNEs. In the third section we describe our approach for getting the desired splits on the top. The fourth section discusses the results of the experiment, followed by the conclusion.

2 Heritage segmenter for NNEs

The first attempt to develop a domain specific segmenter for NNE is reported in Arjuna and Huet (2014). A sample of NNEs was collected from the *Āloka* commentary on *Tarkasaṅgraha* (Varadacharya, 2007) and *Pañcalakṣaṇīsarvasvam* (Sastry, 2005). There were 49 NNEs from the *Āloka* commentary and 352 NNEs from *Pañcalakṣaṇīsarvasvam*. These compounds were split manually into the components, which formed the Gold data. We also extracted the possible combination of secondary derivational suffixes that are found in the selected texts. Figure 2 shows these possible combinations.

Arjuna and Huet (2014) summarize the difficulties in handling NNEs as follows.

1. Long compounds,

2. Technical vocabulary,

3. Productive use of *taddhita* suffixes, and

4. Semi-formal compound structure.

Heritage segmenter was enhanced to handle the first three of these. The salient features of the enhancement are

1. New databanks were added for the inflected forms of the *taddhita* suffixes viz. *-tal* (Fem), *-tva* (Neu), and *-matup* (in all three genders),

2. Technical vocabulary of Navya-Nyāya was acquired in the lexicon,

3. Segmenter transitions were added to accommodate *taddhita* productivity,

4. Word mode for single *pada* was used rather than sentence in order to curb overgeneration, and

5. Lean interface described in Huet and Goyal (2013) was used in order to share the huge solution space.

The recall of the segmenter after this enhancement was 91%.

There are three major problems with this segmenter. The first problem is with the number of solutions. For a typical NNE, this segmenter results with thousands and sometimes even millions of solutions. Typically the topmost row gives the most probable choice, and thus for a compound with n components, n choices by the user results in the proper split of the compound. Thus even if there are thousands of solutions, the user has to look for only a handful of choices. Hence this problem is not that serious.

The second problem with this segmenter is with the granularity. The Heritage segmenter is enhanced with the technical vocabulary of Navya-Nyāya. But still it splits many technical words into components. For example, *nirūpita*, *avacchinna*, *samānādhikaraṇa* etc. are split as *ni-rūpita*, *ava-chinna*, and *samāna-adhi-karaṇa* respectively. In order to understand the NNEs that uses their own specialised technical vocabulary with well-defined meanings, to get a broader picture of a NNE, a Naiyāyika(Indian Logician) prefers to hide the derivation of these technical terms, and would like to see these words as single units without any splits.

Thus while admitting the fact that the term *samānādhikaraṇa* is compositionally equal to *samāna-adhi-karaṇa*, or *vyadhikaraṇa* being compositionally equal to *vi-adhi-karaṇa*, these being technical terms, a *Naiyāyika* would like

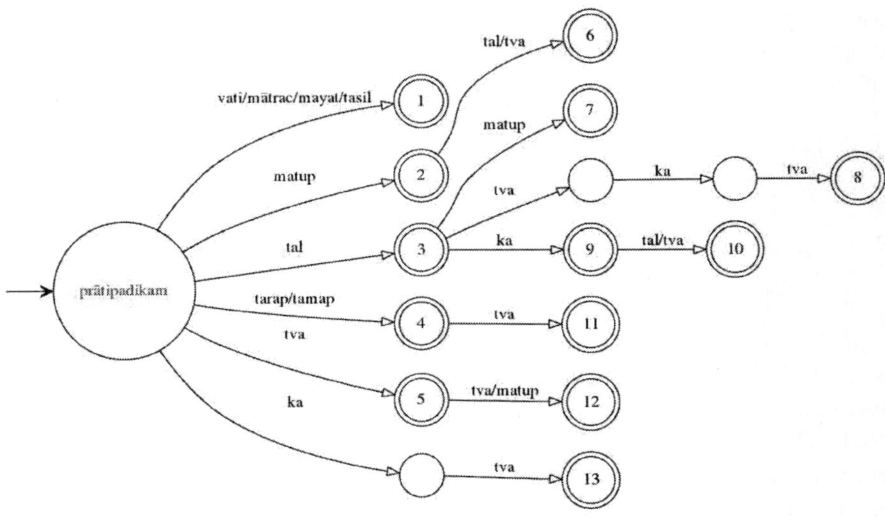

Figure 2: FSA showing possible *taddhita* suffixes in NNE

to look at them as a packaged entry with all the analysis hidden. Treating such technical words as a single unit would also result in lesser choices for user selection.

Finally while the user interface has its own advantages, one would like to reduce the user interaction as far as possible, pushing the correct solution to the top or preferably the first position for further automatic processing of such compounds.

The major focus of the work reported in this paper is on how to take advantage of the specialised vocabulary in order to prune out the bad solutions or push them down and push the better solutions to the top. This time we used Sanskrit morphological analyser developed at the University of Hyderabad, mainly because of more familiarity and easy accessibility. In the next section we describe our approach.

3   Our approach

As a first step we used the same domain specific corpus that was collected by Arjuna and Huet (2014) and enhanced the morphological analyser of University of Hyderabad to handle the *taddhita* suffixes reported in Figure 2. The 49 NNEs obtained from the *Āloka* commentary were used for the development purpose, and we set aside the 352 NNEs for testing purpose. All the collected NNEs were further analysed for their components.

The statistics showed that there are a few nominal stems, which are not typical of NN, but occur frequently as a component in the NNEs. These stems are *artha, ātmaka, pūrvaka, vidha, kara* etc. which occur as a final component of a compound (*in fine compositi* or *samāsa-uttarapada*). Figure 3 shows the sequence of *taddhita* suffixes after which these stems occur.

We extended our morphological analyser to handle the derivational morphology – both the secondary derivations as well as frequent compounds shown in Figures 2 and 3 respectively. We also extended our lexicon with the technical terms in Navya-Nyāya.

The treatment of some *taddhita* suffixes such as 'ka' and the treatment of *kṛt* suffixes (primary derivatives) in compound formation need special mention. The *taddhita* suffix 'ka' results in a *bahuvrīhi* (exo-centric) compound. Such compounds, since have their head external to the compound, they are more like adjectives, and thus can decline in all the three genders. For example, if 'the one which has smoke as the cause' refers to a masculine referent, it will have the form *dhūmahetuka*, and if the referent is a feminine, it will have the form *dhūmahetukā*. But such words when occur as a component of a compound as iics (*in initio compositi* or *samāsa-pūrvapada*), they will always undergo an

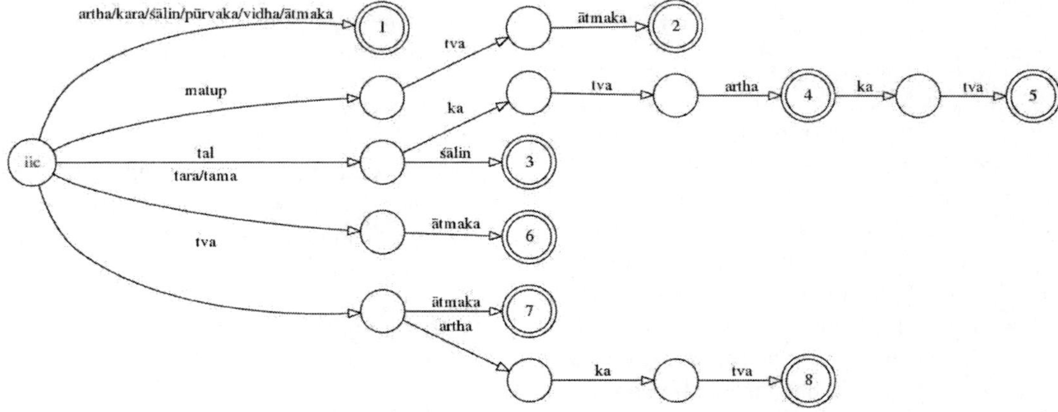

Figure 3: ifcs(*in fine compositi* or *samāsa-uttarapada*) found in NNEs

operation of **puṁvadbhāva**[2] resulting into a word in masculine gender. Thus we get *dhūmahetuka* as an iic form, whatever be the object it refers to.

Similarly, the adjectives formed by the non-finite suffixes (*kṛt* suffixes) such as *ṇvul* (in the sense of an agent), or *kta* (in the sense of an object) also take the base form[3] when they occur in the compounds as iics. For example, a compound 'a lady cook' will be *pācakastrī*, and not *pācikāstrī*.

The Paninian *sūtra* that governs the formation of such compounds is *puṁvatkarmadhārayajātīyadeśīyeṣu* 6.3.42. We have enhanced our morphological analyser to take into account this phenomenon.

With this we were able to split all 49 examples from the development data. The possible splits in each case were in thousands and in 3 cases even in tens of thousands. This was mainly because, though the technical terms were available in the lexicon, machine in addition to this lexical term, also showed all possible splits of such words. For example, for *sambandhāvacchinna* is split as *sambandha+avacchinna*, and also as *sambandha+ava+chinna*, and so on. The second one should be pruned out since in the context of

Navya-Nyāya, *avacchinna* being a technical word need not be split further. So we needed a splitter that discards splits of morphologically analysable long words. We describe below the algorithm of this splitter followed by its performance on the development data as well as the test data.

3.1 SCL-NN splitter

The main aim of this algorithm is to reduce the over-generation ensuring that the imposed conditions do not under-generate, and at the same time push the most preferred solution to the top of the possible solutions. The over-generation and the under-generation are measured only with respect to the NN vocabulary. Thus a split which is an over-generation from the NN point of view, may be a genuine split in the classical Sanskrit. The salient features of the algorithm are stated below.

1. The sandhi rules are of the form $u \rightarrow v + w; f$, where f indicates the number of cases this rule was observed in the Sanskrit Consortium Corpus. Even if u is just a concatenation of v and w, without any underlying phonetic change, then also we treat it as a sandhi rule, in order to use the frequency information.

   The splitter scans the string from the left and looks for the longest match each time. At each juncture, typically more than one sandhi rules are available. In case there are more than one applicable rules, the one with longer u is preferred over the smaller ones, and in case of two rules with matching u of

---

[2]Condition for *puṁvadbhāva* is given in Paninian *sūtra* 6.3.42. It says - In *Karmadhāraya* compound and in those cases where the second component of a compound ends in a *jātīya* or *deśīya* suffix, the word in feminine gender will assume the *bhāṣitapuṁska* 'expressed as a masculine' form.

[3]The technical term for such base forms in Sanskrit is the one with *puṁvadbhāva*

equal length, the one with higher frequency is chosen.

For example, consider a string *adhikaraṇatānirūpaka*. There are two possible splits for this viz. *adhikaraṇatā + nirūpaka*, and *adhikaraṇatā + anirūpaka*. The first split corresponds to a split rule *ān → ā + n*, which involves a window of two phonemes. The second split corresponds to the split rule *ā → ā + a* which involves a context of only one phoneme. The preference for two phoneme rule produces the split *adhikaraṇatā + nirūpaka* before other split *adhikaraṇatā + anirūpaka*. Thus we ensure that the most likely output appears before the other solutions.

There are four ways in which *ā* can be split, viz. *a+a, a+ā, ā+a,* and *ā+ā*, with frequency of occurrence in the Sanskrit Consortium corpus as 3413, 2072, 350 and 233 respectively. Machine uses these rules in the decreasing order of frequency to ensure that the most probable one is reported first.

2. Preference is given to the NN vocabulary over others. The expression *avacchinnakāryatā* is wrongly split as *avacchinnaka+āryatā* as the more preferred one rather than the correct split *avacchinna+kāryatā*, because greedy match prefers the longest component in the beginning. As we notice, the phoneme sequence 'ka' can be potentially a *taddhita* suffix of the first component as well as an initial sequence of a NN technical vocabulary. We resolve such conflicts in favour of the NN technical vocabulary.

3. The splitting is done recursively following the depth first search. The boundaries at which the string is split and the split rule used are remembered. The string is not split twice at the same place with the same split rule. This is to avoid the further splitting of bigger components, and thereby increasing the precision. For example, a string *pratiyogitānirūpaka* is split as *pratiyogitā+nirūpaka* with a rule *ān → ā+n*, and as *pratiyogitā+anirūpaka* with a rule *ā → a+a*. But

the string *pratiyogitā* is not split further as *prati+yogitā*, nor is *nirūpaka* as *ni+rūpaka*.

4. The treatment of *puṁvadbhāva* in the derivational morphology of compounds help in pruning out the wrong splits such as *niṣṭhā+ādheyatā* for *niṣṭhādheyatā*. *Puṁvadbhāva* ensures that we get only the valid split *niṣṭha+ādheyatā*.

5. A split is considered to be an over-generation if it does not contain any NN technical term.

4 Analysis of the Result

Our aim was to improve the precision and also get the correct solution to the top of the list. We first discuss the precision and recall.

4.1 Precision and Recall

We tested 49 NNEs collected from *Āloka* commentary of *Tarkasaṅgraha* on both the Heritage splitter as well as the SCL-NN splitter. The number of possible splits produced by both these splitters is reported in Table 2 and Table 3.

As is obvious from the tables, the number of solutions is reduced drastically, increasing the precision.

The result of the test data of 352 examples (see table 4) from *Pañcalakṣaṇīsarvasvam* also confirms that the new algorithm prunes out all irrelevant splits. The recall is around 91%, which is as good as the recall of Heritage splitter, and at the same time the number of solutions is reduced substantially, increasing the precision almost 100 times.

4.2 Correct Solution

We compared all the generated solutions with the manually tagged Gold data. The table 5 shows

No of Solutions	No of Cases
0-100	10
101-1,000	15
1,001-100,000	18
> 100,000	5
Time-out	1
Total	49

Table 2: Number of solutions of Heritage Splitter

No of Solutions	No of Cases
0-5	14
6-10	11
11-100	18
101-1000	5
> 1000	1
Total	49

Table 3: Number of solutions of SCL-NN Splitter

No of Solutions	No of Cases	Percentage
0-5	196	55.7
6-10	56	15.9
11-100	72	20.4
101-1000	13	3.6
> 1000	3	1
No Split	12	3.4
Total	352	100

Table 4: Number of solutions of SCL-NN Splitter

the number of cases corresponding to the position of the correct solution among the ones produced. In 42 cases, the first solution produced by the machine was the correct one. Later we tested examples from *Pañcalakṣaṇīsarvasvam*. The results are shown in the table 6.

Here is a sample input consisting of 319 phonemes and the first solution with 40 components, which happens to be the correct one.

Input:
*sādhyatāvacchedakasambandhāvacchinna-
sādhyatāvacchedakāvacchinnapratiyogitāka-
sādhyābhāvatvaviśiṣṭhanirūpitasādhyatāvaccheda-
kasambandhāvacchinnasādhyatāvacchedakāva-
cchinnapratiyogitākasādhyābhāvavṛttisādhya-
sāmānyīyapratiyogitvatadavacchedakatvānya-
tarāvacchedakasambandhāvacchinnanirūpakatā-*

Position	No. of Cases	Percentage
1	42	86
2	2	4
3	4	8
7	1	2
Total	49	100

Table 5: Position of the correct solution in the Development data

Position	No. of cases	Percentage
1	264	75
2-5	42	11.9
6-10	6	1.7
11-100	7	2.0
>101	2	0.6
No Split	12	3.4
No-correct solution	19	5.4
Total	352	100

Table 6: Position of the correct solution in the test data

*nirūpitaniravacchinnādhikaraṇatāśrayavṛttitva-
sāmānyābhāvaḥ*

Output:
*sādhyatā- avacchedaka- sambandha- avacchinna-
sādhyatā- avacchedaka- avacchinna- pratiyo-
gitāka- sādhya- abhāvatva- viśiṣṭha- nirūpita-
sādhyatā- avacchedaka- sambandha- avacchinna-
sādhyatā- avacchedaka- avacchinna- pratiyo-
gitāka- sādhya- abhāva- vṛtti- sādhya-
sāmānyīya- pratiyogitva- tad- avacchedakatva-
anyatara- avacchedaka- sambandha-avacchinna-
nirūpakatā- nirūpita- niravacchinna-
adhikaraṇatā- āśraya- vṛttitva- sāmānya-
abhāvaḥ*

5 Conclusion

Thus with the help of domain specific words, greedy approach in selecting the long components, avoiding alternative splits of an already split segment, and selecting the more frequent split rule over the less frequent one, and ensuring that the solution thus produced has at least one NN term in it, we could increase the precision, without compromising the recall, and also we could push the correct solution to the top of the list.

While building this splitter, we took an advantage of the fact that the NNEs are unambiguous. The algorithm does not allow more than one splits at the same position. Thus if a string w is split as $w_0 + w_1 + w_2 + w_4$, it can not be split again as $w_0 + w_5 + w_6 + w_4$. This splitter therefore, can not be used to split the strings that are ambiguous, since it does not allow two different ways of splitting a substring.

References

[Akshar Bharati2006] V Sheeba Akshar Bharati, Amba P Kulkarni. 2006. Building a wide coverage morphological analyser for sanskrit: A practical approach. First National Symposium on Modeling and Shallow Parsing of Indian Languages,IIT Mumbai.

[Arjuna and Huet2014] S. R. Arjuna and Gérard Huet. 2014. Semi-automatic analysis of Navya-Nyāya compounds, SALA-30, Hyderabad. SALA-30, University of Hyderabad.

[Holz and Biemann2008] Florian Holz and Chris Biemann. 2008. Unsupervised and knowledge-free learning of compound splits and periphrases. In *CICLing*, pages 117–127. Lecture Notes in Computer Science - Springer.

[Huet and Goyal2013] Gérard Huet and Pawan Goyal. 2013. Design of a lean interface for Sanskrit corpus annotation. In Dipti Mishra Sharma, Rajeev Sanghal, Karunesh Kr.Arora, and B.K.Murthy, editors, *Proceedings of ICON-2013*, pages 177–186.

[Huet2009] Gérard Huet. 2009. Sanskrit Segmentation, South Asian Languages Analysis Roundtable xxviii, Denton, Texas. South Asian Languages Analysis Roundtable XXVIII.

[Hyman2008] Malcolm D. Hyman. 2008. From Paninian Sandhi to Finite State Calculus. In *Sanskrit Computational Linguistics*, pages 253–265.

[Koehn and Knight2003] Philipp Koehn and Kevin Knight. 2003. Empirical Methods for Compound Splitting. In *Proceedings of the Tenth Conference on European chapter of the Association for Computational Linguistics - Volume 1*, pages 187–193. Association for Computational Linguistics.

[Kulkarni and Shukl2009] Amba Kulkarni and Devanand Shukl. 2009. Sanskrit morphological analyser: Some issues. *Indian Linguistics*, 70(1-4):169–177. in the Festscrift volume of Bh. Krishnamoorty.

[Kumar et al.2010] Anil Kumar, Vipul Mittal, and Amba.P.Kulkarni. 2010. Sanskrit Compound Processor. In *Sanskrit Computational Linguistics*, pages 57–69.

[Macherey et al.2011] Klaus Macherey, Andrew M. Dai, David Talbot, Ashok C. Popat, and Franz Och. 2011. Language-independent Compound Splitting with Morphological Operations. In *Proceedings of the 49th Annual Meeting of the Association for Computational Linguistics: Human Language Technologies - Volume 1*, pages 1395–1404. Association for Computational Linguistics.

[Mittal2010] Vipul Mittal. 2010. Automatic Sanskrit Segmentizer Using Finite State Transducers. In *ACL (Student Research Workshop)*, pages 85–90.

[Natarajan and Charniak2011] Abhiram Natarajan and Eugene Charniak. 2011. S^3 - Statistical Sandhi Splitting. In *IJCNLP*, pages 301–308.

[Sastry2005] Sriram Sastry. 2005. *Pañcalakṣaṇī-sarvasvam*. Bharatiya Vidya Sansthan, Varanasi.

[Varadacharya2007] Varadacharya. 2007. *Tarkasaṅgraha with Āloka commentary*. Arya Grantha Prakashan, Mysore.

Handling Plurality in Bengali Noun Phrases

Biswanath Barik
Innovation Lab Kolkata
Tata Consultancy Services
1B, Ecospace, Rajarhat, Kolkata – 700156
biswanath.barik@tcs.com

Sudeshna Sarkar
Department of Computer Science & Engineering
Indian Institute of Technology Kharagpur
Kharagpur, India -721302
shudeshna@gmail.com

Abstract

Plurality of a Bengali Noun Phrase (NP) is not always determined by the plurality of its governing member (or the *head*). It is often seen that an NP is plural but the plurality is indicated through qualifiers or other means whereas the head noun has the singular form. In such scenarios, the plurality of the NP is determined by analyzing its non-head members or from other components (or context) of the sentence. Classification of Bengali NPs with respect to plurality is important for many applications including Machine Translation (MT) from Bengali to other language (say Hindi). The plurality of NPs in other languages like Hindi and English is always indicated by plurality of head irrespective of the plurality of the qualifiers. In this paper, we have investigated different sources from where the plurality information of head noun (or NP) can be collected and proposed an approach to automatically classify Bengali NPs by analyzing the identified sources.

1 Introduction

Identification of grammatical properties (or features) of different syntactic units of a sentence is a major task of Natural Language Understanding (NLU). Text processing tasks like context-sensitive spell checking, Named Entity Recognition (NER), Word Sense Disambiguation (WSD), parsing etc., which require detail grammatical description of the context, spend a considerable amount of processing time to identify such syntactico-semantic properties of the input sentence. Rule-based MT, on the other hand, not only explores such grammatical properties through multi-level analyses of a source language input sentence to decode the meaning, but also try to map them correctly to the target language so that a grammatically correct target sentence is generated. Therefore, identification of different grammatical properties of interest is a prerequisite for many text processing jobs and associated applications.

Unfortunately, the essential grammatical properties of different components of the sentence are not always directly expressed in a language. Some of them are hidden in the context or are missing. The hidden features can be identified by analyzing the context. For example, the *gender* of an anaphoric personal pronoun can be determined, in general, by the *gender* of the referring noun. In some languages (e. g., Hindi), the *gender* of such pronouns can be traced by analyzing the verb group (VG) as the inflection of the VG is based on the *gender* of the subject.

The problem of identifying hidden grammatical features becomes difficult if the context is very short or is syntactically ambiguous. In such a case, the most logical interpretation of the context has to be identified which requires domain knowledge and pragmatic interpretation of the context.

During the syntactic analysis of Bengali sentences (for developing a rule-based Bengali to Hindi Machine Translation or BHMT), we observe some mismatches on grammatical features between Bengali and Hindi constituents. Bengali and Hindi have strong agreements within/among constituents on some grammatical features like *person* and *case*. In Bengali, these features are identifiable by analyzing the corresponding surface words (nouns and verbs) and, therefore, are also available for target (Hindi) sentence generation. However, some

D S Sharma, R Sangal and J D Pawar. Proc. of the 11th Intl. Conference on Natural Language Processing, pages 295–304,
Goa, India. December 2014. ©2014 NLP Association of India (NLPAI)

other features like *number* and *gender* which play an important role in Hindi sentence generation or agreement are either hidden in some cases or are missing in Bengali side. For example, the *gender* feature is usually missing in Bengali – neither the verb takes *gender* inflection not it can be traced from the morphological analysis of the subject noun phrase. The *number* or plurality information, on the other hand, is sometimes hidden in the context. Such missing/hidden features in source Bengali sentences have to be determined correctly so that they are used in correct target (Hindi) sentence generation which improves the translation accuracy of Bengali-Hindi MT. Figure 1 shows that the Google's Bengali-Hindi translation system fails to handle plurality issue statistically and thus produces incorrect translation.

Figure 1: Incorrect Bengali-Hindi Translation due to plurality

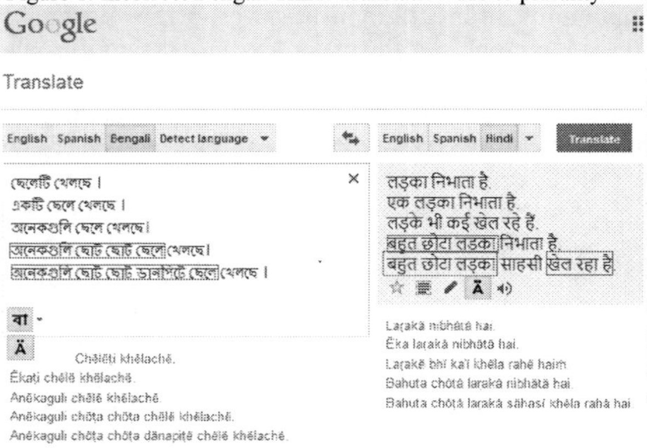

In this work, we discuss how to determine the *plurality*, an implicit morphological feature of Bengali Noun Phrases (NPs). In general, the head nouns of NPs hold the plurality and the NPs are accordingly classified as *singular* or *plural*. However, we have observed that the head nouns of Bengali NPs do not always take plural inflections. In such cases, the plurality of the NP is determined from the contextual information of the sentence. The automatic text processing and allied applications like Machine Translation thus require a computational approach to automatically identify the plurality of Bengali NPs. Sufficient resources like domain knowledge and infrastructures for analyzing large or inter-sentence context are required to handle such issues exhaustively. Using limited available resources, we propose a rule-based approach to classify Bengali NPs as *singular* or *plu-*

ral by analyzing different sources of plurality and have achieved an accuracy of 73.12%.

The paper is organized as follows: Section 2 describes the differences in plurality expression in Bengali and Hindi NPs. Section 3 illustrates a comparison on plural inflection of Bengali and Hindi lexical classes and shows how Bengali to Hindi machine translation is affected due to improper classification of Bengali NPs on plurality. Section 4 investigates different sources of plurality in Bengali sentences. Section 5 describes our approach in three steps to classify NPs by determining the number of the head noun (or equivalent). In the first step, the input sentence is analyzed at different syntactic level and produces some structural representation of the sentence which helps to identify different phrases and their heads, qualifiers of the heads and other necessary information. In the second step, the quantifiers are classified as *singular* or *plural* (as quantifiers are the major source for determining the number of head noun) and, in the last step, the NPs are classified based on the plurality of the quantifiers. Some syntactic patterns are also identified which helps to identify the plurality of NPs. Section 6 shows experimental result of our approach on 1000 sentences chosen randomly from ILMT Bengali corpus[1]. Section 7 categorizes the misclassification errors and justifies why proposed approach fails to classify them properly. Section 8 summarizes our work and concludes with future scope of improvements.

2   Related Work

The difference in plurality expressions in Bengali and Hindi NPs is an example of grammatical divergences between Bengali and Hindi. Some works are found in literature which address such divergence phenomena in specific language pairs. (Dave et al., 2001) addresses the divergence issues between English and Hindi from the perspective of computational linguistics which includes various aspects of syntactic and lexico-semantic divergences. Also, a considerable amount of work is done by the linguistic community on this issue in Indian and Western languages (Bholanath, 1987; Gopinathan, 1993). (Das, 2013) discussed different type of divergences observed in English to Bengali machine translation.

---

[1] ILMT Bengali corpus is created as a resource for Bengali-Hindi MT system under consortium project ILMT Phase I.

In Bengali, a considerable amount of work is done on different morpho-syntactic analyses like morphological analysis/synthesis (Dasgupta et al., 2004; Bhattacharya et al., 2005), Part-of-Speech (POS) tagging (Dandapat, 2009), chunking (Avinesh et al., 2007; Dandapat, 2007), parsing (Ghosh et al., 2009) etc.

The plurality issue in different foreign languages like Chinese (Bošković et al., 2012), Turkish (Walter, 2014) are studied and NP classification on plurality is also reported in (Li, 1999; Dryer, 2005). In Bengali, some work (Chacón. 2011; Biswas, 2012) are reported on the linguistic analysis of plurality.

3   Plurality in Bengali and Hindi NPs

Morphologically, nouns (NNs) and pronouns (PRPs) in Bengali, Hindi and English take null (ø) suffix for *singular* number. The *plurality* is indicated by the plural inflection or suffix attachment with the noun or pronoun. Generally, the plurality of the NP is determined by the plurality of the head noun as the head is the main (or dominating) member of the NP. However, unlike Hindi and English, the plurality of Bengali NP is not always determined by the plurality of the head. Instead, other non-head members of the NP like qualifiers, reduplicative adjectives etc. indicate the plurality of the NP. Examples (1a) and (1b) illustrate the divergences of plurality in Bengali, Hindi and English NPs. Bengali, Hindi and English examples are denoted by B: and H: and E:, respectively.

(1a) B: (সুন্দর/JJ ছেলেগুলো/NN) NP মাঠে   খেলা করছে।
     beautiful <u>boys</u>   ground-in are playing

    H: (सुंदर/JJ लड़के/NN)NP मैदान में खेल रहे हैं।
     beautiful <u>boys</u>   ground in   are playing

    E: (Beautiful/JJ <u>boys/NN</u>)NP are playing in the ground

(1b) B: আজকে (পাঁচজন/QF ছেলে/NN) NP স্কুলে   এসেছে।
     today five-cl <u>boy</u>   school-to   came

    H: आज (पांच/QF लड़के/NN)NP स्कूल में आये हैं।
     today five   <u>boys</u>   school to came

    E: (Five/ QF <u>boys</u>/NN)NP came to school today.

Example (1a) shows that the plurality of NP is kept in the head noun in Bengali, Hindi and English sentences. However, in example (1b), the head noun of Bengali NP does not hold plurality and it is indicated by its quantifier. On the other hand, the head of corresponding Hindi and English NP hold the plurality information although the plural quantifier is present in the NP.

In summary, it can be said that the plurality information is present in the head of a plural Hindi or English NP irrespective of the plurality of the dependents whereas, in Bengali, the head contains the plurality if the other non-head members of a plural NP has no plurality indicator.

4   Number Issues in Bengali-Hindi MT

In Bengali, the nouns and pronominal entities take inflection on *number*. In some cases, the quantifiers also take plural inflection like "গুলো (/gulo/)", "গুলি (/guli/)" etc. or classifiers like "জন (/jan/)" to indicate plurality. The verb forms are not inflected on plurality. Therefore, analyzing verb forms, it is not possible to identify the plurality of the subject (or object) NPs. The other grammatical classes like post-positions, adjectival and adverbial qualifiers etc. do not take plurality inflections. Therefore, the sources of plurality in lexical level are limited to nouns, pronouns or quantifiers. However, in Hindi, if the NP is plural, the plurality information is available in the head, its dependents and the verb group agreeing the subject NP. Table1 shows some representative Hindi and Bengali *singular* and *plural* word-forms taken from different lexical classes where all the plural forms are different than singular forms in Hindi but are not different in Bengali.

Examples (3a) and (3b) show that the plurality differences in lexical level cause higher difference in sentence level. It is observed from the examples that a small difference in Bengali sentences B1 and B2 (i.e., the noun "ছেলে /chhele/" is *singular* in B1 and is *plural* in B2) there has a significant difference in corresponding Hindi sentences H1 and H2 due to strong *number* agreements among/within constituents.

(3a) B1: ওই   ছেলেটি   স্কুলে   পড়ছে ।
      that   boy-cl school-in   studying

    E: 'That <u>boy</u> is studying in the school.'

    H1: वो <u>लड़का</u> स्कूल में पढ़ <u>रहा</u> है।

(3b) B2: ওই <u>ছেলেগুলি</u> স্কুলে পড়ছে ।

      that   boys   school-in   studying

E: 'Those boys are studying in the school.'

H2: वो <u>लड़के</u> स्कूल में पढ़ <u>रहे</u> हैं ।

Table 1: Lexical Categories with Plural Inflection

Lexical Classes	Inflections with Number	
	Singular	Plural
Noun (Hindi)	लड़का (boy)	लड़के (boys)
	कुर्सी (chair)	कुर्सियाँ (chairs)
Noun (Bengali)	ছেলে (boy)	ছেলেগুলো (boys)
	চেয়ার (chair)	চেয়ারগুলো (chair)
Pronoun (Hindi)	मै (I)	हम (we)
	तू (You)	तुम (you)
Pronoun (Bengali)	আমি (I)	আমরা (we)
	তুমি (You)	তোমরা (you)
Adjective (Hindi)	काला (black)	काले (black)
Adjective (Bengali)	কালো (black)	
Post-Position(Hindi)	का ('s)	के ('s)
PostPosition(Bengali)	এর ('s)	দের ('s)
Verb (Hindi)	हूँ (be)	हैं (be)
	था (was)	थे (were)
Verb (Bengali)	হই (be)	
	ছিলে (was)	

Therefore, identifying the correct plurality of each Bengali NP helps in Hindi side agreement among the NP members (head and associated dependents) as well as the inter-constituents agreements like subject-verb, object-verb etc. during the translation from Bengali to Hindi.

5 Plurality Indicators in Bengali NPs

We have discussed in section 2 that the plurality of Bengali NP is not always indicated by the plurality of the head. Plurality can be collected from other sources of the sentence. In this section we investigate different sources (or contextual patterns) from where the plurality information can be collected in Bengali.

5.1 Existence of Quantifiers in NPs

The quantifiers are the major plurality indicators in Bengali noun phrases. NPs containing plural quantifiers are plural.

The quantifiers may appear at different distances from the quantifying nouns. With the increasing distance between a quantifier and a noun, it becomes difficult to relate them without having deep syntactic processing (parsing) of input sentence. To address this issue, we have divided quantifier-noun distance into three categories as described below and try to solve them separately with available resources and infrastructures.

Quantifiers in Short Range (SR) - quantifier appears just before the head noun (4a).

(4a) (কিছু/QC ওষুধ/NN) NP

    Some medicine

    'some medicines'

Quantifier in Medium Range (MR) - other noun modifiers (but not modifying phrases) occur in between the quantifier and the head (4b).

(4b) (কয়েকটা/QC ভালো/JJ ভালো/JJ কথা/NN) NP

    few   good   good   word

    'few good words'

Quantifier in Long Range (LR) – other modifying phrases exists in between quantifier and its noun appear (4c).

(4c) (কয়েকজন/QC (আদিবাসী সম্প্রদায়ভুক্ত) JJP, (অতি সাধারণ মানের,) JJP অস্থায়ী/JJ কর্মচারী/NN) NP

    some   tribal community-belongs-to, very general quality, temporary worker

    'Some temporary workers, belonging to tribal community and of very general quality'

5.2 Quantifiers outside NPs

In some typical cases, it is observed that the *numeral classifiers* are positioned after the head to show strong definiteness (Simpson, 2011) as shown in (5a) and (5b).

(5a) <u>বছর/NN পাঁচেক/QC</u> পরে সে আবার ফিরে এলো ।

    year   five   after he again returned back

'He again retuned back after five years'

(5b) রাজা নাটকের প্রথম সংস্করণে গান/NN ছিল মোট বাইশটি/QC ।

King drama-gen first edition-in song was total twenty-two

'There were a total of twenty-two songs in the first edition of the drama "Raja"'

The major issue in handling such constructions is to dealing with the ambiguity. If a quantifier occurs in between two nouns, then the quantifier may be associated with the previous or the following noun. This causes semantic ambiguity as illustrated in 5(c).

(5c) তার ছেলে/NN দুটো/QC স্কুলে/NN পড়ে ।

his boy two school-in reads

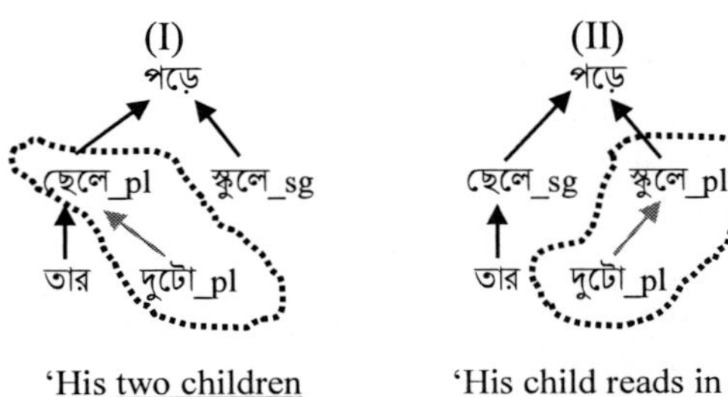

'His two children read in school,

'His child reads in two schools'

In (I), the noun "ছেলে (/chhele/)" is plural (pl) as it is quantified by the following plural quantifier "দুটো (/duto/)" and the other noun "স্কুলে (/skule/)" is singular (sg) whereas in (II) it is reverse as the quantifier modifying the followed noun.

5.3 Plurality Collected from other Nouns

In some constructions, the plural nouns with (optional) modifiers are connected through coordinating conjunctions to form a larger NP unit. In such constructions, none but the last noun contains the plurality information of the NP.

(6) (রাজনৈতিক/JJ নেতা/NN ,/CC মন্ত্রী/NN ও/CC আমলাদের/NN) NP চাপে খুনের কেসটা চাপা পড়ে গেল ।

political   leader   minister and bureaucrats

pressure-due-to murder-gen case-cl suppresses-was

'The murder case was suppressed due to the pressure from political leaders, ministers and the bureaucrats'

In example (6), the plural NP consists of three nouns "নেতা (/netA/)", "মন্ত্রী (/mantrI/)" and "আমলা (/AmalA/)" whereas the plural inflection is visible in the last noun. Plurality of others can be collected from the last noun.

5.4 Reduplication & Compounding

Plurality of the phrase may be determined from the reduplication of the head noun (7a) or its modifiers (7b) and compounding (7c).

(7a) (পথে/NN পথে/NN) NP অবরোধ

road-in   road-in   obstruction

'obstructions in the roads'

(7b) (ছোট/JJ ছোট/JJ নদী/NN) NP

small   small   river

'small rivers'

(7c) (ভালো-মন্দ/JJ কথা/NN) NP

good-bad   word

'good-bad words'

5.5 NP with Elliptic Phenomena

In some typical Bengali constructions (8), the noun is implicit and the inflection of the noun is attached with its modifiers. This phenomenon is an example of *ellipses*. In this type of construction, the resulting quantifier semantically behaves like a plural pronoun if the quantifier is plural.

(8) এই সিনেমাটি অনেকেই দেখেনি ।

This film-cl   many-people seen-not

'Many people did not seen this film'

5.6 Spatio-Temporal Patterns (PAT)

Spatio-temporal entities (also referred as Nouns denoting Space and Time or NST) along with compatible post-position (PSP) holds the plurality of the noun without having any inflection.

(9) বছরের পর বছর ধরে   কাজটা   চলছে ।

year-of after-year   work-cl is-in-porgress

'The working is in progress for many years'

In example (9), instead of taking the plural suffix, the temporal noun "বছর (/bachhar/)" replicate itself with PSPs "পর (/par/)" and "ধরে (/dhare/)". In this type of patterns, the NST is plural.

6 NP Classification Approach

In this section, we will discuss how to identify the plurality of Bengali noun phrases. The NP classification process consists of three steps. In the first step we will analyze the input Bengali sentence and identify different phrases and necessary grammatical (morphological, syntactic) properties associated with the sentence. As we mentioned in section 4 that quantifiers are the major indicators of plurality, we will classify the quantifiers as *singular* or *plural* in the next step. Finally, we will classify NPs by applying some predefined rules on analyzed structure of the sentence. The following sub-sections elaborate the steps.

6.1 Syntactic Analysis of Input Sentence

To solve the plurality issue exhaustively, a detailed, multi-level syntactic analysis of input sentence is required which spans from word level to sentence level. Also, in some ambiguous cases, the analyzed structure needs to be represented in discourse or pragmatic level. In this experiment, we limit the analysis phase in the following steps due to resource constraints.

Morphological Analysis: Input sentences are tokenized and each word-token is analyzed morphologically with a rule-based Bengali Morphological Analyzer (MA) developed at IIT Kharagpur. MA produces all possible analyses of input word. Words having plural suffixes are identified as plural nouns in this step.

Part-of-Speech (POS) Tagging: A CRF based Bengali POS tagger is trained on ILMT POS tagged corpus and used to identify the grammatical functionalities of each word in the sentence.

Chunking: Local dependencies among consecutive words are identified using CRF-based chunking model trained on ILMT corpus with further post-processing (Chatterji et al., 2012).

Morphological Pruning: As a word-token may have more than one morphological interpretation, morphological analyses having context incompati-

bility are pruned out using the method specified in (Barik et al., 2014).

Head of the Chunk Identification: Chunking segments the sentence based on local dependencies and classify each segment. The *head* of each chunk is identified using a rule-based approach.

Dependency Parsing: To identify long range modifiers or modifying phrases, we have used a rule-based Bengali (partial) parser which is developed according to (Bharti et al., 2009).

6.2 Classification of Quantifiers

Quantifiers are the important sources of plurality. The plurality of the quantifier implies the plurality of its quantifying NP. Therefore, each quantifier has to be classified correctly.

The quantifiers are identified in the input sentence during POS tagging. The quantifiers are categorized as follows:

Numerals: Non-negative, integer quantifiers greater than one with (optional) classifiers like ১৮৫৭-জন (1857-cl), ২৫-টা (25-cl) are plural quantifiers.

Cardinal Number: Cardinal numbers without having decimal indicator like পাঁচ (five), দশ (ten), পাঁচশ (five hundreds) etc. are plural.

Ordinal Number: Ordinal quantifiers like প্রথম (first), চতুর্থ (fourth), একাদশ (eleventh) are not plural.

Indefinite Quantifier: For the case of indefinite quantifiers, classifiers play an important role for their plurality. Classifiers are used in Bengali to combine NPs with numerals and quantifiers (Biswas, 2012). For example, the indefinite quantifier "অনেক (/anek/)" with classifier "জন (/jan/)" is plural but with classifiers like "টা (/tA/)" or "খানা (/khana/)" is not plural.

Another observation is that some indefinite quantifiers take regular plural suffixes like "গুলো (/gulo/)", "গুলি (/guli/)" etc. and, thus, are plural. Quantifiers do not take the *associative plurals* (Chacón, 2011) like "রা (/ra/)" as they are special markers for animate nouns (Moravcsik et al., 2013).

Table 2: Plurality of Quantifiers w.r.t Classifiers

	ø	টা/টি	খানা/খানি	জন	গুলো/গুলি
কিছু	Y	×	NA	Y	NA
অনেক	Y	×	×	Y	Y
বহু	Y	NA	NA	Y	NA
কত/যত/এত	Y	×	×	Y	Y
সমস্ত	Y	×	NA	Y	NA
সব	Y	×	NA	×	Y
কতক	Y	×	NA	Y	Y

To determine the plurality of classifier attached indefinite quantifiers, we have prepared a quantifier set (Q) and a classifier set (C) and examined the plurality of each member of Q X C. Some examples are shown in Table 2. Here, "Y" and "×" denote that attachments are valid where the quantifiers are plural for the first case and not for the second. "NA" refers to invalid classifier attachment.

6.3 Rules for Classify NPs

With syntactic analysis of the input sentence, some information of each word-token (or different grammatical units) are found. Each quantifier in the sentence is identified and classified. Other information like measuring units for mass nouns, nouns denoting space or time etc. are listed. Therefore, if any NP is plural, the information is explicitly available in the analyzed structure of the sentence. We have developed sixteen rules to look for the plurality information within chunk members or context. Once the plurality is determined by matching a rule, the plurality information is copied to the head of the chunk so that plurality of the chunk is explicitly identified and it becomes available for grammatical functionalities like agreements. Some of the rules are explained below. Rules are denotes by 'R'.

Case I: *Existence of measuring units like "মিটার"* (meter), *"পাউন্ড"* (pound) *or "ভোল্ট"* (volt) *in NP denotes mass noun and, thus, NP is not plural.*

Case II: *NP having numerals attachment with temporal nouns like "১৬ নভেম্বর"* (16 November) *or "১৭৯৯ সালে"* (in 1799 year) *are not plural.*

Case III: *NPs having plural quantifiers are plural.*

(10) এখানে (পাঁচজন/QC_pl লোকের/NN_sg)NP থাকার ব্যবস্থা আছে।

    here   five-cl   people-gen   accommodating-for arrangement has

    'Here, there is an arrangement for accommodating <u>five people</u>'

R: (QC_pl (.*?) NN_**sg**) NP => (QC_pl (.*?) NN_**pl**) NP

Case IV: *If a NP consists of multiple quantifiers connected with coordinating conjunctions and the rightmost quantifier is plural then the NP is plural.*

(11) (এক/QC_sg, দুই/QC_pl বা পাঁচ/QC_pl মাস/NN_sg) NP বাদেও সে আসতে পারে।

    one, two or five month after-also he come can

    'He can also come after one, two or five years'

R: (QC* QC_pl NN_**sg**) NP => (QC* QC_pl NN_**pl**) NP

Case V: *Reduplications of temporal nouns with certain patterns (i.e., combination of temporal nouns with specific post-position(s)) are considered as plural nouns. If the pattern matches with the rule, the corresponding pattern is modified.*

(12) (বছরের/NN পর/PSP) NP (বছর/NN ধরে/PSP) NP এই রীতি চলে আসছে।

    year-of after-year this ritual continued-over

    'This ritual is continued over years'

R: (NNPSP%পর)NP (NN PSP%ধরে)NP
    => (NN_pl PSP%ধরে)NP

Case VI: *Reduplication of temporal nouns with no post-position attachments are not plural.*

(13) (বছর/NN) NP (বছর/NN) NP দুর্গপূজা হয়।

    year   year   Durgapuja-celebration is

    'Durgapuja is celebrated every year'

Case VII: *Reduplication of animate ('a') and inanimate ('i') nouns (identified during morphological analysis) without having post-position attachments are plural.*

(14) (গাছে/NN) NP (গাছে/NN) NP ফুল ফুটেছে।

    tree-on   tree-on   flower blossomed

'Flowers have blossomed on the trees'

R: (NN_sg && case='এ' && type= 'a' or 'i') NP (NN_sg && case='এ' && type= 'a' or 'i') NP => (NN_pl && case='এ' && type= 'a' or 'i') NP

Case VIII: NPs having *pronouns (PRPs) with reduplications are plurals.*

(15) (যাহা/PRP) NP (যাহা/PRP) NP বলি   মন   দিয়ে   শুন।
  what   what   saying   carefully   listen
  'Listen carefully to what I am saying'

R: (X%PRP_sg) NP (X%PRP_sg) NP => (X%PRP_pl) NP

Case IX: *NPs having adjectival reduplications are plural.*

(16) এই   পুকুরে   (বড়/JJ বড়/JJ মাছ) NP আছে।
  this pond-in big big   fish   have
  'Big fishes are there in this pond'

R:((.*) X/JJ X/JJ (.*) NN_sg)NP=>((.*) X/JJ (.*) NN_pl) NP

7   Evaluation

To evaluate our rule-based NP classification method, we choose 1000 sentences randomly from ILMT corpus as test data. The sentences are analyzed by different steps as specified in section 5.1. The analyzed structures are manually examined and the errors are removed. The 1000 test sentences thus are annotated and are considered as ground truth (or gold standard data).

In the test 1000 sentences, we found 5817 noun chunk (NP) and a total of 5109 nouns which includes both singular (3572), plural (1271) and verbal nouns (39). Among these singular nouns identified by morphological analysis, 227 are actually plural which are detected and marked during manual annotation. The Bengali Morphological Analyzer (MA) fails to analyze them as plural because no plural suffix is attached with these nouns and MA does not consider the context to determine the number of any noun. As a result, 227 NP chunks are misclassified as singular NPs and they are marked in the test data.

Table 3: NP Classification Results

Target Plurals NPs	SR	MR	LR	PAT	SEM	MIS	Total
Ground Truth	141	29	23	17	6	11	**227**
Identified	157	33	7	15	0	0	212
Correctly Identified	129	19	4	15	0	0	**167**

Table 3 shows the distribution NPs having plurality kept in non-head members in ground truth, identified by our approach and correctly identified in different type of plurality sources.

From Table 3, we observe that quantifiers as plurality sources in short range (SR) is solved in most of the cases. The fixed pattern-based (PAT) number acquisition correctly captures all such patterns and classified NPs accordingly. However, plurality determinations of NPs based on the plurality of the quantifiers located in medium (MR) and long range (LR) are solved partially. Plurality determination of NPs where short or no contextual information is available or the context is ambiguous enough (SEM) is not worked. A details summary of the results on 1000 test sentences is given below.

Total NPs	Nouns by MA				After NP Classification	
5817	Sg	Pl	Verbal	Total	Sg -> Pl	Correct
GT	3572	1271	39	5109	-	227
Test	3587	1271	39	5109	212	167

The confusion matrix of the result is given below.

	TRUE	FALSE
Singular	3572	15
Plural	167	55

The overall accuracy is **73.12%**.

8   Errors Analysis of Our Method

8.1   NP Misclassification in Local Level

Classification of NPs on quantifier-noun number agreement depends on the type of the head noun. Some nouns are singular always and NPs with such nouns are also singular. However, with the presence of plural quantifiers, such singular NPs are misclassified as plurals. For example, the specified NP in (17) is singular along with the the singular noun "পৃথিবী (/prithibI/)". The quantifier "সমস্ত (/samasta/)" has two aspects – one is quantitative which means 'all' and it is plural. The other aspect is qualitative which means 'whole'. In this example, the quantifier is realized as plural which is incorrect.

(17) তাজমহল (সমস্ত/QC পৃথিবীর/NN_pl)NP দর্শকদের আকৃষ্ট করে।

    Tajmahal for-all   earth-gen visitors attracts

    'Tajmahal attracts the visitors of the entire world'

To handle this issue, deeper semantic representation of the context is needed.

8.2 Error due to Chunk Level Ambiguity

Quantifier followed by two nouns may quantify either one and, thus, resulting dependency ambiguity as described below.

(18) পাঁচ/QC ছেলের/NN বাবা /NN

    five   boy-gen father

Case1

বাবা/NN_sg

↑

ছেলের/NN_pl

↑

পাঁচ/QC_pl

'Father of <u>five children</u>'

Case2

বাবা/NN_pl

পাঁচ/QC_pl   ছেলের/NN_sg

'<u>five fathers</u> having children'

In case1, the noun "ছেলের (/chhelera/)" is plural due to the plural quantifier "পাঁচ (/panch/)" whereas in case2, the noun "বাবা (/bAbA/)" is plural.

8.3 Long Range Agreement Problems

With the unavailability of good accuracy deep parser in Bengali, the (partial) parser is used to identify long range dependencies which fails to identify some of the relations of long range and causes misclassification of NPs on numbers.

(19) দশটা/QC সুন্দর সুন্দর নক্সা করা নরম কাপড়ের তৈরি আসন/NN দেখিয়ে নন্দিতা বলল - "এখানে আপনারা বসুন"।

ten-cl beautiful beautiful designed soft cotton made seat pointing-to Nandita said – "here you-pl sit down"

'Pointing to <u>ten</u>, beautifully designed, soft, cotton-made seats, Nandita said "please sit down here".

Example (19) is an ambiguous sentence because the quantifier "দশটা(ten)" may attached with either "কাপড় (cloth)" or "আসন(seat)". But in this case by using pragmatics we see that since the sentence addresses a plural number of people are asked to sit, the plurality should be attached with "কাপড় (cloth)".

8.4 Unavailability of Contextual Information

Some cases are found where the given context is not sufficient to determine the plurality of the NP.

(20) জায়গাটা (ছেলেতে/NN_sg) NP ভর্তি হয়ে গেছে।

    place-cl boy-with   filled-up

    '*The place is filled up with the <u>boys</u>*'

The NP with noun "ছেলেতে (/chhelete/)" is plural in (20). However, with available contextual information, our approach fails to identify it as plural.

9 Conclusion and Future Work

In this work, we showed that Bengali NPs cannot be classified on plurality based on the plurality of the head nouns. Also, we showed that the plurality issue in Bengali NPs should be resolved correct as it causes errors in different text processing applications (specifically Machine Translation from Bengali to other language like Hindi or English). Different sources and indicators of plurality are studied in this work and noticed that the quantifiers are the major sources of plurality indicator in Bengali. The quantifiers have been classified on plurality and a rule-based approach is proposed to examine noun phrases as singular or plural.

In error analysis phase, we have noticed that some NPs are not classified properly due to the unavailability of sufficient resources. With correct parsing information, domain knowledge and the facilities for analyzing large context in discourse or pragmatic level, the error rate of our approach can be reduced which is our future scope of work.

Acknowledgments

This work is financially supported by MCIT, Govt. of India through the consortium project "Indian Language to Indian language Machine Translation (IL-ILMT) Systems Phase II" vide order no. 11(1)/2010-HCC(TDIL) dated 27/12/2010. The problem addressed here is explored as a part of performance issues in Bengali-Hindi Machine Translation system. The work is done at the Department of Computer Science & Engineering, IIT Kharagpur during the MS course of the first author.

References

Akshar Bharati, Mridul Gupta, Vineet Yadav, Karthik Gali and Dipti Misra Sharma. 2009. *Simple Parser for Indian languages in a Dependency Framework,* In Proceedings of the Third Linguistic Annotation Workshop, ACL-IJCNLP, Singapore, pp. 162-165

A. Simpson, H. L. Soh and H. Nomoko. 2011. *Bare classifiers and definiteness: A cross-linguistic investigation,* Studies in Languages 35.1, John Benjamins Publishing Company, 168-194.

Biswanath Barik and Sudeshna Sarkar. 2014. *Pattern based Pruning of Morphological Alternatives of Bengali Wordforms,* In Proceedings of International Conference on Advances in Computing, Communications and Informatics (ICACCI), New Delhi.

D. A. Chacón. 2011. *Bangla and company: the distribution of associative plurals in Bangla, Japanese, and Mandarin Chinese,* Handout in Formal Approaches to South Asian Languages (FASAL I), University of Massachussets, Amherst

Aniruddha Ghosh, Pinaki Bhaskar,Amitava Das and Sivaji Bandyopadhyay, *Dependency Parser for Bengali: the JU System at ICON 2009,* Kharagpur, India.

Sandipan Dandapat, *Part of Speech Tagging and Chunking with Maximum Entropy Model,* In Proceedings of IJCAI Workshop on Shallow Parsing for South Asian Languages (SPSAL-2007)

Sandipan Dandapat. 2009. *Part-of-Speech Tagging for Bengali,* MS Thesis submitted at IIT Kharagpur

Niladri Sekhar Dash. 2013. *Linguistic Divergences in English to Bengali Translation,* International Journal of English Linguistics; Vol. 3, No. 1

Edith Moravcšik and Michael Daniel. 2014. *The Associative Plural,* The World Atlas of language Structures Online, http://wals.info/chapter/36, accessed in July 2014

Omkar N. Koul. 2008. *Modern Hindi Grammar,* VA, Dunwoody Press.

Priyanka Biswas. 2012. *Plurality in Classifier Language: Two Types of Plural in Bangla,* In Proceedings of GLOW in Asia IX, Japan

Shachi Dave, Jignashu Parikh and Pushpak Bhattacharyya. *"Interlingua-based English–Hindi Machine Translation and Language Divergence."* Machine Translation 16.4 (2001): 251-304

S. Gopinathan and S. Kandaswamy (eds): 1993, Anauvaad kI samasyaae [Problems of Translation], Lokbharti Prakashan, New Delhi, India.

Tiwari Bholanath and Naresh Kumar: 1987, *Problems of translation from various foreign languages,* Prabhat Prakashan, New Delhi, India

S. Dasgupta and M. Khan. 2004. *Morphological paring of Bangla words using PC-KIMMO,* Proceedings of the 7th International Conference on Computer and Information Technology (ICCIT2004, Dhaka, Bangladesh)

S. Bhattacharya, M. Choudhury, S. Sarkar and A. Basu. 2005. *Inflectional morphology synthesis for Bengali noun, pronoun and verb systems.* In Proc. of the National Conference on Computer Processing of Bangla (NCCPB 05), Dhaka, Bangladesh

Sanjay Chatterji, Nabanita Datta, Arnab Dhar, Biswanath Barik, Sudeshna Sarkar, Anupam Basu. 2012. *Repairing Bengali Verb Chunks for Improved Bengali to Hindi Machine Translation,* In Proceedings of the 10th Workshop on Asian Language Resources, Mumbai, pages 65–74

Avinesh. PVS, Karthik G. 2007. *Part-Of-Speech Tagging and Chunking using Conditional Random Fields and Transformation Based Learning,* In Proceedings of IJCAI Workshop on Shallow Parsing for South Asian Languages (SPSAL-2007)

Ž. Bošković and I. T. C. Hsieh, 2012, *On word order, binding relations, and plurality within Chinese NPs.* In Proceedings of the 13th International Symposium on Chinese Languages and Linguistics (pp. 19-47).

Walter, M. J. (2014). Morphosyntax and semantic type of noun phrases in Turkish

Y. H. A. Li, 1999, *Plurality in a classifier language.* Journal of East Asian Linguistics, 8(1), 75-99

Dryer, Matthew S. 2005. *"33. Coding of Nominal Plurality."*

Making Verb Frames for Bangla Vector Verbs

Sanjukta Ghosh
Department of Linguistics
Banaras Hindu University
Varanasi, INDIA
san_subh@yahoo.com

Abstract

This paper is an initial attempt to make verb frames for some Bangla verbs. For this purpose, I have selected 15 verbs which are used as vectors in the compound verb constructions of Bangla. The frames are made to show their number of arguments as well as case markings on those arguments when these verbs are ued alone and when they form part of compound verb constructions. This work can be extended further to make similar verb frames for all other verbs and can be used as a rich lexical resource.

Keywords: verb frames, compound verbs, Bangla, arguments and case markings, lexical resource.

1 Introduction

Compound verbs had always taken a pivotal role in the linguistic research of Indian languages. They are composed of two verbs and together make a complex predicate. The typical property of the compound verbs in Indian languages is that the second verb or V2 does play a very important role in the meaning composition of the complex predicate and occasionally also retains its own argument while forming a compound verb. For these interesting properties of the compound verbs, they have been studied extensively in almost all major Indian languages (Hook (1974), Kachru and Pandharipande (1980), Butt (1993, 1995), Kachru (1993) on Hindi, Bashir (1993) on Kalasa, Pandharipande (1993) on Marathi, Fedson (1993) on Tamil, Hook (1996) on Gujrarti, Kaul Vijay on Kashmiri (1985), Rajesh Kumar and Nilu (2012) on Magahi, Mohanty (1992) on Oriya and Paul (2004, 2005) on Bangla). The first verb appears in its perfective form in Bangla compound verbs and the second takes the inflection as in other languages.

The vectors of the compound verbs are responsible for providing certain kinds of senses cross-linguistically as shown by Abbi and Gopalkrishnan (1992) with data taking from all four major language families of India. They have categorized these senses into three types: Aspectual, Adverbial and Attitudinal with some sub-types under these. Under aspectual cross-linguistically a sense of perfectivity or completeness of event (telicity) is found. Adverbial is further divided by them into three types: manner, benefactive and others all showing some way the action of the V1 performed. Under attitudinal type, comes the attitude of the speaker or the narrator towards the action mentioned by the V1 such as anger, surprise, contempt, disgust etc. These three senses are observed in Bangla compound verbs also. While aspectual and adverbial are most common senses, some cases are found (vectors *bOS* and *rakh*) with attitudinal sense of undesirability and intention to make the hearer attentive towards the speaker.

D S Sharma, R Sangal and J D Pawar. Proc. of the 11th Intl. Conference on Natural Language Processing, pages 305–314,
Goa, India. December 2014. ©2014 NLP Association of India (NLPAI)

The present paper takes total 15 major vector verbs of Bangla listed in the work of Paul and provides syntactic frames for them when used alone as well as when used as a V2 in a compound verb construction. The goal of the paper is to see whether in a compound verb construction the V2 retains its argument structure and case marking properties or not. The paper as far as my knowledge goes, makes the first attempt to build verb frames for Bangla. The syntactic and semantic information associated with the verb frames can be very useful for classifying and analyzing the verbs as well as for many NLP applications such as information retrieval, text processing, building parser, Machine Translation etc.

2 Syntactic Frames of Bangla Vector Verbs

Attempt for classification of verbs is not a new phenomenon for a resource-rich language like English. Levin's verb classification (Levin 1993), based on syntactic and semantic properties is a gigantic classic work. VerbNet is a broad-coverage freely available online verb lexicon of English based on Levin's classification and provides information about thematic roles and syntactic and semantic representations. It is linked to other lexical resources like FrameNet, PropBank and WordNet. However, Indian languages still lack such kind of broad coverage verb resource. Apart from some initial attempt for making verb frames for Hindi (Rafiya et al, undated online version), we don't find any other work in this direction.[1]

For the present work, to build a frame for a verb, I take the syntactic categories in a sentence where the verb appears. Then the NPs of the sentence are marked with the thematic roles they bear and the case marker or postposition they take. Apart from the traditional thematic roles found in standard GB theory like agent, experience, patient, instrument, benefactive, source, location and goal, I have used some other roles like associative for the accompanying NP with an agent, distinguished between causer, cause and an intermediate agent in case of a verb which provides the semantics of causation. The noun phrases are classified into location, time and matter and they bear locative case markers. Therefore, in the frames these different types of NPs are mentioned. Case markers are very important for Indian languages. For one particular

theta role, there may be more than one case marker. After providing the frame schema, an example sentence of Bangla is given for that particular frame with a gloss and translation in English.

In the following subsections the verb frames are developed and described for each of the vectors found in a compound verb construction.

1. /aSa/ 'come'
Sense 1: Deixis
The deictic verb *aSa* may focus on the source of the movement, the path or the goal. If the source is in focus, the frame has a *theke* marked source location NP, if the goal is in focus the argument is locative *–e* marked and when the path is in focus it is *–die* or *-hoe* marked path NP.

NP1(Agent) NP2-theke (source) V
1. ami baRi theke aSchi.
   I house-from come-pr-prog-1p
   'I am coming from the house.'

NP1-Agent NP2-e(goal) V
2. pOrpOr kotogulo durbOl Sorkar khOmotay aSe.
   Consecutively some weak government power-loc come-pr-3p
   'Some weak governments came to power consecutively.'

NP1(Agent) NP2-hoe/die (Path) V1
3. amra kalna hoe elam.
   We Kalna via come-pt-1p
   'We came via Kalna.'
4. amra   men lain die elam.
   We main line by com-pt-1p
   'We came by main line.'

The verb may also take an associative argument marked with *–r SoMge/Sathe* as in (5).

NP1(agent) NP2-r SOMge (associative) V
5. bacchaTa kar SoMge eSeche?
   Child-cl who-gen with come-pr-pft-3p
   'With whom has the child come?'

The V1 which are compatible with deictic senses are *ghora* 'to roam', *phera* 'to return', *bERano* 'to travel, to stroll'. The frames of the verbs *ghora* and *bERano* require a locative argument. This argument, when combined with *aSa* in a compound verb is merged with the source argument of *aSa*. As a result, there is only one source marked argument in the compound verb frames of *ghure aSa* and *beRie aSa,* which may be dropped occasionally. E.g.

NP1(agent) NP2 –theke(source) V1 V2.
6. amra ladakh theke beRie elam.
  We Ladakh from o travel come-pt-1p
  'We came back travelling from Ladakh.'

When the path is focused in the deictic sense the argument is case marked with postposition *die* as in the next sentence.
NP1(agent) NP2-die(path)   V1 V2
7. je pOth die cole eli, Se pOth Ekhon bhule geli. (Tagore song)
  which way by walk come-pt-2p-NH, that way now forget go-pt-2p-NH
  'Now you forgot the way by which you came past.'

When the goal is in focus, however, the argument of the same compound verb becomes a locative – *e/te* marked place noun.

NP1(agent) NP-e(goal) V1 V2
8. hElheD istinDia kompanir cakri nie bharote cole aSen.
  Halhed East India Company-gen job with India-loc come-pr-3p-hon back
  'Halhed came back to India with a job in East India Company.'

When the source is in focus, the argument will be *theke* marked source.

NP1(agent) NP2(temporal) V1 V2
9. kintu uni jodi ajkaler moddhei phire aSen..
  but he-hon if by today or tomorrow return come
  'What if he comes back by today or tomorrow.'

aSa may also be combined with some verb with one object argument (e.g. *phEla* 'to drop') and in that case that object argument is realized in the frame of the compound verb as the following. However, there is still the deictic sense of the vector retained in such construction. The place of speaking and the place of the first verb cannot be same.

NP1(agent) NP20/ke/re (theme) V1 V2
10. tui phele eSechiS kare?
  You-NH drop come-pr-pft-2p-NH whom (poetic)
  'Whom have you left behind?'

NP1(agent) NP2-ke(patient) V1 V2
11. make bole eSechiS? (alternatively *bOla* may also take locative argument like *baRite*)
  Mother-obj. tell come-pr-pft-2p-NH
  'Have you informed mother?'

Sense 2: Duration
When *aSa* as a V2 is used in the sense of duration of the event of V1, it may have a temporal NP with postpositions like *theke, dhore (kOtodin dhore).*

NP1(agent) NP2 (temporal) V1 V2
12. ami kObe theke bole aSchi.
  I when from say come-pr-prog-3p
  'I have been saying it for a long time.'

NP1(agent) NP2(matter/višay) V1 V2
13. Se tar pitar onukOroNe o nirdeSe ei karjo kore aSche.
  (s)he his/her father-gen following-loc and instruction-e this work do come-pr-prog-3p-NH
  'She has been doing this work following her father's instruction.'

Sense 3: gradualness of the event
When *aSa* is used in the sense of gradualness of the event of V1 it may optionally take a manner adverb phrase like *dhire dhire, aste aste* 'slowly'.

(AdvP) NP1(undergoer) V1 V2
14. (dhire dhire) cokh (ghume) juRe aSche.
  Slowly eyes in sleep close come-3p-pr-prog
  'The eyes have been closing slowing.'

2. *rakha* 'to keep': This verb when used alone takes a locative place argument.

NP1(agent) NP2 (theme) NP3-e/-er +a locative postposition V (locative)
15. boiTa kothay rekhechiS?
  book-cl where keep-pr-pft-2p-NH
  'Where have you kept the book?'

Sense 1: Aspectual

When used in the aspectual sense as a vector, it combines with verbs which take one object argument and that is realized in the frame of the compound verb, aspectual difference of the two senses of *rakha* as a vector is not reflected in the verb frame. In both cases the V1 is verb with one object argument but the difference is in the type of the verb, with the first sense a process verb and with the second sense a perceptual verb resulting some cognitive effect is found as a V1. E.g.

NP1(agent) NP2-0/ke (patient) V1 V2
16. phulTa tule rakhiS.
    flowers pick keep-2p-fut-imp-NH
    'Pick up the flowers (with a telic reading).'
17. benarOs tar oitijjho dhore rekheche.
    Benaras its tradition hold keep-pr-pft-3p 'Varanasi has kept up its tradition.'

Sense 2: to make the hearer attentive/attitudinal sense of the speaker
It is often used in imperative mood and generally comes with the adverbial phrase *bhalo kore* or *mon die* which in this context mean carefully/with attention. E.g.

NP1(agent)NP2-0/ke (patient) AdvP V1(perception verb) V2
18. kOthaTa bhalo kore Sune rakho.
    Word-cl   well   hear keep-pr-imp-2p-NH
    'Listen to the words carefully.'

3. *ana* 'to bring': The basic frame has a subject and an object argument and a source from where the object is brought. The verb *ana* semantically involves a movement of things from one place to another.

NP1(agent) NP2-theke(source) NP2-0/ke (theme) V
19. tumi dilli theke ki enecho?
    you what bring-pr-pft-2p-MH
    'What have you brought?'

When it is combined with another verb with an object argument there is sharing of argument and only one object is realized in the frame of the compound verb.

NP1(agent) NP2-0/ke (theme) V1 V2
20. kake dhore enechi, dEkho.

whom catch bring-pr-pft-1p see-imp-2p
'See, whom have I brought?'

4. *dea* 'to give': It loses its core sense when used as a vector. The frame of *dea* alone is the following.
NP1 (agent) NP2-ke (recipient) NP3 (theme) V
21. ke kake ki dilo?
    Who whom what give-pt-3p-NH
    'Who gave what to whom?'

When used as a vector with any other process verb in complete aspectual sense, it does not retain any of its arguments. The resulting sentence structure has the arguments of V1. The semantics of this vector is the action of V1 will be beneficial for somebody other than the actor.

NP1(agent) NP2-0/ke (patient) V1 V2
22. tumi ki kajTa kore debe?
    you QP work-cl do-give-fut-2p-MH
    'Will you do the work?'

5. nea 'to take'
The basic frame of the verb is the following with a *theke* marked source argument.

NP1(agent) NP-2-theke (source) V
23. eTa kotha theke nile?
    This-cl where from take-pt-3p
    'Where did you take it from?'

However, the source argument is lost when it is used in a compound verb frame as a V2 and the frame follows the first verb completely. The semantics is the action of V1 is done for the benefit of the actor. E.g.

24. taRataRi khee ne, iskuler deri hoe jacche.
    quickly eat take-pr-imp-2p-NH, school-gen. late become go-pr-prog
    'Take the food quickly, (you) are getting late for the school.'

6. *tola* 'to pick up'
The basic frame of the verb consists of an agent of picking up, a source of pick up and the theme/ patient to be picked up.

NP1(agent) NP2- 0/ke (theme) NP3-theke (source) V

25. ami bacchader skul theke tulbo
   I children school from pick up-fut-1p
   ' I will pick up the children from the school.'

The source argument is not found in the frame of the compound verb with an accomplishment V1.

NP1(agent) NP2-0/ke (patient) (AdvP) V1 V2
26. Condrobabu naiDuke notun rajdhani SohorTa dhire dhire goRe tulte hObe.
   Candrababu Naidu-Dat new capital city-cl slowly   build pick be-fut-modal
   'Candrababu Naidu has to build up the new capital city slowly.'

7. /oTha/ 'to rise'
Primary frame of the verb has an agent argument with a locative/temporal argument if it is used in the sense of physical rising or ascending or getting up or some change in the position.

NP1(agent) NP2-0/e (location/temporal) V
27. bacchara chade uTheche.
   kids roof-loc ascend-pr-pft-3p
   'The kids have ascended on the terrace.'
28. amra bhorbEla uThechi.
   We dawn get up-pr-pft-1p
   'We have got up early in the morning.'
29. Surjo purbodike oThe.
   The sun east-loc rise-generic-pr-3p
   'The sun rises in the east.'

This verb when used as a vector with gORa 'to build' makes an unaccusative complex predicate where the subject of the construction is actually the complement of the verb.

NP1(patient) NP2 (location/temporal) V1 V2
30. Sob purono Sobbhotai nodir dhare goRe uThechilo.
   All old civilizations river-gen side-loc build rise-pt-3p
   'All the old civilizations were built in the river banks.'

In the second sense of the vector, it contributes to the modality of the first verb and mostly used with interrogation or negation. The V2 *oTha* in this sense is always with the suffix *–te* with the auxiliary *para* denoting ability.

NP1(agent) NP2(patient) V1 V2-te para
31. ami Ekhono lekhaTa likhe uThte pari ni.
   I so far article-cl write rise can not
   'So far I have not been able to manage to write the article.'

NP1(agent) ki NP2-0(patient) V1 V2 para?
32. tumi ki kajTa kore uThte perecho?
   you QP work-cl do rise can-pr-pft
   'Have you been able to manage to do the work?'

In the third use of the vector *oTha* it is used very commonly with the manner adverb *hOthat* 'suddenly' and denotes the suddenness or unexpectedness of the first event.

NP1(agent) AdvP V1 V2
33. baccaTa hOThat keMde uThlo
   child-cl suddenly cry rise-pt-3p
   'Suddenly the child cried.'

8. pORa 'to fall'
The verb *pORa* as mentioned before denotes a change of place of its subject. The subject undergoes an action of falling from a certain source often marked with *theke*. The location of falling may also be marked in the sentence occasionally with locative *–e*. However, none of these may be present in a sentence. The subject gets the theme theta role and it is actually raised to the position of the subject from the complement position of the verb. Therefore, *pORa* is an unaccusative predicate.

NP1-theke(source) NP2-e(location) NP3 (theme) V
34. kal rate gach theke bagane Onek am poReche.
   last night tree from garden-loc many mangoes fall-pr-pft-3p
   'Many mangoes have fallen in the garden last night.'

When it is used with a stative V1 in a compound verb frame it emphasizes the resulting state of the V1 after certain motion. The frame needs only one compulsory theme argument which is realized as subject NP. The argument is actually a theme can be checked from the fact that in this construction another object is not allowed. For instance, * baccchaTa lOmba ghum ghumie poReche is ungrammatical where *lOmba ghum* 'long sleep' is inserted as an object. However, with the single verb *ghumono* 'sleep' the object argument is perfectly acceptable.

NP1(theme) V1 V2
35. bacchaTa ghumie poReche.
    Child-cl sleep fall-pr-pft-3p
    'The child has fallen asleep.'

9. *bOSa* 'to sit'
The verb frame of the single intransitive verb *boSa* has one compulsory agent argument with one optional (often unrealized in a sentence) location of seating.

NP1(agent) NP2-e/te (location) V
36. tumi maTite boSle kEno?
    You floor-loc sit-pt-2p-NH why
    'Why did you sit on the floor?'

However, when used in a compound verb frame it refers to only aspectual function of the V1, suddenness or unexpected nature of the event. The verbs with which it goes are transitive like *bOla* 'to say', *kOra* 'to do'.

NP1(agent) NP2(time or location) V1 V2 (ke jane)
37. meeTa kOkhon ki bole boSbe ke jane
    girl-cl when what say sit-fut-3p who knows
    'Who knows, when the girl will say what (unexpected)!'

10. phEla 'to drop'
The verb *phEla* when used alone takes an agent argument, a theme and optionally a location of dropping.

NP1(agent) NP2(theme) NP3-e/te (location) V
38. baccaTa cabiTa nice phelechilo
    child-cl key-cl downstairs-loc drop-pt-pft-3p
    'The child had dropped the key downstairs.'

As a vector it is used in the sense of 'to do the event of V1 without hesitation or further consideration' as in *bole phEla* 'speak out', *kore phEla* 'do without hesitation'. The frame has one agent and patient with some manner adverbial.

NP1(agent) NP2(patient) AdvP V1 V2
39. Oto bhabchiS ki, kajTa cOTpOT kore phEl.

Much think-pr-prog-2p-NH what, work-cl fast do drop-imp-2p-NH
    'What are you thinking so much? Do the job quickly.'

The second use in the sense of an unwanted event of V1 can be found with the same set of verbs. The frame typically generally has question words *kOkhon/kothay* and *ki* as time location and patient argument.

NP1(agent) NP2(time or location) NP3(patient) V1 V2
40. o je kOkhon ki kore phelbe tar Thik nei.
    (s)he comp when what do drop-fut-3p its clear not
    'It is not clear, when he will do what (unexpectedly).'

Notice that same verb may be used with both the senses.

The third use is completely aspectual and it indicates the telicity of the event of V1. The transitive verbs with an overt argument go with this reading of phEla. E.g. chuMRe phEla 'to throw out', bheMe PhEla ' to break', gile phEla 'to swallow'.

NP1(agent) NP2(theme) NP3-e/te(location) V1 V2
41. tini phuler toRaTa baje kagojer jhuRite chuMRe phellen.
    (s)he flower-gen bouquet-cl waste paper basket-loc throw drop-pt-3p
    'She threw the bouquet of flowers in the waste paper basket.'

11. *jaoa* 'to go'
As a single verb *jaoa* has an agent of the motion and a goal or destination where the agent goes. It may also alternatively refer to the path of the motion marked by the postposition *–die/hoe*.

NP1(agent) NP2 (goal) V
43. ami dilli jacchi.
    I   delhi go-pr-prog-1p
    'I am going to Delhi.'

When it is used as a vector, it loses the goal argument and it is used with some time adverbial denoting duration of the event. The TAM expressed is either present perfect continuous or habitual present and it is realized by either simple present continuous or simple present in the language.

NP1(agent) NP2(temporal) V1 V2
44. meeTa Sokal theke khele jacche.
   girl-cl since morning play go-pr-prog-3p
   'The girl has been playing (continuously) since morning.'

NP1(agent) NP2(temporal) AdvP V1 V2
45. lokTa Saradin cupcap kaj kore jay.
   man-cl whole day silently work do go-pr-3p
   'The man keeps on working silently for the whole day.' (habitually)

12. *cOla* 'to go on/to work (for a thing)'
cOla as a main verb may mean 'to walk or move' or 'to go on or to work (for a thing)'. In the first sense, it takes an agent and a path or a goal argument as in (44).

NP1(agent) NP2 (path) V
46. amra Onek rasta collam.
   We long way walk-pt-1p
   'We walked a long way.'
47. tumi kothay colle?
   You where go-pt-2p
   'Where are you going?' (past form used in present sense)

When used in the sense of 'to go on', *cOla* takes one theme argument which is realized as the subject. The verb frame may occasionally have a manner adverbial.

NP1(theme) AdvP V
48. purodOme kaj colche.
   in full swing work go on pr-prog-3p
   'The work is going on in full swing'.
49. ghoRiTa ThikThak cloche.
   Clock-cl alright work-pr-prog-3p
   'The clock is working alright.'

The verb when used as a vector provides aspectual information of the main verb. It is used with present perfect continuous TAM realized as present perfect and often has a time adverbial denoting duration of the V1.

NP1(agent) NP2 (temporal) V1 V2
50. cheleTa Sokal theke kaj kore coleche.

   boy-cl morning since work do move-pr-pft-3p
   'The boy has been working continuously since morning.'

13. *paThano* 'to send'
As a main verb *paThano* takes two object arguments one theme and one recipient along with an agent.

NP1(agent) NP2(recipient) NP3(theme) V
51. ami tomake boiTa paThacchi.
   I you-obj book-cl send-pr-prog-1p
   'I am sending you the book.'

As a vector it is used in the sense of causativization. There are causer, causee and an intermediates agent with postposition *die*.

NP1(causer agent) NP2-die (instrument) NP3-ke (causee) V1 V2
52. SahoS dEkho, jhike die amake Deke paThieche.
   audacity look, maid-obj by summon send-pr-pft-3p
   'Look at the audacity, (she) has summoned me through a maid-servant.'

14. *bERano* 'to roam'
When used alone *bERano* takes an agent and a location argument.

NP1(agent) NP2-te(location) V1
53. tOkhon amra bagane beRacchilam.
   Then we garden-loc roam-pt-prog-3p
   'Then we were roaming in the garden.'

When used as a vector it is used in the sense of 'non-directional movement' (Paul (2010) says this as random action of V1 without discretion) and instead of a location may take a temporal or manner adverbial.

NP1(agent) NP2 (temporal) V1 V2
54. ma-mOra meeTa Saradin keMde bERacche.
   mother-died girl-cl whole day cry roam-pr-prog-3p
   'The girl whose mother has died has been crying here and there for the whole day.'

AdvP NP1(agent) V1 V2
55. Sudhu Sudhu ghure bERaccho kEno?

worthlessly wander roam-pr-prog-2p why
'Why are you wandering here and there worth-lessly?'

15. *mOra* 'to die'

mOra is used as an intransitive verb with one undergoer of the event.

NP1(undergoer) V
56. lokTa moreche
    man-cl die-pr-pft-3p 'The man has died.'

When used in a compound verb construction, it denotes futility of the event of V1.
NP1(agent) (AdvP) V1 V2
57. orOkom keMde morchiS kEno?
    Such cry die-pr-prog-3p why
    'Why are you crying such futile?'

When it is combined with a transitive verb like *bhaba* 'to think', it retains the object argument of that verb in the resulting compound verb frame.

NP1(agent) NP2 (patient) V1 V2
58. ami Saradin tomar kOtha bhebe morchi ar tomar kono kheali nei?
    I whole day your word think die-pr-prog-3p and you-gen any concern-emph neg
    'I have been thinking of you only for the whole day and you don't have any concern at all?' and tables below the body, using 10 point text.

3. Findings and Results

From the above data total 45 tokens of verb frames are found and they are listed below together with their respective verbs.

i. NP1(Agent) NP2-theke (source) V
ii. NP1(Agent) NP2-e(goal)V
iii. NP1(Agent) NP2-hoe/die (Path) V
iv. NP1(agent) NP2-r SOMge (associative) V
v. NP1(agent) NP2-0/ke/re (patient) V1   V2 *aSa*
vi. NP1(agent) NP20/ke/re (theme) V1 V2
vii. NP1(agent) NP2(temporal) V1 V2
viii. NP1(agent) NP2((matter/višay) V1 V2
ix. (AdvP) NP1(undergoer) V1 V2
x. NP1(agent) NP2-e/-er +a locative postposition (location) V

xi. NP1(agent) NP2 0/ke/re (patient) V1 V2 rakha
xii. NP1(agent) NP20/ke (patient) AdvP V1 V2
xiii. NP1(agent) NP-theke (source) NP20/-ke/re (theme) V
xiv. NP1(agent) NP2-0/ke/re (theme) V1 V2 ana
xv. NP1(agent) NP2-ke (recipient) NP3 (theme) V
xvi. NP1(agent) NP2-0/ke (patient) V1 V2 dea
xvii. NP1(agent) NP-2-theke (source) NP3 (theme) V
As a vector it follows frame of V1. *Nea*
xviii. NP1(agent) NP2- 0/ke (theme) NP3-theke (source) V
xix. NP1(agent) NP2 (patient) (AdvP) V1(accomplishment) V2 *tola*
xx. NP1(agent) NP2 (location/temporal) V
xxi. NP1(theme) NP2 (location/temporal) V1 V2
xxii. NP1(agent) NP2(patient) V1 V2-te para neg *oTha*
xxiii. NP1(agent) ki (QP) NP2(patient) V1 V2 para?
xxiv. NP1-theke(source) NP2-e(location) NP3(theme) V
xxv.NP1(patient) V1 V2 *pORa*
xxvi. P1(agent) NP2(theme) NP3-e/te(location) V
xxvii. NP1(agent) NP2(patient) AdvP V1 V2
xxviii. NP1(agent) NP2 (temporal/location) NP3(patient) V1 V2
xxxix. NP1(agent) NP2(theme) V1 V2 *phEla*
xxx. NP1(agent) NP2 (goal) V
xxxi. NP1(agent) NP2 (temporal) V1 V2 *jaoa*
xxxii. NP1(agent) NP2 (temporal) AdvP V1 V2
xxxiii. NP1(agent) NP2-0(theme) NP3-ke(recipient) V
xxxiv. NP1(causer) NP2-die (instrument) NP3-ke(causee) V1 V2 *paThano*
xxxv. NP1(agent) NP2-te(location) V1
xxxvi. NP1(agent) NP2(temporal) V1 V2
xxxvii. AdvP NP1(agent) V1 V2 *bERano*
xxxviii. NP1(undergoer) (AdvP/AdvCl) V
xxxix. (AdvP) NP1(agent) NP2 (patient)V1 V2 *mOra*

xl. NP1(agent) NP2-0/te or -r locative postposition (location)V
xli. NP1(agent) NP2(temporal/location) NP3 (patient) V1 V2 (ke jane)   *bOSa*
xlii. AdvP NP1(theme) V
xliii. NP1(agent) NP2 (temporal) V1 V2 *cOla* in the sense of 'go on/work'
xliv. NP1(agent) NP2(path) V
xlv. NP1 (agent) NP2(goal) V *cOla* in the sense of 'move'

We can classify these 45 tokens of verb frames into 17 types.

i. NP1(Agent) NP2-theke (source) V
ii. NP1(Agent) NP2-e(goal)V
iii. NP1(Agent) NP2-hoe/die (Path) V1
iv. NP1(agent) NP2-r SOMge (associative) V
v. NP1(agent) NP2-0/ke/re (patient) V1 V2
vi. NP1(agent) NP20/ke/re (theme) V1 V2
vii. NP1(agent) NP2(temporal) V1 V2
viii. NP1(agent) NP2((matter/višay)) V1 V2
ix. (AdvP) NP1(undergoer) V1 V2
x. NP1(agent) NP2-e/-er +a locative postposition (location) V
xi. NP1(agent) NP20/ke (patient) AdvP V1 V2
xii. NP1(agent) NP-theke (source) NP20/-ke/re (theme) V
xiii.   NP1-theke(source)   NP2-e(location) NP3(theme) V
xiv. NP1(agent) NP2-ke (recipient) NP3 (theme) V
xv. NP1(undergoer) (AdvP/AdvCl) V
xvi. AdvP NP1(theme) V
xvii. NP1(causer) NP2-die (instrument) NP3-ke(causee) V1 V2

The general observation which comes out from these frames are intransitive verbs are generally used with an adverbial phrase or clause which depicts the manner of the event. They may also have a temporal or spatial NP in their frames which denote the time or the location of the event. However, they no longer need their compulsory locative NP argument or manner adverbial phrase or clause in the compound verb structure. The V2s when used in pure aspectual sense as in *jaoa, aSa* (one sense is aspectual), *rakha* (one sense only) and *cOla* or aspectual and some benefactive adverbial sense as in *deoa* and *nea* do not retain their original syntactic arguments in the compound verb structure. With the other adverbial senses like sudden-

ness or unexpectedness of the event with the V2s *phEla* and *bOSa,* the argument and case marking of the vector verb are not retained in the new compound verb structure. The deictic motion verb *aSa* may retain its goal, source or path arguments in a compound verb structure when it is combined with a non-directional motion verb which talks about manner of the motion. The other verb *ana* which has a source deictic motion sense retains it in the compound verb structure also.

3 Conclusion

This work is only a first attempt to build a knowledge-base lexical resource for Bangla verbs and has a very wide scope to extend it to fully develop frames for all the verbs of Bangla and classify them on the basis of syntactic and semantic information. At present, the work does not incorporate any semantic feature in the argument structure of the verbs but a future work can incorporate that to classify the nature of the arguments with same semantic or theta role. Once such a resource is fully developed it can be linked to the Indo Wordnet also.

References

Abbi, A. and Gopalkrishnan, D. 1992. "Semantic Typology of Explicator Compound verbs in South Asian Languages". Paper retrieved online.

Bashir, Elena (1993) "Causal chains and compound verbs." In M. K. Verma ed. (1993) *Complex Predicates in South Asian Languages.* Manohar Publishers and Distributors, New Delhi.

Butt, Miriam (1993) "Conscious choice and some light verbs in Urdu." In M. K. Verma ed.(1993) *Complex Predicates in South Asian Languages.* Manohar Publishers and Distributors, New Delhi.

Butt, M. 1995. The Structures of Complex Predicates in Urdu. Dissertations in Linguistics. Stanford: CSLI.

Fedson, V. J. (1993) "Complex verb-verb predicates in Tamil." In M. K. Verma ed. (1993) *Complex Predicates in South Asian Languages.* Manohar Publishers and Distributors, New Delhi.

Hook, Peter (1974) The compound verb in Hindi. Ann Arbor: University of Michigan center for South and Southeast Asian Studies.

Hook, Peter (1996). The Compound Verb in Gujarati and its Use in Connected Text. R.T. Vyas (ed.) *ConsciousnessManifest: Studies in Jaina Art and Iconography and Allied Subjects in Honour of Dr. U.P. Shah.* Vadodara: Oriental Institute. 339-56.

Kachru, Yamuna (1982) "Pragmatics and compound verbs in Indian languages." O. N. Kaul ed. *Topics in Hindi Linguistics.* Bahari Publications, New Delhi.

Kachru, Yamuna and R. Pandharipande (1980) "Towards a typology of compound verbs in South Asian Languages." *Studies in Linguistic Sciences,* 10:1, 113-24.

Kaul, Vijay. K. (1985) *The Compound Verb in Kashmiri.* Unpublished Ph.D. dissertation. Kurukshetra University.

Levin, B. 1993. English Verb Classes and Alternations: A Preliminary Investigation. The University of Chicago Press.

Mohanty G. 1992.The Compound Verbs in Oriya. PhD dissertation. Deccan College Post-graduate and Research Institute.

Paul, S. 2004. An HPSG Account of Bangla Compound Verbs with LKB Implementation. Ph.D dissertation,University of Hyderabad, Hyderabad.

Paul,S. 2005. The semantics of Bangla Compound Verbs. *Yearbook of South Asian Languages and Linguistics.* 101-112.

Rafiya Begum et al (undated online version). Developing Verb Frames for Hindi. IIITH.

Rajesh Kumar and Nilu. 2012. Magahi Complex Predicates. IJDL.

English to Punjabi Transliteration using Orthographic and Phonetic Information

Kamaljeet Kaur
Guru Nanak Dev Engineering College
Ludhiana-141006, Punjab
meetk.89@gmail.com

Parminder Singh
Guru Nanak Dev Engineering College
Ludhiana-141006, Punjab
parminder2u@gmail.com

Abstract

Machine transliteration is an emerging and a very important research area in the field of machine translation. While the translation system finds the same meaning word/sentence in another language, the transliteration helps us to pronounce them. This paper describes the process of transliteration from English to Punjabi language using a rule based approach. Both source grapheme and phonetic information of words have been considered for rule formation to achieve high performance and more accurate result. Phonetic information proved vital for correct transliteration as well as for ambiguous words. The system is tested on news domain text of more than 10,000 words and achieved accuracy of 95%.

Keywords

Machine translation, transliteration, natural language processing, transliteration rules.

1 Introduction

Transliteration is the conversion of a text from one script to another. It is the process of representing words from one language using the approximate phonetic or spelling equivalents of another language. Machine translation (MT) is the process that takes a message in a source language and transforms it into a target language, keeping the exact meaning. Transliteration is meant to preserve the sounds of the syllables in words. This paper presents the development of English to Punjabi transliteration system that can transliterate English text into equivalent Punjabi text.

The remainder of this paper is organized as follows. Section 2 describes the related work done in machine transliteration. We have described basic character to character mapping and rules for transliteration in section 3. Performance evaluation is discussed in section 4. Finally, we have concluded it in section 5.

2 Related Work

Significant work in the field of machine transliteration has been done for Indian as well as for foreign languages. Three approaches for transliteration being used are: Grapheme based models; Phoneme based models and Hybrid models. Knight and Graehl (1998) have developed a phoneme based statistical model using finite state transducer that implements transformation rules to do backward transliteration. They have proposed method for automatic backward transliteration that can be used for transliteration of words from Japanese back to English. Oh and Choi (2002) have proposed English to Korean transliteration system using pronunciation and contextual rules. They have used phonetic information such as phoneme and its context as well as orthography. Malik (2006) has developed Punjabi Machine Transliteration System that is used to transliterate words from Shahmukhi script to Gurmukhi script using transliteration rules. Saini and Lehal (2008) have proposed a corpus based transliteration system for Shahmukhi script to Punjabi language. The transliteration system has been tested on a small set of poetry, article and story. The average transliteration accuracy of 91.37% has been claimed. Goyal and Lehal (2009) have proposed system in which Hindi words are transliterated into Punjabi words. They have implemented complex rules for accurate transliteration between Hindi-Punjabi language pair. Josan and Lehal (2010) have presented a novel approach to improve Punjabi to Hindi transliteration by combining a basic character to character mapping approach with rule based and Soundex based enhancements. Quite a reasonable improvement can be achieved by small amount of dependency or contextual rules.

D S Sharma, R Sangal and J D Pawar. Proc. of the 11th Intl. Conference on Natural Language Processing, pages 315–320,
Goa, India. December 2014. ©2014 NLP Association of India (NLPAI)

Kaur and Josan (2011) have proposed a system that addresses the issue of statistical machine transliteration from English to Punjabi using MOSES that is a statistical machine transliteration tool. After applying transliteration rules average accuracy of this transliteration system comes out to be 63.31%. Deep and Goyal (2011) have proposed a transliteration system that addresses the problem of forward transliteration of person names from Punjabi to English by set of character mapping rules. The proposed technique achieved accuracy of 93.22%. Josan and Kaur (2011) have developed a statistical model that is used for transliterating the Punjabi text into Hindi text. The proposed system has claimed 87.72% accuracy rate. Dhore et al. (2012) have focused on the specific problem of machine transliteration of Hindi to English and Marathi to English which are previously less studied language pairs using a phonetic based direct approach. Bhalla et al. (2013) have proposed rule based transliteration scheme for English to Punjabi. Some rules have constructed for syllabification. In this probabilities are calculated for name entities (proper names and location). The proposed approach has attained accuracy of 88.19%. Joshi et al. (2013) have proposed system that can do transliteration from Roman script to Devanagari script using statistical machine learning approach.

3 Design and Implementation

3.1 Approach Followed

The proposed system for English to Punjabi transliteration follows rule based approach. A machine transliteration model should reflect the dynamic transliteration behaviors in order to produce the correct transliterations thus we have considered both source grapheme and phonetic information to achieve high performance and more accurate result. The input text goes through various stages, as shown in Figure 1, in order to get transliterated into equivalent Punjabi text.

Preprocessing module identifies language based on Unicode of the words. Segmentation module involves segmentation of source string into transliteration units of source language. Transliteration module transliterates English text to equivalent Punjabi text based on the rules framed. Surrounding characters in a given word are also considered for resolving ambiguities and for more appropriate result.

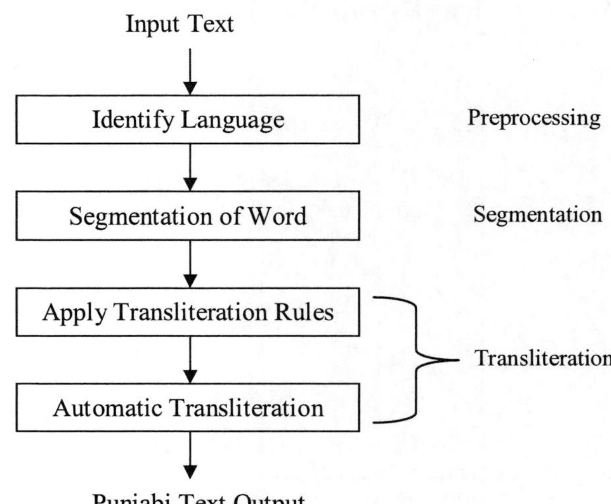

Figure 1. Rule based approach for Transliteration

3.2 English-Punjabi Transliteration Rules

Due to the differences in syntax and vocabulary of both English and Punjabi language, there is need to construct some hard rules. These rules are explained and illustrated in the following subsections.

3.2.1 English-Punjabi Character to Character Mapping

Direct character to character mapping of consonants and vowels for English-Punjabi language pair is shown in Tables 1, 2 and 3 (Deep and Goyal, 2011).

k	kh	g	gh	ng
ਕ	ਖ	ਗ	ਘ	ਙ
ch	chh	j	jh	yan
ਚ	ਛ	ਜ	ਝ	ਞ
t	th	d	dh	n
ਟ	ਠ	ਡ	ਢ	ਣ
t	th	d	dh	n
ਤ	ਥ	ਦ	ਧ	ਨ
p	ph	b	bh	m
ਪ	ਫ	ਬ	ਭ	ਮ
y	r	l	v,w	rh,r
ਯ	ਰ	ਲ	ਵ	ੜ
sh	khh	ghh	z	f
ਸ਼	ਖ਼	ਗ਼	ਜ਼	ਫ਼
lla	s	h		
ਲ਼	ਸ	ਹ		

Table 1. English-Punjabi Consonant Mapping

a ਅ	a, aa ਆ	i, ya ਇ	i ਈ	u ਉ
u ਊ	e, a ਏ	ai ਐ	o ਓ	au ਔ

Table 2. Independent Vowels Mapping

a, aa ਾ	i ਿ	i, ee ੀ	u ੁ	u, oo ੂ
e ੇ	ai, ay ੈ	o ੋ	o, au ੌ	

Table 3. Dependent Vowels Mapping

3.2.2 First Vowel Character in Word

Only direct mapping is not sufficient for transliteration, which may lead to very low accuracy of the system. The vowels in English are mapped to different characters in Punjabi depending on their position in the given word. Following rules are proposed for vowels when they occur at first position in the word:

Rule 1: if first character 'a' is followed by consonant then it is transliterated to 'ਅ'. For example, aman→ਅਮਨ

Rule 2: if 'an' combination is at first position then it is transliterated to 'ਅੰ'. For example, ankit→ਅੰਕਿਤ

Rule 3: if 'ea' combination is at first position then it is transliterated to 'ਈ'. For example, eagle→ਈਗਲ

Rule 4: if 'ei' combination is at first position then it is transliterated to 'ਏ'. For example, eight→ਏਟ

Rule 5: if 'in' combination is at first position then it is transliterated to 'ਇੰ'. For example, india→ਇੰਡੀਆ

Rule 6: if 'oi' combination is at first position then it is transliterated to 'ਉ'+'ਇ'. For example, oil→ਉਇਲ

Rule 7: if first character 'u' is followed by 'double consonant' then 'u' is transliterated to 'ਉ'+'ੱ'. For example, utter→ਉੱਤਰ

3.2.3 Last Vowel Character in Word

Vowels are mapped to different characters when they occur at last position. In order to achieve more accurate result there is need to refer to previous characters because their pronunciation is also affected by the consonants or vowels, they follow. The following rules are proposed to handle last vowel character in a word:

Rule 1: if 'ia' combination occurs at last then 'a' is transliterated to 'ਆ'. For example, sonia→ਸੋਨੀਆ

Rule 2: if last character 'a' is preceded by consonant then 'a' is transliterated to 'ਾ'. For example, samrala→ਸਮਰਾਲਾ

Rule 3: if 'nu' combination occurs at last then 'u' is transliterated to 'ੰ' + 'ੁ'. For example, sonu→ਸੋਨੂੰ

Rule 4: if 'oa' combination occurs at last then it is transliterated to 'ੋ'+ 'ਆ'. For example, goa→ਗੋਆ

Rule 5: if last character is 'e' and second last character is 'i' then 'e' is usually skipped in that case. For example, like→ਲਾਈਕ

3.2.4 CVCC Pattern (Double Consonants)

In phonetics, gemination or consonant elongation happens when a spoken consonant is pronounced for an audibly longer period of time than a short consonant. In transliteration, double consonants in English are mapped with Punjabi gemination symbol 'Addak'. The two geminates 'mm' and 'nn' are written with 'Tippi' in many cases because they represent nasalized sound (Gill and Gleason, 1986). Proposed rules for gemination are described in Table 4.

Word Combinations	English Word	Punjabi Mapping	Punjabi Word
'a' + double consonant	bhatt	'ੱ'	ਭੱਟ
'e' + double consonant	dress	'ੇ' + 'ੱ'	ਡਰੇੱਸ
'i' + double consonant	gill	'ਿ' + 'ੱ'	ਗਿੱਲ
'o' + double consonant	boss	'ੋ'	ਬੋਸ
'u' + double consonant	full	'ੁ' + 'ੱ'	ਫੁੱਲ

Table 4. Rules for Gemination

3.2.5 CVVC Pattern (Long Vowels)

When two vowels are adjacent, they form a vowel combination. There are two vowels between consonants that create either one or two sounds. For example, word 'hair' and 'poor' creates two sounds and word 'four' creates one sound. Table 5 shows mapping of various vowel combinations.

'a' Vowel Combinations (aa, ae, ai, ao, au)	'o' Vowel Combinations (oa, oe, oi, oo, ou)
'ao' → '◌ਾ' + 'ਓ' (Sarao → ਸਰਾਓ)	'oa' → '◌ੋ' (Road → ਰੋਡ)
'aun' → '◌ੌ' + '◌ਂ' (Launch → ਲੌਂਚ)	'ook'/'ood' → '◌ੁ' + '◌ੋ' (Took → ਟੁੱਕ)
'au' → '◌ੌ' (Author → ਔਥਰ)	'oo' → '◌ੁ' (Stool → ਸਟੂਲ)
'aa' → '◌ਾ' (Taal → ਤਾਲ)	'oi' → '◌ੋ' + 'ਇ' (Spoil → ਸਪੋਇਲ)
'ai' → '◌ੈ' (Train → ਟਰੇਨ)	'ou' → '◌ੋ' (Four → ਫੋਰ)
'ae' → '◌ਾ' + 'ਏ' (Rae → ਰਾਏ)	'oe' → '◌ੋ' + 'ਏ' (Poem → ਪੋਏਮ)

'e' Vowel Combinations (ea, ee, ei, eo, eu)	'u' Vowel Combinations (ua, ue, ui, uo)
'ei' → '◌ੈ' (Veil → ਵੇਲ)	'lue'/'rue' at last → '◌ੂ' (True → ਟਰੂ)
'ee' → '◌ੀ' (Mandeep → ਮਨਦੀਪ)	'ue' → '◌ੀ' + 'ਊ' (Continue → ਕੌਂਟੀਨੀਉ)
'eo' → '◌ੋ' + 'ਓ' (Deol → ਦੇਓਲ)	'ua' → '◌ਾ' (Guard → ਗਾਰਡ)
'ea' → '◌ੀ' (Heat → ਹੀਟ)	'ui_e' → '◌ਾ' + 'ਈ' (Guide → ਗਾਈਡ)
'eu' → '◌ੋ' + 'ਊ' (Heuristic → ਹੀਉਰੀਸਟੀਕ)	'uit'/'uice'/ 'uise' → '◌ੁ' (Fruit → ਫਰੂਟ)

'i' Vowel Combinations (ia, ie, io, iu)	
'ia' → '◌ੀ' + 'ਆ' (Pia → ਪੀਆ)	
'io' → '◌ੀ' + 'ਓ' (Jio → ਜੀਓ)	
'ie' at last → '◌ਾ' + 'ਈ' (Die → ਡਾਈ)	
'ie' → '◌ੀ' (Piece → ਪੀਸ)	
'iu' → '◌ੀ' + 'ਆ' (Celcius → ਸੈਲਸੀਆਸ)	

Table 5. Rules for CVVC Pattern

3.2.6 Silent Letters

A silent letter is a letter that, in a particular word, does not correspond to any sound in the word's pronunciation. Some rules have been constructed for the most common silent letters- ck, wr, kn, mn, mb, mp, dg, gh, wh etc. Following are some English words examples with silent letters and their corresponding transliteration in Punjabi: Trick→ਟਰਿੱਕ, whole→ਹੋਲ, write→ਰਾਈਟ, know→ਨੋ, column→ਕੋਲਮ, company→ਕੰਪਨੀ etc.

3.2.7 CVCe Pattern

There are somewhat different rules for syllables with CVCe pattern. An 'e' is found at the end of the word. These words are transliterated according to the matching rules, as shown in Table 6.

Word Combinations	English Word	Punjabi Mapping	Punjabi Word
current_char is 'a' second_next_char is 'e'	grace	'◌ੇ'	ਗਰੇਸ
current_char is 'i' second_next_char is 'e'	like	'◌ਾ' + 'ਈ'	ਲਾਈਕ
current_char is 'o' second_next_char is 'e'	vote	'◌ੋ'	ਵੋਟ
current_char is 'u' second_next_char is 'e'	tune	'◌ੀ' + 'ਊ'	ਟੀਉਨ

Table 6. Rules for CVCe Pattern

3.2.8 Ambiguity Resolution

There are certain characters in English those correspond to more than one pronunciation. For example, the word 's' can be pronounced as 'ਸ' or 'ਜ' as in case of 'house' or 'resume'. Other ambiguous word is 'g'. In order to resolve this problem following rules have been proposed:

Rule 1: if 'g' is followed by 'en'/'in'/'ic'/'im' then 'g' is transliterated to 'ਜ'. For example, general/ margin/ logic→ਜਨਰਲ/ ਮਾਰਜਨ/ ਲੋਜਿਕ

Rule 2: if there is 'ange'/'enge' combination then 'g' is transliterated to 'ਜ'. For example, orange/challenge→ਓਰੇਂਜ਼/ਚੈਲੇਂਜ਼

318

Rule 3: if 'g' is preceded by 'a'/'d' and followed by 'e' then 'g' is transliterated to 'ਜ'. For example, page/bridge→ਪੇਜ/ਬਰਿੱਜ

Rule 4: if 's' is preceded by 'ou'/'a' and followed by 'e' then 's' is transliterated to 'ਸ'. For example, mouse/base→ਮਾਊਸ/ਬੇਸ

Rule 5: otherwise if 's' is followed and preceded by vowel then it is transliterated to 'ਜ਼'. For example, visit/season→ਵਿਜ਼ੀਟ/ਸੀਜ਼ਨ

3.2.9 CVC Pattern (Short Vowels)

A short vowel word is any word that does not allow the vowel within it to generate that vowel's long vowel sound. Table 7 shows proposed rules for short vowels.

Short Vowel	English Word	Punjabi Mapping	Punjabi Word
'a'	fan, scan	'ੈ'	ਫੈਨ, ਸਕੈਨ
'e'	bed, pen	'ੈ' + 'ੱ'	ਬੈੱਡ, ਪੈੱਨ
'i'	big, swim	'ਿ' + 'ੱ'	ਬਿੱਗ, ਸਵਿੱਮ
'o'	dog, stop	'ੋ'	ਡੋਗ, ਸਟੋਪ
'u'	cut, bus	'ੱ'	ਕੱਟ, ਬੱਸ

Table 7. Rules for Short Vowels

3.2.10 Unreduced Vowel (Schwa + Consonant)

English language has certain words with unstressed syllables that are often pronounced with full vowels like care→ਕੇਅਰ, fire→ਫਾਇਰ, clear→ਕਲੀਅਰ, affair→ਅੱਫੇਅਰ, real→ਰੀਅਲ etc.

3.2.11 Schwa Reduction

The main problem in machine transliteration system is mainly due to the existence of schwa vowel that is sometimes considered and sometimes not. Figure 2 illustrates the schwa sound deletion and retention process in general.

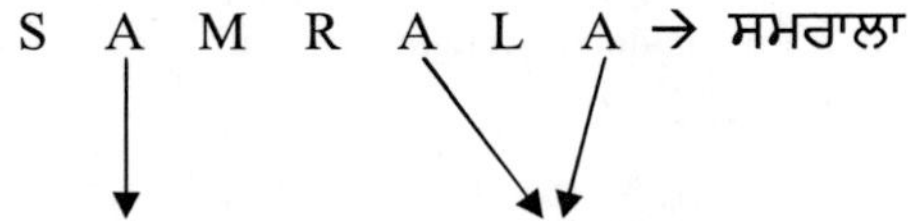

Figure 2. Process of Schwa Deletion

To find out when to retain schwa sound is not a trivial task. Some rules have been constructed to handle schwa sound:

Rule 1: if 3rd_last_char and last_char is 'a' then both are transliterated to 'ੋ'. For example, batala/samrala→ਬਟਾਲਾ/ ਸਮਰਾਲਾ

Rule 2: if 2nd_last_char is 'a' and 4th_last_char is vowel then skip 'a'. For example, sonam→ਸੋਨਮ

Rule 3: if 'a' is followed by 'rt'/ 'ph'/ 'th'/ 'rk'/ 'sk'/ 'st' then it is transliterated to 'ੋ'. For example, part/ graph/ dark/ flask/ last→ਪਾਰਟ/ਗਰਾਫ/ਡਾਰਕ/ਫਲਾਸਕ/ਲਾਸਟ

Rule 4: if 'a' is followed and preceded by same consonant then 'a' is transliterated to 'ੋ'. For example, brar→ਬਰਾੜ

4   Performance Evaluation

The evaluation of machine transliteration system can be found using Word Accuracy Rate that is used to capture the performance at word level. The word accuracy rate of proposed system is found to be 95% as shown in Table 8.

Language	Transliteration Units			Accuracy (%)
	Total	Wrong	Right	
English	10,000	495	9505	95%

Table 8. Accuracy of Transliteration System

We have manually evaluated the proposed transliteration system on news data published on a web site and the output is shown in Table 9.

Input Text
chief minister parkash singh badal had approved the agriculture power tube wells policy stipulating guide lines for the release of electric connections for agricultural pump sets in the state the punjab state electricity regulatory commission had mandated the state government to decide the number of agricultural pump connections to be released each year in the state citing reasons of ecology inadequate ground water potential declining water table among others well before the process for parliamentary elections was set in motion 593 farmers in the abohar electricity division were issued notices to deposit whopping amounts ranging between 3 lakh to get tube well connections only six of them have paid the demand notices during the recent visit of the chief minister at bahadurkhera village small farmers charan singh bhupinder singh and tejinder singh minced no words in telling him that they feel cheated since sharomani akaali dal leaders had given them an impression

during the recent elections that substantial subsidy would be made available whereas the corporation authorities had told them to bear the total cost of tube well connections
Output Text
ਚੀਫ ਮਿਨੀਸਟਰ ਪਰਕਾਸ਼ ਸਿੰਘ ਬਾਦਲ ਹੈਡ ਅੱਪਰੁਵਡ ਦ ਐਗਰੀਕੱਲਚਰ ਪਾਵਰ ਟੀਊਬ ਵੈੱਲਸ ਪੋਲਿਸੀ ਸਟੀਪੁਲੇਟਿੰਗ ਗਾਈਡ ਲਾਈਨਸ ਫੋਰ ਦ ਰੀਲੀਜ਼ ਆਫ ਇਲੈੱਕਟਰਿਕ ਕਨੈਕਸ਼ਨਜ਼ ਫੋਰ ਐਗਰੀਕੱਲਚਰਲ ਪੰਪ ਸੈੱਟਸ ਇਨ ਦ ਸਟੇਟ ਦ ਪੰਜਾਬ ਸਟੇਟ ਇਲੈੱਕਟਰੀਸਿਟੀ ਰੇਗੁਲੇਟਰੀ ਕੋਮਿਸ਼ਨ ਹੈਡ ਮਨਡੇਟਡ ਦ ਸਟੇਟ ਗਵਰਨਮੈਂਟ ਟੂ ਡੇਸਾਈਡ ਦ ਨੰਬਰ ਆਫ ਐਗਰੀਕੱਲਚਰਲ ਪੰਪ ਕਨੈਕਸ਼ਨਜ਼ ਟੂ ਬੀ ਰੀਲੀਜ਼ਡ ਈਚ ਈਅਰ ਇਨ ਦ ਸਟੇਟ ਸਾਈਟਿੰਗ ਰੀਜ਼ਨਸ ਆਫ ਏਕੋਲੋਜੀ ਇੰਨਏਡੁਕੁਏਟ ਗਰਾਊਂਡ ਵਾਟਰ ਪੋਟੈਂਸ਼ੀਅਲ ਡੇਕਲਾਈਨਿੰਗ ਵਾਟਰ ਟੇਬਲ ਅਮੰਗ ਅਦਰਸ ਵੈੱਲ ਬੀਫੋਰ ਦ ਪ੍ਰੇਸੈਂਸ ਫੋਰ ਪਰਲਿਆਮੈਂਟਰੀ ਇਲੈੱਕਸ਼ਨਜ਼ ਵਾਜ਼ ਸੈਂਟ ਇਨ ਸੈਸ਼ਨ 593 ਫਾਰਮਰਸ ਇਨ ਦ ਅਬੇਹਰ ਇਲੈੱਕਟਰੀਸਿਟੀ ਡੀਵੀਜ਼ਨ ਵਰ ਇੱਸੁਡ ਨੋਟੀਸਜ਼ ਟੂ ਡੀਪੋਜ਼ਿਟ ਵੇਰਿੰਗ ਅਮਾਉਂਟਸ ਰੈਂਜ਼ਿੰਗ ਬੇਟਵੀਨ 3 ਲਖ ਟੂ ਗੈਂਟ ਟੀਊਬ ਵੈੱਲ ਕਨੈਕਸ਼ਨਜ਼ ਉਨਲੀ ਸਿੱਕਸ ਆਫ ਦੈੱਮ ਹੈਵ ਪੇਡ ਦ ਡੇਮਾਂਡ ਨੋਟੀਸਜ਼ ਡੀਉਰਿੰਗ ਦ ਰੀਸੈਂਟ ਵਿਜ਼ੀਟ ਆਫ ਦ ਚੀਫ ਮਿਨੀਸਟਰ ਐਟ ਬਹਦੁਰਖੇਰਾ ਵਿੱਲੇਜ ਸਮਾਲ ਫਾਰਮਰਸ ਚਰਨ ਸਿੰਘ ਭੁਪਿੰਦਰ ਸਿੰਘ ਐਂਡ ਤੇਜਿੰਦਰ ਸਿੰਘ ਮਿੰਸਡ ਨੇ ਵਰਡਸ ਇਨ ਟੈੱਲਿੰਗ ਹਿੰਮ ਦੈਟ ਦ ਫੀਲ ਚੀਟਡ ਸ੍ਰੋਮਨੀ ਅਕਾਲੀ ਦਲ ਲੀਡਰਸ ਹੈਡ ਗਿਵਨ ਦੈੱਮ ਐਨ ਇੰਪ੍ਰੈੱਸ਼ਨ ਡੀਉਰਿੰਗ ਦ ਰੀਸੈਂਟ ਇਲੈੱਕਸ਼ਨਜ਼ ਦੈਟ ਸੁਬਸਟੈਂਸ਼ੀਅਲ ਸਬਸਿਡੀ ਵੁੱਡ ਬੀ ਮੇਡ ਅਵੇਲੇਬਲ ਵੇਅਰਾਐਜ਼ ਦ ਕੋਰਪੋਰੇਸ਼ਨ ਐਥੋਰੀਟੀਜ਼ ਹੈਡ ਟੇਲਡ ਦੈੱਮ ਟੂ ਬੀਅਰ ਦ ਟੇਟਲ ਕੋਸਟ ਆਫ ਟੀਊਬ ਵੈੱਲ ਕਨੈਕਸ਼ਨਜ਼

Table 9. Result of Proposed System

5 Conclusion and Future Scope

In this paper we have described transliteration system for English-Punjabi language pair using a rule based approach. There are certain syllable patters in English such as CVC, CVVC, CVCC, CVCe etc. Only a single rule is not applicable to all these patterns so different rules have been proposed for the transliteration of such syllable patterns. Also various rules have been proposed to handle ambiguous words, unstressed vowels and schwa sound. The proposed system is also applicable for transliteration of some person names and locations.

The existing work done in English to Punjabi transliteration emphasis on transliteration of named entities. In our work we have considered all possible English words for transliteration.

Still schwa sound deletion and multiple representation of same word need to be more explored. There are many English words that are spelled the same but pronounced differently. To resolve this issue, the future work can be based on referring to the context of the words in order

to choose correct transliteration. We can say that accuracy of proposed system is depends on the rules framed so it can be furthered improved by adding new rules when identified.

References

Bhalla, D. and Joshi, N. (2013), *"Rule Based Transliteration Scheme For English To Punjabi"*, International Journal on Natural Language Computing, Vol. 2, No. 2, pp. 67-73.

Deep, K. and Goyal, V. (2011), *"Development of a Punjabi to English Transliteration System"*, International Journal of Computer Science and Communication, Vol. 2, No. 2, pp. 521-526.

Dhore, M., Dixit, S. and Dhore, R. (2012), *"Hindi and Marathi to English NE Transliteration Tool using Phonology and Stress Analysis"*, in proceedings of 24th International Conference on Computational Linguistic, Mumbai, India, pp. 111-118.

Gill, H. and Gleason, H. (1986), *"A Reference Grammar of Punjabi"*, Publication Bureau, Punjabi University, Patiala, India, pp. 38-42.

Goyal, V. and Lehal, G. (2009), *"Hindi-Punjabi Machine Transliteration System (For Machine Translation System)"*, George Ronchi Foundation Journal, Italy, Vol. 64, No. 1, pp. 1-7.

Josan, G. and Kaur, J. (2011), *"Punjabi To Hindi Statistical Machine Transliteration"*, International Journal of Information Technology and Knowledge Management, Vol. 4, No. 2, pp. 459-463.

Josan, G. and Lehal, G. (2010), *"A Punjabi to Hindi Machine Transliteration System"*, Computational Linguistics and Chinese Language Processing, Vol. 15, No. 2, pp. 77-102.

Joshi, H., Bhatt, A. and Patel, H. (2013), *"Transliterated Search using Syllabification Approach"*, Forum for Information Retrieval Evaluation, Delhi, India.

Kaur, J. and Josan, G. (2011), *"Statistical Approach to Transliteration from English to Punjabi"*, International Journal on Computer Science and Engineering, Vol. 3, No. 4, pp. 1518-1527.

Knight, K. and Graehl, J. (1998), *"Machine transliteration"*, in proceedings of the 35th annual meetings of the Association for Computational Linguistics, Madrin, Spain, pp. 128-135.

Malik, M. (2006), *"Punjabi Machine Transliteration"*, in proceedings of the 21st International Conference on Computational Linguistics and 44th Annual Meeting of the ACL, Sydney, pp. 1137-1144.

Oh, J. and Choi, K. (2002), *"An English-Korean Transliteration Model Using Pronunciation and Contextual Rules"*, in proceedings of the 19th International Conference on Computational Linguistics, Taipei, Taiwan, pp. 758-764.

Saini, T. and Lehal, G. (2008), *"Shahmukhi to Gurmukhi Transliteration System: A Corpus based Approach"*, Research in Computing Science (Mexico), Vol. 33, pp. 151-162.

Evaluating Two Annotated Corpora of Hindi Using a Verb Class Identifier

Neha Dixit
Centre for Technology Studies,
MGAHV, Wardha
bhunehadixit@gmail.com

Narayan Choudhary
ezDI, LLC.
choudharynarayan@gmail.com

Abstract

[In the past few years, Indian languages have seen a welcome arrival of large parts of speech annotated corpora, thanks to the DIT funded projects across the country. A major corpus of 50,000 sentences in each of the 12 of major Indian languages is available for research purposes. This corpus has been annotated for parts of speech using the BIS annotation guideline. However, it remains to be seen how good these corpora are with respect to annotation itself. Given that annotated corpora are also prone to human errors which later affect the accuracies achieved by the statistical NLP tools based on these corpora, there is a need to open evaluation of such a corpus. This paper focuses on finding annotation and other types of errors in two major parts of speech annotated corpora of Hindi and correcting them using a tool developed for the identification of verb classes in Hindi.]

1 Introduction

This paper emerges from a task meant to automatically identify the syntactico-semantic class of Hindi verbs occurring in a sentence. A verb class identifier was developed that took the parts of speech annotated text as input and identified the class of the verbs marked as main verbs in the text. Section 1 and 2 details the development of this automated identifier. This tool was run against two corpora, first the Hindi corpus developed by Microsoft Research India (MSRI) (Bali et al., 2010) and distributed by the Linguistic Data Consortium (LDC)[1] and second, the Hindi corpus developed under the consortia project called Indian Language Corpora Initiative (ILCI) (Choudhary et al., 2011) and distributed by the TDIL[2]. While the MSRI corpus is annotated in the IL-PoST framework (Baskaran et al., 2008) of parts of speech annotation, the ILCI corpus is annotated using a tagset now commonly known as the BIS (Bureau of Indian Standards) tagset. Both of these tagsets are conceptually hierarchical and therefore have top level categories for each of the classes of words. For verbs, both of these tagsets categorize them as either main verb or auxiliary verb. While the IL-POST also includes the morphological information for each of the verbs annotated, the BIS tagset requires only the top level categorization of main or auxiliary verb. We show that both of these corpora have a high number of errors of both omission and commission which should be taken care of before these corpora are used as gold data for further NLP tasks such as statistical parts of speech tagging and so on.

The second section gives an overview of the verb classification used to develop the verb class identifier followed by the third section detailing the development of the knowledge base. The fourth and fifth sections detail the ambiguities arising out of the use of a knowledge base for verb classification and provide a solution for the most frequent cause of the ambiguities. The last sections present the results achieved after evaluating the verb class identifier against the LDC and the ILCI corpora followed by an error analysis.

---

[1] https://catalog.ldc.upenn.edu/LDC2010T24
[2] http://tdil-dc.in

D S Sharma, R Sangal and J D Pawar. Proc. of the 11th Intl. Conference on Natural Language Processing, pages 321–327,
Goa, India. December 2014. ©2014 NLP Association of India (NLPAI)

2 Verb Classification

While we base the classification of verbs on the traditional classification into transitive and intransitives, we extend the category into multiple sub-classifications. Verbs are classified into a total of 13 categories. The classification we use emanates from the practical use envisaged for such a knowledge base. While the major categories are traditionally four in number (namely, intransitive, transitive, causative and double causative), we further classify the intransitives into 7 sub-classes based on some diagnostic tests which govern their syntactic function and affect or validate what constructions they allow in a sentence.

2.1 Classification of Intransitive Verbs

There are three diagnostic tests applied to classify the intransitive verbs. These diagnostic tests are as follows.

2.1.1 Allows ergative –ne

We know that some verbs require the marking of ergative case marker –ne in the simple past sentences in Hindi while with the others the same is not allowed. While this is always required with the transitive, causative and double causative verbs, the same does not always happen with the intransitive verbs.

For example, in the following two sentences where the main verb is intransitive, the use of –ne makes the sentence ungrammatical:

*Hindi	मोहन	ने	बहुत	सोया
IPA:	mohən	ne	bahut	soja:
Gloss:	Mohan	ERG	very	sleep-PST-MSG
Meaning:	Mohan slept a lot			

*Hindi	सुमन	के	सिर	ने	बहुत	चकराया
IPA:	sumən	ke	sir	ne	bahut	cəkra:ja:
Gloss:	Suman	POS	head	ERG	a lot	reel
Meaning:	Suman's head reeled a lot.					

But in the sentences below where again the main verb is intransitive, the use of –ne marking is perfectly fine:

Hindi	शेर	ने	जोर	से	दहाड़ा
IPA:	sher	ne	dʒor	se	dəha:ɖa:
Gloss:	lion	ERG	strong	ASSOC	roar-PST-MSG
Meaning:	The lion roared strongly.				

Hindi	राम	ने	जोर	से	छींका
IPA:	ra:m	ne	dʒor	se	cʰĩːka:
Gloss:	Ram	ERG	strong	ASSOC	sneeze-PST-MSG
Meaning:	Ram sneezed heavily.				

2.1.2 Allows Adjectival Use of the Perfective Form

All the intransitive verbs in their perfective forms cannot be used as an adjective. While some verbs allow this, others do not. For example, in the following sentences, the perfective forms of the verbs are being used as adjectives to modify nouns or noun phrases following it:

*Hindi	तीर्थ	यात्रा	पर	गए	हुए	लोगों	की..
IPA:	ti:rtʰa:	ja:tra:	pər	gəe	hue	logon	ki: …
Gloss:	pilgrimage	on	go-PFT	be-PFT	peopl e	of	
Meaning:	People who have gone on a pilgrimage…						

Hindi	संत	गिरे	हुए	लोगों	को	उठा ते	हैं
IPA:	sənt	gire	hue	logon	ko	utʰa ʈe	hɛ̃
Gloss:	saint	fall-PFT	be-PFT	peo-ple	ACC	pick IMPF	be-PL
Meaning:	Saints help the fallen people.						

Hindi	झाड़ी	में	अटका	गेंद	खो	गया
IPA:	dʒʰaɖi	mẽ	əʈka:	gẽɖ	kʰo	gəja:
Gloss:	bush	LOC	stick-PST	ball	lose-PST	go-PST
Meaning:	The ball stuck in the bush got lost.					

But if we use the same form of some other verbs as adjectives, the sentence becomes ungrammatical or sounds awkard:

*Hindi	कांपा	हुआ	लड़का	गिर	गया
IPA:	kã:pa:	hua:	ləɖka:	gir	gəja:
Gloss:	shiver-PST	be-PST	boy	fall	go-PST
Meaning:	The boy, who had shivered, fell.				

*Hindi	घाटी	में	चीखा	लड़का	मर	गया
IPA:	gʰa:ʈ	mẽ	ci:kʰa:	ləɖk	mə	gəja:

	i:			a:	r
Gloss:	val-ley	LO C	shriek-PST	boy	die	go-PST
Meaning:	The boy, who had shrieked in the valley, died.

*Hindi	दौड़ा	हुआ	लड़का	जीता
IPA:	dəuɖa:	hua:	ləɖka:	ʤi:ʈa:
Gloss:	run-PFT	be-PFT	boy	win-PFT
Meaning:	The boy, who had run, won.

2.1.3 Passivization Selection

Similar to other constraints, some intransitive verbs does not allow passivization while other intransitives do. For example, in the following sentences the passive use of the main verb is alright:

Hindi	अब	उठा	जाए
IPA:	əb	utʰa	ʤae
Gloss:	now	stand-PFT	go-OPT
Meaning:	Let's stand up now.

Hindi	शेर	से	गुर्राया	नहीं	गया
IPA:	ʃer	se	gurraja:	nəhĩ:	gəja:
Gloss:	lion	ASSOC	roar-PFT	NEG	go-PFT
Meaning:	The lion could not roar.

But the same does not hold true for the intransitive verbs as used in the following sentences:

Hindi	अब	उजड़ा	जाए
IPA:	əb	uʤɖa:	ʤa:e
Gloss:	now	wreck-PFT	go-OPT
Meaning:	Let's get wrecked now.

Hindi	उससे	घबड़ाया	नहीं	गया
IPA:	usəse	gʰəbɖa:ja:-PFT	nəhī:	gəja:
Gloss:	he-DAT	bewilder-PFT	NEG	go-PFT
Meaning:	He could not get bewildered.

Taking these three diagnostics test as the base of the sub-classification within intransitive verbs, we come with a total of 13 classes of verbs as noted in the table below:

Verb Class	Verb Class Label
Causative	CAUS
Copular Verb	COP
Second Causative	DB_CAUS
Intransitive (+Adjectival)	INTR_ADJ

Intransitive (+Adjectival +Passivization)	INTR_ADJ_PAS
Intransitive (+Ergative)	INTR_ERG
Intransitive (+Ergative + Adjectival)	INTR_ERG_ADJ
Intransitive (+Ergative + Adjectival +Passivization)	INTR_ERG_ADJ_PAS
Intransitive (+Ergative +Passivization)	INTR_ERG_PAS
Intransitive (+Passivization)	INTR_PAS
Intransitive	INTR
Intransitive/Transitive	TRAN_INTR
Transitive	TRAN

Table 1: Classification of Verbs

3 Developing a Verb Class Knowledge Base

Identification of verbs and their classes bases itself mainly on what we consider the largest ever knowledge base of Hindi verbs collected from various sources such as dictionaries, corpus and others. The knowledge base contains a total of 3240 verbs and all of their morphological forms, including spelling variations and common mistakes. The morphological forms and the spelling variations are further given their own labels in the knowledge base itself along with the class for each of the verbs and their forms. The structure of knowledge base has been illustrated in the following table:

ID	Word	morph_type	verb_class
86727	पीना	inf_msg	Transitive
86728	पीनी	inf_fsg	Transitive
86729	पीने	inf_pl	Transitive
86730	पीता	impf_msg	Transitive
86731	पीती	impf_fsg	Transitive
86732	पीतीं	impf_fsgh	Transitive
86733	पीते	impf_pl	Transitive
86734	पिया	pft_msg	Transitive
86735	पियी	pft_fsg_var1	Transitive

Table 2: Structure of Knowledge Base

With inclusion of 3240 verbs, we get a total of 149,518 words present in the knowledge base.

4 Types of Ambiguities in Verb Classification

The knowledge base forms as main base for the assignment of verb classes in a given sentence. However, the knowledge base itself cannot cover all the cases as there are verbs which can fall into more than one class depending on the context in which they appear. An analysis of the verbs present in the knowledge shows that it has 1260 words that occur twice in the corpus. These words are possible causes of ambiguity resulting into incorrect assignment of class to the verbs. Our analysis shows that these ambiguities could be of 5 different types as mentioned below.

4.1 Ambiguity: Verb Root vs. Perfective Verb

This occurs mainly because of a derivational process used in Hindi and several other Indian languages where a valency is added by vowel lengthening. For example while the verb जग/ʤəg, an intransitive verb, means "to wake up" the verb root जगा/ʤəga, a transitive verb, means "to awaken". While जगा/ʤəga is a verb root, it is also the perfective inflectional form of the verb root जग/ʤəg and this way जगा/ʤəga gets two verb classes which need to be resolved.

While a solution to disambiguate this type of ambiguity has been implemented as described in by analysing the verb group patterns (as mentioned in the section below), the other types of ambiguities (described below) have to be taken care of at the word level.

4.2 Ambiguity: Conjunctive Participle vs. Perfective Verb

Another type of ambiguity which has a chance of becoming frequent if the genre of the corpus under test is of non-formal kind is that conjunctive participles can get confused with the perfective of the verbs ending on consonant -क/-k. Conjunctive participles are usually formed by adding the auxiliary verb –कर/-kər to any verb root and give a sense of perfective aspect to the verb. While the formal way of creating the conjunctive participle is to either attach -कर-/-kər to the verb root itself or juxtaposing it afterwards, informally the variant -के/-ke is used. Thus we can have खाकर/kʰa:kər and खाके/kʰa:ke having the same sense and used interchangeably. Except for a few frequent use of this variant such as खाके//kʰa:ke, रोके/roke, कसके/kəske, etc. most of the time this variant is not used. And this is why we have ignored finding out a rule-based solution to disambiguate this.

4.3 Ambiguity: Perfective Verb vs. Infinitive Verb

Some verbs that end with consonant –न/-n as in छान/cʰa:n, मान/ma:n, जान/ʤa:n etc. may be sharing the same grapheme and may be homophonous with some other verb's infinitive form. Thus a verb like छाना/cʰa:na: may have two meanings, the first being the perfective of the verb root छान/cʰa:n (to filter) and another as the infinitive form of the verb root छा/cʰa: (which means "to cover the roof"). However, this type of ambiguity is also limited and count only 3 in Hindi. For this very reason, we have also ignored disambiguating this for the time being.

4.4 Ambiguity: Perfective Verb vs. Imperfective Verb

There are also a couple of verbs which can be interpreted as imperfective of a verb root and perfective of another. There are two verb root pairs that create this problem. The first pair is जीतना/ʤi:tna: and जीना/ʤina:, meaning respectively "to win" and "to live". The second pair is बरतना/bərətna बरना/bərna, meaning respectively "to follow" and "to choose".

4.5 Ambiguity: Verbs in multiple classes

While it is very common in other languages such as English that the same verb is used both as transitive and intransitive, the same is very rare in Indo-Aryan languages like Hindi. Out of all the verbs that we have analysed, we found only one verb that can be used both as transitive and intransitive. This verb is ऐंठना/ɛ̃tʰna: (meaning "to writhe" or "to snatch by deceit").

5 Root vs. Perfective: Disambiguation

Taking a cue from the work done on identification of verb groups in Hindi by Choudhary et al. (2011a), we perform an analysis of the total verb group templates as defined here. Choudhary identifies a total of 675 templates covering all the verb groups possible in Hindi, including the compound verb constructions. As we know that for each of the verb groups found in Hindi, the class is defined by the main verb and this main verb occurs at the start of the verb groups. If we know the morphological type of the main verb (knowing whether it is verb root or a perfective form), we can identify the class of the verb with the help of the verb groups.

An analysis of the 675 verb group templates shows that there are only 30 such templates where both verb root (VR) and perfective verb (VR_pft) can stay. This means we basically have to find out the disambiguation rules for only these verb groups. The rest are taken care of automatically as proper, grammatical structure of Hindi would not allow them. These verb group templates are noted in the table below:

Template with First word as either VR or VR_pft	Ambiguity
VR_pft+ja+rah_pft+ho_fut	Yes
VR_pft+ja_pft+ho_impf+prs_aux	Yes
VR_pft+ja+rah_pft+prs_aux	Yes
VR_pft+ja_inf+cahiye+pst_aux	Yes
VR_pft+ja+rah_pft+pst_aux	Yes
VR_pft+ja_inf+cahiye	Yes
VR_pft+ja_impf+prs_aux	Yes
VR_pft+ja_pft+prs_aux	Yes
VR_pft+par_pft+prs_aux	Yes
VR_pft+ja_pft+pst_aux	Yes
VR_pft+par_pft+pst_aux	Yes
VR_pft+ja+rah_pft	Yes
VR_pft+ja_fut	Yes
VR_pft+ja_impf	Yes
VR_pft+ja_opt	Yes
VR_pft+ja_pft	Yes
VR_pft+rah_pft	Yes
VR_pft+VINF	Yes
VR_pft+VINF_imp	Yes
VR_pft+ho_fut	No
VR_pft+ho_impf	No
VR_pft+ho_opt	No
VR_pft+ho_pft	No
VR_pft+kar_fut	No
VR_pft+kar_imp	No
VR_pft+kar_impf	No
VR_pft+rah_fut	No
VR_pft+rah_imp	No
VR_pft+rah_opt	No
VR_pft+rakh_pft	No

Table 3: Possible Ambiguous Verb Group Templates

Now, if we closely analyse these auxiliary verbs in the given templates, we find that these auxiliaries actually do not allow perfective verbs to occur as their main verbs. This conclusion is based on a corpus study done on the EMILLE (McEnery et al., 2000) corpus and the Gyan-Nidhi corpus as well as some exact searches done on a prominent search engine. For example, in the phrase जगा जाएगी/ʤga: ʤa:egi:, the main verb जगा/ʤga: or for that matter any other verb can never be inflected for the perfective aspect. Similar is the case with the place of other main verbs in the templates having ambiguity (noted with "yes" in table V above).

6 Evaluating against Corpora

The tool was given two corpora as input– the LDC and the ILCI. A summary of the error analysis on the results achieved has been provided here.

6.1 The LDC Corpus

LDC corpus contains a total of 4839 sentences annotated in the IL-PoST framework. When run against the verb class identifier, we get the following results:

Total Main Verbs Found	8,386
Total Main Verbs Classified	8,048
Unclassified Main Verbs	338
Error Percentage	4.030527

The 4% of error in identifying a verb class for a verb marked as VM emerges due to four different reasons as noted below:

Error Types	Frequency
Spelling Error	258
Annotation Error	39
Tokenization Error	18
Echo-Words	23
Total Errors	338

6.2 The ILCI Corpus

The Hindi corpus of ILCI contains 50,000 sentences from two domains of health and tourism. Summary of the error analysis done on the output of this corpus is given below:

Total Main Verbs in ILCI	87,801
No. of Main Verbs Classified in ILCI	82,232
No. of Main Verbs Unclassified in ILCI	5,569
Accuracy on the ILCI Corpus	93.66
Error Percentage	6.34

Further analysis breaks down the types of errors found in this evaluation. This has been shown in the table below:

Error Type	Tour-ism	Heal-th	Over-all	% of Errors
Annotation	3396	1721	5117	0.91604

Error				
Echo word	104	144	248	0.044397
Spelling Error	31	96	127	0.022735
KB Error	74	8	82	0.01468
Pre-Processing Error	3	9	12	0.002148

Table 4: Error Types in the ILCI Corpus

7 Error Types

Evaluating against the ILCI corpus and following the error analysis, we find that there are four types of errors in the annotated text. "KB errors" are errors of knowledge base used in the verb classification tool itself. A summary of the errors for each of the tokens at the annotation level are shown below:

Correct Tag for VM	Unique Words	Frequency of Errors
JJ	420	3,543
NN	660	1,868
Echo	120	254
KB	41	213
Spelling	109	127
Tokenization	26	30
PP	7	28
RB	6	11
RPD	2	9
DMD	5	5
FW	1	1
PRP	1	1
CCD	1	1
DMR	1	1

Table 5: Error Types and their Frequency in the ILCI Corpus

The four major types of errors are mentioned below.

7.1 Annotation Error

Annotation errors are the errors in the assignment of the parts of speech tags to the text. As seen in the table above, the highest number of words marked incorrectly as main verb adjectives which should have been marked as JJ. This is followed by words that should have been marked as NN but are marked as VM. Some prepositions, adverbs, particles and demonstratives are also marked as VM. Some examples such errors are noted below:

Actual Tag	Example Words
JJ	स्थित, पैदा, उपलब्ध, पता, स्थापित, प्राप्त, खड़े, प्रदान, घिरा, शुरू, तैयार, सेवन, निर्मित
NN	सेवन, प्रयोग, आराम, नजर, ध्यान, लाभ, काम, निर्माण, मालिश, याद, इस्तेमाल, बढ़ावा, बढ़ावा
PP	पर, बाहर, सामने, पास, अंदर, आर-पार, का, पारकर
RB	खासकर, नहीं, रूबरू, ऐसे, खड़े-खड़े, सिर्फ
RPD	वाला, ही
DMD	इससे, यह, यहाँ, वहाँ, वहीं

Table 6: Examples of Annotation Errors

7.2 Echo word

Echo-words are a type of reduplication used as a method of word formation for emphasis and other semantic purposes. Using the echo-formation as the word formation process, a non-word is used together with the actual word to add a meaning to it. This phenomenon is seen all the content class words of Indian languages.

However, when it comes to be captured at the level of language computation, this has not been covered yet in most of the cases. The current knowledge base used in the verb class identifier also does not cover the echo-words. Therefore, the main verbs when used in their echo-formation forms do not get detected. Some examples of such words as shown in the examples below:

खाने-पीने, चलने-फिरने, कूट-पीसकर, आने-जाने, घूमने-फिरने, आना-जाना, चलते-चलते, पहुँचते-पहुँचते, उठने-बैठने, मिलता-जुलता

7.3 Spelling Error

The ILCI corpus contains text that is usually corrected for any spelling errors. But some errors have still been found in our analysis. Some of these spelling errors are as follows:

होगें, धों, बढने, भिगों, रखनें, करेगें, करों, चढ़कर, छुपे

7.4 Pre-Processing Error

Parts of speech annotation is usually done after the text is pre-processed and tokenized properly. The same is true with the ILCI corpus as well. However, some errors of pre-processing/tokenization are still left in the text itself. Some examples are shown below:

"(बोलना, ", "बहना'", "```देखने```", "```देखो",
"```सुनने```", "```सूँघने```", "आना'", "आने'", "करें-",
"काँट", "किया।", "खायें/खिलायें", "जाँचे,"

8   Conclusion

NLP community in India must be elated to have
received a big annotated corpus in many Indian
languages, including Hindi. These corpora really
help a lot in developing next generation of NLP
tools for various purposes. However, these cor-
pora are labor intensive tasks and prone to hu-
man errors. Errors have been noted in almost all
of the human annotation tasks including the Penn
Treebank (Manning, C., 2011), the same is true
also for other corpora. We have shown here a
method to check the accuracy of the tags as-
signed to main verbs, done the error analysis and
pointed out the errors that should be taken care
of in the next release of the ILCI corpus and the
LDC corpus so that users of the corpora do not
need to do the same task again. The verb class
identifier tool we used to mark the possible er-
rors can also be used to check the accuracy of
any other Hindi corpus annotated for parts of
speech tags, thereby alleviating the time taken
for error analysis.

Reference

Bali, Kalika, Monojit Choudhury, Priyanka Biswas,
Girish Nath Jha, Narayan Kumar Choudhary and
Maansi Sharma. 2010. Indian Language Part-of-
Speech Tagset: Hindi. Linguistic Data Consortium,
Philadelphia.

Baskaran, Sankaran, Kalika Bali, Monojit Choudhury,
Tanmoy Bhattacharya, Pushpak Bhattacharyya, Gi-
rish Nath Jha, S. Rajendran, K. Saravanan, L. Sob-
ha and K.V. Subbarao. 2008. A Common Parts-of-
Speech Tagset Framework for Indian Languages.
In: Nicoletta Calzolari (Conference Chair), Khalid
Choukri, Bente Maegaard, Joseph Mariani, Jan Od-
jik, Stelios Piperidis, Daniel Tapias (Eds.) Proceed-
ings of the Sixth Inter-national Language Re-
sources and Evaluation (LREC'08), Marrakech,
Morocco.

Choudhary, Narayan and Girish Nath Jha. 2011.
Creating Multilingual Parallel Corpora in Indian
Languages.   In: Proceedings of 5th Language
Technology Conference, Poznan.

Choudhary, Narayan, Girish Nath Jha, Pramod Pan-
dey. 2011a. A Rule based Method for the Identifi-
cation of TAM features in a PoS Tagged Corpus.
In: Proceedings of 5th Language Technology Con-
ference, Fundacja Uniwersytety im. A. Mickiewic-
za, Poznan.

Manning, Christopher D. 2011. Part-of-Speech Tag-
ging from 97% to 100%: Is It Time for Some Lin-
guistics? In: Alexander Gelbukh (ed.), Computa-
tional Linguistics and Intelligent Text Processing,
12th International Con-ference, CICLing 2011,
Proceedings, Part I. Lecture Notes in Computer
Science 6608, Springer

Hindi Word Sketches

Anil Krishna Eragani[1], Varun Kuchibhotla[1], Dipti Misra Sharma[1], Siva Reddy[2], and Adam Kilgarriff[3]

[1]IIIT Hyderabad, India; [2]University of Edinburgh; [3]UK, Lexical Computing Ltd., UK

`{anil.eragani,varun.k}@research.iiit.ac.in, dipti@iiit.ac.in,`
`siva.reddy@ed.ac.uk, adam@lexmasterclass.com`

Abstract

Word sketches are one-page automatic, corpus-based summaries of a word's grammatical and collocational behaviour. These are widely used for studying a language and in lexicography. Sketch Engine is a leading corpus tool which takes as input a corpus and generates word sketches for the words of that language. It also generates a thesaurus and 'sketch differences', which specify similarities and differences between near-synonyms. In this paper, we present the functionalities of Sketch Engine for Hindi. We collected HindiWaC, a web crawled corpus for Hindi with 240 million words. We lemmatized, POS tagged the corpus and then loaded it into Sketch Engine.

1   Introduction

A language *corpus* is simply a collection of texts, so-called when it is used for language research. Corpora can be used for all sorts of purposes: from literature to language learning; from discourse analysis to grammar to language change to sociolinguistic or regional variation; from translation to technology.

Corpora are becoming more and more important, because of computers. On a computer, a corpus can be searched and explored in all sorts of ways. Of course that requires the right app. One leading app for corpus querying is the Sketch Engine (Kilgarriff et al., 2004). The Sketch Engine has been in daily use for writing dictionary entries since 2004, first at Oxford University Press, more recently at Cambridge University Press, Collins, Macmillan, and in National Language Institutes for Czech, Dutch, Estonian, Irish, Slovak and Slovene. It is also in use for all the other purposes listed above. On logging in to the Sketch Engine, the user can explore corpora for sixty languages. In many cases the corpora are the largest and best available for the language. For Indian languages, there are the corpora for Bengali, Gujarati, Hindi, Malayalam, Tamil and Telugu. The largest is for Hindi with

कर *(verb)*
HindiWaC Sketches - Grammar_70% freq = 4955783 (18,246.1 per million)

pof	1,345,592	6.6	lwg cont	1,027,372	5.2	k2	283,996	3.6	k7	161,837	5.7	k1	114,164	2.7
प्राप्त	50,479	10.16	है	629,115	11.08	कि	41,434	9.96	तौर	4,268	9.01	लोग	3,437	7.23
बंद	33,516	9.6	था	151,263	10.6	लोग	4,837	7.43	आधार	3,600	8.93	सरकार	2,592	7.91
तैयार	33,110	9.58	सक	61,025	10.13	कार्य	2,396	7.63	बात	3,250	7.44	पुलिस	1,869	8.03
प्रस्तुत	25,295	9.23	रह	54,961	9.12	बात	2,192	6.61	स्तर	2,517	8.24	सिंह	1,254	7.21
पैदा	24,767	9.18	हो	22,890	6.65	मन	1,581	6.98	विषय	1,804	7.79	कुछ	955	5.94
पूरा	24,715	9.1	गया	22,153	8.66	काम	1,370	6.74	स्थान	1,697	7.53	जी	926	6.75
तय	23,929	9.15	जा	19,941	7.93	जीवन	1,277	6.41	नाम	1,681	7.27	विभाग	672	6.77
स्थापित	23,403	9.12	चाह	17,318	8.6	कमी	1,110	6.87	पद	1,610	7.79	अधिकारी	597	6.47
जारी	23,322	9.09	गई	6,716	7.36	समाज	1,064	6.25	मुद्दा	1,338	7.63	कंपनी	588	6.46
पेश	23,064	9.1	पहले	5,268	7.18	बच्चा	1,050	6.18	समय	1,243	6.37	वह	537	6.44

Figure 1. Word sketches for the verb कर (do)

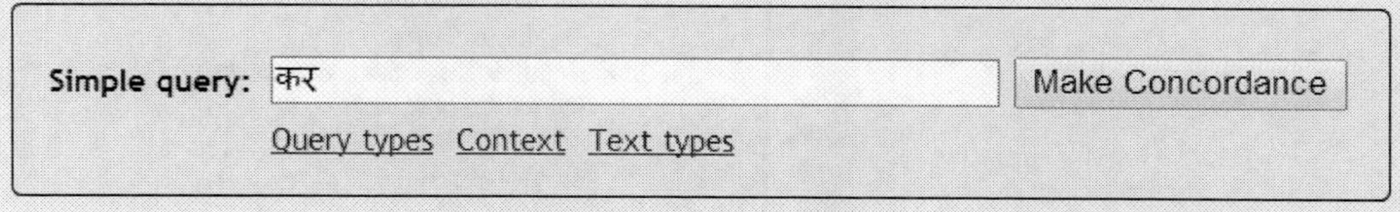

Figure 2. Simple concordance query

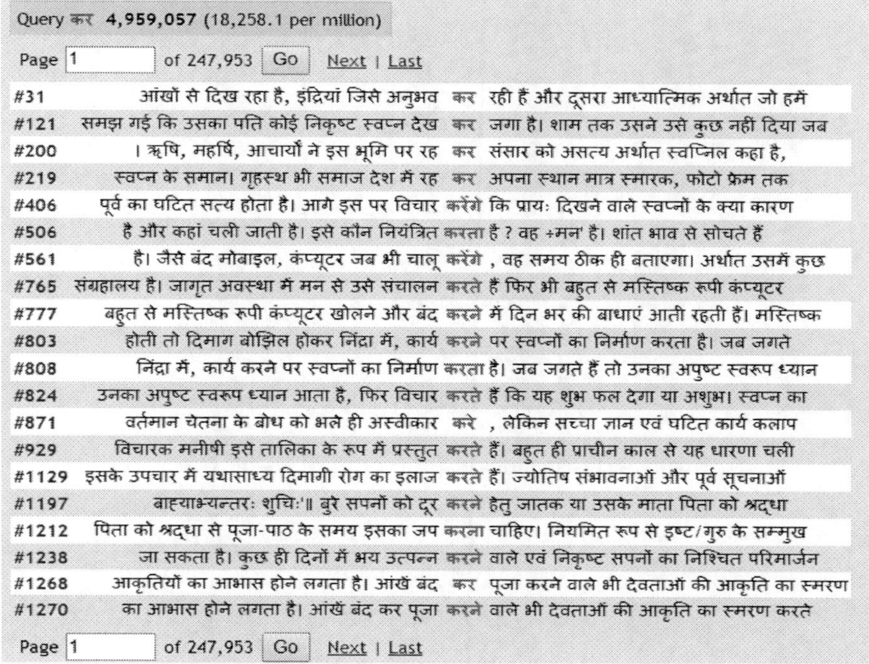

Figure 3. The resulting concordance lines

240 million words – we would be referring to it as HindiWaC in the rest of the paper.

The function that gives the Sketch Engine its name is the **'word sketch'**, a one-page, automatically-derived summary of a word's grammatical and collocational behaviour, as in Figure 1. Since the images in this paper are screen shots taken from Sketch Engine, translations and gloss have not been provided for the Hindi words in the images.

In this paper we first introduce the main functions of the Sketch Engine, with Hindi examples. We then describe how we built and processed HindiWaC, and set it up in the Sketch Engine.

2 The Sketch Engine For Hindi

2.1 The Simple Concordance Query Function

A Simple concordance query shows the word as it is used in different texts. Figure 2 shows the query box, while Figures 3 shows its output. A simple search query for a word such as कर (do) searches for the lemma as well as the words which have कर (do) as the lemma, so कर (do), किया (did), करन (to do), करत ([they] will do), etc. are all retrieved. Figure 3 shows the first 20 results out of the retrieved ~5 million results.

2.2 The Frequency Functions

The Sketch Engine interface provides easy access to tools for visualizing different aspects of the word frequency (see Figure 4). The *Frequency Node forms* function on the left hand menu in Figure 4 shows which of the returned forms are most frequent.

Thus we have immediately discovered that the commonest forms of the lemma कर (do) are कर (do), किया (did) and करन (to do).

The **p/n** links are for positive and negative examples. Clicking on **p** gives a concordance for the word form, while clicking on **n** gives the whole concordance *except* for the word form.

329

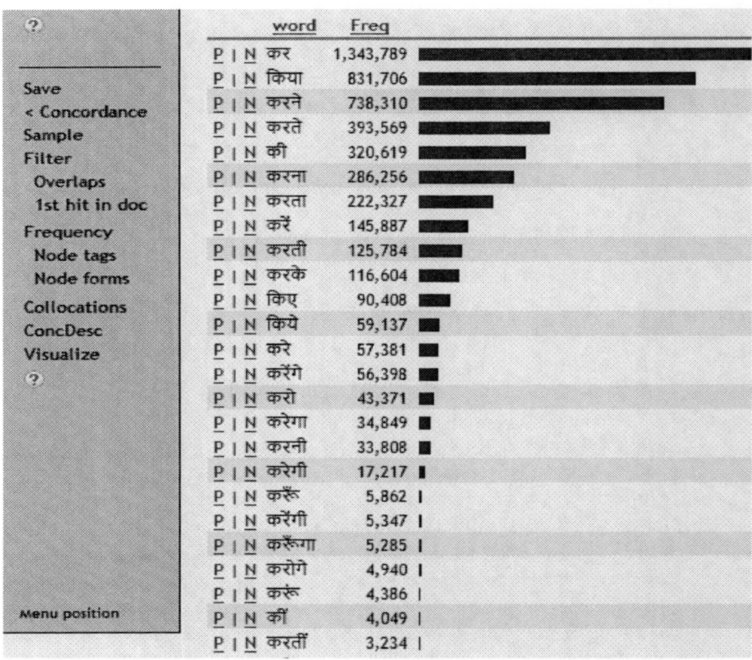

Figure 4. Frequency of word forms of कर (do)

Word list

Corpus: HindiWaC Sketches - Grammar_70%

Page 1 [Go] Next >

word	Freq
के	8,231,422
है	6,874,255
में	6,320,120
की	5,300,482
से	4,155,505
और	3,878,405
को	3,684,171
का	3,557,923
हैं	2,506,724
पर	2,348,155
भी	2,219,652
कि	1,925,263
नहीं	1,838,022
एक	1,767,536
ने	1,715,933
ही	1,655,169
तो	1,637,519
हो	1,398,617

word	Hindi Election Corpus		HindiWaC		Score
	Freq	Freq/mill	Freq	Freq/mill	
केजरीवाल	234	7801.8	2,097	31.9	8.5
पार्टी	209	6968.3	17,336	263.6	6.3
मोदी	161	5367.9	4,884	74.3	5.9
सरकार	222	7401.7	59,774	908.8	4.4
कांग्रेस	130	4334.3	18,838	286.4	4.1
चुनाव	115	3834.2	11,435	173.9	4.1
राहुल	105	3500.8	8,324	126.6	4.0
सम्मेलन	84	2800.7	4,093	62.2	3.6
गुजरात	83	2767.3	5,203	79.1	3.5
कहा	285	9502.2	136,695	2078.3	3.4
भाजपा	82	2734.0	9,501	144.5	3.3
गांधी	88	2934.0	15,291	232.5	3.2
दिल्ली	107	3567.5	30,665	466.2	3.1
प्रधानमंत्री	75	2500.6	12,890	196.0	2.9
मंत्री	74	2467.2	17,495	266.0	2.7
वाराणसी	54	1800.4	1,499	22.8	2.7
उन्होंने	130	4334.3	65,402	994.4	2.7
नरेंद्र	44	1467.0	1,502	22.8	2.4
मुख्यमंत्री	53	1767.1	10,822	164.5	2.4
विधानसभा	44	1467.0	3,764	57.2	2.3

Figures 5 & 6. Frequency list of the whole corpus for Words and Keywords extracted automatically from Hindi Election Corpus by comparing it with Hindi Web Corpus

2.3 The Word List function

The Word List function allows the user to make frequency lists of many types (words, lemmas, tags). Figure 5 shows the most frequent words in the corpus. In addition to most frequent words, keywords of any target corpus can be extracted. This is done by comparing frequent words from the target corpus with the frequent words from a general purpose corpus. Figure 6 displays the keywords of a Hindi Election corpus, where this is the target corpus, and the general purpose corpus is the HindiWaC.

Almost every keyword closely relates to the trend of news articles in the 2014 Indian Parliament elections. Since the Hindi Election Corpus is of small size, the frequency-per-million column contains projected values. These are signifi-

लोग *(noun)*
HindiWaC Sketches - Grammar_70% freq = 568946 (2,094.7 per million)

nmod_adj	240,145	4.3	k1_inv	22,290	6.4	nmod	12,337	9.8
कुछ	24,854	10.33	जम	159	7.05	मानसिकता	104	7.01
उन	11,086	10.12	मान	1,117	6.42	ज्यादातर	52	6.04
ऐसे	10,530	9.98	कह	2,606	6.0	मुताबिक	73	6.04
कई	11,367	9.66	मार	265	5.83	अधिकतर	40	5.83
सभी	7,664	9.28	मर	152	5.77	जी	86	5.8
सब	5,960	9.21	जता	76	5.73	रसूख	21	5.73
आम	5,412	9.16	सोच	277	5.72	सोच	65	5.51
जिन	4,453	9.1	मचा	57	5.56	आय	37	5.49
लाख	4,871	9.1	समझा	141	5.53	राशि	86	5.45
इन	7,082	9.02	बता	616	5.53	रख	550	5.36
अन्य	4,844	8.76	सराह	36	5.5	गुजर	57	5.29
स्थानीय	3,444	8.72	पूछ	172	5.48	पहुंचने	33	5.22
यह	11,814	8.67	घेर	48	5.42	बस	30	5.11
कम	3,329	8.46	देख	727	5.14	मर	81	5.03
हजारा	2,322	8.22	थाना	49	5.08	विचारधारा	29	5.03
सारा	2,851	8.2	उठा	166	5.02	विपरीत	24	4.99
ज्यादातर	1,958	7.98	चुन	68	4.99	आमदनी	15	4.86
अधिक	2,581	7.97	बोल	193	4.99	पैसा	49	4.83
अनेक	2,215	7.93	बैठ	142	4.95	छवि	25	4.8
ज्यादा	2,257	7.87	बजा	42	4.95	कमा	31	4.78

Figure 7. Word Sketch results for लोग (people)

Word sketch item 12,337 (45.4 per million)

Page 1 of 617 Go Next | Last

#19929	के अनुसूचित जाति की बस्ती में *रहने* वाले लोगों को ज़मीन का प
#27749	बचने के उपाय इंटरनेट का इस्तेमाल *करने* वाले लोगों में से 91 प्रतिश
#41844	कभी दुकानदारों के सामान आवागमन *करने* वाले लोगों से सट जाने से ट
#46724	ज्यादा झटके बहुमंजिला भवनों में *रहने* वाले लोगों को महसूस हुए।
#65638	है। उनका लक्ष्य पहली बार मतदान *करने* वाले लोगों और छात्रों को रि
#128970	मान लेती हैं. साथ ही वह हमें उन *अजीब* वाले लोगों के बारे में भी बत
#133700	हो रहा है जिसमें आवास निर्माण *करने* वाले लोग डीपू से लकड़ी ख
#148608	जाता है, इसी वजह से यह उपाय *अपनाने* वाले लोगों को काफी लाभ प
#149334	समय में उन धर्म का झंडा बुलंद *करने* वाले लोगों की ज़बान भी शं
#163854	ठिकानों में रहनेवाले परिवारों की मदद *करने* वाले लोगों के नाम सामान्य
#233242	लिए इंटरनेट बैंकिंग का इस्तेमाल *करने* वाले लोगों को यह सुनिश्चि
#237487	खुला उल्लंघन है। कानून के तहत ऐसे *करने* वाले लोग व कंपनी के ऊपर
#238735	हाइवे के रास्ते साइबर ग्रीन में *आने* वाले लोग कुछ आगे से ही
#311386	उन्हें यकीन था कि सिर्फ कॉलेज *आने* वाले लोग ही शुक्राणु दान प
#313981	प्रदीप व उसके पिता की मदद के लिए आगे *आने* वाले लोग परिजनों के लि
#379140	नियमित करता है। अधिक शारीरिक मेहनत *करने* वाले लोगों को मैग्नेशियम
#414958	बताते हैं कि लहसुन का नियमित सेवन *करने* वाले लोगों को कैंसर होने क
#452814	साथ जुड़ेंगे कि 'हास्य रहित *अभिरुचि* वाले लोगों के लिए, विकिपी
#497244	का हर हिस्सा तथा हर वस्तु उसमें *रहने* वाले लोगों के जीवन को कि
#559618	अगुवाई में अमल में लाई गई।पुलिस के *मुताबिक* इन लोगों ने एक लाख पांच

Page 1 of 617 Go Next | Last

Figure 8. Concordance lines for लोग (people) in combination with its gramrel "nmod"

cantly higher than the same words in the Hindi-WaC since the Election Corpus is domain specific.

2.4 The Word Sketch and Collocation Concordance functions

The Word Sketch function is invaluable for finding collocations. The word sketches of the word लोग (people) for three dependency relations are shown in Figure 7.

The dependency relations that we use are based on the Paninian framework (Begum et al., 2008). Three of the most common dependency relations given by this model are as follows:

- k1: agent and/or doer

- k2: object and/or theme

- k3: instrument

These relations are syntactico-semantic in nature, and differ slightly from the equivalent thematic roles mentioned above. More about how we get the word sketches shown in Figure 7 is explained in Section 3.

In figure 7, the three dependency relations shown are:

- nmod_adj: noun-modifier_adjective

- k1_inv: doer_inverse

- nmod: noun-modifier

The word sketch function assigns weights to each of the collocates and also to the dependency relations.

Clicking on the number after the collocate gives a concordance of the combination (Figure 8).

2.5 The Bilingual Word Sketch function

A new function has been added recently to the Word Sketch, which is the Bilingual Word Sketch. This allows the user to see word sketches for two words side by side in different languages. Figure 9 shows a comparison between लाल (red) and *red*. Interestingly, the usage of word red in Hindi and English are very diverse. The only common noun which is modified by *red* in both languages is गुलाब (*rose*).

लाल *(adjective)* Alternativ
HindiWac Sketches - G   **red** *(noun)*   ukWaC freq

modifier of	6,082	7.8	modifies	76,712	3.1
मिर्च	579	10.95	squirrel	1,549	9.12
रंग	938	10.64	tape	2,781	9.11
किला	337	10.53	wine	2,668	8.63
किताब	303	9.83	herring	853	8.4
शास्त्री	168	9.6	deer	952	8.26
चंदन	160	9.51	brick	1,070	8.14
बत्ती	112	9.12	sandstone	753	8.09
वस्त्र	148	9.08	pepper	818	8.04
फूल	136	8.64	flag	1,087	7.9
तुम	62	8.15	cell	2,590	7.81
धागा	54	8.01	meat	938	7.62
गुलाब	54	8.01	carpet	639	7.59
यादव	64	7.87	kite	434	7.37
डोरा	45	7.86	onion	528	7.36
कपड़ा	76	7.86	light	2,350	7.34
बल्ब	47	7.68	rose	375	7.03

Figure 9. Adjective results of a bilingual word sketch for Hindi लाल (red) and English red
English translations of some of the Hindi words are: chilli, colour, fort, flower, rose, cloth, Shastri

2.6 Distributional Thesaurus and Sketch Diff

The Sketch Engine also offers a distributional thesaurus, where, for the input word, the words 'sharing' most collocates are presented. Figure 10 shows the top entries in similarity to कर (do). The top result is हो (be). Clicking on it takes us to a 'sketch diff', a report that shows the similarities and differences between the two words in Figure 11.

कर *(verb)* HindiWac Sketches - G

Lemma	Score	Freq
हो	0.653	4,452,572
दे	0.594	1,714,785
ले	0.52	1,020,412
रह	0.491	2,086,780
रख	0.485	316,618
आ	0.476	978,940
है	0.468	9,658,560
बना	0.467	440,902
देख	0.444	527,703
था	0.411	2,460,144
लगा	0.403	355,352
जान	0.389	506,661
कह	0.372	914,047
मिल	0.344	431,473
लग	0.337	483,869
मान	0.335	233,821

कर/हो HindiWac Sketches - Grammar_70% freqs = 4,955,783 | 4,452,572

कर 6.0 4.0 2.0 0 -2.0 -4.0 -6.0 हो

nmod_inv	41,209	24,626	2.7	1.9
नुकसान	0	398	–	8.4
खर्च	0	287	–	7.8
आय	0	239	–	7.6
भीत	0	234	–	7.5
न्यायालय	0	178	–	7.5
क्रांति	0	152	–	7.3
परिवर्तन	0	236	–	7.1
भांति	0	119	–	7.0
परेशानी	0	153	–	6.9
आमदनी	0	105	–	6.9
बीमारी	24	283	3.3	7.2
लोग	2,641	200	7.0	3.3
व्यक्ति	1,541	102	7.8	4.0
मजदूर	220	0	6.9	–
संस्था	448	0	7.3	–

lwg__vaux_inv	376,082	777,605	0.8	1.9
कर	9,931	147,999	5.3	9.2
दे	4,489	31,036	6.0	8.5
भर	2,942	10,521	7.6	8.6
रख	6,341	18,095	8.0	8.9
बना	8,434	18,068	8.0	8.7
बन	7,042	14,564	8.0	8.5
लगा	6,370	11,432	8.0	8.3
देख	18,411	23,626	9.2	9.1
बैठ	5,532	5,851	8.5	7.7
मिल	4,486	3,056	8.3	6.8
डाल	4,873	2,529	8.2	6.5
सुन	5,010	2,426	8.4	6.5
हासिल	4,809	1,892	8.6	6.3
निकाल	6,084	1,262	8.7	5.5
गिरफ्तार	8,607	474	9.5	4.3

pof	1,345,592	1,284,066	6.6	7.4
समाप्त	10,420	16,955	8.0	8.7
साबित	10,394	16,615	8.0	8.7
शामिल	17,310	22,322	8.6	9.1
पैदा	24,767	29,186	9.2	9.5
प्राप्त	50,479	33,391	10.2	9.6
बंद	33,516	16,418	9.6	8.6
तैयार	33,110	15,056	9.6	8.5
पूरा	24,715	10,938	9.1	8.0
महसूस	22,439	9,613	9.1	7.9
तय	23,929	6,343	9.1	7.3
स्थापित	23,403	4,693	9.1	6.9
जारी	23,322	3,175	9.1	6.3
पेश	23,064	1,591	9.1	5.3
व्यक्त	16,658	1,102	8.6	4.8
प्रस्तुत	25,295	1,138	9.2	4.8

Figure 10 & 11. Thesaurus search showing entries similar to कर (do) (left) and Sketch Diff comparing collocates of कर (do) and हो (be) (right)

332

The red results occur most frequently with हो (be), the green ones with कर (do). The ones on white occur equally with both.

3 Building and processing HindiWaC and loading it into the Sketch Engine

HindiWaC was built using the Corpus Factory procedure (Kilgarriff et al., 2010). A first tranche was built in 2009, with the crawling process repeated and more data added in 2011, and again in 2014. Corpus Factory method can be briefly described as follows: several thousands of target language search queries are generated from Wikipedia, and are submitted to Microsoft Bing search engine. The corresponding hit pages for each query are downloaded. The pages are filtered using a language model. Boilerplate text is removed using body text extraction, deduplication to create clean corpus. We use jusText and Onion tools (Pomikálek, 2011) for body-text extraction and deduplication tools respectively.

The text is then tokenized, lemmatized and POS-tagged using the tools downloaded from http://sivareddy.in/downloads (Reddy and Sharoff, 2011). The tokenizer found here is installed in the Sketch Engine.

3.1 Sketch Grammar for Hindi

A sketch grammar is a grammar for the language, based on regular expressions over part-of-speech tags. It underlies the word sketches and is written in the Corpus Query Language (CQL). Sketch grammar is designed particularly to identify head-and-dependent pairs of words (e.g., खा [eat] and राम [Ram]) in specified grammatical relations (here, k1 [doer]), in order that the dependent can be entered into the head's word sketch and vice versa.

Sketch Grammars are popular with lexicographic and corpus linguistics community, and are used to identify collocations of a word with a given grammatical relation (Kilgarriff and Rundell, 2002). We use Sketch Grammar to identify words in syntactic relations in a given sentence. For example, a grammar rule for the relation "k1" (doer) is 2:"NN" "PSP\:ने" "JJ"? 1:"VM", which specifies that if a noun is followed by a PSP and an optional adjective and followed by a verb, then the noun is the kartha/subject of the verb. The head and child are identified by 1: and 2: respectively. Each rule may often be matched

by more than one relation creating ambiguity. Yet they tend to capture the most common behavior in the language.

Writing a full-fledged sketch grammar with high coverage is a difficult task even for language experts, as it would involve capturing all the idiosyncrasies of a language. Even though such hand-written rules tend to be more accurate, the recall of the rules is very low. In this paper, the grammar we use is a collection of POS tag sequences (rules) which are automatically extracted from an annotated Treebank, Hindi Dependency Treebank (HDT-v0.5), which was released for the Coling2012 shared task on dependency parsing (Sharma et al., 2012). This treebank uses IIIT tagset described in (Bharati et al., 2006). This method gives us a lot of rules based on the syntactic ordering of the words. Though these rules do not have all the lexical cues of a language, the hope is that, when applied on a large-scale web corpus, the correct matches (sketches) of the rules automatically become statistically more frequent, and hence more significant.

From the above mentioned treebank (HDT) we extract dependency grammar rules (i.e. sketch grammar) automatically for each dependency relation, based on the POS tags appearing in between the dependent words (inclusive). For example, from the sentence,

राम(Ram)　ने(erg.)　कमरे(room)　में(inside) आम(mango) खाया(eat), Ram ate [a] mango in [the] room, we extract rules of the type: **(k1[doer], k2 [object], k7[location])**

k1 - 2:[tag="NNP"] [tag="PSP\:ने"] [tag="NN"] [tag="PSP\:में"] 1:[tag="VM"]
k2 - 2:[tag="NN"] 1:[tag="VM"]
k7 - 2:[tag="NN"] [tag="PSP\:में"] [tag="NN"] 1:[tag="VM"]

In the above example, relation names are in bold with one of the corresponding rules for each of them.

We do include a few lexical features associated with the POS tags **PSP** (post-position) and **CC** (conjunction) in order to disambiguate between different dependency relations. For example, in both the relations **k1 (doer)** and **k2 (object)** we have the rules (1) and (2) given below respectively in Figure 12:

बच्चे (NN) ने (PSP) आम (NN) खाया (VM)
(child) (erg.) (mango) (eat.pst) (the child ate a mango)
2:[tag="NN"] [tag="PSP\:ने"] [tag="NN"] 1:[tag="VM"] ------- (1)

कागज़ (NN) को (PSP) बाहर (NN) फेंका (VM)
(paper) (acc.) (outside) (throw.pst) ([Someone] threw the paper outside)
2:[tag="NN"] [tag="PSP\:को"] [tag="NN"] 1:[tag="VM"] ------- (2)

Figure 12. A sample of similar rules for different dependency relations

In (1), the ergative marker indicates that the noun (NN) is the *doer* of the verb (VM). In (2), the accusative marker indicates that the noun (NN) is the *object* of the verb (VM). Also, (2) is not a complete sentence – the *doer* has not been mentioned, and only the part of the sentence that the rule is applied to is shown.

If in the rules, the **PSP** POS tags didn't contain the lexical features, both the rules would have been the same, and hence both the rules have been applied on both the sentences, making the word sketches erroneous.

By lexicalizing the **PSP** POS tag, the rule(s) formed are now less ambiguous, and more accurate.

After extracting all the dependency rules, we apply each rule on the annotated Treebank (HDT), and compute its precision. For example, if the rule "**k7 (location)** - 2:[tag="NN"] [tag="PSP\:में"] [tag="NN"] 1:[tag="VM"]" is applied on the HDT, we get all the [2:NN, 1:VM] pairs where the rule holds, say **N** pairs. Out of these **N** pairs, if **M** of them are seen correctly with k7 (place) relation in the training data then the precision of the rule is $\frac{M}{N}$.

Conditions that need to be satisfied for a rule to be included in the sketch grammar:

- The rule must have a precision of at least 70%. A higher cut-off gives us rules with better precision, but less recall, and it is the reverse for lower cut-off limits.

- The frequency of the tag sequence (N) must be greater than 4, to ensure some amount of statistical significance of the rules.

The context size – the maximum allowed length of the tag sequence (rule), is set to 7 to limit the number of rules generated.

4   Error Analysis

The word sketches may not always be accurate due to the ambiguous nature of rules, and POS tagging errors. For example, when a rule such as 1:[tag="NN"] [tag="PSP: ने"] 2:[tag="VM"] is applied on sentences which have nouns ending with the honorific जी in the data, जी is likely to be a collocate of the words. This is an error due to the POS tagger that we use to tag the Hindi-WaC. The tagger tags the honorific जी as **NN** and not **RP**. These word sketches can be improved further by improving the POS tagger, or the grammar, for example by involving local word group information. The other related errors are due to **UNK** POS tag which is generally assigned to the words that are unknown to the tagger.

As the length of a rule increases so does its sparsity, i.e. the number of sentences on which the rule can be applied since all the POS tags in the rule have to occur in that particular order. Hindi being a free word order language the possibility of all the POS tags occurring in that order is even less.

5   Conclusion and Future Work

Corpora are playing an increasing role in all kinds of language research as well as in language learning, lexicography, translation, literary studies and discourse analysis. The requirements are, firstly, a suitable corpus, and secondly, a corpus query tool. We have presented HindiWaC, a large corpus of Hindi, which has been prepared for use in the Sketch Engine. We have described how we used Hindi Dependency Treebank to develop the grammar underlying the word sketches. And we have shown the core features of the Sketch Engine, as applied to Hindi.

Our current grammar is prone to data sparseness as the length of rule increases. A future direction of this work could be on building compact grammars using regular expressions.

Additionally, one could also explore the usefulness of morphological features in grammar rules to make them semantically accurate.

Reference

Adam Kilgarriff, Pavel Rychly, Pavel Smrz and David Tugwell. *The Sketch Engine*. Proceedings of EURALEX 2004.

R. Begum, S. Husain, A. Dhwaj, D. Sharma, L. Bai and R. Sangal. *Dependency annotation scheme for Indian languages*. Proceedings of International Joint Conference on Natural Language Processing 2008

Adam Kilgarriff, Siva Reddy, Jan Pomikálek and Avinesh PVS. *A Corpus Factory for many languages*. In *LREC*. 2010

Jan Pomikálek. *Removing Boilerplate and Duplicate Content from Web Corpora*. 2011

Siva Reddy and Serge Sharoff. *Cross Language POS Taggers (and other Tools) for Indian Languages: An Experiment with Kannada using Telugu Resources*. Proceedings of IJCNLP workshop on Cross Lingual Information Access 2011.

Adam Kilgarriff and Michael Rundell. *Lexical Profilng Software and its Lexicographic Applications – a Case Study*. In A. Braasch et al. (eds.) EURALEX Proceedings 2002 807-818.

A. Bharati, R. Sangal, D. Sharma and L. Bai. "Anncorra: Annotating corpora guidelines for pos and chunk annotation for Indian languages." LTRC-TR31 2006

D. Sharma, P. Mannem, Joseph van Genabith, Sobha Lalitha Devi, Radhika Mamidi and Ranjani Parthasarathi. *Workshop on Machine Translation and Parsing in Indian Languages (MTPIL-2012)*. Proceedings of International Conference on Computational Linguistics (COLING) 2012

Kilgarriff, Adam, et al. "Itri-04-08 the sketch engine." *Information Technology*105 (2004): 116.

Pearce, Michael. "Investigating the collocational behaviour of man and woman in the BNC using Sketch Engine 1." *Corpora* 3.1 (2008): 1-29.

Extracting and Selecting Relevant Corpora for Domain Adaptation in MT

Lars Bungum
Norwegian University of Science and Technology
Dept. of Computer and Information Science
Sem Sælands vei 7
N-7490 Trondheim, Norway
`larsbun@idi.ntnu.no`

Abstract

The paper presents scheme for doing Domain Adaptation for multiple domains simultaneously. The proposed method segments a large corpus into various parts using self-organizing maps (SOMs). After a SOM is drawn over the documents, an agglomerative clustering algorithm determines how many clusters the text collection comprised. This means that the clustering process is unsupervised, although choices are made about cut-offs for the document representations used in the SOM.

Language models aren then built over these clusters, and used as features while decoding a Statistical Machine Translation system. For each input document the appropriate auxiliary Language Model most fitting for the domain is chosen according to a perplexity criterion, providing an additional feature in the log-linear model used by Moses. In this way, a corpus induced by an unsupervised method is implemented in a machine translation pipeline, boosting overall performance in an end-to-end experiment.

1 Introduction

Broadly viewed, the problem of Domain Adaptation (DA) is relevant to many computer applications, not only Artificial Intelligence (AI) and Machine Translation in (MT), the focus of this research. A MT system fit for a specific or generic domain or purpose, often has trouble is translating text from another domain, consisting of different input data, a claim backed by Carpuat et al. (2012).

To illustrate, suppose a MT system trained on- or tuned for a certain text domain, say archery, is used on a text about a completely different field such as string quartets. One would, among other things, assume that the meaning of the word *bow* is different in the two domains, and is likely to require different translations into some other languages. (Differences in text domains can also pertain to other features of language, such as punctuation and grammar.) Furthermore, the assumption is that a small in-domain system is already built, and the characteristics of this model and its training data are used for selecting more domain specific text from a larger, general source.

Alternatively, a system is built on a general corpus, and needs to be adapted to domain-specific text as it comes in. In this paper we will present a method that allows for a general-purpose MT system to be adapted to multiple domains online. This is achieved by using an unsupervised method to cluster unorganized text into segments and combining Language Models (LMs) built on these segments via log-linear feature functions. As new text is input to the MT system, an assessment is done at the document level to select the appropriate domain-specific LM.

In Statistical Machine Translation (SMT) contexts, data-driven MT systems are trained on parallel and monolingual training data. When in need of translating text belonging to a certain domain, domain specific training material is often hard to come by, whereas general (other) text exists in abundance. Using the web as a corpus has an obvious appeal, as Kilgarriff and Grefenstette (2003) effectively demonstrated, but since data from the web is usually not structured, effectively making use of this knowledge source is difficult. While finding more *in*-domain monolingual text is easier than bi-lingual text, it is still not trivial.

When faced with a translation task where the training material for a specific domain to be translated (the *in*-domain) is scarce, one answer to the problem is using refined machine learning methodologies such as active learning (see Rai et

336

D S Sharma, R Sangal and J D Pawar. Proc. of the 11th Intl. Conference on Natural Language Processing, pages 336–343,
Goa, India. December 2014. ©2014 NLP Association of India (NLPAI)

al. (2010) for a discussion of Active Learning and Domain Adaptation) to exploit the (often little) domain specific training material available and building a new SMT model trained on it. Another approach is to use scarce in-domain data as a starting point to collect more in-domain training material with bootstrapping methods, similar to the little one begins with, from a larger source such as the Internet. It is possible to expand the available *in*-domain data, be it mono- or bi-lingual text, and to use the *in*-domain data more efficiently, or both. (See Wu et al. (2009) who employ bootstrapping for Domain Adaptation in a Named-Entity Recognition task).

We employed an unsupervised algorithm, the Self-Organizing Map (SOM), to create order in an otherwise unorganized body of text and used this to create auxiliary Language Models (LMs) for SMT decoding. Decisions had to be taken on how the documents were represented as vectors, and we used an agglomerative algorithm to decide how many clusters should be created from the SOM with bottom-up hierarchical clustering.

The algorithm provides *n* separate clusters of text, from which standard n-gram LMs were built. With this method, the number of auxiliary text corpora (and later LMs) are determined by the agglomerative clustering algorith, enabling Domain Adaptation into the *available* domains, which is why an unsupervised method was chosen. The LMs were used in a SMT pipeline (Moses), implemented as features in Moses' log-linear decoder. When a document is input for translation, it was matched against the *n* LMs created above, ranked after perplexity. The LM with the lowest perplexity was selected by the Moses feature to provide additional information for the decoder. This setup creates a platform in which a system can do adaption to multiple domains, as the additional feature in the SMT decoding phase can select the most appropriate auxiliary LM on-the-fly. Additionally the SOM-approach to Domain Adaptation is evaluated in an end-to-end MT context, although with rudimentary evaluation on just one dataset.

2   Technical Overview

The implementation consists of two stages, (i) the segmentation of a large corpus with a SOM and (ii) the utilization of language models built on the basis of these corpus segments in an SMT system . The first phase is conducted offline, whereas the employment of the language models is done while decoding a SMT model given input sentences.

The steps in the offline and online parts of the system are summarized in Figure 1. Once the first offline phase is completed, the system is able to adapt to any number of incoming text domains, via the Moses feature that selects the most appropriate LM depending for the input document based on a perplexity measure.

2.1   SOM-Induced Corpora

When Kohonen et al. (1996) introduced Self-Organizing Maps (SOMs) they were used to cluster USENET (newsgroup) data. Later, the same methodology was used to cluster patent data (Kohonen et al., 2000) and the Encyclopedia Britannica (Lagus et al., 2004).

SOMs are maps of vectorized data that can cluster high-dimensional data within a lower (most often 2 or 3-dimensional) topology. It is a way of showing similarities between high-dimensional data (such as documents represented with tens of thousands of dimensions) in a low-dimensional space. The algorithm is summarized in the following steps:

1. Create *n* random nodes in the low-dimensional map according to some topology.

2. Pick an input (document) vector.

3. Associate with the node that is closest according to a distance measure.

4. Update the node and its neighbors to be more like the vector.

The corpus used in the experiments was the SdeWac (Faa and Eckart, 2013) corpus of German text, consisting of parsable sentences. Each document in the collection was vectorized with Scikit-learn (Pedregosa et al., 2011), which has many different vectorizers available, such as TF-IDF and N-gram vectorizers, on word and character level. In these experiments, a mostly unigram TF-IDF vectorizer was used, some tests were also run using it in combination with N-gram frequencies and for bigrams.

The SOM algorithm was implemented in MPI (mpi4py) and Python, and run on a PBS scheduler. This means that no changes to the SOM algorithm as presented by Kohonen (2001) were needed. A

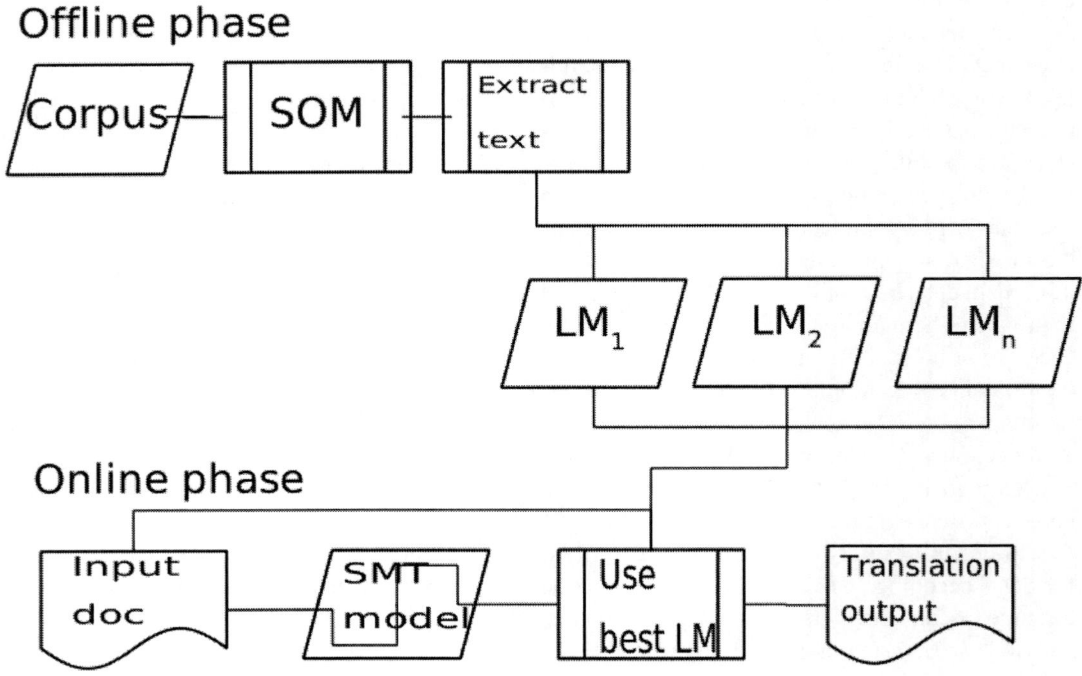

Figure 1: Overall architecture

quadratic layout of nodes was used in the experiments, and for each sample, the comparisons with all the different vectors in the node were done in parallel, as was the updating of the nodes in the next stage. But the traversal of the samples was done serially, so that the SOM was updated according to the information supplied in each sample after it had found its winning node.

After a maximum number of iterations was reached (usually set to 100 or 1000), the last run of the input samples was kept, which left similar samples with the same winning node. An agglomerative clustering algorithm was then run on the nodes to cluster them by similarity. The algorithm chose a cut-off point in the clustering according to the relative change in the similarity measure.

The development of the SOM from its randomized beginning is displayed in Figure 2. Each of the nodes contains a vector of the dimensionality printed in the caption. These vectors are then scaled down to four dimensions with Principal Component Analysis (Jolliffe, 2005), that Matplotlib (Hunter, 2007) allows for as input to its color printing (four dimensions were preferred over three to allow for one more component). It can be seen on the figures that areas of similar

documents (as indicated by reducing to about the same color) arise towards the end of the cycle.

2.2 Selection of Relevant Corpora

Finally, each of the n clusters resulting from the agglomerative clustering had a certain number of samples belonging to them. The samples (text documents) were then output and placed in the same directory. When the files were concatenated they were again text corpora over which normal n-gram models were constructed.

Hierarchical agglomerative clustering algorithms are algorithms that successively merge clusters from the bottom up. Whereas the top-down approach would need metrics to split clusters, the bottom-up approach needs criteria to merge clusters. We used the algorithms provided by the Scipy package (Jones et al., 2001). Running the algorithm, a distance metric to determine similarity between clusters is picked, as well as a selection of which data points to measure distances between. Distance metrics, for instance Euclidean or Chebychev distances, are combined with a a choice of nodes in the grid to calculate distance between to determine the distance between clusters (comprised of more and more nodes in the

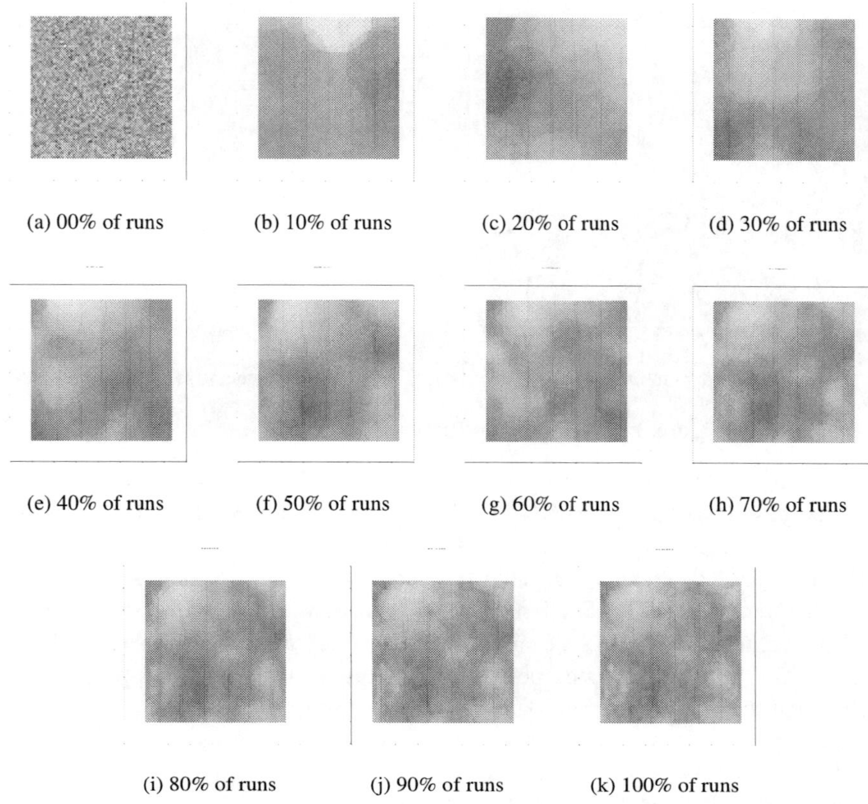

(a) 00% of runs   (b) 10% of runs   (c) 20% of runs   (d) 30% of runs

(e) 40% of runs   (f) 50% of runs   (g) 60% of runs   (h) 70% of runs

(i) 80% of runs   (j) 90% of runs   (k) 100% of runs

Figure 2: Development of SOM with 77,733 dimensions, 4096 nodes and 100 iterations

agglomerative algorithm). The average distance was used in these experiments, the distance between the closest, or the most separated once are alternatives. A dendrogram of the agglomerative clustering is shown in Figure 3, next to a plot of the distance between the clusters on the vertical axis against the possible clusterings on the horizontal. The number of clusters was chosen by finding a knee-point in this curve, where the marginal gain of adding another cluster is the highest. (This is hard to interpret visually on a curve with this many points.)

2.3 Multiple Language Models as a Feature in Moses

The Moses (Koehn et al., 2007) SMT system allows for the use of user-defined features in its log-linear model. A feature was created using one of the SOM-induced LMs created in the above step for scoring the sentences, depending on what LM gave the lowest perplexity score to the document that any given input sentence belonged to. As each SL sentence was read, it would leave a number designating which LM to use for the feature in decoding its translation.

This way, information at the document level provided information about which LM is the best to use for the documents as they come in. The SRILM kit was used to create the LMs and using corresponding libraries were used to score hypotheses inside the Moses feature.

3 Preliminary Results

A preliminary evaluation was done on sentence-level WMT12 data as proof of concept. An SMT model was trained on the Europarl (Koehn, 2005) and News Commentary[1] corpora combined and tested on the newstest2012 dataset. One of the LMs generated with the method presented in Section 2.1 was used for the entire test set. After hav-

---

[1]The WMT News Commentary parallel corpus contains news text and commentaries from the Project Syndicate and is provides as training data for the series of WMT translation shared tasks (See http://statmt.org/).

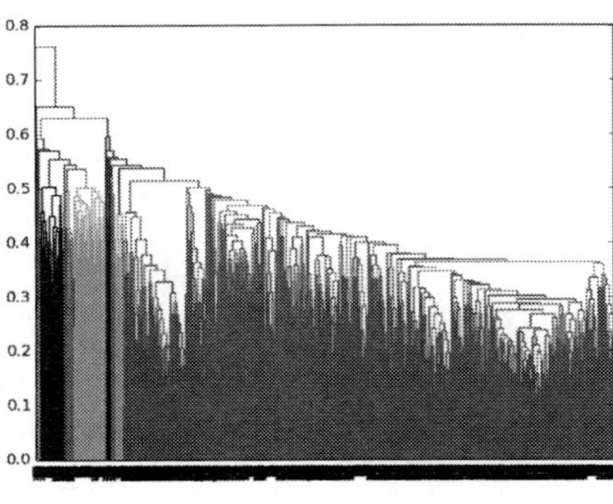

(a) Dendrogram of clusters

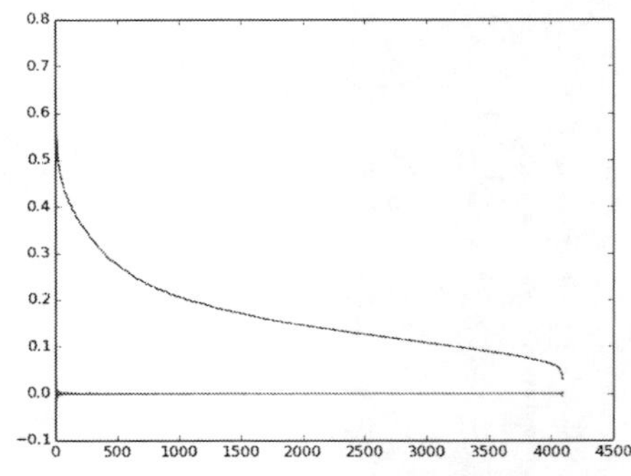

(b) Agglomerative clustering of SOM

Figure 3: Illustrations of how the SOM map is clustered

ing used the newstest2011 data for MERT (Och, 2003) tuning of the feature weights, a gain of 2.44 BLEU (Papineni et al., 2002) points was achieved when using the feature presented in Section 2.3.

The full implementation is yet to be evaluated, as we are still working on preparing corpora that can be processed at the document level. This can be done by processing the newstest corpora provided in the WMT datasets as the provided *sgml* files are included with document IDs, making it possible to identify separate documents, unlike some other available parallel corpora. This is also the case for the biography dataset created by Louis and Webber (2014).

4 Related Research

Domain Adaptation generalizes beyond the scope of Machine Translation, and can be viewed as a general Machine Learning task. Blitzer (2008) performed a rigorous analysis of Domain Adaptation algorithms and under what conditions they perform well, conducting experiments in sentiment classification and part-of-speech (POS) tagging. Hildebrand et al. (2005) employed information retrieval techniques for DA in MT by selecting the sentences in the training material that were similar to the ones used in the test set.

Xu et al. (2007) built separate SMT models based on little *in*-domain data for building both translation and language models. The models were used in combination with a larger, general SMT system, as the *in*-domain training data was limited. The authors performed DA as a classification task, where a document is classified before translation to belong to a certain domain, and the

corresponding SMT model was used. The authors found that classifying the right domain for an input document was more accurate when measuring their perplexity on a Language Model than other, Information Retrieval-based methods.

While their work mainly focused on adapting translation models, Sennrich et al. (2013) also investigated the idea of using unsupervised methods to classify text, combining them with mixture models to perform Domain Adaptation. Louis and Webber (2014) used cache models to store domain specific information in language modeling, also implemented as features in the Moses SMT system, that was also used in this work.

Moore and Lewis (2010) used a perplexity criterion to select the best corpus for building an auxiliary LM by testing the available extra data on the sentence level to extract the relevant parts at the sentence level according to a cross-entropy threshold. They showed that it is not necessary to use the whole additional text in order to obtain improvement in performance. Building on this idea, our work also uses only segments of the total corpus on which the SOM is drawn, but selects the auxiliary LM based on the perplexity of the *input* document at decode time.

Axelrod et al. (2011) did a similar extraction of what they term *pseudo-in-domain* sentences based on cross-entropy measures; pseudo because they are similar, but not identical to the in-domain data. Their measures of perplexity and cross-entropy is also done at sentence level. They demonstrated increased performance in an end-to-end experiment using only parts of a large, general corpus. With the firepower of modern computers, however, it is well feasible to build large LMs efficiently ((Bungum and Gambäck, 2012)) on quite standard equipment, so a comparison with the performance of the entire general corpus on the end-to-end task would be interesting.

5 Discussion

The methodology in the present work stipulates a solution to the Domain Adaptation problem that looks for external sources to increase the available training data. The SOM approach is a way of finding similarities in unorganized data collections that has been applied successfully in other application areas. This is the first stage in creating separate language models from a large web corpus, to aid translation of a specific language domain.

In Machine Translation history there are several accounts of systems working well for a specific domain, but very hard to build a system working in any domain (general-purpose) while retaining high quality. Since it is feasible to translate text for one specific domain well, but very hard to translate general text with the same high quality, bridging the gap between these two processes is a possible way forward.

The work presented here needs to be tested more rigorously, as it is hard to find datasets consisting of many different domains, sorted on document level that are needed to test the idea fully. Otherwise, while the scale of the project is large, and it requires significant computer resources, it is still well within what it is possible to incorporate into one SMT model, simply by adding the corpus that we are doing clustering on to the training material. In principle though, given the scale of the Internet and the growth of content added, it is not possible to add all new text that can be crawled from online resources in any system, and some sort of segmentation is desirable.

Our approach builds on earlier work in segmenting a large corpus into relevant parts and using this to aid the overall MT task. Relating to other work on DA it presents a method where a general MT system can be adapted to multiple target domains at the same time. As discussed in (Bungum and Gambäck, 2011) it is not always obvious how to separate text domains from each other, where to draw the line between them, and what dimensions (such as writing style, topic, author or target age groups) through which to separate them. Using an unsupervised approach segmentation of a vast data source is a way of enabling a MT system to respond to various input domains also along such dimensions.

6 Future Work

Looking forward, we would like to test this method on more languages and more parallel corpora to see if it generalizes well. There is also extensive literature on language domains and sublanguages as they can be characterized not only by thematic variance and genre, but also differences in the properties of the author (age, style, emotional state). It is not obvious that this method works equally well for all such situations.

The method proposed here integrates many parts in the two stages of the process. Especially in the SOM step there are many choices to be made regarding how documents are represented, and how the number of clusters are chosen as the nodes are joined together in the final step. The system is implemented with Scikit-learn so that alternative similarity measures both in running vector comparisons in the SOM and cluster similarity can be used. In many runs the resulting text corpora varied greatly in size with one big corpus dominating the others. Trying to skew the agglomeration towards more equal-sized partitions is an interesting avenue to pursue.

There has also been interesting work on trying to mine more text based on a little in-domain corpus from the web. Such approaches could also be integrated in these experiments by using quantitative data on the in-domain corpus to compute vector representations. Finally, extending the SOM approach to also mine parallel and not just monolingual corpora is a goal that can further advance Machine Translation performance. More monolingual data certainly helps, but more high-quality parallel text would arguably help even more.

Acknowledgements

I thank Björn Gambäck for valuable feedback on this article.

References

Amittai Axelrod, Xiaodong He, and Jianfeng Gao. 2011. Domain adaptation via pseudo in-domain data selection. In *Proceedings of the Conference on Empirical Methods in Natural Language Processing*, EMNLP '11, pages 355–362, Edinburgh, United Kingdom. Association for Computational Linguistics.

John Blitzer. 2008. *Domain Adaptation of Natural Language Processing Systems*. Ph.D. thesis, University of Pennsylvania.

Lars Bungum and Björn Gambäck. 2011. A survey of domain adaptation in machine translation: Towards a refinement of domain space. In *Proceedings of the India-Norway Workshop on Web Concepts and Technologies*, Trondheim, Norway. Tapir Academic Press.

Lars Bungum and Björn Gambäck. 2012. Efficient N-gram Language Modeling for Billion Word Web-Corpora. Workshop on Challenges in the Managment of Large Corpora, LREC 2012.

Marine Carpuat, Hal Daumé III, Alexander Fraser, Chris Quirk, Fabienne Braune, Ann Clifton, Ann Irvine, Jagadeesh Jagarlamudi, John Morgan, Majid Razmara, Aleš Tamchyna, Katharine Henry, and Rachel Rudinger. 2012. Domain adaptation in machine translation: Final report. In *2012 Johns Hopkins Summer Workshop Final Report*.

Gertrud Faa and Kerstin Eckart. 2013. Sdewac – a corpus of parsable sentences from the web. In Iryna Gurevych, Chris Biemann, and Torsten Zesch, editors, *Language Processing and Knowledge in the Web*, volume 8105 of *Lecture Notes in Computer Science*, pages 61–68. Springer Berlin Heidelberg.

Almut Silja Hildebrand, Matthias Eck, Stephan Vogel, and Alex Waibel. 2005. Adaptation of the translation model for statistical machine translation based on information retrieval. In *Proceedings of the 10th Annual Conference of the European Association for Machine Translation*, pages 133–142, Budapest, Hungary, May. European Association for Machine Translation.

J. D. Hunter. 2007. Matplotlib: A 2d graphics environment. *Computing In Science & Engineering*, 9(3):90–95.

Ian Jolliffe. 2005. *Principal component analysis*. Wiley Online Library.

Eric Jones, Travis Oliphant, Pearu Peterson, et al. 2001–. SciPy: Open source scientific tools for Python. [Online; accessed 2014-07-17].

Adam Kilgarriff and Gregory Grefenstette. 2003. Introduction to the special issue on the web as corpus. *Comput. Linguist.*, 29(3):333–347, September.

Philipp Koehn, Hieu Hoang, Alexandra Birch, Chris Callison-Burch, Marcello Federico, Nicola Bertoldi, Brooke Cowan, Wade Shen, Christine Moran, Richard Zens, Chris Dyer, Ondřej Bojar, Alexandra Constantin, and Evan Herbst. 2007. Moses: Open source toolkit for statistical machine translation. In *Proceedings of the 45th Annual Meeting of the ACL on Interactive Poster and Demonstration Sessions*, ACL '07, pages 177–180, Stroudsburg, PA, USA. Association for Computational Linguistics.

Philipp Koehn. 2005. Europarl: A Parallel Corpus for Statistical Machine Translation. In *Conference Proceedings: the tenth Machine Translation Summit*, pages 79–86, Phuket, Thailand. AAMT.

Teuvo Kohonen, Samuel Kaski, Krista Lagus, and Timo Honkela. 1996. Very large two-level SOM for the browsing of newsgroups. In C. von der Malsburg, W. von Seelen, J. C. Vorbrüggen, and B. Sendhoff, editors, *Proceedings of ICANN96, International Conference on Artificial Neural Networks, Bochum, Germany, July 16-19, 1996*, Lecture Notes in Computer Science, vol. 1112, pages 269–274. Springer, Berlin.

Teuvo Kohonen, Samuel Kaski, Krista Lagus, Jarkko Salojrvi, Vesa Paatero, and Antti Saarela. 2000. Organization of a massive document collection. *IEEE Transactions on Neural Networks, Special Issue on Neural Networks for Data Mining and Knowledge Discovery*, 11(3):574–585, May.

Teuvo Kohonen. 2001. *Self-organizing maps*. Springer series in information sciences, 30. Springer, Berlin, 3rd edition, December.

Krista Lagus, Samuel Kaski, and Teuvo Kohonen. 2004. Mining massive document collections by the WEBSOM method. *Information Sciences*, 163(1-3):135–156.

Annie Louis and Bonnie Webber. 2014. Structured and unstructured cache models for smt domain adaptation. In Israel Shuly Wintner, University of Haifa, Germany Stefan Riezler, Heidelberg University, and UK Sharon Goldwater, University of Edinburgh, editors, *Proceedings of the 14th Conference of the European Chapter of the Association for Computational Linguistics, volume 2: Short Papers*. Association for Computational Linguistics, April.

Robert C. Moore and William Lewis. 2010. Intelligent selection of language model training data. In *Proceedings of the ACL 2010 Conference Short Papers*, pages 220–224, Uppsala, Sweden, July. Association for Computational Linguistics.

Franz Josef Och. 2003. Minimum error rate training in statistical machine translation. In *Proceedings of the 41st Annual Meeting on Association for Computational Linguistics - Volume 1*, ACL '03, pages 160–167, Stroudsburg, PA, USA. Association for Computational Linguistics.

K. Papineni, S. Roukos, T. Ward, and W. J. Zhu. 2002. BLEU: A method for automatic evaluation of machine translation. In *Proceedings of the 40th Annual Meeting of the Association for Computational Linguistics*, pages 311–318, Philadelphia, Pennsylvania, July. ACL.

F. Pedregosa, G. Varoquaux, A. Gramfort, V. Michel, B. Thirion, O. Grisel, M. Blondel, P. Prettenhofer, R. Weiss, V. Dubourg, J. Vanderplas, A. Passos, D. Cournapeau, M. Brucher, M. Perrot, and E. Duchesnay. 2011. Scikit-learn: Machine learning in Python. *Journal of Machine Learning Research*, 12:2825–2830.

Piyush Rai, Avishek Saha, Hal Daumé III, and Suresh Venkatasubramanian. 2010. Domain adaptation meets active learning. In *Proceedings of the NAACL HLT 2010 Workshop on Active Learning for Natural Language Processing*, pages 27–32. Association for Computational Linguistics.

Rico Sennrich, Holger Schwenk, and Walid Aransa. 2013. A multi-domain translation model framework for statistical machine translation. In *ACL (1)*, pages 832–840. The Association for Computer Linguistics.

Dan Wu, Wee Sun Lee, Nan Ye, and Hai Leong Chieu. 2009. Domain adaptive bootstrapping for named entity recognition. In *Proceedings of the 2009 Conference on Empirical Methods in Natural Language Processing: Volume 3 - Volume 3*, EMNLP '09, pages 1523–1532, Stroudsburg, PA, USA. Association for Computational Linguistics.

Jia Xu, Yonggang Deng, Yuqing Gao, and Hermann Ney. 2007. Domain dependent statistical machine translation. In *In Proceedings of the MT Summit XI*, pages 515–520.

Merging Verb Senses of Hindi WordNet using Word Embeddings

Sudha Bhingardive   Ratish Puduppully   Dhirendra Singh   Pushpak Bhattacharyya
Department of Computer Science and Engineering,
IIT Bombay, Powai, Mumbai, 400076.
{sudha, ratishp, dhirendra, pb}@cse.iitb.ac.in

Abstract

In this paper, we present an approach for merging fine-grained verb senses of Hindi WordNet. Senses are merged based on gloss similarity score. We explore the use of word embeddings for gloss similarity computation and compare with various WordNet based gloss similarity measures. Our results indicate that word embeddings show significant improvement over WordNet based measures. Consequently, we observe an increase in accuracy on merging fine-grained senses. Gold standard data constructed for our experiments is made available.

1   Introduction

Hindi WordNet[1] (HWN) is the first Indian language WordNet. It was created manually from Princeton WordNet[2] (Christiane Fellbaum, 1998) using expansion approach and similarly other 16 Indian language WordNets were created from Hindi. This linked structure of Indian language WordNets is known as IndoWordNet[3] (Bhattacharya P., 2010) . It is as shown in Figure 1.

The structure of HWN is similar to the Princeton WordNet. It is composed of synsets and semantic relations. Synset is a set of synonyms representing the same concept. Synsets are linked with basic semantic relations *viz., hypernymy, hyponymy, meronymy, holonymy, troponymy etc*. In comparison with Princeton WordNet, HWN provides extra relations *e.g., gradation, causative,*

---

[1]http://www.cfilt.iitb.ac.in/wordnet/webhwn/wn.php

[2]http://wordnet.princeton.edu/

[3]IndoWordNet is available in following Indian languages: Assamese, Bodo, Bengali, English, Gujarati, Hindi, Kashmiri, Konkani, Kannada, Malayalam, Manipuri, Marathi, Nepali, Punjabi, Sanskrit, Tamil, Telugu and Urdu. These languages cover three different language families, Indo Aryan, Sino-Tibetan and Dravidian. http://www.cfilt.iitb.ac.in/indowordnet

compounds, conjunction etc. HWN is widely used

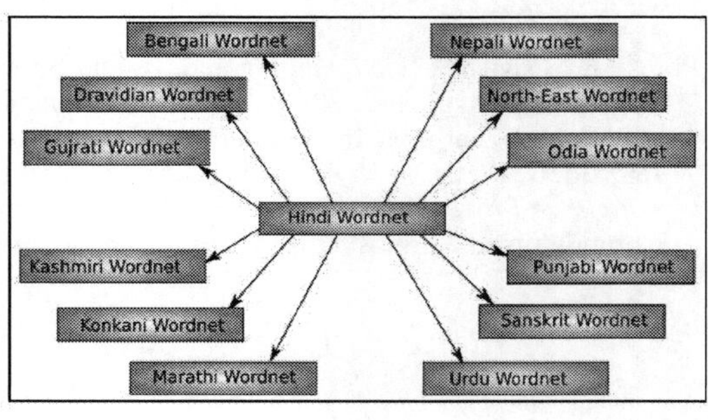

Figure 1: IndoWordNet

in Natural Language Applications (NLP) *viz.*, Machine Translation (Ananthakrishnan et al., 2008; Kunchukuttan et al., 2012), Word Sense Disambiguation (Khapra et al., 2010; Bhingardive et al., 2013), Sentiment Analysis (Balamurali et al., 2012; Popat et al., 2013) *etc*. Over-specified sense distinctions in HWN may not be useful for certain applications. Hence, generating a coarse-grained version of HWN is a crucial task in order to get better results for such applications. In this paper, we present a method for merging the fine-grained senses of HWN using gloss similarity. Word embeddings are used for computing this similarity. The presented method performs better as compared to baselines.

The paper is organised as follows. Section 2 describes the sense granularity that exists in HWN. Section 3 presents the related work. Section 4 gives details about Word Embeddings. Sense merging approach is given in section 5. Experiments and results are presented in section 6. Error analysis is given in section 7. Section 8 concludes the paper and points to the future work.

2   Hindi WordNet Sense Granularity

Different applications need different types of sense granularity. Fine-grained sense distinctions

D S Sharma, R Sangal and J D Pawar. Proc. of the 11th Intl. Conference on Natural Language Processing, pages 344–352,
Goa, India. December 2014. ©2014 NLP Association of India (NLPAI)

to blow	1	मुँह बहुत थोडा खुला रखकर हवा बाहर निकालना (mumha bahuta thodA khulA rakhakar havA bAhar nikAlanA) **(blow air through a very small opening of mouth)**
	2	मुख से बजाए जाने वाले बाजों को फूँककर बजाना (mukha se bajAye jAne wAle bAjom ko phumkakara bajAnA) **(blowing the instruments that are played by mouth)**
to ignite	3	फूँक मार कर दहकाना या प्रज्वलित करना (phUmka mAra kara dahakAnA yA prajjvalita karanA) **(ignite by blowing)**
	4	आग के संयोग से किसी वस्तु को जलने में प्रवृत्त करना (Aga ke sanyoga se kisI vastu ko jalane mem pravarutt karanA) **(to burn something with fire)**
	5	आग लगाना (Aga lagAnA) **(to burn)**
to smoke	6	तम्बाकू गाँजे आदि का धुआँ मुँह से खींचकर बाहर निकालना (tambAkU, gAnje Adi kA dhumA mumha se khINcakara bAhara nikAlanA) **(to exhale the smoke of tobacco etc after inhaling)**

Table 1: Fine-grained senses of the verb फूंकना (*phUmkanA*); six senses can be merged into three sense groups

are suitable for language learners and applications like Document Categorization, Information Retrieval, Information Extraction *etc*. However, coarse-grained senses are sufficient for applications like Machine Translation and Word Sense Disambiguation. The main difficulty arises in finding the consistent criteria for making accurate sense distinctions.

HWN has many fine-grained senses. For example, there are six senses of word फूंकना (*phumkanA*), which can be merged into three sense groups as shown in Table 1. Hindi senses are distinguished depending on different types of linguistic properties like *properties of subject, object, time variations, compulsion, mode of communication, visibility, acts, existence etc.* Some of them are listed in Table 2 and explained below:

- **Subject property :** Senses can be distinguished depending on the properties of the subject. Consider the word काटना (*kAtanA*) which has two senses S_1 (to cut) and S_2 (insect bite) as shown in Table 2. In S_1, subject will always be an animate entity (a human being) while in S_2, it will always be an insect.

- **Object property :** Object property can also help in making sense distinction. For example, the word रखना (*rakhanA*) has two senses S_1 (to put) and S_2 (to present) as shown in Table 2, in which S_1 can take either animate or inanimate object while S_2 can take only abstract object.

- **Compulsion :** In some cases, senses are distinguished depending on the force of action.

For example, the word निकालना (*nikAlanA*) has two senses S_1 (to remove from a post) and S_2 (forcefully remove from a post) are distinguished by the force of action. Word Sense Disambiguation algorithms often fail in making such fine distinction.

- **Time period :** Consider the senses of word दिन (*dina*). There are total nine senses out of which three senses (ref Table 2) differ only in time period.

Fine grained sense distinctions are very difficult to capture programmatically. Sometimes even humans fail in making such distinctions. Hence, for applications which do not need fine-grained senses, a coarse-grained version of HWN is essential.

3 Related Work

Recently, a large number of sense clustering techniques have been proposed. These techniques rely on various information resources like ontological structure, external corpora, translation similarities, supervision *etc*.

WordNet ontology structure is very helpful for merging fine-grained word senses. Various synset similarity measures have been proposed *viz.*, Path Based Similarity (Wu and Palmer, 1994), (Leacock and Chodorow, 1998), Information Content Based Measures (Resnik, 1995) (Lin, 1998) (Jiang and Conrath, 1997), Gloss Based Heuristics (Lesk, 1986) (Banerjee and Pedersen, 2003) *etc*. These measures were used for creating coarse-grained

Linguistic Properties	Target word	Senses	Gloss/Definition in Hindi WordNet
Subject property (animate/inanimate)	काटना (kAtnA)	S_1	धारदार शस्त्र आदि से किसी वस्तु आदि के दो या कई खंड करना या कोई भाग अलग करना (dhArdAr shastra Adi se kisI vastu Adi ke do yA kaI khanda karnA ya koI bhAg alag karnA) **[cutting into two or more pieces using a sharp instrument]**
		S_2	विषैले कीडो जन्तुओ आदि का दाँत से काटना (vishaile kido, jantu aadi ka dat se kAtnA **[biting with teeth by poisonous insects and creatures]**
Object property (Knowledge/Experience)	रखना (rakhnA)	S_1	स्थित करना (sthit karnA) **[to put]**
		S_2	प्रस्तुत करना (prastuta karnA) **[to present]**
Compulsion	निकालना (nikAlnA)	S_1	स्थान स्वामित्व अधिकार पद आदि से अलग करना (sthAn, swAmitva, adhikAr, pad Adi se alag karnA) **[to remove from a place, ownership, rights, position etc.]**
		S_2	स्थान छोडने पर विवश करना (sthAn chodane ke liye vivash karnA) **[to force to leave a place]**
Time period	दिन (dina)	S_1	सूर्य निकलने से उसके अस्त होने तक का समय (surya nikalne se uske asta hone tak kA samay) **[the time after sunrise and before sunset]**
		S_2	एक सूर्योदय से लेकर दूसरे सूर्योदय तक का समय जो चौबीस घंटे का माना जाता है (ek suryoday se lekar dusre suryoday tak kA samay jo choubis ghante kA maana jAtA hai) **[time between two sunrise which considered as of 24 hours]**
		S_3	चौबीस घंटे में से वह समय जो सोने के बाद काम करने में गुजरता है (choubis ghante me se vaha samay jo sone ke bad kaam karane se gujaratA hai) **[within 24 hours, the time apart from sleeping that is spent working]**

Table 2: Hindi WordNet Sense Distinction

senses. Dolan (1994) first used ontological information for sense clustering. He presented a heuristic based algorithm for clustering senses of Longman's Dictionary of Contemporary English (LDOCE). Peters (1998) addressed different ways for reducing the fine-grainedness of EuroWordNet. In his approach, senses were grouped depending on the semantic relations like *sisters, twins, cousins, autohyponymy etc.*

Mihalcea and Moldovan (2001) derived a set of semantic and probabilistic rules for reducing average polysemy. This was the first attempt of grouping synsets rather than word senses. The resulting version of WordNet leads to reduction of polysemy by around 26% with an error rate of 2.1%. Tomuro (2001) used a similar approach but introduced more principled algorithms.

Agirre and Lacalle (2003) presented a clustering technique which uses confusion matrices, translation similarities, hand-tagged examples of the target word senses and other web information. McCarthy (2006) used combination of word-to-word distributional similarity along with WordNet based similarity measures for sense clustering.

Bhagwani et. al., (2013) proposed a semi-supervised approach which learns synset similarity by using graph based recursive similarity. Resulting coarse-grained sense inventory boosts performance of noun sense disambiguation.

Chugur et. al., (2002) used translational equivalences of word senses for sense merging. Two word senses are expected to be similar, if they lead to the same translation in other languages.

Several sense clustering attempts were made by mapping WordNet to other sense inventories either manually or automatically. Navigli (2006) proposed a sense clustering method by mapping WordNet senses to Oxford English Dictionary (OED). Martha Palmer (2007) suggested a semi-automatic technique for verb sense grouping by using Levin class theory.

Snow et. al., (2007) proposed a supervised approach using Support Vector Machine in which features were derived from WordNet and other lexical resources.

Due to shallow hierarchy of verbs in WordNet, the knowledge based measures which exploit ontology structure are ineffective for sense merging. We therefore make use of gloss to infer fine-grained senses. We investigate usage of word embeddings for gloss similarity computation.

4 Word Embeddings

Word Embeddings are increasingly being used in variety of NLP tasks. Word Embeddings represent each word with low-dimensional real valued vector. Such models work under the assumption that similar words occur in similar context (Harris, 1968). (Collobert et al., 2011) used word embeddings for POS tagging, Named Entity Recognition and Semantic Role Labeling. Such embeddings have also been used in Sentiment Analysis (Tang et al., 2014), Word Sense Induction (Huang et al., 2012), Dependency Parsing (Bansal et al., 2014) and Constituency Parsing (Socher et al., 2013).

Word embeddings have been used for textual similarity computation (Mihalcea et al., 2006). We are using word embeddings for finding gloss similarity between synsets. The fine-grained senses can be merged based on the similarity values. Word embeddings have been trained using *word2vec*[4] tool (Mikolov et al., 2013). *word2vec* provides two broad techniques for word vectors generation: Continuous SkipGram and Continuous Bag of Words (CBOW). CBOW predicts current word based on surrounding context, whereas Continuous SkipGram model tries to maximize classification of word based on another word in the same sentence (Mikolov et al., 2013). The approach followed here is using SkipGram model by varying context window size (w). Like (Bansal et al., 2014) we find that lower window size results in syntactically similar words. As the window size increases, more semantically similar words are listed. For the experiments we performed, we fixed window size as $w = 7$ as we are interested in more semantically similar words. The word vectors have been trained on 44M sentence corpus (Bojar et al., 2014). The time taken to create word embeddings on the corpus was few minutes on a 2X2 GHz machine.

5 Gloss-based Semantic Similarity Measure used for Sense Merging

Let us consider the following example:

Example: Target Word: डरना (darnA)

- Sense 1: "किसी चीज का डर होना (kisI cheez kA dar honA)" **[to fear of something]**

- Sense 2: "अनिष्ट या हानि की आशंका से आकुल होना (anishta yA hAni kI aAshankA se Akul honA)" **[nervousness due to feeling of loss or premonition]**

Above two senses of word डरना (daranA) are too fine-grained. Lesk similarity (Lesk, 1986) and Extended Lesk similarity (Banerjee and Pedersen, 2003) comes out to be zero as there is no gloss overlap and no relation between these two senses in HWN. Therefore, instead of finding the gloss overlap, the approach followed here is to find whether words from two glosses are semantically related or not.

5.1 Mihalcea Text Similarity using Word Embeddings

We used word embeddings generated using *word2vec* (ref Section 4) for finding the semantic similarity between words from two glosses. We leverage the text similarity measure proposed by (Mihalcea et al., 2006) for gloss similarity computation. It considers both word-to-word similarity and word specificity. Word specificity indicates whether the word is specific or generic. Specificity of a word is measured using Inverse document frequency (idf) (Sparck-Jones et al., 1972). idf is defined as the total number of documents in the corpus divided by the total number of documents including that word. We used hindi wikipedia dump[5] for obtaining idf. Each wikipedia page is treated as single document.

The text similarity measure given in Equation 1 compares two text segments T_1 and T_2 for semantic similarity. For each word w in T_1, it finds the respective word in T_2 with which it has maximum similarity $maxSim(w, T_2)$.

$$sim(T_1, T_2) = \frac{1}{2} * \left(\frac{\sum_{w \in T_1} (maxSim(w, T_2) * idf(w))}{\sum_{w \in T_1} idf(w)} + \frac{\sum_{w \in T_2} (maxSim(w, T_1) * idf(w))}{\sum_{w \in T_2} idf(w)} \right)$$

(1)

---

[4]https://code.google.com/p/word2vec/

[5]http://dumps.wikimedia.org/hiwiki/20140814/

Sense Merging Techniques	Precision	Recall	F-measure
Mihalcea Text Similarity Using Word Embeddings	**0.97**	0.39	0.56
Compositional Text Similarity using Word Embeddings	0.89	**0.43**	**0.58**
Lesk with idf	**0.97**	0.27	0.42
Lesk without idf	0.91	0.14	0.25
Path Similarity	0.89	0.22	0.36
WUP	0.86	0.087	0.16
LCH	0.53	0.24	0.33

Table 3: Sense Merging Results with similarity threshold ≥ 0.7

Sense Merging Techniques	Precision	Recall	F-measure
Mihalcea Text Similarity Using Word Embeddings	0.95	**0.54**	**0.69**
Compositional Text Similarity Using Word Embeddings	0.75	**0.54**	0.63
Lesk with idf	**0.97**	0.29	0.45
Lesk without idf	0.86	0.29	0.44
Path Similarity	0.90	0.24	0.38
WUP	0.82	0.21	0.33
LCH	0.43	0.28	0.34

Table 4: Sense Merging Results with similarity threshold ≥ 0.6

Sense Merging Techniques	Precision	Recall	F-measure
Mihalcea Text Similarity Using Word Embeddings	0.74	0.58	0.65
Compositional Text Similarity Using Word Embeddings	0.67	**0.69**	**0.68**
Lesk with idf	**0.96**	0.36	0.52
Lesk without idf	0.76	0.38	0.51
Path Similarity	0.82	0.27	0.41
WUP	0.61	0.24	0.35
LCH	0.39	0.34	0.36

Table 5: Sense Merging Results with similarity threshold ≥ 0.5

where, $maxSim(w, T_i)$ is computed on word embeddings by finding the maximum cosine similarity between w and words in T_i. The process is repeated for each word in T_2 w.r.t T_1. The similarities are weighted by *idf* values, summed up and normalized w.r.t to the length of the text segment. Similarity scores obtained are values between 0 and 1, where 0 indicates least similarity and 1 indicates maximum similarity.

5.2 Compositional Text Semantic Similarity Using Word Embeddings

In this approach, we consider the word embedding of the text segment T as compositionally obtained from that of its words. The principle behind the same is that the meaning of the sentence is derived from its constituent words. This is the Weighted

Addition model in (Mitchell and Lapata, 2008). For this system, we construct word embeddings for each text segment as in Equation 2:

$$vec(T_1) = \sum_{w \in T_1} (vec(w) * idf(w)) \quad (2)$$

$$sim(T_1, T_2) = cosine(vec(T_1), vec(T_2)) \quad (3)$$

where $vec(T)$ is the word embedding for text segment T.

6 Experiments and Results

For the purpose of experiments, we created gold standard data. It consists of 250 verbs each with two senses. The test set verbs were tagged as mergeable or not. Five annotators worked independently and created this data with 0.8 inter annotator agrrement. This data is released for further

348

experimentation [6].

We compare our approach with WordNet based gloss similarity measures listed below:

- Lesk with idf: Senses are merged based on the word overlap between glosses (Lesk, 1986) with idf weighting applied on them. For this, we use the Equation 1 with $maxSim$ defined as follows:

$$maxSim(w, T_i) = 1 \quad if\, w \in T_i$$
$$= 0 \quad if\, w \notin T_i$$

- Lesk without idf: In this method, senses are merged based on the word overlap between glosses (Lesk, 1986) without applying idf weighting on them. The following equation is used which is derived from the Equation 1.

$$sim(T_1, T_2) = \frac{1}{2} * \left(\frac{\sum_{w \in T_1}(maxSim(w, T_2))}{count(T_1)} + \frac{\sum_{w \in T_2}(maxSim(w, T_1))}{count(T_2)} \right)$$

(4)

where $maxSim$ is as defined in Lesk with idf.

- Path Length Measure: It measures the similarity between two synsets depending on the number of links existing in the is-a hierarchy of WordNet.

This measure is defined as follows:

$$sim_{path} = \frac{1}{shortest\_path\_length(S1, S2)}$$

(5)

where $S1$, $S2$ are synsets.

The shorter the length of the path between them, the more related they are considered. Thus there is an inverse relation between the length of the path between the synsets and the similarity between them. This sim_{path} value is substituted into Equation 1.

- The Leacock Chodorow (Leacock and Chodorow, 1998) similarity is determined as:

$$sim_{LCH} = -log\frac{shortest\_path\_length(S1, S2)}{2 * D}$$

(6)

where D is the maximum depth of the taxonomy. This sim_{LCH} value is substituted into Equation 1.

[6]https://github.com/sudhabh/SenseMerging

- (Wu and Palmer, 1994) similarity metric measures the depth of two given synsets in the WordNet taxonomy, and the depth of the least common subsumer (LCS), and combines these figures into a similarity score:

$$sim_{WUP} = \frac{2 * depth(LCS)}{depth(S_1) + depth(S_2)}$$

(7)

This sim_{WUP} value is substituted into Equation 1.

Table 3, Table 4 and Table 5 present Precision, Recall and F-measure for sense merging techniques with similarity threshold as 0.7, 0.6 and 0.5. Here threshold is value above which the two candidate verb senses are considered similar. The similarity values range from 0 to 1. From the results, we observe that decreasing the value of similarity threshold leads to increase in recall with corresponding decrease in precision. Figure 2 and Figure 3 show the variation in F-measure across range of similarity thresholds. From the figures, again we observe that techiques based on Word Embeddings performs much better than techniques based on WordNet similarity measures with regard to F-measure.

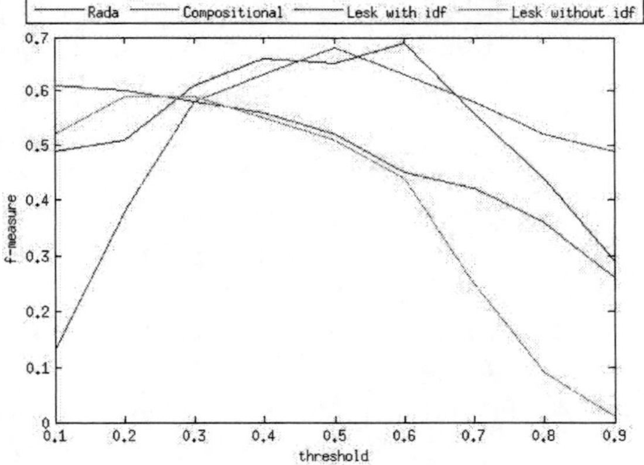

Figure 2: Plot of F-measure of Word embedding based measures (Rada and Compositional) and WordNet similarity based (Lesk with idf and Lesk without idf) figures against various threshold values

7 Error Analysis

Our approach suffers from some limitations listed below.

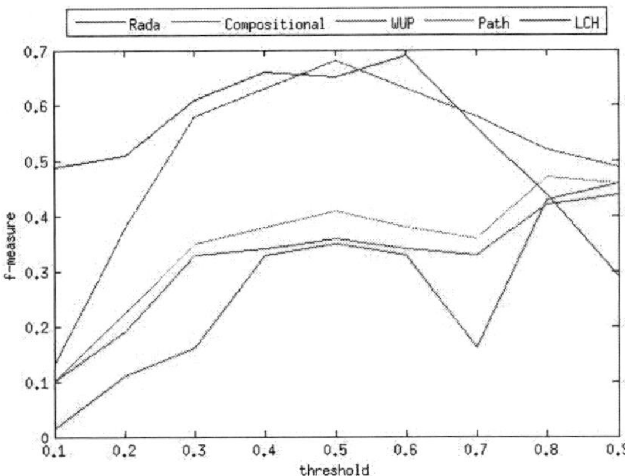

Figure 3: Plot of f-measure of Word embedding based measures (Rada and Compositional) and Wordnet based measures (WUP, Path and LCH) against various threshold values

1. Sometimes gloss semantic similarity score is very high, even though the word senses are not similar. This leads to an incorrect sense merging. Consider the two senses of the word पहुँचना (pahuchanA) listed below.

   - S_1: {पहुँचना, पहुंचना , फैलना } (pahumchanA, pahunchanA, failenA) - किसी स्थान तक फैलना (kisI sthAn tak failenA) [**to extend upto a place**]
   - S_2:   {पहुँचना, पहुंचना} (pahumchanA, pahunchanA) - किसी पद स्थान आदि तक पहुँचना (kisI pad, sthAn aadI tak pahunchanA) [**to reach a position or a place**]

   Senses S_1 and S_2 are not similar, but they have high semantic similarity score resulting in an incorrect sense merging. This might have happened because स्थान ($sthAn$) is common between the two gloss and पहुँचना ($pahunchanA$) is semantically similar to फैलना ($failenA$) in the corpus.

2. Another source of error is disparity in idf values due to multiple ways of expressing Hindi word forms. For example, as seen in S_1, S_2 above, पहुँचना (pahumchanA), पहुंचना (pahunchanA) are two ways of saying the same word. This results in split in their counts and consequent change in idf value.

8 Conclusion and Future Work

We conclude that word embeddings are indeed effective in computing gloss similarity and can be used to merge fine-grained senses of Hindi WordNet. We report significant performance improvement with word embeddings over WordNet based similarity measures. The resulting coarse-grained verb senses of Hindi WordNet are important resources in applications which do not prefer the fine-grained sense distinctions.

In future, we will perform evaluation on verbs having more than two senses. Also, the same technique can be applied for merging senses of other Indian language WordNets. We plan to use the coarse grained senses in both Rule Based Machine Translation and Statistical Machine Translation systems and conduct experiments to verify increase in accuracy of translation. The Weighted Addition model for compositional meaning is agnostic to syntax of the sentence. We plan to explore additional models of representing phrases and sentences such as lexical function model in (Paperno et al., 2014).

References

Agirre E. and Lacalle. 2003. *Clustering wordnet word senses*, In RANLP, volume 260, pages 121-130.

Ananthakrishnan R., Hegde J., Bhattacharyya P. and Sasikumar M. 2008. *Simple Syntactic and Morphological Processing Can Help English-Hindi Statistical Machine Translation*, International Joint Conference on NLP (IJCNLP08), Hyderabad, India.

Balamurali A.R., Joshi A. and Bhattacharyya P. 2012. *Cross-Lingual Sentiment Analysis for Indian Languages using WordNet Synsets*, COLING, Mumbai.

Banerjee S. and Pedersen T. 2003. *Extended Gloss Overlaps as a Measure of Semantic Relatedness*, Proceedings of the Eighteenth International Joint Conference on Artificial Intelligence, Acapulco, Mexico.

Bansal, Mohit and Gimpel, Kevin and Livescu, Karen 2014. *Tailoring Continuous Word Representations for Dependency Parsing*, Proceedings of ACL 2014.

Bhagwani S., Satapathy S. and Karnick H. 2013. *Merging Word Sense*, Association for Computational Linguistics, Proceedings of the TextGraphs-8 Workshop, USA.

Bhattacharya P. 2010. *IndoWordNet*, Lexical Resources Engineering Conference (LREC 2010), Malta.

Bhingardive S., Shaikh S. and Bhattacharyya P. 2013. *Neighbor's Help: Bilingual Unsupervised WSD Using Context*, ACL 2013, Sofia, Bulgaria.

Bojar Ondřej and Vojtěch Diatka and Pavel Rychlý and Pavel Straňák and Vít Suchomel and Aleš Tamchyna and Daniel Zeman 2014. *HindEnCorp - Hindi-English and Hindi-only Corpus for Machine Translation*, Proceedings of the Ninth International Conference on Language Resources and Evaluation (LREC'14)

Christiane Fellbaum. 1998. *WordNet: An Electronic Lexical Database*, MIT Press.

Chugur I., Gonzalo J. and Verdejo F. 2002. *Polysemy and sense proximity in the senseval-2 test suite*, In Proceedings of the ACL 2002 WSD workshop.

Collobert Ronan , Jason Weston, Leon Bottou, Michael Karlen, Koray Kavukcuoglu, and Pavel Kuksa 2011. *Natural language processing (almost) from scratch*, Journal of Machine Learning Research, 12:2493–2537.

Dolan W. 1994. *Word sense ambiguation: clustering related senses*, In Proceedings of the 15th conference on Computational linguistics - Volume 2, COLING,, pages 712-716, Stroudsburg, PA, USA. Association for Computational Linguistics.

Harris. Z. 1968. *Mathematical Structures of Language.*, Wiley, New York.

Huang Eric H. , Richard Socher, Christopher D. Manning, and Andrew Y. Ng. 2012. *Improving Word Representations via Global Context and Multiple Word Prototypes*, Proceedings of the 50th Annual Meeting of the Association for Computational Linguistics: Long Papers - Volume 1 Pages 873-882

Jiang J. and Conrath D. 1997. *Semantic similarity based on corpus statistics and lexical taxonomy*, In Proceedings on International Conference on Research in Computational Linguistics.

Khapra M., Shah S., Kedia P. and Bhattacharyya P. 2010. *Domain-Specific Word Sense Disambiguation Combining Corpus Based and WordNet Based Parameters*, 5th International Conference on Global WordNet (GWC 2010), Mumbai.

Kunchukuttan A., Roy S., Patel P., Ladha K., Gupta S., Khapra M. and Bhattacharyya P. 2012. *Experiences in Resource Generation for Machine Translation through Crowdsourcing*, Lexical Resources Engineering Conference (LREC 2012), Istanbul, Turkey.

Leacock C., and Chodorow M. 1998. *Combining local context and WordNet similarity for word sense identification*, In Fellbaum, C., ed., WordNet: An electronic lexical database. MIT Press, pages 265–283.

Lesk M. 1986. *Automatic sense disambiguation using machine readable dictionaries: how to tell a pine cone from and ice cream cone*, In Proceedings of the ACM SIGDOC Conference, pages 24–26, Toronto, Canada.

Lin D. 1998. *An information-theoretic definition of similarity*, In Proceedings of the International Conference on Machine Learning.

McCarthy D. 2006. *Relating WordNet Senses for Word Sense Disambiguation*, In proceedings of ACL Workshop on Making Sense of Sense.

Mihalcea Rada and Moldovan Dan 2001. *Ez.wordnet: principles for automatic generation of a coarse grained wordnet*, In Proceedings of Flairs 2001, pages 454-459.

Mihalcea Rada, Courtney Corley, Carlo Strapparava 2006. *Corpus-based and Knowledge-based Measures of Text Semantic Similarity*, In Proceedings of the American Association for Artificial Intelligence (AAAI 2006), Boston, July 2006.

Mikolov Tomas , Kai Chen, Greg Corrado, and Jeffrey Dean 2013. *Efficient Estimation of Word Representations in Vector Space*, In Proceedings of Workshop at ICLR, 2013.

Mitchell Jeff and Mirella Lapata 2008. *Vector-based models of semantic composition*, In Proceedings of ACL, pages 236–244, Columbus, OH.

Navigli R. 2006. *Meaningful clustering of senses helps boost word sense disambiguation performance*, In Proceedings of COLING-ACL, pages 105-112.

Palmer M., Dang H. and Fellbaum C. 2007. *Making Fine-grained and coarse-grained sense distinctions, both manually and automatically*, Natural Language Engineering.

Paperno Denis and Nghia The Pham and Marco Baroni 2014. *A practical and linguistically-motivated approach to compositional distributional semantics*, Proceedings of ACL 2014.

Pedersen T., Patwardhan S. and Michelizzi J. 2004. *WordNet::Similarity - Measuring the Relatedness of Concepts*, Proceedings of Fifth Annual Meeting of the North American Chapter of the Association for Computational Linguistics (NAACL-04), pages 38-41, Boston, MA.

Peters W., Peters I. and Vossen P. 1998. *Automatic sense clustering in Eurowordnet*, Proceedings of first international conference on language resource and evaluation : Granada, Spain, pages 409-416.

Popat K., Balamurali A., Bhattacharyya P. and Haffari G. 2013. *The Haves and the Have-Nots: Leveraging Unlabelled Corpora for Sentiment Analysis*, ACL 2013, Sofia, Bulgaria.

Resnik P. 1995. *Using information content to evaluate semantic similarity in a taxonomy*, In Proceedings of the 14th international joint conference on Artificial intelligence - Volume 1, IJCAI'95, pages 448-453, San Francisco, CA, USA.

Snow R., Prakash S., Jurafsky D. and Andrew Ng. 2007. *Learning to Merge Word Senses*, In Proceedings of the Joint Meeting of the Conference on Empirical Methods on Natural Language Processing and the Conference on Natural Language Learning.

Socher Richard, John Bauer, Christopher D. Manning and Andrew Y. Ng. 2013. *Parsing With Compositional Vector Grammars*, In Proceedings of the ACL conference. 2013

Sparck-Jones, K. 1972. *A statistical interpretation of term specificity and its application in retrieval.*, Journal of Documentation 28(1):11–21

Tang, Duyu and Wei, Furu and Yang, Nan and Zhou, Ming and Liu, Ting and Qin, Bing 2014. *Learning Sentiment-Specific Word Embedding for Twitter Sentiment Classification*, Proceedings of the 52nd Annual Meeting of the Association for Computational Linguistics (Volume 1: Long Papers)

Tomuro M. 2001. *Tree-cut and a lexical based on systematic polysemy*, proc. Of the second meeting of the North America Chapter of the Association for Computational Linguistics, (NAACL).

Wu Z. and Palmer M. 1994. *Verb semantics and lexical selection*, In 32nd Annual Meeting of the Association for Computational Linguistics, pages 133–138.

Hierarchical Recursive Tagset for Annotating Cooking Recipes

Sharath Reddy Gunamgari[*]
Samsung Research India
Bangalore, India - 560037
gsharathreddy77
@gmail.com

Sandipan Dandapat
CNGL, DCU
Dublin 9, Ireland
sdandapat
@computing.dcu.ie

Monojit Choudhury
Microsoft Research India
Bangalore, India - 560001
monojitc
@microsoft.com

Abstract

Several natural language annotation schemas have been proposed for different natural language understanding tasks. In this paper we present a hierarchical and recursive tagset for annotating natural language recipes. Our recipe annotation tagset is developed to capture both syntactic and semantic information in the text. First, we propose our hierarchical recursive tagset that captures cooking attributes and relationships among them. Furthermore, we develop different heuristics to automatically annotate natural language recipes using our proposed tagset. These heuristics use surface-level and syntactic information from the text and the association between words. We are able to annotate the recipe text with 91% accuracy in an ideal situation.

1 Introduction

Cooking or cookery is the art or practice of preparing food for consumption. Our motivation is to aid the applications useful for cooking process like recipe search, recipe recommendation etc. The first step required for these applications is to extract the information from a given recipe by annotating that recipe. Annotating natural language text is an important step towards the process of natural language understanding. Many such annotations schemas have been proposed for different NLP applications. Annotation schemas are often designed to capture a wide range of linguistic informations. These include morphological,

syntactic and semantic information. Some such well known annotation schemas include POS tagging, NE tagging, syntactic tree etc. All annotation schemas are developed towards solving a real world problem. In this paper, we aim towards arriving at an annotation scheme for cooking recipes.

Large number of cooking recipes are available in the web. People often follow these recipes while cooking. Annotation of cooking recipes can aid applications like complicated recipe search (e.g.,"find chicken pizza recipes that do not use mushrooms and can be baked in an electric oven"). It can also be used in recipe recommendation and adaptation. Our aim is to develop an annotation scheme for cooking recipes which can be used in above mentioned applications.

The rest of the paper is organized as follows. In Section 2, the related work in this domain is discussed. In Section 3, cooking recipes format is described briefly. Sections 4 and 5 discusses the features and structure of the proposed annotation scheme. In Section 6, completeness of the tagset is discussed. Section 7 describes the heuristics for automatically annotating the recipe text. Conclusions are drawn in Section 9.

2 Related Work

Many efforts have been done for extracting important information from recipes e.g. cooking ingredients, utensils, cooking actions, recipe recommendation (Teng et al., 2012), finding replaceable ingredients (Shidochi et al., 2009), recipe retrieval (Wang et al., 2008) etc. Ziqi et al. (2012) proposed different methods for automatically acquiring procedural knowledge in machine interpretable formats from natural language instructions like recipes. Shinsuke et al. (2014) used

---

* This work was done during the author's project work in IIT Guwahati.

D S Sharma, R Sangal and J D Pawar. Proc. of the 11th Intl. Conference on Natural Language Processing, pages 353–361,
Goa, India. December 2014. ©2014 NLP Association of India (NLPAI)

flow graphs to annotate the recipes. These flow graphs are directed acyclic graphs in which vertex labels are named entities in the recipe, such as foods, tools, cooking actions etc and arc labels denote relationships among them. Valmi et al. (2012) proposed a semantic representation of cooking recipes using graphs. This representation is used for cooking recipes search and adaptation of new recipes according to user constraints. In this paper, we adopted a hierarchical and recursive schema for annotating the cooking recipes. Tagsets and recipe representation languages like Recipe Markup Language (RML),[1] RecipeBook XML[2] were defined earlier, but the primary goal of these representations is to allow people to create, store and share recipes in a variety of electronic formats and to convert from one format to another. Moreover, these tagsets capture linguistic information only at a shallow level and miss out the richer information present in the recipe text. Thus, we need a framework to describe the finer details of a cooking recipe text. The new framework proposed here addresses these deficiencies in an efficient and principled manner. The hierarchical and recursive schema enables us to capture various relations among the ingredients, devices/utensils and cooking actions and other attributes related to cooking action.

3 Cooking Recipes Format

Large number of recipe formats are available in the web describing the process of cooking. In general, there exist two main sections in a cooking recipe specification – ingredients list and procedure (directions). The *ingredients* section consists of various materials needed in preparing the dish and additional information like quantity, size, name of the items, preprocessing actions to be performed etc. *Procedure* includes various steps to be performed to prepare a particular dish. Each step contains cooking actions performed on the ingredients or intermediate materials formed from previous cooking steps, using utensils or devices. An example snippet of a cooking recipe taken from a popular website[3] is given below.

Ingredients:

1. *7 tablespoons olive oil, divided*

2. *Kosher salt, freshly ground pepper*

3. *2 garlic cloves, coarsely chopped*

Procedure: *Preheat oven to 350F. Toss bread and 3 tablespoons oil on a large rimmed baking sheet, squeezing bread so it absorbs oil evenly; season with salt and pepper. Spread out bread pieces in an even layer and bake, tossing occasionally, until crisp on the outside but still chewy in the center, 10 to 15 minutes. Let croutons cool......*

4 Features of the Proposed Tagset

In this section we discuss the principles behind our tagset framework. The tagset proposed is hierarchical and recursive. Flat tagsets just list down the categories applicable for each unit of text without any provision for modularity or feature reusability (Baskaran et al., 2008). Hierarchical tagsets on the other hand are structured relative to one another and offer a well-defined mechanism for finding semantic relations between ingredients, utensils/devices, cooking actions and time.

4.1 Recursive and Hierarchical

The framework is recursive and forms a tree-structure. This ensures that instead of having a large number of independent categories, a recursive tagset contains a small number of broad categories at the top level, tagging larger units of text. Each broad category text has a number of sub-categories in a tree-structure. The finer details of recipe text are captured in the separate layers of the hierarchy; beginning from the major categories in the top and gradually progressing down to cover specific features. This hierarchical arrangement helps in forming semantic relations between various elements of a recipe text.

5 Structure of the Tagset

In this section we describe our proposed framework where each node of the tree structure is explained. The tree starts with initial levels which describe the higher levels of the hierarchy.

5.1 Initial Levels

The framework has many layers organized in a tree structure. The initial levels cover broad categories. The root of the tree is the entire cooking

---

[1]http://www.formatdata.com/recipeml/
spec/recipeml-spec.html
[2]http://www.happy-monkey.net/
recipebook/
[3]http://www.epicurious.com

procedure, which is divided into ingredients section and procedure in the second level. The ingredients section contains descriptions of various ingredients used in the procedure. The procedure section is divided into number of individual steps. The details of the tagset are given in figure 1 and figure 2.

5.2 Ingredient Description

The subtree starts with ingredient description as the root. It describes Name of the Ingredient (NOI), Properties of Ingredients (POI), Total Size of the Ingredient (TSOI), Total Quantity of the Ingredient (TQOI), preprocessing actions performed on the Ingredients (IAOI). Properties (POI) is further divided into size, color, odor etc. Quantity (TQOI) is divided into number and units.

5.3 Step

Each step contains cooking actions performed on the ingredients or intermediate materials formed from previous steps, using utensils or devices. Time may also be specified in the step. Step is further divided into cooking actions, ingredients, utensils/devices, time specifications.

5.3.1 Cooking Action Specifications (ca)

Specifications are tagged under *ca* tag. They describe the verb of action, its purpose and how the action is to be performed.
(1) Stir the potatoes gently to make them soft.
Verb of action - *stir*
How the action is to be performed - *gently*
Purpose of action - *to make them soft.*

5.3.2 Utensils Specifications (uca)

Specifications of utensils or devices used in a cooking action like name, purpose, properties, usage are tagged under *uca* tag. The usage is specified using prepositions like *to, into, through, with, using, in, on, from* etc.
(1) through the mesh sieve, using the knife, from the bowl, into the jar.

5.3.3 Ingredients Specifications (ica)

Specifications of ingredients or materials used in a cooking action like name, quantity, size, properties are tagged under *ica* tag.
(1) Mix *3 tablespoons of kosher salt* with *potatoes* and stir the *mixture* using spatula.

5.3.4 Time Details (time)

Specifications of the time taken for performing a cooking action are tagged under *time* tag.
(1) Stir the eggs gently *until they turn into golden yellow color.*
(2) Stir *for 5 minutes.*

5.4 An Illustrative Example

An example of a recipe snippet annotated with the above defined framework is given below.
Snippet: 2 tablespoons , unsalted butter, divided

```
⟨ingredient description ingr
id=''1''⟩
    ⟨TQOI⟩
        ⟨number⟩2⟨/number⟩
        ⟨units⟩tablespoons⟨/units⟩
    ⟨/TQOI⟩
    ⟨POI⟩
        ⟨state⟩unsalted⟨/state⟩
    ⟨/POI⟩
    ⟨NOI⟩butter⟨/NOI⟩
    ⟨IAOI⟩
        ⟨action⟩divided⟨/action⟩
    ⟨/IAOI⟩
⟨/ingredient description⟩
```

Snippet: Cook eggs, stirring gently about 3 minutes.

```
⟨step step-id=''4''⟩
    ⟨ca id = ''1''⟩
        ⟨action⟩Cook⟨/action⟩
    ⟨/ca⟩
    ⟨ica⟩
        ⟨NOI⟩eggs⟨/NOI⟩
    ⟨/ica⟩
    ⟨ca id = ''2''⟩
        ⟨action⟩stirring⟨/action⟩
        ⟨how-adv⟩gently⟨/how-adv⟩
    ⟨/ca⟩
    ⟨time⟩
        ⟨tnca⟩about
            ⟨number⟩3⟨/number⟩
            ⟨units⟩minutes⟨/units⟩
        ⟨/tnca⟩
    ⟨/time⟩
⟨/step⟩
```

6 Completeness of the Tagset

In this section, we discuss the completeness of our tagset. In general, an object is complete if nothing needs to be added to it. This notion is made more specific in various fields. In this context, it

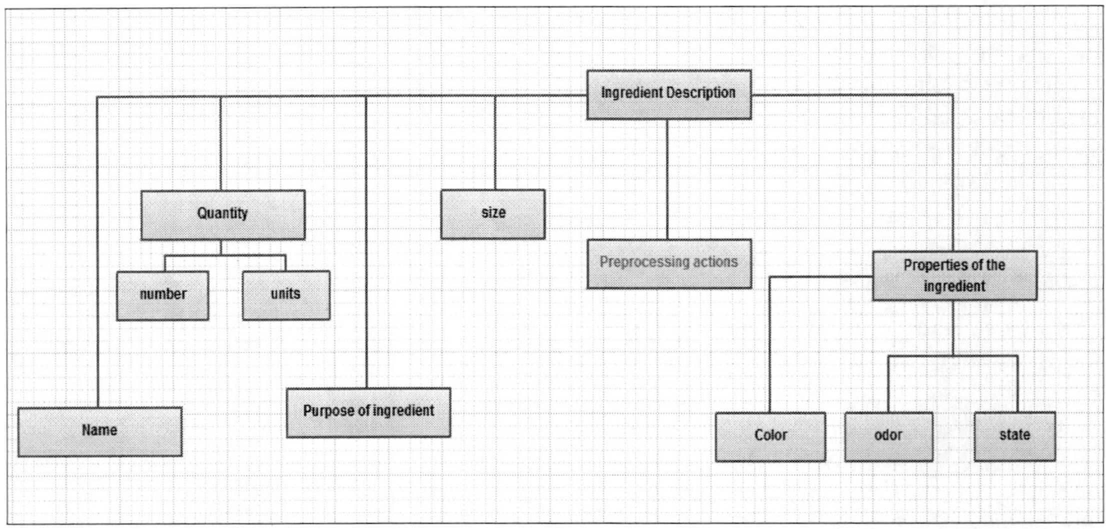

Figure 1: Ingredient Section. The nodes in red are not expanded further.

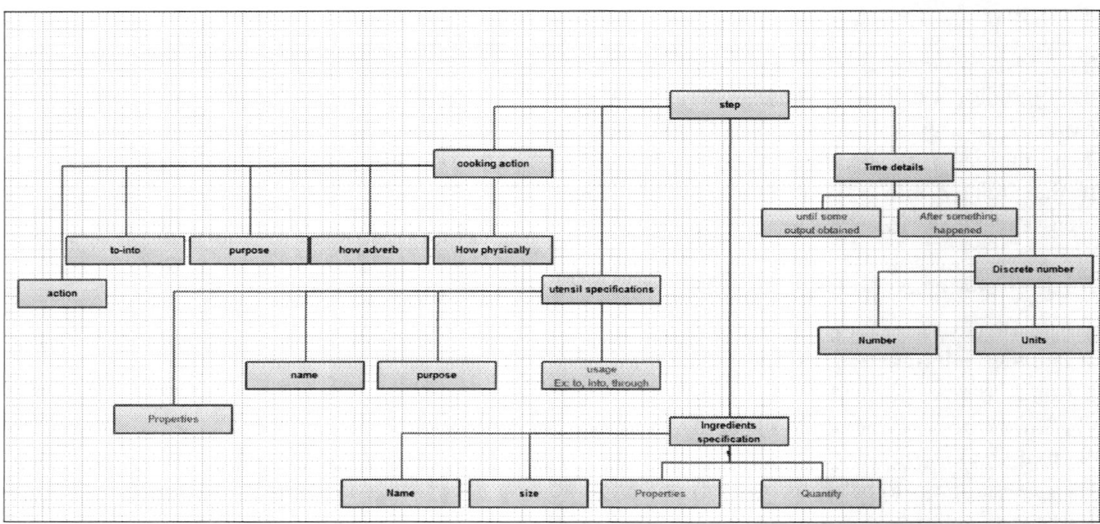

Figure 2: Procedure Section. The nodes in red are not expanded further.

means that, all the recipes can be annotated with the provided framework.

The smallest unit of a cooking procedure consists of performing a cooking action using utensils and ingredients to produce an output. The entire cooking procedure is the combination of these smallest units. Let us define this smallest unit as **atomic action.** Atomic action may include actions like stirring, cutting, heating, transferring etc. Each such action may require utensils or devices and materials or ingredients. Time taken for the atomic action may also be specified in the recipe text. We describe how these attributes are specified in a cooking recipe.

6.1 Specifications of Atomic action

Following are the different attributes under *cooking action*.

1. Main verb of action, which specifies action to be done

2. Purpose of the action

3. How the action is to be done

Following are the different attributes under *Ingredients* used in atomic action.

356

1. Name of the ingredient, size of the ingredient, quantity of the ingredient, properties of the ingredient

2. Direct ingredients - Taken from the Ingredients list

3. Intermediate ingredients - These are formed in previous steps as an intermediate product

Following are the different attributes under *utensils* used in atomic action.

1. Name of the utensil, size, properties

2. Usage of utensils is specified using prepositions like with, to, into etc

Following are the different attributes under *time* specifications used in atomic action.

1. Discrete values say, 5 minutes or

2. Until some desired output is obtained

3. Time is not specified or defined for some atomic actions

We have annotated and studied many recipes written in English language from a recipe website.[4] We found that all the above specifications of an atomic action can be tagged using the tagset defined earlier. Also the tagset framework is language independent and must be applicable to all languages as we are annotating semantic relations only.

7 Heuristics for Tagging the Recipe

We have defined heuristics to tag the input recipe based on the parts of speech of the words, parse structures of the sentences and lexical association measures. Heuristics for annotating ingredient section is based on the parts of speech(POS) of various tokens in the ingredient description. Parse trees are used for tagging procedure section. In addition, there are some bigrams which are to be tagged combinedly, like for example *olive oil*, *kosher salt* etc. We use a collocation measure, **salience score** (Pecina, 2010), as the lexical association measure for bigram modeling. The process of combining words into phrases and sentences of natural language is governed by a complex system of rules and constraints. In general, basic rules

are given by syntax, however there are also other restrictions (semantic and pragmatic) that must be adhered to in order to produce correct, meaningful, and fluent utterances. These constraints form important linguistic and lexicographic phenomena generally denoted by the term collocation . Salience score is used to decide whether to tag bigrams combinedly or not. The salience score of a bigram is given by,

$$Salience(xy) = \log \frac{p\,(xy)^2}{p\,(x*)\,p\,(*y)} \cdot \log f\,(xy)$$

where *p(xy)* is the probability of xy occuring together

f(xy) is the frequency of bigram xy

Here * means any token.

7.1 Ingredients Description

Usually ingredient section has a semi structured data. First, annotate the ingredient description using Stanford POS tagger[5] (Toutanova et al., 2003). Then scan through all the tokens formed from the input line in a linear fashion and annotate based on the heuristics. We describe some heuristics below. The heuristics given here are in a broad sense. Exact implementation details are omitted.

H1: Let k be the current token in the linear scan. If tag(k) is a **number** then annotate token k and $k + 1$ as **quantity**. Inside this quantity tag, annotate k as **number** and $k + 1$ as **units**.

H2: Let k be the current token in the linear scan. If tag(k) is a **adverb** and if it is followed by verb or noun or adjective, then annotate k and $k + 1$ under **ca** tag. Inside the **ca**, annotate k as **how** and $k + 1$ as **verb**.

H3: Let k be the current token in the linear scan. If tag(k) is a **adjective** and if tag($k + 1$) is **noun** with salience($k, k + 1$) >threshold then annotate the bigram ($k, k + 1$) as **NOI**.
Else annotate all the following adjectives under **properties** and next noun as **NOI**.

[4]http://www.epicurious.com

[5]http://nlp.stanford.edu/software/
tagger.shtml

H4: Let k be the current token in the linear scan. If tag(k) is a **preposition**, such as *for* or *to* and if tag($k + 1$) is **verb**, then annotate the pair (k, $k + 1$) under purpose of ingredient tag.

Below is the sample output obtained using above heuristics.

```
⟨TQOI⟩
    ⟨number⟩2⟨/number⟩
    ⟨units⟩tablespoons⟨/units⟩
⟨/TQOI⟩
⟨POI⟩
    ⟨p1⟩golden⟨/p1⟩
⟨/POI⟩
⟨NOI⟩butter⟨/NOI⟩
⟨POI⟩
    ⟨color⟩brown⟨/color⟩
⟨/POI⟩
⟨NOI⟩flaxseeds⟨/NOI⟩
```

7.2 Procedure

The procedure section consists of natural language text. We used tools like natural language parser and WordNet (2010) in the process of annotating the recipe. A natural language parser is a program that works out the grammatical structure of sentences, for instance, which groups of words go together (as "phrases") and which words are the subject or object of a verb. Parse tree gives a complete picture of relations between various phrases in the sentence. These relations can be used to form semantic relations in our analysis, which will be helpful in annotating the recipe. Stanford Parser[6] (Socher et al., 2013), a statistical parser is used for our purpose. WordNet gives the sense of various words in the recipe text. For example, if we query WordNet with the word *avocado*, the output contains *noun.food*. This information can be used for classifying words into utensils, ingredients and cooking actions etc.

The first step involves the tokenization of procedure into many individual sentences. Each sentence is annotated as *step*. Each step is then parsed and the parse tree is analyzed to annotate various details inside that step.

7.2.1 Handling Various Phrases

The most common phrases to be handled includes noun phrases (NP), verb phrases (VP), adjective phrases (ADJP), adverb phrases (ADVP),

---

⁶`http://nlp.stanford.edu/software/lex-parser.shtml`

prepositional phrases (PP) and some intermediate nodes of the parse tree like S (sentence), SBAR (Subordinate clause), WHADVP (Wh-adverb phrase) etc. These phrases and nodes are handled recursively. The recursion stops at the leaves of the tree. The modules for handling NP, VP, PP, ADVP, ADJP are described below. Below is the parse tree for the sentence "Add crushed black peppercorns and lemon juice and mix well".

```
(ROOT
    (S
        (VP
            (VP (VB Add)
                (NP
                    (NP (JJ crushed) (JJ black)
(NNS peppercorns))
                    (CC and)
                    (NP (JJ lemon) (NN juice))))
            (CC and)
            (VP (VB mix)
                (ADVP (RB well))))
    (. .)))
```

Noun phrases:

A noun phrase can consist of one word (for example, the pronoun *it* or the plural noun *apricots*), or it can consist of a noun with a number of dependents. The dependents occur before or after the noun head depending on their function. All noun phrases (NPs) have a noun or pronoun as the head. The noun is the anchor of the phrase and the phrase will not be grammatical without it. Noun phrases often function as complements to the verb.

In the NP, *crushed black peppercorns*, peppercorns is the head word (Noun) and crushed, black are dependants (adjectives). This NP is the complement of the verb *Add*, which is the cooking action. First we find the sense of the head word and depending upon the sense we carry out further analysis. For example, if sense shows it is an ingredient then annotate as name of the ingredient(noi), its properties (poi), quantity and units in that NP. Similarly other cases are covered.

Prepositional Phrase:

A prepositional phrase has a preposition as its head and this is usually followed by a noun phrase. A PP relates the dependent NP to other constituents in a sentence in terms of place (for example, *in the flour*).

Verb Phrase:

Each verb phrase contains one main verb. This is most probably the cooking action. Each VP contains only one main verb that functions as the head of the VP. Eg: *Add* is the head of the VP given in above example. The main verb is tagged as cooking action and the surrounding adverb phrases and adjective phrases tells how the action is performed.

Adverb Phrase:

An adverb phrase takes an adverb as its head. **AdvP**s typically modify a verb within a VP (for example, Mix *well*). They usually describe how the cooking action is to be performed.

Adjective Phrase:

An adjective phrase has an adjective as its head. An AdjP can function as a modifier within a noun phrase (for example, the *brown* flaxseeds) in which case it is annotated under property.

The following are some issues which are taken care while automatically tagging the input recipe.

1. **Co-reference**: In linguistics, co-reference occurs when two or more expressions in a text refer to the same person or thing. Ingredients or intermediate outputs and utensils from the previous steps are co-referenced in the current step. Usually pronouns refer to nouns. We are using Stanford Deterministic Coreference Resolution System[7] (Lee et al., 2013) to resolve the coreferences.

2. **Distance references**: The tags corresponding to a particular subtree may not be at consecutive positions in the input recipe. So for an individual tag, if it is not inside its subtree, we have to keep a reference to its parent using an attribute called *ref*.

   In the example below, *action, how-adv* have same parent *ca*. But they are not present in consecutive positions, so *how-adv* makes a reference to *ca* using *ref* attribute.

   Cut potatoes smoothly using knife

```
⟨step step-id=``4''⟩

    ⟨ca id = ``1''⟩

        ⟨action⟩Cut⟨/action⟩

    ⟨/ca⟩

    ⟨ica⟩
```

```
        ⟨NOI⟩potatoes⟨/NOI⟩

    ⟨/ica⟩

        ⟨how-adv
ref=``ca-1''⟩smoothly⟨/how-adv⟩

        ⟨uca⟩

            ⟨using-uca⟩using⟨/using-uca⟩

            ⟨nuca⟩knife⟨/nuca⟩

        ⟨/uca⟩

⟨/step⟩
```

8 Results

The above heuristics are tested on over 100 recipes collected from the web and results are compared with manually annotated recipes. Results on only 20 recipes are shown below. These recipes are collected from an Indian website[8] and a foreign website.[9] The evaluation is done as follows.

1. **Scheme A:** Each step in the procedure can get a maximum score of 1. This maximum score is divided equally among various *ca, ica, uca, time* tags present in that step. For example, if a step has 2 *ca* tags, 1 *uca* tag, 2 *ica* tags and 1 *time* tag, the maximum score each tag can get is $1/6$, as there are 6 of them present in that step. The score is further divided among their children. In addition to dividing score among the children, score is also divided for coreferencing the pronouns. Then evaluation is done at each tag. If the annotation is correct, it gets the maximum score it was assigned. The score of the step is calculated by adding scores of individual tags in that step. Once the score for each step is calculated, mean of scores of all the steps in the recipe is calculated. This mean score is called the *score of the recipe*. Average of the scores of all the tested recipes gives the accuracy of the system.

2. **Scheme B:** Some errors in the annotated output are due to the wrong output of the Stanford parser. In this scheme we want to find out how much gain in accuracy can be obtained if no parser error exist. So if an error occurs in annotation because of the wrong

---

[7]http://nlp.stanford.edu/software/dcoref.shtml

[8]http://www.sanjeevkapoor.com/

[9]http://www.epicurious.com/

parse tree of the sentence, that part of the annotation is not considered while scoring the sentence i.e, score is not divided among those tags.

Table 1: Results of evaluation of some recipes

Recipe Number	Scheme A	Scheme B
1	0.63	0.9
2	0.74	0.98
3	0.78	0.83
4	0.85	0.9
5	0.81	0.96
6	0.89	0.96
7	0.72	0.75
8	0.82	0.94
9	0.82	0.95
10	0.71	0.94
11	0.65	0.98
12	0.74	0.94
13	0.77	0.94
14	0.75	0.85
15	0.77	0.90
16	0.68	0.85
17	0.81	0.98
18	0.72	0.86
19	0.72	0.95
20	0.72	0.94
Avg. Accuracy	0.75	0.91

8.1 Inferences

Given a step in a procedure, the accuracy scores in Table 1 signifies that the step can be annotated with an accuracy of 75% in scheme A evaluation and an accuracy of 91% in scheme B evaluation. We observe in bar graph of Figure 3 that scheme A scores are less than Scheme B scores. This infers that if the accuracy of the Stanford parser is increased we can annotate the recipe with greater accuracy.

9 Conclusion and Outlook

In this paper we have presented a tagset framework designed for cooking recipes and a system which automates the recipe annotation process using the proposed framework. The hierarchical recursive tagset framework captures relations among different attributes through linguistic analysis. Furthermore, we have shown that the automatic annotation with out tagset framework achieves reasonably good accuracy using language tools and heuristics.

The heuristics used for the current system required language specific analysis which may not be available for many languages. In order to make the system language independent, we plan to use machine learning-based approach to identify different attributes and relationship from the recipe text for automatic annotation.

References

Sankaran Baskaran and Kalika Bali and Tanmoy Bhattacharya and Pushpak Bhattacharyya and Girish Nath Jha and Rajendran S and Saravanan K and Sobha L and Kvs Subbarao. 2008. *A Common Parts-of-Speech Tagset Framework for Indian Languages* In Proc. of LREC 2008.

Heeyoung Lee, Angel Chang, Yves Peirsman, Nathanael Chambers, Mihai Surdeanu and Dan Jurafsky. 2013. Deterministic coreference resolution based on entity-centric, precision-ranked rules. *Computational Linguistics*, 39(4), pages. 885-916,

Shinsuke Mori and Hirokuni Maeta and Yoko Yamakata and Tetsuro Sasada. 2014. Flow Graph Corpus from Recipe Texts, In *Proceedings of the Ninth International Conference on Language Resources and Evaluation (LREC'14), European Language Resources Association (ELRA)*.

Pavel Pecina. 2010. Lexical association measures and collocation extraction *Language resources and evaluation*, Vol.44, pages. 137-158, Springer.

Princeton University "About WordNet". WordNet. Princeton University. 2010. ⟨http://wordnet.princeton.edu⟩

Yuka Shidochi, Tomokazu Takahashi, Ichiro Ide, and Hiroshi Murase. 2009. Finding Replaceable Materials in Cooking Recipe Texts Considering Characteristic Cooking Actions. In *Proceedings of the ACM Multimedia 2009 Workshop on Multimedia for Cooking and Eating Activities*, ACM, pages. 9-14.

Richard Socher, John Bauer, Christopher D. Manning and Andrew Y. Ng 2013. Parsing With Compositional Vector Grammars, In *Proceedings of the 51st Annual Meeting of the Association for Computational Linguistics*, Sofia, Bulgaria, pages. 455-465.

Kristina Toutanova, Dan Klein, Christopher Manning, and Yoram Singer. 2003. Feature-Rich Part-of-Speech Tagging with a Cyclic Dependency Network In *Proceedings of HLT-NAACL 2003*, pp. 252-259.

Chun-Yuen Teng, Yu-Ru Lin, and Lada A. Adamic. 2012. Recipe Recommendation Using Ingredient

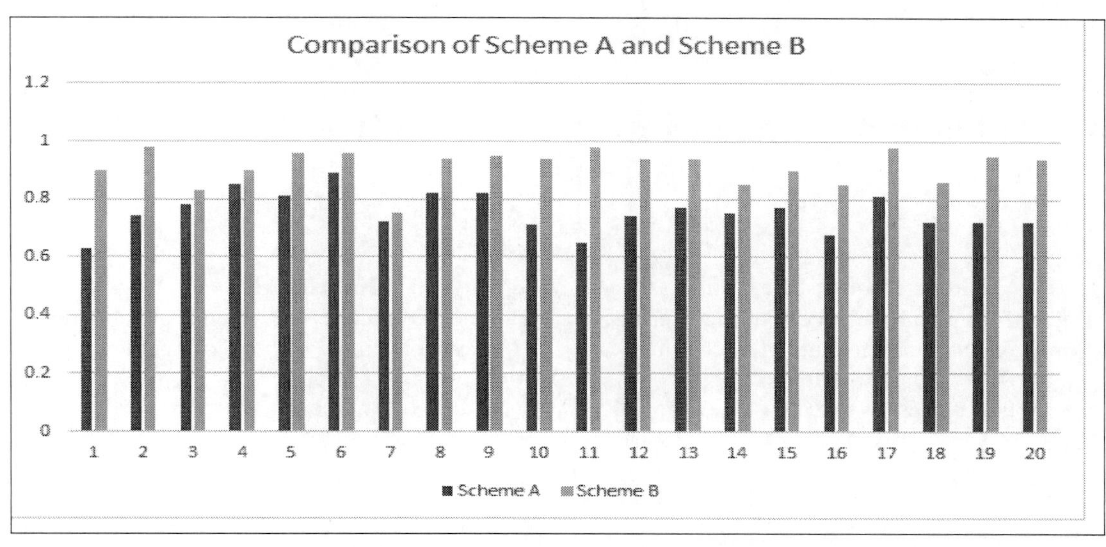

Figure 3: Comparison of results in Scheme A and Scheme B.

Networks. In *Proceedings of the 3rd Annual ACM Web Science Conference*, ACM, pages. 298-307.

Dufour-Lussier Valmi, Le Ber Florence, Lieber Jean, Meilender Thomas and Nauer Emmanuel. 2012. Semi-automatic annotation process for procedural texts: An application on cooking recipes.

Liping Wang, Qing Li, Na Li, Guozhu Dong, and Yu Yang. 2008. Substructure Similarity Measurement in Chinese Recipes. In *Proceedings of the 17th International Conference on World Wide Web*, ACM, pages. 979-988.

Ziqi Zhang and Philip Webster and Victoria Uren and Andrea Varga and Fabio Ciravegna. 2012. Automatically Extracting Procedural Knowledge from Instructional Texts using Natural Language Processing. In *Proceedings of the Eight International Conference on Language Resources and Evaluation (LREC'12)*.

Named Entity Based Answer Extraction form Hindi Text Corpus Using n-grams

Lokesh Kumar Sharma
Dept. of Computer Science and Engineering
Malaviya National Institute of Technology
Jaipur, India
2013rcp9007@mnit.ac.in

Namita Mittal
Dept. of Computer Science and Engineering
Malaviya National Institute of Technology
Jaipur, India
Nmittal.cse@mnit.ac.in

Abstract

Most existing systems, are constructed for the English language, such as state-of-art system Watson that win the Jeopardy challenge. While working with Indian languages (i.e. Hindi), a richer morphology, greater syntactic variability, and less number of standardized rules availability in the language are just some issues that complicate the construction of systems. It is also considered a resource-poor language since proper gazetteer lists and tagged corpora is not available for it. In this paper, Named Entity (NE) based n-gram approach is used for processing questions written in Hindi language and extract the answer from Hindi documents. Combination of classical information retrieval term weighing model with a linguistic approach mainly based on syntactic analysis is used. We use a corpus of 420 questions and 300 documents containing around 20,000 words as a back-end for closed-domain (World History) Question Answering. A Named Entity Recognizer is employed to identify answer candidates which are then filtered according their usage. Results obtained using this technique outperforms the previously used techniques (e.g. Semantic Based Query Logic).

1 Introduction

With the advancement in technology, Question Answering has become a major area of research. Question Answering systems enable the user to ask questions in natural language instead of a query and retrieve one or many valid and accurate answers in natural language. The explosion of information on Internet, Natural language QA is recognized as a capability with great potential (Hirschman and Gaizauskas, 2001). Information retrieval systems allow us to locate full documents or best matching passages that might contain the pertinent information, but most of them leave it to the user to extract the useful information from a ranked list. Therefore, professionals from various areas are beginning to recognize the usefulness of other types of systems, such as QA systems, for quickly and effectively finding specialist information. The QA technology takes both IR and IE a step further, and provides specific and brief answers to the user's questions formulated naturally. Hindi holds 5th position among top 100 spoken languages in the world, with no. of speakers being close to 200 million (Shachi et al., 2001) but comparing Indian languages with other languages, word segmentation is a key problem in Indian question answering. As per our knowledge not much work has been done in Hindi as compared to various other languages like English (Ittycheriah et al., 2008), Chinese etc. This motivates for developing a Hindi question answering system (Vishal and Jaspreet, 2013). Our dataset consists of 420 questions and 300 documents containing around 20,000 words chosen from a specific domain (World History). Our model involves three general phases which are as follows. The first phase, Question Processing, involves analyzing and classifying the questions into different categories. This classification later helps in Answer type Detection. Further, in this module, a query is formulated which is passed on to the next phase for searching the relevant documents which might contain the answer. In the second phase, Information Retrieval, we have applied an algorithm called Term Frequency-Inverse-Document-Frequency

D S Sharma, R Sangal and J D Pawar. Proc. of the 11th Intl. Conference on Natural Language Processing, pages 362–367,
Goa, India. December 2014. ©2014 NLP Association of India (NLPAI)

(TF-IDF) (Ramos, 2003), which uses dot product and cosine similarity rule to find the probability of a given text in a given set of documents. This gives us the list of relevant documents. The next phase, Answer Extraction, uses bigram forming approach (Wang et al., 2005) to retrieve the answer from a given document. In this we have also used a pre-built Hindi named entity recognition model which categorizes the given text into different categories.

2 Related Work

Specific research in the area of question answering has been prompted in the last few years in particular by the Question Answering track of the Text Retrieval Conference (TREC-QA) competitions (Satoshi and Ralph, 2003). Recently IBM Watson defeated two human winners and win the Jeopardy game show. Watson uses very complex algorithm to read any given clue. At the first stage in question analysis Watson does parsing and semantic analysis using a deep Slot Grammar parser, a named entity recognizer, a co-reference resolution component, and a relation extraction component (Lilly et. al 2012). Our work uses similar approach by using named entity taggers and parsing. Research work has been done in Surprise Language Exercise (SLE) within the TIDES program where viability of a cross lingual question answering (CLQA) (Shachi et al., 2001) has been shown by developing a basic system. It presents a model that answers English questions by finding answers in Hindi newswire documents and further translates the answer candidates into English along with the context surrounding each answer (Satoshi and Ralph, 2003). Another approach taken by some researchers (Praveen et al., 2003) presents a Hindi QA system based on a Hindi search engine that works on locality-based similarity heuristics to retrieve relevant passages from the corpus over agriculture and science domain. Some researchers (Sahu et al., 2012) discusses an implementation of a Hindi question answering system "PRASHNOTTAR". It presents four classes of questions namely: "when", "where", "what time" and "how many" and their static dataset includes 15 questions of each type which gives an accuracy of 68%. In addition to the traditional difficulties with syntactic analysis, there remains many other problems to be solved, e.g.,

semantic interpretation, ambiguity resolution, discourse modeling, inference, common sense etc.

3 Proposed Approach

Question Processing is the first phase of our proposed question answering model in which we analyze the question and create a proper IR query which is further used to retrieve some relevant documents which may contain the answer of the question. Another task is question classification to classify a question by the type of answer it requires. The former task is called Question Classification and the latter one is known as Query Formulation. Both these aspects are equally important for Question Processing.

3.1. Question Classification

The goal of Question Classification is to accurately assign labels to questions based on expected answer type. Hence, we detect the category of a given question.

Question Phrase	Answer Type (AT)
क्या	AT:Desc, Single type cannot be decided
कब	Date
कहाँ	Location
कितनी कितना कितने	Number
कौनसा कौनसी	Answer type depends on next following word
किसका किसकी कौन किसे किसने	Person
क्यों	AT:Desc, Single type cannot be decided
कैसे	AT:Method, Single type cannot be decided
किस	Answer type depends on next following word

Table 1. Possible Answer Type Based on Question Phrase

In English there are 6 main categories namely LOCATION, PERSON, NUMERIC, ENTITY, ABBREVIATION and DESCRIPTION and but for

Hindi we have taken only 4 categories for our categorization process includes PERSON, COUNT, DATE and LOCATION. We applied proposed algorithm over the following answer types highlighted in table 1. The output file contains the previously mentioned category of question to which it belongs followed by the question itself and thus mapping from questions to answer types is done here. After categorization of the question, we store it in a file, so that it can be used later for answer extraction. Here is an example. Suppose we have the following question, लोक अदालत की शुरुआत राजस्थान में सबसे पहले कहां हुई ? Then the output file will contain: LOCATION: लोक अदालत की शुरुआत राजस्थान में सबसे पहले **कहां** हुई।

3.2. Query Formation

Query Formation is a technique to make the question format such that it can be passed on to a system which takes the input in the form of a query and searches out the relevant documents i.e. the documents which have the maximum probability of containing the answer. For this purpose, we have formulated a query by extracting the main or focus words (Haung, 2008) of the question by removing the stop words occurring in the question. For this, we have used a file containing a prebuilt list of stop words. Examples of some stop words are: (के, का, हुई, है, पर, इस, होता, , बनी, नहीं, तो, ही, या, एवं, दिया, हो, इसका, था, द्वारा, हुआ, तक, साथ, करना, कुछ, सकते, किसी, हुई) After stop words removal, the text looks like this: लोक अदालत शुरुआत राजस्थान पहले After removal of these less important words from the question, the resultant output can be used as a query for the information retrieval system which involves the next part of the model.

3.3. Relevant Information Extraction

The task of Information Retrieval phase is to query the IR Engine, find relevant documents and return candidate passages that are likely to contain the answer. In our model, our dataset is scattered over various documents, each containing question re-

lated text along with its answer. Then we performed a search within these documents in order to find out such documents which may contain the answer. And for this purpose, we have applied an algorithm called TF-IDF; it gives as output the list of various documents which may contain any of the given words from the query. The term frequency (TF) for a given term t_i within a particular document d_j is defined as the number of occurrences of that term in the d_j^{th} document, which is equal to $n_{i,j}$: the number of occurrences of the term t_i in the document d_j.

$$TF_{i,j} = n_{i,j}$$

$IDF(t_i) = \log_e$(Total number of documents / Number of documents with term t in it).

$$IDF_i = \frac{\log |D|}{|\{d : ti \in d\}|}$$

With $|D|$: total number of documents in the collection and $|\{d : t_i \in d\}|$: number of documents where the term t_i appears. To avoid divide-by-zero, we can use $1 + |\{d : t_i \in d\}|$. For a given corpus D, then the TF-IDF is then defined as:

$$(TF\text{-}IDF)_{i,j} = TF_{i,j} \times IDF_i.$$

The input of TF-IDF is the file which contains focus words of the question i.e. the output of query processing. When TF-IDF algorithm was applied on this file, it gave as output the relevant documents i.e. documents having maximum probability of containing the answer. TF-IDF numbers imply a strong relationship with the document they appear in, suggesting that if that word were to appear in a query, the document could be of interest to the user (Ramos, 2003). For our given example, the given method extracted the following:

औधोगिक विवादों के त्वरित निपटारे के किए जयपुर स्थित राजस्थान उच्च-न्ययालय में 20 जुलाई को मेगा लोक अदालत का आयोजन किया जाएगा । लोक अदालत की शुरुआत राजस्थान में सबसे पहले कोटा में हुई । </146.txt>

146 is the document number from which it extracts the passage. Then we take the mentioned documents and retrieve all its content in a separate file which is further used to find answers in the answer extraction phase.

3.4. Answer Extraction

The final task of a QA system is to process the relevant Passages (which we get after Information Retrieval phase) and extract a segment of word(s) that is likely to be the answer of the question. Question classification comes handy here. There are various techniques for answer extraction. We have used the following steps to extract answer.

Step 1: Take the file containing the text and remove all of its stop words.

Step 2: Take the file which contains the question and form its bigrams i.e. form words taking twice a time and stored it in a file.

Step 3: Then take the output file and form the bigram of the text it contains and match it with the file which contains the question's bigrams.

Step 4: Save the number of bigrams matched for each line to the question's bigrams.

Step 5: Output the line which contains the maximum number of bigrams matched.

We have the following output after removing stop words from the passage:

औधोगिक विवादों त्वरित निपटारे जयपुर स्थित राजस्थान उच्च-न्ययालय 20 जुलाई मेगा लोक अदालत आयोजन जाएगा लोक अदालत शुरुआत राजस्थान पहले कोटा

After storing this output file as a target document. The questions are stored in a separate file of their bigrams i.e. taking two words together (Wang and McCallum, 2005). Storing the outcome in a file called QBigram-feature file. This gave us the following output,

$\textbf{Q-Bi-gram}_{(feature)}$ = {(लोक अदालत)$_1$, (अदालत शुरुआत)$_2$, (शुरुआत राजस्थान)$_3$, (राजस्थान पहले)$_4$, (पहले हुई)$_5$}

The given passage will have following bigrams,

$\textbf{P-Bi-gram}_{(feature)}$ = {(लोक अदालत)$_1$, (अदालत शुरुआत)$_2$, (शुरुआत राजस्थान)$_3$, (राजस्थान पहले)$_4$, (पहले कोटा)$_5$, (कोटा हुई)$_6$}

Now these bigrams will be matched with the question's bigram as per our designed algorithm. The concept in this is, the line which contains the maximum number of two words same at a time will have maximum probability of containing the answer. So when we do this we will get following line as output:

लोक अदालत की शुरुआत राजस्थान में सबसे पहले कोटा में हुई I </146.txt>

Now we pass the question containing file to the prebuilt Hindi Named Entity Recognition (NER) System (Maksim and Andrey, 2012) which will tag the given text into the aforementioned 5 categories. The NER gives output as following:

लोक	o	both
अदालत	o	both
शुरुआत	o	both
राजस्थान	LOCATION	GAZETTEER
पहले	o	both

As we know the possible type of answer from the question classification method which we have applied earlier, we can remove those named entities which are present in both answer and the question, as they will not be the required answer. And hence, the remaining tagged entity will be our required answer. After removing the named entities which are tagged in the question, following words are left in the text: लोक अदालत शुरुआत पहले कोटा Now running the NER on the output line again, getting the tagged output:

लोक	o	both
अदालत	o	both
शुरुआत	o	both
पहले	o	both
कोटा	LOCATION	GAZETTEER

Through this output, we extract the entities which matches the Answer Type which we have detected earlier i.e. Answer Type Detection (Roberts and Hickl, 2008) is done on the output. For example in our case here the Answer Type is LOCATION, so we extract the entity which is tagged as location which is <कोटा>.

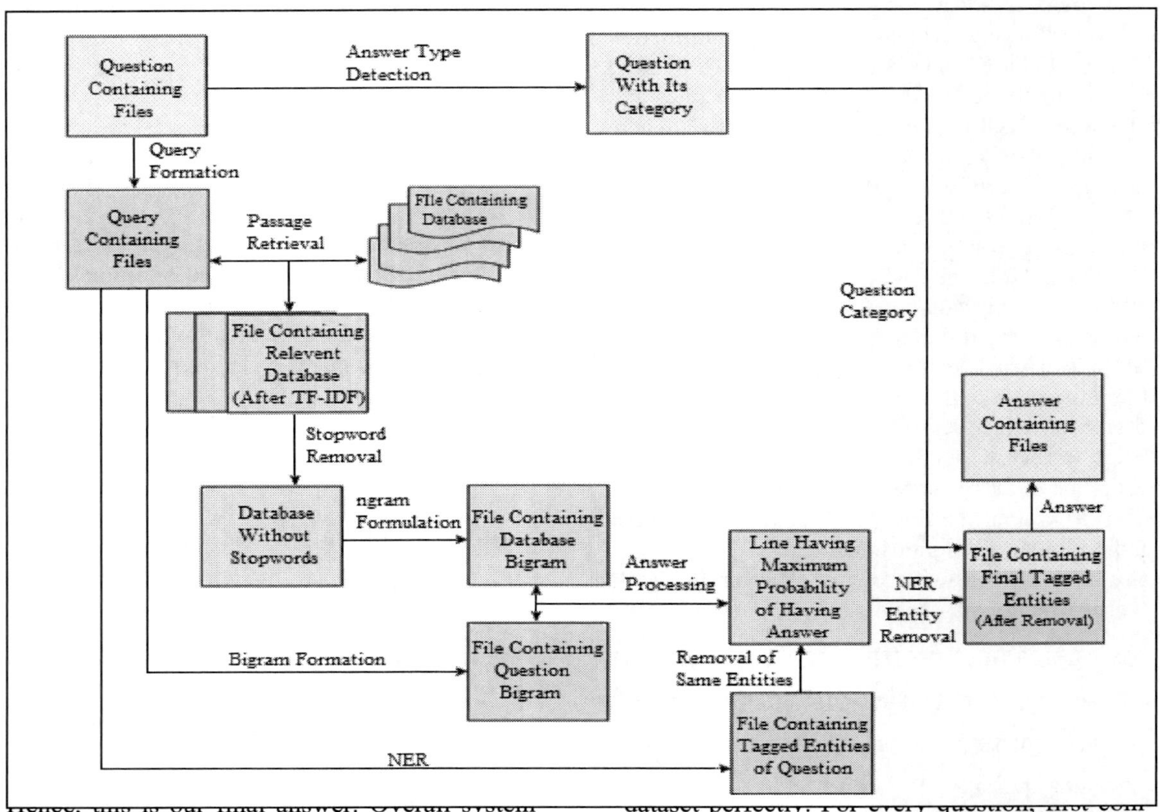

architecture is shown in figure 1.

4. Experimental Setup and Analysis

To evaluate the effectiveness of the proposed methods for answer extraction from Hindi corpus, 300 standard documents datasets is used. The accuracy for the questions of category 'कब', 'कहाँ', 'कितनी, कितना, कितने', and 'किसका, किसकी' is satisfactory in proposed approach shown in table 2. The accuracy of question type 'किस समय' is not considered by the proposed approach because the answer type of this question has been not considered. The accuracy of the question type 'कब', 'कहाँ', and 'किसका किसकी' is highly accurate. Some question has low syntactic information to reach the answer, and it is difficult for the system to answer. For such a questions it may have multiple documents and multiple matches in these documents, an algorithm may not extract every answer in the dataset perfectly. For every question, first compute its precision (P) and its recall (R) by taking the dataset as gold standard answers as the relevant answer and the predicted answer at the retrieved set. Now, taking an average of P and R over all Topics. Now, calculating macro F1 using the harmonic mean of the average P and R,

$$macro\ F1 = \frac{2PR}{(P + R)}$$

Where,

$$P = \frac{correct}{retrieved} \text{ and } R = \frac{correct}{retrieved}.$$

Accuracy (F1-measure) is calculated which outperforms existing Semantic Based Query Logic approach comparison results are highlighted in the Table 2.

Type of Question (Total 420 Question)	Accuracy (macro F1)	
	(Semantic Based Query Logic)	(Proposed Approach- NE Based n-gram)

कब	66.66%	**74.33%**
कहाँ	53.00%	**86.66%**
कितना कितने कितनी	73.33%	**72.50%**
किसका किसकी	-	**82.75%**
Total	64.33%	**79.06%**

Table 2. Accuracy of the proposed approach

The question set of 420 questions[1] and supported answer documents used in this work are manually collected from web. The documents have answer for every question still it is not easy to extract correct answers for all questions.

5. Conclusion and Future Work

In this paper, Question answering for Hindi language has been experimented on 420 natural language questions. Results outperforms the previously used semantic based logic query approach. Using this approach, we achieved state-of-art results for most of the question types namely Person, Location, Date and Count. But as this approach is syntactic, so using this approach we able to get answers for factoid questions. Text where usage of synonyms or hyponyms of words is seen, accurate answers could not be extracted. Such issues can be dealt by introduction of the semantic approach. Results can be improved by adding features like entailment, co-reference etc in the answer extraction phase. Improving the accuracy of Hindi NER will also help in improving the accuracy of the system. Also, as our model is domain based, one can extend its domain by using a searching algorithm over the Wikipedia or other online resources.

References

Hirschman L., Gaizauskas R., *"Natural language question answering: the view from here"*, Natural Language Engineering, v.7 n.4, p.275-300, December, 2001.

Ittycheriah et al., *"IBM's Statistical Question Answering System"*, In Proceedings of the Ninth Text Retrieval Conference (TREC-9), 2000. Roberts, K., & Hickl, A, "Scaling Answer Type Detection to Large Hierarchies", In Proceedings of LREC, May 2008.

Lally A., Prager J. M., McCord M. C., Boguraev B. K., S. Patwardhan, Fan J., Fodor P., and Chu-Carroll J., *"Question analysis: How Watson reads a clue"*, IBM J. Res. Dev., vol. 56, no. 3/4, Paper 2, pp. 2:1–2:14, May/Jul. 2012.

Maksim Tkachenko, Andrey Simanovsky, *"Named Entity Recognition: Exploring Features"*. In Proceedings of KONVENS 2012, Vienna, September 20, 2012.

Praveen Kumar, Shrikant Kashyap and Ankush Mittal, *"A Query Answering System for E-Learning Hindi Documents"*, South Asian Language Review Vol. XIII, Nos. 1&2, January-June,2003.

Ramos J., *"Using TF-IDF to determine word relevance in document queries"*. In Proceedings of the First Instructional Conference on Machine Learning, December 2003.

Roberts K. and Hickl A, *"Scaling Answer Type Detection to Large Hierarchies"*, In Proceedings of LREC, May 2008.

Sahu S., Vasnik N., and Roy D., *"Prashnottar: A Hindi Question Answering System"*, International Journal of Computer Science and Technology, Vol 4, pp. 149-158, 2012.

Satoshi Sekine and Ralph Grishman, *"Hindi-English cross-lingual question-answering system"*, ACM Transactions on Asian Language Information Processing (TALIP), v.2 n.3, p.181-192, September 2003.

Shachi Dave, Pushpak Bhattacharya & Dietrich Klakowya, *"Knowledge Extraction from Hindi Text"*, Journal of Institution of Electronic and telecommunication engineers, 18(4), 2001.

Vishal G. and Jaspreet K., *"Comparative Analysis of Question Answering System in Indian Languages"*, International Journal of Advanced Research in Computer Science and Software Engineering" 3(7) pp.584-592, July 2013.

Wang X. and McCallum A., *"A note on topical n-grams"*, Massachusetts University Amherst Dept of Computer Science, 2005.

---

[1] https://code.google.com/p/hindiqset/

"ye word kis lang ka hai bhai?"

"ye word kis lang ka hai bhai?"
Testing the Limits of Word level Language Identification

Spandana Gella[*]
University of Edinburgh
Microfost Research Lab, India
t-spgell@microsoft.com

Kalika Bali, Monojit Choudhury
Microsoft Research Lab, India
{kalikab,monojitc}@microsoft.com

Abstract

Language identification is a necessary pre-requisite for processing any user generated text, where the language is unknown. It becomes even more challenging when the text is code-mixed, i.e., two or more languages are used within the same text. Such data is commonly seen in social media, where further challenges might arise due to contractions and transliterations. The existing language identification systems are not designed to deal with code-mixed text, and as our experiments show, perform poorly on a synthetically created code-mixed dataset for 28 languages.We propose extensions to an existing approach for word level language identification. Our technique not only outperforms the existing methods, but also makes no assumption about the language pairs mixed in the text - a common requirement of the existing word level language identification systems.This study shows that word level language identification is most likely to confuse between languages which are linguistically related (e.g., Hindi and Gujarati, Czech and Slovak), for which special disambiguation techniques might be required.

1 Introduction

As the World Wide Web is constantly being inundated by user-generated content in many languages, automatic *Language Identification* (LI) of text fragments has become an extremely important

---

The work was done during authors internship at Microsoft Research Lab India

problem. Since mid 90s, this problem has attracted the attention of researchers (Prager,), and by 2005 it was thought to be a solved problem (McNamee, 2005). However, there is a renewed interest in LI over last few years (Lui and Baldwin, 2011; Tromp and Pechenizkiy, 2011; Bergsma et al., 2012; Lui and Baldwin, 2012; Goldszmidt et al., 2013; King and Abney, 2013; Carter et al., 2013; Lui et al., 2014) primarily due to a surge in user-generated content in social media, given the rising popularity of Twitter, Facebook and several other online social networking platforms.

Short length, presence of non-standard spelling variations, idiomatic expressions and acronyms are the most commonly cited reasons that make LI for social media content, such as tweets, a challenging problem (Carter et al., 2013; Goldszmidt et al., 2013). However, there are two other frequently observed phenomena in social media (and also in other forms of user-generated content such as blogs and discussion forums) which have received very little attention: *Code-mixing* and *Transliteration*.

Code-mixing, loosely speaking, is the process of mixing more than one language in a single conversation. In the context of social media, code-mixing can be defined as using more than one, usually only two, languages in a single tweet or post. For instance, in the following comment posted on Facebook, the user has *mixed* Hindi (in italics) and English words in a single sentence.

```
love affection lekar salose
se sunday ke din chali aarahi
divine parampara ko age badhha
rahe ho
```

Translation: With love and affection, (you) are carrying forward the divine tradition that

D S Sharma, R Sangal and J D Pawar. Proc. of the 11th Intl. Conference on Natural Language Processing, pages 368–377,
Goa, India. December 2014. ©2014 NLP Association of India (NLPAI)

has been going on on Sundays for years.

This example also illustrates the phenomenon of *transliteration*; the Hindi text is not written using the Devanagari script; the user has transliterated it in Roman script. Code-mixing and transliteration are not mere challenges for LI, rather these phenomena demand a new definition of LI. It is no longer sufficient to identify the language of a tweet or microblog or even a sentence. One needs to identify the language of every word.[1] Transliteration adds to the complexity of the problem because there is no notion of correct transliteration (the same word can be spelled as *badhha, badha, badhaa* and so on), which then can be further contracted according to the norms of computer mediated communication.

How common are these phenomena? In a separate study by us (to appear, reference removed for anonymity), we found that 50% of the sentences on a Hindi film discussion forum are code-mixed (mainly between Telugu-English and Hindi-English); we also found that 17% of the posts on Facebook public pages of Indian celebrities have code-mixing, and more than 90% of the Indian language texts were Romanized. In fact, code-mixing and transliteration are not unique to social media; Gupta et al (2014) have shown that 6% of Bing queries from India has Roman transliterated Hindi words mixed with English terms. Neither is code-mixing unique to Indian languages. In a recently conducted shared task on LI for codeswitched text[2], tens of thousands of tweets were released that had code-mixing between English and Spanish, English and Nepali, English and Mandarin, and between standard and dialectal Arabic. Thus, LI at word level in the presence of code-mixing and transliteration (wherever relevant) is an essential task that needs to be solved before any further analysis of user-generated text in social media.

In this paper, we study the performance of word-level LI for code-mixed text of several state-of-the-art and off-the-shelf LI systems. Since these systems were not designed for tackling code-mixed text, the performance, as expected, is less than satisfactory. We propose extensions to an existing LI technique for language labeling at word level. In the absence of sufficient data across many languages annotated with language labels for words, we created a synthetic dataset by mixing natural language text fragments in 28 languages. Our dataset included three cases of transliterated text, for Hindi, Bengali and Gujarati. The proposed extensions outperform all the existing LI systems evaluated by a significant margin for all 28 languages.

Previous work on LI at word level presumes an a priori knowledge of the *two languages* mixed and the task mostly reduces to a binary classification problem (Solorio and Liu, 2008a; Nguyen and Dogruoz, 2013; Gella et al., 2013). However, this is not the case in practice. The languages to be identified are usually not known in advance and the set of potential language labels can span all the languages represented on the World Wide Web. The primary contribution of the current work is to highlight the challenges in such a scenario and present a few techniques to deal with these.

The rest of the paper is organized as follows. In Sec. 2 we review related work with special reference to the existing LI systems evaluated in this work. Sec. 3 describes the synthetic dataset creation. In Sec. 4 we propose different extensions and baselines for word level LI, and in the next section, we present the results of the evaluation experiments. Sec 6 discusses the various implications of these results. We conclude with some future directions in Sec 7.

2 Related Work

Code-Mixing (CM) or the embedding of linguistic units such as phrases, words and morphemes of one language into an utterance of another language (Gumperz, 1982; Myers-Scotton, 1993; Myers-Scotton, 2002) is a well-studied linguistic phenomenon of multilingual speech communities. As mentioned earlier,the wide-spread use of computer mediated communication like email, chat, and more recently, on social media like Facebook and Twitter (Herring, 2003; Cardenas-Claros and Isharyanti, 2009; Paolillo, 2011) has ensured that code-mixed data is fairly prevalent on the web. In the case of social-media content where there are additional complications due to contractions, non-standard spellings, and non-standard constructions as well as mixing of

---

[1]Sometimes, in certain languages, even the same word can be composed of parts taken from different languages. E.g., the word *housinalli* is composed of an English root *house* and Kannada suffix *nalli* meaning "in the house". This kind of usage is not uncommon for morphologically rich languages, but is beyond the scope of the current work.

[2]`http://www.emnlp2014.org/workshops/CodeSwitch/call.html`

scripts, processing of the data poses major challenges. Further, many languages that use non-Roman scripts, like Hindi, Bangla, Chinese, Arabic etc. are often present in a Romanized form. (Sowmya et al., 2010). Not a lot of work has been done on computational models of code-mixing (Solorio and Liu, 2008a; Solorio and Liu, 2008b; Nguyen and Dogruoz, 2013) , primarily due to the paucity of CM data in conventional text corpora which makes data-intensive methods hard to apply. (Solorio and Liu, 2008a) in their work on English-Spanish CM use models built on smaller datasets to predict valid switching points to synthetically generate data from monlingual corpora. While natural language processing like POS tagging, normalization, etc remain hard problems to solve, any processing of code-mixed text, first needs to deal with the identification and labeling of the parts of text which are in different languages.

Monolingual language identification has been worked on intensively in NLP where the task is to assign a language to every document according to the language it contains. There are existing methods which show high accuracies on large (Xia et al., 2009) and short (Tromp and Pechenizkiy, 2011; Lui and Baldwin, 2012) documents when tested against a small set of languages. However, for Code-mixed text, especially those involving transliterations and orthographic variation, this is far from a solved problem. In their work, (King and Abney, 2013) use a weakly supervised n-gram based model trained on monolingual data for labeling languages in a mixed-language document. In their experiments with language-labels of words in multilingual online discussions using language models and dictionaries, (Nguyen and Dogruoz, 2013) show that spelling variations, similarity between words in the two languages, as well as Named Entities, are the biggest source of errors, though they show some improvement with the incorporation of context. Gella et al. (2013) built the system with the best performance for the shared task on language identification and back transliteration for English mixed with Hindi, Bangla and Gujarati in FIRE 2013 (Saha Roy et al., 2013). The system uses a source language with a confidence probability for each word similar to (King and Abney, 2013), and incorporates context information through a code-switching probability. The thing to be noted in all these cases is that the LI

systems have a priori information on the languages that they have to disambiguate,making this essentially a binary classification task.

Some of the commonly used as well as state-of-the-art LI techniques used that we evaluate in our work are:

linguini: This was one of the early systems proposed by (Prager,) to identify multiple languages and their proportions in a single document. This is based on vector space model, where the languages in a document are determined by the similarity scores of the document vector with the language feature vector.

langid.py: `langid.py`[3] is an off-the-shelf language identification tool trained over naive bayes classifier with a multinomial event model over a mixture of byte 1,2,3,4-grams. It supports 97 languages and has shown high accuracy scores over both long and short documents.

polyglot: This system is designed to detect multilingual documents, their constituent languages and to estimate the portion of each constituent language. This was achieved with a generative mixture model combined with the document representation developed for monolingual language identification. (Lui and Baldwin, 2011).

CLD2: `CLD2`[4] is a compact language detection tool designed to target mono/multi lingual web pages of at least 200 characters. It uses Naive Bayes classifier over unigrams, with quadgrams as features.

3 Synthetic Dataset for Code-Mixed Text

In order to conduct a comprehensive evaluation of LI systems on code-mixed text, we need a dataset of short text fragments, which we shall refer to as *document* (even though they are no longer than a sentence), spanning a large number of languages. Ideally, a good proportion of these sentences should feature code-mixing between various language pairs. Most importantly, the words in every sentence must be annotated with the appropriate language label, so that we can automatically evaluate the performance of various LI systems on this collection.

We are not aware of any such publicly available dataset. There are monolingual LI testbenches, but none of these features code-mixing at the word level. The dataset used by (King

---

[3]https://github.com/saffsd/langid.py
[4]https://code.google.com/p/cld2/

and Abney, 2013) has language mixing at inter-sentential level; typically there are stretches of 20 or more words in a single language before switching. However, tweets and social media posts are shorter, and code-mixing in such context often means embedding one to three word phrases of one language inside a sentence in another language (such as the example cited in Sec. 1). Recently, around 500 code-mixed Web search queries with language labels for words were released as a part of the FIRE shared task on transliterated search (Roy et al., 2013). The dataset contains Bengali-English, Hindi-English and Gujarati-English mixed queries, where all the Indian language words are Romanized. We shall refer to this dataset as the **FIRE-data**, which will be used later for some of our experiments.[5]

Code-mixed text in only four languages is not sufficient for a realistic evaluation of Web-scale systems. Nevertheless, it is also a very effort intensive task to gather and annotate code-mixed text for a large number of language pairs. Hence, we decided to create a synthetic code-mixed dataset spanning 28 languages listed in Table 2.

3.1 Design Principles

Artificially generating code-mixed text from monolingual text data is a non-trivial problem for several reasons. First, code-mixed text is not a random mixture of two languages; rather there are strict syntactic and semantic rules that govern the code-switching points as well as the structure of the sentence. Second, while theoretically one could mix any subset of languages, in practice code-mixing is commonly observed only between certain pairs of languages which have a sizeable bilingual population with active Web presence. Therefore, we came up with the following design principles for creating a synthetic dataset:

1. *Every document consists of words from at most two languages.* This is based on a practical observation that people rarely mix more than two languages in a single sentence. Whenever they apparently mix more than two languages, words of one of the languages can almost always be explained away as *borrowing* rather than mixing.

2. *All the documents are in a single script, which we chose as the Roman script because of its popularity.* If in a code-mixed text, each language is written in their native script (say Hindi words in Devanagari and English words in Roman script), LI becomes a trivial problem. Therefore, we choose languages which either use Roman script (like most of the West European languages) or languages which are quite commonly Romanized on the Web such as the Indian languages.

3. *Whenever code-mixing happens, one of the languages is always English.* This principle is also based on the empirical observation that code-mixing happens mostly between English and other languages (Vyas et al., 2014). However, this is not necessary; there are examples of code-mixing between Turkish and Dutch, Arabic and French, Chinese and Malay, and so on. Since selecting a representative set of language pairs is difficult, and mixing between all pairs would not only lead to impractical cases, but also make it cumbersome to analyze and represent the experimental data, we decided to only experiment with mixing between English and other languages. Note that this choice does not limit the generality of the conclusions of this study as none of the algorithms exploit the fact that one of the languages is English.

4. *The length of the documents vary from 4 to 12 words, roughly equivalent to 20-135 characters.* This choice is again motivated by the typical length of tweets and social media posts.

5. *There is only one codeswitching point per document.* Thus, for every code-mixed document, the words from each language appear together (see Table 1 for examples). This is not true in reality. For instance, the code-mixed sentence cited in Sec. 1 has 5 codeswitching point. Nevertheless, code-mixing does not allow a random set of words chosen from two languages to be permuted in any fashion. The distribution of words as well as codeswitching points are governed by a complex interplay of the syntactic rules of the two languages and semantic constraints; while some of the constraints are known, how they interact with each other and between language pairs are open questions. In absence of such knowledge, we thought as a first study, it will be a better to have as much coherent text fragments in a document as possible. This is achieved through this one codeswitching principle, of course, at the expense

---

[5]As a part of the Code-switching shared task at EMNLP 2014, large datasets for English-Spanish, English-Mandarin, English-Nepali and Dialectal-Standard Arabic have been released recently. But those were not available during this study.

of losing some generality.

3.2 Dataset Creation

As a testbench for our experiments, we created a synthetic dataset following the above design priciples. The monolingual text samples have been collected from the dataset used by (King and Abney, 2013). These are texts from the Wikipedia and various other resources, such as The Universal Declaration of Human Rights, Rosetta project and Jehovah's Witness website[6]. We selected 25 languages, including English, from this sample, all of which use Roman script.

We created 954 short documents for each language in the following manner. First, a real valued random variable γ is sampled uniformly at random from the interval $[0, 1]$. γ defines the fraction of words in the document that are in English. Another integer valued random variable L is sampled, again uniformly at random from the interval $[4, 12]$. L is the number of words in the document. We define two integer dependent variables $X = \text{round}(\gamma L)$ and $Y = \text{round}((1 - \gamma)L)$. Here, $\text{round}(\cdot)$ is the rounding-to-nearest-integer function. A sequence of X words are chosen from the English monolingual corpus (i.e., an X-gram is sampled from the corpus following the X-gram frequency distribution of English). Let us denote this sequence (potentially null) as Z_{en}. Similarly, a sequence of Y words are sampled, again at random from the text corpus of the other language. Let this (again potentially null) sequence be denoted by Z_{l*}. Finally, a binary variable s is sampled from $\{0, 1\}$. If $s = 1$, we generate the document $Z_{en}Z_{l*}$, else we generate the document $Z_{l*}Z_{en}$. Thus, we created 22896 documents spanning 25 languages, most of which are code-mixed with English.

For transliterated text in Gujarati, Bengali and Hindi, we used the test and development sets of the **FIRE-data**. This dataset has naturally code-mixed text mostly derived from Web search queries, and we will report the performance of our system directly on this data.

In Table 1 we show few sample test documents.

3.3 Limitations

It is important to understand the limitations of this synthetic dataset, so that we can appropriately draw our conclusions on the basis of the

---

[6]http://www.watchtower.org

experimental results on this testbench. As we shall see in the next section, none of the LI algorithms proposed here explicitly assume that at most two languages are mixed and there is only one codeswitching point. Therefore, we believe that these features of the synthetic dataset are not expected to lead to any misleading conclusions. On the other hand, real code-mixed data can have richer distributional patterns, for instance often single words or short phrases are embedded, which if appropriately exploited can lead to better performance. This dataset, however, lacks contractions and non-standard spellings because most of the text fragments come from Wikipedia. Therefore, performance of the algorithm on tweets or social media data could be lower than what we observe here, unless the training data is appropriately modified.

4 Language Identification Algorithms

Following the ideas of (King and Abney, 2013) and (Gella et al., 2013), we first build binary classifiers for each language. The classifier for a language l takes a word as input and returns a score between 0 and 1, which can be loosely interpreted as some sort of probability that the input word is of language l. We combine the outputs of these 28 classifiers and the context of a word to decide the final label of the word. We use character n-gram based classifiers as they are more efficient, robust to noisy data and save us the effort of collecting lexicons.

In this section, first we describe the binary classifier, followed by two simple baselines and one simple disambiguation strategy. We also describe a method to compute the accuracy if we had an optimal disambiguation strategy.

4.1 Binary classifier for Words

For each language l, we built a binary classifier using character n-gram features. We experimented with character n-grams for $n = 1$ to 5, and two standard classifiers – *Naive Bayes* and *Logistic Regression*, for which we used the Mallet tool box (McCallum, 2002) set to the default settings. The positive examples consisted of a random set of words of l and an equal number of negative examples were constructed by choosing words from all the other 27 languages. The training data for 25 languages were collected from the respective Wikipedias; since user-generated transliter-

372

Language	L	γ	Sentence
Spanish	8	0.50	do nicely Switch off *efectivos tanto entre los*
Turkish	11	0.45	*safhalarnda paraszdr lk retim mecburidir Teknik* be delighted to meet them
French	12	0.25	Vasili knew this *une libert plus grande Considrant que les tats Membres*
Hindi	5	0.60	to reinvent Michigan *chandini badarava*
Bangla	9	0.60	*swadhinatar sutre smritituku pasei* sailing in from another room
Latvian	5	0.10	*ierobeojumu un apmakstu periodisku atvainjumu*
Swahili	11	0.90	*ya Magharibi kwenye pwani la Bahari Atlantiki Imepakana na Benin* finger

Table 1: Sample of synthetic test data; the non-English part is in italics

ated content is not available on Wikipedia, for the three Indic languages the training data was obtained from the development set of the **FIRE-data**. Table 2 shows the number of positive training examples used for each language. An equal number of negative examples were used as well.

We found that for all languages, logistic regression gave the best performance when we use a combination of n-gram features for all $n = 1$ to 5. The accuracy on the training set of the best binary classifiers varied from 0.866 for Catalan to 0.992 for Gujarati with an average of 0.941. These findings and numbers are in good agreement with those mentioned in (King and Abney, 2013; Gella et al., 2013).

Language	Size	Language	Size
Catalan (ca)	908	Czech (cs)	1318
Danish (da)	1054	German (de)	1108
Estonian (et)	1304	Finnish (fi)	1435
French (fr)	1038	Irish (ga)	1002
Hunharian (hu)	1379	Indonesian (in)	1055
Italian (it)	1342	Latvian (lv)	1519
Lithuanian (lt)	1258	Maltese (mt)	1369
Dutch (nl)	1160	Polish (pl)	1652
Portuguese (pt)	1228	Romanian (ro)	1278
Slovak (sk)	1410	Slovene (sl)	1136
Spanish (es)	905	Swahili (sw)	931
Swedish (sv)	1051	Turkish (tr)	1363
Hindi (hi)	9486	Bangla (bn)	3140
Gujarati (gu)	384	English (en)	3276

Table 2: Languages tested and number of unique words in the training samples used for training the binary classifiers for words.

4.2 Baselines

Let $d = w_1, w_2 \ldots w_{|d|}$ be a document, where w_i's are the words. The task of word-level LI is to assign each word w_i with a language label $\lambda(w_i)$ chosen from $\mathbf{L} = \{l_1, l_2 \ldots l_{28}\}$, the set of all languages. Let us denote the confidence score of the classifier for language l_j on input w_i as $conf\_score(w_i, l_j)$.

MaxWeighted: In this method we simply assign the label of the language classifier that has the highest confidence score.

$$\lambda(w_i) = \mathrm{argmax}_{j=1}^{n} conf\_score(w_i, l_j)$$

Thus, this is a completely context agnostic model.

Random: In this model, a randomly chosen label from the possible set of labels is assigned to the w_i, where the possible set of labels is obtained by setting a threshold value t on the confidence scores of the classifiers.

$$\lambda(w_i) = rand\{l_j : conf\_score(w_i, l_j) \geq t\}$$

where $rand\{\cdot\}$ selects a random element from the set.

4.3 CoverSet Method

The CoverSet method is based on the assumption that code-mixing, whenever it happens, happens only with a few languages, though it assumes no hard upper bound on the number of languages that can be mixed in a document. Thus, we want to choose as few labels from $\mathbf{L}$ as possible so as to label or *cover* all the words w_1 to $w_{|d|}$, without compromising on accuracy. Since this in essence is similar to the *minimum set cover* problem, we call this technique the CoverSet.

Like Random, we define a hard threshold t, such that the only labels that are considered valid for w_i are those for which $conf\_score(w_i, l_j) \geq t$. Let us define this subset of languages as $\mathbf{L}^i \subset \mathbf{L}$. We define the *minimal coverset* of d as $\mathbf{L}_d^*$ if and only if the following two conditions are satisfied:

1. $\mathbf{L}_d^* \cap \mathbf{L}^i \neq \phi \quad \forall 1 \leq i \leq 28$

2. There does not exist a set $\mathbf{L}'_d$ that satisfies condition 1, and $|\mathbf{L}'_d| < |\mathbf{L}^*_d|$.

Once the *minimal coverset* is determined through iterative search, λw_i is assigned the label from the set $\mathbf{L}^*_d \cap \mathbf{L}^i$ that has the highest confidence score. Note that there can be more than one *minimal coverset* for d, in which case, we do the labeling for all the sets and the one that yields the highest $\sum_i conf\_score(w_i, \lambda(w_i))$ is selected as the final output.

4.4 Optimal Labels

In order to estimate the maximum achievable accuracy in such an extreme LI problem with our language classifiers, we designed the following optimal method. For each word w_i, we first compute the set of possible labels $\mathbf{L}^i$ based on a threshold t. If the actual (gold standard) label of w_i, $\lambda^*(w_i) \in \mathbf{L}^i$, then we assign $\lambda(w_i) = \lambda^*(w_i)$, else any random label is selected for $\mathbf{L}^i$. Note that this is not a practical system because it assumes the knowledge of the gold standard labels; but it will be studied to understand the maximum achievable accuracy of a word label LI system.

5 Experiments and Results

We evaluated the four existing LI systems as well as the four proposed word level LI strategies on the synthetic testbench. Since the existing LI systems output language labels only for the entire document, we evaluated them on document labeling accuracy, and only on the 25 non-Indic languages because they cannot handle transliterated content. However, the strategies that we proposed were evaluated on both document and word labeling accuracies for all the languages.

5.1 Document label accuracy

Table 3 we present the document label accuracies for the 8 systems. For a given document, **Lang1** refers to the language which has the higher proportion of words. The other language is denoted as **Lang 2**. In other words, if for a document $\gamma > 0.5$, **Lang1** is English and **Lang2** is the other language, else **Lang1** is the other language and **Lang2** is English.

The 4 existing systems output a single language as the label for an input document. But `linguini`, `polyglot` and `langid.py` also output a second or more languages with some

System	Lang1	Lang2	Code Mixing		
			P	R	F
linguini	0.589	0.084	0.817	0.846	0.831
polyglot	0.827	0.308	0.990	0.426	0.590
langid.py	0.781	0.058	0.790	1.000	0.885
CLD2	0.817	NA	NA	NA	NA
Random-0.8	0.635	0.235	0.814	0.991	0.894
MaxWeighted	0.832	0.468	0.814	0.993	0.895
CoverSet-0.5	0.888	0.717	0.868	0.991	0.920
Optimal-0.5	0.968	0.882	0.910	0.990	0.953

Table 3: Document label accuracies for the existing and the proposed LI systems. The value of t shown after hyphen.

scores whenever the system identifies that the document could consist of more than one language. Thus, for these systems, we compare their first or primary output with **Lang1** and the second output, whenever present, with **Lang2** to compute the respective accuracies. For our approaches, we count the word labels and assign the language with the highest and the second highest number of labels in the document as **Lang1** and **Lang2** respectively. We tuned the parameter t for three of the proposed systems for maximum word labelling accuracy. These values are also shown in the Table 3, for which the document labeling accuracies have been reported.

We also report the precision (P), recall (R), f-score (F) of the systems in identifying code-mixed documents. While computing these values, we did not consider the language labels, but only whether the output was a single (implying monolingual document) or multiple (implying code-mixed document) languages.

System	Hindi	Gujarati	Bangla	English
Random-0.8	0.170	0.103	0.180	0.812
MaxWeighted	0.419	0.105	0.399	0.797
CoverSet-0.5	0.569	0.017	0.394	0.814
Optimal-0.5	0.792	0.714	0.719	0.864

Table 4: Language accuracies on **FIRE-data**

Table 4 presents the document labeling accuracies for the 3 Indic languages evaluated on the **FIRE-data**. The numbers are lower than the corresponding figures for the other languages.

5.2 Word Labeling Accuracy

We define the word labeling accuracy as the fraction of words (tokens) in the entire synthetic dataset (including Indic language data) that have been labeled with the correct language. Figure 1 plots the word labeling accuracy of the four systems for different values of t. Since MaxWeighted does not depend on t, its value is constant (0.67). As expected, Optimal presents an upper-bound on the accuracy, which is close to 0.94, and the Random baseline provides a lower-bound on the accuracies, which varies between 0.3 and 0.5. Performance of CoverSet is always better than MaxWeighted, and reaches 0.82 for optimal value of $t = 0.5$.

L	A	Top n confused languages			
it	.815	en (.096)	ca (.018)	ro (.012)	pt (.010) es (.009)
es	.733	pt (.071)	en (.060)	it (.038)	ca (.027) ro (.013)
mt	.889	en (.039)	nl (.007)	fr (.005)	ro (.004) it (.004)
tr	.809	en (.094)	hi (.015)	bn (.014)	da (.011) lv (.007)
fr	.681	en (.201)	ca (.029)	ro (.017)	pt (.017) it (.008)
hu	.884	en (.024)	bn (.011)	hi (.009)	da (.009) pt (.007)
ca	.618	en (.199)	es (.040)	ro (.025)	pt (.025) fr (.023)
sk	.690	cs (.164)	en (.062)	sl (.031)	pl (.009) bn (.006)
lt	.869	en (.032)	lv (.021)	bn (.012)	id (.007) pt (.006)
de	.775	en (.122)	nl (.041)	da (.016)	sv (.007) fr (.006)
ga	.811	en (.112)	pt (.018)	fr (.012)	hu (.007) bn (.006)
sl	.737	en (.065)	sk (.063)	cs (.030)	bn (.017) hi (.015)
pl	.871	en (.043)	sk (.013)	ro (.010)	mt (.009) pt (.006)
ro	.740	en (.127)	it (.027)	fr (.021)	ca (.019) es (.010)
nl	.730	en (.153)	de (.039)	da (.032)	hu (.007) sv (.007)
pt	.800	en (.070)	es (.050)	it (.023)	ca (.015) bn (.007)
sv	.803	en (.082)	da (.061)	de (.008)	nl (.007) it (.006)
cs	.599	sk (.218)	en (.069)	sl (.030)	hu (.018) mt (.011)
da	.702	en (.177)	sv (.060)	nl (.015)	mt (.011) de (.007)
fi	.681	et (.169)	en (.037)	hi (.022)	sv (.020) bn (.011)
et	.848	en (.050)	hi (.024)	ro (.009)	nl (.009) id (.009)
lv	.848	en (.041)	lt (.026)	pl (.013)	sl (.008) id (.006)
sw	.714	en (.069)	tr (.039)	hi (.032)	bn (.026) pl (.017)
id	.810	hi (.045)	en (.040)	bn (.016)	es (.014) tr (.014)
hi	.738	bn (.148)	en (.040)	id (.014)	gu (.006) nl (.006)
bn	.878	en (.042)	hi (.041)	pt (.003)	it (.003) id (.003)
gu	.712	hi (.146)	bn (.087)	en (.017)	id (.006) mt (.005)
en	.897	pt (.008)	it (.008)	fr (.007)	hu (.006) ga (.006)

Table 5: Confusion matrix between languages. L:Language, A: Accuracy

5.3 Error Analysis

Figures 2a and 2b show the variation of the word labeling accuracy of three of the proposed systems (results for Random ommited) with the parameters L (document length) and γ (fraction

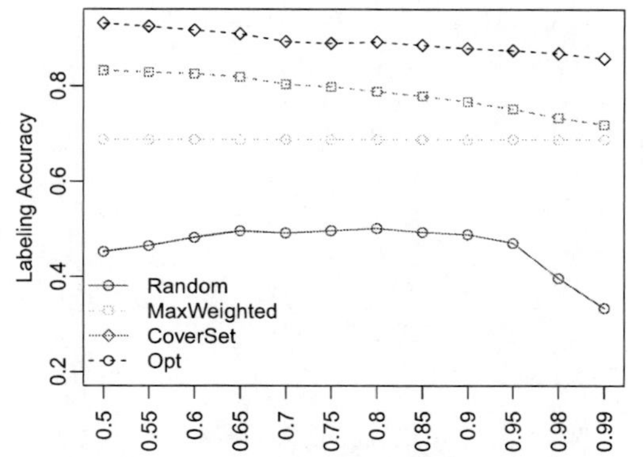

Figure 1: Word labeling accuracy vs. t

of words in English). Again, as expected, performance of Optimal is not affected by variation of these parameters, and that of CoverSet is also quite robust though we see slight decrease in performance when L drops below 6. Performance of MaxWeighted is mostly unaffected by L, but improves linearly with γ, which implies that there is a high tendency for this system to label words as English.

We also computed the language label confusion matrix for these strategies. Table 5 shows the five most common confused languages for each of the languages, along with the fraction of tokens so confused by the CoverSet approach. From the table we can infer that English is the least confused language and Czech, Catalan and Finnish are the most confused languages. This table also shows that (Czech, Slovak), (Gujarati, Hindi), (Hindi, Bangla) and (Finnish, Estonian) are some of the most confused language pairs.

6 Discussion

As can be seen from the results presented in the previous section, three of the four extensions proposed by us outperform all of the existing LI systems (Table 3). While polyglot and CLD2 are comparable to the three proposed extensions in labelling accuracies for Lang1, they fail to a varying degree in labelling Lang2. This is not unexpected as none of the existing systems are designed to identify and label languages in a code-mixed text. The low accuracies of the Random0.8 are also not surprising as this algorithm randomly assigns la-

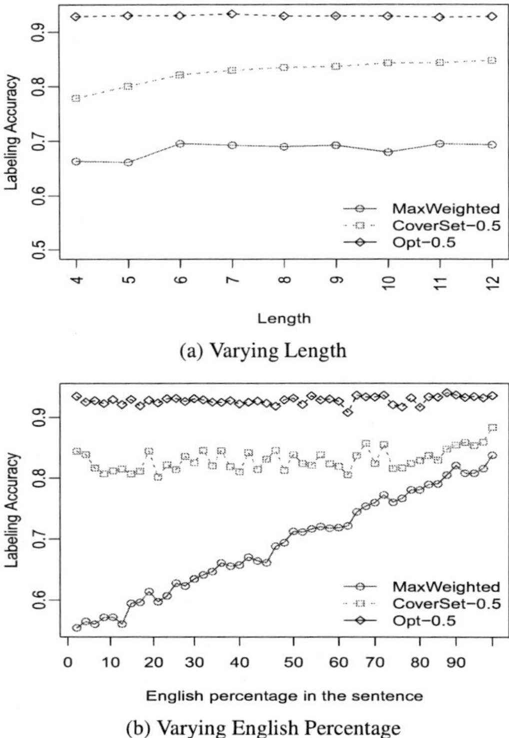

(a) Varying Length

(b) Varying English Percentage

Figure 2: Effect of L and γ on the performance.

bels from a set without taking any context information into consideration.

All the three extensions are robust to length, i.e., the number of words in a text fragment (Fig. 2a). The `Optimal` method provides an upper-bound on the accuracy that can be achieved using the current set of binary classifiers. `CoverSet` uses context information and achieves higher accuracies for labeling both Lang1 and Lang2 confirming the importance of context in identifying languages in code-mixed text. Further, `CoverSet` technique is also stable with respect to γ. Thus, from the results the `CoverSet` technique seems the most promising for identifying and labeling languages in a code-mixed text.

It is interesting to note that the language-pairs that are confused the most (e.g., Hindi-Gujarati, Slovak-Czech etc.) are linguistically related and very close to each other. In fact, the very poor performance of the `CoverSet` meythod for Gujarati as opposed to that of `Optimal` in Table 4 is due to the fact that most of the Gujarati words were also identified as Hindi words. Hence, these are likely to be confused by the LI systems. It therefore seems that different techniques and features would be required to disambiguate between these languages.

The fall in accuracies for all the proposed extensions when tested on **FIRE-data** could be attributed to the fact that this data is not synthetic and shows all the variations we might expect in real code-mixed data, but more importantly the data is in Roman transliteration. As previous studies have shown (Sowmya et al., 2010; Ahmed et al., 2011) there is a lot of variation in transliterations of Indian languages due to one-to-many mappings at character level, regional variations and lack of any universally applicable standard conventions. The difficulty for LI systems to disambiguate transliterated Indian languages, thus, increases manifold. It should be noted, however, that the overall trend followed by the proposed extensions remains the same as that on the synthetic data for other languages.

7   Conclusion

In this paper we considered language identification task for short code-mixed documents containing one or two languages. We analyzed the word-level LI accuracy of some off-the-shelf systems on code-mixed synthetic dataset. We extended these algorithms to identify word-labels across 28 languages. The results show that our extensions outperform the existing systems significantally. However, most of the methods used consider a binary classification for a language pair.

An important area to work on is the code-mixing of transliterated text where standard techniques do not work and lexicons are not available. Our results also show that linguistically close or related languages are more difficult to disambiguate and further work is required to specifically address this problem.The biggest bottleneck, as always, remains the unavailability of suitable datasets and we will continue to explore new ways to collect, generate and annotate code-mixed data. In conclusion, we would like to mention that language identification is far from a solved problem; issues like code-mixing, transliteration and non-standard usage not only make it a more difficult problem, but also demands fundamental modifications in the definition of LI. It is an area that is likely to attract a lot more interest from researchers in the near future.

References

U. Ahmed, K. Bali, M. Choudhury, and V. B. Sowmya. 2011. Challenges in designing input method editors for indian languages: The role of word-origin and context. In *Proceedings of IJCNLP Workshop on Advances in Text Input Methods*.

S. Bergsma, P. McNamee, M. Bagdouri, C. Fink, and T. Wilson. 2012. Language identification for creating language-specific Twitter collections. In *Proceedings of the Second Workshop on Language in Social Media*, pages 65–74.

MS Cardenas-Claros and N Isharyanti. 2009. Code-switching and code-mixing in internet chatting: Between yes, ya, and si a case study. In *The JALT CALL Journal, 5*.

S. Carter, W.Weerkamp, and E. Tsagkias. 2013. Microblog language identification: Overcoming the limitations of short, unedited and idiomatic text. *Language Resources and Evaluation Journal*, 47:195–215.

Spandana Gella, Jatin Sharma, and Kalika Bali. 2013. Query word labeling and back transliteration for indian languages: Shared task system description. In *FIRE Working Notes*.

Moises Goldszmidt, Marc Najork, and Stelios Paparizos. 2013. Boot-strapping language identifiers for short colloquial postings. In *Proc. of ECMLPKDD*. Springer Verlag.

J. Gumperz. 1982. *Discourse Strategies*. Oxford University Press.

Parth Gupta, Kalika Bali, Rafael E. Banchs, Monojit Choudhury, and Paolo Rosso. 2014. Query expansion for mixed-script information retrieval. In *Proc. of SIGIR*, pages 677–686. ACM Association for Computing Machinery.

S. Herring. 2003. *Media and Language Change: Special Issue*.

Ben King and Steven Abney. 2013. Labeling the languages of words in mixed-language documents using weakly supervised methods. In *Proceedings of NAACL-HLT*, pages 1110–1119.

Marco Lui and Timothy Baldwin. 2011. Cross-domain feature selection for language identification. In *In Proceedings of 5th International Joint Conference on Natural Language Processing*. Citeseer.

Marco Lui and Timothy Baldwin. 2012. langid. py: An off-the-shelf language identification tool. In *Proceedings of the ACL 2012 System Demonstrations*, pages 25–30.

Marco Lui, Jey Han Lau, and Timothy Baldwin. 2014. Automatic detection and language identification of multilingual documents. *Transactions of the Association for Computational Linguistics*, 2:27–40.

Andrew Kachites McCallum. 2002. Mallet: A machine learning for language toolkit. *http://mallet.cs.umass.edu*.

P. McNamee. 2005. Language identication: A solved problem suitable for undergraduate instruction. *Journal of Computing Sciences in Colleges*, 20(3).

C. Myers-Scotton. 1993. *Dueling Languages: Grammatical Structure in Code-Switching*. Claredon, Oxford.

C. Myers-Scotton. 2002. *Contact linguistics: Bilingual encounters and grammatical out-comes*. Oxford University Press, Oxford.

Dong Nguyen and A. Seza Dogruoz. 2013. Word level language identification in online multilingual communication. In *Proceedings of the 2013 Conference on Empirical Methods in Natural Language Processing*, pages 857–862.

John C. Paolillo. 2011. "conversational" codeswitching on usenet and internet relay chat. *Language@Internet*, 8(3).

John M Prager. Linguini: Language identification for multilingual documents. In *Systems Sciences, 1999. HICSS-32. Proceedings of the 32nd Annual Hawaii International Conference on*.

Rishiraj Saha Roy, Monojit Choudhury, Prasenjit Majumder, and Komal Agarwal. 2013. Overview and datasets of fire 2013 track on transliterated search. In *FIRE Working Notes*.

T Solorio and Y. Liu. 2008a. Learning to predict code-switching points. In *Proceedings of the Empirical Methods in natural Language Processing*.

T Solorio and Y. Liu. 2008b. Parts-of-speech tagging for english-spanish code-switched text. In *Proceedings of the Empirical Methods in natural Language Processing*.

V. B. Sowmya, M. Choudhury, K. Dasgupta Bali, T., and A. Basu. 2010. Resource creation for training and testing of transliteration systems for indian languages. In *Proceedings of the LREC 2010*.

Erik Tromp and Mykola Pechenizkiy. 2011. Graph-based n-gram language identification on short texts. In *Proc. 20th Machine Learning conference of Belgium and The Netherlands*, pages 27–34.

Yogarshi Vyas, Spandana Gella, Jatin Sharma, Kalika Bali, and Monojit Choudhury. 2014. Pos tagging of english-hindi code-mixed social media content. *Proceedings of the First Workshop on Codeswitching, EMNLP*.

Fei Xia, William D Lewis, and Hoifung Poon. 2009. Language id in the context of harvesting language data off the web. In *Proceedings of the 12th EACL*, pages 870–878.

Identifying Languages at the Word Level
in Code-Mixed Indian Social Media Text

Amitava Das
University of North Texas
Denton, Texas, USA
amitava.santu@gmail.com

Björn Gambäck
Norwegian University of Science and Technology
Trondheim, Norway
gamback@idi.ntnu.no

Abstract

Language identification at the document level has been considered an almost solved problem in some application areas, but language detectors fail in the social media context due to phenomena such as utterance internal code-switching, lexical borrowings, and phonetic typing; all implying that language identification in social media has to be carried out at the word level. The paper reports a study to detect language boundaries at the word level in chat message corpora in mixed English-Bengali and English-Hindi. We introduce a code-mixing index to evaluate the level of blending in the corpora and describe the performance of a system developed to separate multiple languages.

1 Introduction

An essential prerequisite for any kind of automatic text processing is to be able to identify the language in which a specific segment is written. Here we will in particular address the problem of word level language identification in social media texts. Available language detectors fail for these texts due to the style of writing and the brevity of the texts, despite a common belief that language identification is an almost solved problem (McNamee, 2005). Previous work has concentrated on identifying the (single) overall language of full documents or the proportions of different languages appearing in mixed-language documents. Longer documents tend to have fewer code-switching points, caused by loan words or author shifts. The code-mixing addressed here is more difficult and novel: we only have access to short (Facebook chat) utterances.

Looking at code-mixing in social media text is also overall a new research strand. These texts are characterised by having a high percentage of spelling errors and containing creative spellings (*gr8* for *'great'*), phonetic typing, word play (*goooood* for *'good'*), and abbreviations (*OMG* for *'Oh my God!'*). Non-English speakers do not always use Unicode to write social media text in their own language, frequently insert English elements (through code-mixing and Anglicisms), and often mix multiple languages to express their thoughts, making automatic language detection in social media texts a very challenging task, which only recently has started to attract attention.

Different types of language mixing phenomena have, however, been discussed and defined by several linguists, with some making clear distinctions between phenomena based on certain criteria, while others use 'code-mixing' or 'code-switching' as umbrella terms to include any type of language mixing — see, e.g., Muysken (2000) or Gafaranga and Torras (2002) — as it is not always very clear where word loaning stop and code-mixing begins (Alex, 2008). In the present paper, we will take 'code-mixing' as referring to the cases where the language changes occur inside a sentence (which also sometimes is called intra-sentential code-switching), while we will refer to 'code-switching' as the more general term and in particular use it for inter-sentential phenomena.

The next section discusses the concept of code-switching and some previous studies on code-mixing in social media text. Section 3 then introduces the data sets that have been used for investigating code-mixing between English and Hindi as well as between English and Bengali. Section 4 describes the methods used for word level language detection, based on character n-grams, dictionaries, and support vector machines, respectively. The language detection experiments are reported in Section 5, while Section 6 discusses the results. Finally, Section 7 sums up the discussion and points to some areas of future research.

D S Sharma, R Sangal and J D Pawar. Proc. of the 11th Intl. Conference on Natural Language Processing, pages 378–387,
Goa, India. December 2014. ©2014 NLP Association of India (NLPAI)

2 Background and Related Work

In the 1940s and 1950s, code-switching was often considered a sub-standard use of language. However, since the 1980s it has generally been recognised as a natural part of bi- and multilingual language use. Linguistic efforts in the field have mainly concentrated on the sociological and conversational necessity behind code-switching (Auer, 1984) and its nature (Muysken, 1995), for example, on whether it is an act of identity in a group or competence-related (i.e., a consequence of a lack of competence in one of the languages), and on dividing switching into sub-categories such as *inter-* vs *intra-sentential* (if it occurs outside or inside sentence / clause boundaries); *intra-word* vs *tag* (if switching occurs inside a word, e.g., at a morpheme boundary, or by inserting a tag phrase or word from one language into another).

Following are examples of each type of code-switching between English and Bengali. Bengali segments are in boldface and each example has its corresponding English gloss on a new line.

Inter-sentential switching

Fear cuts deeper than sword ....
Fear cuts deeper than a sword ....

bukta fete jachche   ... :(
it seems my heart will blow up ... :(

Intra-sentential switching

dakho sune 2mar kharap lagte pare
You might feel bad hearing this

but it is true that u   r   confused.
but it is true that you   are   confused.

Tag switching

ami majhe majhe *fb*   ***te on hole ei***
While I get on   facebook I do visit

confession page   ***tite aasi.***
(the) confession page   very often.

Intra-word switching

tomar osonkkhho   *admirer* ***der***
Among your numerous   admirer-s,

modhhe ami ekjon nogonno manush
I'm the inconsiderable one
In the intra-word case, the plural suffix of *admirer* has been Bengalified to *der*.

2.1 Characteristics of Code-Mixing

Several researchers have investigated the reasons for why code-mixing appear. Studies on Chinese-English code-mixing in Hong Kong (Li, 2000) and Macao (San, 2009) indicated that mainly linguistic motivations were triggering switches in those highly bilingual societies, with social motivations being less salient. However, this contrasts with studies on other language pairs and user groups in various social media, indicating that code-mixing often takes place at the beginning of messages or through simple insertions, and mainly to mark in-group membership: in short text messages (Sotillo, 2012), chat messages (Bock, 2013), Facebook comments (Shafie and Nayan, 2013), and emails (Negrón Goldbarg, 2009)

Other studies have investigated the types and frequency of code-mixing in social media. Hidayat (2012) showed that facebookers tend to mainly use inter-sentential switching (59%) over intra-sentential (33%) and tag switching (8%), and reports that 45% of the switching was instigated by real lexical needs, 40% was used for talking about a particular topic, and 5% for content clarification. The predominance of inter-sentential code-switching in social media text was also noted by San (2009), who compared the switching in blog posts to that in the spoken language in Macao.

2.2 Automatic Analysis of Code-Switching

The problem of language identification has been investigated for half a century (Gold, 1967) and that of computational analysis of code switching for several decades (Joshi, 1982), but there is little previous work on automatic language identification for multilingual code-mixed texts, although there have been some related studies on identifying code-switching points in speech (Chan et al., 2009; Solorio et al., 2011; Weiner et al., 2012). Notably, this work has mainly been on artificially generated speech data, with the simplification of only having 1–2 code-switching points per utterance. The spoken Spanish-English corpus used by Solorio and Liu (2008) is a small exception, with 129 intra-sentential language switches. They looked at part-of-speech tagging for this type of data in part by utilising a language identifier as a pre-processing step, but with no significant improvement in tagging accuracy.

Previous work on text has mainly been on identifying the (one) language (from several possible) of documents or the proportion of a text written in a language, often restricted to 1–2 known languages; so even when evidence is collected at word level, evaluation is at document level (Prager, 1997; Singh and Gorla, 2007; Yamaguchi and Tanaka-Ishii, 2012; Rodrigues, 2012; King and Abney, 2013; Lui et al., 2014). Other studies have looked at code-mixing in different types of short texts, such as information retrieval queries (Gottron and Lipka, 2010) and SMS messages (Rosner and Farrugia, 2007), or aimed to utilize code-mixed corpora to learn topic models (Peng et al., 2014) or user profiles (Khapra et al., 2013).

Most closely related to the present work are the efforts by Carter (2012), Lignos and Marcus (2013), Nguyen and Doğruöz (2013), and Voss et al. (2014). Carter collected Twitter messages (tweets) in five different European languages and manually inspected the multilingual micro-blogs for determining which language was the dominant one in a specific tweet. He then performed post level language identification, experimenting with a range of different models and a character n-gram distance metric, reporting a best overall classification accuracy of 92.4%. Evaluation at post level is reasonable for tweets, as Lui and Baldwin (2014) note that users that mix languages in their writing still tend to avoid code-switching within a tweet. However, for this is not the case for the chat messages that we address in the present paper.

Nguyen and Doğruöz (2013) investigated language identification at the utterance level on randomly sampled mixed Turkish-Dutch posts from an online chat forum, mainly annotated by a single annotator, but with 100 random posts annotated by a second annotator. They compared dictionary-based methods to language models, and adding logistic regression and linear-chain Conditional Random Fields. Their best system reached a high word accuracy (97.6%), but with a substantially lower accuracy on post level (89.5%), even though 83% of the posts actually were monolingual. Similarly, Lignos and Marcus (2013) also only addressed the bi-lingual case, looking at Spanish-English tweets. The strategy chosen by Lignos & Marcus is interesting in its simplicity: they only use the ratio of the word probability as information source and still obtain good results, the best being 96.9% accuracy at the word-level. However, their corpora are almost monolingual, so that result was obtained with a baseline as high as 92.3%. Voss et al. (2014) on the other hand worked on quite code-

Number	EN-BN1	EN-HN1
Utterances	2,309	1,743
Words	71,207	66,494
Unique tokens	15,184	10,314

Table 1: Details of corpus collection

mixed tweets (20.2% of their test and development sets consisted of tweets in more than one language). They aimed to separate Romanized Moroccan Arabic (Darija), English and French tweets using a Maximum Entropy classifier, achieving F-scores of .928 and .892 for English and French, but only .846 for Darija due to low precision.

3   Code-Mixed Corpora

Most research on social media texts has so far concentrated on English, whereas the majority of these texts now are in non-English languages (Schroeder, 2010). Fischer (2011) provides an interesting insight on Twitter language usages in different geographical regions. Europe and South-East Asia are the most language-diverse areas of the ones currently exhibiting high Twitter usage. It is likely that code-mixing is frequent in those regions, where languages change over short geo-spatial distances and people generally have basic knowledge of the neighbouring languages.

Here we will concentrate on India, a nation with close to 500 spoken languages (or over 1600, depending on what is counted as a language) and with some 30 languages having more than 1 million speakers. India has no national language, but 22 languages carry official status in at least parts of the country, while English and Hindi are used for nation-wide communication. Language diversity and dialect changes instigate frequent code-mixing in India. Hence, Indians are multi-lingual by adaptation and necessity, and frequently change and mix languages in social media contexts.

3.1   Data Acquisition

English-Hindi and English-Bengali language mixing were selected for the present study. These language combinations were chosen as Hindi and Bengali are the two largest languages in India in terms of first-language speakers (and 4th and 7th worldwide). In our study, we include corpora collected both by ourselves for this study and by Utsab Barman (Burman et al., 2014), hereforth called EN-BN1 and EN-HN1 resp. EN-BN2 and EN-HN2. Various campus Facebook groups

Tag	Description	Tag	Description
`en`	English word	`en+bn_suffix`	English word + Bengali suffix
		`en+hi_suffix`	English word + Hindi suffix
`bn`	Bengali word	`bn+en_suffix`	Bengali word + English suffix
`hi`	Hindi word	`hi+en_suffix`	Hindi word + English suffix
`ne`	Named Entity (NE)	`acro`	Acronym
`ne+en_suffix`	NE + English suffix	`acro+en_suffix`	Acronym + English suffix
`ne+bn_suffix`	NE + Bengali suffix	`acro+bn_suffix`	Acronym + Bengali suffix
`ne+hi_suffix`	NE + Hindi suffix	`acro+hi_suffix`	Acronym + Hindi suffix
`univ`	Universal	`undef`	Undefined / Others

Table 2: Word level code-mixing annotation tagset

Corpus	Code Switching Types			Total
	Intra	Inter	Word	
EN-BN2	60.23%	32.20%	7.58%	56.51%
EN-HN2	54.71%	37.33%	7.96%	28.51%

Table 3: Code-switching categorisation

were used for data acquisition. In both cases, the English-Bengali data came from Jadavpur University in Eastern India where the native language of most students is Bengali. For English-Hindi, the data came from the Indian Institute of Technology Bombay in the West of the country where Hindi is the most common language. Table 1 presents statistics for our corpora for both language pairs.

The languages of the corpora were tagged at the word-level with the tag-set displayed in Table 2. The `univ` tag stands for emoticons (:), : (, etc.) and characters such as ", ′, >, !, and @, while `undef` is for tokens that are hard to categorise.

3.2 Types of Code-Switching

The distribution of code-switching types is reported in Table 3, under the hypothesis that the base language is English with the non-English words (i.e., Hindi/Bengali) having been mixed in. Named entities and acronyms were treated as language independent, but assigned the language for multilingual categories based on suffixes.

The figures for inter- and intra-sentential code-switching were calculated automatically and are based on the total code-switching found in the corpus: if the language of a sentence was fully tagged either as Bengali or Hindi, then that sentence was considered as a type of inter-sentential code-switching, and all words in that sentence contribute to the inter-sentential code-switching percentage. For the word-internal code-mixing identification, only the "* + * suffix" tags were considered. Tag-mixing was not considered or annotated as it either is a semantic category or can be further described as a subcategory of intra-sentential code-switching.

The 'total' percentage in Table 3 has been calculated at the word level, that is, as

$$\frac{\textit{total number of words found in non-English}}{\textit{total number of words in the corpus}}$$

The distributions of different mixing types were then calculated based on the total code-mixing found for the particular language pair.

3.3 A Code-Mixing Index

A typical inter-sentential code-switching example:

> *Yaar tu to,* GOD *hain.*
> Dude you are GOD.
> ***tui JU te ki korchis?***   Hail u man!
> What you are doing in JU?   Hail u man!

This comment was written in three languages: English, Hindi (italics), and Bengali (boldface italics; JU is an abbreviation for Jadavpur University, but we treated named entities as language independent). The excerpt stems from the "JU Confession" Facebook group, which in general is English-Bengali; however, it has some 3–4% Hindi words mixed in (since Hindi is India's primary nation-wide language it has strong influence on the other languages of the country). The example shows how closely languages co-exist in social media text, making language detection for these types of text a very complex task.

When comparing different code-mixed corpora to each other, it is desirable to have a measurement of the level of mixing between languages. To this end we introduce a *code-mixing index*, CMI. At the utterance level, this amounts to finding the most frequent language in the utterance and then counting the frequency of the words belonging to all other languages present, that is,

$$\text{CMI} = \frac{\sum\limits_{i=1}^{N}(w_i) - max\{w_i\}}{n - u} \tag{1}$$

Tag	EN-BN1
CMI mixed	24.48
CMI all	5.15
Non-mixed (%)	78.95
Mixed (%)	21.05

Table 4: Level of code-mixing in a corpus

where $\sum_1^N(w_i)$ is the sum over all N languages present in the utterance of their respective number of words, $max\{w_i\}$ is the highest number of words present from any language (regardless of if more than one language has the same highest word count), n is the total number of tokens, and u is the number of tokens given language independent tags (in our case that means tokens tagged as "universal", as abbreviations, and as named entities),

If an utterance only contains language independent tokens, we define its index to be zero. For others, we multiply by 100 to get digits in the range $0 : 100$. Further, since $\sum_1^N(w_i)$ in fact is equivalent to $n - u$, Equation 1 can be rewritten as

$$\text{CMI} = \begin{cases} 100 \times [1 - \frac{max\{w_i\}}{n-u}] & : n > u \\ 0 & : n = u \end{cases} \quad (2)$$

where w_i is the words tagged with each language tag ($w_{en}, w_{hi}, w_{bn}, ...$; hence excluding items tagged `univ`, `acro`, `ne`, `undef`, etc., while including those with language tags and language-based suffix tags) and $max\{w_i\}$ thus is the number of words of the most prominent language (so for mono-lingual utterances, we will get $\text{CMI} = 0$, since then $max\{w_i\} = n - u$).

As an example, we utilize this index to evaluate the level of code-mixing in our English-Bengali corpus both on average over all utterances and on average over the utterances having a non-zero CMI, that is, over the utterances that contain some code-mixing, as shown in Table 4. It is also important to give the fraction of such utterances in a corpus, so we include those numbers as well.

4   Word-Level Language Detection

The task of detecting the language of a text segment in mixed-lingual text remains beyond the capabilities of classical automatic language identification techniques, e.g., Cavnar and Trenkle (1994) or Damashek (1995). We have tested some of the state-of-the-art systems on our corpora and found that they in general fail to separate language-specific segments from code-switched texts.

Instead we experimented with a system based on well-studied techniques, namely character n-gram distance measures, dictionary-based information, and classification with support vector machines, as further described in this section. The actual experiments and results with this system are reported in Section 5, where we also discuss ways to improve the system by adding post-processing.

4.1   N-gram Language Profiling and Pruning

The probably most well-known language detection system is *TextCat* (Cavnar and Trenkle, 1994), which utilises character-based n-gram models. The method generates language specific *n-gram* profiles from the training corpus sorted by their frequency. A similar text profile is created from the text to be classified, and a cumulative "out-of-place" measure between the text profile and each language profile is calculated. The measure determines how far an n-gram in one profile is from its place in the other profile. Based on that distance value, a threshold is calculated automatically to decide the language of a given text. Since the work of Beesley (1988), this approach has been widely used and is well established in language identification (Dunning, 1994; Teahan, 2000; Ahmed, 2005). Andersen (2012) also investigated n-gram based models, both in isolation and combined with the dictionary-based detection described below, as well as with a rule-based method utilising manually constructed regular expressions.

An *n-gram* model was adopted for the present task, too, but with a pruning technique to exclude uninformative n-grams during profile building. Common (high-frequency) n-grams for language pairs are excluded, as they are ambiguous and less discriminative. So is, for example, the bigram "*to*" very common in all the three languages, so less discriminative. To achieve this, a weight w_i^a is calculated for each n-gram g_i in language l_a by the formula $w_i^a = f_i^a / m_a$ where f_i^a is the frequency of the n-gram g_i in language l_a and m_a the total number of n-grams in language l_a. A particular n-gram g_i is excluded if its discriminative power when comparing languages l_a and l_b is lower than an experimentally chosen threshold value θ, i.e., if the condition $|w_i^a - w_i^b| \leq \theta$ is true.

There are various trade-offs to consider when choosing between character n-grams and word n-grams, and when deciding on the values of n and θ, i.e., the size of the n-grams and the discrimination threshold. Using Romanization for the Hindi and Bengali, and converting all text to lower-case, the alphabet of English is limited to 26 characters, so the set of possible character n-grams remains manageable for small values of n. White-spaces between words were kept for n-gram creation, in order to distinctly mark word boundaries, but multiple white-spaces were removed.

We carried out experiments on the training data for $n = \{1, 2, 3, 4, 5, 6, 7\}$, and found 3-grams and 4-grams to be the optimum choices after performance testing through 10-fold cross validation, with $\theta = 0.2$. The value of θ was not varied: n-grams with the same presence in multiple languages are less discriminating. The presence ratio should be $> 2\%$, so that value was selected for θ. N-gram pruning helps reduce the time it takes the system to converge by a factor 5 and also marginally increases performance (by 0.5).

4.2 Dictionary-Based Detection

Use of most-frequent-word dictionaries is another established method in language identification (Alex, 2008; Řehůřek and Kolkus, 2009). We incorporated a dictionary-based language detection technique for the present task, but were faced with some challenges for the dictionary preparation, in particular since social media text is full of noise. A fully edited electronic dictionary may not have all such distorted word forms as are used in these texts (e.g., 'gr8' rather than 'great'). Therefore a lexical normalisation dictionary (Han et al., 2012) prepared for Twitter was used for English.

Unfortunately, no such dictionary is available for Hindi or Bengali, so we used the Samsad English-Bengali dictionary (Biśvās, 2000). The Bengali part of the Samsad dictionary is written in Unicode, but in our corpus the Bengali texts are written in transliterated/phonetic (Romanized) form. Therefore the Bengali lexicon was transliterated into Romanized text using the Modified-Joint-Source-Channel model (Das et al., 2010). The same approach was taken when creating the Hindi dictionary, using Hindi WordNet (Narayan et al., 2002). In order to capture all the distorted word-forms for Hindi and Bengali, an edit distance (Levenshtein, 1966) method was adopted. A Minimum Edit Distance (MED) of ± 3 was used as a threshold (chosen experimentally).

The general trend in dictionary-based methods is to keep only high-frequency words, but that is for longer texts, and surely not for code-mixing situations. Our language detection solution is targeted at the word level and for short texts, so we cannot only rely on the most-frequent word lists and have thus instead used the full-length dictionaries. Again, words common in any of the language pairs were excluded. For example, the word *"gun"* (ENG: weapon, BNG: multiplication, HND: character/properties/competence/talent) was deleted from all three dictionaries as it is common and thus ambiguous. Another example is the word *"din"* which is common in English (loud) and Hindi (day) dictionaries, and therefore removed. The Hindi-Bengali dictionary pair was not analysed because there are huge numbers of lexical overlaps between these two languages. Words that cannot be found in any of these dictionaries are labelled as **undef** and passed for labelling to the SVM module (described next), which can consider language tags of the contextual words.

4.3 SVM-based Word-Language Detection

Word level language detection from code-mixed text can be defined as a classification problem. Support Vector Machines (SVM) were chosen for the experiment (Joachims, 1999). The reason for choosing SVM is that it currently is the best performing machine learning technique across multiple domains and for many tasks, including language identification (Baldwin and Lui, 2010). Another possibility would be to treat language detection as sequence labelling and train the word level language tag sequences using the best performing sequence labelling techniques, e.g., Hidden Markov Models (HMM) or Conditional Random Fields (CRF). For the present system, the SVM implementation in Weka v3.6.10 (Hall et al., 2009) was used with default parameters. This linear kernel SVM was trained on the following features:

N-gram with weights: Implemented using the bag-of-words principle. If there after pruning are n unique n-grams for a language pair; there are n unique features. Assume, for example, that *"in"* is the ith bigram in the list. In a given word w (e.g., *painting*), a particular n-gram occurs k times (twice for *"in"* in *painting*). If the pre-calculated weight of *"in"* is t_w^i, the feature vector is $1, 2, ..., (t_w^i * k), .., (n-2), (n-1), n$. Weights are set to 0 for absent n-grams. Weighting gives 3–4% better performance than binary features.

Dictionary-based: One binary feature for each of the three dictionaries (ENG, BNG, HND).

MED-based weight: Triggered if a word is out-of-vocabulary (absent in all dictionaries). The Minimum Edit Distance is calculated for each language, choosing the lowest MED as feature value. To simplify the search, radix sort, binary search and hash map techniques were incorporated.

Word context information: A 7-word window feature (including ± 3 words) was used to incorporate contextual information. Surface-word forms for the previous three words and their language tags along with the following three words were considered as binary features. For each word there is a unique word dictionary pre-compiled from all corpora for both language pairs, and only three features were added for language tags.

5 Experiments and Performance

A simple dictionary-based method was used as baseline, hypothesising that each text is bilingual with English as base language. An English dictionary was used to identify each word in the text and the undefined words were marked either as Hindi or Bengali based on the corpus. In a real-world setting, location information could be extracted from the social media and the second language could be assumed to be the local language. For both languages, the base performance is below 40% (38.0% and 35.5% F-score for ENG-HND and ENG-BNG, resp.), which gives a clear indication of the difficulty.

To understand the effect of each feature and module, experiments were carried out at various levels. The n-gram pruning and dictionary modules were evaluated separately, and those features were used in the SVM classification. The performance at the word level on the test set is reported in Table 5. In addition, we run 10-fold cross-validation on the training set using SVM on both the language pairs and calculated the performance. The results then were quite a lot higher (around 98% for ENG-HND and 96% for ENG-BNG), but as can be seen in the table, evaluation on the test set made performance drop significantly. Hence, though using 10-fold cross-validation, the SVM certainly overfits the training data, which could be addressed by regularization and further feature selection. The N-gram pruning was an attempt at feature selection, but adding other features or filtering techniques is definitely possible.

Looking at the system mistakes made on the development data, a post-processing module was designed for error correction. The most prominent errors were caused by language in continuation: Suppose that the language of the words w_n and w_{n+2} is marked by the system as l_a and that the language of the word w_{n+1} is marked as $\neg l_a$, then the post-processor's role is to restore this language to l_a. This is definitely not a linguistically correct assumption, but while working with word-level code-mixed text, this straightforward change gives a performance boost of approximately 2–5% for both language pairs, as can be seen in the last line of Table 5.

There are also a few errors on language boundary detection, but to post-fix those we would need to add language-specific orthographic knowledge.

6 Discussion

Social media text code-mixing in Eurasian languages is a new problem, and needs more efforts to be fully understood and solved. This linguistic phenomenon has many peculiar characteristics, for example: *addaing*, *jugading*, and *frustu* (meaning: being frustated). It is hard to define the language of these words, but they could be described as being examples of *"Engali"* resp. *"Engdi"*, along the lines of Benglish and Hinglish, (see Section 3.1), i.e., the root forms are English, but with suffixes coming from Bengali and Hindi.

Another difficult situation is reduplication, which is very frequent in South-East Asian languages. The social media users are influenced by the languages in their own geo-spaces, so reduplication is quite common in South-East Asian code-mixed text. The users in these regions are also very generative in terms of reduplication and give birth to new reduplication situations that are not common (or even valid) in any of the local languages or in English; for example: *affair taffair*.

It is also difficult to compare the results reported here to those obtained in other media and for other types of data: While previous work on speech mainly has been on artificially generated data, previous work on text has mainly been on language identification at the document level, even when evidence is collected at word level. Longer documents tend to have fewer code-switching points.

The code-mixing addressed here is more difficult and novel, and the few closely related efforts cannot be directly compared to either: the multi-lingual Twitter-setting addressed by Voss et al. (2014) might be closest to our work, but their

	System	Precision		Recall		F$_1$-Score	
		HND	BNG	HND	BNG	HND	BNG
	N-Gram Pruning	70.12%	69.51%	48.32%	46.01%	57.21%	55.37%
	+ Dictionary	82.37%	77.69%	51.03%	52.21%	63.02%	62.45%
SVM	Word Context	72.01%	74.33%	50.80%	48.55%	59.57%	58.74%
	+ N-Gram Weight	89.36%	86.83%	58.01%	56.03%	70.35%	68.11%
	+ Dictionary + MED	90.84%	87.14%	65.37%	60.22%	76.03%	74.35%
	Post Processing	94.37%	91.92%	68.04%	65.32%	79.07%	76.37%

Table 5: System word-level performance for language detection from code-mixed text

results were hurt by very low precision for Morrocan Arabic, possibly since they only used a Maximum Entropy classifier to identify languages. The solution used by Carter (2012) is based on Twitter-specific priors, while the approach by Nguyen and Doğruöz (2013) utilises language specific dictionaries (just as our approach does), making a comparison across languages somewhat unfair. The idea introduced by Lignos and Marcus (2013), to only using the ratio of the word probability, would potentially be easier to compare across languages.

Our work also substantially differs from Nguyen and Doğruöz (2013) and Lignos and Marcus (2013) in that we address a multilingual setting, while their work is strictly bilingual (with the first authors making the assumption that words from other languages — English — appearing in the messages could be assumed to belong to the dominating language, i.e., Dutch in their case). Further, even though they also work on chat data, Nguyen and Doğruöz (2013) mainly investigated utterance (post) level classification, and hence give no actual word-level baseline, just stating that 83% of the posts are monolingual. 2.71% of their unique tokens are multilingual, while in our case it is 8.25%. Nguyen & Dogruoz have gratefully made their data available and testing our system on it gives a slightly increased accuracy compared to their results (by 1.0%).

7 Conclusion and Future Work

The social media revolution has added a new dimension to language processing, with the borders of society fading, and the mixing of languages and cultures increasing. The paper has presented an initial study on the detection of code-mixing in the context of social media texts. This is a quite complex language identification task which has to be carried out at the word level, since each message and each single sentence can contain text and words in several languages.

The experiments described in here have focused on code-mixing only in Facebook posts written in the language pairs English-Hindi and English-Bengali. In the future, it would be reasonable to experiment with other languages and other types of social media text, such as tweets. Although Facebook posts tend to be short, they are commonly not as short as tweets, which have a strict length limitation (to 140 characters). It would be interesting to investigate whether this restriction induces more or less code-mixing in tweets (as compared to Facebook posts), and whether the reduced size of the context makes language identification even harder.

Furthermore, the present work has concentrated on code-mixing in romanized Indian social media texts, but there are other possible code-mixing cases such as Unicode and romanized Indian language text plus English, or with English words transliterated in Unicode. The following examples are collected from Twitter.

kishe poren ?

In which department you are studying ?

আমি – mechanical engineering তে ।

I am in mechanical engineering .

আউটিঙ এ এসেও এত *বোরিং* কাটবে সময়!

I am getting bored even in outing!

The language identification system described here mainly uses standard techniques such as character n-grams, dictionaries and SVM-classifiers. Incorporating other techniques and information sources are obvious targets for future work. For example, to use a sequence learning method such as Conditional Random Fields to capture patterns of sequences containing code switching, or combinations (ensembles) of different types of learners.

Acknowledgements

Thanks to Utsab Barman, Dublin City University, Ireland, for helping us in corpus collection-annotation, and to Dong Nguyen and Seza Doğruöz (University of Twente resp. Tilburg University, The Netherlands) for making their data set available.

References

Bashir U. Ahmed. 2005. *Detection of Foreign Words and Names in Written Text*. PhD Thesis, School of Computer Science and Information Systems, Pace University, New York, USA.

Beatrice Alex. 2008. *Automatic Detection of English Inclusions in Mixed-lingual Data with an Application to Parsing*. PhD Thesis, School of Informatics, University of Edinburgh, Edinburgh, UK.

Gisle Andersen. 2012. Semi-automatic approaches to Anglicism detection in Norwegian corpus data. In Cristiano Furiassi, Virginia Pulcini, and Félix Rodríguez González, editors, *The Anglicization of European lexis*, pages 111–130. John Benjamins.

Peter Auer. 1984. *Bilingual Conversation*. John Benjamins.

Timothy Baldwin and Marco Lui. 2010. Language identification: The long and the short of the matter. In *Proceedings of the 2010 Human Language Technology Conference of the North American Chapter of the Association for Computational Linguistics*, pages 229–237, Los Angeles, California, June. ACL.

Kenneth R. Beesley. 1988. Language identifier: A computer program for automatic natural-language identification of on-line text. In *Proceedings of the 29th Annual Conference of the American Translators Association*, pages 47–54, Medford, New Jersey.

Śailendra Biśvās. 2000. *Samsad Bengali-English dictionary*. Sahitya Samsad, Calcutta, India, 3 edition.

Zannie Bock. 2013. Cyber socialising: Emerging genres and registers of intimacy among young South African students. *Language Matters: Studies in the Languages of Africa*, 44(2):68–91.

Utsab Burman, Amitava Das, Joachim Wagner, and Jennifer Foster. 2014. Code-mixing: A challenge for language identification in the language of social media. In *Proceedings of the 2014 EMNLP*, pages 13–23, Doha, Qatar, October. ACL. 1st Workshop on Computational Approaches to Code Switching.

Simon Carter. 2012. *Exploration and Exploitation of Multilingual Data for Statistical Machine Translation*. PhD Thesis, University of Amsterdam, Informatics Institute, Amsterdam, The Netherlands, December.

William D. Cavnar and John M. Trenkle. 1994. N-gram-based text categorization. In *Proceedings of the 3rd Annual Symposium on Document Analysis and Information Retrieval*, pages 161–175, Las Vegas, Nevada, April. UNLV Publications/Reprographics.

Joyce YC Chan, Houwei Cao, PC Ching, and Tan Lee. 2009. Automatic recognition of Cantonese-English code-mixing speech. *International Journal of Computational Linguistics and Chinese Language Processing*, 14(3):281–304.

Marc Damashek. 1995. Gauging similarity with n-grams: Language-independent categorization of text. *Science*, 267(5199):843–848.

Amitava Das, Tanik Saikh, Tapabrata Mondal, Asif Ekbal, and Sivaji Bandyopadhyay. 2010. English to Indian languages machine transliteration system at NEWS 2010. In *Proceedings of the 48th ACL*, pages 71–75, Uppsala, Sweden, July. ACL. 2nd Named Entities Workshop.

Ted Dunning. 1994. Statistical identification of language. Technical report, Computing Research Laboratory, New Mexico State University, Las Cruces, New Mexico, March.

Eric Fischer. 2011. Language communities of Twitter, October. http://www.flickr.com/photos/walkingsf/6277163176/in/photostream/.

Joseph Gafaranga and Maria-Carme Torras. 2002. Interactional otherness: Towards a redefinition of codeswitching. *International Journal of Bilingualism*, 6(1):1–22.

E. Mark Gold. 1967. Language identification in the limit. *Information and Control*, 10(5):447–474.

Thomas Gottron and Nedim Lipka. 2010. A comparison of language identification approaches on short, query-style texts. In *Advances in Information Retrieval: 32nd European Conference on IR Research, Proceedings*, pages 611–614, Milton Keynes, UK, March. Springer.

Mark Hall, Eibe Frank, Geoffrey Holmes, Bernhard Pfahringer, Peter Reutemann, and Ian H. Witten. 2009. The WEKA data mining software: An update. *ACM SIGKDD Explorations Newsletter*, 11(1):10–18, November.

Bo Han, Paul Cook, and Timothy Baldwin. 2012. Automatically constructing a normalisation dictionary for microblogs. In *Proceedings of the 2012 Joint Conference on Empirical Methods in Natural Language Processing and Computational Natural Language Learning*, pages 421–432, Jeju Island, Korea, July. ACL.

Taofik Hidayat. 2012. An analysis of code switching used by facebookers (a case study in a social network site). BA Thesis, English Education Study Program, College of Teaching and Education (STKIP), Bandung, Indonesia, October.

Thorsten Joachims. 1999. Making large-scale support vector machine learning practical. In Bernhard Schölkopf, Christopher J.C. Burges, and Alexander J. Smola, editors, *Advances in Kernel Methods: Support Vector Learning*, chapter 11, pages 169–184. MIT Press, Cambridge, Massachusetts.

Aravind K. Joshi. 1982. Processing of sentences with intra-sentential code-switching. In *Proceedings of the 9th International Conference on Computational Linguistics*, pages 145–150, Prague, Czechoslovakia, July. ACL.

Mitesh M. Khapra, Salil Joshi, Ananthakrishnan Ramanathan, and Karthik Visweswariah. 2013. Offering language based services on social media by identifying user's preferred language(s) from romanized text. In *Proceedings of the 22nd International WWW*, volume Companion, pages 71–72, Rio de Janeiro, Brazil, May.

Ben King and Steven Abney. 2013. Labeling the languages of words in mixed-language documents using weakly supervised methods. In *Proceedings of the 2013 Conference of the North American Chapter of the Association for Computational Linguistics: Human Language Technologies*, pages 1110–1119, Atlanta, Georgia, June. ACL.

Vladimir I. Levenshtein. 1966. Binary codes capable of correcting deletions, insertions and reversals. *Soviet Physics Doklady*, 10(8):707–710, February.

David C. S. Li. 2000. Cantonese-English code-switching research in Hong Kong: a Y2K review. *World Englishes*, 19(3):305–322, November.

Constantine Lignos and Mitch Marcus. 2013. Toward web-scale analysis of codeswitching. In *87th Annual Meeting of the Linguistic Society of America*, Boston, Massachusetts, January. poster.

Marco Lui and Timothy Baldwin. 2014. Accurate language identification of twitter messages. In *Proceedings of the 14th Conference of the European Chapter of the Association for Computational Linguistics*, pages 17–25, Göteborg, Sweden, April. ACL. 5th Workshop on Language Analysis for Social Media.

Marco Lui, Jey Han Lau, and Timothy Baldwin. 2014. Automatic detection and language identification of multilingual documents. *Transactions of the Association for Computational Linguistics*, 2:27–40, February.

Paul McNamee. 2005. Language identification: A solved problem suitable for undergraduate instruction. *Journal of Computing Sciences in Colleges*, 20(3):94–101, February.

Pieter Muysken. 1995. Code-switching and grammatical theory. In Lesley Milroy and Pieter Muysken, editors, *One speaker, two languages: Cross-disciplinary perspectives on code-switching*, pages 177–198. Cambridge University Press, Cambridge, England.

Pieter Muysken. 2000. *Bilingual speech: A typology of code-mixing*. Cambridge University Press, Cambridge, England.

Dipak Narayan, Debasri Chakrabarti, Prabhakar Pande, and Pushpak Bhattacharyya. 2002. An experience in building the Indo WordNet — a WordNet for Hindi. In *Proceedings of the 1st International Conference on Global WordNet*, Mysore, India, January.

Rosalyn Negrón Goldbarg. 2009. Spanish-English codeswitching in email communication. *Language@Internet*, 6:article 3, February.

Dong Nguyen and A Seza Doğruöz. 2013. Word level language identification in online multilingual communication. In *Proceedings of the 2013 EMNLP*, pages 857–862, Seattle, Washington, October. ACL.

Nanyun Peng, Yiming Wang, and Mark Dredze. 2014. Learning polylingual topic models from code-switched social media documents. In *Proceedings of the 52nd ACL*, volume 2, short papers, pages 674–679, Baltimore, Maryland, June. ACL.

John M. Prager. 1997. Linguini: Language identification for multilingual documents. In *Proceedings of the 32nd Hawaii International Conference on Systems Sciences*, pages 1–11, Maui, Hawaii, January. IEEE.

Radim Řehůřek and Milan Kolkus. 2009. Language identification on the web: Extending the dictionary method. In Alexander Gelbukh, editor, *Computational Linguistics and Intelligent Text Processing: Proceedings of the 10th International Conference*, number 5449 in Lecture Notes in Computer Science, pages 357–368, Mexico City, Mexico, March. Springer-Verlag.

Paul Rodrigues. 2012. *Processing Highly Variant Language Using Incremental Model Selection*. PhD Thesis, Indiana University, Dept. of Linguistics, Bloomington, Indiana, February.

Mike Rosner and Paulseph-John Farrugia. 2007. A tagging algorithm for mixed language identification in a noisy domain. In *Proceedings of the 8th Annual INTERSPEECH Conference*, volume 3, pages 1941–1944, Antwerp, Belgium, August. ISCA.

Hong Ka San. 2009. Chinese-English code-switching in blogs by Macao young people. MSc Thesis, Applied Linguistics, University of Edinburgh, Edinburgh, Scotland, August.

Stan Schroeder. 2010. Half of messages on Twitter aren't in English [STATS], February. http://mashable.com/2010/02/24/ half-messages-twitter-english/.

Latisha Asmaak Shafie and Surina Nayan. 2013. Languages, code-switching practice and primary functions of Facebook among university students. *Study in English Language Teaching*, 1(1):187–199, February.

Anil Kumar Singh and Jagadeesh Gorla. 2007. Identification of languages and encodings in a multilingual document. In *Proceedings of the 3rd Workshop on Building and Exploring Web Corpora*, pages 95–108, Louvain-la-Neuve, Belgium, September. Presses universitaires de Louvain.

Thamar Solorio and Yang Liu. 2008. Part-of-speech tagging for English-Spanish code-switched text. In *Proceedings of the Conference on Empirical Methods in Natural Language Processing*, pages 1051–1060, Honolulu, Hawaii, October. ACL.

Thamar Solorio, Melissa Sherman, Yang Liu, Lisa M. Bedore, Elisabeth D. Peña, and Aquiles Iglesias. 2011. Analyzing language samples of Spanish-English bilingual children for the automated prediction of language dominance. *Natural Language Engineering*, 17(3):367–395, July.

Susanna Sotillo. 2012. *Ehhhh utede hacen plane sin mi???:@ im feeling left out:(* form, function and type of code switching in SMS texting. In *ICAME 33 Corpora at the centre and crossroads of English linguistics*, pages 309–310, Leuven, Belgium, June. Katholieke Universiteit Leuven.

William John Teahan. 2000. Text classification and segmentation using minimum cross-entropy. In *Proceedings of the 6th International Conference on Computer-Assisted Information Retrieval (Recherche d'Information Assistée par Ordinateur, RIAO 2000)*, pages 943–961, Paris, France, April.

Clare Voss, Stephen Tratz, Jamal Laoudi, and Douglas Briesch. 2014. Finding romanized Arabic dialect in code-mixed tweets. In *Proceedings of the 9th International Conference on Language Resources and Evaluation*, pages 188–199, Reykjavík, Iceland, May. ELRA.

Jochen Weiner, Ngoc Thang Vu, Dominic Telaar, Florian Metze, Tanja Schultz, Dau-Cheng Lyu, Eng-Siong Chng, and Haizhou Li. 2012. Integration of language identification into a recognition system for spoken conversations containing code-switches. In *Proceedings of the 3rd Workshop on Spoken Language Technologies for Under-resourced Languages*, Cape Town, South Africa, May.

Hiroshi Yamaguchi and Kumiko Tanaka-Ishii. 2012. Text segmentation by language using minimum description length. In *Proceedings of the 50th ACL*, volume 1, pages 969–978, Jeju, Korea, July. ACL.

Unsupervised Detection and Promotion of Authoritative Domains for Medical Queries in Web Search

Manoj K. Chinnakotla[*]
Microsoft, Hyderabad, India
manojc@microsoft.com

Rupesh K. Mehta
Microsoft, Hyderabad, India
rupeshme@microsoft.com

Vipul Agrawal
Microsoft, Bellevue, USA
vipulag@microsoft.com

Abstract

Medical or Health related search queries constitute a significant portion of the total number of queries searched everyday on the web. For health queries, the *authenticity* or *authoritativeness* of search results is of utmost importance besides relevance. So far, research in automatic detection of authoritative sources on the web has mainly focused on - a) link structure based approaches and b) supervised approaches for predicting *trustworthiness*. However, the aforementioned approaches have some inherent limitations. For example, several content farm and low quality sites artificially boost their link-based authority rankings by forming a syndicate of highly interlinked domains and content which is algorithmically hard to detect. Moreover, the number of positively labeled training samples available for learning trustworthiness is also limited when compared to the size of the web.

In this paper, we propose a novel unsupervised approach to *detect* and *promote* authoritative domains in health segment using click-through data. We argue that standard IR metrics such as NDCG are relevance-centric and hence are not suitable for evaluating authority. We propose a new authority-centric evaluation metric based on side-by-side judgment of results. Using real world search query sets, we evaluate our approach both quantitatively and qualitatively and show that it succeeds in significantly improving the authoritativeness of results when compared to a standard web ranking baseline.

1 Introduction

The web is growing at an enormous rate with information spread across billions of web pages. Medical and Health related web sites constitute a significant portion of the web and its growth. The Pew Internet Project, one of the largest national surveys undertaken in the U.S, reveals that 59% of U.S adults have looked online for health information in the past year (Pew , 2013). Moreover, the study states that 35% of the U.S adults were *"Online Diagnosers (OD)"* - people who turn to the internet to figure out which medical condition they have. Interestingly, 41% of ODs had their condition confirmed by the clinician. As per the study, 80% of the people with a health information need start off their inquiry with a web search engine. Not just patients, recent studies (AMA , 2002) show that physicians too rely on the web for their research and studies. In view of its impact on decisions related to people's health, it's highly imperative for search engines to provide information which is not just relevant and accurate but also *authoritative*. We define *authoritativeness* of a search result as follows:

Definition 1. A search result is said to be authoritative for a query if:

- It is widely accepted to be an authentic source of information by experts in the domain

- It is the site of an organization or corporation vested with the right to give first-hand information on the entity or topic

The quality of content available on the web poses a serious challenge to search engines while trying to provide accurate and reliable information. The content quality varies a lot, ranging from shallow content written by amateurs, automatic content generated by engines, plagiarized and spammy content to deep and authentic articles written by domain experts. Besides, many low

____
Corresponding Author

D S Sharma, R Sangal and J D Pawar. Proc. of the 11th Intl. Conference on Natural Language Processing, pages 388–394,
Goa, India. December 2014. ©2014 NLP Association of India (NLPAI)

Domain	Type of Site	PageRank
`ehow.com`	Content Farm	64,678
`ezinearticles.com`	Content Farm	61,566
`webmd.com`	Authoritative	65,504
`mayoclinic.com`	Authoritative	63,832

Table 1: Comparison of PageRank values of a few popular content farm sites and authoritative sites.

quality sites employ a variety of Search Engine Optimization (SEO) techniques to trick search engines and artificially boost their rankings. Hence, attempts have been made (Spink et al. , 2004) to aid information seekers by identifying and accrediting web sites which provide high quality, well-researched, reliable and trust-worthy information. For example, "Health on Net (HON)" logo on web sites helps in identifying reliable health information sources. However, since it is a manual effort, it is not scalable for the web.

So far, research in automatic detection of authoritative sources on the web has mainly focused on - a) link structure based approaches and b) supervised approaches for predicting trustworthiness. Link based approaches such as PageRank, HITS, SALSA (Sergey and Larry , 1998; Kleinberg , 1999; Lempel and Moran , 2001) analyse the hyperlinking structure of the web graph for identifying the authoritative sources. In PageRank, which is the most popular variant, the notion of authority is similar to the notion of citations in scientific literature. The authority of a page is proportional to the number of incoming hyperlinks and to the authority of the pages which point to it. However, since links are created by content curators, it is easy to manipulate them. Bianchini *et. al.* (Bianchini et al. , 2003) point to one such limitation of link based algorithms - it's possible to artificially boost the authority scores of pages through the creation of artificial communities which are algorithmically hard to detect. Many low quality information sources, such as content farms, exploit this weakness to gain decent PageRank scores by forming a syndicate of highly interlinked content. Table 1 shows a comparison of PageRank values for a few content farm and authoritative domains. It can be observed that their PageRanks are almost comparable. On the other hand, supervised approaches for learning trustworthiness of domains rely on the availability of gold standard labeled data which is hard to obtain in large quantities.

In this paper, we propose a novel unsupervised approach to automatically detect authoritative domains in the medical query segment using user click logs. We aggregate the click signals at a domain level and assign an authority score which is based on - a) popularity of the domain and b) specificity of content with respect to the query segment. Although click signals are noisy, the advantage of relying on clicks for authority computation is that it is hard to manipulate them, and they provide a user-centric view of authority. In practice, a search engine has to optimize both *relevance* and *authority*. Hence, we fire the initial query to get the top k documents and then rerank them based on a combination of relevance and domain authority scores. We also show that the standard NDCG metric is not sensitive to authority and hence can't be used to measure it. In our current work, we define a measure based on side-by-side authority-centric judging of ranking results and show that our approach improves the authoritativeness of results when compared to a standard web ranking baseline.

2 Related Work

Several researchers have reported the presence of unreliable and low quality information, especially in the context of medical domain, on the web (Matthews et al. , 2003; Tang et al. , 2006; Marriott et al. , 2008).

(A1 et al. , 2007b; A1 et al. , 2007a; Sondhi et al. , 2012; Olteanu et al. , 2013) have employed supervised machine learning techniques to learn the notion of trustworthiness or credibility of web pages. (A1 et al. , 2007b; A1 et al. , 2007a) use the Health On Net (HoN) label data as gold standard and learn a prediction model based on content and URL based features. (Sondhi et al. , 2012) use both content based features and link based features. (Olteanu et al. , 2013) further experimented with social features from popular sources such as Facebook and Twitter and web page design. However, the main problem with supervised methods is the lack of training samples. The number of web sites which apply and refresh their HoN rat-

389

Domain	Popularity	Focus	Authority Score
www.webmd.com	0.02997	0.863161	*0.025869*
www.livestrong.com	0.039595	0.629975	*0.024944*
www.drugs.com	0.027413	0.811211	*0.022237*
www.mayoclinic.com	0.023445	0.904002	*0.021195*
www.medicinenet.com	0.015026	0.871997	*0.013102*

Figure 1: Top 5 Medical Domains identified through Authority Scores defined in Section 3

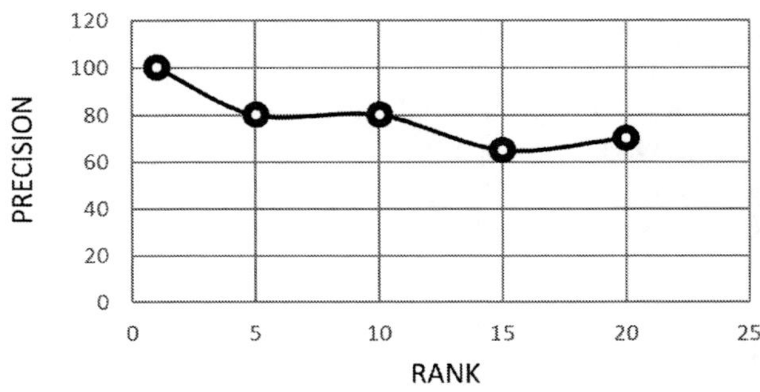

Figure 2: Precision vs. Rank for Authority Scores defined in Section 3

ings regularly is usually very less. Due to this, curating enough number of training samples to learn reasonably accurate models is hard. Our approach differs from the other approaches discussed so far in the following ways:

- We propose an *unsupervised technique* to detect and score segment-specific authoritative domains using click data

- We also propose a re-ranking technique to promote the authoritative domains in the ranking

3   Segment Authority

In this section, we describe our approach to score domains based on their authority. The main intuition behind the technique is that typically content farm and other low-quality sites such as eHow, ezinearticles, create shallow and generic content across a wide variety of query segments. This is mainly done to maximize their revenue through ad monetization. On the other hand, authoritative sites curate high-quality and deep content for a particular segment. There are very few sites which do both of the above with notable exceptions such as wikipedia (i.e. deep content spread across a wide variety of segments). Hence, for each do-

main, we model this notion of "generic" vs "specific" and popularity and combine them as a single score for authority. We define *Focus* and *Popularity* of a domain d with respect to a query segment *seg* as follows:

Definition 2. Focus of a domain d with respect to query segment *seg*, is defined as the probability of a user choosing a query from segment *seg* when there is a click on the domain d.

$$Focus(d, seg) = Pr(seg|d) \qquad (1)$$

Definition 3. Popularity of a domain d within the query segment *seg*, is defined as the probability of a user clicking on the domain d when the user query belongs to the segment *seg*.

$$Popularity(d, seg) = Pr(d|seg) \qquad (2)$$

Given the click logs, we first run query classifiers (Cao et al. , 2009) to classify each query into segments such as health, movies, sports, technology, finance, *etc.* Later, the probability scores mentioned above are computed as follows:

$$Score(seg|d) =$$

$$\frac{\text{No. of queries on d where seg classifier is ON}}{\text{Total no. of queries on d}}$$

$$(3)$$

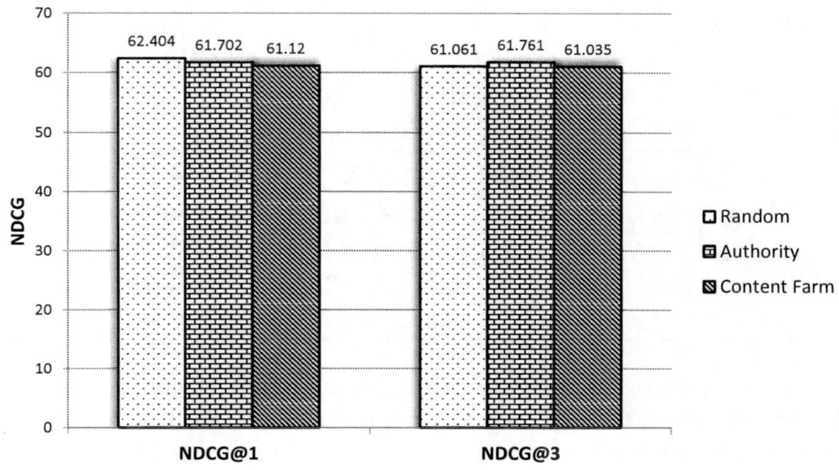

Figure 3: Sensitivity of NDCG Metric to Authority

The above score is unnormalized since the query classifiers were independently trained. The normalized probability is given below:

$$Pr(seg|d) = \frac{Score(seg|d)}{\Sigma_{seg} Score(seg|d)} \quad (4)$$

$$Pr(d|seg) = \frac{Pr(seg|d) \times Pr(d)}{\Sigma_{seg} Pr(seg|d) \times Pr(d)} \quad (5)$$

$$Pr(d) = \frac{\text{No. of queries on d}}{\text{Total no. of queries}} \quad (6)$$

$$Authority(d) = Pr(seg|d) \times Pr(d|seg) \quad (7)$$

Figure 1 shows the top five authoritative domains, when sorted using the authority score, for the medical segment. These scores were generated using three months of click logs from the commercial search engine Microsoft Bing. We perform a simple validation of our authority scores by checking how many of the top ranked domains have valid HON certification. The results are shown in Figure 2. We can observe that the automatically mined top domains correlate well with the HON labels given by medical experts.

4 Authority Based Reranking of Results

Although, both relevance and authority are both important, Jones *et. al.* (Jones et al. , 2011) show that users prefer relevant information from a spammy domain than irrelevant results. We combine our domain authority score with relevance score of web ranker to promoting both relevant and authoritative pages.

We take the top 'k' results from the initial retrieval and re-rank them using a function designed to factor in both relevance and authority. Let $U = \{u_1, u_2, \ldots, u_k\}$ be the set of top 'k' URLs retrieved by the initial ranker. Let $S = \{s_1, s_2, \ldots, s_k\}$ be their corresponding scores assigned by the ranker. Let $D = \{d_1, d_2, \ldots, d_k\}$ be the corresponding domains of these URLs. The new scoring function for re-ranking is:

$$Score(u_i, s_i, q) = s_i \times (1 + \alpha \times \text{Authority}(d_i)) \quad (8)$$

The above function ensures that sites with good relevance and authority scores are boosted higher in the ranking. The above function also ensures that irrelevant results from authoritative domains do not trump a relevant result from a less authoritative source by adjustiing the value of α.

5 Evaluation Metrics for Authority

Standard web ranking metrics such as NDCG (Järvelin and Kekäläinen , 2000) are measures of *graded relevance*. The guidelines which are typically used to grade the web result sets is based purely on relevance. Hence, it can't be directly used to measure authority. To prove this point, from a standard evaluation set for web (size around 13K, where judgments are available), we sampled three equal sized query sets of size 100 with the following variations - a) random queries b) queries with authoritative URLs appearing in top 3 c) queries with content farm sites appearing

Query Set	No. of Queries /Judgment Queries	$Surplus_{strong}$ (W/L/T)	$Surplus_{weak}$ (W/L/T)
HealthQuery Set	462/181	+5.52 (24/14/143)	*+14.36** (88/62/31)*
HealthTestSet-1K	1K/1K	+1.2 (41/29/930)	*+6.9** (264/195/541)*

Table 2: Results comparing the performance of Authority Based Reranking with Baseline web ranker on two query sets. Results marked as ** indicate that the surplus was found to be statistically significant over the baseline at 95% confidence level ($\alpha = 0.05$). W/L/T denote the number of Wins, Losses and Ties observed.

in top 3 (b and c are identified manually). We computed NDCG@1 and NDCG@3 on top of these three sets and the results are shown in Figure 3. One can notice that NDCG@1 and NDCG@3 remain almost the same for all three query sets, and hence they are not sensitive to the notion of authority. In view of the above, we define a new metric called "Surplus" which is based on relative comparison of baseline and treatment rankers with respect to their relevance and authoritativeness. The procedure is as follows:

- We show the first page (top 10) of baseline and treatment results to a judge in two separate tabs in a single window.

- For each query, the baseline and treatment results are randomly placed in the left (L) and right (R) tabs of window to avoid any identification and biased judgments.

- Each judge is given detailed guidelines on how to identify authoritative sites[1].

- The ratings are given on a seven-point scale - a) Left Much Better b) Left Better c) Left Slightly Better d) Neutral e) Right Slightly Better f) Right Better g) Right Much Better.

- A technique scores a *Strong Win* for a query if it gets a Better or Much Better rating with respect to the baseline. It scores a *Weak Win* if it gets Slightly Better, Better or Much Better ratings with respect to baseline and a *Tie* if it gets a Neutral rating. *Strong Loss* and *Weak Loss* are similarly defined.

---

[1] http://bit.ly/1uOJeVw

A pool of 25 judges were hired and trained (using the guidelines) specifically for providing these judgments.

Given a query set with n queries, if a technique scores n_W wins, n_L losses and n_T ties, the surplus of a technique is defined as follows:

$$Surplus = \frac{n_W - n_L}{n_W + n_L + n_T} \times 100 \qquad (9)$$

The final metric used for measurement is $Surplus_{strong}$, where strong win/losses are used, and $Surplus_{weak}$ where weak win/losses are used. We also check for the statistical significance of the surplus to ensure more robustness of the metric. A good surplus on a large query set implies that the technique is performing well with respect to the baseline. As discussed in Section 4, a technique has to also ensure that it does not hurt relevance - it should not decrease the NDCG metric significantly.

6 Experimental Setup

We evaluate the performance of our system on a real world dataset from Microsoft Bing search engine. The dataset consists of around 13,711 English queries sampled from one year query logs. From these, we apply query classifiers and filter out only "health" segment queries which are around 462. We call this query set as *Health-QuerySet*. For these queries, we also have human generated relevance ratings available on a five-point scale (0-4) where 4 means most relevant and 0 means irrelevant. This judgement data is useful for computing the NDCG metric. We train a LambdaMART (Burges , 2010) baseline

Query	Top 3 Results in Baseline	Top 3 Results in Authority Ranker	Description
flaxseed oil health benefits ??? *(Strong Win)*	1. www.ehow.com/about_4587396_health-benefits-flaxseed-oil.htm 2. www.webmd.com/diet/features/benefits-of-flaxseed 3. www.livestrong.com/article/112063-benefits-flaxseed-oil-capsules/	1. www.webmd.com/diet/features/benefits-of-flaxseed 2. www.livestrong.com/article/112063-benefits-flaxseed-oil-capsules/ 3. www.ehow.com/about_4587396_health-benefits-flaxseed-oil.htm	*"webmd.com"* and *"livestrong.com"* are much more authoritative sites than *"ehow.com"* which is a content farm site.
high calcium symptoms *(Weak Win)*	1. www.ehow.com/list_6197078_signs-high-calcium-levels-blood.html 2. www.mayoclinic.org/diseases-conditions/hypercalcemia/basics/symptoms/CON-20031513 3. www.emedicinehealth.com/hypercalcemia_elevated_calcium_levels/page3_em.htm	1. www.mayoclinic.org/diseases-conditions/hypercalcemia/basics/symptoms/CON-20031513 2. www.ehow.com/list_6197078_signs-high-calcium-levels-blood.html 3. www.emedicinehealth.com/hypercalcemia_elevated_calcium_levels/page3_em.htm	*"mayoclinic.com"* is much more authoritative than *"ehow.com"* which is a content farm site.
infected sebaceous cyst *(Strong Loss)*	1. mackinven.com/sebaceous-cyst-treatment-how-to-treat-an-infected-sebaceous-cyst-at-home/ 2. en.wikipedia.org/wiki/Sebaceous_cyst 3. www.webmd.com/skin-problems-and-treatments/guide/epidermoid-sebaceous-cysts	1. www.webmd.com/skin-problems-and-treatments/guide/epidermoid-sebaceous-cysts 2. en.wikipedia.org/wiki/Sebaceous_cyst 3. mackinven.com/sebaceous-cyst-treatment-how-to-treat-an-infected-sebaceous-cyst-at-home/	Result #1 from *"mackinven.com"* gives the most relevant page. The pages from *"webmd"* and *"wikipedia"* are not relevant.

Table 3: Qualitative comparison of Authority Based Reranking and Baseline through a few representative queries from the query sets.

with standard text based features and document level features defined in the LETOR dataset (Qin et al. , 2010). We use this as the baseline, which does not have any authority oriented features, for comparing with our approach. The baseline was trained on a separate set of 12,124 queries for which judgments (for URLs per query) were available on a five-point scale. We tune the value of α in Equation 8 such that the number of wins is maximised. In order to show that our technique performs well on completely unseen queries as well, we sample a new test set of 1000 queries, called *HealthTestSet-1K*, from only health segment and show our performance on this. While submitting queries for judgments, we only consider queries where both the technique and the baseline rankings differ in some way in the top five positions. This is mainly to save judgement cost and does not have any impact on the evaluation. However, in the HealthTestSet-1K query set, we remove this constraint as well and submit the entire 1K subset for judgments to enable much clearer and straightforward interpretation.

7 Results and Discussion

As mentioned in Section 6, we tune the value of α in Equation 8 using the *HealthQuerySet* such that the number of wins is maximised. The optimal value of α was found to be 0.6.

The results of our technique with respect to the baseline is shown in Table 2. The results show that Authority Based Reranking technique shows significant gains in weak surplus over the baseline web ranker. Since our technique does not lead to any relevance improvements, similar surplus gains were not observed for the strong surplus metric. We also noticed that the NDCG@3 for the baseline ranker was 51.57 whereas it was 52.78 for the treatment authority ranker. This shows that the technique leads to improvements in authority while minimally affecting NDCG@3 which is indicative of relevance. Moreover, the technique also scores significant improvements on the unseen *HealthTestSet-1K* query set.

Table 3 illustrates the qualitative improvement achieved by our technique through some actual examples from the dataset. The first two query examples show the cases where the technique scored wins by promoting authoritative sites which are equally relevant in the top 3. The last case shows a loss where due to the promotion of authoritative site, the relevance was hurt. Since, our technique just does a interpolation of relevance score and domain authority score, this is sometimes bound to happen.

8 Conclusion and Future Work

We proposed a novel unsupervised approach to automatically detect authoritative medical domains using user click logs. We also proposed a technique, which making use of the domain authority scores, reranks the top *'k'* search results from the initial retrieval and promotes the results from top authoritative domains. We argued and experimentally showed that standard web IR metrics such as NDCG are not suitable for measuring authority. Hence, we propose a new authority-centric metric which is based on side-by-side judging of results. Through experiments on different query sets sampled from real web query logs, we showed that our proposed technique significantly improves the *authoritativeness* of results over a standard web ranker baseline. As part of future work, we plan to - a) further refine the concept of authority at a topic-level within each segment and b) come up with a notion of query dependent authority.

References

[A1 et al. 2007a] Gaudinat A1, Grabar N, and Boyer C. 2007a. Automatic Retrieval of Web Pages with Standards of Ethics and Trustworthiness within a Medical Portal: What a Page Name Tell Us. In *Bellazzi, R., Abu-Hanna, A., Hunter, J. (eds.) AIME 2007. LNCS (LNAI)*, pages 185–189.

[A1 et al. 2007b] Gaudinat A1, Grabar N, and Boyer C. 2007b. Machine Learning Approach for Automatic Quality Criteria Detection of Health Web Pages. In *Proc. of the World Congress on Health (Medical) Informatics Building Sustainable Health Systems*, pages 705–709.

[AMA 2002] AMA. 2002. Study of physicians' use of the world wide web. *American Medical Association*.

[Bianchini et al. 2003] M. Bianchini, M. Gori, and F. Scarselli. 2003. Pagerank and Web Communities. In *IEEE International Conference on Web Intelligence*, pages 365–371.

[Burges 2010] Christopher J. C. Burges. 2010. From RankNet to LambdaRank to LambdaMART: An Overview. Technical report, Microsoft Research.

[Cao et al. 2009] Huanhuan Cao, Derek Hao Hu, Dou Shen, Daxin Jiang, Jian-Tao Sun, Enhong Chen, and Qiang Yang. 2009. Context-Aware Query Classification. In *SIGIR '09*, pages 3–10, New York, NY, USA. ACM.

[Järvelin and Kekäläinen 2000] Kalervo Järvelin and Jaana Kekäläinen. 2000. IR Evaluation Methods for Retrieving Highly Relevant Documents. In *SIGIR'00*, pages 41–48, New York, NY, USA. ACM.

[Jones et al. 2011] Timothy Jones, David Hawking, Paul Thomas, and Ramesh Sankaranarayana. 2011. Relative Effect of Spam and Irrelevant Documents on User Interaction with Search Engines. In *CIKM '11*, pages 2113–2116, New York, NY, USA. ACM.

[Kleinberg 1999] Jon M. Kleinberg. 1999. Authoritative Sources in a Hyperlinked Environment. *J. ACM*, 46(5):604–632, September.

[Lempel and Moran 2001] R. Lempel and S. Moran. 2001. Salsa: The Stochastic Approach for Link-Structure Analysis. *ACM Trans. Inf. Syst.*, 19(2):131–160, April.

[Pew 2013] The Pew Internet and American Life. Health Online 2013. http://www.pewinternet.org/2013/01/15/health-online-2013/.

[Marriott et al. 2008] JV1 Marriott, Stec P, El-Toukhy T, Khalaf Y, Khalaf P, and Coomarasamy A. 2008. Infertility Information on the World Wide Web: A Cross-Sectional Survey of Quality of Infertility Information on the Internet in the UK. *Human Reproduction*, pages 1520–1525.

[Matthews et al. 2003] "Scott C. Matthews, Alvaro Camacho, Paul J. Mills, and Joel E. Dimsdale". "2003". "The Internet for Medical Information about Cancer: Help or Hindrance? ". "*Psychosomatics* ", "44"("2"):"100 – 103".

[Olteanu et al. 2013] Alexandra Olteanu, Stanislav Peshterliev, Xin Liu, and Karl Aberer. 2013. Web Credibility: Features Exploration and Credibility Prediction. In *ECIR '13*, pages 557–568, Berlin, Heidelberg. Springer-Verlag.

[Qin et al. 2010] Tao Qin, Tie-Yan Liu, Jun Xu, and Hang Li. 2010. Letor: A Benchmark Collection for Research on Learning to Rank for Information Retrieval. *Inf. Retr.*, 13(4):346–374.

[Sergey and Larry 1998] Brin Sergey and Page Larry. 1998. The Anatomy of a Large-Scale Hypertextual Web Search Engine. In *Computer Networks and ISDN Systems*, pages 107–117.

[Sondhi et al. 2012] Parikshit Sondhi, V. G. Vinod Vydiswaran, and Cheng Xiang Zhai. 2012. Reliability Prediction of Webpages in the Medical Domain. In *ECIR '12*, pages 219–231, Berlin, Heidelberg. Springer-Verlag.

[Spink et al. 2004] Amanda Spink, Yin Yang, Jim Jansen, Pirrko Nykanen, Daniel P. Lorence, Seda Ozmutlu, and H. Cenk Ozmutlu. 2004. A Study of Medical and Health Queries to Web Search Engines. *Health Information and Libraries Journal*, 21(1):44–51.

[Tang et al. 2006] ThanhTin Tang, Nick Craswell, David Hawking, Kathy Griffiths, and Helen Christensen. 2006. Quality and Relevance of Domain-Specific Search: A Case Study in Mental Health. *Information Retrieval*, 9(2):207–225.

Significance of Paralinguistic Cues in the Synthesis of Mathematical Equations

Venkatesh Potluri, SaiKrishna Rallabandi, Priyanka Srivastava, Kishore Prahallad

```
International Institute of Information Technology - Hyderabad
{venkatesh.potluri, saikrishna.rallabandi}@research.iiit.ac.in
{priyanka.srivastava, kishore}@iiit.ac.in
```


Abstract

Text to speech (TTS) systems hold promise as an information access tool for literate and illiterate including visually challenged. Current TTS systems can convert a typical text into a natural sounding speech. However, auditory rendering of mathematical content, specifically equation reading is not a trivial task. Mathematical equations have to be read so that appropriate bracketing such as parentheses, superscripts and subscripts are conveyed to the listener in an accurate way. Earlier works have attempted to use pauses as acoustic cues to indicate some of the semantics associated with the mathematical symbols. In this paper, we first analyse the acoustic cues which human-beings employ while speaking the mathematical content to (visually challenged) listeners and then propose four techniques which render the observed patterns in a text-to-speech system. The evaluation considered eight aspects such as listening effort, content familiarity, accentuation, intonation, etc. Our objective metrics show that a combination of the proposed techniques could render the mathematical equations using a TTS system as good as that of a human-being.

1 Introduction

Mathematical equations comprise of different types of visual cues to convey their semantic meaning. Some of these visual cues are superscripts, subscripts, parentheses,etc. Despite advances in screen reading and text to speech technologies, the problem of speaking complex math remains majorly unsolved. Speaking the equation just as any other string of text, a line, or a sentence will not suffice to effectively render mathematics in speech. For instance, $e^{x+1} - 1$ denotes that the value "e" should be multiplied "x+1" times before subtracting 1 from it. However, when it is rendered in speech like a general string, it is difficult to identify the portion of the equation in the superscript and the remainder of it after the superscript. To effectively resolve such ambiguities and identify such demarcations in mathematical content, information presented through visual cues such as spatialisation must be mapped to their auditory equivalent. Mathematics, in its visual form, gives the reader a very high level granularity in perceiving the equation. Mathematical equations, when presented in audio must be able to match the advantage in granularity provided in visual representation of mathematics. The typical issues in audio rendering of mathematical equations include quantification, superscripting and subscripting, and fractions.

1.1 Quantification

Most of mathematical equations contain expressions in parentheses. For instance, considering the equation $(A+B)*(C+D)+E$, it may seem that the equation can just be treated as a general string of text while speaking. However, this will create a confusion in the listener, as there are two ways of expressing.

- "left parenthesis A plus B right parenthesis times left parenthesis C plus D right parenthesis plus E"

- "A plus B times C plus D plus E".

In the former case, the listener will have to keep a track of all the parentheses when he or she listens to the equation. This becomes a hectic task for bigger equations and also results in deviating the listener's attention from concentrating on the actual contents of the equation. On the other hand,

D S Sharma, R Sangal and J D Pawar. Proc. of the 11th Intl. Conference on Natural Language Processing, pages 395–402,
Goa, India. December 2014. ©2014 NLP Association of India (NLPAI)

in the latter case, the listener gets an ambiguous representation of the equation. The spoken form of the equation should have additional information to the equation to solve this ambiguity.

1.2 Superscript and subscript

Today's screen readers and TTS engines do not effectively convey the equations with superscript and subscript content. They often do not speak out the parts of the equation contained in the superscript and subscript. They often speak out such content continuously, with the rest of the equation. For instance, let us say the expression is E^X. With the currently available technologies, the expression may be rendered as "EX". This does not give the listener the information that X is in the superscript and the listener may understand the expression as $E * X$. In expressions where there are at least 2 variables that cause a phonetic sound when spoken together, the general TTS may treat the expression as a complete word. consider the expression A^B. The TTS may speak it as "ab". In case of numbers, say we have an expression 5^{2^5}, the TTS reads it as "five hundred twenty five" or "five two five". We come across the same issues while trying to render subscript text. If a human speaks the expression, he may not make such mistakes. The challenge to the human speaker lies in effectively conveying the spatial orientation of the different parts of the equation. That is, the equation, presented in audio must give the listener a clear picture of what content is in the superscript and the subscript. The listener must also be able to observe the end of the super script or subscript part of a mathematical expression. The listener should understand that any thing that he listens to after the end is in the baseline or the general part of the equation, unless specified. To overcome this challenge, the spoken form of an equation should provide the listener with different cues for superscript and subscript content.

1.3 Fractions

Fractions, like the other mathematical concepts discussed above can not be treated like a general string of text. The key information that has to be conveyed to the listener in addition to the contents of the fraction is the beginning of the fraction, the content of the fraction in numerator and denominator and the end of the fraction. The audio equivalent of the equation should effectively be able to convey nested fractions in addition to the regular fractions to the listener.

There have been several attempts to present mathematical content through alternative modes to vision. Efforts have been made to formulate standards for presenting math through Braille and speech. Nemeth Code(Nemeth et al., 1973) is a special type of Braille used for math and science notations. With Nemeth Code, one can render all mathematical and technical documents into six-dot Braille. This code could also be used to speak mathematical content. Dr T.V Raman has developed an audio system for technical readings (ASTER)(Raman, 1998). ASTER is a computing system for producing audio renderings of electronic documents. The present implementation works with documents written in the TEX family of markup languages: TEX, LaTeX and AMS-TEX. A more recent attempt has been made by a company called design science. They developed an internet explorer plugin called Math-Player that displays and speaks out mathematical content marked up in MathML(Soiffer, 2005). There have been attempts to form a set of guidelines to effectively speak mathematics in audio. The handbook for spoken mathematics (Chang et al., 1983) gives an account of such an attempt. An article on how to speak math also describes the challenges in speaking mathematics to and by a computer (Fateman, 1998). The ChromeVox project (Raman et al., 2012) is a screen reader built for Google Chrome browser and the Chrome OS. It has basic support for mathematical expressions encoded using the MathML language on web pages. The expressions are verbally presented during normal text navigation. The screen reader announces that the spoken text is a mathematical expression and it can further be explored. Navigation support is based on the MathML tree.

Earlier works discussed so far, have not effectively used paralinguistic cues and variations in the equation. However, humans use a lot of cues when reading out a mathematical equation which helps in understanding the semantics of it. Usage of the cues similar to the humans would result in more effective rendering of the equations.

The objective of this paper is to analyse the way these visual cues are presented in an auditory format by human speakers who are well acquainted with speaking the mathematical content especially to visually challenged individuals. A subjective and objective analysis is performed on the equations recorded by the speakers. Based on this analysis, we make an attempt to form specific rules to map the visual cues to their auditory equivalents to programatically and unambiguously render the mathematical content in audio using a text-to-speech system.

Section 2 discusses the basis for the study. Section 3 has the inferences drawn form the initial listening tests . Section 4 discusses the proposed ideas. Section 5 presents the analysis of the qualitative study performed.

2 Cues in spoken equations

Our study is based on the preposition that treating a mathematical expression as a regular English sentence while speaking is not an effective way to present mathematical content in an auditory form. In order to test this observation, we asked a set of 15 people to rate mathematical equations spoken by a traditional TTS system. Then we conducted the same experiment on spoken equations (i.e., equations spoken by a human-being). The details of the listening tests are as follows.

2.1 Procedure for the listening tests

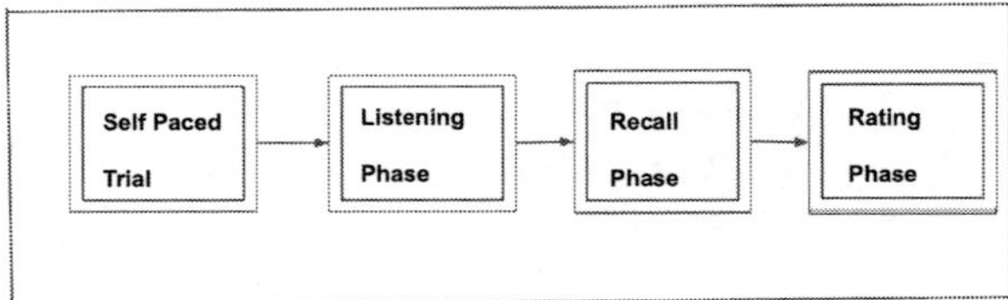

Fig: Evaluation procedure

A set of 15 participants were made to listen to the recorded equations. Each participant was made to listen to the equations using headphones and the responses were recorded. The listening test was self paced and also the users were informed that they were free to listen to the equation any number of times till they felt comfortable that they could recall the equation. Similarly, the same participants were also made to listen to speech of mathematical equations generated by a TTS system. The participant will have to reproduce the equation he/she listens to. In addition to reproducing the equation, the participant will have to evaluate the spoken equation based on eight other parameters, i.e., perform objective analysis. We arrived at these parameters partly by following the

Table 1: Evaluation of Spoken Math vs TTS

Parameter	Spoken	Synthesized (Current TTS)
Listening Effort	2.5	4.4
Content Familiarity	2.7	2.7
Effectiveness of additional cues	3.2	1.2
Accentuation	4.3	2.5
Intonation	4.26	1.6
Pauses	3.1	2.15
Number of repetitions (Mode)	2	4
Mean Opinion Score	4.42	1.89

listening test procedures followed in the Blizzard challenges (Hinterleitner et al., 2011) and our own analysis.

2.2 Selection of the equations

Selection of suitable equations is a critical component to analyse the auditory presentation of mathematical content. We hand picked a few equations which had variations in number of variables, number of sub expressions and length of the equation. The equations can be found in appendix A. Each of the equations is semantically unrelated, that is, the equations have mathematical content but the listener may not have come across the exact same equation prior to listening to them from our recordings . The reason behind choosing the equations in such a way is to ensure that the listener's prior knowledge does not influence the ability to recall the equation. If the listener is able to recall the equation even before he or she listens to it completely, the listener is benefitting from memory, not the spoken equation.

2.3 Parameters for objective analysis

On a scale of 1 to 5, the participants were asked to evaluate the spoken equations on the following parameters.

- Listening effort (1 = low, 5 = high)

- Intonation (1 = ineffective and 5 = very effective)

- Acceptance (1 = poor, 5 = good).

- Speech pauses (1= not noticeable and 5 = very prominent)

- Accentuation (1 = poor and 5 = very prominent).

- Content familiarity (1 = totally new concept and 5 = very familiar). Here 1 indicates that the user is not acquainted to the terminology used in the equation. In this case, the participants' response for that particular equation can not be considered completely as he may have entered a wrong response due to the lack of domain knowledge, not due to the lack of understanding of the audio.

- Effectiveness of additional cues such as sounds, pitch and rate variations, change in direction, etc. (1 = hardly noticeable and 5 = very helpful).

- Number of repetitions of each equation.

3 Inferences from the listening tests

The results of this experiment, shown in the Table 1 indicate that the equations are not intelligible enough if it is spoken as a plain text using a text-to-speech system. The mean opinion scores of spoken equations indicate a human-being use several acoustic cues to manifest the semantics of the mathematical symbols in audio mode. It was noticed that the trained speakers brought certain variations in their speech while speaking specific aspects of the mathematical expression. The variations are noticed in pauses and pitch variations (intonation). A careful analysis revealed that the acoustic variations were introduced by the speakers to unambiguously speak 1) quantification, 2) superscripting and subscripting and 3) handling fractions in mathematical equations.

Based on the feedback received from participants, we can infer that the use of these additional cues can effectively and unambiguously present mathematical content in audio. The question is how to introduce such cues to synthesise a mathematical equation using a text-to-speech system.

4 Proposed techniques

With the advent of languages like MathML, it is possible to programatically identify different attributes and visual cues of a mathematical expression. This possibility can in turn be leveraged to make some modifications while generating speech for mathematical content. We propose four techniques that could enhance the way mathematical content is rendered in audio.

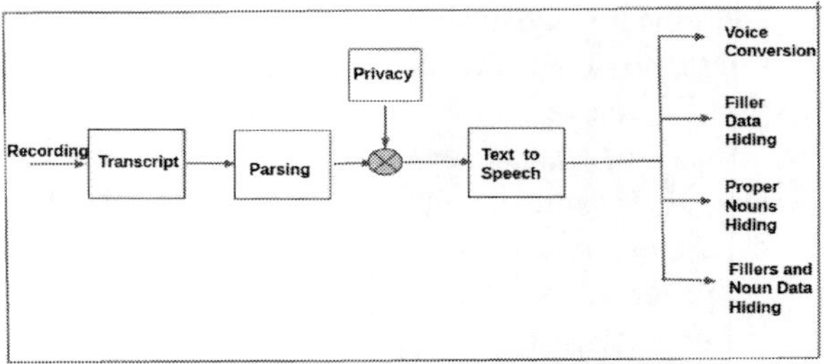

Fig: Overall framework for the proposed techniques

An example depicting the workflow of the entire algorithm is shown in the Figure 1. For the sake of illustration, a simple expression , $(X+Y)^{4-2}$ was taken :

The Equation was first converted into the Math Markup Language format. We chose "Presentation" Markup style to represent the equations. It is then text processed to identify and segregate the different terms occurring in the equation. The following terms have been segregated.

- Subscripts and superscripts

- Fractions

- Square root terms

- Overscripts and underscript

The MathML representation is processed to convert it into natural language and the acoustic cues such as pauses, intonation are incorporated to generate a file in the SABLE[1] markup language. The SABLE file is input to the speech synthesis system which generates the audio form of the equation with specified pauses and intonation. We have generated the audio files using the Festival Speech Synthesis System(Black et al., 2002). Sections 4.1 through 4.4 discuss each of the four proposed techniques.

4.1 Technique 1 : Rendering equations with pauses and special sounds

In visual communication, icons and symbols are used as indications for some types of information. In the context of mathematical expressions, the user can perceive the type of elements (

---

[1]SABLE is mark up language due to collaboration between Sun, AT&T, Bell Labs, Edinburgh and CMU to devise a standard cross synthesizer standard mark up language. The language is XML-based and allows users to add addition controlling commands in text to affect the output. An implementation exists in Festival speech synthesis system.

Figure 1: Example Synthesis using a simple expression

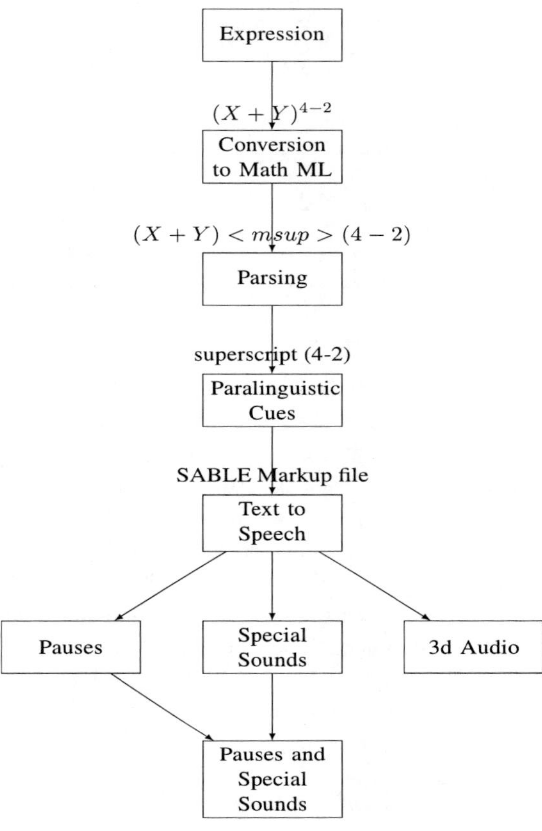

superscripts, subscripts, etc) by getting a glance at the equation. A person has the advantage of perceiving a lot of information of the equation even before looking at the actual contents of the equation. This technique attempts to present the equation in a manner that a person gets a similar advantage when he listens to it.

In this concept, we made use of special sounds or ear cons while presenting the equations. However, replacing speech with sounds alone is not the most effective way to tackle the problem of presenting mathematic equations in audio. We made use of paralinguistic cues including, but not limited to sounds.

The cues presented in this method include:

- **Pauses** to convey certain parts of an equation. These pauses are mainly used to separate the parts of mathematical expressions. Consider $(A + B)^2$ and $(A + B^2) + 1$. It would sound more natural and intuitive if the expressions

Table 2: Pitch and rate variations

Term	Pitch variation	Rate variation
Superscript	50	20
Subscript	-50	-20
Fraction	25	-25
Underscript	-60	-25
Overscript	60	25

are spoken as "the quantity A + B pause superscript 2 " and "the quantity A + B superscript 2 pause + 1" .

- **Sounds** to indicate certain symbols and mathematical operations. Sounds are used to indicate superscripts, subscripts, roots, under scripts, over scripts and under script-over script combination.

We chose the sounds(such as the sound "ding") such that would be pleasant to the ear and that are passively noticed by a listener so as not to distract too much, at the same time, are loud enough not to go unnoticed. The sounds show a transition from high to low and low to high when there is a subscript and superscript respectively. Any other type of sounds and their variations could also be applied in this technique.

4.2 Technique 2 : Rendering equations with pitch and rate variations

Screen Reader users are familiar to pitch changes. Generally, a high pitch is used to denote capitals and a low pitch is used to denote tool tip messages. On observing the human recorded equations explained in Section 2, we observed that speakers tend to modulate the pitch as they read aloud certain parts of a mathematical expression. It has been observed that certain parts of a mathematical expression are spoken at a faster rate to indicate that it is a sub expression and to isolate it from the rest of the expression.

In this technique, we use pitch and rate changes to denote the presence of certain mathematical attributes. The pitch and rate increase while speaking out the superscript text and decrease while speaking the subscript text. A similar method can be employed to properly render fractions. The numerator is spoken in a higher pitch and the denominator is spoken in a lower pitch. Similarly, quantities in a root are spoken at a faster rate. Table

Table 3: Evaluation of the proposed techniques

Parameter	Technique#1	Technique#2	Technique#3	Technique#4
Intonation Variation	2.3	**4.7**	4.32	4.68
Pitch Variation	1.4	4.43	**4.82**	4.36
Pauses	**4.15**	3.7	3.7	3.87
Listening Effort	3.5	**2.3**	2.64	2.47
Content Familiarity	2.7	2.7	2.7	2.7
Effectiveness of additional cues	1.82	4.32	**4.37**	4.23
Accentuation	**3.47**	2.3	3.2	3.6
Number of repititions(Mode)	3	2	2	2
Mean Opinion Score	2.27	4.37	**4.62**	4.35

2 shows the pitch and rate variation(in percentage) that are applied to the Mathematical equation. The variation is with respect to the base pitch and rate of the TTS.

4.3 Technique 3: Rendering equations with audio spatialisation

In this technique, we made an attempt to draw a closer analogy to the spatial positioning of various variables and numbers of a mathematical equation. The listener can be given the illusion that the superscript part of the math expression is spoken from above his head and the rest at the usual level using the Head Related Transfer Function (HRTF) (Geronazzo et al., 2011). Table 4 shows the sets of angles chosen for the different parts of the equation such as superscript, etc.

Table 4: Sets of HRTF angles for audio spatialisation

Term	Elevation Angle	Azimuth Angle
Superscript	90	30
Subscript	-90	30
Fraction	270	45
Underscript	-90	45
Overscript	90	30

We identify the portions of a mathematical expression that require modification in spatial orientation of sound. Based on the attribute, we apply the HRTF function with the required angles.

4.4 Technique 4 : Rendering equations with pitch variations and special tones

In this technique, we render the equations in audio by varying the pitch, adding pauses, emphasising the speech and adding sounds at required parts of a mathematical expression. As explained in 4.3, we can make pitch and rate manipulation while rendering superscripts, subscripts, fractions, under scripts and over scripts. In addition to the variations in speech, we have also added sounds to indicate the listener before hand that he must expect one of the above mentioned variations (superscripts, subscripts, etc). The sounds used here are the same as the ones mentioned in section 4.2. The Pitch and rate variations that are introduced are the same as the percentage values given in table 2.

5 Analysis of the listening test

A system was built to render mathematical expressions implementing each of the proposed ideas. An experiment procedure similar to the one explained in Section 2 was followed. 30 participants were made to participate in the experiment. The table contains the normalised scores(1 to 5) calculated over the responses for the equations. The number of repetitions of the equation has the mode value(most occurring value).

On analysing the experiment as described in Section 2, it is observed that the participants are able to understand the human spoken equations. More over, it can be clearly understood that generating spoken forms of mathematical equations without making any enhancements is not capable of rendering math effectively. It can also be inferred that making use of just a few paralinguistic cues, sounds and pauses as explained in section 4.1 will not suffice either. The pitch and rate changes while rendering certain parts of the mathematical expressions have proven to be helpful to the participants in comprehending the expression. In the method described in section 4.3, the listener has been able to draw an analogy to the print form of mathematics. It has been observed that the method explained in section 4.1 did not prove to be helpful to the listeners. However, from the table 3 and the values corresponding to the technique explained in section 4.4, it is evident that use of cues (pauses and rate variations) in addition to special sounds can be significantly effective in helping a listener.(see the demonstration of the listening test on the webpage associated to this paper: http://goo.gl/FLTIOv).

6 Conclusion

From the analysis and the proposed ideas, we can say that there is a possibility to unambiguously render mathematics in audio. With the increase in voice driven interfaces and information access through audio, rendering mathematical content in audio could also help more effectively present such content in these interfaces. Personal assistance or any other voice driven UIs can more effectively render mathematical content to the listener. In addition to this, effectively rendering mathematical content in audio can be of a great advantage for people with print disabilities including, but not limited to vision impairment, dyslexia and cognitive impairment. With currently available assistive technology, understanding mathematical content is very difficult and almost impossible. the ideas explained in sections 4.1 to 4.3 improve the scenario of understanding mathematical content through a non visual input mode. as explained in section 4.4, There is also a chance that a combination of the proposed ideas are more effective than each of the ideas alone.

Acknowledgements

We thank Prof Peri Bhaskararao for his contributions in our initial discussions related to this research effort.

References

Alan W Black, Paul Taylor, Richard Caley, and Rob Clark. 2002. The festival speech synthesis system. *University of Edinburgh*, 1.

Larry A Chang, CM White, and L Abrahamson. 1983. Handbook for spoken mathematics. *Lawrence Livermore National Laboratory*.

Richard Fateman. 1998. How can we speak math. *Journal of Symbolic Computation*, 25(2).

Michele Geronazzo, Simone Spagnol, and Federico Avanzini. 2011. A head-related transfer function model for real-time customized 3-d sound rendering. In *Signal-Image Technology and Internet-Based Systems (SITIS), 2011 Seventh International Conference on*, pages 174–179. IEEE.

Florian Hinterleitner, Georgina Neitzel, Sebastian Möller, and Christoph Norrenbrock. 2011. An evaluation protocol for the subjective assessment of text-to-speech in audiobook reading tasks. In *Proceedings of the Blizzard challenge workshop, Florence, Italy*. Citeseer.

Abraham Nemeth, National Braille Association, et al. 1973. *The Nemeth Braille Code for mathematics and science notation*. American Print. House for the Blind.

TV Raman, Charles L Chen, and Dominic Mazzoni. 2012. Rachel shearer, chaitanya gharpure, james deboer, david tseng google inc 1600 amphitheatre parkway.

TV Raman. 1998. *Audio system for technical readings*. Springer.

Neil Soiffer. 2005. Mathplayer: web-based math accessibility. In *Proceedings of the 7th international ACM SIGACCESS conference on Computers and accessibility*, pages 204–205. ACM.

A Equations recorded by Human voice

$$X + Y = z \tag{1}$$

$$\frac{X + Y}{K} = \alpha \tag{2}$$

$$(X+Y)^{P+Q} = X^{P*Q}+Y^P*Q-P+\frac{Q}{Y}-\frac{P}{Q-X} \tag{3}$$

$$\frac{(P + X) * (Q - Y)}{(X + Y)^K} = \frac{P}{X + K} - Q * \left(\frac{K^x}{Y - P}\right) \tag{4}$$

$$(X + Y)^K = 3 * X^K + 4 * X^y - 5Y^{K+X} \tag{5}$$

$$(X+Y)^{P+Q} = X^{P*Q}+Y^P*Q-P+\frac{Q}{Y}-\frac{P}{Q-X} \tag{6}$$

$$\frac{(P+X)*(Q-Y)}{(X+Y)^K} = \frac{P}{X+K} - Q*\left(\frac{K^x}{Y-P}\right) \tag{7}$$

$$\frac{X+Y}{K} = \alpha \tag{8}$$

$$(X+Y)^K = 3*X^K + 4*X^y - 5Y^{K+X} \tag{9}$$

B Equations for testing the Systems

$$1+2+3-5+4+2+3 = (3+2)*(1+1) \tag{10}$$

$$\lim_{x\to+\infty} \frac{3x^2+7x^3}{x^2+5x^4} = 3. \tag{11}$$

$$\frac{\partial}{\partial x}x^2 y = 2xy \tag{12}$$

$$\frac{\partial u}{\partial t} = h^2 - E^{n+1} - 1 \tag{13}$$

$$\int_0^R \frac{2x\,dx}{1+x^2} = \log(1+R^2) \tag{14}$$

$$\int_0^{+\infty} x^n e^{-x}\,dx = n!. \tag{15}$$

$$(P+Q)^K + R = P^K*Q + Q^K*P + R^{P*Q}*K + \frac{P^Q*K+1}{R} \tag{16}$$

$$(P+Q)*(R+K) = (P+R)^Q - (K+R^Q) + \frac{R+Q^K}{(R+Q)^K+1} \tag{17}$$

$$(P+Q)*(R+K) = (P+R)^Q - (K+R^Q) + \frac{R+Q^K}{(R+Q)^K+1} \tag{18}$$

$$\frac{X_1^K + X_2^K}{P_3^X * 5_4^x} + E^X = e^{\frac{X_{K+1}+X_{K+2}}{(X+Y)}} \tag{19}$$

$$\sqrt[P+Q]{A + K^P + A^{K+P}} = \frac{(K+P)(K-P)}{K*(P+K)} \tag{20}$$

$$\sum_{i=1}^{\infty} \frac{1}{i^2} + 5i + \sqrt[3]{i+1} = \frac{\pi^2 + 4\pi^3 + \sqrt[\pi+i]{9*\pi}}{6} \tag{21}$$

$$\left(\frac{X+Y}{K}+1\right)^3 = \sqrt[3]{X}+\sqrt[3]{Y}+(X*Y)/3+\frac{X+Y}{3+K}+3 \tag{22}$$

Author Index